THINKING, PROBLEM SOLVING, COGNITION

THINKING, PROBLEM SOLVING, COGNITION

SECOND EDITION

Richard E. Mayer

University of California, Santa Barbara

W. H. Freeman and Company
New York

Library of Congress Cataloging-in-Publication Data

Mayer, Richard E., 1947–
    Thinking, problem solving, cognition / Richard E. Mayer. — 2nd ed.
        p.   cm.
    Includes bibliographic references and index.
    ISBN 0-7167-2214-3. — ISBN 0-7167-2215-1 (pbk.)
    1. Thought and thinking.   2. Problem solving.   3. Cognition.
    I. Title.
    BF441.M35 1991
    153.4′2—dc20   91-18492
                                                                                    CIP

Printed in the United States of America

1 2 3 4 5 6 7 8 9 0 VB 9 9 8 7 6 5 4 3 2

Dedicated to
Beverly
and Kenny, David, and Sarah

CONTENTS

PREFACE

"Why is it that some people, when they are faced with problems, get clever ideas, make inventions and discoveries? What happens, what are the processes that lead to such solutions?" These questions were asked by the famous Gestalt psychologist Max Wertheimer (Luchins & Luchins, 1970, p. 1) more than a half century ago, but only recently have psychologists and cognitive scientists possessed the tools to seek to answer them. This book introduces you to what researchers have learned about human problem solving. If you are interested in how people solve problems, then this book is for you.

This second edition of *Thinking, Problem Solving, Cognition* retains the same goal as the first: to introduce the reader to our current understanding of the cognition side of cognitive psychology. It retains the same friendly style and still asumes that the reader has no prior experience in cognitive psychology. This book contains the same kinds of pedagogic aids as the previous edition: each chapter begins with an engaging introductory problem and ends with an integrative summary; many concrete examples and illustrations are presented in each section; and the reader is encouraged to participate in numerous problem-solving activities. The book's intended audience is also the same: students in such courses as cognitive psychology, learning and memory, problem solving, critical thinking, and educational psychology, as well as courses in professions that involve problem solving. Since this book emphasizes the cognition side of cognitive psychology, it can be used in conjunction with books that emphasize the perception side of cognitive psychology.

Thinking, Problem Solving, Cognition: Second Edition is divided into four parts:

Historical Perspective (Chapters 1 to 3) introduces the classic theories of problem solving: associationism and Gestalt theory.

Basic Thinking Tasks (Chapters 4 and 5) discusses research and theories concerning two specific types of reasoning—induction and deduction.

Information-Procesing Analysis of Cognition (Chapters 6 to 9) presents techniques for analyzing problem-solving strategies, cognitive skills, categorical knowledge, and verbal knowledge.

Implications and Applications (Chapters 10 to 16) gives examples of how the techniques and findings of cognitive psychology can be applied to such real problems as human cognitive development, individual differences in problem-solving ability, teaching and transfer of creative problem solving, mathematical problem solving, and everyday thinking.

Three new chapters have been added to this second edition, representing areas that have developed rapidly during the past decade: "Expert Problem Solving" (Chapter 13) compares the problem solving of experts and novices in fields such as medical diagnosis and computer programming, "Analogical Reasoning" (Chapter 14) examines how people transfer what they have learned from one situation to another, and "Everyday Thinking" (Chapter 16) examines how people solve problems that occur in the context of working or shopping. In addition, the two chapters in the first edition on Gestalt approaches to problem solving have been reorganized into a single chapter (Chapter 3). Each of the remaining chapters has been rewritten, reorganized, and updated to reflect changes over the past decade.

In the years since publication of the first edition of *Thinking, Problem Solving, Cognition,* the field of human thinking and problem solving has matured and been enriched by developments in cognitive science—the interdisciplinary study of cognition which Gardner (1985) calls "the mind's new science." Over the past decade, three important directions of growth in the study of problem solving have been a focus on *thinking in real problem-solving situations,* such as how shoppers determine the best buy in a supermarket (Chapter 16) or how physicians diagnose a patient's symptoms (Chapter 13); a focus on *individual differences in thinking,* such as comparisons between experts and novices (Chapter 13) or between students of high verbal and low verbal ability (Chapter 11); and a focus on *problem-solving transfer* from solving one problem to another (Chapters 12 and 14). In short, the study of problem solving has become more concrete, more individualized, and more practical. In comparing the research focus of this edition to that of the previous one, the most obvious change has been a movement away from studying general thinking in context-free environments to studying real thinking in specific situations. For example, instead of studying the general strategies that people use to solve puzzles, current research focuses on the specific knowledge people use to write computer programs or to determine the most efficient way to complete a work assignment.

As with the previous edition, readers will need a tolerance for lack of closure. Although the field of human (and machine) cognition has received much attention lately, it remains in a state of change. No single approach can bring order to the entire field. Instead of trying to artificially organize the book around a theme that has not yet emerged, I have attempted to present an honest assessment of what we know about human problem solving. Rather than writing an encyclopedia, I have tried to choose representative theories and research studies. I have written each chapter as a self-contained survey of a specific topic, and at the same time I have pointed out interrelations among chapters.

Over the years, I have developed a continuing interest in the study of human problem solving because I believe that the ability to solve problems is the hallmark of human survival. Accordingly, I have been thinking about the revisions needed for this edition for almost ten years, and I am pleased to finally have them all on paper. My hope is that you enjoy reading *Thinking, Problem Solving, Cognition* as much as I have enjoyed writing it.

In addition to the acknowledgments I offered in the previous edition, I would like to thank Jonathan Cobb, Janet Tannenbaum, Karen Osborne, and the staff of W. H. Freeman and Company for helping create this book. I appreciate the advice of the reviewers: Emanuel Donchin, Mary Gick, Diane F. Halpern, Robert Kail, Lance Rips, Robert S. Siegler, Robert J. Sternberg, and Robert Weisberg. Although they cannot be held responsible for the shortcomings in the book, they clearly are responsible for many improvements. I also appreciate the dozens of suggestions for improving the book that I have received over the years from instructors and students; in this regard I am particularly pleased to acknowledge the detailed feedback from Anne Bovenmyer Lewis and Erika L. Ferguson. This book has profited from my graduate education at the University of Michigan, as well as visiting appointments at Indiana University, the University of Pittsburgh, and the University of Illinois. In particular, I am indebted to Jim Greeno, who introduced me to and engaged my interest in the psychology of problem solving. I am also grateful for the intellectual stimulation provided by my colleagues and students in the Department of Psychology at the University of California, Santa Barbara. Finally, I appreciate the support of my family: my thanks go to my parents, James and Bernis Mayer, and my brothers, Bob and Bernie Mayer, for their continued interest in this book; and to Beverly and to Kenny, David, and Sarah for their patience and understanding as I worked on it. Again, I dedicate this book to them, with love.

May 1991   *Richard E. Mayer*
Santa Barbara

PART · I

HISTORICAL PERSPECTIVE

CHAPTER 1

BEGINNINGS

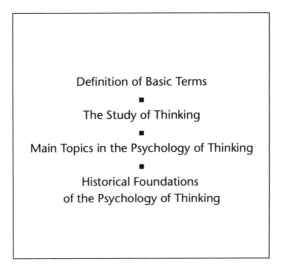

Definition of Basic Terms

■

The Study of Thinking

■

Main Topics in the Psychology of Thinking

■

Historical Foundations
of the Psychology of Thinking

INTROSPECTION TASK

In a moment you will be given a word and a question about the word. Your job is to say the first answer that comes to your mind and then to describe all the details of the thought process that led to it.

Your test word is BITE, and your question is, What is the CAUSE? Now describe the thinking process that led you to whatever word you answered.

If the word "dog" came to your mind, your response corresponds to that obtained by the German psychologist Otto Selz in the early 1900s (Humphrey, 1963). Check the top of Box 1-1 to see how Selz's subject described his chain of thought. Note that an image of a wounded leg came first, followed by the conscious words, "dogs bite." Did you also experience an image while you were thinking?

BOX 1 • 1   Method of Introspection

Problem 1

Bite. Cause?

"As soon as I had read the [words] the search was on. I had also a picture of a leg with a wound on it and saw nothing else. Then 'dog' came to me in the form of an idea, with the consciousness: dogs bite" (1963, p. 138).

Problem 2

Poem. In what *larger category* does it belong?

"Once again, immediately a full understanding of the [question]. Then again an intensive glance, the symbolic fixation of that which is sought; then at once the flitting memory of art, poetry, and so on appeared. The word 'art,' I think, in auditory-motor terms. Then the thought that I cannot subsume poetry under art but only under artistic production. With this, I am certain, no words and images; then I said, 'work of art' " (p. 137).

Problem 3

Parson. What is an *equivalent occupation?*

"I read the words successively and with understanding. Immediately came the consciousness that something [equivalent] was very familiar. Then came the word 'chaplain,' internally spoken. It is certain that the consciousness of the familiarity of a solution preceded the, as yet, uneffected appearance of the word 'chaplain' " (p. 134).

From Humphrey (1963)

Now try the word—and question: POEM. In what LARGER CATEGORY does it belong? A typical response from Selz's experiment is "work of art," and the introspections of one subject about how the answer was derived are given in Box 1-1. Note that no images were involved in the subject's thinking about this problem. Did you experience an image?

Finally, try to describe your thought process for: PARSON. What is an EQUIVALENT OCCUPATION? The introspections of a typical subject appear in Box 1-1. The answer this subject made was "chaplain" (remember these introspections are translations from German), and again no imagery was involved.

These tasks are examples of the first type of experimental studies on human thought processes ever carried out. The method is called *introspection* because the thinker must inspect his or her own mental events and report them to the experimenter. Long before the birth of psychology, human beings undoubtedly introspected, perhaps trying to understand themselves, but it was not until the beginning of this century that the method of introspection was taken into the experimental laboratory and systematically applied to the study of human thought. We shall talk more about introspection later in this chapter.

■
DEFINITION OF BASIC TERMS
■

To study human cognitive processes effectively, it is useful to define the basic terms such as *problem* and *thinking*.

PROBLEM

Although they express the terms differently, most psychologists agree that a problem has certain characteristics:

Givens—The problem begins in a certain state with certain conditions, objects, pieces of information, and so forth being present at the onset of work on the problem.

Goals—The desired or terminal state of the problem is the goal state, and thinking is required to transform the problem from the given to the goal state.

Obstacles—The thinker has at his or her disposal certain ways to change the given state or the goal state of the problem. The thinker, however, does not already know the correct answer; that is, the correct sequence of behaviors that will solve the problem is not immediately obvious.

In short, any definition of "problem" should consist of the three ideas that (1) the problem is presently in some state, but (2) it is desired that it be in another state, and (3) there is no direct, obvious way to accomplish the change. This definition is broad enough to include problems ranging from geometry (Greeno & Simon, 1988; Polya, 1957) and chess (Newell & Simon, 1972) to riddles (Reitman, 1965).

Reitman (1965) has further analyzed four categories of problems according to how well the given and goal states are specified:

Well-defined given state and well-defined goal state: "How can you turn a sow's ear into a silk purse?" Note, however, that although the given state (sow's ear) and the goal state (silk purse) are clearly specified in this problem, there is a serious lack of possible ways to solve it.

Well-defined given state and poorly defined goal state: "How can you redesign a Cadillac El Dorado to get better gas mileage?" The given state, the automobile, is clearly designated, but what does "better gas mileage" mean exactly?

Poorly defined given state and well-defined goal state: "Explain the mechanisms responsible for sun spots. " The goal, "sun spots," is clear, but the initial state that causes this goal is not.

Poorly defined given state and poorly defined goal state: "What is red and goes put-put?" The answer is "an outboard apple," and you can blame Reitman for this one.

Greeno (1978a) suggested a three-part typology of problems, and more recently a fourth problem type has been added (Greeno & Simon, 1988).

1. *Problems of transformation:* Given a well-defined initial state and goal state, the problem solver must find a sequence of operations that produces the goal state. Greeno and Simon (1988, p. 627) describe the problem-solving process as "searching through a set of possibilities." Examples include water jug problems (Chapter 3), Tower of Hanoi problems (Chapters 3 and 6), and math word problems (Chapter 15).

2. *Problems of arrangement:* Given all the elements and a general description of the goal, the problem solver must arrange the elements in a way that solves the problem. Greeno and Simon (1988, p. 627) also refer to these as design problems and describe the problem-solving process as "narrowing the set of possibilities." Examples include anagram problems (Chapter 2), cryptarithme tic problems (Chapters 3 and 6), and insight problems (Chapters 3 and 12).

3. *Problems of inducing structure:* Given several examples or instances, the problem solver must discover a general rule or pattern that is consistent with the information. Greeno and Simon (1988, p. 627) refer to these as induction problems and describe the problem-solving process as "find[ing] a general principle or structure." Examples include series completion problems (Chapter 4), analogy problems (Chapter 14), and problems of scientific reasoning (Chapter 4).

4. *Evaluation of deductive arguments:* Given premises, determine whether or not a conclusion logically follows. Although logical deduction has been heralded by some philosophers as the basis for human rationality, Greeno and Simon (1988, p. 660) contend that "psychological analyses provide no evidence for a belief in deductive reasoning as a category of thinking processes different from other thinking processes." Examples of deduction problems include judging the validity of categorical, conditional, and linear syllogisms (Chapter 5).

As Greeno points out, however, not all problems can be neatly classified into one of these types. Instead, many of the most interesting problems include aspects of several types of problems.

THINKING AND PROBLEM SOLVING

There are many definitions of *thinking, problem solving,* and *cognition,* but this book will use these three terms interchangeably, based on a single, general definition common to them all. Unfortunately, we begin with a serious lack of agreement among psychologists about whether thinking should be generally defined as an external, behavioral process or an internal, cognitive process. The behavioral argument is that the science of psychology must deal only with empirical, observable behaviors as its primary data; internal states or processes cannot be directly observed and therefore cannot be part of psychology. Behaviorists consider a view of thinking as an internal process with no relationship to behavior to be useless; for example, a famous critique of an early cognitive theory of rat maze learning was that the rat was "left buried in thought at the choice point"—there was no relationship between internal mechanisms and external observable events. In this view, psychological definitions must be tied firmly to behavior. The cognitive argument, on the other hand, is that behavior is merely the manifestation or result of thinking and therefore psychological definitions must be tied firmly to the mechanisms that underlie behavior.

A compromise that most, but not all, psychologists who study thinking might accept is that concepts such as internal, cognitive processes have a place in psychology if and only if they generate clearly testable predictions, that is, if they suggest observable predictions concerning human behavior. In short, a general definition of thinking includes three basic ideas:

1. Thinking is *cognitive,* but is inferred from behavior. It occurs internally, in the mind or cognitive system, and must be inferred indirectly.

2. Thinking is a *process* that involves some manipulation of or set of operations on knowledge in the cognitive system.

3 . Thinking is *directed* and results in behavior that "solves" a problem or is directed toward solution.*

---

* Some types of thinking may not be directed, such as autistic thinking, daydreaming, or the fragmented thinking of schizophrenics; however, this book will deal mainly with normal, directed thinking.

In other words, thinking is what happens when a person solves a problem, that is, produces behavior that moves the individual from the given state to the goal state—or at least tries to achieve this change. Thus Johnson (1972) defined thinking as "problem solving," and similarly Polya (1965, p. ix) suggested that problem solving is based on cognitive processing that results in "finding a way out of a difficulty, a way around an obstacle, attaining an aim that was not immediately attainable. " The remainder of this book aims at making the general definition of thinking more specific, although, as you will see, currently there is agreement neither on a definition of thinking nor on exactly what mechanisms underlie thinking.

Other terms used in the study of thinking, such as *induction, deduction,* and *reasoning,* have more restricted meanings than those we have discussed and can be considered as subsets of thinking. Induction, which we shall examine in Chapter 4, refers to a situation in which a thinker is given a series of examples and must "leap" to the creation of a general rule; deduction refers to a situation in which a thinker is given a set of general rules and must draw a logical conclusion, as we shall see in Chapter 5. Induction and deduction are both types of reasoning.

■
THE STUDY OF THINKING
■

People are endowed with a number of basic cognitive processes that, although closely related, have been separated and studied individually by psychologists. These cognitive processes include: sensation and perception (reception and recognition of input stimuli), learning (encoding of input information), memory (retrieval of input information), and thinking (manipulation of perceived, learned, and remembered information). These topics form the core of what has been called *cognitive psychology,* and to the extent that each involves active manipulation of information, each involves thinking. Bruner (1973) emphasized the role of problem solving in perception by suggesting that perception involves "going beyond the information given." Bartlett (1932) stressed the role of problem solving in memory and learning by suggesting that learning and recall require an "effort after meaning." Thinking has also been investigated in many other contexts in psychology, including social psychology (attitude formation and change), developmental psychology (cognitive development), personality (cognitive style), and testing and measurement (intelligence tests).

Thinking is thus a component of experimental psychology; while the main focus is on a complex cognitive process, thinking depends on and is part of simpler processes. Because thinking is so complex and because it may be based on lower cognitive processes, many psychologists have argued that we should understand the simpler or lower cognitive processes before trying to study the complex or higher processes. However, there have always been some psychologists who ignored these warnings and who were challenged by the prospect of studying one of the supreme achievements of the human species, the ability to think and deal with complex learning:

> The topic has fascinated psychologists in and out of the laboratory. They have worried it as a dog worries a bone. It was always there, sometimes buried, sometimes dug up again and brought to a high sheen, never quite cracked or digested, and never forgotten. Even the Wundts and the Hulls promised themselves to get back to the problem sooner or later while they counseled patience and attention to simpler problems that seemed to contain the principles needed to unlock the complexities of human thought. But for every Wundt psychology had a Buhler, for every Hull a Wertheimer—psychologists impatient with the programmatic building-block approach, unwilling to wait for the solution of the simple, and eager to plunge into the complexities and wonders of full-blown human thought. (Mandler & Mandler, 1964, p. 1)

■
MAIN TOPICS IN THE PSYCHOLOGY OF THINKING
■

The psychology of thinking and complex learning has held a regular, albeit modest, position in the mainstream of psychology ever since William James (1890) included a chapter on reasoning in his famous textbook. Yet the subject has never been completely unified or well understood, and the basic knowledge has remained hard to define. There are now, however, encouraging signs that some progress has been made since Humphrey's assessment (1963, p. 308) of the first fifty years of work by experimental psychologists on thinking: "Fifty years' experiments on the psychology of thinking or reasoning have not brought us very far, but they have at least shown the road which must be traversed.

New roads that have been traversed since Humphrey's critique include exciting developments in an information-processing approach to cognition such as computer simulation of human thinking (Chapter 6), new theories of semantic memory representation (Chapter 9), and the fresh interest of American psychologists in cognitive development motivated largely by Piaget's work (Chapter 10). Older roads that have continued to stimulate further travel include the Gestalt approach to problem solving based on the idea that thinking involves "restructuring" a problem (Chapter 3), the study of concept learning, which suggests that the testing of "hypotheses" may be a part of thinking (Chapter 4), and the associationist approach to thinking, which is based on the principle of learning by reinforcement (Chapter 2).

This book, then, is organized into sixteen chapters, each covering a main road or side road of the study of thinking. The first three chapters provide a historical perspective by showing you the oldest paths:

- *Chapter 1 (Beginnings)* defines key terms and summarizes the early history of research on thinking.
- *Chapter 2 (Associationism)* investigates the idea that thinking is based on the principle of learning by reinforcement. It includes such classic research as Thorndike's work on cats in a puzzle box as well as more recent research, such as the analysis of anagram solving and the physiological correlates of thinking.
- *Chapter 3 (Gestalt)* investigates the idea that thinking involves restructuring the elements of the problem in a new way; the famous Gestalt experiments on insight and rigidity in problem solving and current work on the analysis of stages in problem solving are covered.

Part II provides two chapters on thinking tasks that have been heavily studied by psychologists:

- *Chapter 4 (Inductive Reasoning)* examines the idea that thinking involves forming and testing hypotheses. It describes original research on concept learning by Hull and Heidbreder plus up-to-date work on strategies in concept learning, serial pattern learning, visual prototype formation, and errors in induction.
- *Chapter 5 (Deductive Reasoning)* investigates how people draw conclusions from premises. It presents the classic work on deduction and emphasizes ongoing work on models of deductive reasoning.

The chapters in Part III examine the information-processing approach to the analysis of cognition processes and structures:

- *Chapter 6 (Computer Simulation)* presents an information-processing analysis of problem-solving strategies; the computer simulation of human thinking is highlighted.
- *Chapter 7 (Mental Chronometry)* analyzes cognitive skills; the use of process models such as flow charts is emphasized.
- *Chapter 8 (Schema Theory)* provides an analysis of verbal knowledge, focusing on how meaningful information is comprehended and stored in memory.
- *Chapter 9 (Question Answering)* explores the problem of how people search their existing semantic memory to answer questions. The

topics covered include recent work on psycholinguistics and categorization of objects in memory.

Part IV covers recent implications and applications of research on problem solving, including individual differences in problem solving and problem solving within specific contexts:

- *Chapter 10 (Cognitive Development)* presents Piaget's theory and information-processing theories of cognitive development. It also examines the degree to which cognitive development can be taught.
- *Chapter 11 (Intelligence)* investigates techniques for measuring and understanding individual differences in intellectual ability.
- *Chapter 12 (Creativity Training)* considers whether creative thinking can be taught just like any practical skill.
- *Chapter 13 (Expert Problem Solving)* examines the differences between how experts and novices solve problems in physics, computer programming, and medical diagnosis.
- *Chapter 14 (Analogical Reasoning)* examines the thorny issue of how people transfer what they know about solving one problem to solving a new related problem.
- *Chapter 15 (Mathematical Problem Solving)* analyzes how people solve mathematics problems, such as those found in mathematics classrooms.
- *Chapter 16 (Everyday Thinking)* explores the strategies people use for solving problems encountered while working or shopping.

■
HISTORICAL FOUNDATIONS OF THE PSYCHOLOGY OF THINKING
■

ASSOCIATIONIST PHILOSOPHY: PHILOSOPHERS ANALYZE HUMAN COGNITION

Before psychology began as an experimental science in the late nineteenth century, the issues of psychology were already well established within the domain of mental philosophy. The dominant philosophy of human mental processes then was *associationism,* the belief that mental life can be explained in terms of two basic components: ideas (or elements) and associations (or links) between them. Associationism is usually traced back to three laws of learning and memory expressed by the Greek philosopher Aristotle:

Doctrine of association by contiguity—Events or objects that occur in the same time or space are associated in memory, so that thinking of one will cause thinking of the other.

Doctrine of association by similarity—Events or objects that are similar tend to be associated in memory.

Doctrine of association by contrast—Events or objects that are opposites tend to be associated in memory.

In addition, Aristotle claimed that thinking involves moving from one element or idea to another via a chain of associations and that such thought is impossible without images: "We cannot think without imagery" (quoted in Humphrey, 1963, p. 31). Aristotle's dogma about imagery later became a key issue when the psychology of thinking was first subjected to empirical rather than philosophical study.

The British associationists, led by Hobbes and Locke in the seventeenth and eighteenth centuries, reformulated the concepts and principles of associationism, including the three laws of Aristotle. Their theory of mental life can be summarized as containing four main characteristics:

Atomism—The unit of thinking is the association between two specific ideas. All mental life can be analyzed into specific ideas and associations.

Mechanization—The process of thinking or of moving from one idea to another is automatic and based solely on strength of associations.

Empiricism—All knowledge, that is, all ideas and associations, come from sensory experience. The mind begins as a "blank slate" and is filled by reproducing the world exactly as it is received through the senses.

Imagery—Thus thinking is merely the automatic movement from point to point along mental paths established through learning, and since each point is a sensory experience, thinking must involve imagery (or some other sensory experience).

WUNDT: PSYCHOLOGY BEGINS WITHOUT THINKING

By the late nineteenth century, people were increasingly applying the methods of empirical science to the study of the physical world all around them—to the planets and space (astronomy), to moving objects and weights (physics), to the makeup of earth, water, and fire (chemistry), to the world of plants and animals (biology), and even to their own bodies (physiology and medicine). One of the last areas to be subjected to scientific study was what Wilhelm Wundt called the "new domain of science": the human mind and behavior.

Wundt is often identified as the "father" of psychology, and his opening of a psychology laboratory at the University of Leipzig in 1879 is generally considered the beginning of psychology as a science. Wundt subjected some of the old issues of mental philosophy to the rigors of empirical science and experimental study and created the new science on the principle that "all observation implies . . . that the observed object is independent of the observer" (quoted in Mandler & Mandler, 1964, p. 132). His approach evolved into structuralism, the goal of which was to break human consciousness into its elementary parts.

Wundt also influenced the study of thinking when he divided the subject matter of psychology into two classes. One class is simple psychical processes—such as physiological reflexes and sensation and perception that could be studied by direct experimental methods; the other is higher psychical processes, about which "nothing can be discovered in such experiments" (Wundt, 1911/1973). Thus Wundt decreed that higher-level mental processes *could not* be studied in the scientific laboratory; instead they could be studied by looking at the mental products of an entire society such as its art, stories, and so on. Although Wundt had shown that science could be directed at ourselves, our own mental processes and behaviors, he drew the line at studying thinking and complex learning. The nineteenth century ended with no major experimental work having yet begun on the psychology of human thinking.*

WURZBURG GROUP: PSYCHOLOGISTS STUDY THINKING

Working against Wundt's dogma forbidding the study of thinking, a group of German psychologists in the city of Wurzburg finally did attempt to study human cognitive processes experimentally in the early part of this century. This Wurzburg group set out to refine the old associationist theory of the philosophers by using the new experimental method of introspection.

In a typical early experiment, the psychologists would present a word to a subject, ask the subject to give a free association to the word, and then ask the person to describe the thought process that led to the response; or they might ask a subject to describe the thought process of answering some question (see Marbe [1901], Mayer & Orth [1901], and Messer [1906] in Mandler & Mandler, 1964). A major finding of these studies was a sort of negative result—many of the subjects reported that they were not consciously aware of any images in their associations (see Box 1-1). This finding was called "imageless thought."

---

* A notable exception is Ebbinghaus's (1885/1964) exciting monograph *Memory,* which provided a solid study of learning and memory of verbal material.

A second type of experiment used different questions for the same stimulus words. For example, Watt (1905/1964) found a different pattern of response for a word if he presented flash cards that said "name a whole of" rather than "name an example of." In a more elaborate experiment, Ach (1905/1964) hypnotized subjects and, while they were under hypnosis, instructed them to add, subtract, multiply, or divide numbers. Then he brought them out of the hypnotic state and gave them cards with number pairs such as 4,2 and asked the subjects to respond. Answers such as 2 or 8 came instantly, depending on the hypnotic suggestion, in this case to divide or to multiply. A major conclusion of this line of research was that thought is directed by some "determining tendency" that is relevant for a particular problem (Kulpe, 1912/1964).

The work of the Wurzburg group has been justly criticized: their method of introspection was challenged as being based on subjective experience rather than observable data; their results were largely negative; they had no theory. However, they did show it was possible to study human thinking, and their work began to cast doubts on the foundations of the associationist philosophy, as their results showed:

Antiatomism—Preliminary reports indicated that the elements of thought change as they are combined.

Antimechanization—Evidence showed that thought is directed and guided by some human motive or purpose.

Antiempiricism—Evidence began to mount that experience is not reproduced or copied in the mind exactly as it occurs in the world.

Antiimagery—Images are particular, but the Wurzburgers found examples of general and abstract thought and also of "imageless thought."

SELZ: PSYCHOLOGY RECEIVES A THEORY OF THINKING

Although the early research of the Wurzburg group began to challenge associationist philosophy, alternative theories did not develop until the work of Otto Selz (1913/1982a, 1922/1982b). He used the method of introspection and examples like those shown in Box 1-1, but unlike his predecessors, he developed a theory independent of images and associations. The main concepts in Selz's theory were that the unit of thought is a structural complex of relations among thoughts rather than a string of particular responses and that the process of thinking involves filling in or completing a gap in the structural complex rather than following a chain of associations.

For example, in Benjamin Franklin's problem of how to bring electricity from a lightning bolt to the ground, Selz claimed the solution involved the development of a complex of ideas, in this case a kite as a means of producing contact between the earth and the storm clouds. The solution involved filling in the complex with "kite" to build an organized structure in which objects had certain relationships to each other. Thus thinking is simply the tendency of a "complex toward completion."

In Selz's writings (Frijda & de Groot, 1982), we find the beginnings of psychology's first nonassociationist theory of thinking. Selz's pioneering ideas are now recognized as anticipating some of the major concepts in modern cognitive psychology (Simon, 1982), including the following:

The unit of thought is the directed association. Selz argued that mental activity was based on directed associations rather than the simple associations of associationist philosophy. A directed association has two terms (such as dog and cat) and a specific relation between them (such as coordinate) and can be expressed as X is the R of Y (dog is the coordinate of cat); in contrast, a simple association involves only a connection between two terms, such as dog and cat and can be expressed as X is associated with Y (dog is associated with cat). Simon (1982, p. 151) points out that modern information-processing theories, especially computer-based simulations of human thinking, use directed rather than simple associations: "In replacing associations with directed associations, Selz achieved a fundamental insight into the requirements of memory for an information-processing system that would be capable of thinking like a human."

Understanding a problem involves forming a structure. Instead of taking the associationist view of thinking as an automatic chain of associations, Selz argued that thinking involved forming a relational structure that included the givens and the goal, such as "Dog—coordinate—_____?" Accordingly, thinking consists of finding a response term (i.e., dog) that completes the structure—a process that Selz called *schematic anticipation*. This idea is a forerunner of schema theories in modern cognitive psychology, such as those discussed in Chapter 8.

Solving a problem involves testing for conditions. Selz argued that mental processing was based on condition-action pairs, which he called *couplings*, rather than on stimulus-response associations. Thinking involves testing for a "specific condition of elicitation" and carrying out the appropriate "partial operation," with the success or failure of one operation serving as the condition for the next operation. Instead of saying "X is related to Y," thinking is driven by saying "*If* condition X is met, *then* carry out action Y." Simon (1982) notes that these ideas —although stated vaguely—foreshadowed *productions* and *means-ends analysis* in modern theories of thinking, as described in Chapter 6.

Unfortunately, Selz's career was cut short by Nazi policies in Europe that banned him from his profession and ultimately took his life. His works remained largely untranslated into English until recently (Frijda & de Groot, 1982).

MODERN PSYCHOLOGY: THINKING IS BANISHED, BASHED, AND REBORN

The next phase, which takes us from Otto Selz's unfinished work to the present, can be broken into three parts: behaviorism, Gestalt psychology, and the cognitive revolution. The rise of behaviorism in America during the 1910s, partly brought on as a reaction against the abuses of the method of introspection, emphasized the study of observable stimuli and observable responses only; to some psychologists this meant that internal mental events such as thinking could not be observed and therefore should not be studied in psychology. For forty years, American psychologists largely accepted J. B. Watson's "denial of the legitimacy of mental concepts such as thinking" and his call to "eradicate such terms as *thought* . . . from the whole of psychological theorizing" (Dellarosa, 1988, p. 6). Remnants of this approach can be found in Chapter 2.

While behaviorism was completing its stranglehold on the psychology of thinking in America, research on thinking was beginning in Germany by the Gestalt psychologists who were trying to take Selz's ideas one step further. The rise of Nazism during the 1930s put an end to the work of many Gestalt psychologists, although some did continue their work elsewhere, mostly in the United States. Chapter 3 summarizes the contributions of the Gestaltists to the psychology of thinking.

With the life of Gestalt psychology cut short, research on thinking did not reemerge on a large scale until what Gardner (1985) calls "the cognitive revolution." The development of electronic computers, cognitive theories of development and language, and a shift from studying laboratory animals to humans all converged to produce modern *cognitive psychology* during the late 1950s and 1960s. During the 1970s and 1980s, the scope was broadened by the emergence of *cognitive science* as an interdisciplinary study of cognition. For those interested in the psychology of thinking, Gardener (1985, pp. 4–5) paints an optimistic picture of the future:

> Today, armed with tools and concepts unimaginable even a century ago, a new cadre of thinkers called cognitive scientists has been investigating many of the same issues that first possessed the Greeks some twenty-five hundred years ago. . . . Proceeding well beyond armchair speculation, cognitive scientists are fully wedded to the use of empirical methods for testing their theories and their hypotheses, of making them susceptible to disconfirmation.

These events are summarized on Box 1-2.

BOX 1 • 2   Historical Events in the Psychology of Thinking

400 B.C.	Aristotle proclaims the doctrine of association by contiguity, similarity, and contrast.	
A.D. 1700	British associationists reformulate associationism.	
1800	1879. Wundt opens the first psychology laboratory, but thinking is not studied.	
1900	The Wurzburg group brings thinking into the laboratory, discovers imageless thought and determining tendencies.	
1910	1913. Selz proposes the first nonassociationist theory of thinking.	
1920	Behaviorism develops in America. Gestalt psychology develops in Germany.	
1930	Behaviorism stifles American research on thinking. Nazism destroys Gestalt psychology in Germany; some Gestaltists move to the United States.	
1940		
1950		
	Cognitive psychology is reborn.	
1960		
1970		
	Cognitive science emerges.	
1980		
1990		

EVALUATION

One major criticism of the early work in thinking is methodological. The method of introspection is a very difficult one since the experimenter must rely on the subject's self-reports. It fits the requirements of science only if we assume that the data are the subjects' reports rather than the subjects' experiences: the reports are observable for all to see and hear, but the experiences are not. The real problem is that these reports may not have much to do with the actual mental processes involved; that is, subjects may not be able to report on their own cognitive experiences accurately. Since the days of the early twentieth century, many clever methods have been developed to study thinking. In addition, the method of introspection has been ingeniously used and refined in recent work on computer simulation in an attempt to program computers to behave the way humans do during problem solving.

A second criticism of the early work in thinking is theoretical. The associationist theory of the philosophers was inconsistent with some of the findings of the Wurzburg group, but the early psychologists proposed no real alternative and Selz's theory was vague. The clash between the associationist theory and the pre-Gestalt work of Selz is still far from resolved, although many current theories such as information processing may be seen as compromises.

Finally, we are left with the question of legitimacy. Although there is currently a renewed interest in cognitive psychology, some question of the place of thinking and complex learning in psychology remains. Ultimately, the question of whether we can find out how the human mind works will be answered in the laboratory.

Suggested Readings

FRIJDA, N. H., & DE GROOT, A. D. (Eds.). (1982). *Otto Selz: His contribution to psychology.* The Hague: Mouton. An edited collection of Otto Selz's papers along with commentaries by contemporary cognitive psychologists.

GARDNER, H. (1985). *The mind's new science: A history of the cognitive revolution.* New York: Basic Books. A detailed but enjoyable history of the development of cognitive science.

HUMPHREY, G. (1963). *Thinking: An introduction to its experimental psychology.* New York: Wiley. An excellent introduction to the historical ideas and findings underlying modern cognitive psychology.

MANDLER, J. M., & MANDLER, G. (1964). *Thinking: From association to Gestalt.* New York: Wiley. A set of condensed readings from early studies in the psychology of thinking.

MAYER, R. E. (1981). *The promise of cognitive psychology.* New York: Freeman. (Reprinted in 1990 by University Press of America.) A brief overview of modern cognitive psychology.

CHAPTER · 2

ASSOCIATIONISM
Thinking as Learning by Reinforcement

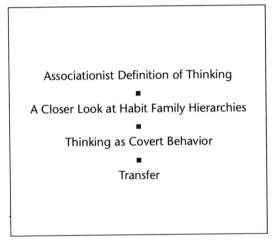

Associationist Definition of Thinking
■
A Closer Look at Habit Family Hierarchies
■
Thinking as Covert Behavior
■
Transfer

ANAGRAM TASK

Suppose someone gave you the following letters and asked you to rearrange them to form a word: GANRE. Get a piece of paper and work on this one.

There are two solutions to this anagram (that we know of). Most college students give the answer RANGE, and their median response time is about 8 seconds A less frequent answer is ANGER, which takes about 114 seconds (median solution time). If you cheated on GANRE, here's another to try before you read on: TARIL

This anagram also has two solutions, so try to find both. Don't read on until you have found both words or until you give up. The easiest answer seems to be TRAIL, which takes about 7 seconds, and the more difficult is TRIAL, which takes about 240 seconds.

For more anagrams and median solution times to amuse yourself and your friends, see Tresselt and Mayzner (1966). Anagrams like these have long been enjoyed as mental puzzles, but recently their solutions have been analyzed in psychological experiments. Since each five-letter anagram has 120 possible letter arrangements, solving anagrams may be viewed as trying arrangements until one works.*

PUZZLE BOX TASK

Another favorite task that has been studied closely involves problem solving in a puzzle box—a closed box with an escape hatch like the one shown in Box 2-1—in which an animal must perform a certain response to solve the problem. In 1898, Edward Thorndike published his famous monograph, "Animal Intelligence," in which he described the process of thinking and problem solving. Thorndike placed a cat into what he called a puzzle box; if the cat performed a certain response, such as clawing down a loop of string or pushing a lever, a trap door opened and allowed it to escape and eat food set out nearby. Thorndike supposed (correctly) that cats do not like being cooped up in a box and do like the chance to get out and have a snack.

From his observations of cats in the puzzle box, Thorndike developed a theory of thinking and problem solving that formed the basis for further ideas that we call in this book *associationist theories* of thinking. One of Thorndike's most famous observations was that his cats solved the puzzle box problem by trial and error—that is, they responded in a seemingly almost random fashion without much evidence at all of any thinking. The cat might meow, or squeeze a bar, or claw at a loose object, or jump onto things in the box until it would hit

---

* If you are baffled trying to figure out how there can be 120 possible arrangements for a five-letter anagram, then read this footnote: otherwise you can skip it. Suppose you have five letters, *a, b, c, d, e,* and five blank spaces to fit one letter each: — — — — —. Pick one letter and place it in any one of the five spaces; you have five choices as to where to put it. Let's say you pick the second blank: — *a* — — — . Now there are four spaces left for the next letter, so you have only four choices. Let's say you decide to put *b* in space five: — *a* — — *b*. No matter where you put a, you have four places to put *b*; and no matter where you put *b*, you have three places to put the next letter. You may pick the following arrangement: *c a* — — *b;* there are now two choices for the next letter. When you pick one, say *c a d* — *b*, there is one blank left for the last letter: *c a d e b*. Therefore, there are always 5 first choices, 4 second choices, 3 third choices, 2 fourth choices, and 1 last choice; this yields 5 x 4 x 3 x 2 x 1, or 120 ways to arrange five letters in five spaces. The number of ways to arrange X things in X spaces is called the number of permutations, and the general formula for calculating it is: Number of permutations = $X!$ The "!" is read "factorial" and simply means to multiply the number times one less than the number, times two less than the number, times three less, and so on down to one. In this example: $5! = 5 \times 4 \times 3 \times 2 \times 1 = 120$.

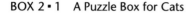

BOX 2 • 1   A Puzzle Box for Cats

"When put into the box the cat would show evident signs of discomfort and of impulse to escape from confinement. It tries to squeeze through any opening; it claws
and bites at the wire; it thrusts its paws out through any opening and claws at everything it reaches . . . . It does not pay very much attention to the food outside but
seems simply to strive instinctively to escape from confinement . . . . The cat that is
clawing all over the box in her impulsive struggle will probably claw the string or
loop or button so as to open the door. And gradually all the other unsuccessful im-
pulses will be stamped out and the particular impulse leading to the successful act
will be stamped in by the resulting pleasure, until, after many trials, the cat will, when
put in the box, immediately claw the button or loop in a definite way."

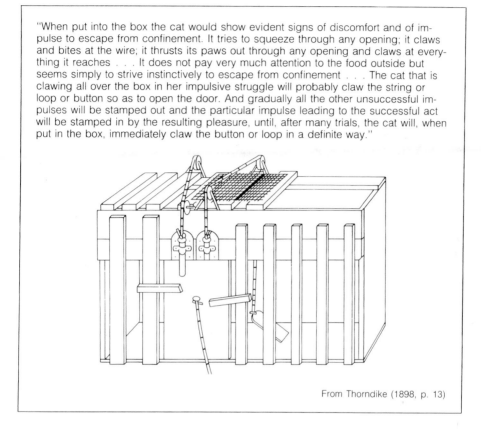

From Thorndike (1898, p. 13)

accidentally upon the required solution to open the escape hatch. Thorndike
observed that the next time the cat was put in the box, it still performed by *trial
and error*—by trying various responses until one accidentally worked—but as
practice increased the animal had a tendency to perform the responses that didn't
work less often and to perform the responses that did work sooner. Eventually,
after being placed in the box many times, the cat would go to the string and pull
it almost immediately. According to Thorndike, the cat was learning "by trial, and
error, and accidental success."

Both solving anagrams and the puzzle box task may require a subject to try
many responses until one solves the problem, and the thinking process may,
among other things, be conceived of as *response learning*.

■
ASSOCIATIONIST DEFINITION OF THINKING
■

TRIAL AND ERROR APPLICATION OF HABIT FAMILY HIERARCHY

According to the associationist view, thinking can be described as the trial and error application of the preexisting response tendencies called "habits." This view is called associationist because it assumes that for any problem situation, S, there are associations or links to many possible responses, R_1, R_2, R_3, and so on. Thus the three elements in an associationist theory of thinking are: the stimulus (a particular problem-solving situation), the responses (particular problem-solving behaviors), and the associations between a particular stimulus and a particular response. The links are assumed to be in the problem solver's head, where they form a family of possible responses associated with any given problem situation. In addition, the responses may vary in strength, with some associations being very strong and some being very weak. Thus the responses for any given situation may be put into a hierarchy in order of their strength.

A typical habit family hierarchy for Thorndike's puzzle box is shown in Box 2-2. A similar hierarchy could be constructed for behavior in the anagram problem since there are 120 possible responses for a five-letter anagram, some of which are initially stronger than others. In the problem-solving situation, the problem solver (either overtly or covertly) tries the most dominant response, R_1, in the habit family hierarchy for that situation and, if that fails, tries R_2, and so on until one works.

LAWS OF EXERCISE AND EFFECT

Two laws of learning, which Thorndike termed the *law of exercise* and the *law of effect*, are required to describe the solution process.

The *law of exercise* states that responses that have been previously practiced many times with a given situation are more likely to be performed when that situation is presented again, or, to state it another way, practice tends to increase the specific S-R link.

The *law of effect* states that responses to a problem that do not help solve the problem lose strength and are demoted in the hierarchy, while the responses that do solve the problem increase in strength and go up in the hierarchy until, after many trials, they reach the top.

BOX 2 • 2   Habit Family Hierarchy for Puzzle Box Problem

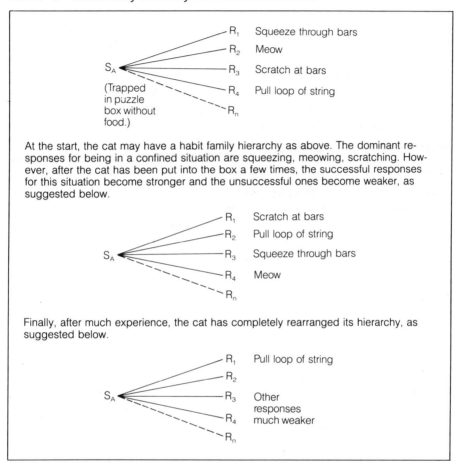

At the start, the cat may have a habit family hierarchy as above. The dominant responses for being in a confined situation are squeezing, meowing, scratching. However, after the cat has been put into the box a few times, the successful responses for this situation become stronger and the unsuccessful ones become weaker, as suggested below.

Finally, after much experience, the cat has completely rearranged its hierarchy, as suggested below.

Thus the associationists describe problem solving as the trial and error application of a thinker's existing habit family hierarchy. In a new situation, such as the puzzle box or anagrams, subjects try their most dominant response first, then their second strongest, and so on. Maltzman (1955) summarizes this view as follows: "thinking is not a response" but thinking results in a change in "a new combination of habit strengths" within a habit family hierarchy.

COVERT RESPONDING

Thorndike observed cats in his puzzle box and saw trial and error learning of solution responses. When the Gestalt psychologist Kohler (1925) presented similar problems to apes, he did not observe trial and error performance or activity at all but rather was sure that his animals solved by a flash of *insight*—as they thought about the problem, the solution suddenly fell into place. We shall talk more about the Gestalt interpretation of problem solving in Chapter 3, but it is puzzling that two psychologists observing a similar kind of problem-solving task in animals saw such different things and were inspired to develop such different theories.

Let's assume for a moment that both Thorndike and Kohler were correct, at least in their observations of trial and error learning and of insight. How would an associationist explain the phenomenon of insight? That question was solved by the associationists in an ingenious way. Sometimes, especially with humans, trial and error may be *covert*. In other words. people tend to try out various solutions *in their minds* (or sometimes even in their muscles). According to this view, thinking is simply covert action: thinking involves trying all the likely responses mentally until the one that will work is found. Since this form of the trial and error process cannot be seen, the solution therefore appears to be achieved suddenly, as by a flash of insight.

STEREOTYPED RESPONSES

Another premise of Thorndike's habit family hierarchy theory is that the responses are quite specific—the cat opens the door with the same movement each time. As a follow-up to Thorndike's famous observations, a more thorough study was conducted by Guthrie and Horton (1946) half a century later. These researchers filmed cats in a puzzle box and analyzed the behaviors of a given cat on each successive trial. Each specific behavior was carefully defined in detail, and the order of behaviors was tallied for each trial. The results showed that the movements of a given cat were almost identical for a particular response from trial to trial; for example, it pulled the string in the same way. Since the behaviors were stereotyped, Guthrie and Horton concluded that the cats had specific response tendencies that changed in strength during problem solving rather than general plans.

The habit family hierarchy or trial and error description proposed by Thorndike and by Guthrie and Horton for cats in the puzzle box has also been observed in human beings. For example, Ruger (1910) provided subjects with mechanical puzzles like the heart and bow problem shown in Box 2-3. At first the subjects tended to exhibit a series of apparently random behaviors, often not realizing what brought about the solution. Solution times fell from trial to trial, but the subjects in this experiment also tended to persist in using certain specific behaviors on several trials until finally only the successful twist response remained.

BOX 2 ▪ 3   The Heart and Bow Problem

The heart and bow problem is a typical mechanical puzzle used to study trial and error problem solving in humans. The problem is to disentangle the two pieces. Usually time to solution decreases for each successive trial since unsuccessful responses are weakened and the successful "twist" response becomes dominant.

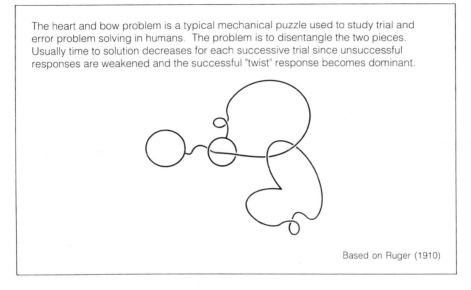

Based on Ruger (1910)

A CLOSER LOOK AT HABIT FAMILY HIERARCHIES

A few cats locked into puzzle boxes may not seem like much to build a theory of human problem solving upon. However, there is further evidence in support of the associationist theory, some of which has come from studying how people solve anagrams. One reason there has not been more research may be that the associationists have concentrated their efforts on the psychology of learning; you probably have sensed that Thorndike's theory is also the basis of theories of learning and memory. On the other hand, the Gestaltists—the main competitors of the associationists—have focused on the psychology of thinking and perception; their chapter will be longer than this one.

FAMILIARITY OF GOAL WORD

One nice thing about the S-R association representation of thinking is that it makes precise predictions that can be tested. For example, suppose you presented a subject with one of the five-letter anagrams shown in Box 2-4. Each way of arranging the letters can be considered a response in the habit family hierarchy. Of course, for any given subject some potential responses should be stronger than

BOX 2 • 4   Median Solution Times in Seconds for Selected Anagrams

Familiar Words	Time	Unfamiliar Words	Time
beahc *to* beach	3.0	hroac *to* roach	9.5
odelm *to* model	4.5	ypeon *to* peony	12.0
ntrai *to* train	5.0	patoi *to* patio	22.0
chari *to* chair	10.0	tanog *to* tango	45.0
ugars *to* sugar	10.5	obrac *to* cobra	50.5

Low LTP Anagrams	Time	High LTP Anagrams	Time
rhtae *to* heart	28.5	ahter *to* heart	168.5
oeshr *to* shore	8.5	osher *to* shore	39.0
ietdr *to* tried	18.0	dteri *to* tried	71.0
aephs *to* phase	11.0	hesap *to* phase	115.5
aecrt *to* crate	18.0	atcer *to* crate	48.5

Familiar words occur 100 times per million or more, and unfamiliar words occur one or fewer times per million. Both familiar and unfamiliar word solutions require moving only one letter, yet familiar words are generally easier, presumably because they are higher in the habit family hierarchy. Solving anagrams made of pairs of letters that seldom occur together (low letter transition probability, or low LTP) is generally easier than high LTP anagrams for the same solution words, presumably due to the difficulty in breaking up dominant letter pairs.

Based on Tresselt and Mayzner (1966)

others and thus higher on the hierarchy and more likely to be tried. The solution for an anagram, should come faster if the solution is a common word.

To test this prediction, Mayzner and Tresselt (1958, 1966) constructed anagrams based on rearranging either common five-letter words or uncommon five-letter words in the same way. To measure how common a word was, they used the lists compiled by Thorndike and Lorge (1944) that contained a tally of how many times each of 30,000 words appeared in books, magazines, newspapers, and other randomly selected printed sources. Mayzner and Tresselt found that anagrams were generally solved more than twice as fast if the solution word occurred frequently in print—more than 100 times per million words—than if it occurred infrequently. Examples are given in Box 2-4. For example, TANGO, PEONY, or COBRA, which occurred less than once per million words, took much more time to solve than CHAIR, SUGAR, or TRAIN, which occurred more than 100 times per million. In addition, with anagrams that have two solutions, such as TABLE (more than 100 per million) and BLEAT (7 per million), the more common word was usually found first. These results are consistent with the idea of habit family hierarchy, since the most dominant response—assuming past experience with word frequencies influences dominance—occurred before the weaker response in problem solving.

LETTER TRANSITION PROBABILITY OF GOAL WORD

The associationist theory also predicts that past experience with the way one letter usually follows another letter should influence the response hierarchy. Certain letter pairs have high *transition probabilities* because the second letter often follows the first in normal English words, such as *ch, th, es,* and others. Since each five-letter word has four successive pairs of letters, word transition probabilities can be generated for them based on how common each of the four two-letter pairs are in ordinary English (Mayzner & Tresselt, 1959, 1962, 1966). For example, RANCH, TRAIN, and BEACH contain letters in a more common order (higher transition probability) than ENJOY, KNIFE, and TRIBE. In general, solution words with high letter transition probabilities are solved faster than those with low. Again, these results are consistent with the idea that problem solving involves trial and error rearrangement of the letters based on 120 responses, but beginning with the most dominant responses first.

NUMBER OF MOVES

The order of letters in anagrams influences problem solving (Mayzner & Tresselt, 1958, 1963). This finding is consistent with the finding that dominant responses are given first. In general, the fewer the number of letters that must be moved, the faster the solution. If two solution words are possible, such as TABLE and BLEAT, or ANGER and RANGE, the order in which the anagram letters are presented can influence which word is discovered. Again, subjects tend to make dominant responses such as moving just one or two letters first; if that doesn't work, they try weaker responses such as moving all five letters.

LETTER TRANSITION PROBABILITY OF PRESENTED WORD

Finally, a fourth typical result with anagram problem solving is that if the anagram is already in the form of a word or if it has a high transition probability, it is more difficult to solve than if it is in the form of a nonsense syllable or if it has a low transition probability (Mayzner & Tresselt, 1959; Devnich, 1937; Beilin & Horn, 1962). Typical results are given in Box 2-4. For example, discovery of KANGAROO is generally easier if the subject is given OAG KRNOA than if given AGO KORAN. Beilin and Horn's subjects required about 17 seconds to solve word anagrams like CAUSE to SAUCE but only 9 seconds for nonsense anagrams matched for frequency and other variables, such as ERTEN to ENTER. Mayzner and Tresselt (1966) also found that going from low transition probability words as anagrams (BOARD, TRIAL, ANGER, EARTH) to high transition probability solution words (BROAD, TRAIL, RANGE, HEART) was much easier than the reverse. However, Dominowski and Duncan (1964) found that anagrams with high transition probabilities (such as NILEN, GSEAT, HECAB) were more difficult than low transition probabilities (such as LNNIE, TSGAE, AEBHC) only when the solution words had high transition probabilities (LINEN, STAGE, BEACH). In general, these results seem to indicate that subjects have trouble breaking up letter combinations that occur frequently together. This kind of inflexibility can be compared to what the Gestaltists call rigidity or mental set. In the anagram experiments, subjects try the dominant response of rearranging loose letters first before they begin on the more complex responses, which involve breaking up frequent letter combinations.

In summary, experiments with anagrams offer four different lines of support for the idea that problem solving involves trial and error application of a subject's habit family hierarchy. With many possible ways to arrange a five-letter anagram, it is clear that subjects do not try solutions at random but rather begin with the most dominant responses and go on to the weaker ones if those don't work. Thus frequently used words, high transition probability solution words, words that require only minor rearrangement, or words that do not require breaking up a combination of high transition probability letters are solved more quickly than others.

PROBLEM-SOLVING SET

In solving problems, not only is the general past experience of a subject important in determining the response hierarchy, but so are his or her experiences just prior to and during problem solving. These experiences form the subject's *problem-solving set.*

For example, Rees and Israel (1935) gave subjects ambiguous anagrams that could be solved by either one or two words. When the subjects were instructed to look for a certain type of word, such as "nature words," they found more words in this category than the subjects in a control group found. Subjects who found a high number of nature words in one block of anagrams were also more likely to find more nature words in the next block than were the controls. Maltzman and Morrisett (1952, 1953) also found that giving instructions to look for a certain class of words to subjects who had previous experience with anagrams soluble by that set strongly influenced the solutions of the ambiguous anagrams in the direction of the set.

Safren (1962) used two methods of dividing thirty-six anagrams into six sets of six anagrams each. In one grouping, solution words often associated with one another (like MILK, CREAM, SUGAR, COFFEE, SWEET, and DRINK) appeared on the same list. The other grouping of anagrams was in unorganized lists, with the associated words appearing on each of the six different lists. Overall, the median solution time for the organized lists was about 7 seconds, compared with 12 seconds when the same anagrams were presented in separate lists.

In terms of the response hierarchy framework, these results indicate that several different habit family hierarchies (or response hierarchies) may exist for a given problem. According to Maltzman (1955, p. 281), problem solving "may involve the selection of habit family hierarchies as well as the selection of specific response sequences within a hierarchy." Thus the response hierarchy shown in Box 2-2 must now be changed into a "compound habit family hierarchy" to account for the effects of set. Thinking about nature words may lead to response hierarchy A, thinking about beverage words may lead to hierarchy B, thinking about no particular category of words may lead to hierarchy C, and so on.

■
THINKING AS COVERT BEHAVIOR
■

MEDIATION

The idea that thinking involves a chain of covert responses has led to changes in the traditional associationist idea that a stimulus (S) goes in, a response (R) comes out, and everything that goes on in between can be summarized by a hyphen (S-R). How, then, does the habit family hierarchy change? Or, to put it another way, what comes between, or *mediates* between, the overt problem-solving situation (S) and the solution response (R)? A mediational theory suggests that the S evokes a miniature internal response called a *mediational response* or r_m; the r_m creates a new internal state or s_m, this new s_m may evoke another different r_m followed by a new s_m and so on until an s_m finally evokes an overt solution response, R. For example, Berlyne (1965) presents a comprehensive mediational theory based on the principle that thinking is a chain of symbolic responses; thus, the "train of thought" may be represented as a series of internal responses and stimuli mediating an S and R:

$$S - r_{m1} - s_{m1} - r_{m2} - s_{m2} - r_{m3} - s_{m3} - \ldots - r_{mn} - s_{mn} - R$$

The capital S is the overt problem situation, the capital R is the overt response, and the lowercase s's and r's represent internal covert responses and stimulus situations.

Mediational theories such as Berlyne's are generally extensions of Hull's (1943) claim that animals make tiny responses in anticipation of the goal as they learn to solve a maze; he called these responses "fractional goal responses." For example, rats made miniature licking movements as they ran down a maze toward a liquid reward. These fractional goal responses helped the animal mediate between being put in the maze and performing the needed solution behavior. Kendler and Kendler (1962a, 1962b) used the idea of mediating responses to describe developmental changes in discrimination learning; Osgood (1957, 1966) used "mediating reaction" to explain the human use of language meanings; and Underwood (1965) developed "implicit associative responses" to explain the course of human verbal learning. These theories are examples of mediational theory because they are based on the idea that tiny, covert responses mediate between a stimulus and a response.

TWO VIEWS OF COVERT THINKING

There are various ways to interpret how covert or mediational responses relate to the habit family hierarchy approach to thinking. A relatively liberal interpretation, such as that cited by Maltzman (1955), is that the habit family hierarchy represents a set of dispositions and that thinking can be conceived of as changes in the state of the hierarchy. According to this view, thinking is not a chain of responses, but "responses may be taken as a criterion or manifestation of thinking" (p. 282). In other words, covert responses may occur as a result of thinking, but they are not equivalent to thinking.

A more strict and literal interpretation that is probably less popular today than the one just given is that thinking *is* covert responding, especially covert verbal responding. This view received serious attention during the 1920s and 1930s because it was consistent with the behaviorist revolution in psychology—the idea that psychologists must study only what can be directly observed (behavior) and should not hypothesize about unseen phenomena (thoughts). One focus of this interest was to determine where in the human body the covert responses occur: the peripheralists tended to study muscle changes during thinking because they claimed that responses occurred in the muscles; the centralists tended to study electrical brain activity during thinking because they claimed that responses occurred in the brain.

PERIPHERAL THEORY: MUSCLE ACTIVITY

The behaviorist psychologist Watson (1930) claimed that since human problem solving involves language, silent thinking is subvocal speech. In other words, thinking is simply "talking to oneself," and the locus of thinking behavior should be in the muscles related to talking. For example, Jacobson (1932) measured electrical activity in the muscles of human subjects during various periods of intellectual activity. When the subjects were relaxed and not concentrating on anything, their muscles showed little electrical activity. However, when he asked them to *think* about picking up a heavy object with their left hands, changes occurred in readings for muscles in their left arms. Similarly, when Jacobson asked a subject to imagine a certain object, he noted increased electrical activity from the muscles around the eyes.

Max (1935, 1937) investigated the muscle activity of deaf mutes when they were thinking. Since his subjects normally used sign language to communicate, he thought that perhaps subvocal speech could be detected by changes in electrical activity in the arm muscles even if no overt signs were made. As Max expected, he did find increased electrical activity in the arm muscles of these deaf mute subjects when they were thinking about how to solve a problem or about a past conversation, and even when they were asleep and apparently dreaming.

Although the peripheral theory of thinking has not received much attention since Max's interesting study, McGuigan (1966, 1973) has done further work on the subject. For example, McGuigan, Keller, and Stanton (1964) measured the muscle activity of students while they read silently. As these researchers predicted, changes occurred in chin and lip muscle activity and in the breathing rates of the students during the reading period but not during rest. Unfortunately, a major problem with this study, as with earlier studies by the peripheralists, is that muscle changes may be caused by the awareness of the subjects that they are being studied or by factors other than thinking. McGuigan (1966) has suggested that a more convincing test of the peripheralist theory might be to inject subjects with a chemical (curare) that numbs both the smooth and the skeletal muscles and then ask them to solve problems. If injected subjects were still able to solve problems, it would follow that something must be wrong with the theory that thinking occurs in the muscles.

The peripheral correlates of thinking are not limited to muscle movements in speech. Another behavior that seems related to thinking is *laterality of gaze*—the direction in which your eyes gaze when you answer a question. For example, suppose you are asked a question that required a moment's reflection before answering. As you think about the question, you might briefly gaze to one side. Kinsbourne (1972) has hypothesized that the direction of the gaze is related to which side of the brain is being most heavily used. A gaze to the right indicates that the problem solver is using the left side of the brain, an area that may be specialized for verbal and mathematical thinking; a gaze to the left indicates that the responder is using the right side of the brain, an area that may be specialized for spatial thinking.*

---

* In some subjects, such as most left-handed subjects, the brain functions are specialized in the reverse order, that is, left for spatial and right for verbal. For additional information about brain lateralization, see Wittrock's (1980) *The Brain and Psychology* or Kolb and Whishaw's (1990) *Fundamentals of Human Neuropsychology*.

To test these ideas, Kinsbourne observed subjects' gazes as they answered difficult questions. Some questions were verbal, such as having to explain a proverb. These questions tended to elicit gazes to the right, suggesting that the left side of the brain was being used. Some questions were spatial, such as deciding which way the Indian faces on a nickel. These questions tended to elicit gazes to the left, suggesting that the right half of the brain was being used. Similar results obtained by Kocel, Galin, Ornstein, and Merrin (1972) support Kinsbourne's theory.

However, before you try these experiments on your friends, you should know that the methodology and theory are still far from perfect. First, there are individual differences among subjects, with some people "preferring" to gaze right (or left) regardless of the type of question (Bakan, 1969). Second, results may be influenced if you emphasize that you are watching eye gazes, if you stand in front rather than behind the subject, or if you ask complex questions. These events seem to increase the anxiety of the subject, and when the subject is anxious you can destroy the usefulness of the very sensitive measure of laterality of gaze (Ehrlichman, Weiner, & Baker, 1974; Gur, Gur, & Harris, 1975). Although there have been attempts to relate work on brain lateralization to practical issues in learning and problem solving (for example, Wittrock, 1980), the underlying theory concerning laterality of gaze is still vague.

CENTRALIST THEORY: BRAIN ACTIVITY

The next logical step is to look for thinking inside the brain. In a review of the role of the brain in problem solving, Holyoak (1990, p. 126) points to the frontal lobes of the cerebral cortex—including the area behind the forehead—as having "special importance in problem solving." People with damage to their frontal lobes, while showing no impairment on IQ tests, perform poorly on tasks that

BOX 2 • 5   The Tower of London Problem

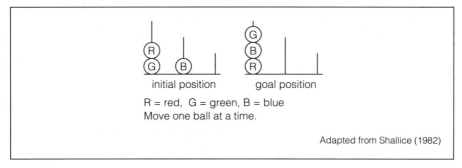

initial position   goal position

R = red, G = green, B = blue
Move one ball at a time.

Adapted from Shallice (1982)

BOX 2 • 6   Proposed Lateralization of Cognitive Activities

Left Hemisphere (Verbal)	Right Hemisphere (Spatial)
Seeing words	Seeing pictures
Hearing words	Hearing music
Remembering words	Remembering pictures
Reading books	Reading maps
Solving arithmetic problems	Solving geometry problems
Writing words	Drawing pictures

Modified from Kolb and Whishaw (1990, p. 373)

involve planning, executing, and monitoring a series of actions (Stuss & Benson, 1986) and on tasks requiring a novel answer (Shallice, 1988).

To test planning in problem solving, Shallice (1982, 1988) asked brain-damaged patients to solve the Tower of London problem, as shown in Box 2-5. The task is to change the problem from the initial position (i.e., red ball on top of green ball on the first peg and blue ball on second peg) to the goal position (i.e., green ball on top of blue ball on top of red ball on first peg) by moving one ball at a time (placing no more than one ball on the third peg, two balls on the second peg, and three balls on first peg). Patients with damage to their left frontal lobe performed more poorly on this task than patients with other forms of brain damage; frontal-lobe damage was related to difficulty in control of cognition processes, including inability to establish and maintain a series of subgoals.

To test originality in problem solving, Shallice and Evans (1978) asked brain-damaged patients to answer questions that required thinking, such as, "How fast do horses gallop?" or "How long is an average man's spine?" Patients with frontal-lobe damage gave more bizarre answers than patients with brain damage in other areas. Using a similar procedure, Smith and Milner (1984) asked patients to estimate the cost of toys, such as a toy trumpet or a cup. Patients with damage to the right frontal lobe produced more bizzare answers than patients with damage to other areas of the brain.

Kolb and Whishaw (1990) summarize evidence indicating that damage to the frontal lobe of the right hemisphere is more strongly related to decrements in visual problem solving, while damage to the frontal lobe of the left hemisphere is more strongly related to decrements in verbal problem solving. Based on a summary of research on brain-damaged people, Box 2-6 shows the dominant hemisphere (for most right-handers) for some typical cognitive activities (Kolb & Whishaw, 1990).* For example, typical spatial cognition tasks require a person to mentally rotate an object or visualize a scene from someone else's perspective. In a review of clinical reports, Kolb and Whishaw (1990, p. 662) conclude that "right hemisphere damage results in more frequent and more obvious spatial deficits than left hemisphere damage." Similarly, specific language difficulties are associated with damage to specific areas of the left hemisphere. For example, when asked to name a picture of an anchor, a person suffering from *aphasia*—damage to a language area of the brain—may say "I know what it does . . . you use it to anchor a ship" but still may not be able to produce the name "anchor" (Kolb & Whishaw, 1990, p. 578).

Does research on brain-damaged people prove that thinking is nothing more than chemical-electrical activity in a specific portion of the brain? Unfortunately, the emerging field of *cognitive neuroscience,* concerned with identifying the neurological basis of cognition, has focused more on language, visual, and motor performance than on problem solving (Cacioppo & Tassinary, 1990; Coles, Donchin, & Porges, 1986). However, it is doubtful that finding the biological site of thinking in the brain would eliminate the need for a psychological theory of thinking.

The search for the biological site of thinking has been aided by an ever-increasing set of sophisticated techniques for measuring physiological correlates of mental activity, including some that focus on the electrical activity of brain neurons (Brandeis & Lehmann, 1986; Kutas & Hillyard, 1984; Squires & Ollo, 1986) and on blood flow in the brain (Roland, Eriksson, Stone-Elander, & Widen, 1987; Roland & Friberg, 1985). Although a complete review of psychophysiological research is beyond the scope of this book, let's briefly explore the usefulness of recording electrical brain activity during cognitive tasks.

In order to record general brain activity, electrodes are placed on the scalp. These electrodes can record gross changes in electrical brain activity, analogous to estimating changes in the flow of freeway traffic by listening from an overpass. An electroencephalogram (EEG) is a record of electrical brain activity over a period of time; event-related potentials (ERPs) are changes in electrical activity associated with specific stimulus or response events (Allison, Wood, & McCarthy, 1986). In many problem-solving tasks, such as deciding if two stimuli are the same, the following sequence of ERP components has been identified (Coles et al., 1986; Donchin & Coles, 1988; Donchin & Israel, 1980; John & Schwartz, 1978):

---

* It is incorrect to assume that language and mathematical thinking cannot occur in the right hemisphere or that spatial thinking cannot occur in the left hemisphere; Kolb and Whishaw (1990) warn that "the question of what is lateralized does not have a simple or generally accepted answer" (p. 375) and that "laterality is relative, not absolute because both hemispheres play a role in nearly every behavior" (p. 347).

BOX 2 • 7   Event-Related Potentials (ERPs)

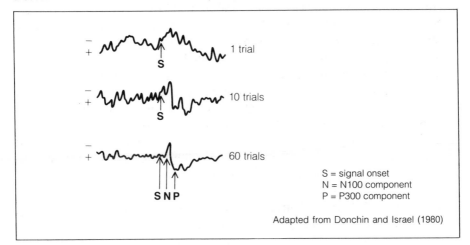

1 trial

10 trials

60 trials

S N P

S = signal onset
N = N100 component
P = P300 component

Adapted from Donchin and Israel (1980)

Contingent negative variation refers to a slowly increasing negativity that occurs in expectation of the stimulus.

N100 refers to an increase in negative potential that occurs about 100 milliseconds after the problem is presented and may reflect the initial arrival of the information in short-term memory.

P300 refers to an increase in positive potential that occurs about 300 milliseconds after a problem is presented. This component may reflect a sort of "aha!" experience in which the problem solver understands the significance of the information; evidence suggests that "P300 is a manifestation of activity occurring whenever one's model of the environment must be revised" (Donchin & Coles, 1988, p. 355).

Box 2-7 shows a typical EEG recording for the presentation of a stimulus generated by averaging one, ten, and sixty trials. The arrows show the point at which the stimulus was presented, followed by an increase in negative activity and then an increase in positive activity. As you can see, the sequence of ERP components is much clearer when activity is averaged over many trials.

Donchin and Israel (1980), following earlier work (Sutton, Braren, Zubin, & John, 1965), point out that there are two basic kinds of ERP components. *Exogenous components* are obligatory responses to the stimulus based on activation of the sense organs. *Endogenous components* are not obligatory and are related to internal cortical processing imposed by the demands of the task. For example, the P300 component and other late positive components are influenced by the amount of information and instructions in the problem. In a typical study (Heffley, Wickens, & Donchin, 1978), subjects watched a screen with moving geometrical figures and counted the number of times one of those objects increased in brightness (that is, flashed). For example, a subject might be asked to count the number of times that a square flashed but to ignore a flashing triangle. In this study, there was a strong P300 component for the target stimulus—when a square flashed—but almost no change in potential for the ignored stimulus—when a triangle flashed. Thus the P300 component seems to be an endogenous component that is related to internal processing rather than an immediate sensory response. Interestingly, the typical P300 component is not found in children with learning disabilities (Preston, Guthrie, & Childs, 1974; Shields, 1973) or patients with frontal-lobe brain damage (Knight, 1984; Shallice, 1988).

You may be tempted to suppose that we will soon be able to describe thinking as a specific chain of electrical changes, clearly localized in the brain. However, John and Schwartz (1978) point out that it is "experimentally and logically untenable" to try to locate specific cells or brain areas that correspond directly to specific thoughts. Instead, the global or Gestalt aspects of the nervous system need to be taken into account. John and Schwartz conclude that "the neurophysiology of information processing and cognition is still in the early stages of infancy. . . . Much work remains to be done, even at the level of defining questions that are to be asked and experimental techniques that are to be used" (1978, p. 25). Thus it seems unlikely that an analysis of brain activity will provide a definitive theory of human thinking, although such work provides an increasingly important approach.

McGuigan (1966) has suggested that since the centralist theory predicts that electrical stimulation of specific brain neurons should cause spontaneous thinking, further research using these new techniques is needed. McGuigan concluded: "If the peripheralist theory that thinking is a behavioral phenomena is confirmed, thinking can be studied directly by recording responses. . . . If the centralist theory is confirmed . . . brain events can often be indirectly studied by recording their consequent responses. . . . In either case we should get on with the measurement of covert responses" (pp. 294–295). At this time, most psychologists assume biological bases for thinking and concede that physiological changes are probably correlated with thinking, but very few are willing to accept the extreme position that physiological activity *is* thinking.

■

TRANSFER

■

The aspect of Thorndike's work that has perhaps the greatest implications for the psychology of thinking concerns the nature of *transfer*. Transfer refers to the effects of prior learning on new learning, such as the effects of learning to solve addition problems on the ease of learning to solve multiplication problems. If learning task A helps you to learn task B (as compared to learning B without A), we have a case of *positive transfer*. Conversely, if learning task A hurts your learning of task B (as compared to learning B without A), then we have *negative transfer*. The main focus of Thorndike's work concerned whether positive transfer occurred because specific elements in A and B were identical (called *specific transfer*) or because learning A provided a general cognitive skill that also somehow helped in learning B (called *general transfer*).

Thorndike's theory of *transfer through identical elements* is quite specific: positive transfer occurs because some of the elements in the to-be-learned task (B) are identical to elements that the learner has already learned from a previous task (A). For example, consider the situation of learning Latin and then learning something else such as French: "One mental function or activity improves others . . . because it contains elements in common to them. . . . [K]nowledge of Latin gives increased ability to learn French because many of the facts learned in one case are needed in the other" (Thorndike, 1906, pp. 243–248). In contrast, the *doctrine of formal discipline,* the prevailing view when Thorndike began his work, proposed that transfer was quite general: studying subjects such as Latin and geometry taught "proper habits of mind" that would improve a person's ability to learn and think in general (Mayer, 1987a; Singley & Anderson, 1989).

In order to determine whether transfer was specific or general, Thorndike conducted a series of experiments. For example, in one study he compared students who took Latin and students who did not take Latin on the learning of other subjects, finding no differences (Thorndike & Woodworth, 1901). Follow-up studies showed that learning supposedly mind-broadening subjects such as Latin and geometry in high school had no greater effect on solving various reasoning problems than taking less celebrated subjects such as bookkeeping and shopwork (see Singley & Anderson, 1989, p. 25). Even within a subject domain, Thorndike (1922) found evidence that students who learned to solve one kind of algebra problem—such as factoring $(x^2 - y^3)$—were much more likely to have difficulty when the problem was presented in a different format—such as $1/x^3 - 1/y^2$.

Although Thorndike's research helped to put the doctrine of formal discipline to rest, contemporary theories of thinking are still haunted by what Singley and Anderson (1989, p. 24) call "the ghost of general transfer." After nearly a century of empirical research on transfer, Singley and Anderson (1989, p. 25) were forced to conclude that "the evidence for the existence of general transfer is not good." In spite of this, the "elusive search" (Mayer, 1987a, p. 327) for transferable aspects of problem-solving skill continues—as will be seen later in our review of the Gestalt concept of productive thinking (Chapter 3), discussion of cognitive skills (Chapter 6), examination of the teaching of thinking skills (Chapter 12), and analysis of thinking by example (Chapter 14).

■

EVALUATION

■

The associationist approach offers a means of representing thinking and problem solving that allows for clear predictions. Perhaps for this reason, associationist concepts are reappearing in some contemporary theories of human learning and thinking. Examples of contemporary associationist theories include production system models that describe cognitive skills (Chapter 6) and parallel distributed processing models that describe cognitive processing (Chapter 6). In addition, advances in *cognitive neuroscience*—the study of the biological bases of cognition—may eventually clarify the nature of covert responding during thinking.

However, the associationist approach may fail to capture the full-blown powers of creative human thought: Is all thinking simply the trial and error application of past habits? Some kinds of thinking can be explained by the response hierarchy model, but there seems to be much more to human thinking than trial and error. The following chapters explore some other theories and possibilities.

Suggested Readings

DUNCAN, C. P. (Ed.). (1967). *Thinking: Current experimental studies*. Philadelphia: Lippincott. Contains classic research on anagrams.

MCGUIGAN, F. J., & SCHOONOVER, R. A. (1973). *The psychophysiology of thinking*. New York: Academic Press. A book of readings concerning early research on cognitive correlates of thinking.

THORNDIKE, E. L. (1911). *Animal intelligence*. New York: Macmillan. Describes Thorndike's classic research on cats in puzzle boxes.

SHALLICE, T. (1988). *From neuropsychology to mental structure*. Cambridge, England: Cambridge University Press. Summarizes recent research on the biological bases of thinking.

GESTALT

Thinking as Restructuring Problems

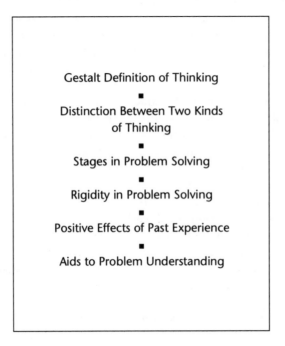

Gestalt Definition of Thinking

▪

Distinction Between Two Kinds
of Thinking

▪

Stages in Problem Solving

▪

Rigidity in Problem Solving

▪

Positive Effects of Past Experience

▪

Aids to Problem Understanding

REORGANIZATION TASKS

Suppose you were given six identical matchsticks and asked to make four identical, equilateral triangles with them. Find six matchsticks (or toothpicks) and try it. What are you doing? According to the Gestalt psychologists, you are trying to *reorganize* the problem-solving elements—in this case, the six sticks—so they fit together in a new way.

An important contribution of the Gestaltists is the idea that people get stuck solving problems because they cannot change their *problem-solving set*—since they cannot look at the situation in a new way, they cannot see a new way to fit the elements together. For example, when trying to solve the six-stick problem, many people have trouble changing their problem-solving set from two dimensions to three. Giving a hint like this (or as some Gestaltists have called it, giving *direction*) is important in problem solving because it helps people to break out of their old ways of organizing the situation. The new way of looking at this problem afforded by thinking in three dimensions is called *insight*—the sudden flash that occurs when you finally see how to fit the sticks together. Some Gestaltists have pointed out that the solution and flash of insight are often accompanied by the exclamation, "aha!", although critics have questioned the existence of insight (Weisberg, 1986).

If you still have not solved the problem, leave it for a while and come back to it later. This process is called *incubation*. Although it has been difficult to verify incubation in experimental research (Olton, 1979; Olton & Johnson, 1976), proponents claim that the time lapse allows confusing ideas to be forgotten. See if this helps you, but if you cannot solve it, then you may "cheat" by looking at Box 3-1.

Let's try another example. Wolfgang Kohler, one of the founders of the Gestalt school of psychology, spent the years of 1913 to 1917 at an animal research station on the island of Tenerife in the Atlantic Ocean. Determined not to waste his time as war raged in Europe, Kohler studied problem solving in the island's most willing subjects, some chimpanzees. Eventually he published a monograph on his research, *The Mentality of Apes* (1925). Here was a typical problem as he reported it: given that you are an ape in a cage, that there are some crates in your cage, and that there is a banana hanging from the ceiling out of reach, how do you get the banana?

What Kohler wanted was for the apes to place the crates on top of each other to form a stairway to the banana. This solution, like the solution to the six-stick problem, required that the problem elements be reorganized. Kohler reported that solutions were preceded by a period of intense thinking by the ape, followed by what appeared to be a flash of insight.

These two problems—the six-stick problem and Kohler's banana problem—are examples of the type of problem solving the Gestalt psychologists tried to understand. Their problems usually supply all the needed parts—either in the form of pieces of information or as concrete objects—and the solver's task is to arrange them in a certain way to solve the problem. The Gestaltists felt that these kinds of problems involved creative or novel solutions—although some later evidence has indicated that without appropriate past experience (in the case of the apes, for example, moving crates) such problems cannot be solved (Birch, 1945).

BOX 3 • 1   The Six-Stick Problem

The Problem

Given six sticks, arrange them to form four triangles that are equilateral and with each side one stick long.

The Solution

Some subjects take the six sticks,

and form a square with an X in it, such as,

However, this solution is not acceptable because the triangles are not equilateral—each has a 90 degree angle. In order to solve the problem, the solver must think in three dimensions, making a pyramid with a triangle base. For example, an overhead view is,

with the middle point raised from the triangle base.

■

GESTALT DEFINITION OF THINKING
■

What is problem solving? According to Gestalt psychologists, the process of problem solving is a search to relate each aspect of a problem situation to each, and it results in *structural understanding*—the ability to comprehend how all the parts of the problem fit together to satisfy the requirements of the goal. This involves *reorganizing* the elements of the problem situation in a new way so that they solve the problem.

Thus, although the Gestaltists limit themselves to one class of problems and use certain imprecise terms such as "insight" and "structural understanding," they are trying to comprehend and explain a very high level and creative type of mental process. Their emphasis on *organization*—on how elements fit together to form a *structure*—is consistent with the contributions of the Gestalt psychologists to the study of perception. The famous laws of perceptual organization, for

BOX 3 • 2   Differences Between Gestalt and Associationist Theories

	Associationist	Gestalt
1. Type of Task	Reproductive	Productive
2. Mental Activity	Try stimulus-response links	Reorganize elements
3. Unit of Thought	Stimulus-response links	Organizations
4. Detail of Theory	Precise	Vague

example, were based on the Gestalt idea that perception involves the mind imposing an order or structure on incoming stimuli.

The differences between the Gestalt approach to thinking and the associationist approach are summarized in Box 3-2. These two approaches do not deal with the same kinds of problems—Gestaltists are concerned with creating novel solutions to new situations, while the associationists are concerned with applying solution habits from past experience. Where the Gestalt theory views thinking as rearranging problem elements, the associationist view is that problem solving involves trying possible solutions until one works. In analyzing thinking into its component parts, the Gestaltists rely on mental structures or organizations as the unit of thought, while the associationists describe thinking in terms of associations among stimuli and responses. And finally, although the Gestaltists deal with a more complicated kind of thinking than do the associationists, their theory is more vague and thus more difficult to test scientifically.

■
DISTINCTION BETWEEN TWO KINDS OF THINKING
■

One of the basic concepts in the Gestalt approach is that there are two kinds of thinking. One, based on creating a new solution to a problem, is called *productive* thinking because a new organization is produced; the other, based on applying past solutions to a problem, is called *reproductive* thinking because old habits or behaviors are simply reproduced. The distinction between productive and reproductive thinking (Maier, 1945; Wertheimer, 1959) has also been called a distinction between "insight" and "trial and error" (Kohler, 1925, 1929), "meaningful apprehension of relations" versus "senseless drill and arbitrary associations" (Katona, 1940), and "structural understanding" versus "rote memory" (Wertheimer, 1959). Unfortunately, however, the Gestaltists have never clarified their various distinctions, have often confused differences in instructional method with differences in a subsequent problem-solving approach, and have provided little or questionable empirical support for their claims.

The flavor of the Gestalt distinction between productive and reproductive thinking can be found in an example by Wertheimer suggesting two methods of teaching students how to find the area of a parallelogram. One method emphasizes the geometrical or structural property—the triangle on one end of the figure could be placed on the other end of the figure, thus forming a rectangle (see Box 3-3). The other method emphasizes a sort of recipe of steps to calculate the area by dropping the perpendicular and multiplying its height times the length of the base.

Although students taught by both methods should perform equally well on criterion tasks that involve finding the area of parallelograms like those they had learned about, Wertheimer reported that they differed in their ability to transfer what they had learned to new tasks. For example, the students who learned "by understanding" (the first method) were able to find the areas of unusual parallelograms and shapes and to recognize uncalculable situations such as are shown in the figure, while the students who learned in a mechanical way (the second method) usually said something like, "We haven't had this yet."

In an example of memorizing digit strings, Katona (1940) claimed that learning by "understanding the structural relationships" not only improved subjects' ability to transfer but also improved their ability to retain information over time. He had one group learn the digit string 581215192226 by understanding the structural pattern of, "add 3, add 4" as indicated by the organization 5-8-12-15-19-22-26, while another group learned by rote memorization of the string organized as 581-215-192-226. Although both groups performed equally well on immediate retention, Katona reported that the first group remembered the string longer.

Katona (1940) provided another set of problem-solving situations in the form of card tricks and matchstick problems. A typical card trick problem (trick 3 in the series) involved figuring out how to arrange eight cards in such a way that if the subject dealt the top card of the deck face up on the table, put the next card from the remaining seven in the pack at the bottom without determining what it was, placed the next card face up on the table, the one after that at the bottom, and so on until all the cards were dealt, the cards put on the table would follow the sequence: red, black, red, black, red, black, red, black. The problem was to find the order of the red and black cards in the original deck.

The solution was taught by two methods: (1) *learning by memorizing*, in which the specific order of the cards required for solution (RRBRRBBB) was given in its entirety for the solver to memorize, and (2) *learning by understanding*, in which the solver was given a diagram to help him figure out the "structure" of the problem

BOX 3 ▪ 3   Two Approaches to Wertheimer's Parallelogram Problem

Understanding Method

The understanding method encouraged students to see the structural relations in the parallelogram, for example, that the parallelogram could be rearranged into a rectangle by moving a triangle from one side to the other. Since the students knew how to find the area of a rectangle, finding the area of a parallelogram was easy once they discovered the appropriate structural relations.

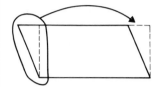

Rote Method

In the rote method, students were taught to drop a perpendicular and then apply the memorized solution formula.

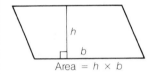

Area $= h \times b$

Transfer

Both groups performed well on typical problems asking for the area of parallelograms; however, only the understanding group could transfer to novel problems, such as finding the area of the three figures below

or distinguishing between solvable and unsolvable problems such as

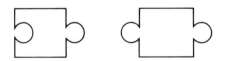

The response of the "rote" group to novel problems was, "We haven't had that yet."

Based on Wertheimer (1959)

BOX 3 ▪ 4   Two Approaches to Katona's Card Problem

The Problem

Deal out every other card onto the table, putting every skipped card on the bottom of the deck until all eight cards are on the table. The order of appearance on the table is RBRBRBRB. What was the order of the original deck?

Rote Method (Group Mem)

Subjects may be taught the solution by rote memorization: "The order of the original deck was RRBRRBBB."

Meaningful Method (Group Und)

Or they may learn by a more meaningful method involving a diagram:

1st run	R	?	B	?	R	?	B	?
2nd run		R		?		B		?
3rd run				R				?
4th run								B
Original	R	R	B	R	R	B	B	B

Results

Typical proportions correct on retention and transfer tests were as follows:

Group	Transfer Problems			Retention Problems		
	No. 1	No. 2	No. 3	No. 3	No. 4	No. 5
Mem	.23	.08	.42*	.32*	.36*	.18
Und	.44	.40	.44*	.48*	.62	.52
Control	.09	.03	.09	.09	.14	.09

*Subjects had practice on the problem prior to the test.

Adapted from Katona (1940)

for himself. The diagram system involved writing down the required color for each card for each run through the deck as shown in Box 3-4.

In one experiment, subjects in the memorization group learned this card trick and card trick 4 (in which they produced a chain of spades from ace to eight by dealing out every other card) by memorizing the required order during 4 minutes. Subjects in the understanding group had the same time to learn, by means of the suggested diagram, how to arrange the deck for trick 3 only. A control group received no training. An immediate transfer task consisted of the previously learned task (trick 3), an easy variation of trick 3 (trick 1, output BRBRBR by dealing every other card), and a difficult variation (trick 2, output same as trick 3 by dealing every third card); a 4-week retention transfer task consisted of tricks 3, 4, and 5 (same output as trick 1 but by dealing out every third card).

The results summarized in Box 3-4 show the proportion correct. As you can see, the memorization subjects (Group Mem) performed slightly better on immediate retention but much worse on transfer and long-term retention than understanding subjects (Group Und).

Katona also reported studies in which subjects learned to solve matchstick problems by several instructional methods. Two of these methods were: (1) Group Mem, in which the experimenter presented the complete series of solution steps in order, moving one stick at a time, and repeating the series six times, and (2) Group Help, in which the experimenter presented a series of hints to help the subjects understand the structure of the problem, such as by shading in the squares that were essential and pointing to the sticks that had to be moved. For example, in the problem shown in Box 3-5, the subject was shown five squares made of matchsticks and was required to move three sticks to make four squares; no sticks could be removed and all squares had to be one stick wide and one stick long. The first method (memorization) involved showing the required moves to the subject repeatedly, and the second method (understanding) encouraged the subject to discover the principle that some sticks served as the sides of one square and some bordered two squares, by the experimenter's giving a series of hints and saying, "Try to understand what I am doing."

In a typical experiment, all the subjects were given (1) a pretest to ensure their initial state of inexperience, (2) practice on two tasks by one of the two methods, and (3) delayed tests (some after 1 week and others after 3 weeks) on the learned problems as well as on the two new transfer tasks.

The results, in terms of percent correct, are given in Box 3-5. The Group Mem subjects performed quite well—better than the Group Help subjects—on retention of the solution for practiced tasks both after 1 week and after 3 weeks; however, Group Help subjects excelled (as did Group Und subjects with card tricks) on transfer tasks.

The experimental design, the lack of clear definitions, and, particularly, the lack of statistical analysis have all been criticized (Melton, 1941; Katona, 1942), and to the extent that these criticisms are justified, an interpretation of Katona's results is difficult. However, there is some evidence for the idea that giving solvers hints so they can discover the "structure of the problem situation" does aid in transfer—what the Gestaltists would call productive problem solving. For example, in a similar experiment performed under more controlled conditions, Hilgard, Irvine, and Whipple (1953) found that the understanding group took

BOX 3 · 5   Two Approaches to Katona's Matchstick Problem

The Problem

Given matchsticks that form five squares, move three sticks to form four squares.

Rote Method (Group Mem)

The complete solution steps are presented to the subject in order, moving one stick at a time and repeating six times. For the above problem, the required moves shown are:

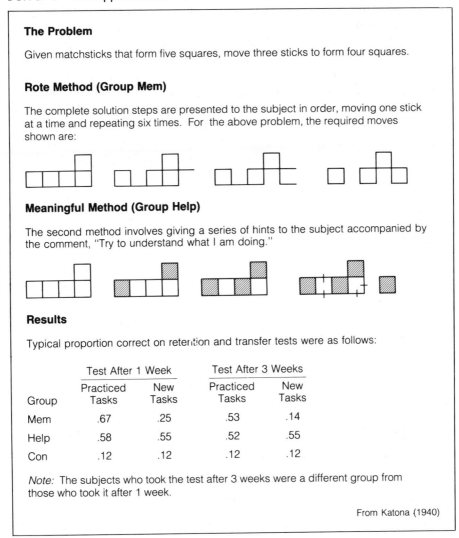

Meaningful Method (Group Help)

The second method involves giving a series of hints to the subject accompanied by the comment, "Try to understand what I am doing."

Results

Typical proportion correct on retention and transfer tests were as follows:

	Test After 1 Week		Test After 3 Weeks	
Group	Practiced Tasks	New Tasks	Practiced Tasks	New Tasks
Mem	.67	.25	.53	.14
Help	.58	.55	.52	.55
Con	.12	.12	.12	.12

Note: The subjects who took the test after 3 weeks were a different group from those who took it after 1 week.

From Katona (1940)

significantly longer than the memorizing group to solve the two practice problems, performed no differently from the memorizing subjects on a 1-day retention test, and performed significantly better on a set of transfer problems.

A major practical question raised by this work is how to help learners "understand" so they will be productive thinkers who are able to transfer their experience to novel problems. For example, Hilgard, Irvine, and Whipple (1953) pointed out that many so-called understanding subjects did not really understand the diagraming device in the full sense. In another experiment, Hilgard, Ergren, and Irvine (1954) taught subjects by one of five variations of learning by understanding. Although there were no overall differences on a transfer task, the errors the subjects made were related to the type of method used, suggesting a mechanical or rote application of the various helps. Similarly, Corman (1957) found that giving subjects a statement of the "double function principle"—that a stick can be a part of one square or of two squares—did not aid in productive thinking on transfer, although the diagram method did. Apparently, a supposedly meaningful principle such as the diagram or double function method can be learned in a mechanical way.

■
STAGES IN PROBLEM SOLVING
■

GENERAL PHASES

There have been many attempts to break the thinking process down into several smaller stages. In his classic book *The Art of Thought,* Wallas (1926) suggested four phases:

1. *Preparation*—information is gathered and preliminary attempts at solution are made.

2. *Incubation*—the problem is put aside to work on other activities or sleep.

3. *Illumination*—the key to the solution appears (this is where the "flash of insight" and the "aha!" occur).

4. *Verification*—the solution is checked out to make sure it "works."

Unfortunately, these four stages are based on introspections by Wallas and others about what they think they are doing when they solve problems, rather than on psychological experimentation. However, McKeachie and Doyle (1970) have shown how the analyses can be applied with partial success to reports of thinking processes, such as the introspections of the mathematician Henri Poincaré (1913) shown in Box 3-6. The first 15 days of thinking are Poincaré's preparation period; preparation continues as ideas "collided until pairs interlocked" and is followed immediately by illumination and verification. In the second phase, preparation is followed by illumination and verification, apparently without a sudden burst of insight. The third part of the introspection

BOX 3 • 6 Wallas's Phases of Problem Solving: An Example from Poincaré

"For fifteen days I strove to prove that there could not be any functions like those I have since called Fuchsian functions. I was then very ignorant; every day I seated myself at my work table, stayed an hour or two, tried a great number of combinations and reached no results. One evening, contrary to my custom, I drank black coffee and could not sleep. Ideas rose in crowds; I felt them collide until pairs interlocked, so to speak, making a stable combination. By the next morning I had established the existence of a class of Fuchsian functions, those which come from the hyper-geometric series; I had only to write out the results which took but a few hours.

"Then I wanted to represent these functions by the quotient of two series; this idea was perfectly conscious and deliberate, the analogy with elliptic functions guided me. I asked myself what properties these series must have if they existed, and I suc-ceeded without difficulty in forming the series I have called theta-Fuchsian.

"Just at this time time I left Caen, where I was then living, to go on a geologic excur-sion under the auspices of the school of mines. The changes of travel made me for-get my mathematical work. Having reached Countances, we entered an omnibus to go some place or other. At the moment when I put my foot on the step the idea came to me, without anything in my former thoughts seeming to have paved the way for it, that the transformations I had used to define the Fuchsian functions were identical with those of non-Euclidean geometry. I did not verify the idea; I should not have had time, as, upon taking my seat in the omnibus, I went on with a conversation already commenced, but I felt a perfect certainty. On my return to Caen, for conscience' sake I verified the result at my leisure."

From Poincaré (1913)

completes Wallas's four stages, including an incubation period (during the geological excursion) and a sudden burst of insight in the illumination period.

More recently, Polya (1957, 1965) has introduced a series of steps in problem solving based on observations he has made as a teacher of mathematics. Polya's four steps—first described in *How to Solve It* (1957)—are:

Understanding the problem—the solver gathers information about the problem and asks, "What do you want (or what is unknown)? What have you (or what are the data and conditions)?"

Devising a plan—the solver tries to use past experience to find a method of solu-tion and asks, "Do I know a related problem? Can I restate the goal in a new way based on my past experience (working backwards) or can I restate the givens in a new way that relates to my past experience (working forward)?" (Here's where insight flashes.)

Carrying out the plan—the solver tries out the plan of solution, checking each step.

Looking back—the solver tries to check the result by using another method, or by seeing how it all fits together, and asks, "Can I use this result or method for other problems?"

Polya's steps are similar to Wallas's in general form. Polya's "understanding" step is similar to Wallas' preparation phase, his "devising a plan" step includes some of Wallas's preparation phase and both the incubation and illumination phases, and the "carrying out the plan" and "looking back" steps relate to Wallas's verification.

Box 3-7 gives an example of Polya's (1965) four phases of problem solving based on a mathematical problem. The "understanding the problem" phase requires that the solver ask what is given (*a*, *b*, and *h* are given) and what is unknown (*F* is unknown). The "devising a plan" phase requires the solver to "look around for an appropriate related problem." (Let's assume the solver already knows how to find the volume of a pyramid.) In addition, the solver must try to restate either the goal or the givens to fit the related problem. In the frustum problem, the solver may restate the goal as to find the volume of the big pyramid minus the volume of the smaller pyramid and to then use the givens to produce the needed variables. The "carry out plan" phase requires the solver to make the calculations by using the formula for volume of a pyramid. The "looking back" phase requires the solver to see the logic of what he or she has done and to check to see if the method works on other problems.

As you can see, Polya's ideas of restating the goal (working backward from the unknown to the givens) and restating the givens (working forward from the givens to the goal) are examples of the Gestalt idea of "restructuring." While Polya gives many excellent intuitions about how the restructuring event occurs and how to encourage it, the concept is still a vague one that has not been experimentally well studied.

FUNCTIONAL SOLUTIONS AND REFORMULATIONS

Duncker (1945) attempted to study the stages in solving a problem empirically by giving a problem to a subject and asking him to report his thought process aloud as he was thinking. The problem Duncker used was the tumor problem illustrated at the top of Box 3-8 and was stated as follows: "Given a human being with an inoperable stomach tumor, and rays which destroy organic tissue at sufficient intensity, by what procedure can one free him of the tumor by these rays and at the same time avoid destroying the healthy tissue which surrounds it?" The protocol of a typical subject led Duncker to conclude that problem solving proceeds by stages, going from general solutions to more specific ones, with the original problem being continually reformulated. An example of how problem solving moves from *general solutions* to

BOX 3 ▪ 7   Stages in the Solution of Poly's Frustum Problem

The Problem

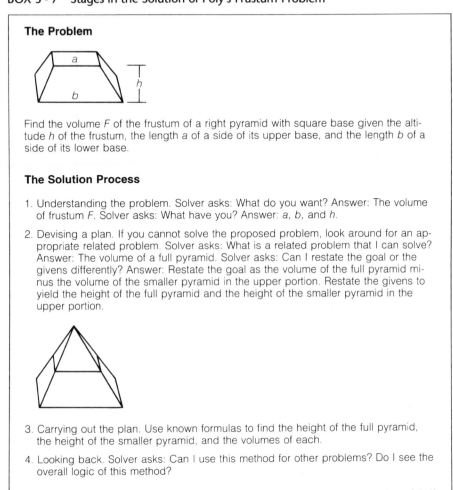

Find the volume F of the frustum of a right pyramid with square base given the altitude h of the frustum, the length a of a side of its upper base, and the length b of a side of its lower base.

The Solution Process

1. Understanding the problem. Solver asks: What do you want? Answer: The volume of frustum F. Solver asks: What have you? Answer: a, b, and h.

2. Devising a plan. If you cannot solve the proposed problem, look around for an appropriate related problem. Solver asks: What is a related problem that I can solve? Answer: The volume of a full pyramid. Solver asks: Can I restate the goal or the givens differently? Answer: Restate the goal as the volume of the full pyramid minus the volume of the smaller pyramid in the upper portion. Restate the givens to yield the height of the full pyramid and the height of the smaller pyramid in the upper portion.

3. Carrying out the plan. Use known formulas to find the height of the full pyramid, the height of the smaller pyramid, and the volumes of each.

4. Looking back. Solver asks: Can I use this method for other problems? Do I see the overall logic of this method?

Based on Polya (1965)

functional solutions to *specific solutions* is shown in the solution tree for the tumor problem in Box 3-8. For example, a general solution might be "avoid contact between rays and healthy tissue"; once solvers had thought of this they would generally hit upon several functional solutions, such as "use free path to the stomach," or "insert protecting wall," or "remove healthy tissue from path," and ultimately reach specific solutions, such as "use esophagus" or "insert a cannula." If that general plan or those functional solutions failed, solvers would think up new

BOX 3 • 8   Solution Tree for One Subject Working on Duncker's Tumor Problem

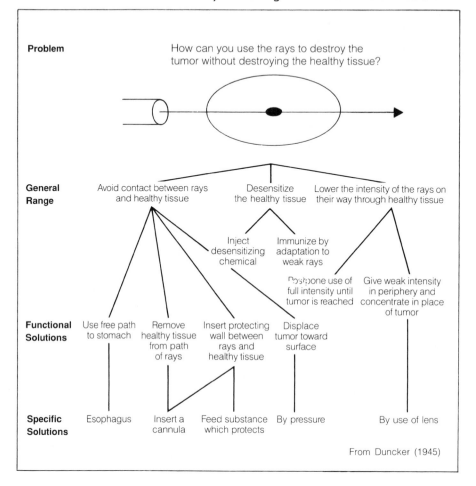

Problem   How can you use the rays to destroy the tumor without destroying the healthy tissue?

General Range   Avoid contact between rays and healthy tissue | Desensitize the healthy tissue | Lower the intensity of the rays on their way through healthy tissue

Inject desensitizing chemical   Immunize by adaptation to weak rays

Postpone use of full intensity until tumor is reached   Give weak intensity in periphery and concentrate in place of tumor

Functional Solutions   Use free path to stomach | Remove healthy tissue from path of rays | Insert protecting wall between rays and healthy tissue | Displace tumor toward surface

Specific Solutions   Esophagus | Insert a cannula | Feed substance which protects | By pressure | By use of lens

From Duncker (1945)

general and functional solutions, such as "lower intensity of rays on their way through healthy tissue"; more specific ideas that followed from this general idea were "turn down ray when it gets near healthy tissue and turn it up when it gets to the tumor" (wrong) or "use focused lens" (right).

Like Polya and the Gestalt psychologists, Duncker noted several basic phenomena in the process of problem solving:

Functional solution or value—elements of the problem must be seen in terms of their general or functional usefulness in the problem, and general or functional solutions precede specific solutions.

Reformulating or recentering—problem solving involves successive stages of reformulating (or restructuring) the problem with each new partial solution creating a new, more specific problem. In this example, the general solution of desensitizing healthy tissue is a reformulation of the original goal.

Suggestion from above—reformulating the goal to make it closer to the givens, for example, thinking of protecting the healthy tissue by somehow desensitizing it, similar to Polya's "working backward."

Suggestion from below—reformulating the givens so they more closely relate to the goal, for example, thinking of using the rays somehow in a weak form, similar to Polya's "working forward."

Another example comes from Duncker's (1945) 13 problem; "Why are all 6 place numbers of the form 276,276 or 591,591 or 112,112, and so on, divisible by 13?" The solution, according to Duncker, involves a suggestion from below to reformulate or recenter the originally given material from *abcabc* to *abc* × 1001. Once the solver restates the givens in this form, it can be argued that any number divisible by 1001 is also divisible by 13. In his experiments, Duncker found that when he told subjects that "the numbers are divisible by 1001," over 59 percent of the subjects solved the problem, but when he gave the general rule or no help the solution rate was 15 percent or below. Thus, as Duncker (p. 34) noted, "the real difficulty of the 13 problem is overcome as soon as the common divisor 1001 emerges"—that is, as soon as the givens are reformulated.

According to Duncker (1945, p. 29), major reformulations of a problem are preceded by sudden and unexpected flashes of insight: "The decisive points in thought-processes, the moments of sudden comprehension, of *Aha!*, of the new, are always at the same time moments in which a sudden restructuring of the thought-material takes place."

Until recently, there was not convincing research evidence for the Gestalt concept of insight—that is, sudden and unexpected restructuring of problems (Weisberg, 1986). In an important series of experiments, however, Metcalfe (1986a, 1986b; Metcalfe & Wiebe, 1987) found evidence for insight in nonroutine but not in routine problems. The routine problems, which were taken from a high school algebra textbook, included the following:

$$\text{Factor: } 16y^2 - 40yz + 25z^2$$

The nonroutine problems were classic insight problems, such as the following:

> A landscape gardener is given instructions to plant four special trees so that each one is exactly the same distance from each of the others. How could the trees be arranged?

As a first test of the concept of insight, Metcalfe (1986b) asked problem solvers to predict whether or not they would be able to solve each of several routine and nonroutine problems. If nonroutine problems require insight—sudden and unexpected reformulations of the problem—but routine problems do not, then problem solvers should perform poorly in predicting how well they will perform on nonroutine problems but well in predicting their performance on routine problems. The results confirmed these predictions (Metcalfe, 1986b).

As a second test of the concept of insight, Metcalfe and Wiebe (1987) asked subjects to solve some routine and nonroutine problems; at 15-second intervals during their solution processes, the subjects rated how close they felt they were to solving the problem on a scale from 1 (cold) to 7 (hot). If nonroutine problems involve insight but routine problems do not, then ratings of warmth should increase as problem solvers get closer to solving routine problems but should not be related to progress on nonroutine problems. The results confirmed this prediction: when solving routine problems, the majority of students gave "warm" ratings (i.e., above 4) when they were 15 seconds away from solution but not at 60 seconds prior to solution; in contrast, when solving nonroutine problems the majority of students gave "cool" ratings (i.e., below 4) both when they were 15 seconds away from solution and at 60 seconds prior to solution. These results show that problem solvers do not have accurate "feelings of knowing" when they solve insight problems—a finding that is consistent with the Gestalt idea that insight involves surprise. Holyoak (1990, p. 136) concludes that "Metcalfe's results thus provide empirical evidence that insight is a real psychological phenomenon."

■
RIGIDITY IN PROBLEM SOLVING
■

PROBLEM-SOLVING SET

Another major contribution of the Gestalt psychologists is their finding that prior experience can have negative effects in certain new problem-solving situations. The idea that the reproductive application of past habits inhibits productive problem solving has been called *functional fixedness* (Duncker, 1945), *Einstellung* (German for *attitude*) or *problem-solving set* (Luchins, 1942), and *negative transfer* (Bartlett, 1958).

The Luchins' work (Luchins, 1942; Luchins & Luchins, 1950) provides an often-cited example of how prior experience can limit an individual's ability to develop a solution rule of sufficient breadth and generality. Their water jar problems involved presenting subjects with the hypothetical situation of three jars of varying sizes and an unlimited water supply and asking them to figure out

BOX 3 • 9   Water Jar Problems

| Problem | Given Jars of the Following Sizes | | | Obtain the Amount |
	A	B	C	
1.	29	3		20
2. Einstellung 1	21	127	3	100
3. Einstellung 2	14	163	25	99
4. Einstellung 3	18	43	10	5
5. Einstellung 4	9	42	6	21
6. Einstellung 5	20	59	4	31
7. Critical 1	23	49	3	20
8. Critical 2	15	39	3	18
9.	28	76	3	25
10. Critical 3	18	48	4	22
11. Critical 4	14	36	8	6

Possible Answers for Critical Problems (7, 8, 10, 11)

Problem	Einstellung Solution	Direct Solution
7	$49 - 23 - 3 - 3 = 20$	$23 - 3 = 20$
8	$39 - 15 - 3 - 3 = 18$	$15 + 3 = 18$
10	$48 - 18 - 4 - 4 = 22$	$18 + 4 = 22$
11	$36 - 14 - 8 - 8 = 6$	$14 - 8 = 6$

Performance of Typical Subjects on Critical Problems

Group	Einstellung Solution	Direct Solution	No Solution
Control (Children)	1%	89%	10%
Experimental (Children)	72%	24%	4%
Control (Adults)	0%	100%	0%
Experimental (Adults)	74%	26%	0%

Adapted from Luchins (1942)

how to obtain a required amount of water. The problems, in order of presentation (with about 2 minutes allowed for each), are reproduced in Box 3-9.

Item 1 is an example-practice problem. The experimental group was given problems 2 through 11 in order, one at a time, to be solved by each subject without aid from the experimenter. The control group was given the same introduction and practice problem but began working on problems 7 through 11. Luchins called problems 2 through 6 *Einstellung* problems because they all evoked the same problem-solving set of $b - a - 2c$ as a solution. Problems 7, 8, 10, and 11 were critical problems because they could be solved by either a shorter, more productive method ($a - c$ or $a + c$) or by the longer method used to solve 2 through 6. Problem 9 was inserted to help the subjects "recover" from their mechanized or *einstellung* response, since the $b - a - 2c$ formula would not work on this problem; the recovery, if any, could be noted by a greater tendency to use the shorter solution on 10 and 11 than on 7 and 8. Luchins performed this experiment on more than 900 subjects ranging from elementary school students to students in his graduate seminars.

Typical results are shown in Box 3-9. The control group almost always discovered the short, direct solution, whereas the experimental group frequently used the *longer, einstellung* solution even on problems 10 and 11. Luchins summarized the findings as follows (Luchins & Luchins, 1950, p. 281): "This basic experiment and its variations have been administered by the author to over 9000 subjects. Most of these subjects showed considerable einstellung effect. Recovery from mechanization was in general not large for adult groups and was negligible in most elementary school groups." Based on these findings, Luchins (1942, p. 15) noted the consequences of mechanized thought: "*Einstellung* —habituation—creates a mechanized state of mind, a blind attitude toward problems; one does not look at the problem on its own merits but is led by a mechanical application of a used method."

This monumental work supports the Gestalt claim that reproductive application of past habits could be a detriment to effective and productive problem solving in a new situation. There is, of course, another explanation that is often cited by associationist-oriented psychologists: that the experimental subjects who used the *einstellung* method to solve new problems were actually more efficient because they did not have to waste time trying to create a new method for each problem. However, the Luchins' results provide evidence that past experience can limit the type of solution a subject devises in a new situation.

Bartlett (1958) noted a similar effect, which he called *negative transfer*, when he observed how subjects solved the DONALD + GERALD = ROBERT problem shown in Box 3-10. The task was to substitute numbers for the letters, given that D = 5, that every number from 0 to 9 has its corresponding letter, and that each letter must be given a number different from any other letter. In observing his subjects, Bartlett (1958, p. 59) noted that much of the difficulty they had was due to their past habits or methods of solving addition and subtraction problems, such as working from right to left: "Several more students tried the problem, but couldn't do it. They substituted 5 for D and zero for T, but since no direct clue is provided for L and R, they said they couldn't get any farther. It seems that the habit of

BOX 3 ▪ 10   Donald + Gerald = Robert Problem

```
    DONALD
  + GERALD
    ROBERT
```

"This is to be treated as an exercise in simple addition. All that is known is: (1) that
D = 5; (2) that every number from 0–9 has a corresponding letter; (3) that each
letter must be assigned a number different from that given for any other letter. The
operation required is to find a number for each letter, stating the steps of the processes and their order."

From Bartlett (1958, p. 51)

---

starting to make an addition sum from the right-hand column and continuing to
the left with succeeding columns was so deeply ingrained that they couldn't
conceive of any other method of approach, and they soon tired of trying to find
L and R by trial and error."*

FUNCTIONAL FIXEDNESS

Using a slightly more experimental approach, Duncker (1945) also investigated
how past experience could limit problem-solving productivity. For example, he
devised a diagram for his tumor problem with an arrow (representing the ray)
going through a black dot (representing the tumor) surrounded by a circle
(representing the healthy tissue). When the diagram was shown with the
problem, the solution rate was 9 percent compared to 37 percent when no
diagram was given. This finding suggested to Duncker that the diagram helped to
fix the function of the ray as a single line going through the body and thus
blocked the ability of the subject to think of it as several rays focused on the
tumor. Duncker called this phenomenon *functional fixedness* because the past
experience of seeing the diagram limited the number of different functions a
subject could devise for the ray.

Duncker thus defined functional fixedness as a mental block against using an
object in a new way that is required to solve a problem. To investigate this
phenomenon more carefully, he devised a series of problems that he thought
might involve functional fixedness and presented them to subjects in his
laboratory. For example, in the box problem (see Box 3-11), the subject was given

---

* The solution, by the way, is: T = 0, G = 1, O = 2, B = 3, A = 4, D = 5, N = 6, R = 7, L = 8, E = 9.

BOX 3 • 11   Materials in Duncker's Box Problem

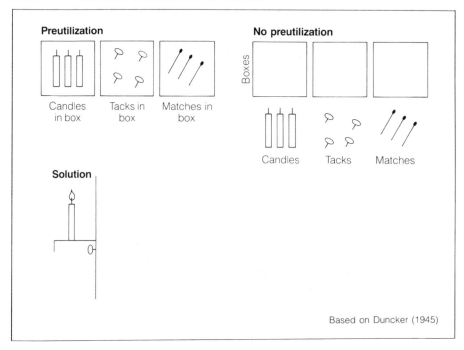

Based on Duncker (1945)

three cardboard boxes, matches, thumbtacks, and candles. The goal was to mount a candle vertically on a nearby screen to serve as a lamp. Some subjects were given a box containing matches, a second box holding candles, and a third one containing tacks—preutilization of the boxes—while other subjects received the same supplies but with the matches, tacks, and candles outside the boxes—no preutilization. The solution—to mount a candle on the top of a box by melting wax onto the box and sticking the candle to it and then tacking the box to the screen—was much harder to discover when the boxes were given filled rather than empty. Duncker's explanation, like those of Luchins and Bartlett, was that the placement of objects inside a box helped to fix its function as a container, thus making it more difficult for subjects to reformulate the function of the box and think of it as a support.

In the paper-clip problem, the subject was given one large square, four small squares, several paper clips, and an eyelet screwed to an overhead beam. The task was to attach the small squares to the large one and hang it from the eyelet. The preutilization group had to use some of the paper clips to attach the small squares to the large one first, but for the group without preutilization the small squares were already stapled to it. The solution—bending one paper clip to form a hook from which to hang the large square—was much harder for the preutilization group to discover. Again, Duncker suggested that using the clip as an attacher made it more difficult for subjects to conceive of it in a different function, namely, as a hook. In all, half a dozen tasks of this sort were given; typical results were for the preutilization group to solve 58 percent and the group without preutilization to solve 97 percent of the tasks.

Although these results are consistent with the Luchins', they are suspect because there were only fourteen subjects in Duncker's original study, the experiment was poorly specified, and no statistical analysis was performed. To overcome some of these problems, Adamson (1952) reran several of Duncker's experiments, including the box problem and the paper-clip problem. Fifty-seven subjects were divided into two groups—preutilization and no preutilization—and each subject received three different problems for a maximum of 20 minutes each. The results were similar to those in Duncker's original study. For example, with the box problem, 86 percent of the subjects solved the problem within 20 minutes when the boxes were presented empty, but only 41 percent solved the problem when the boxes were presented as containers. All subjects solved the paper-clip problem, but those in the preutilization group (the group that had to first use the paper clips to attach the squares together) took almost twice as much time.

Adamson's replication seemed to confirm Duncker's original idea—that subjects who utilize an object for a particular function will have more trouble in a problem-solving situation that requires a new and dissimilar function for the object. There is one drawback to the Duncker and Adamson experiments: since the same situation was used both for preutilization and for the new task, it was difficult to pinpoint the difficulties that the preutilization subjects had; furthermore, there was no control for the experience the subjects had with the objects prior to the experiments. Birch and Rabinowitz (1951) conducted an experiment that attempted to overcome these two criticisms with a problem different from those used by Duncker. The two-cord problem, adapted from an experiment by Maier (1930, 1931), is shown in Box 3-12. In this experiment a subject was put in a room with two cords hanging from the ceiling to the floor just out of reach of one another and two heavy objects, an electrical switch and an electrical relay, placed nearby. The goal was to tie the cords together. Some subjects, Group S, were given a pretest task of completing an electrical circuit on a "breadboard" by using a switch; other subjects, Group R, were given the same pretest task, but were given a relay to use to complete the circuit; and a third group, the control Group C, was given no pretest experience. The solution required a subject to tie one of the cords to a heavy object, swing it as a pendulum, and, while holding the other cord, catch the pendulum on the upswing. If the subjects had not solved the problem within 9 minutes the

BOX 3 ▪ 12   Functional Fixedness in the Two-Cord Problem

The Problem

Given two cords hanging from the ceiling and two heavy objects around the room, tie the cords together.

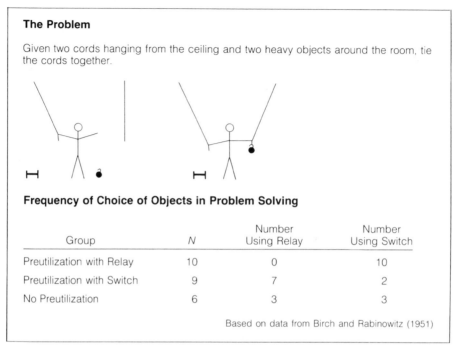

Frequency of Choice of Objects in Problem Solving

Group	N	Number Using Relay	Number Using Switch
Preutilization with Relay	10	0	10
Preutilization with Switch	9	7	2
No Preutilization	6	3	3

Based on data from Birch and Rabinowitz (1951)

---

experimenter gave a helpful hint by walking by one of the cords and "accidentally" setting it in motion. The results are shown in Box 3-12. All of the subjects solved the problem, but the Group R subjects tended to use the switch as a weight and the Group S subjects tended to use the relay as a weight. When asked why they used one heavy object instead of the other, subjects in both groups replied, "Anyone can see this one is better."

These results seem to fit nicely with those of Duncker and with the idea of functional fixedness. Previous experience with the object as a relay made it much more difficult to think of it as a weight—previous experience had fixed the function of the object. The Gestalt psychologists would not, of course, claim that all previous experience is detrimental to problem solving. Broad, nonspecific, general experience and certain basic past learning "represents an essential repertoire of behavior which must be available for restructuring when the new situation demands"; however, "productive thinking is impossible if the individual is chained to the past," and in cases where a subject relies on very specific, limited habits, "past experience may become a hindrance" (Birch & Rabinowitz, 1951, p. 121).

There are the additional questions of how long the effects of functional fixedness last and whether functional fixedness with respect to a certain object tends to affect similar objects. Adamson and Taylor (1954) investigated these questions with a variation of the two-cord problem just described. Before the subjects tackled this problem, they were given a task of working on an electrical circuit board with a pair of pliers. Then, when they tried to solve the two-cord problem, Adamson and Taylor found they were far less likely than control subjects to use those same pliers as a weight for the pendulum; in addition, they had more difficulty than control subjects in using another pair of pliers or even a pair of scissors as weights—which, however, they preferred to using the original pliers. Apparently the effect of functional fixedness does spread to objects that are similar to the fixed object. However, the effect seems to fade with time, as Adamson and Taylor (1954) showed by giving the two-cord problem at varying intervals following the initial experience of their subjects with the pliers and the circuit board. They tested subjects immediately following the experience, 1 hour later, 1 day later, and 1 week later. The longer the time elapsed between the use of the pliers on the circuit board and the introduction of the two-cord problem, the larger the number of subjects who used the pliers as the weight.

Another series of experiments (Glucksberg & Danks, 1968; Glucksberg & Weisberg, 1966; Weisberg & Suls, 1973) has provided information concerning the role of labeling problem-solving elements. In the box problem, for example, subjects were more likely to generate the preferred answer of using the box as a platform if the instructions explicitly named the box as part of the given materials. Apparently, when only the tacks, matches, and candles were labeled in the instructions, the boxes that held them were not thought of as separate elements.

In another study, subjects were given elements for an electric circuit (such as a switch, bulb, battery, and wrench) and asked to make a complete circuit. In contrast to the box experiment, when the wrench was explicitly named in the instructions, subjects were less likely to use it to conduct electricity and complete the circuit. Why does labeling an object help problem solving in the box problem but hinder problem solving in the circuit problem? Apparently, thinking of an object as a box is compatible with using it as a platform, but thinking of an object as a wrench is not compatible with using it as an electrical conductor. Thus labels that might be associated with the desired use of an object in a problem are helpful in breaking functional fixedness, but labeling objects with names that are not associated with the desired use are likely to promote functional fixedness.

More recently, researchers have shown that problem solvers are unlikely to use previously given hints effectively unless they are explicitly told to do so. For example, Weisberg, DiCamillo, and Phillips (1978) required students to learn a list of word pairs, including *candle–box*, prior to attempting to solve the candle problem. Subjects performed poorly on the candle problem unless they were explicitly told that one of the previously given word pairs was relevant to the problem. In follow-up experiments, the usefulness of previously provided hints depended on whether or not subjects could spontaneously remember the needed information during problem solving (Adams et al., 1988; Lockhart, Lamon, & Gick, 1988; Perfetto, Bransford, & Franks, 1983).

■
POSITIVE EFFECTS OF PAST EXPERIENCE
■

The work of Luchins, Duncker, and others has often been cited as evidence that reapplication of very specific, rigid past habits can hinder productive problem solving. There is, of course, complementary evidence that in some cases specific past experience may aid problem solving. For example, Maier (1945) asked subjects to solve the string problem as shown in Box 3-13: given several wooden poles, clamps, and a string, subjects had to hang the string from the ceiling without damaging it. The solution consisted of tying the string around one stick and bracing it horizontally against the ceiling at both ends with two long sticks made by clamping the wooden poles together. Another problem asked subjects to make a hatrack given objects similar to those in the preceding experiment. The solution to the hatrack problem consisted of clamping two sticks together to make a pole that reached from the floor to the ceiling and using the handle of the clamp to hang the hat. Of subjects who had no prior experience with the string structure, only 24 percent solved the hatrack problem; of subjects who had solved the string problem, which had been removed from their sight, 48 percent solved the hatrack problem; and of subjects who had solved the string structure problem and could still see the solution, 72 percent solved the new problem.

Maier's results seem to conflict directly with those of Duncker and the others who found that past experience limited future problem-solving effectiveness. Instead of negative transfer, Maier found strong evidence for *positive transfer*—the fact that past experience with the string structure helped subjects in a new problem-solving situation. In trying to reconcile the Maier experiment with those in the previous section, three facts are important: (1) the change from function one to function two is very small in Maier's experiment since the hatrack is part of the string structure, but the two functions of box as container and box as support are very different in the experiments by Duncker; (2) the change from the normal use to function one is great in Maier's experiment in that using a braced pole to hang a string is uncommon, but small in Duncker's experiments because boxes are often used as containers; (3) the first function facilitates the second function in Maier's experiment, but in the Duncker experiment the functions are mutually exclusive. Apparently, specific habits and experiences are useful in

BOX 3 ▪ 13   Materials in Maier's String and Hatrack Problems

String Problem

Given several wooden poles, clamps, and string, hang the string from the ceiling to the floor without defacing the ceiling.

The solution is to tie the string around a pole and then brace the pole against the ceiling using poles clamped together.

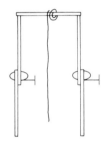

Hatrack Problem

Given poles and clamps, make a hatrack.

The solution is to clamp two poles together from floor to ceiling and use a clamp as a hook from which to hang a hat.

Based on Maier (1945)

BOX 3 ▪ 14   Materials in Saugstad and Raaheim's Transfer Problem

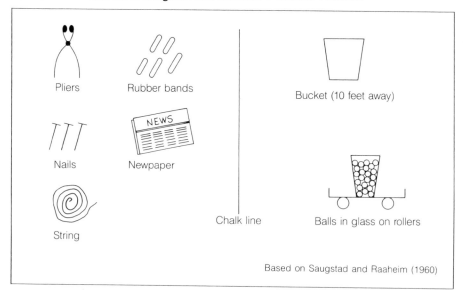

Pliers

Rubber bands

Bucket (10 feet away)

Nails

Newpaper

String

Chalk line

Balls in glass on rollers

Based on Saugstad and Raaheim (1960)

situations that require those specific ideas applied in much the same form but are a hindrance in situations that require using objects in a new way.

One interpretation of the value of past experience is that in some cases it can make functions of objects available, especially if the past experience with a certain function of an object and the required function in a new situation are similar. Saugstad and Raaheim (1960; Raaheim, 1965) presented subjects with the following problem: given newspapers, string, pliers, rubber bands, and a nail, figure out a way to transfer a few steel balls from a glass jar on a wheeled platform to a bucket about 10 feet away from you without crossing a chalk line. (See Box 3-14.) The solution, believe it or not, is to bend the nail with the pliers to make a hook, attach the hook to the string, throw it out to catch the movable glass full of steel balls and pull it toward you, roll the newspapers into tubes that you hold in shape with the rubber bands, and drop the balls through the tubes into the bucket.

Suppose you gave the subjects, before starting the experiment, a bent nail and said, "This object could be used to catch things with. Could you give some examples?"; and suppose you showed them the newspaper rolled into a tube and said, "This object you may use to conduct something through. Can you give me some examples?" Saugstad and Raaheim (1960, p. 97) called this "making the functions of objects available"; Duncker would probably have called it giving the problem away. After 30 minutes on this problem, 95 percent of the subjects solved it if they had the experience described above, but only 22 percent of the subjects solved the problem if they had not been familiarized with the two new functions of the nail and the newspaper.

In a similar, slightly more subtle experiment. subjects were given the nail and the newspaper prior to the experiment and asked to think of all possible uses for them. They were then given the task of transporting the steel balls. Of the subjects who mentioned both the hook as a possible function of the nail and the tube as a possible function of the newspaper during the pretest, 89 percent solved the problem; of subjects who mentioned either the hook or the tube function during the pretest but not both, 42 percent solved the problem; and of subjects who thought of neither function during the pretest, only 19 percent solved the problem. Again, Saugstad and Raaheim claimed that success in problem solving sometimes depends on appropriate functions being available to the solvers at the appropriate time.

"Making the functions available" may result from general experience with the solution objects. For example, Birch (1945) examined the role of insight in apes—over 20 years after Kohler—by placing some food out of reach outside the cage and giving them a hoe with which to rake it in. Only two out of four chimpanzees could solve this task, so Birch allowed them to play with short sticks for the next few days. The chimps invented many new uses for the sticks while playing with them, including prying, shoveling, and noise making. After a few days of such play, the apes were given the hoe problem again, and this time they solved it quite easily. Apparently, insight is aided by and builds on useful past experiences.

Taken together, the work of Maier, of Saugstad and Raaheim, and of Birch seems to supplement the idea of functional fixedness described by Duncker: in situations where similar functions are required, past experience is an aid. Note, however, that the type of problem solving that Maier and Saugstad and Raaheim are discussing is very close to the definition of reproductive thinking. What these results indicate is that problems that seem to require productive solutions—reorganization of the problem elements—are more easily solved by a mind that is prepared with appropriate general past experiences. On the other hand, if those past experiences specifically tend to fix the function of objects in one way, creative problem solving can be hurt.

One way to resolve this problem, and one that most good teachers aim for, is to provide learners with certain basic, specific facts coupled with more general problem-solving techniques. Although Luchins successfully demonstrated that past experience in solving problems can limit problem-solving ability, there is also evidence that such practice can lead to a more general ability to deal with all sorts of problems. For example, Harlow (1949) gave monkeys problems (Box 3-15) in which they were given two (or three) objects on a tray and had to pick

BOX 3 ▪ 15   Materials Used in a Study of Learning Sets

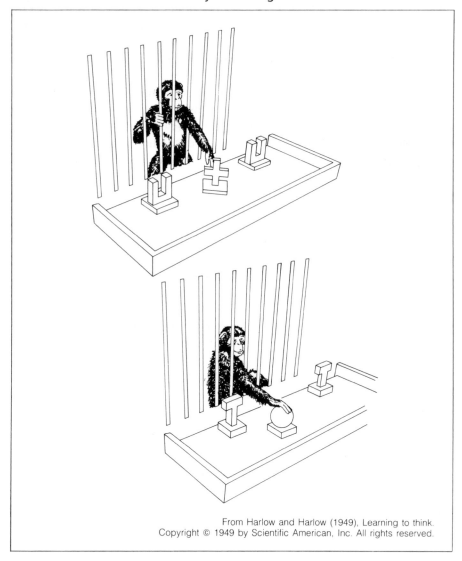

one up. If they picked up the "correct" object, they received a piece of banana. (When three objects were presented, the correct object was the odd object.) The monkeys were given the same problem over and over again, with the position of the objects randomly arranged on each trial. Then a new problem was presented with variations for hundreds of repetitions (monkeys are more patient than human subjects). Harlow found that the monkeys performed better on new problems as the experiment progressed; although it took them many trials to respond consistently to the early problems, they never made a mistake after the second trial on the problems presented toward the end of the experiment. Specific aspects of problems at the end were different or even opposite from those at the beginning, but the monkeys had apparently picked up a *general* strategy for responding. They seemed to follow a rule that we can express as, "If you get food for picking that object keep picking it, and if you do not, then pick the other object." Harlow called this use of general past experience "learning set" or "learning to think." His work shows that general as well as specific experience can be an aid in problem solving if the problem situation resembles prior problems.

The experiments by Maier, by Saugstad and Raaheim, and by Harlow indicate that part of solving a problem is finding out how it relates to past experience. Polya cited "finding a related problem" as a main factor in devising a solution plan, and Birch and Rabinowitz talked about using "an essential repertoire" of past behaviors and experiences in solving Duncker's problems. How does a problem solver find the relationship between past experience and the needed reformulation of the problem? According to Maier (1930, 1931, 1933), the leap to solution requires *direction.*

Since past experience alone is not enough for an original solution, a subject needs some organizing principle, some new way of looking at the problem situation, in short, some direction. Maier provided an example of the crucial importance of direction in his two-cord problem. In one experiment, he waited some time as the subject tried to solve the problem and then provided the first hint: he walked by the string, thus setting it in gentle motion. He waited a little more time, and if there was still no solution, gave a second hint: he handed the subject a pair of pliers and said, "This is all you need."

He waited again, and if no solution occurred, repeated hint one. Of 61 college student subjects, 39 percent solved the problem before any hints were given and 38 percent solved it with hints. Those in the group who solved it with hints generally did so almost immediately after the hints were given—an average of 42 seconds from the last hint to solution. The solution appeared suddenly and in complete form, and many subjects were not consciously aware of the hint. From this experiment, Maier concluded that direction is needed in problem solving— that subjects need some clue, which may be either externally or internally generated, about how to reformulate the problem. Putting the string in motion helped the subjects to reformulate the function of the string as a swing on a pendulum. Apparently, direction can be very subtle, and in some cases the problem solver does not realize it has occurred: "When an idea suddenly appears, what sets it off may be lost to consciousness" (Maier, 1931, p. 192).

In a more subtle use of direction, Cofer (1951) used the same two-cord situation but had his subjects memorize lists of words before they were given the problem. Subjects who had memorized lists with words such as *rope, swing,* and *pendulum* produced more solutions than subjects who had memorized neutral words.

In another variation of the same problem, Battersby, Teuber, and Bender (1953) provided direction by restricting the number of potential solution objects among three groups of subjects. The restricted group could only use objects the experimenter put on the table; the objects were added to the table every two minutes for a total of five objects, with any one capable of serving as a weight for the pendulum. The less restricted group could use any object in the room, including the five objects the experimenter was adding at the same rate. Finally, the unrestricted group could use any object in the room, including the five objects that had already been placed upon the table with no attention drawn to them. The average solution times were much faster for the restricted group (2.4 minutes) than for the less restricted (7.5 minutes) or the unrestricted group (15.2).

■
AIDS TO PROBLEM UNDERSTANDING
■

In Gestalt theory, problem representation rests at the heart of problem solving—the way you look at the problem can affect the way you solve the problem. For example, consider the horse problem given at the top of Box 3-16. Subjects in an experiment by Maier and Burke (1967) performed quite poorly on this problem, getting the right answer less than 40 percent of the time. However, now try the second problem in Box 3-16. When Maier and Burke gave this problem to a new group of subjects, 100 percent of the subjects gave the correct answer ($20). Specfically, the first representation encouraged subjects to think of a chain of transactions about *one* horse, whereas the second representation encouraged them to interpret the problem as two separate and independent transactions.

The Gestalt approach to problem solving has fostered numerous attempts to improve creative problem solving by helping people represent problems in useful ways. In this section, we explore three aids to understanding problems: concretizing, discovering, and blockbusting.

CONCRETIZING

First, one way to make a problem more understandable is to convert it from abstract form to concrete form. For example, Luchins and Luchins (1950) presented the water jar problems (as in Box 3-9) using real cups and water that could actually be poured. When sixth-graders were given the water jar problems

BOX 3 ▪ 16   The Horse Problem

Representation 1

A man bought a horse for $60 and sold it for $70. Then he bought it back again for $80 and sold it for $90. How much did he make in the horse business?

a. lost $10
b. broke even
c. made $10
d. made $20
e. made $30

Representation 2

A man bought a white horse for $60 and sold it for $70. Then he bought a black horse for $80 and sold it for $90. How much money did he make in the horse business?

a. lost $10
b. broke even
c. made $10
d. made $20
e. made $30

Adapted from Maier and Burke (1967)

---

in concrete form, almost all of them calculated the solution with paper and pencil before they used the cups and water, and 68 percent gave the *Einstellung* solution on the first two critical problems. When college students were given the problems in concrete form, 60 percent showed the *einstellung* effect on the first two critical problems if they were allowed to use paper and pencil, and 55 percent showed the same effect if they were not. Apparently, concretizing the situation reduced but did not eliminate the *einstellung* effect. One reason for the difficulty in eliminating the *einstellung* effect, according to Luchins and Luchins, was that the students carried over school-learned attitudes toward problem solving that counteracted the experimental manipulations.

In another attempt to foster better problem-solving performance by concretizing a problem, Brownell and Moser (1949) taught children the procedure for two-column subtraction using either the standard method or a concrete method. In the standard method, children were taught the subtraction procedure in words, as shown in the top of Box 3-17. In the concrete method, children were taught the subtraction procedure using concrete objects such as bundles of sticks, as shown in the bottom of Box 3-17. Although both groups learned to perform equally well on the exercise problems, the children who had

BOX 3 ▪ 17   How to Make Arithmetic Meaningful

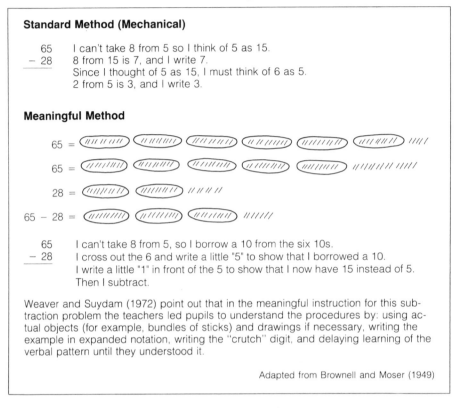

Standard Method (Mechanical)

    65   I can't take 8 from 5 so I think of 5 as 15.
− 28   8 from 15 is 7, and I write 7.
             Since I thought of 5 as 15, I must think of 6 as 5.
             2 from 5 is 3, and I write 3.

Meaningful Method

    65   I can't take 8 from 5, so I borrow a 10 from the six 10s.
− 28   I cross out the 6 and write a little "5" to show that I borrowed a 10.
             I write a little "1" in front of the 5 to show that I now have 15 instead of 5.
             Then I subtract.

Weaver and Suydam (1972) point out that in the meaningful instruction for this subtraction problem the teachers led pupils to understand the procedures by: using actual objects (for example, bundles of sticks) and drawings if necessary, writing the example in expanded notation, writing the "crutch" digit, and delaying learning of the verbal pattern until they understood it.

Adapted from Brownell and Moser (1949)

learned with bundles of sticks performed much better on later tests with different kinds of subtraction problems. These results are consistent with Brownell's (1935) call for a meaning theory of arithmetic learning—the idea that students should understand how problem-solving rules relate to meaningful experiences, not simply memorize automatic responses. Unfortunately, however, the effectiveness of concrete materials for mathematical problem solving has "not been adequately validated by research" (Resnick & Ford, 1981, p. 126).

There is growing evidence that under appropriate conditions concrete representations, including illustrations and animations, can improve problem-solving performance (Mayer, 1989a, 1989b). For example, Mayer (1975) taught a simple computer programming language to subjects using a standard ten-page text. Some of the subjects were introduced to a concrete model of the concepts, which were expressed in familiar terms, prior to reading the text and were allowed to use this model during their reading (the before group); other subjects were given the same model only after they had read the text (the after group). The model represented the computer's memory as an erasable scoreboard, the program as a shopping list with an arrow, input as a ticket window, and output as a telephone message pad. On a subsequent transfer test, the after group was better at writing simple programs such as those taught in the booklet, but the before group was better at tasks not specifically taught, such as interpreting what a program would do or writing complex programs. One explanation is that the model helped the subjects to relate new information to other knowledge they already had in memory; this broader learning outcome produced better transfer performance.

DISCOVERING

A second technique for increasing the understandability of problem-solving procedures is to encourage students actively to discover for themselves how to solve problems. For example, Gagné and Smith (1962) asked subjects to solve the disk problem (Ewert & Lambert, 1932), or what Newell and Simon (1972) called the Tower of Hanoi problem. As shown in Box 3-18, given three disks on peg 1, arranged in order of size with the smallest on top, your job is to move the disks to peg 3 in the least number of moves, moving them one at a time and never putting a larger disk on top of a smaller one.

Subjects solving this problem used two, three, four, and five disks under one of the following conditions: group 1 (verbalize-and-think group) was instructed to state the reason for each move and to think of a general principle involved, group 2 (verbalize group) received instructions only to verbalize, group 3 (think group) were told only to think of a general principle, and group 4 (control) received none of these instructions. All the subjects eventually found the solutions to all four problems, with groups 3 and 4 taking less time and making more moves. However, on a transfer problem using six disks in which no verbalizations were required, the subjects who had verbalized during the previous four problems performed significantly better than the nonverbalizing subjects. The instruction to think of a general principle had no significant effect on transfer. Apparently, the active verbalizations given for each move provoked subjects to relate the problem solution to their general knowledge. Similar results were obtained by Gagné and Brown (1961) and Roughead and Scandura (1968) using series sum problems.

During the 1960s, Bruner (1961, 1966, 1968) became a major proponent of the discovery method of learning. For example, Box 3-19 shows how children can be encouraged to discover the quadratic equation using concrete shapes corresponding to x^2, x, and 1. According to Bruner and Kenney (1965), by manipulating the blocks, a child can discover that $(x + 2)^2$ equals $x^2 + 4x + 4$, and so on. The discovery method shares with the Gestalt learning by understanding

BOX 3 ▪ 18   The Disk Problem

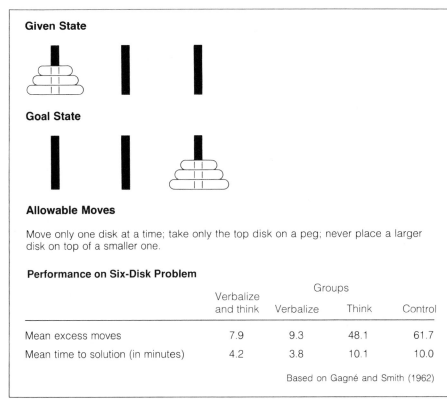

Given State

Goal State

Allowable Moves

Move only one disk at a time; take only the top disk on a peg; never place a larger disk on top of a smaller one.

Performance on Six-Disk Problem

	Verbalize and think	Groups		
		Verbalize	Think	Control
Mean excess moves	7.9	9.3	48.1	61.7
Mean time to solution (in minutes)	4.2	3.8	10.1	10.0

Based on Gagné and Smith (1962)

method the promise of superior transfer. Unfortunately, the claims for discovery were not based on a strong base of research support (Mayer, 1987a; Shulman & Keisler, 1966). As Wittrock (1966, p. 33) pointed out, "Many strong claims for learning by discovery are made . . . but almost none of these has been empirically substantiated or even clearly tested in an experiment."

A guided discovery approach, however, has been shown to improve problem-solving performance (Mayer, 1987a). For example, Mayer and Greeno (1972) taught students to solve binomial probability problems using inductive and deductive sequences. The inductive group began by learning about concepts such as trial, success, and probability of success in terms of familiar experiences with batting averages or the probability of rain and worked up to constructing parts and eventually all of the formula. The deductive group began with the formula for computing binomial probability and gradually learned how the

BOX 3 • 19   Discovery Learning of Quadratic Equation

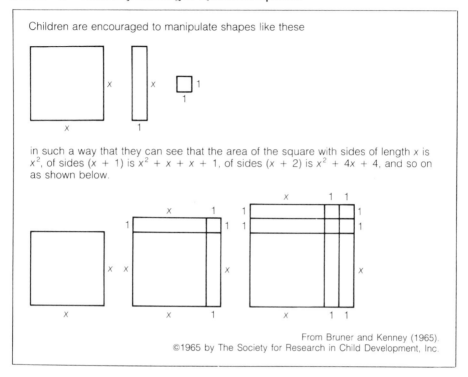

Children are encouraged to manipulate shapes like these

in such a way that they can see that the area of the square with sides of length x is x^2, of sides $(x + 1)$ is $x^2 + x + x + 1$, of sides $(x + 2)$ is $x^2 + 4x + 4$, and so on as shown below.

From Bruner and Kenney (1965).
©1965 by The Society for Research in Child Development, Inc.

components figured in calculating with it. Although both groups received the same general information—albeit in different order—and the same examples, they showed completely different patterns of performance on a subsequent problem-solving test. The deductive group performed best on solving problems that were like those in the instruction booklet (near transfer) but very poorly on questions about the formula and on problems they should have recognized as impossible to solve (far transfer); the inductive group showed the reverse pattern. These results suggest that the inductive group was encouraged to connect the newly learned procedure to their existing knowledge, whereas the deductive group connected the procedure to a narrow range of experience with computations and formulas.

BLOCKBUSTING

The third approach is to learn how to look at a problem in a new way. As an example of self-imposed constraints on problem representation, consider the nine-dot problem shown in the top of Box 3-20. Your job is to connect all nine dots with four straight lines, without lifting your pencil from the paper. If you are like most people who are not already familiar with this task, you will not be able to solve this problem. Why is this problem so difficult? According to Gestalt theory, the answer is *fixation:* problem solvers tend to see the problem in only one way. In his book *Conceptual Blockbusting,* Adams (1974, p. 17) observes that most people "delimit the problem too closely" by assuming that the lines must remain within the square bounded by the dots: "A surprising number of people will not exceed this imaginary boundary . . . even though it is not in the definition of the problem at all." Newell and Simon (1972, p. 91) note that "most subjects adopt a representation . . . that assumes the straight lines must all terminate on the dots and cannot continue outside the boundaries of the square." For example, the middle portion of Box 3-20 shows three incorrect solutions based on this unneeded restriction (Wickelgren, 1974).

The correct solution requires drawing lines that extend beyond the square, as shown in the bottom of Box 3-20. Where does the solution come from? According to Gestalt theory, the solution emerges from *insight*—a sudden reorganization in the way that the problem solver understands the problem. For example, Newell and Simon (1972, p. 91) propose that "if the subject at any time considers the possibility of generating lines that extend outside the square, he finds the solution very quickly." Similarly, Wickelgren (1974, p. 64) predicts that once a person realizes that "it is permissible to attempt solutions in which the lines extend beyond the perimeter of the array of dots . . . the solution is readily achieved."

Weisberg and Alba (1981) tested the idea that removing the problem solver's fixation on the square bounded by the dots would result in sudden solution of the problem, a prediction that they attributed to Gestalt theory. In the experiment, subjects were given a maximum of twenty attempts to solve the nine-dot problem. After the first ten attempts, some subjects (hint group) were told that they would have to extend lines outside the square to solve the problem, and other subjects (control group) were not given any hints. The results show that almost all of the hint subjects drew lines extending beyond the square, while none of the control subjects did; however, none of the subjects in either group ever solved the problem! In contrast, all subjects who were shown the first two lines of the solution after ten tries solved the problem before the twentieth trial. Weisberg & Alba (1981, p. 169) conclude that "the terms *fixation* and *insight* are not useful in describing the processes involved in the solution of these problems" and that successful problem solvers need to know responses that are specific to the problem.

Coming to the rescue of Gestalt theory, Dominowski (1981, p. 193) suggested that fixation is not necessarily "the sole obstacle to problem solving" and that

BOX 3 ▪ 20   The Nine-Dot Problem

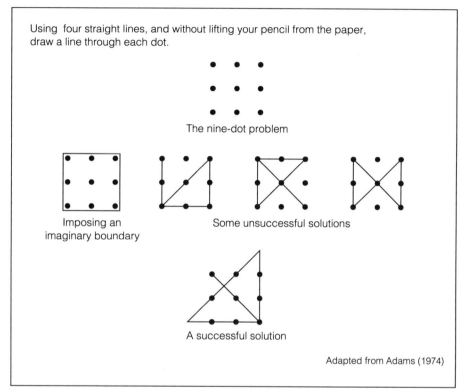

Using four straight lines, and without lifting your pencil from the paper, draw a line through each dot.

The nine-dot problem

Imposing an imaginary boundary

Some unsuccessful solutions

A successful solution

Adapted from Adams (1974)

problem solving is "not necessarily restricted to direct transfer of past experience." In support of this rebuttal, Lung and Dominowski (1985) gave subjects a maximum of forty chances to solve the nine-dot problem. Some subjects (control group) attempted to solve the problem without any help, and other subjects (hint-and-practice group) received prior practice in solving the six-dot problems shown in Box 3-21 as well as the following hint (Lung & Dominowski, 1985, p. 807):

> In order to solve each of these problems, you must extend some of the solution lines beyond the dots, i.e. you should not always regard a dot as the place where you stop a line just drawn and where you start a new line. On the contrary, sometimes, it is necessary to extend a line beyond the last dot on the line, to a point where you can start a new line connecting other dots. At least one line must end beyond the last dot on the line, and the next line will start beyond the dots on that line.

BOX 3 ▪ 21   Practice Problems with Solutions

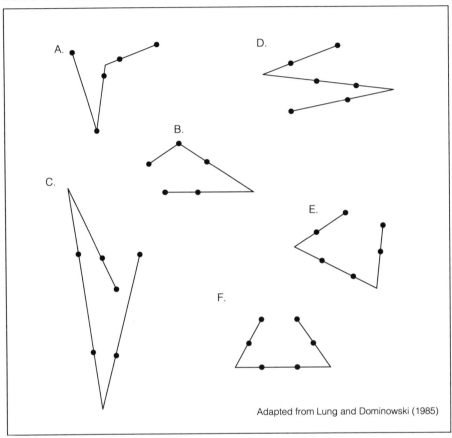

Adapted from Lung and Dominowski (1985)

In contrast to Weisberg and Alba's results, the nine-dot problem was solved by 60 percent of the students given the hint and practice and 9 percent of the control subjects. Lung and Dominowski concluded that hint-and-practice subjects learned a general strategy that they could apply to the nine-dot problem, rather than specific responses as suggested by Weisberg and Alba.

The role of fixation and insight in problem solving, however, is still not resolved. Dominowski (1981, p. 198) suggests that "insight" can refer to a person's understanding of a problem—an idea that "can serve a central role in the development of improved theories of problem solving." In contrast, Weisberg (1986, pp. 45–46) criticizes "the Gestalt view that a solution can occur in an Aha! experience if one simply breaks away from past experience" because "attractive as this view may be . . . the results of several experimental studies lead one to question it." Again, we are faced with a situation in which the Gestaltists offered psychology an interesting phenomenon—how people come to understand a problem—and challenged others to develop an adequate theoretical explanation.

■
EVALUATION
■

The Gestaltists attempted to understand some highly complex mental processes— what they called "productive thinking." They enriched the study of thinking by introducing several provocative ideas: the distinction between productive and reproductive thinking, the idea that thinking occurs in stages, and the demonstration of rigidity of problem-solving set. Their main tool for understanding such processes was the idea that problem solving involves reorganizing or restructuring the problem. Critics point out, however, that the theory is much too vague to be tested directly in experiments (Dellarosa, 1988; Ohlsson, 1984a; Weisberg, 1986). Dellarosa (1988, p. 7) correctly concludes that the Gestaltists "simply did not possess the tools and techniques for building models of the level of complexity they required," but that "the Gestalt school foreshadowed the cognitive revolution . . . carving out the domains that would be explored later" as the necessary tools and techniques were invented. More recently, cognitive scientists have been partially successful in clarifying some of the ideas of the Gestaltists; for example, Ohlsson (1984b) has related *restructuring* to the information-processing approach to thinking (see Chapter 6), and Gick and Holyoak (1980, 1983) have examined the role of transfer using Duncker's tumor problem (see Chapter 14).

Suggested Readings

DUNCKER, K. (1971). *On problem-solving*. Westport, CT: Greenwood. A reprint of Duncker's classic 1945 *Psychological Monographs* paper.

KATONA, G. (1940). *Organizing and memorizing*. New York: Columbia University Press. Describes Katona's experiments on learning to solve matchstick and card problems.

KOHLER, W. (1925). *The mentality of apes*. New York: Harcourt Brace Jovanovich. A famous study of problem solving and insight in apes.

LUCHINS, A. S., & LUCHINS, E. H. (1959). *Rigidity of behavior: A variational approach to Einstellung*. Eugene: University of Oregon Press. Discusses research on rigidity in problem solving.

POLYA, G. (1957). *How to solve it*. Garden City, NY: Doubleday Anchor. A mathematician explains how to solve problems.

WASON, P. C., & JOHNSON-LAIRD, P. N. (1968). *Thinking and reasoning.* Baltimore: Penguin. An excellent collection of classic research articles in problem solving, including works by Adamson, Duncker, Luchins, and Maier.

WERTHEIMER, M. (1959). *Productive thinking.* New York: Harper & Row. A Gestalt view of problem solving and how to teach it.

PART II

BASIC THINKING TASKS

CHAPTER · 4

INDUCTIVE REASONING

Thinking as Hypothesis Testing

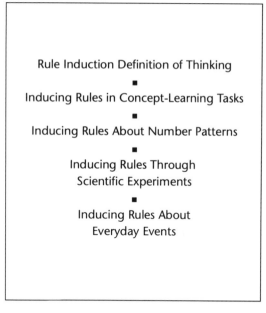

Rule Induction Definition of Thinking
■
Inducing Rules in Concept-Learning Tasks
■
Inducing Rules About Number Patterns
■
Inducing Rules Through
Scientific Experiments
■
Inducing Rules About
Everyday Events

CONCEPT FORMATION TASK

Suppose you have in front of you a pile of cards with pictures of different colors, shapes, sizes, and number of objects. The colors are RED or GREEN, the shapes are CIRCLE or SQUARE, the sizes are SMALL or LARGE, and the number of objects is ONE or TWO. The experimenter picks out one card and places it in one of two boxes—Box Yes or Box No. Each time the experimenter picks out a card you must "guess" which box it belongs in. The cards and their group, Yes or No, are shown in Box 4-1. Cover the column marked "Correct Group" with a piece of paper and try to guess the group membership for each card, then check the correct answer and go on. See how long it takes you to predict group membership without error.

In another example of this kind of task, an experimenter enters the room, points down to the metal legs of a table, and says, "Oogle." Then he goes to a wooden chair, lifts it for all to see, points up to it and says, "Aagle." Having accomplished these two "scientific" tasks, he moves toward a door, points down to the metal doorknob and again utters, "Oogle." Next he points up to the top half of the wooden door and says, "Aagle." Suppose you were in a classroom experiencing all this; by now you might be sitting a little higher in your seat with your eyes brightening up a bit. When the experimenter points to the spout of a water fountain, what response do you suppose fills the room?

A chorus of "Oogle" you say? To this the experimenter smiles and replies, "No, it's an aagle." This process of pointing to things and telling to which category they belong continues until the people in the room are getting long runs of correct anticipations. The rule, the subjects later report, is based on which way the experimenter s finger points: if it points up, the object is an "oogle," if it points down, the object is an "aagle."

Consider another example. Young Billy is looking out the window and sees a poodle. His mother points to the poodle and says, "Dog." Then a German shepherd walks by and again mom points and says, "Dog." Next, a terrier wanders down the street and again mom points and says, "Dog." By now Billy is beginning to catch on, so when a new creature strolls into view he jumps up and down wildly, pointing to the little animal and shouting, "Dog!" However, this time his mom says, "No, Billy, that's a cat."

All these tasks are examples of *concept learning* because the subject must learn a rule for classifying objects into mutually exclusive categories. In general, each particular presentation of a to-be-classified stimulus is called a *trial* or *instance* (for example, one-red-large-circle is the first instance of a No category), each instance may have several *dimensions* (number, color, size, and so on), and each dimension may have several possible *values* or *features* (red or green color, large or small size, and so on).

These examples illustrate two main types of concept-learning tasks. When all the basic stimulus dimensions are described in advance to the subject who must then identify the relevant rule, this type of concept learning is called *concept*

BOX 4 ▪ 1   A Concept-Learning Task

You will be given a series of stimuli, individually, with each item varying in shape (circle or square), size (large or small), color (red or green), and number (one or two). Cover the column labeled "Correct Group" with a folded piece of paper. For each item listed on the left, guess its group (either Group Yes or Group No), then slide the folded paper down one notch to check the correct answer, and so on.

Instance	Your Prediction	Correct Group
1 red large square	_____	No
1 green large square	_____	No
2 red small squares	_____	Yes
2 red large circles	_____	No
1 green large circle	_____	No
1 red small circle	_____	Yes
1 green small square	_____	Yes
1 red small square	_____	Yes
2 green large squares	_____	No
1 red large circle	_____	No
2 green small circles	_____	Yes
2 red small circles	_____	Yes
2 green large circles	_____	No
2 green small squares	_____	Yes
2 red large squares	_____	No
1 green small circle	_____	Yes

identification: in the first example, for instance, you were told all the dimensions such as red versus green color, large versus small shape, and so on. When the subject does not know the basic set of potentially important stimulus dimensions and must develop or produce it in addition to identifying the relevant rule, the task is called *concept formation;* the oogle-aagle problem, in which you were not told that the dimensions included wood versus metal, up versus down finger, and so on, is an example of that kind of concept learning. Note that when people try to solve problems like any of these, they sometimes begin by forming rules or hypotheses that are based on the wrong or too few dimensions—for example, small = yes; metal = oogle; animal = dog—but as more experience is acquired, correct performance increases. The remainder of this chapter will investigate the thinking process that underlies this improvement.

■

RULE INDUCTION DEFINITION OF THINKING

■

The concept-learning example provides a basis for a theory of thinking that can go beyond the simple response hierarchy model. The thinking process required in concept learning has been characterized in a number of ways, including two basic classes of theories:

The continuity theory views concept learning as a direct extension of the S-R associationist model. Each feature of an instance serves as a stimulus, and the particular response is strengthened for all presented features on each trial. Thus, after many instances are presented, only the relevant features will have consistent (and therefore strong) responses associated with them. Thinking is simply building response hierarchies.

The noncontinuity theory views concept learning as *inducing rules* (or hypotheses) and *testing* them. If the rule can predict class membership for any instance, it is retained, but if it cannot predict class membership, a new hypothesis is generated. Thinking is hypothesis testing.

The continuity or S-R associationist view and the noncontinuity or hypothesis-testing view yield different predictions about subject behavior, which the next two sections of this chapter will investigate in more detail.

CONTINUITY THEORY

The most obvious and straightforward theory of thinking is that the concept-learning task is a simple extension of the response (or habit) hierarchy model described in Chapter 2. During concept learning, the subject forms a response hierarchy for each attribute in the problem by tallying the number of times each category response has been or has not been associated with a given attribute. When a new example is given, the subject simply adds the response strengths for all the attributes present in the new example.

For example, consider the situation in Box 4-1 in which subjects are shown cards with drawings that are either red or green in color, large or small in size, round or square in shape, and one or two in number. The continuity theory assumes that each type of color, size, number, and shape builds its own response hierarchy (with the associated responses either Yes or No) based on past experience, as shown in Box 4-2. For example, suppose that the subject has just been shown the first six objects described in Box 4-1 and now must determine whether one green small square is a Yes or a No. In Box 4-2, the response hierarchy for green favors a No response since it has been associated with No many times and few times with Yes; similarly the hierarchy for one favors No; the

BOX 4 • 2   Continuity Theory of Concept Learning

Using the example given in Box 4-1, the continuity theory suggests that subjects keep a tally of the number of times each attribute (for example, red, circle, and so on) has been associated or not associated with a Yes or a No. For the first few instances the tally could be as follows.*

Instance	Group	Number		Color		Size		Shape	
		1	2	R	G	L	S	C	S
1 red large square	No	−	+	−	+	−	+	+	−
1 green large square	No	−	+	+	−	−	+	+	−
2 red small squares	Yes	−	+	+	−	−	+	−	+
2 red large circles	No	+	−	−	+	−	+	−	+
1 green large circle	No	−	+	+	−	−	+	−	+
1 red small circle	Yes	+	−	+	−	−	+	+	−

*Minus means the attribute was part of an object put into Group No or not part of an object put into Group Yes; plus means that the attribute was part of an object put into Group Yes or not part of an object put into Group No.

To determine the response hierarchy for each new instance, the tendency to say Yes or No for each attribute must be added up for all previous instances. For example, after the first three instances, the response tendencies for the fourth instance are:

Two: 3 Yes and 0 No
Red: 2 Yes and 1 No
Large: 0 Yes and 3 No
Circle: 2 Yes and 1 No

To determine the response for 2 red large circles, the total is 7 Yes and 5 No, so there may be a weak tendency to say Yes, the wrong answer. However, after more experience the irrelevant dimensions become neutral. If the seventh instance is 1 green small square, the tallies are:

One: 2 Yes and 4 No
Grow: 2 Yes and 4 No
Small: 6 Yes and 0 No
Square: 3 Yes and 3 No

The totals are 13 Yes and 11 No, so the response may be a mild Yes.

hierarchy for small is strongly Yes, and there is equal preference for Yes and No for square. The individual tendencies for one, green, small, and square add (or subtract) to yield a weak Yes response as shown in Box 4-2. If one green small square turns out to be a Yes, the response strength for Yes for each attribute would

BOX 4 · 3   Hull's Concept-Learning Experiment

Six of the Chinese radicals that Hull used are shown here. First, the subject was shown a Chinese character and guessed its "name" (for example, oo), then the experimenter gave the correct name, and so on. Characters with the same radicals always were given the same name so that after going through several packs of characters, the subjects improved their performances and were eventually able to correctly name characters they had never seen before.

From Hull (1920)

be modified and so on. As practice continues, the difference between Yes and No response strengths will become closer to zero for all nonsize attributes and the differences for large versus small size will continue to grow.

Hull (1920) was the first to investigate this abstraction process in concept learning experimentally. Subjects learned to give one of twelve responses to twelve Chinese characters like those in Box 4-3. First the character was shown, then the subject made a response such as "oo," "li," "ta," and then the correct response was given to the subject. Once a subject had correctly responded to all twelve characters, a second pack of twelve was shown but the same twelve responses were associated with each character as with the first group. This process continued with several different packs. Chinese characters contain certain basic features called "radicals," and in the experiment the same radical was always associated with the same response. Subjects showed much improvement with later packs of characters and were often able to guess the correct response for characters they had never seen before. Hull concluded that they had abstracted the basic radicals and had developed strong tendencies to respond to them as described by the continuity theory. The relevant attributes, in this case the radicals, strongly evoked different responses while the irrelevant features around the radicals tended to become neutral. The abstraction process could be speeded up by coloring the radicals red, thus drawing the subject's attention to the relevant dimension. This speeding up is an example of "cue salience"—the idea that certain aspects of the stimulus are more salient than others.

NONCONTINUITY THEORY

Can concept learning be explained by this straightforward view of the thinker as passively and gradually tallying past experience into multiple response hierarchies? An alternative view is that concept learning is not a process of gradually strengthening associations at all, but rather a noncontinuous or discontinuous process of constructing and testing hypotheses until one works. According to the hypotheses-testing view, individuals actively try to formulate rules and then stick with their rule until it fails to work. This has been called the "win stay, lose switch" strategy.

For example, in the task shown in Box 4-1, a subject who is first told that one red large circle is No might hypothesize that "red is No, green is Yes," and when shown one green large square, will guess Yes. Since that is a wrong guess, the subject will make up a new hypothesis such as "one is No, two is Yes" which works for two red small squares, but when this fails on two red large circles may change the hypothesis to "small is Yes, large is No" and from then on make no more errors. In this noncontinuity view, thinking involves making a hypothesis and keeping it until it is disconfirmed rather than being a gradual learning of associations. Finding the correct solution is an "all or none" process.

The Kendlers (Kendler & D'Amato, 1955; Kendler & Kendler, 1959, 1962a, 1962b, 1975) attempted to investigate the two theories of concept learning in a series of experiments involving shifts in the rules. Stimuli were presented in pairs, the subject picked one, and the experimenter then gave the correct answer. For example, suppose a subject learns the set of responses given in Box 4-4: Yes for black-large and white-large and No for black-small and white-small. The rule can then be switched in two ways: a *reversal shift*, in which the two larges become No and the two smalls become Yes, or a *nonreversal shift*, in which a new dimension is used, such as labeling black as Yes and white as No. If concept learning involves strengthening single S-R

BOX 4 · 4   Reversal and Nonreversal Shifts

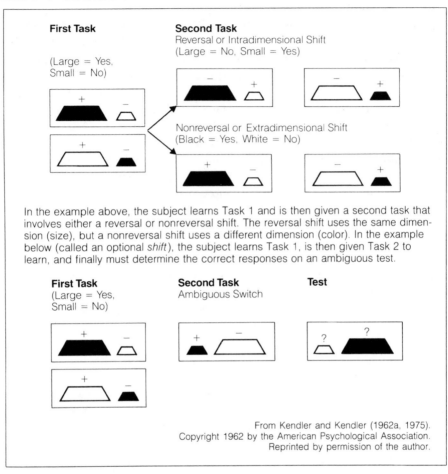

In the example above, the subject learns Task 1 and is then given a second task that involves either a reversal or nonreversal shift. The reversal shift uses the same dimension (size), but a nonreversal shift uses a different dimension (color). In the example below (called an optional *shift*), the subject learns Task 1, is then given Task 2 to learn, and finally must determine the correct responses on an ambiguous test.

associations (continuity theory), then the reversal shift should be more difficult to learn since it requires changing four associations while the nonreversal shift requires changing only two links. However, if concept learning involves forming a rule that *mediates* between the stimulus and the response (noncontinuity theory), then in a reversal shift the same dimension mediates and only new labels need be added while in the nonreversal shift a new dimension and new labels must be found. A long series of studies showed that the reversal shift was easier to learn than the nonreversal shift for college students and verbal children (children over 5 years of age), but that the nonreversal shift was easier for preverbal children (children under 5 years of age) and for laboratory animals.

In another set of experiments, subjects were taught that the appropriate responses for figures such as black-large and white-large were Yes and for black-small and white-small were No. Then there was an ambiguous switch—for example, subjects learned black-small was now Yes and white-large was now No. What was black-large or white-small? If the subject responded that black-large was Yes and white-small was No, that was a nonreversal shift—two of the original associations were retained and the classification rule was based on a new dimension, color. If the subject said No for black-large and Yes for white-small, that was a reversal shift—all four of the original associations were changed but the original dimension, size, was retained. Since a nonreversal shift required changing fewer new associations, it could be predicted by the continuity view; the noncontinuity theory would predict that since thinking is based on rules instead of individual associations, a reversal shift was more likely. Younger children typically preferred nonreversal shifts, but older children and adults tended to prefer reversal shifts. This is illustrated by the percentages of reversal shifts: 37 percent for 3-year-olds, 50 percent for 5-year-olds, and 62 percent for 10-year-olds. Kendler and Kendler concluded that as age increases, thinking in the concept-learning situation is more likely to be mediated by a general rule rather than by individual associations.

Another test of the continuity-noncontinuity argument was conducted by Bower and Trabasso (1963; Trabasso & Bower, 1964, 1968). They gave college student subjects a concept-learning task similar to the one shown in Box 4-1, made up of six dimensions, each with two attributes: color (red or blue), size (large or small), shape (square or hexagonal), number (three or four), position (right or left), and shaded area (upper right and lower left or upper left and lower right). The stimuli were presented one at a time, with the subject asked to anticipate which of two classes each stimulus belonged to, the experimenter then giving the correct answer, and so on. In observing the performance of their subjects, Bower and Trabasso noted that the pattern of performance remained at chance level for a long time, then jumped suddenly to 100 percent correct. This observation seemed consistent with the noncontinuity theory, but to test the theory more closely, Bower and Trabasso performed a further experiment in which the solution rule was changed while the subjects were still responding at chance level, that is, before they had learned the original rule: red = 1, blue = 2. The continuity theory predicts that such a switch would seriously hurt learning since associative strengths have been slowly getting stronger for the relevant cues; the noncontinuity theory predicts that the switch will not make any difference since the problem solver has not yet induced the classification rule. The results clearly supported the noncontinuity view: changing the solution rule prior to learning did not slow learning in a group of subjects compared with another group that retained the same rule throughout the experiment. Apparently these subjects formed a hypothesis, tested it on new stimuli, and changed it on the basis of negative feedback without the need to tally past experiences with particular attributes. The Bower and Trabasso results indicate that when these subjects picked a new hypothesis they did not benefit at all from a long chain of past experience; each new selection of a hypothesis may have been made independent of previous hypotheses. Mathematical models based on this idea are discussed by Restle and Greeno (1970).

On the basis of these findings, the noncontinuity theory seems to be the better description of the thinking of college students and some verbal children. Oster and Fivel (1961) investigated the pattern of performance before solution on a concept identification task with high school students. They observed that the students with IQs over 110 showed the same sudden learning noted by Bower and Trabasso—a period of chance performance, presumably while incorrect hypotheses were being selected, followed by 100 percent performance when the correct hypothesis was finally chosen. However, students of average and below-average intelligence displayed a pattern in which the rate of correct response for each individual rose gradually. One interpretation of these findings is that the bright students made successive hypotheses while the strategy of the other students was learning by association.

■
INDUCING RULES IN CONCEPT-LEARNING TASKS
■

STRATEGIES FOR HYPOTHESIS TESTING

What strategies do people use to solve concept-learning tasks? Probably the best known and most often cited concept-learning experiment was conducted by Bruner, Goodnow, and Austin (1956) and published in their classic monograph, *A Study of Thinking.* They used a set of eighty-one stimuli, shown in Box 4-5, which consisted of four *dimensions* with three *values* (or attributes) per dimension: *shape*—circle, square, cross; *color*—red, green, black; *number of borders*—one, two, or three; and *number objects*—one, two, or three.

Classification rules could be formulated in several ways, but the three main classes of rules used by Bruner, Goodnow, and Austin were: (1) *single-value concepts,* in which the concept was defined as having one particular value on one particular dimension, ignoring all other dimensions (for example, red); (2) *conjunctive concepts,* in which the concept was defined as having one value on one dimension *and* another value on another dimension (red crosses, for example); and (3) *disjunctive concepts,* in which the concept was defined as having one value on one dimension *or* a different value on another dimension (red or cross).

BOX 4 • 5   Stimuli Used in Concept-Learning Experiments

Subjects either selected or were given one card at a time. Then they "guessed" whether it was a positive or negative instance and were told the correct answer. The cards varied in shape, color, number of borders, and number of objects.

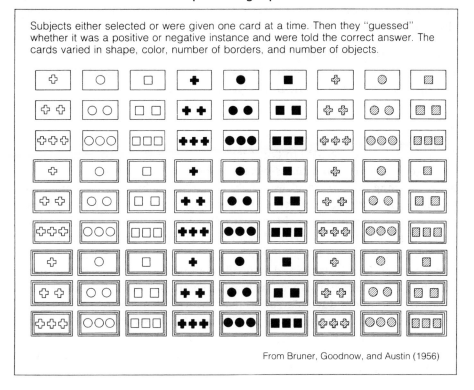

From Bruner, Goodnow, and Austin (1956)

Once a classification rule had been selected, a method was needed for presenting the desired positive *instances* (or exemplars) of the concept and the negative instances (or nonexemplars) to the subject. The two most important methods used were: (1) the *reception method,* in which the experimenter picked the stimulus cards one at a time, the subject said whether she thought each card was a negative or positive instance, and the experimenter told her whether or not she was correct, and (2) the *selection method,* in which the subject looked at the entire board of eighty-one stimuli, picked the cards one at a time and said for each whether she thought it was a positive or negative instance of the rule, and the experimenter indicated whether or not the answer was correct.

In observing the solution process of concept-learning problems under these conditions, Bruner, Goodnow, and Austin noted that their subjects seemed to use certain strategies. With the reception method, for example, two distinct *reception strategies* were noted:

Wholist strategy—with this the subject had to remember all the attributes common to those instances where the response was correct and ignore everything else, thus eliminating attributes that were not part of a positive instance.

Partist strategy—here the subject focused on one hypothesis at a time (for example, color green = Yes), kept the hypothesis if it correctly predicted the membership of a stimulus card, and formed a new one based on all past experience if it did not.

These strategies are specified in Box 4-6.

In general, Bruner and his associates found that wholist strategy resulted in better learning performance, especially when the subjects were under time pressure. The partist strategy requires the subject to retain all prior information and select a hypothesis consistent with this information, while the wholist strategy incorporates a record of all past instances within the current hypothesis. The subject using a wholist strategy remembers all the values of the first correct response or positive instance and gradually eliminates those that fail to reappear on subsequent positive instances. Although negative instances have not been an important part of our discussion of Bruner's theory, other researchers have found that subjects can learn equally well with negative instances as with positive (Freibergs & Tulving, 1961).

With the selection method of presentation, Bruner, Goodnow, and Austin noted several selection strategies:

Simultaneous scanning, in which the subject began with all possible hypotheses and eliminated the untenable ones after each instance.

Successive scanning, in which the subject began with one hypothesis, kept it if it correctly predicted class membership, and changed it to another based on all past experience if it did not.

Conservative focusing, in which the subject picked one positive instance and selected subsequent cards that changed one attribute value at a time.

Focus gambling, in which the subject picked one positive instance and selected subsequent cards that changed several attribute values at a time.

The scanning strategies are similar to the partist strategies and the focusing strategies are similar to the wholist. Again, focusing is usually far more efficient because it does not require as much memorization.

BOX 4 • 6   Strategies in Concept Learning

When subjects are presented with a series of instances selected from those shown in Box 4-5 and told whether each is a positive or negative instance, they may adopt one of the following strategies or a mixed combination

Wholist Strategy

Take the first positive instance and retain all the positive attributes as the initial hypothesis. Then, as more instances are presented, eliminate any attribute in this set which does not occur with a positive instance:

	Positive Instance	Negative Instance
Confirming	Maintain the hypothesis now in force	Maintain the hypothesis now in force
Infirming	Take as the next hypothesis what the old hypothesis and the present instance have in common	Impossible unless one has misreckoned. If one has misreckoned, correct from memory of past instances and present hypothesis

Partist Strategy

Begin with part of the first positive instance as a hypothesis (for example, choose just one attribute). Then retain or change it in the following way:

	Positive Instance	Negative Instance
Confirming	Maintain the hypothesis now in force	Maintain the hypothesis now in force
Infirming	Change hypothesis to make it consistent with past instances; that is, choose a hypothesis not previously infirmed	Change hypothesis to make it consistent with past instances; that is, choose a hypothesis not previously infirmed

From Bruner, Goodnow, and Austin (1956)

MODELS OF HYPOTHESIS TESTING

The strategies by Bruner, Goodnow, and Austin suggest that subjects create and test hypotheses based on all relevant past instances. However, Restle (1962) and

BOX 4 • 7   Hypothesis-Testing Models

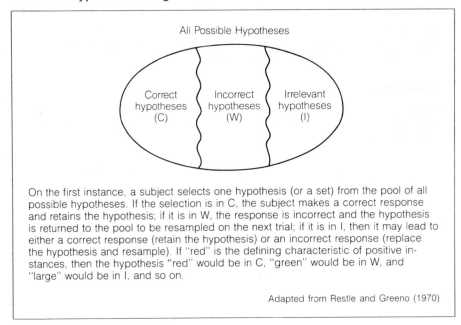

All Possible Hypotheses

Correct
hypotheses
(C)

Incorrect
hypotheses
(W)

Irrelevant
hypotheses
(I)

On the first instance, a subject selects one hypothesis (or a set) from the pool of all possible hypotheses. If the selection is in C, the subject makes a correct response and retains the hypothesis; if it is in W, the response is incorrect and the hypothesis is returned to the pool to be resampled on the next trial; if it is in I, then it may lead to either a correct response (retain the hypothesis) or an incorrect response (replace the hypothesis and resample). If "red" is the defining characteristic of positive instances, then the hypothesis "red" would be in C, "green" would be in W, and "large" would be in I, and so on.

Adapted from Restle and Greeno (1970)

Bower and Trabasso (1964; Trabasso & Bower, 1968) have proposed a basic model to account for hypothesis testing. Represented in Box 4-7 this model has two ideas: (1) the *sampling idea* that the subject samples one hypothesis (or set of hypotheses) from a pool of all possible hypotheses that may be correct, incorrect. or irrelevant and (2) the *no-memory idea* that if the hypothesis results in correct classification of an instance it is retained, otherwise it is replaced in the pool and a new hypothesis (or set of hypotheses) is selected.

To test this kind of model, Levine (1966) used a new approach to determine what strategy a subject was using in concept learning. In Levine's experiments subjects had to choose between two letters on a stimulus card like those shown in Box 4-8. The letters differed in color (black or white), position (left or right), size (large or small), and form (X or T). The subjects were told that they could choose from only eight possible hypotheses—right, left, large, small, black, white, T, or X—and were given four trials without being told if they were correct, followed by a fifth trial in which the experimenter randomly said either "Correct" or "Wrong." Levine noted it was clear that the subjects used hypotheses, since their responses on any set of

BOX 4 • 8   Levine's Blank Trial Procedure

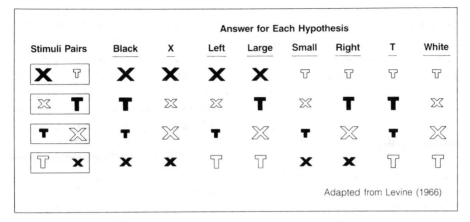

Adapted from Levine (1966)

four nonfeedback trials were consistent with one of the eight hypotheses more than 92 percent of the time. Based on the prior four responses, their choices on the fifth trial could be correctly predicted 97 percent of the time. Furthermore, the subjects tended to retain the same hypothesis if they were given positive feedback (95 percent of the time) and to change to another hypothesis if given negative feedback on the fifth trial (98 percent of the time). Levine's experiment is consistent with the idea that subjects use strategies, that they sample hypotheses one at a time, and that they use the win-stay, lose-switch policy, but it does not support the no-memory assumption of the model. For example, if the subjects sampled with replacement, they had a 12.5 percent chance (one in eight) of picking the same hypothesis after an "error"; yet the retention rate was only 2 percent. Levine's results indicate that subjects used some of their past experience, but certainly not all of it.

In a further experiment, Wickens and Millward (1971) gave their subjects large amounts of practice on a concept-learning task and tried to describe performance in terms of a hypothesis-testing model. The results were consistent with the idea that subjects tend to consider a small number of dimensions simultaneously, that a dimension paired inconsistently with the correct response is eliminated, and that when all the dimensions in a set are eliminated the subject samples a new set. These subjects apparently retained some information about previous dimensions that had been tested, but there were large individual differences in how many prior hypotheses could be remembered. It was always more than zero—indicating some memory load—but it was definitely limited.

FACTORS THAT INFLUENCE DIFFICULTY

There have been many studies investigating the factors make concept problems more or less difficult. One question concerns the role of positive and negative instances. In general, a subject who has developed a hypothesis tends to pick test cards that confirm it—that is, subjects tend to rely on positive instances to test their hypotheses and may be less able to use the information from a negative instance they have correctly predicted. In a typical experiment, Freibergs and Tulving (1961) gave twenty different concept-learning problems to a group of subjects. With each problem the subjects were given either all positive or all negative instances of the concept to be learned. For the first few problems, the subjects solved much faster with all positive instances (the median solution times were 50 to 140 seconds) than with all negative (no solutions within 210 seconds). However, after about fifteen problems there was no difference between the groups. Apparently these subjects had a preference for using information in positive instances but could learn, in a relatively short time, to effectively use the information in negative instances as well.

Another important factor that influences the difficulty of concept-learning problems is the complexity of the concept rule that must be induced. For example, several experiments have shown that increasing the number of relevant dimensions tends to decrease solution time since a subject can use any dimension to solve the problem; increasing the number of irrelevant dimensions makes the problem more difficult because it allows the subject more chances to pick a useless hypothesis (Bourne, 1966; Bourne, Ekstrand, & Dominowski, 1971; Walker & Bourne, 1961). In addition, solution performance was made more difficult under some conditions by increasing the number of values per dimension (Battig & Bourne, 1961) and by using disjunctive rather than conjunctive classification rules (Haygood & Stevenson, 1967).*

Hunt, Marin, and Stone (1966) have represented classification rules as sequential decision trees such as the one shown in Box 4-9. Since decisions about new instances are based on a series of tests going down the tree, more complex trees should be harder to learn. Evidence to support this idea came from a study by Trabasso, Rollins, and Shaughnessy (1971) in which the subjects read statements like "large triangle and red circle" and were shown a triangle and circle on a slide. The task was to verify the statement by responding Yes or No to the slide. Reading times were longer for complex trees than for simple ones, and decision times were also longer. Apparently, the classification can be represented

---

* Haygood, Herbert, and Omlor (1970) have defined the limited conditions under which increasing the number of values per dimension increases problem difficulty.

BOX 4 ▪ 9   A Sequential Decision Tree

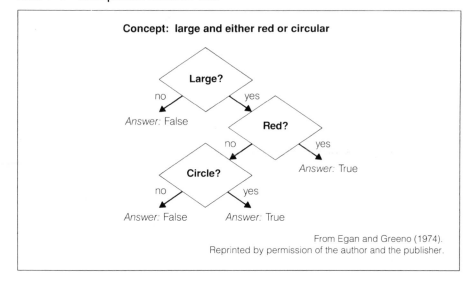

Concept: large and either red or circular

Large?

no   yes

Answer: False

Red?

no   yes

Answer: True

Circle?

no   yes

Answer: False   *Answer:* True

From Egan and Greeno (1974).
Reprinted by permission of the author and the publisher.

as a sequential decision tree, and as more decisions are needed the problem becomes more difficult.

Bourne (1970) obtained similar results in a concept-learning task in which subjects were presented with objects that varied in shape (square, circle, triangle) and color (red, green, blue) and were asked to classify them as Yes or No. The experimenter provided feedback based on either very complex or on short rules that were not stated to the subject. For example, a complex rule that defined red triangle and red circle as No and all others as Yes took an average of forty-five trials to learn: "If an object is red and is also a square, answer yes; if an object is red and is not a square, answer no; if an object is not red, answer yes." A simpler rule that defined red triangle as Yes and all others as No took an average of eighteen trials to learn: "If an object is red and is also a triangle, answer yes; otherwise answer no." Bourne (1970) suggested that concept learning may require learning a hierarchy of rules and subrules with complex problems incorporating several lower-level rules.

ABSTRACTION OF VISUAL PROTOTYPES

An alternative, or refinement, to the hypothesis-testing models of concept learning comes from a series of studies on learning to classify visual patterns. In previous sections, concept learning was broken down into two phases—learning

BOX 4 ▪ 10   Prototype Pattern of Dots and Various Degrees of Distortion

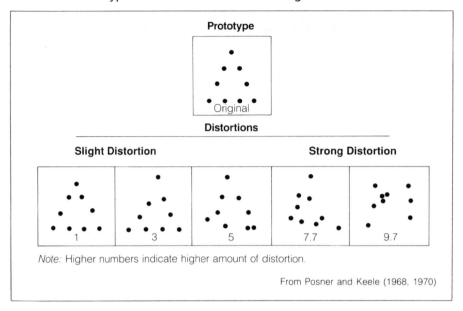

Note: Higher numbers indicate higher amount of distortion.

From Posner and Keele (1968, 1970)

to attend to the relevant attributes and learning the rule that should be applied to the attributes. However, another way of characterizing this initial process involves averaging all the instances of each category into a schematic or prototypical instance. For example, consider how someone learns to classify cars into categories such as Chevrolet, Ford, or Dodge, regardless of year or model, or how we learn to sort pocket change into pennies, nickels, dimes, and so on, regardless of mint year or amount of wear. There are several alternative theories to explain this, one of which is the *abstraction of prototype.* In the automobile example, an individual might have a mental image of a typical Chevy or Ford and compare any car against this ideal image. Another classification theory is *feature differentiation.* Here the subject learns to attend to particularly distinguishing cues, such as, say, the square headlights of Chevrolets versus the round headlights of Fords. Although the feature-differentiation view, which is an aspect of discrimination learning, is an implicit part of several models of concept learning, some subjects may use the prototype strategy in certain types of concept-learning tasks. Eventually, these two approaches must be reconciled to a theory of concept learning.

In a set of studies, Posner and Keele (1968, 1970) presented dot patterns like those shown in Box 4-10. Each pattern was constructed by distorting a nine-dot prototype; for example, to create a distortion, several of the dots, randomly selected, would be moved on the prototype either to the right or left or up or down. In a typical experiment, subjects were shown four different distortions of three separate prototypes and asked to classify each of these twelve dot patterns into one of three categories. Although the subjects never saw the actual prototypes, they were able to learn to classify their exemplars. More importantly, once the subjects had learned to classify the initial set of distorted patterns, they were given a test that consisted of classifying "new" distorted patterns made in the same way as the original ones, "old" distorted patterns, which were identical to those already learned, and the actual prototypes, which had never been presented. The results were that the old patterns were classified quite well (about 87 percent correct) and the new patterns were a bit more difficult (about 75 percent correct); however, the most striking finding was that the prototypes were classified correctly just as well as the old patterns, that is, the subjects behaved as if the prototypes were old patterns even though they had never been presented before. These results are consistent with the conclusion that the subjects *abstracted* the general prototype of the categories by averaging the characteristics of the distortions they saw and that they created the prototypes in their own memories.

Additional support for the prototype-abstraction idea comes from a similar study by Posner (1969) in which the subjects looked at a set of dot patterns that were distortions of a prototype. On a subsequent recognition test, they showed strong tendencies to classify the prototype as having been in the initial set although it had not been presented before. Apparently, the prototype-abstraction process occurs automatically even when deliberate concept learning is not called for.

Similar studies (Franks & Bransford, 1971; Reed, 1972) provide additional evidence that people sometimes use a prototype-abstraction strategy for learning to classify visual stimuli. In addition, people can use a variety of strategies; situational factors influence whether we average the features into a prototype or focus on distinctive features (Neumann, 1977).

■
INDUCING RULES ABOUT NUMBER PATTERNS
■

An extension, or refinement, of the hypothesis-testing models of concept learning comes from examining how people perform on Wason's (1960) 2–4–6 task, such as shown in the top of Box 4-11. For example, suppose I gave you a set of three numbers (e.g., 2, 4, 6) that conform to some rule and ask you to discover the rule. You may generate sets of three numbers, along with the rule you are

BOX 4 ▪ 11   Confirmation Bias on the 2–4–6 Task

Task

You will be given three numbers that conform to a simple rule. The rule is concerned with a relation between the numbers, not with their absolute magnitude. Your job is to discover the rule by writing down three numbers along with the reason for your choice. I will tell you whether or not the numbers conform to the rule. There is no time limit, but you should try to discover the rule using the minimum sets of numbers. When you feel highly confident that you have discovered the rule, and not before, you should write down the rule and circle it. The first set that conforms to the rule is 2-4-6.

Trial	Subject's Example	Feedback	Subject's Current Hypothesis	Strategy
1	4–6–8	Yes	Increasing by 2s	Confirmatory
2	10–12–14	Yes	Increasing by 2s	Confirmatory
3	6–8–10	Yes	Evens increasing by 2s	Confirmatory
4	20–22–24	Yes	Evens increasing by 2s	Confirmatory
5	32–34–36	Yes	Evens increasing by 2s	Confirmatory
6	8–10–12	Yes	Evens increasing by 2s	Confirmatory
7	Rule is "three even numbers that increase by 2s"			

testing, and I will tell you whether or not you are correct. When you are highly confident that you know the rule, stop and tell me the rule.

In this task, you must generate a hypothesis (such as "all triples that increase by twos") and test it. One way to test your hypothesis is to try to prove it by generating positive examples that conform to your hypothesized rule, such as 6–8–10 or 1–3–5; in contrast, another way is to try to falsify your hypothesis by generating negative examples, such as 10–8–6 or 5–3–1. As you can see, positive feedback for a confirmatory strategy provides ambiguous information—your hypothesis may be correct or another one may be correct; however, positive feedback for a disconfirmatory strategy provides conclusive evidence that your hypothesis is wrong. For this reason, scientists are encouraged to try to falsify rather than confirm their theories (Popper, 1959).

Do people behave like scientists on the 2–4–6 task? When Wason presented this task to adults, he found that the most commonly used strategy was to test a hypothesis by generating a positive rather than negative example; that is, people preferred to prove rather than disprove their hypotheses. If you are like the subjects in Wason's (1960) original study and in the many subsequent replications, you selected a hypothesis and tested it mainly by generating examples that conformed to it—a strategy Wason called *confirmation bias*.

For example, the bottom of Box 4-11 shows the performance of a typical subject on the 2–4–6 task. The subject begins by hypothesizing that the rule is "increasing by 2s". To test this hypothesis, the subject generates 4–6–8 and is told that this set conforms to the rule. Then the subject tests to see whether the rule works for two-digit numbers, 10–12–14, and again is told that the set conforms to the rule. Next, the subject tries 6–8–10 and again is given positive feedback. The subject tries three more examples in which even numbers increase by 2s and receives positive responses for each. The subject now is very confident that she knows the rule and announces it proudly: "any three even numbers that increase by 2s." Unfortunately, the subject is wrong; the experimenter's rule was "any three numbers in ascending order." Only now does the subject realize that a sequence such as l–2–3 or 5–16–27 also conforms to the rule. Like the subjects in Wason's study and in many replication studies, our subject shows a strong confirmation bias—she selects positive examples to test her hypothesis. How effective is this strategy? Wason found that 79 percent of the subjects confidently discovered a rule that was incorrect.

Why does a confirmation strategy lead people to believe they have proved a rule that actually is incorrect? Klayman and Ha (1989, p. 601) argue that in the 2–4–6 task, the tendency to try to confirm one's hypothesis "means it is easier for a tester to see ways of restricting a current hypothesis than ways of expanding it." Unfortunately, in most cases subjects begin with or soon develop a hypothesis that is more restricted than the experimenter's rule. For example, Klayman and Ha (1987, 1989) identified three common relations between the experimenter's rule and the subject's rule: the subject's rule (e.g., even numbers that increase by 2s) may be a subset of the experimenter's rule (e.g., all triples in increasing order); the subject's rule (e.g., even numbers that increase by 2s) may overlap with the experimenter's rule (e.g., three single-digit numbers); the subject's rule (e.g., even numbers that increase by 2s) may be a superset of the experimenter's rule (e.g., single-digit even numbers that increase by 2s). Box 4-12 shows that the only unambiguous information in the subset situation comes from generating a negative example, that is, using a disconfirmatory strategy; if your negative example leads to positive feedback, then you know that your rule is incorrect and should be changed. Box 4-12 also shows that the only unambiguous information

BOX 4 • 12   Three Common Relations Between Subject's Rule (S) and
Experimenter's Rule (E)

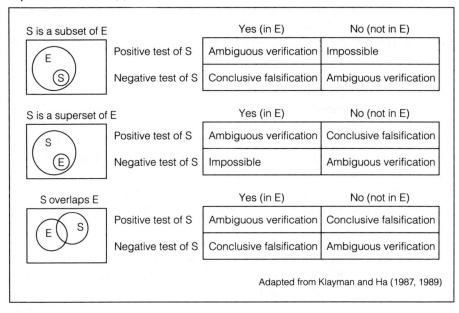

S is a subset of E		Yes (in E)	No (not in E)
	Positive test of S	Ambiguous verification	Impossible
	Negative test of S	Conclusive falsification	Ambiguous verification

S is a superset of E		Yes (in E)	No (not in E)
	Positive test of S	Ambiguous verification	Conclusive falsification
	Negative test of S	Impossible	Ambiguous verification

S overlaps E		Yes (in E)	No (not in E)
	Positive test of S	Ambiguous verification	Conclusive falsification
	Negative test of S	Conclusive falsification	Ambiguous verification

Adapted from Klayman and Ha (1987, 1989)

in the superset situation comes from receiving negative feedback for a positive example of one's rule; in this case, you know to change your rule. Finally, Box 4-12 shows that for the overlap situation, unambiguous information is obtained for both of these situations. Klayman and Ha (1987) concluded that generating positive tests of a hypothesis—which they call a *positive test strategy*—can lead to successful reasoning in certain cases, such as when there is a high probability that the positive tests will fail and when the tests are conducted on alternative hypotheses.

Over the course of eighteen trials, Klayman and Ha (1989) noted that the subjects stated an increasing number of rules that were subsets of the experimenter's rule while stating a decreasing number of overlap and superset rules. But once a subject develops a rule that is a subset of the experimenter's rule, she cannot expand her rule unless she tests alternative hypotheses. Consistent with Wason's results, subjects in Klayman and Ha's experiment strongly preferred to test hypotheses by generating positive rather than negative examples. In addition, Klayman and Ha (1989) found that subjects rarely tested alternative hypotheses that could help to expand a rule.

What do successful reasoners do that unsuccessful reasoners do not do? Let's consider four possible strategies for testing your current hypothesis (e.g., "even numbers increasing by 2s"): a *confirmatory strategy* in which you select an example that conforms (e.g., 4–6–8) to your current hypothesis, a *disconfirmatory strategy* in which you select an example that conflicts (e.g, 8–6–4) with your hypothesis, a *positive counterfactual strategy* in which you select an example that conforms (e.g., 1–3–5) to an alternative hypothesis (e.g., "odd numbers that increase by 2s"), and a *negative counterfactual strategy* in which you select an example (e.g., 5–3–1) that conflicts with an alternative hypothesis (e.g., "odd numbers that increase by 2s"). If negative feedback is useful in shaping a correct hypothesis, then we can predict that successful reasoners are more likely than unsuccessful reasoners to generate examples that lead to "this does not conform to the rule." Consistent with this prediction, Farris and Revlin (1989) found that students who successfully discovered the correct rule received negative feedback three times more often and required approximately 50 percent more trials than unsuccessful reasoners. A closer examination of students' performance showed that counterfactual reasoning was far more common than disconfirmation and that successful reasoners were twice as likely as unsuccessful reasoners to engage in counterfactual reasoning—that is, to test alternative hypotheses. Klayman and Ha (1989) obtained complimentary results: use of alternative (or counterfactual) hypotheses was far more common than disconfirmation, and successful reasoners were three times more likely than unsuccessful reasoners to use counterfactual strategies. For example, 81 percent of the examples generated by unsuccessful reasoners involved confirming their current hypothesis, compared to 52 percent for successful reasoners. The picture that emerges is that successful reasoners are more likely than unsuccessful reasoners to entertain alternative hypotheses, but they tend to test these alternative hypotheses by choosing positive examples.

■
INDUCING RULES THROUGH SCIENTIFIC EXPERIMENTS
■

Scientific reasoning involves designing experiments to test hypotheses and analyzing the results of experiments to form hypotheses (Inhelder & Piaget, 1958; Klahr & Dunbar, 1988). Although concept-learning and rule induction tasks form the basis for current theories of human inductive reasoning, you might wonder whether these theories also apply to the discovery of rules in more realistic scientific situations.

Klahr and Dunbar (1988) examined how students discover how to operate a six-wheeled toy robot tank called BigTrak. Box 4-13 shows the keypad used to program the actions of BigTrak. You begin by pressing CLR to clear the memory; then enter up to sixteen instructions, each consisting of a function key followed

BOX 4 ▪ 13   Keypad from BigTrak

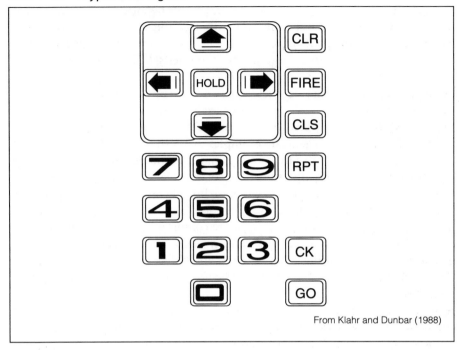

From Klahr and Dunbar (1988)

by a one- or two-digit number; and then press GO to have BigTrak execute your program. For example, suppose that you press the following buttons: CLR ↑ 5 ← 7 ↑ 3 → 15 HOLD 50 FIRE 2 ↓ 8 GO. If you enter a syntactically correct command (such as ↑ 5 or HOLD 50), BigTrak responds with a beep; if you enter an illegal command (such as ↑→ or ↓ 444), no beep is given and the offending keystrokes are ignored. Here's what BigTrak does as soon as you press GO: move forward 5 feet, rotate counterclockwise 42 degrees, move forward 3 feet, rotate clockwise 90 degrees, pause for 5 seconds, fire twice, and back up 8 feet. By entering commands and seeing what BigTrak does, you may discover the following:

↑ means to move forward and must be followed by 1 to 99 (with each unit indicating 1 foot)

↓ means to move backward and must be followed by 1 to 99 (with each unit indicating 1 foot)

← means to rotate counterclockwise and must be followed by 1 to 99 (with each unit indicating 6 degrees)

→ means to rotate clockwise and must be followed by 1 to 99 (with each unit indicating 6 degrees)

HOLD means to pause and must be followed by 1 to 99 (with each unit indicating one-tenth of a second)

FIRE means to make a loud blast sound and must be followed by 1 to 99 (with each unit indicating one blast)

CLS clears the last step

CK executes the last step in isolation

CLR clears all instructions

GO executes the program

In Klahr and Dunbar's (1988) experiments, subjects were taught how to use each of these ten instructions and were then asked to figure out how the RPT key worked. They could enter and run any programs until they were sure they had discovered what RPT did. They were asked to "think aloud" by stating their current hypothesis and telling what they were thinking as they pressed keys and watched BigTrak respond.

Box 4-14 gives the protocol of a subject in this experiment. As you can see, the subject begins with a hypothesis (lines 19–20) that RPT 1 means to repeat the last step one time and confirms this hypothesis by typing in a simple program (lines 21–22). Then the subject tests the hypothesis that RPT 4 means to repeat the last step four times (lines 25–26) but seems to disconfirm this theory by typing in a new program (lines 26–28). In lines 30–38 the subject develops the hypothesis that RPT 2 means to repeat the last two steps, testing this idea in lines 40 and 43. In the remainder of the protocol, the subject continues to test this hypothesis until he is convinced he knows how the RPT key works.

In analyzing subjects' protocols, Klahr and Dunbar (1988) noted that people had to make two kinds of selections. First, subjects must select a hypothesis. The most common hypotheses in order of preference were that RPT n means: repeat the last instruction n times, repeat the entire program n times, repeat the entire program one time, repeat the last instruction one time, repeat the nth instruction one time, repeat the first n instructions one time, repeat the last n instructions one time, repeat the next instruction one time. Second, subjects had to select an experiment to test their hypothesis. The experiments varied the number of steps before RPT (e.g., ↑ 2 → 15 FIRE 2 RPT 2 has three steps before RPT) and varied the argument for the repeat command (e.g., ↑ 2 → 15 FIRE 2 RPT 2 has the argument 2 immediately after RPT).

Consistent with previous research on the 2–4–6 task, subjects often failed to seek disconfirming evidence. Instead they used what Klayman and Ha (1987, 1989) call a *positive test strategy* of the form: "according to my hypothesis, BigTrak

BOX 4 • 14   Protocol from Subject Solving Big Trak Problem

002	EXP: SO HOW DO YOU THINK IT MIGHT WORK?
003	Uh. . . it would repeat all of the steps before it, however many times
004	I told it to repeat it.
005	EXP: WELL . . . SO START WORKING ON IT NOW THEN.
006	OK.
007	EXP: AND TELL ME EVERYTHING THAT'S GOING ON IN YOUR MIND.
008	OK.
009	EXP: NOW PRESS CLEAR.
010	OK, um . . . I'm gonna make it go
011	forward two, and then I'm gonna make it repeat that twice.
012	00:30 ↑2 RPT 2

$$\uparrow 4$$

013	Maybe not, uh . . . . . . repeat once
014	02:00 ↑1 ←15 ↑1 HOLD 2 RPT 1

$$\uparrow 1 \leftarrow 15 \; \uparrow 1 \; \text{HOLD } 4$$

015	*Hmm . . . guess that as it.*
016	EXP: SO WHAT ARE YOU THINKING?
017	Um . . . actually I have no idea now.
018	I'm trying to figure out what it is.
019	Um . . . maybe it repeats the last step.
020	OK, I'm gonna try that . . . . . . repeat once.
021	03:30 ↑2 ←30 RPT 1

$$\uparrow 2 \leftarrow 60$$

022	All right, that backs up my theory.
023	Let me see if I can somehow make sure that that's what it does
024	is repeats the last step however many times that I tell it to,
025	so I'm gonna . . . repeat it four times . . .
026	04:00 ↑2 ←30 RPT 4

$$\uparrow 2 \leftarrow 30 \; \uparrow 2 \leftarrow 30$$

027	
028	That was strange, hmm . . . um . . . let me see that again.
029	04:30 ↑2 ←30 RPT 4

$$\uparrow 2 \leftarrow 30 \; \uparrow 2 \leftarrow 30$$

030	OK, maybe it means repeat the last number . . .
031	however many steps before it that I put in,
032	that'll be the number after the repeat. For instance,
033	if I put repeat two, it'll repeat the last two steps.
034	If I put repeat five, it'll repeat the last five steps,
035	and if there's too many . . .
036	if the five is more than the number of steps in the program,
037	it'll just end it at whatever number of steps in the program,
038	so . . . repeat one, no, repeat two.
039	
040	06:00 ↑2 ←15 ↑2 FIRE 3 RPT 2

(continued)

BOX 4 · 14, *continued*

↑2 ←15 ↑2 FIRE 3 ↑2 FIRE 3

041   All right, I think I might have gotten it.
042
043   06:30 ↑2 ←15 ↑2 FIRE 3 RPT 3

↑2 ←15 ↑2 FIRE 3 ←15 ↑2 FIRE 3

044   OK, I think I've gotten it. I'm gonna make it repeat four times.
045   . . . wanna repeat four . . .
046   07:30 ↑2 ←15 ↑2 FIRE 3 RPT 4

↑2 ←15 ↑2 FIRE 3 ↑2 ←15 ↑2 FIRE 3

047   OK, now I'm trying to figure out which order the repeat step goes.
048   If it does the first part of the program or if it does . . . if it starts
049   from the last part of the program, where repeat . . .
050   if I say repeat one, does it repeat the first step in the program,
051   or does it repeat the last step I pressed in? Um . . . repeat that
052   step . . .
053
054   09:00 ↑2 ←15 ↑2 FIRE 3 RPT 1

↑2 ←15 ↑2 FIRE 6

055
056   It goes from the last step
057   and I don't understand why it doesn't go backwards.
058   Maybe it counts back two steps.
059   If I put repeat two, it would count back two steps,
060   starting from there and go until the last step. Alright,
061   . . . um . . . the last two steps were forward two and fire three,
062   so let me try and repeat that again.
063   10:00 ↑2 ←15 ↑2 FIRE 3 RPT 2

↑2 ←15 ↑2 FIRE 3 ↑2 FIRE 3

064   All right, now if I . . . repeat five . . .
065   so if I repeat four, it should do the whole program over again.
066   11:00 ↑2 ←15 ↑2 FIRE 3 RPT 4

↑2 ←15 ↑2 FIRE 3 ↑2 ←15 ↑2 FIRE 3

067   Well, I think I figured out what it does.
068   EXP: SO HOW DOES IT WORK?
069   OK, when you press the repeat key and then the number,
070   it comes back that many steps and then starts from there
071   and goes up to, uh . . . it proceeds up to the end of the program
072   and then it hits the repeat function again.
073   It can't go through it twice.
074   . . . . . .
075   EXP: GREAT

From Klahr and Dunbar (1988)

should do this." However, in 60 percent of the experiments, subjects received disconfirming evidence. Even though the subjects tended to generate programs they thought would confirm their hypothesis, their hypotheses were usually falsified. This finding is consistent with Klayman and Ha's argument that positive test strategies can lead to effective reasoning in cases when the probability pool of obtaining confirmation is low.

Also consistent with previous research, subjects frequently tolerated disconfirming evidence; approximately half the time they retained a hypothesis that had just been disconfirmed by an experiment. One reason for this behavior seems to be that the subjects think there may have been a mistake in the way the commands were received or executed; so they often replicate the identical experiment. Another reason is that subjects want to be very sure a hypothesis has been disconfirmed; when it has been disconfirmed in one experiment, they want to see it disconfirmed again before rejecting it.

Klahr, Dunbar, and Fay (1990) distinguished between successful and unsuccessful strategies in the RPT task. Strategies that lead to faster discovery of the rule include testing alternative hypotheses of different types (e.g., viewing n as determining the number of repetitions versus viewing n as the number of commands to be repeated) and designing experiments to explain surprising results; strategies that slow down progress include searching for confirmation of a hypothesis and focusing on a single hypothesis of one type. Interestingly, successful strategies in the RPT task are similar to successful strategies observed in computational models of scientific discovery (Kulkari & Simon, 1988; Langley, Simon, Bradshaw, & Zytkow, 1987). These results show that humans can be successful scientific reasoners, but further research is needed to determine the strategies that are most efficient for various situations.

■
INDUCING RULES ABOUT EVERYDAY EVENTS
■

In everyday life you often must make judgments based on your past experience. How likely is it that the bus will be late? How many times will you have to visit a doctor during the next year? What are your chances of dying in a plane crash? When we answer questions like these, we must base our answers on previous experience with frequencies or probabilities of certain events occurring.

FREQUENCY JUDGMENTS

Tversky and Kahneman (1974) have provided many examples of the mistakes that people make when they try to make predictions based on past experience.

For example, suppose I asked you to think of all the words you have ever read or heard spoken. Based on your experience, answer the following question. Consider the letter *r*. Is *r* more likely to appear in the first position of a word or in the third position? When Tversky and Kahneman posed this question to a large number of subjects, the great majority of people said that letters such as *r* (or *k* or *d*) occurred more frequently as the first letter of a word. However, an actual count of real words shows that these letters are more likely to occur in the third position.

How did people come up with the wrong generalization? According to Tversky and Kahneman (1973, 1974; Kahneman & Tversky, 1973), words that begin with r are easier to think of than words that have *r* as the third letter. In short, words that begin with *r* are more *available*. Apparently, people make generalizations about frequency based on the *availability* of the instances in memory rather than by an accurate count of actual past experience—a shortcut called the *availability heuristic*.

To test this idea in a controlled experiment, Tversky and Kahneman (1973) asked subjects to read a list of thirty-nine names of well-known people. Some of the lists contained nineteen female and twenty male names, but the women on the list were more famous than the men. Other lists contained nineteen male and twenty female names, but the men on the list were more well known. Later, when subjects were asked whether there were more men or women on the list they read, frequency estimates were heavily influenced by the fame of the names. Subjects overwhelmingly decided that there were more female names on the list that contained famous women and overwhelmingly decided that there were more males on the list that contained famous men. Again, as with the previous study, people's generalizations about frequency of events seemed to be influenced by the *availability* of the items; since the famous names were easier to remember, there seemed to be more of them.

As a final example of how availability influences judgments about frequency, consider what Tversky and Kahneman (1974) call "illusory correlation"—the generalization that two events occur together more often than they really do in actual life. For example, Chapman and Chapman (1967, 1969) asked subjects to read diagnoses of mentally ill patients; the subjects were also shown a picture of each patient. Later, subjects were asked to estimate how often certain diagnoses went with certain characteristics of the pictures. Subjects tended to overestimate related occurrences of salient associates, such as suspiciousness with peculiar eyes. Even when they were presented with contradictory evidence, subjects were reluctant to revise their judgments. Apparently, the expectation of a correlation between two attributes was so strong that people greatly overestimated how often the two occurred together in a given situation. Again, the association was highly *available* and thus influenced the subjects' judgments of frequency of co-occurrence.

PROBABILITY JUDGMENTS

Tversky and Kahneman (1974, 1982, 1983; Kahneman & Tversky, 1973) have also identified errors people make in judging the probabilities of events. The *gambler's fallacy* is based on the idea that the probability of a random event will be influenced by a previous string of events. For example, say that you flipped a fair coin and it came up heads five times in a row. What do you think the next outcome will be? Most people feel that tails is due to occur. According to statistical theory, of course, the probability of obtaining heads or tails is always the same 50 percent on each flip, regardless of previous results. However, Tversky and Kahneman (1974) reported that students think that some sequences, such as HTHTHT, are far more likely to occur than others, such as HHHHHT. Why do people think a long string of the same outcome is unlikely? One explanation is that people use what Tversky and Kahneman call the *similarity heuristic*—people base their judgments on the idea that HTHTHT seems similar to typical patterns but long runs do not resemble many previous experiences.

As an example of a fallacy involving sample size, consider the urn problem:

> Imagine an urn filled with balls, of which two-thirds are of one color and one-third are of another. One person has drawn 5 balls from the urn, and found that 4 were red and 1 was white. Another individual has drawn 20 balls and found that 12 were red and 8 were white. Which person should feel more confident that the urn contains twice as many red balls as white balls rather than the opposite? What odds should each individual give? (Tversky & Kahneman, 1974, p. 1125)

Most of Tversky and Kahneman's (1974) subjects believed that getting four out of five was stronger evidence than getting twelve out of twenty red balls. However, statistically computed odds favor the latter as better evidence. These results suggest that people have trouble taking sample size into account when make an inference. People seem to ignore the fact that you can be more sure of your generalization if it is based on a larger pool of past experience. When you ignore sample size, you are left with the conclusion that 80 percent red seems like better evidence than 60 percent red.

Next, consider the following medical problem described by Tversky and Kahneman (1982, p. 154):

> If a test to detect a disease whose prevalence is 1/1000 has a false positive rate of 5%, what is the chance that a person found to have a positive result actually has the disease, assuming you know nothing about the person's symptoms or signs?

When this problem was given to faculty and students at the Harvard Medical School, the most common answer was 95 percent. The correct answer, however, is 2 percent, an answer given by about one-fifth of the Harvard respondents. (To answer the question, suppose 1000 people were given the test; 1 of them would have the disease and would test positive and 5 percent of the remaining 999 people—or about 50 people—would not have the disease but would test positive; therefore, of the 51 people who test positive only 1 has the disease—yielding a probability of about 2 percent.) Tversky and Kahneman call this the *base rate fallacy* and, as in the previous examples, attribute it to the use of logical shortcuts, called *heuristics*. In this case, the subject seems to ignore the 1 in 1000 base rate and focus only on the false positive rate.

Finally, let's consider the Linda problem (Tversky & Kahneman, 1983, p. 299):

> Linda is 31 years old, single, outspoken, and very bright. She majored in philosophy. As a student, she was deeply concerned with the issues of discrimination and social justice and also participated in anti-nuclear demonstrations.
>
> Based on this information, which of the following two alternatives is more probable?

> (a) Linda is bank teller
> (b) Linda is a bank teller and is active in the feminist movement

Tversky and Kahneman (1983) found that most students chose (b) although (a) is the correct answer; subjects who believe that two concurrent events are more likely to happen that one of the events alone are said to commit the *conjunction fallacy.* According to Tversky and Kahneman, the prevalence of the conjunction fallacy suggests that people do not reason logically about the probabilities of everyday events. Instead they choose (b) because it describes a person who seems more typical of or similar to the description given. Again, subjects appear to use shortcut heuristics—such as picking the most representative alternative—rather than basing their judgments on the rules of statistical logic.

MAKING COGNITIVE BIASES DISAPPEAR

The picture that emerges from Tversky and Kahneman's line of research is that people often use shortcut heuristics rather than logical reasoning when they think about the probabilities of everyday events. However, Gigerenzer (in press) has recently summarized some studies that seriously challenge this interpretation. Gigerenzer argues that humans find it more natural to reason about how frequently an event occurs than about how probable an event is. When probability questions are restated as frequency questions, the fallacies in judgment seem to disappear.

Consider, for example, what happens to the conjunction fallacy in the Linda problem when we change the question to:

There are 100 persons who fit the description above (i.e., Linda's). How many of them are

(a) bank tellers
(b) bank tellers and active in the feminist movement?

The answer is that the conjunction fallacy largely disappears (Fiedler, 1988)—people no longer choose (b) more often than (a).

As another example, let's see what happens to the base rate fallacy in the disease problem when the question is changed to:

How many people who test positive for the disease will actually have the disease? _____ out of _____

Cosmides and Tooby (1990) found that the overwhelming majority of the students gave the correct answer when they were asked to give a judgment of frequency rather than probability, that is, to think about how many people will test positive and how many of those will actually have the disease.

These results call into question the claim that humans generally rely on shortcut heuristics rather than logical reasoning processes. Gigerenzer (in press) argues that the heuristics that were proposed in the early 1970s—such as availability and similarity (or representativeness)—were promising but have failed to develop into a theory of human reasoning. Instead, Gigerenzer (in press) notes that "in the 20 years of heuristics and biases research since then, a lack of theoretical progress is possibly the most striking result." In spite of this critique, we should note that the judgment research has extended work on inductive reasoning to real-world problems and has produced a large collection of reasoning errors that deserve further study. During the next decade, research is likely to focus on the conditions under which errors occur, and ultimately a coherent theory of human reasoning may emerge.

■
EVALUATION
■

Traditionally, concept-learning tasks have been targeted by researchers interested in human inductive thinking. One advantage of concentrating on an agreed-upon task is that researchers have been able to amass an impressive amount of detailed information about how humans solve concept learning problems. A disadvantage, however, is that the concept-learning task is just one kind of problem-solving situation. It is not clear how far one can generalize from laboratory studies on learning of artificial categories to the full range of human thought. For these reasons, it is useful that research on rule induction has begun to examine other situations, including how people induce rules in other artificial problems (such as the 2–4–6 task), in scientific hypothesis testing (such as in the BigTrak problem), and about everyday experiences (such as making judgments about frequencies and probabilities).

We can analyze research on rule induction according to three distinct stages. Early work prior to 1950 was concerned largely with how laboratory animals learned in discrimination tasks (see Levine, 1975). Then, during the 1950s and 1960s, concept-learning paradigms designed for animals were adapted to humans. Results indicated that the continuity theory was adequate for describing some animal learning but inadequate for describing how humans induce rules. In particular, humans came to be seen as hypothesis generators and hypothesis testers. More recently, attention has shifted to how humans form and test hypotheses in more natural situations. This line of research on the development of "natural categories" is described in Chapter 9, and research on inducing rules about series completion problems—a common intelligence test item—is described in Chapter 11.

Suggested Readings

BRUNER, J. S., GOODNOW, J. J., & AUSTIN, G. A. (1956). *A study of thinking.* New York: Wiley. Describes a classic set of experiments on concept learning.

KAHNEMAN, D., SLOVIC, P., & TVERSKY, A. (Eds.). (1982). *Judgement under uncertainty: Heuristics and biases.* Cambridge, England: Cambridge University Press. Contains an edited collection of research papers on how people induce rules about everyday events.

LANGLEY, P., SIMON, H. A., BRADSHAW, G. L., & ZYTKOW, J. M. (1987). *Scientific discovery: Computational explorations of the creative process.* Cambridge, MA: M.I.T. Press. Presents an analysis of scientific problem solving from a cognitive science viewpoint.

CHAPTER · 5

DEDUCTIVE REASONING

Thinking as Logically Drawing Conclusions

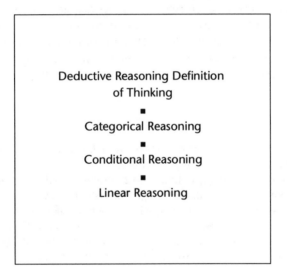

Deductive Reasoning Definition
of Thinking

▪

Categorical Reasoning

▪

Conditional Reasoning

▪

Linear Reasoning

SYLLOGISMS

Consider the three problems in Box 5-1 and then pick the conclusion that logically follows each one.

If you think like most people—or at least like most people who participate in psychology experiments—problem 1 was probably the easiest for you (Answer: A).

BOX 5 • 1   Sample Syllogisms

Pick the conclusion you can be sure of.

1. All S are M
   All M are P
   Therefore,
   A. All S are P
   B. All S are not P
   C. Some S are P
   D. Some S are not P
   E. None of these conclusions is valid

2. As technology advances and natural petroleum resources are depleted, the secur-
   ing of petroleum from unconventional sources becomes more imperative. One
   such source is the Athabasca tar sands of northern Alberta, Canada. Since some
   tar sands are sources of refinable hydrocarbons, these deposits are worthy of
   commercial investigation. Some kerogen deposits are also sources of refinable hydrocarbons. Therefore:
   A. All kerogen deposits are tar sands.
   B. No kerogen deposits are tar sands.
   C. Some kerogen deposits are tar sands.
   D. Some kerogen deposits are not tar sands.
   E. None of the above.

3. The delicate Glorias of Argentina, which open only in cool weather, are all Sas-
   soids. Some of the equally delicate Fragilas, found only in damp areas,
   are not Glorias. What can you infer from these statements?
   A. All Fragilas are Sassoids.
   B. No Fragilas are Sassoids.
   C. Some Fragilas are Sassoids.
   D. Some Fragilas are not Sassoids.
   E. None of the above.

Adapted from Stratton (1967)

However, problems 2 and 3 generate much higher error rates—75 percent errors for
problem 2, with most errors due to subjects picking C instead of E, and 90 percent
errors in problem 3, mainly due to subjects picking D instead of E.

Although these results (based on data from Stratton, 1967, and reported by
Johnson, 1972) do not suggest that people are stupid, they do indicate that formal
logic and individual mental or psycho-logic are not necessarily the same.

Now try the syllogisms in Box 5-2, indicating for each one whether the conclusion
logically follows.

If you are like most of Lefford's (1946) subjects, you had much more difficulty
answering Yes to problem 1 than to problem 3 and more difficulty answering No
to problem 2 than to problem 4. Although problems 1 and 3 have the same
formal characteristics and length (all A are B, all B are C, therefore all A are C), and
2 and 4 have the same formal characteristics and length (all A are B, all C are B,

BOX 5 ▪ 2   Questionable Conclusions

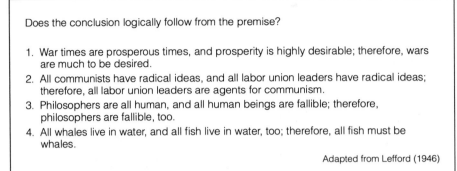

Does the conclusion logically follow from the premise?

1. War times are prosperous times, and prosperity is highly desirable; therefore, wars are much to be desired.
2. All communists have radical ideas, and all labor union leaders have radical ideas; therefore, all labor union leaders are agents for communism.
3. Philosophers are all human, and all human beings are fallible; therefore, philosophers are fallible, too.
4. All whales live in water, and all fish live in water, too; therefore, all fish must be whales.

Adapted from Lefford (1946)

therefore all C are A), problems 1 and 2 are far more difficult. Apparently, human reasoning or psycho-logic is influenced not only by the form of the argument but also by the desirability or amount of agreement with the conclusion.

Syllogisms like the ones just given require deductive thinking—deducing or deriving a conclusion from given premises. This contrasts with inductive thinking, discussed in Chapter 4, which involves inducing or formulating or extrapolating a rule based on limited information. In deductive thinking, the propositions or rules are given and the thinker uses this given information to derive a conclusion that can be proven correct. Mathematical proofs, for example, are deductive. Inductive thinking, however, such as concept learning, can never result in a provable rule because new information may come along that violates the induced rule; since induced rules are based on a limited set of information, they require the thinker to go beyond that information, to generalize. Since human beings and many other kinds of animals are capable of solving both induction and deduction tasks, such tasks have received much research attention in psychology. Although induction and deduction are tasks rather than theories of thinking, each has an implied view of human thinking. In Chapter 4 we investigated the idea—fostered by examining induction—that thinking involves a constant searching (sampling) for a rule. In this chapter, we shall focus on the perspective—suggested by work in deduction—that thinking involves combining information by using a set of psychological and mathematical operations.

■
DEDUCTIVE REASONING DEFINITION OF THINKING
■

Although deductive reasoning is not a theoretical approach in the same sense that associationism and Gestalt are, deduction implies that thinking involves the combining of existing information by following specific mental operations as in addition or subtraction. This approach, consistent with the information-processing approach, interprets thinking as the processing of premises by using specifiable operators—similar but not identical to formal logical operators.

William James (1890) devoted nearly an entire chapter of his classic textbook on psychology to describing the two main processes involved in deductive reasoning: analysis and abstraction. Analysis refers to the process of breaking down an object into its parts and then substituting a part for the object, whereas abstraction refers to subsuming a specific property under a broader, more general rule. As an example of analysis, to process the proposition "Socrates is a man," a thinker must think of Socrates only in terms of one property. James argued that analysis requires a "mode of conceiving"—a way of referring to Socrates (as a man). As an example of abstraction, the thinker, to process the proposition "All men are mortal," must subsume Socrates as a man under the general heading of "mortality." Although James's conception of the analysis and abstraction processes may not necessarily be the best or the most precise (this is really an empirical question to be answered by sound experimental research), it does suggest that deduction may be viewed as a series of specific processes or operations performed on information.

The main focus of this approach is the *syllogism,* which consists of two premises and a conclusion. Three types of syllogisms will be discussed in this chapter: (1) *categorical syllogisms,* such as, "All A are B; All B are C; Therefore, All A are C"; (2) *linear syllogisms,* such as, "A is greater than B; B is greater than C; Therefore, A is greater than C"; and (3) *conditional syllogisms,* such as "If p, then q; p is true; Therefore, q is true." In each case, you are given some premises that you must accept as true; then you draw a logical conclusion. Aristotle claimed that syllogistic reasoning represented the highest achievement in human rational thought. Thus many psychologists have focused on human performance in syllogistic tasks, with hopes of providing information about a task that may be fundamental to human rationality.

■
CATEGORICAL REASONING
■

DEFINITIONS

There are four types of propositions that describe the relationship between two sets (or categories) of things:

Universal affirmative (UA), such as "All A are B."

Universal negative (UN), such as "No A are B."

Particular affirmative (PA), such as "Some A are B."

Particular negative (PN), such as "Some A are not B."

Venn diagrams of each of these four basic categorical propositions are given in Box 5-3. Note that most of the propositions are ambiguous—you are able to generate more than one possible Venn diagram. For example, the universal affirmative proposition may result if set A and set B are identical or if set A is a subset of set B. Thus "All A are B" does not necessarily imply "All B are A," but it does not rule it out either. Note also that "some" means "at least one and possibly all." Thus the particular negative proposition may result from either set A and set B overlapping, from set A and set B being disjoint, or from set B being a subset of set A. "Some A are not B" does not necessarily imply "Some B are not A," although it does not rule it out either.

A categorical syllogism consists of two premises and a conclusion with each being any one of the four types of categorical propositions, For example, the syllogism

> All magnificent things are preposterous.
> All syllogisms are magnificent.
> Therefore, all syllogisms are preposterous.

consists of two universal affirmative premises and a universal affirmative conclusion. The subject of the conclusion ("syllogism") is the S term, the predicate of the conclusion ("preposterous") is the P term, and the middle term, which is in both premises but not in the conclusion ("magnificent"), is the M term. The *major premise* gives the relationship between the predicate (P) and middle (M) term; the *minor premise* gives the relation between the subject (S) and the middle (M) term. There are 4 ways of organizing the major and minor premises, called *figures*, as shown in Box 5-4. In addition, since any of the 4 types of premises may be the major premise and any of the 4 types of premises may be the minor premise, there are 16 possible combinations, called *moods*. Each of the 16 moods may appear in any of the 4 figures.

BOX 5 • 3   Possible Venn Diagrams for Four Types of Propositions

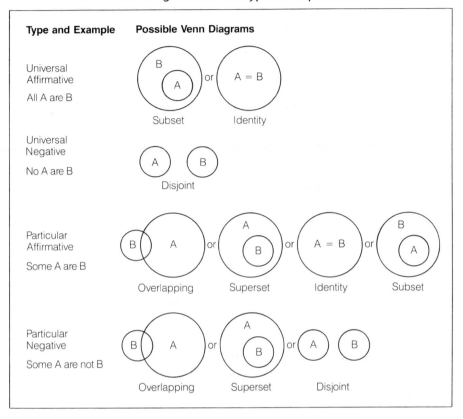

Type and Example   **Possible Venn Diagrams**

Universal
Affirmative

All A are B

    B / A   or   A = B
    Subset   Identity

Universal
Negative

No A are B

    A   B
    Disjoint

Particular
Affirmative

Some A are B

    B A   or   A / B   or   A = B   or   B / A
    Overlapping   Superset   Identity   Subset

Particular
Negative

Some A are not B

    B A   or   A / B   or   A   B
    Overlapping   Superset   Disjoint

Consequently there are 64 possible pairs of premises; however, if you try to solve them you will find that only 19 of them are valid, that is, only 19 lead to an unambiguous conclusion. For each of the 64 premise pairs, there are 4 possible conclusions, yielding a total of 256 possible syllogisms.

Johnson-Laird and Steedman (1978) have argued that the conclusion for a pair of premises can concern the S–P relation—such as All S are P, Some S are P, Some S are not P, or No S are P—as in traditional logic summarized in Box 5-4. They also suggest that the conclusion for a pair of premises can concern the P–S relation—such as All P are S, Some P are S, Some P are not S, No P are S. Using this approach, there are 512 possible syllogisms: 64 premise pairs with 4 possible S–P conclusions and 4 possible P–S solutions for each. If we assume that each of the 64 premise pairs has 8 possible conclusions, then Johnson-Laird and Steedman are able to locate 27 valid syllogisms.

BOX 5 ▪ 4   Examples of Four Figures of Categorical Syllogisms

---

Figure 1

M–P	All humans are mortals
S–M	All psychologists are humans
S–P	All psychologists are mortals

Figure 2

P–M	All mortals are humans
S–M	All psychologists are humans
S–P	All psychologists are mortals*

Figure 3

M–P	All humans are mortals
M–S	All humans are psychologists
S–P	All psychologists are mortals*

Figure 4

P–M	All mortals are humans
M–S	All humans are psychologists
S–P	All psychologists are mortals*

*Conclusion is not valid.

Box 5-5 gives examples of three types of categorical syllogisms that are particularly susceptible to some common errors in deductive reasoning. Although the conclusions are often accepted as valid by people, they are nevertheless invalid. The first two exemplify two common *form errors:* errors due to the format of the premises, such as undistributed middle errors and particular premises errors. Syllogism 1 involves an undistributed middle error in which subjects may overgeneralize the breadth of the middle term. This form creates ambiguity in which logically combining all correct interpretations of the first and second premises leads to many possible conclusions, of which the reasoner selects only one. Syllogism 2 involves a particular premises error in which subjects may overgeneralize "some" to mean "all." The third syllogism exemplifies a *content error,* namely a belief-bias error in which the believability of the premises or conclusions influences the reasoner's answer.

Errors attributable to form and to content may both be present in any one situation, thus increasing the tendency to error. For example, any of the form errors presented in the box may be more plentiful when the incorrect conclusion

BOX 5 • 5   Three Types of Errors on Categorical Reasoning Problems

Undistributed Middle Errors

Wallonians dance the polka
My worthy opponent dances the polka
Therefore, it is obvious that my worthy opponent is a Wallonian

Form: All A are B; All C are B; Therefore, All C are A

Particular Premises Errors

Some Republicans have inherited oil wells
Some Wallonians are Republicans
Hence, we know that some Wallonians have inherited oil wells

Form: Some A are C; Some C are A; Therefore, Some C are B

Content Errors

Any form of recreation that constitutes a serious health menace will be outlawed
  by the City Health Authority
The increasing water pollution in this area will make swimming at local beaches
  a serious health menace
It does not follow that swimming at local beaches will be outlawed by the
  City Health Authority

Content: undesirable conclusion

Adapted from McGuire (1960) and Wilkins (1928)

is also highly believable than when it is neutral. Since these kinds of errors are quite common, they have a practical value for propagandists and others who wish to affect public opinion. However, they are also of theoretical interest because they suggest that human logic and formal logic are not the same; thus errors in human reasoning have received much research attention.

Two basic theoretical explanations for human errors in syllogistic reasoning are:

Encoding theories—in which errors are attributed to incomplete or incorrect interpretations of the premises and/or conclusions, and

Processing theories—in which errors are attributable to incomplete or nonlogical processing of the premises.

In this section, we explore research aimed at determining the existence of form and content errors and the usefulness of encoding and processing theories to account for them.

FORM ERRORS

In analyzing the psychological mechanisms underlying form errors, both encoding theories and processing theories have been proposed. In this section we explore *atmosphere theory,* a processing theory that attributes errors to nonlogical processing; *conversion theory,* an encoding theory that attributes errors to incorrect encoding of premises; what could be called *ambiguity theory,* an encoding theory that attributes errors to incomplete encoding of premises; and *mental model theory,* a processing theory that attributes errors to incomplete processing.

Atmosphere Theory.   Atmosphere theory (Sells, 1936; Woodworth & Sells, 1935) was the first important psychological theory aimed at explaining errors due to logical form. According to this theory, errors resulted from an atmosphere effect in which the form of the two premises set an atmosphere favorable to accepting conclusions of certain forms. For example, two universal affirmative premises create an atmosphere for the acceptance of a universal affirmative conclusion, while two particular negative premises lead to a particular negative conclusion. In addition, any one negative premise creates a negative atmosphere, and any one particular premise creates a particular atmosphere. Predictions based on the atmosphere theory have been fairly accurate (Morgan & Morton, 1944; Sells, 1936).

Begg and Denny (1969, p. 351) restated the atmosphere theory as two principles: "Whenever the quality of at least one premise is negative, the quality of the most frequently accepted conclusion will be negative; when neither premise is negative, the conclusion will be affirmative. Whenever the quantity of at least one premise is particular, the quantity of the most frequently accepted conclusion will be particular; when neither premise is particular, the conclusion will be universal." Based on an analysis of errors in syllogistic reasoning, they concluded that the atmosphere theory was the best predictor of results.

The information-processing approach has encouraged the reformulation of old theories and the development of new ones based on the operation of specific models of the reasoning processes for various tasks. These models may be represented as computer programs, as mathematical equations, or as flow charts. For example, Box 5-6 shows a flow diagram of the processes involved in syllogistic reasoning based on a reformulation of the idea of atmosphere effect (Revlis, 1975).

In the first stage of the model, the subject extracts two pieces of information from each premise—whether the premise is *universal* (All A are B) or *particular* (Some A are B), and whether the premise is *affirmative* (are) or *negative* (are not). In stage 2, the subject determines the same two characteristics of the composite

BOX 5 ▪ 6 An Information-Processing Model of Atmosphere Theory

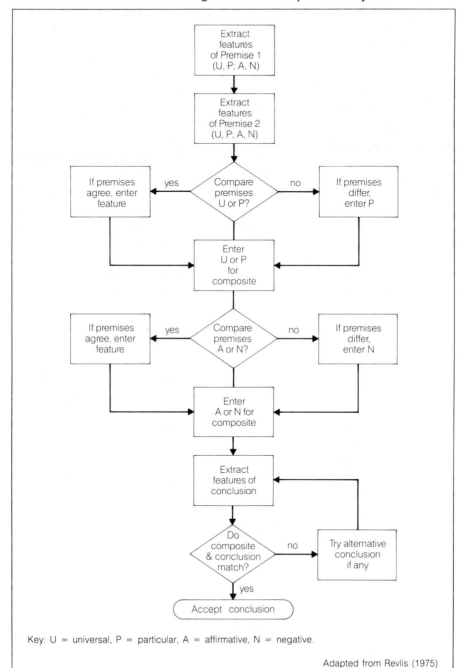

Key: U = universal, P = particular, A = affirmative, N = negative.

Adapted from Revlis (1975)

of the two premises based on two rules: (1) if both premises are universal, the composite is universal; if one or both are particular, then the composite is particular; (2) if both premises are affirmative, the composite is affirmative; if one or both are negative, the composite is negative. The subject then extracts the two characteristics of the conclusion (stage 3). Finally, in stage 4, the subject compares the two characteristics of the conclusion with the two characteristics of the composite and answers Yes if they match and No if they do not.

The advantage of specifying the atmosphere effect as a precise model of information-processing stages and rules is that it provides specific predictions that can be tested; as Revlis (p. 180) notes, "The model is sufficiently detailed to make predictions concerning solutions to every syllogism." For example, the model predicts that subjects would never respond that no valid conclusion could be drawn even though many premises were invalid, such as All P are M, Some M are S. Further, of the syllogisms that have valid conclusions, errors are predicted for the following forms: All M are P, All M are S; All P are M, All M are S; No M are P, No M are S; and No P are M, No M are S. Thus, the model can make predictions about error rates in syllogistic reasoning; such predictions are easily tested. In this way, information-processing models help in creating testable theories—one of the main conditions for the advance of science (Popper, 1959).

Conversion Theory. In contrast to atmosphere theory's assumption that people do not process syllogisms logically, conversion theory holds that people tend to make logically correct deductions based on incorrectly encoded premises (Chapman & Chapman, 1959). In particular, errors occur because of *invalid conversion* of propositions—the tendency to assume that if "All A are B" then "All B are A" or if "Some A are not B" then "Some B are not A ." You should note that conversion of universal affirmative and particular negative propositions (i.e., the respective examples in the previous sentence) is not valid, whereas conversion of universal negative and particular affirmative propositions is valid. Chapman and Chapman (1959) gave two premises, in letter form, and asked their subjects to choose the correct conclusion:

> Some L's are K's.
> Some K's are M's.

Therefore,

> 1. All M's are L's.
> 2. Some M's are L's.
> 3. No M's are L's.
> 4. Some M's are not L's.
> 5. None of these.

BOX 5 • 7   Subject's Conclusions for Six Syllogisms

Which conclusions can you be sure of?

	Proportion of Subjects' Conclusions				
Premises	All S are P	Some S are P	No S are P	Some S are not P	None of these
All P are M, All S are M	.81	.04	.05	.01	.09
All M are P, No S are M	.02	.03	.82	.05	.08
All P are M, Some M are S	.06	.77	.02	.06	.07
Some M are P, No S are M	.01	.06	.62	.13	.18
Some M are not P, No M are S	.03	.07	.41	.19	.30
No M are P, Some S are not M	.03	.10	.24	.32	.32

Based on data from Chapman and Chapman (1959)

Although the correct answer was always "none of these" for each of 42 experimental syllogisms, the subjects chose other conclusions over 80 percent of the time. Some typical responses are shown in Box 5-7. As you can see, many of the responses, like the first three in the box, seemed to fit both the atmosphere effect explanation and the invalid conversion explanation; however, the atmosphere effect would predict that the main error for the latter three syllogisms should be "Some S are not P," while the more preferred response was often "No S are P"—a response that could be derived if subjects made invalid conversions. Thus, the results indicated that invalid conversion could account for a large proportion of errors, including some that could not be accounted for by atmosphere effect.

You may note that the problems taken from Stratton in Box 5-1 result in errors that can be described as resulting from atmosphere effect (syllogism 2 has particular affirmative premises that encourage the particular affirmative conclusion, C) or invalid conversion (syllogism 3's statements that "All Glorias are Sassoids" may be converted to "All Sassoids are Glorias," thus encouraging conclusion D). Apparently, some errors are explained by atmosphere and some by conversion, but while the former is a superficial attempt on the part of the thinker to be consistent, the latter reflects an attempt to be logical that simply is not quite right. Although conversions may be formally illogical, Chapman and Chapman (1959, p. 224) point out that they may be based on consistency with practical past experience, since invalid conversions "although logically invalid often correspond to our experience of reality, and being guided by experience are usually regarded as justifiable procedures." One may realistically accept the converse of many, perhaps most particular negative propositions about qualities of objects; for example, "some plants are not green" and "some greens are not plants." The acceptance of the converse of universal affirmative propositions is also often appropriate, for example, "all right angles are 90 degrees" and "all 90 degree angles are right angles."

Revlin and his colleagues (Revlin & Leirer, 1978; Revlis, 1975) have developed a formal model of syllogistic reasoning based on conversion theory. The model assumes that, under some circumstances, the reasoner translates each premise into its converted form and then reasons logically using the misencoded premises and conclusions. In order to test the model, Revlin (Revlis, 1975) asked subjects to solve a series of abstract syllogisms under some time constraint, such as a limit of 30 seconds. For some of the problems, the conversion model and logic produced the same answer—called *sames*—whereas on other problems, conversion and logic produced different answers—called *differents*. As predicted by the conversion model, error rates were higher for differents than for sames.

Ambiguity Theory. In contrast to conversion theory's claim that people encode premises incorrectly, an alternative that could be called ambiguity theory assumes that people encode premises incompletely. As shown in Box 5-3, there are two correct interpretations of "All A are B," three correct interpretations of "Some A are not B," and four correct interpretations of "Some A are B." To reason logically, a person has to combine each possible interpretation of the first premise with each possible interpretation of the second premise. However, given the limits of working memory, people may fail to consider all possible interpretations of each premise.

As an example of the memory demands of categorical syllogisms, consider the ambiguous syllogism shown in the top of Box 5-8. First, I hold up a red block with a hole in it and say, "All red blocks have holes." You should interpret this universal affirmative premise in two ways: as an identity relation (every red block has a hole, and every block with a hole is red) and as a set-subset relation (all red blocks have holes, but some blocks with holes are not red). Then I hold up a triangular block and say, "All triangular blocks have holes." Again, you must interpret this universal affirmative premise as expressing an identity and a set-subset relation. Now I ask you to determine the relation between red blocks and triangular blocks that unambiguously follows from the premises. You should combine each possible interpretation of the first premise with each possible interpretation of the second premise. If you combine the two identity interpretations of the premises, you can conclude that there is an identity relation between red and triangular blocks—all red blocks are triangular. If you combine the identity interpretation of the first premise with the set-subset interpretation of the second premise, you can deduce that some red blocks are triangular. In fact, as shown in Box 5-8, five different conclusions about red blocks and triangular blocks are possible—so the correct answer is, "Can't say." As you can see, to correctly solve the problem, a reasoner must be able to keep in mind all of the possible interpretations of the premises and then consider all possible combinations of these premises. When Ceraso and Provitera (1971) gave this problem to college students, only 22 percent selected the correct answer, "Can't say."

In contrast, the unambiguous syllogism shown in the bottom of Box 5-8 specifies a single interpretation for each premise: the first premise specifies an identity in which red blocks are identical to blocks with holes, and the second premise specifies that triangular blocks are a subset of blocks with holes. Consequently, only one conclusion logically follows—that triangular blocks are a subset of red blocks. In this case, 93 percent of the students chose the correct answer, "Some A are C." Over a set of thirteen problems, students given traditional syllogisms generated errors 42 percent of the time, whereas students given syllogisms that allowed only one interpretation per premise generated errors 20 percent of the time. Ceraso and Provitera conclude that errors occur when people fail to encode all the possible interpretations of each premise or fail to consider all the possible outcomes produced by combining all interpretations of the first premise with all interpretations of the second premise. According to this view, reasoning errors arise out of the limitations of human memory rather than a lack of human capacity for rational thought.

Erickson (1974, 1978) has proposed a model in which subjects are limited in translating premises into internal mental representations and, in some cases, subjects are also limited in how they combine these representations to generate a conclusion. During the translation of premises, subjects may focus on just one interpretation of each premise, although several interpretations may be possible. For example, consider the premise, "All A are B." To deal correctly with this premise, you must be able to simultaneously interpret this premise to mean "A and B are identical" (called *set identity*) and "A is a subset of B" (called *set inclusion*). In order to study how subjects interpret premises, Erickson asked subjects to draw Venn diagrams to represent various premises. For a statement such as "All A are B," 60 percent opted for set identity diagrams and 40 percent preferred set inclusion diagrams, as shown in Box 5-9. Furthermore, subjects were very consistent, almost always drawing the same kind of representation for the same kind of premise. For example, if subjects are given pairs of premises like the ones in Box 5-9, they represent them either as two set identities or as two set

BOX 5 ▪ 8   Reasoning from Ambiguous and Unambiguous Premises

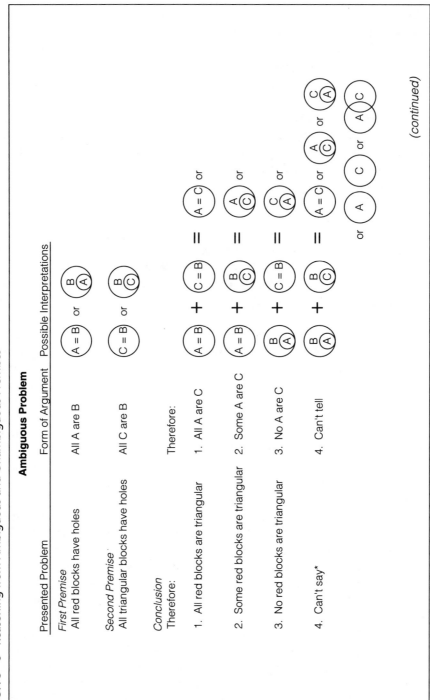

(continued)

BOX 5 · 8, *continued*

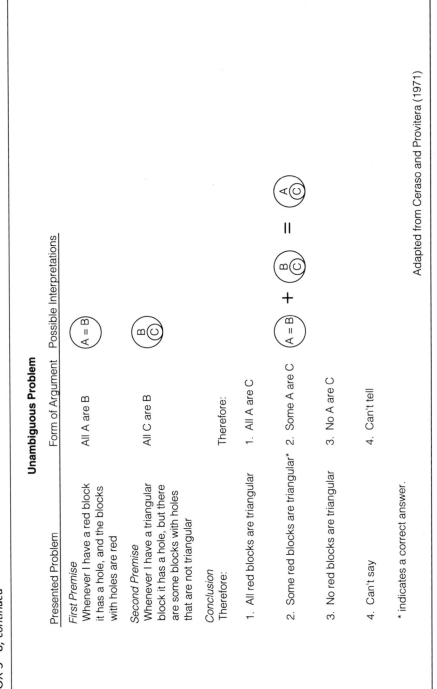

Unambiguous Problem

Presented Problem	Form of Argument	Possible Interpretations
First Premise Whenever I have a red block it has a hole, and the blocks with holes are red	All A are B	(A = B)
Second Premise Whenever I have a triangular block it has a hole, but there are some blocks with holes that are not triangular	All C are B	(B C)
Conclusion Therefore:	Therefore:	

1. All red blocks are triangular   1. All A are C

2. Some red blocks are triangular*   2. Some A are C   (A = B) + (B C) = (A C)

3. No red blocks are triangular   3. No A are C

4. Can't say   4. Can't tell

* indicates a correct answer.

Adapted from Ceraso and Provitera (1971)

BOX 5 ▪ 9 Subjects' Interpretation of Premise Pairs

		Possible Interpretation of Premises		Possible Conclusions					
Premises				(AC)	(A)C	(C)A	A(C)	(A) (C)	None
All B are C All A are B	60%	(BC)	(AB)	100%	0	0	0	0	0
	40%	(B) C	(A) B	0	90%	0	10%	0	0
All C are B All A are B	60%	(BC)	(AB)	100%	0	0	0	0	0
	40%	(C) B	(A) B	20%	0	0	20%	10%	50%
All B are C All B are A	60%	(BC)	(AB)	100%	0	0	0	0	0
	40%	(B) C	(B) A	20%	5%	5%	70%	0%	0%
All C are B All B are A	60%	(BC)	(AB)	100%	0	0	0	0	0
	40%	(C) B	(B) A	5%	0	85%	10%	0%	0%

Based on Erickson (1974)

inclusions. Apparently, subjects are able to choose one possible interpretation and ignore the others.

When combining the premises, subjects may focus on just one logical conclusion, although there may be several possible logical conclusions. For example, the premises

All C are B

All A are B

can generate five different conclusions. To study how subjects combine premises, Erickson and his colleagues gave two Venn diagrams to subjects and then asked them to draw the conclusion. Examples are given in Box 5-9. As you can see, two identity diagrams always lead to an identity conclusion. However, set inclusion diagrams lead to a variety of conclusions. For example, "C as a subset of B" and "A as a subset of B" lead to an identity conclusion for 20 percent of the subjects, to a disjoint diagram as a conclusion for 10 percent, to an overlap for 20 percent, and to none for 50 percent. Thus subjects seem to reduce information. When there are many possible interpretations for how to combine premises or for how to interpret a premise, they tend to choose just one.

Importantly, Erickson's (1974, 1978) theory accurately predicts the percentage of people who select each conclusion on several categorical syllogisms. In critique, other researchers have obtained different data concerning how people interpret premises as Venn diagrams (Neimark & Santa, 1975), and other theories may be able to account for more of the data. However, Erickson provides an important account of human reasoning in which people are logical but overly restrictive in how they handle ambiguous information.

Mental Model Theory. Finally, errors can be accounted for by assuming that people fail to completely process the information. According to Johnson-Laird's (1988; Johnson-Laird & Steedman, 1978) mental model theory, people try to mentally create and analyze a meaningful situation to represent the premises. In short, reasoners "imagine the situation described in the premises," "formulate an informative conclusion that is true for the situation," and "consider if there is a way that it could be false" (Johnson-Laird, 1988, p. 227). For example, what can you conclude from the following premises:

None of the archaeologists is a biologist

All the biologists are chess players

According to mental model theory, your first step is to understand the premise information as a meaningful situation. The top portion of Box 5-10 presents a concrete model of the situation (mental model 1). As you can see, the disjoint

BOX 5 • 10   Three Mental Models for the Archeologist/Chess Player Problem

The Problem

Given the premises:

None of the archaeologists is a biologist
All of the biologists are chess-players

What conclusion(s) are valid?

Mental Model 1

archaeologist
archaeologist

	biologist	=	chess player
	biologist	=	chess player
			(chess player)

Mental Model 2

archaeologist
archaeologist   =   chess player

	biologist	=	chess player
	biologist	=	chess player
			(chess player)

Mental Model 3

archaeologist   =   chess player
archaeologist   =   chess player

	biologist	=	chess player
	biologist	=	chess player
			(chess player)

Adapted from Johnson-Laird (1988)

relation between archaeologists and biologists is consistent with the first premise: there are some archaeologists (indicated by listing this term in the first column) and some biologists (indicated by listing this term in the second column), but no one is both an archaeologist and a biologist (as indicated by the horizontal line separating the two). Similarly, the set-superset relation between biologist and chess player comes from the second premise and is indicated by = between all of the biologists in column 2 and some of the chess players in column 3. Because the horizontal line serves as a barrier, people do not realize that a chess player who is not a biologist (indicated in parentheses in mental model 1) could possibly be an archaeologist. Failure to fully process this model yields the conclusion reached by 60 percent of the college students who were tested: "None of the archaeologists is a chess player."

This conclusion, however, is refuted by the mental model 2 in Box 5-10. As you can see, this model includes the possibility that a chess player who is not a biologist (in the top of the third column) may also be an archaeologist (as indicated by the =) and that a different archaeologist is not a chess player. This model allows the reasoner to conclude that "Some archaeologists are not chess players," an answer given by 10 percent of the reasoners.

Finally, mental model 3 in Box 5-10 presents a third possible interpretation that is consistent with the information in the premises. In this case, all of the archaeologists are chess players. Reasoners who find that none of the archaeologists are chess players in model 1 and that all archaeologists are chess players in model 3 may be moved to conclude that "There is no valid conclusion," a response produced by 20 percent of the reasoners. However, there is one conclusion that is consistent with all three models: "Some of the chess players are not archaeologists." Although this conclusion follows from all three models, none of the students in Johnson-Laird's study produced it.

Where do errors come from? According to the mental model theory, the major source of errors is incomplete processing of the information, such as considering only one model when the premises actually are consistent with two or three models, or failing to consider all of the possible conclusions from each model. For example, college students were asked to solve syllogisms that required constructing and analyzing one, two, or three alternative models. Mental model theory predicts that "the greater the number of different models that have to be constructed the harder the task will be" (Johnson-Laird, 1988, p. 228). As predicted, the correct conclusion was found 92 percent of the time when students needed to construct only one model, 46 percent of the time when two models needed to be analyzed, and 28 percent of the time when they had to create and analyze three models.

In short, Johnson-Laird (1988; Johnson-Laird & Steedman, 1978) shows how errors can occur when reasoners fail to completely process the information. Guyote and Sternberg (1981) offer another detailed theory that accounts for performance of their subjects on reasoning tasks by assuming that people encode the premises correctly but do not process the encoded information completely.

Which theory is best? By now, you probably suspect that there is at least a grain of truth in each. Under some circumstances a person might incorrectly encode a premise, as suggested by conversion theory, and under other circumstances nonlogical processing is more likely, as suggested by atmosphere theory. At still other times, as suggested by the two more recent theories, ambiguity theory and mental model theory, incomplete encoding and incomplete processing seem to characterize human thinking. We are left with the view of the human reasoner as neither a perfect logician nor an irrational animal: rather than solely and diligently applying the general rules of logic to all syllogisms, humans may attempt to understand the situation being presented in terms of their existing knowledge, if possible, and sometimes attempt to minimize the amount of work needed to derive an answer.

CONTENT ERRORS

According to traditional views of logic, the content of the syllogism is irrelevant to the reasoning process. If people apply the same general rules of logic to every syllogism regardless of its content, then performance should be about the same on syllogisms with neutral propositions as on those with more controversial propositions. However, some of the earliest psychological research on syllogistic reasoning contradicted this rule-based theory of reasoning by demonstrating strong context effects—conclusions that were consistent with beliefs or desires were more likely to be accepted as valid regardless of deductive logic.

In a classic study of belief-bias, Janis and Frick (1943) presented syllogisms as short paragraphs and asked subjects to indicate whether they agreed or disagreed with the conclusion and whether or not the conclusion was valid based on the premises. As expected, a high number of errors were obtained on the second measure, with the subjects showing a strong tendency to judge the conclusions they agreed with as valid and the conclusions they disagreed with as invalid. In addition, the four syllogisms listed in Box 5-2 produced similar results, with more errors made for logically identical syllogisms containing high emotional content than those containing low emotional content (Lefford, 1946). These results clearly contradict the rule-based reasoning theory. They suggest that deductive syllogisms are not processed in a vacuum; rather they are assimilated or fitted into the existing knowledge of the problem solver. *Cognitive consistency*—the tendency for information in a person's memory to be internally consistent—may play a role in deduction.

A similar study of the belief-bias effect was conducted by Parrott (1969, cited in Johnson, 1972). According to the rule-based theory, people's performance should be about the same on syllogisms involving abstract symbols (e.g., All A are B), sentences that are true (i.e., consistent with the subject's past experience), and sentences that are false (i.e., inconsistent with the subject's past experience). However, even when instructions made it clear that subjects were to assume that the premises were true in judging the validity of the conclusions, Parrott (1969, cited in Johnson, 1972) found large differences in performance: syllogisms with false premises were more difficult than syllogisms with true premises, which in turn were more difficult than syllogisms using symbols. The results contradict the idea that humans always engage in rule-based reasoning. Apparently, the content-free syllogisms allowed subjects to be less influenced by the need for consistency with other information in their memories.

In a classic study of desirability-bias, McGuire (1960) asked a group of subjects to rate a list of propositions for probability of occurrence and for desirability. Nested within the list were the components of several syllogisms with premises and conclusions separated by other propositions. If the subjects were entirely rational (i.e., engaging in logical thinking), the probability of a conclusion should be equal to the probability of premise 1 times the probability of premise 2. If the subjects were entirely irrational (i.e., engaging in wishful thinking), there should be a high correlation between desirability and probability judgments—the subjects should rate highly desirable conclusions as highly probable regardless of the premises. As might be expected, McGuire found evidence for both logical and wishful thinking, with a correlation of 0.48 between the judged probabilities of the conclusions and the products of the judged probabilities of the premises, and a correlation of 0.40 between the rated desirabilities of events and their rated probabilities of occurrence.* These results seem to indicate that deductive reasoning involves more than applying logical rules to the premises of a syllogism; rather, humans seem to try to fit the propositions within their existing knowledge structures. In order to preserve the cognitive consistency of their great mass of existing knowledge and beliefs, reasoners may process inconsistent or undesirable propositions in ways that violate the rules of logic for a particular syllogism.

Although classic research on reasoning had demonstrated content effects, such as belief-bias, the next step was to specify the reasoning process that people use. In short, if people do not always process syllogisms according to the rules of formal logic, what sort of theory can account for errors in reasoning? As with form errors, psychologists have proposed two major classes of theories— *encoding theories,* in which people misinterpret or incompletely interpret the material and then reason logically, and *processing theories,* in which people do not use complete and/or logical operations.

Emphasizing incorrect encoding, Revlin, Leirer, Yopp, and Yopp (1980) have provided evidence that reasoners may misinterpret controversial premises. For example, consider the (somewhat distasteful) syllogism:

> No black people in Newton are residents of Sea Side
> All black people in Newton are welfare recipients

---

* Correlations such as 0.40 and 0.48 indicate a moderately strong positive relation between variables.

Therefore:

1. All welfare recipients in Newton are residents of Sea Side
2. No welfare recipients in Newton are residents of Sea Side
3. Some welfare recipients in Newton are residents of Sea Side
4. Some welfare recipients in Newton are not residents of Sea Side
5. None of the above is proven

In this situation the conclusion is relatively neutral but the premises are not. Sadly, some subjects tended to believe the converse of the second premise—that is, "All welfare recipients are black." People who misinterpret the second premise in this way and then reason logically will conclude that "No welfare recipients in Newton are residents of Sea Side." In contrast, the correct answer is, "Some welfare recipients in Newton are not residents of Sea Side." Revlin and colleagues (1980) found that college students gave the correct answer 22 percent of the time for syllogisms such as these. When converting controversial premises would lead to an incorrect conclusion, the students usually erred; but when conversion would not give an incorrect conclusion, they usually answered correctly. Approximately 80 percent of the errors could be accounted for by assuming that reasoners converted controversial premises to a form more consistent with their beliefs. Revlin and colleagues (1980, p. 584) conclude that "students do not suspend rational choice, but rather, their decisions are judicious ones, flowing logically from their idiosyncratic understanding of the materials reasoned about."

In contrast, Evans, Barston, and Pollard (1983) offer an alternative explanation that is an example of a *processing theory*: reasoners engage in nonlogical processing such as evaluating a conclusion on the basis of its correspondence to their beliefs. For example, they found that subjects who selected valid conclusions that conflicted with their beliefs referred to the premises more than subjects who selected invalid conclusions that corresponded to their beliefs. Apparently, some subjects used logical processes based on processing the premises, whereas others used nonlogical strategies based on finding a believable conclusion.

One way to encourage subjects to pay more attention to the premises is to given them a production task rather than an evaluation task. In a production task, the reasoner is given two premises and must generate a conclusion; in an evaluation task, the reasoner is given the premises along with one or more possible conclusions. However, when Oakhill and Johnson-Laird (1985) used a production task, reasoners still displayed a high level of belief-bias—by generating invalid conclusions that were believable. For example, 88 percent of the incorrect conclusions produced by subjects were believable. To test whether the errors could be explained solely by assuming that reasoners had converted the premises, Oakhill and Johnson-Laird used syllogisms for which the same correct answer would be produced if reasoners converted or did not convert the premises. Even in this case reasoners produced many invalid conclusions—89 percent of which were believable. Oakhill and Johnson-Laird (1985, p. 566) conclude that beliefs affect reasoning by "influencing the processes of deduction and conclusion" rather than by "leading to distortions in the interpretation of the premises." One possibility is that the reasoning process is stopped prematurely when a reasoner produces either an unbelievable conclusion —resulting in a "no conclusion" response—or a believable conclusion —resulting in acceptance of that conclusion without further processing.

Markovits and Nantel (1989) attempted to clarify the role of nonlogical processing by comparing students' performances on syllogisms with neutral and believable conclusions in both production and evaluation tasks. For example, in the following two evaluation tasks, do the conclusions follow from the premises?

> All things that have a motor need oil
> Automobiles need oil
> Therefore, automobiles have motors

> All things that have a motor need oil
> Opprobines need oil
> Therefore, opprobines have motors

Although the correct answer in both cases is that no conclusion can be proved, many people accept the conclusions that are shown—especially for the first syllogism (Markovits & Nantel, 1989). You may recognize this as an undistributed middle error: All A are B; All C are B; Therefore, All C are A. In particular, Markovits and Nantel (1989) found that people were almost twice as likely to make an undistributed middle error when the conclusion corresponded with their beliefs (as in the first syllogism) than when the conclusion was neutral (as in the second syllogism). If reasoners' errors occur because they ignore the premises, relying instead on their beliefs to choose a conclusion, then people should make fewer errors on production tasks—which force reasoners to attend to the premises—than on evaluation tasks. However, Markovits and Nantel found the same pattern of performance for both tasks. They suggest a two-stage process in which reasoners first generate possible conclusion(s) from the premises and then evaluate them, sometimes using extralogical methods, including belief-bias methods.

In summary, there is overwhelming evidence for content effects in deductive reasoning, with belief-bias as the best example. Clearly, people are more likely to err by accepting conclusions they believe than by accepting conclusions that they do not believe. This research also shows that although content errors are prevalent, they are clearly not the only kind of errors that reasoners make. In trying to account for content errors, a comprehensive theory will likely include both encoding and processing mechanisms: some reasoners under some circumstances may misinterpret the information (such as encoding a premise or conclusion as its converse or encoding only one possible interpretation of a premise), and some reasoners under some circumstances may use nonlogical strategies (such as selecting conclusions on the basis of believability or failing to completely process all alternatives).

CONDITIONAL REASONING

SOURCES OF ERROR ON THE CONDITIONAL REASONING TASK: ENCODING OR PROCESSING?

Conditional syllogisms consist of two premises and a conclusion. The first premise is an implicative sentence of the form "If p, then q," where p is some antecedent condition and q is some consequent condition. The second premise is either an affirmation of the antecedent (p is true), a denial of the antecedent (p is not true), an affirmation of the consequence (q is true), or a denial of the consequence (q is not true). For example, consider the conditional syllogism:

> If there is a solar eclipse, then the streets will be dark
> There is a solar eclipse
> Therefore, the streets are dark

Does the conclusion follow from the premises? If you are like most students (Braine, Reiser, & Rumain, 1984; Markovits, 1987, 1988; Rips, 1990; Rips & Marcus, 1977), you gave the logically correct answer—Yes. In this example, the first premise is of the form "If p, then q," with "solar eclipse" as the antecedent condition and "dark streets" as the consequent condition. The second premise affirms the antecedent condition, and the conclusion—which logically follows—affirms the consequent condition.

We begin with a dilemma. People do not perform very well on conditional reasoning tasks, such as evaluating the validity of conditional syllogisms. For example, Rips and Marcus (1977) found that people made mistakes about 25 percent of the time on some basic conditional syllogisms, and Staudenmayer (1975) reported similar results.

Why do people make errors in conditional reasoning? Staudenmayer and his colleagues (Staudenmayer, 1975; Staudenmayer & Bourne, 1978; Taplin & Staudenmayer, 1973) have found that many errors in conditional reasoning can be attributed to subjects' misinterpretations of the first premise rather than errors in logic. For example, many subjects appear to interpret the conditional statement "If p, then q" as a *biconditional* relation that includes the assertion "If q, then p."

BOX 5 • 11   Answers for Eight Conditional Syllogisms Based on Conditional and Biconditional Interpretations

Example	Form	Answer for Conditional Interpretation	Answer for Biconditional Interpretation
1. If the switch is turned on, then the light will go on. The switch is turned on. ∴ The light goes on.	If p, then q p is true ∴ q is true	True	True
2. If the switch is turned on, then the light will go on. The switch is turned on. ∴ The light does not go on.	If p, then q p is true ∴ q is not true	False	False
3. If the switch is turned on, then the light will go on. The switch is not turned on. ∴ The light goes on.	If p, then q p is not true ∴ q is true	Sometimes	False
4. If the switch is turned on, then the light will go on. The switch is not turned on. ∴ The light does not go on.	If p, then q p is not true ∴ q is not true	Sometimes	True
5. If the switch is turned on, then the light will go on. The light goes on . ∴ The switch is turned on.	If p, then q q is true ∴ p is true	Sometimes	True
6. If the switch is turned on, then the light will go on. The light goes on . ∴ The switch is not turned on.	If p, then q q is true ∴ p is not true	Sometimes	False
7. If the switch is turned on, then the light will go on. The light does not go on . ∴ The switch is turned on.	If p, then q q is not true ∴ p is true	False	False
8. If the switch is turned on, then the light will go on. The light does not go on . ∴ The switch is not turned on.	If p, then q q is not true ∴ p is not true	True	True

Adapted from Staudenmayer (1975)

Actually, in formal logic you should assume that "If p, then q" signifies only a *conditional relation;* thus whether "If q, then p" is true or not is unknown.

Box 5-11 provides examples of eight major conditional syllogisms. The column labeled "Answer for Conditional Interpretation" gives an evaluation of the validity of the conclusion assuming that the first premise is interpreted as containing only a conditional relation. The column labeled "Answer for Biconditional Interpretation" gives an evaluation of the validity of the conclusion assuming that the first premise is interpreted as containing a biconditional relation. As you can see, both interpretations yield the same answers for syllogisms 1, 2, 7, and 8, but they differ on problems 3, 4, 5, and 6. For example, in syllogism 5, a biconditional interpretation adds a second way of stating the first premise—that is, "If the light goes on, then the switch is turned on."

In a series of experiments by Staudenmayer (1975; Staudenmayer & Bourne, 1978), subjects were given conditional syllogisms such as those in Box 5-11 and were asked to evaluate whether the conclusion was "true," "false," or "sometimes true." Most of the subjects behaved as if they consistently and exclusively used *either* a conditional interpretation *or* a biconditional interpretation for all syllogisms. For example, when presented with premises in the form "If p, then q," 59 percent of the subjects behaved as if they had consistently used a biconditional interpretation; for premises of the form "p causes q," 77 percent of the subjects behaved as if they had consistently used a biconditional interpretation. The experiments also found that more people used biconditional interpretations for abstract material (such as single letters) than they did for concrete material (such as sentences). Staudenmayer concluded that errors in conditional reasoning can be attributed to people's misinterpretations of the premises rather than to a faulty reasoning process.

Rips and Marcus (1977) asked subjects to judge conditional syllogisms such as those given in Box 5-12. The results indicated perfect performance on syllogisms 1 and 2, but many errors on the others. Rips and Marcus were able to develop a model that accounts for the error patterns shown in the box by assuming that some subjects use a biconditional interpretation of the first premise (which accounts for errors in problems 3 through 6) and some subjects misinterpret the negatives in the second premise (which accounts for errors in problems 7 and 8). In summary, this line of research provides evidence that one reason for errors in conditional reasoning tasks is that people may misinterpret the premises—that is, they appear to make errors in encoding the premises rather than in applying the rules of logic.

SOURCES OF ERROR ON THE SELECTION TASK: RULES, INSTANCES, OR SCHEMAS

In order further to examine conditional reasoning, let's modify the conditional reasoning situation into what has been called a *selection task*. I will give you a conditional rule along with several ways to test the rule. Your job is to select the

BOX 5 • 12   Performance on Eight Conditional Syllogisms

Example	Form	True (Always)	Sometimes	False (Never)
1. If the card has an A on the left, it has a 7 on the right. The card has an A on the left. ∴ The card has a 7 on the right.	If p, then q p is true ∴ q is true	100%	0%	0%
2. If the card has an A on the left, it has a 7 on the right. The card has an A on the left. ∴ The card does not have a 7 on the right.	If p, then q p is true ∴ q is not true	0%	0%	100%
3. If the card has an A on the left, it has a 7 on the right. The card does not have an A on the left. ∴ The card has a 7 on the right.	If p, then q p is not true ∴ q is true	5%	79%	16%
4. If the card has an A on the left, it has a 7 on the right. The card does not have an A on the left. ∴ The card does not have a 7 on the right.	If p, then q p is not true ∴ q is not true	21%	77%	2%
5. If the card has an A on the left, it has a 7 on the right. The card has a 7 on the right. ∴ The card has an A on the left.	If p, then q q is true ∴ p is true	23%	77%	0%
6. If the card has an A on the left, it has a 7 on the right. The card has a 7 on the right. ∴ The card does not have an A on the left.	If p, then q q is true ∴ p is not true	4%	82%	14%
7. If the card has an A on the left, it has a 7 on the right. The card does not have a 7 on the right. ∴ The card has an A on the left.	If p, then q q is not true ∴ p is true	0%	23%	77%
8. If the card has an A on the left, it has a 7 on the right. The card does not have a 7 on the right. ∴ The card does not have an A on the left.	If p, then q q is not true ∴ p is not true	57%	39%	4%

Adapted from Rips and Marcus (1977)

tests that are needed to determine whether the rule is true or false. Here is a conditional rule, along with four possible tests; put a checkmark next to the tests that you would like done:

> If there is a solar eclipse, then the streets will be dark.

☐ There is a solar eclipse; I will tell you whether or not the streets are dark.

☐ There is not a solar eclipse; I will tell you whether or not the streets are dark.

☐ The streets are dark; I will tell you whether or not there is a solar eclipse.

☐ The streets are not dark; I will tell you whether or not there is a solar eclipse.

In this case, you begin with a rule of the form "If p, then q," and you have four possible tests: p, not p, q, and not q. The correct answer is to select the first (p) and last (not q) tests.

If you are like most students you did not produce the logically correct answer (Wason, 1966). In this section, we explore three views of how people reason:

By rules—people use general logical rules that are applied to all conditional reasoning problems,

By instances—people use their experience with specific instances such as those described in the problem, and

By schemas—people use reasoning strategies (either learned or innate) that are based on certain kinds of conditional reasoning situations, such as permissions or social exchange.

Analysis of people's performance on the selection task provides a vehicle for understanding human conditional reasoning (Johnson-Laird & Wason, 1977; Wason, 1966, 1968; Wason & Johnson-Laird, 1972). For example, Box 5-13 shows a problem in which subjects are given a conditional statement: "If a card has a vowel on one side, then it has an even number on the other side." In addition, subjects are given four cards corresponding to an affirmed antecedent (A), a denied antecedent (D), an affirmed consequent (4), and a denied consequent (7). The subject's job is to determine which cards should be flipped over to test the truth of the statement.

Let's assume that you use a biconditional interpretation of the statement and that, due to difficulty in interpreting negatives, you ignore denied conditions. You would accept both the given conditional statement and its reversed interpretation: "If a card has an even number on one side, then it has a vowel on

BOX 5 ▪ 13   Card-Turning Problem

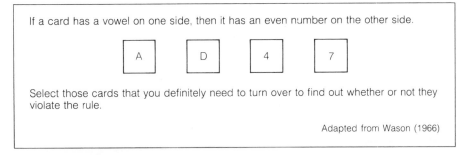

If a card has a vowel on one side, then it has an even number on the other side.

A   D   4   7

Select those cards that you definitely need to turn over to find out whether or not they violate the rule.

Adapted from Wason (1966)

the other." To test the given statement, you would flip over the A card; if it lacked an even number, you would know that the statement is false. To test the reversed version, you would flip over the 4 card to make sure it had a vowel on the other side. This was the most popular strategy among Wason's subjects: 46 percent asked to flip over card A and card 4.

In contrast, let's assume that you use only a conditional interpretation of the premise and that you will not rule out the use of denied conditions. In this case, you would select card A because you know that the premise says there must be an even number on the other side. In addition, you would choose card 7; if it had a vowel on the other side, you would know that the statement cannot be true. Only 4 percent of the subjects selected cards A and 7, although this is the logically correct answer. Note that flipping over card 4 does not test the if–then statement, because either a vowel or a consonant would be consistent with the statement. Similarly, flipping over the D card adds no information because neither an even number nor an odd number violates the if–then statement. As you can see, Wason's subjects appeared to opt for biconditional interpretations of conditional statements and were unable to use negative (that is, denied) conditions.

Is there any way to combat these misinterpretations of conditional statements? In one study (Johnson-Laird, Legrenzi, & Legrenzi, 1972; Johnson-Laird & Wason, 1977), subjects were given a concrete version of the previous task. The conditional statement was: "If an envelope is sealed, then it has a 50-lira stamp on it." Four tests that could be carried out are to turn over a sealed envelope (affirmed antecedent), an unsealed envelope (denied antecedent), an envelope with a 50-lira stamp (affirmed consequent), and an envelope with a 40-lira stamp (denied consequent). The subject's job was to pretend to be working in a post office and to determine which envelopes should be flipped over to test the conditional statement. A version of the task is summarized in Box 5-14. Unlike in the abstract version of this task, the majority

BOX 5 ▪ 14   Envelope Problem

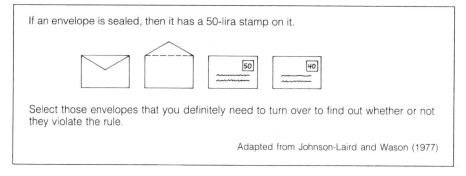

If an envelope is sealed, then it has a 50-lira stamp on it.

Select those envelopes that you definitely need to turn over to find out whether or not they violate the rule.

Adapted from Johnson-Laird and Wason (1977)

of subjects in the envelope experiment said that the sealed envelope and the envelope with the 40-lira stamp should be turned over. Thus most subjects appear to have behaved logically, using a conditional interpretation and negative conditions. This study suggests that when a concrete context is used, the tendency to make incorrect interpretations is decreased; however, as you will see, this result has not always been easily replicated and other theories have been proposed.

In summary, early work on the selection task produced two interesting effects. First, people performed very poorly on the task, contradicting the idea that humans are naturally logical reasoners; apparently interpreting and/or using the general rules of logic in all situations is not a basic human characteristic. Instead, humans make errors which suggest that they incorrectly interpret conditional statements as biconditionals and that they fail to adequately process information about negatives. Second, in some cases there is a *thematic-materials effect* whereby people make fewer errors—and presumably fewer biconditional interpretations— for concrete situations than for abstract situations. This line of research allows us to eliminate the rule theory, which predicts that people should make few errors and make the same kind of errors on abstract and concrete versions.

The next step was to gain a better understanding of the thematic-materials effect. Several researchers (Griggs & Cox, 1982; Manktelow & Evans, 1979) have found that concrete materials lead to better performance than abstract materials only under certain circumstances—namely, when the concrete materials are familiar enough to remind the reasoner of past experience with the conditional rule. For example, when Griggs and Cox (1982) presented the envelope problem (as in Box 5-14) to American students who were unfamiliar with Italian postal rules, they performed about the same on this concrete problem as on an abstract version of the problem (as in Box 5-13). In contrast, when the American students

BOX 5 ▪ 15   The Drinking-Age Problem

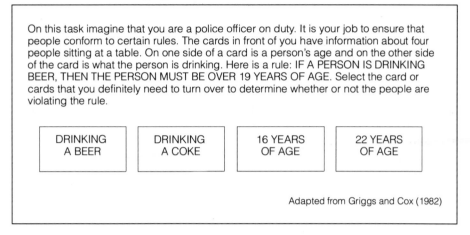

On this task imagine that you are a police officer on duty. It is your job to ensure that people conform to certain rules. The cards in front of you have information about four people sitting at a table. On one side of a card is a person's age and on the other side of the card is what the person is drinking. Here is a rule: IF A PERSON IS DRINKING BEER, THEN THE PERSON MUST BE OVER 19 YEARS OF AGE. Select the card or cards that you definitely need to turn over to determine whether or not the people are violating the rule.

| DRINKING A BEER | DRINKING A COKE | 16 YEARS OF AGE | 22 YEARS OF AGE |

Adapted from Griggs and Cox (1982)

were given a problem that was familiar to them—such as the drinking-age problem in Box 5-15—they performed much better than on an abstract version of the problem. Griggs and Cox (1982, p. 419) concluded that successful performance on the selection task occurs when the reasoner understands the rule within the context of specifically relevant past experience:

> In referring to some of the studies on the thematic-materials effect, Wason (1977, p. 132) comments, "it is a little depressing too because it suggests that the critical appreciation of falsification is aroused, not by invoking a calculus, but by assimilation to more mundane experience." It is this "mundane experience" that we feel is responsible for the thematic-materials effect.

Research on the drinking-age problem suggests that it is the *familiarity* of the material rather than the *concreteness* that affects reasoning performance. Consistent with the *instance theory* and in contrast to the *rule theory*, successful conditional reasoning seems to depend on the reasoner's use of prior knowledge about the conditional rule rather than on applying general rules of logic to all problems.

The next question we might ask concerns the specificity of the experience: Do people remember specific instances or general schemas? The *instance theory*, which has been attributed to Griggs and Cox (1982), holds that people remember specific examples and counterexamples about the rule; for example, when confronted with the drinking-age rule, reasoners may remember an episode in which they were not allowed to drink because they were underage. In contrast,

Cheng and Holyoak (1985; Cheng, Holyoak, Nisbett, & Oliver, 1986, p. 294) suggest a *pragmatic reasoning schema theory,* in which people use "clusters of rules that are highly generalized and abstracted but nonetheless defined with respect to classes of goals and types of relations"; an example of a pragmatic reasoning schema is permission—rules in which permission must be obtained before some action or event may occur.

To test the distinction between specific instances and general schemas as the basis for conditional reasoning, Cheng and Holyoak (1985) compared how people solved two versions of the envelope problem (as in Box 5-14). In the standard version, American subjects (who were unfamiliar with this kind of rule) were told the following:

> You are a postal clerk working in some foreign country. Part of your job is to go through letters to check the postage. The country's postal regulation requires that <u>if a letter is sealed, then it must carry a 20-cent stamp.</u> In order to check that the regulation is followed, which of the following four envelopes would you turn over? Turn over only those that you need to check to be sure.

Along with this paragraph, subjects received four drawings of envelopes: the back of a sealed envelope, the back of an unsealed envelope, the front of an envelope carrying a 20-cent stamp, and the front of an envelope carrying a 10-cent stamp. The rationale version of the problem was identical except that the following sentences were inserted immediately after the underlined rule:

> The rationale for this regulation is to increase profit from personal mail, which is nearly always sealed. Sealed letters are defined as personal and must therefore carry more postage than unsealed letters.

According to Cheng and Holyoak (1985), the rationale version is more likely than the standard version to remind reasoners of their general experience with permission rules—that is, the rationale version is more likely to elicit the permission schema and thus lead to improved reasoning performance. In contrast, the specific instance theory might predict that both versions would produce the same low performance, because American subjects lack specific experience with postal regulations involving sealed-versus-unsealed envelopes. The results provide support for the pragmatic reasoning schema theory: the correct answer was achieved by approximately 57 percent of the subjects given the standard version and 87 percent of the subjects given the rationale version.

In an interesting follow-up, Cheng and Holyoak (1985) gave the standard version of Wason's original selection task (as shown in Box 5-13) or a revised version that emphasized permission. The standard version of the problem stated

> Below are four cards. Every card has a letter on one side and a number on the other. Your task is to decide which of the cards you need to turn over in order to find out whether or not a certain rule is being followed. The rule is: "If a card has an A on one side, then it must have a 4 on the other side." Turn over only those cards that you need to check to be sure.

Along with this statement were drawings of four cards: A, D, 4, and 7. In contrast, the permission version stated

> Suppose you are an authority checking whether or not people are obeying certain regulations. The regulations all have the general form: "If one is to take action A, then one must first satisfy precondition P." In other words, in order to be permitted to do A, one must first have fulfilled prerequisite P. The cards below contain information about four people: one side of the card indicates whether or not a person has taken action A, the other side indicates whether or not the same individual has fulfilled precondition P. In order to check that a certain regulation is being followed, which of the cards below would you turn over? Turn over only those that you need to check to be sure.

These instructions were followed by four cards inscribed as follows: "has taken action A," "has not taken action A," "has fulfilled precondition P," and "has not fulfilled precondition P."

In this study, both versions are abstract, although Cheng and Holyoak argue that the permission version is even more abstract than the standard version. According to the instance theory, performance should be very low on both problems, with the permission version eliciting the poorest performance. In contrast, if the permission version is successful in reminding reasoners about their general experience with permission rules, then reasoning should be considerably better on the permission version than on the standard version. Consistent with the pragmatic reasoning schema theory, the correct answer was given by 61 percent of the subjects on the rationale version and 19 percent on the standard version. Cheng and Holyoak (1985, p. 391) conclude that "people reason using knowledge structures that we term pragmatic reasoning schemas."

The next issue addressed in the research literature concerns the origins of general reasoning schemas: Are they learned from experience (Cheng & Holyoak, 1985, 1989; Cheng et al., 1986) or are they innate (Cosmides, 1989)? In a lengthy series of experiments, Cosmides (1989, p. 187) tested the idea that "natural selection has shaped how humans reason." In contrast to the view that reasoning schemas are abstracted from experience, Cosmides (1989) suggests *social contract theory*—the idea that humans have evolved innate strategies for reasoning about social exchange contracts of the form, "If you take the benefit, then you must pay the cost." Cosmides (1989, p. 196) asserts that "evolutionary biology places tight

BOX 5 • 16   The High School Problem

Permission Version

The secretary you replaced at the local Board of Education may have made some mistakes when she processed student documents. It is important that certain rules for assigning students from various towns to the appropriate school district be followed, because the population statistics they provide allow the Board of Education to decide how many teachers need to be assigned to each school. If these rules are not followed, some schools could end up with too many teachers, and other schools with too few.

Students are to be assigned either to Grover High School or to Hanover High School.

Some students live in the town of Grover City, some live in Hanover, and some live in Belmont. There are rules that determine which school a student Is to be assigned to; the most important of these rules is:

> If a student is to be assigned to Grover High School, then that student must live in Grover City.

Shortly before she retired, the secretary you replaced was supposed to sort through the documents that specify what town the students live in and make school assignments according to this rule. She was a sweet little old lady who had become rather absent-minded and who often made mistakes when categorizing student documents.

The cards below have information about the documents of four students. Each card represents one student. One side of a card tells what school the retired secretary assigned the student to, and the other side of the card tells what town that student lives in.

You suspect the retired secretary may have inadvertently categorized some of the students' documents incorrectly so you decide to see for yourself whether she ever violated the rule. Indicate only those card(s) you definitely need to turn over *to see if the documents of any of these students violate the rule.*

| GROVER HIGH SCHOOL | HANOVER HIGH SCHOOL | GROVER CITY | TOWN OF HANOVER |

(continued)

constraints on how humans must process information regarding social exchange," including "algorithms that produce and operate on cost-benefit representations of exchange interactions" and "procedures that make one very good at detecting cheating on social contracts." In other words, when it comes to social exchange rules, evolution has provided us with powerful procedures for catching cheaters and assessing benefits.

For example, consider the two versions of the high school problem shown in Box 5-16: a social contract version and a permission version. Both present the same

BOX 5 • 16, *continued*

Social Contract Version

You supervise four women who volunteered to help out at the local Board of Education. When you came into work today, you found the place abuzz with rumor and innuendo. Your volunteers were supposed to follow certain rules for assigning students from various towns to the appropriate school district. Each volunteer is the mother of a teenager who is about to enter high school, and each processed her own child's documents. So now rumors are flying that your volunteers cheated on the rules when it came to assigning their own children to a school. Here is the situation:

Students are to be assigned either to Grover High School, which is located in Grover City, or to Hanover High School, which is located in the town of Hanover. Grover High is a great school with an excellent record for getting students placed in good colleges. In contrast, Hanover High is a mediocre school with poor teachers and decrepit facilities.

The reason the schools are so different is how willing the parents of each community are to financially support their schools through taxes. Although both communities are equally prosperous, the parents in Grover City have always cared about the quality of their schools, including Grover High, and have been willing to pay for it. In contrast, the parents in the neighboring towns of Hanover and Belmont have never wanted to spend the money and have opposed any taxes to improve Hanover High.

The Board of Education took these factors into account when it created rules to determine which school a student is to be assigned to; the most important of these rules is:

> If a student is to be assigned to Grover High School, then that student must live in Grover City.

Your volunteers were supposed to follow this rule when processing *all* student documents—including the documents of their own children. You must find out if the rumors are true: Did any of your volunteers cheat on this rule when it came to processing their own children's documents?

The cards below have information about the documents of the four volunteers' children. Each card represents the child of one volunteer. One side of a card tells what school the volunteer assigned her son or daughter to, and the other side of the card tells what town that student lives in.

Most parents want their children to get the best education possible; however, some are not willing to pay for it. It Is easy to imagine that your volunteers, being ambitious mothers, might have been tempted to cheat on the rule. Indicate only those card(s) you definitely need to turn over *to see if the documents of any of these students violate the rule.*

Adapted from Cosmides (1989)

permission rule: "If a student is to be assigned to Grover High School, then that student must live in Grover City." The social contract version embeds the rule within a story showing that being assigned to Grover High School (rather than Hanover High School) is a benefit and that living in Grover City (rather than Hanover) is a cost. The permission version embeds the rule within a story that gives the rule a rationale, without making it a social contract; subjects are told that the rule allows the school administration to assign the proper number of teachers to each school.

If people use learned schemas, we can predict that both versions should produce good reasoning, because both elicit a permission schema. In contrast, social contract theory predicts that only the social contract version will produce good reasoning, because it is the only version that elicits reasoning about social exchange. The results clearly favored the predictions of social contract theory: the correct answer was produced by 75 percent of the people given the social contract version and 30 percent of the people given the permission version. Similar results were obtained in additional experiments.

In defense of their pragmatic reasoning schema theory, Cheng and Holyoak (1989) argue that the two versions of Cosmides's high school problem differ in many uncontrolled ways, that the permission version does not match their definition, and that the permission version's wording promotes a biconditional interpretation. In short, Cheng and Holyoak (1989, p. 306) state "not only is Cosmides empirically incorrect in claiming that social exchange situations have some uniquely privileged status in human reasoning, but it is unclear why one would believe this erroneous prediction follows from considerations of importance for survival."

Even if the methodology was flawless, would Cosmides's work prove that there is a "social contract reasoning gene" or that there are "cheater detector neurons" in the brain specialized for reasoning about social contracts? Obviously, the answer is No. However, her approach is provocative because it relates the psychology of thinking to the wider context of human life and reminds us that humans developed means of reasoning in order to adapt. Certainly, it makes sense to assume that humans have evolved certain mental capacities that increase their likelihood of survival.

As we close this section on conditional reasoning, let's review the chain of research. First, early research demonstrated that humans are not particularly good at applying general, context-free rules to a wide variety of conditional reasoning tasks. The tendency to misinterpret conditional statements as biconditionals and to ignore negative terms conflicts with the rule-based reasoning theories implied by formal logic. Second, research comparing familiar and unfamiliar versions of problems suggested that we use our existing knowledge to guide our reasoning; this led to theories of instance-based reasoning. Third, research on pragmatic reasoning schemas seemed to show that people use generalized schemas in reasoning, rather than specific instances; and research on social exchange theory suggested that the capacity to engage in schema-based reasoning has been determined through human evolution. Although progress has been made in determining the sources of error in human reasoning, the final chapter is yet to be written.

■
LINEAR REASONING
■

THE THREE-TERM SERIES TASK

Suppose I gave you the following linear reasoning problem:

> Bill is shorter than Allen
> Bill is taller than Charles
> Who is tallest?

If you answered that Allen is the tallest, you have correctly solved the problem.

How do people solve linear syllogisms such as this three-term series problem? In this section we focus on two issues concerning how people represent and process linear syllogisms. One issue concerns whether people process the syllogism visually or verbally. For example, which of the following descriptions best matches your strategy?

> *Visual strategy.* I formed a mental image.
> *Verbal strategy.* I did not form a mental image.

If you formed some sort of a mental image, we can say you used a visual (or spatial) strategy; if you focused only on the words, without using imagery, we can say you used a verbal (or linguistic) strategy.

A second issue concerns whether people integrate the information in the two premises into a single unified representation or whether they encode individual facts. For example, which of the following descriptions best matches your strategy?

> *Integrated strategy.* After I read the first sentence I arranged the two terms in order, Allen taller than Bill, and after I read the second sentence I added Charles next to Bill, forming three terms in order: Allen, Bill, and Charles.
> *Separate strategy.* After I read the first sentence, I stored information that Bill is shorter than Allen, and after I read the second sentence I stored information that Bill is taller than Charles. I did not make the inference that Allen is taller than Charles until I read the question.

For example, if you formed a visual array with the three boys in order from tallest to shortest, then you used an integrated strategy (and also a visual strategy); if you formed individual images of Allen as tall and Charles are short, then you used a separate strategy (and also a visual strategy). In this section we explore research aimed at determining strategies people use to represent and process linear syllogisms.

Evidence for Visual Versus Verbal Strategies. One of the first theoretical battles concerns whether people represent the premises visually or verbally. For example, DeSoto, London, and Handel (1965) allowed their subjects 10 seconds to respond Yes or No to conclusions based on premises such as those shown in Box 5-17. According to a traditional view of logical reasoning, problems that proceed from one extreme to the middle term in the first premise and from the middle term to the other extreme in the second premise (such as problems 1 and 4) should be easiest, and problems that proceed in one direction for one premise and the opposite direction in the second premise (such as problems 5 and 6) should be most difficult. However, in contrast to these predictions, Box 5-17 shows that problem 4 is among the most difficult, whereas problems 5 and 6 are among the easiest. DeSoto and colleagues (1965, p. 515) concluded that formal logic is not necessarily the system that human beings use to reason: "Clearly, an altogether different paralogic is required to account for the findings."

How can we account for the pattern of performance on the eight problems shown in Box 5-17? Consistent with the integrated and visual strategies described above, DeSoto and colleagues proposed that people form a visual image of the three terms in order. Further, they proposed two *paralogical principles* that describe how people form mental images (p. 515): "people learn orderings better in one direction than the other" and "people end-anchor orderings" by focusing on end terms (i.e., terms on the two extreme ends of the ordering). The first principle is demonstrated by the fact that the subjects performed better on an evaluative ordering when the terms were presented from better-to-worse (as in problem 1) than on a mixed ordering (as in problems 2 and 3), and worst of all when terms were presented from worse-to-better (as in problem 4). The second principle is indicated by the fact that the subjects performed better when the premises stated an end term (that is, best or worst) followed by a middle term rather than a middle term followed by an end term. For example, problems 5 and 6 have two propositions that go from ends-to-middle and are much easier than problems 7 and 8, which have two propositions that go from middle-to-ends.

DeSoto and colleagues described the reasoning process as involving spatial paralogic in which an up-down or left-right series of spaces is imagined and the terms of the ordering (A, B, C) are placed in the spaces. Similar results were obtained using the continuums better-worse, above-below, lighter-darker, and

BOX 5 • 17   Proportion of Correct Responses for Eight Deduction Problems

Premises	Proportion of Correct Responses	Form of Premises	
		Within Premises	Between Premises
1. A is better than B B is better than C	.61	Better-to-worse	Better-to-worse
2. B is better than C A is better than B	.53	Better-to-worse	Worse-to-better
3. B is worse than A C is worse than B	.50	Worse-to-better	Better-to-worse
4. C is worse than B B is worse than A	.43	Worse-to-better	Worse-to-better
5. A is better than B C is worse than B	.62	Ends-to-middle	Better-to-worse
6. C is worse than B A is better than B	.57	Ends-to-middle	Worse-to-better
7. B is worse than A B is better than C	.41	Middle-to-ends	Better-to-worse
8. B is better than C B is worse than A	.38	Middle-to-ends	Worse-to-better

The question for the subjects was stated in each of four ways:
Is A better than C? Is C better than A? Is A worse than C?
Is C worse than A?

From DeSoto, London, and Handel (1965). Copyright 1965 by The American
Psychological Association. Reprinted by permission of the author

left-right, although performance was generally poorer for left-right, possibly
because it is more difficult to imagine horizontal than vertical ordering.
Performance was poorer with the descriptor "more" than "better," with "below"
than "above," and with "right of" than "left of," which suggests that the
direction of filling the spatial ordering is important.

Huttenlocher (1968) has summarized a series of experiments that replicated
the DeSoto findings, using orderings of the form: "Tom is shorter than Sam; Sam
is shorter than Pete; Who is tallest?" As a refinement of DeSoto's theory,
Huttenlocher proposed that reasoners use the first premise to set up a relation
between two terms (e.g., to place X above Y or Y above X) and use the second
premise to determine where to place the third term (e.g., either above or below
the other terms). As predicted by this theory, reasoners performed faster and more

BOX 5 • 18   A Block Problem

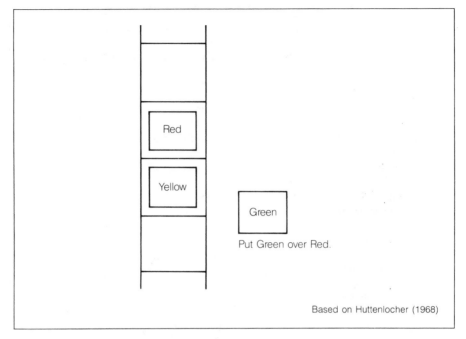

Put Green over Red.

Based on Huttenlocher (1968)

accurately when the subject of the second premise was the third term (e.g., "Tom is taller than John; Sam is shorter than John; Who is tallest?") than when the third term was the object of the second premise (e.g., "John is shorter than Tom; John is taller than Sam; Who is tallest?"). Even when the premises were given in the passive voice, reasoning was better when the third term was the logical subject and grammatical object of the second premise. For example, "Tom is leading John; Tom is led by Sam; Who is the winner?" was easier than "Tom is leading John; Sam is led by John; Who is the winner?" Apparently, the ability to process the second proposition depends on how it fits into the fixed relation established by the first premise.

Huttenlocher's emphasis on the subject-object grammar of the mobile third term in the second premise added a new approach to DeSoto's principle of end-anchoring. In experiments with children, Huttenlocher found that it was easier for the children to place a block in a concrete ladder or array, as shown in Box 5-18, if the subject of the instruction sentence was the block to be placed. For example, if the ladder had a red block above a yellow block, the children could more easily place the third block (green) in the ladder when they were given sentences in which the green block was the subject, as in "Put green over red" or

BOX 5 ▪ 19   Mean Solution Time in Seconds for 16 Deduction Problems

Premises	Who is Best?	Who is Worst?	Mean
1a. A better than B; B better than C	5.4	6.1	5.8
1b. B better than C; A better than B	5.0	5.5	5.2
2a. C worse than B; B worse than A	6.3	6.5	6.4
2b. B worse than A; C worse than B	5.9	5.0	5.5
3a. A better than B; C worse than B	5.4	5.3	5.3
3b. C worse than B; A better than B	4.8	5.8	5.3
4a. B worse than A; B better than C	5.0	6.0	5.5
4b. B better than C; B worse than A	6.1	5.4	5.8
1'a. A not as bad as B; B not as bad as C	6.8	6.0	6.3
1'b. B not as bad as C; A not as bad as B	7.2	6.6	6.8
2'a. C not as good as B; B not as good as A	5.6	6.6	6.1
2'b. B not as good as A; C not as good as B	6.1	6.6	6.4
3'a. A not as bad as B; C not as good as B	6.3	6.7	6.5
3'b. C not as good as B; A not as bad as B	6.7	6.3	6.5
4'a. B not as good as A; B not as bad as C	6.1	6.2	6.1
4'b. B not as bad as C; B not as good as A	5.5	7.1	6.2

From Clark (1969). Copyright 1969 by The American Psychological Association. Reprinted by permission of the author.

"Put green under yellow" than when the mobile block was the object of the sentence, as in "Put red under green" or "Put yellow over green." The deductive reasoning process in adults may involve mentally placing objects into an imaginary array, with the first proposition setting the fixed relation between two terms and the second proposition telling the reasoner where in the array to place the third term. Answering questions about who is the tallest or shortest involves referring to the constructed array. Thus, while Huttenlocher retained the idea that reasoners construct a spatial linear ordering, she suggested that the difficulty in placing items into the imaginary array was influenced by the grammar of the second premise, or what DeSoto called "ends-to-middle" end-anchoring.

Although DeSoto and Huttenlocher described linear reasoning as constructing a spatial image, using principles such as end-anchoring, Clark (1969) attempted to show that linear reasoning can better be described in terms of nonspatial linguistic processes. Clark asked subjects to respond to problems such as "If John isn't as good as Pete, and Dick isn't as good as John, then who is the best?" The overall response times for sixteen problem types are summarized in Box 5-19. Overall performance on the first eight problems seems to correspond nicely with the results of DeSoto and Huttenlocher. Performance was better on problems where the propositions went from better-to-worse (such as problem 1a and 1b) than on those that went from worse-to-better (such as problem 2a and 2b); and performance was better when the third term was the subject of the second premise (that is, when it was end-anchored, as in problems 1b, 2b, 3a, and 3b) than when the third term was the object of the second premise (as in problems 1a, 2a, 4a, and 4b). However, based on the new information provided by examining the negative problems shown in the bottom half of Box 5-19 and by comparing the questions "Who is best?" and "Who is worst?", Clark was able to propose three new principles to describe reasoning in terms of linguistic processes:

1. *The primacy of functional relations* is the idea that the logical (or functional) relations in a sentence are stored rather than the grammatical relations of voice and negatives; for example, "A is led by B" may be encoded as "B leads A," or "A is not as good as B" may be translated as "B is better than A."

2. *Lexical markings* is the idea that relational terms that imply both a scale and a position on a scale (i.e., *marked* terms such as "bad" or "short") require more effort to encode than adjectives that imply only the scale name but no position on the scale (i.e., *unmarked* terms such as "tall" or "good"). (To test whether an adjective such as "tall" or "short" is marked, you can ask whether there is a difference between "How tall is X?" versus "How short is X?" The marked term implies that X is short.) A simpler lexicon, such as "X is better than Y," is easier to store and process than "Y is worse than X."

3. *The principle of congruence* states that thinkers compare the question with the information they have encoded in memory and, if necessary, reformulate the question to make it congruent with this information.

The principle of functional relations correctly predicts that the problems with negatives in the premises will take longer to solve than the problems without negatives, presumably due to an extra translation step. Similarly, the principle of lexical marking predicts that problems with "bad" or "worse," such as problems 2 and 1', should be more difficult than those with "good" or "better," such as problems 1 and 2'. The principle of congruence predicts that if the propositions are given in terms of "worse than," then the question "Who is worst?" will be easier, but if the propositions are given in terms of "better than," then "Who is best?" will be easier. This finding is generally upheld. In addition, the principles of congruence and functional relation suggest that problems 3 and 4' should be easier than problems 4 and 3', because in the former if A is worse than B then A is worst, and if A is better than B then A is best, but not in the latter. Most of Clark's results are consistent with those of Huttenlocher and of DeSoto, and his linguistic interpretation provides a different—albeit not completely contra-dictory—analysis of the reasoning process. The differences between the a-form and b-form of the eight problem types, however, are not well explained by Clark and seem to be best interpreted by the principle of end-anchoring. For example, problem 2b presents the terms in the order B, A, C, so that the third term, C, is anchored into A > B; in contrast, problem 2a presents the terms in the order C, B, A, so that the C > B relation is established first but the end term, A, is not mentioned next. As predicted by the end-anchoring principle, 2a takes more time to solve than does 2b.

We can close the first phase of psychological research on linear reasoning by noting that the patterns of errors and response times across problem types are consistent with both visual and verbal strategies in most cases, the verbal strategy alone in some other cases, and the visual strategy alone in other cases. Among the most salient findings are

Directional effect/marked relation effect—Problems are easier when the relational terms in the premises and questions describe better-to-worse rather than worse-to-better relations.

End-anchoring effect—Problems are easier when the subject of each premise is an end term rather than the middle term.

Translation effect—Problems are easier when the premises and questions contain no passives or negatives than when they do.

However, this line of research has not succeeded in proving that all people use only a visual strategy or all people use only a verbal strategy.

Evidence for Integrated Versus Separate Strategies. Although the debate on visual versus verbal strategies for linear reasoning produced some important findings, a second phase of research was needed to determine whether reasoners form integrated or separate representations of the information in the premises. For example, Potts (1972) focused on the cognitive representation that a reasoner builds and the cognitive processes a reasoner goes through to answer a question about a linear ordering. As shown in Box 5-20, Potts asked subjects to read a paragraph about a linear ordering in the form A > B, B > C, C > D and then answer questions about the adjacent pairs, such as A > B, B > C, C > D, and about the remote pairs, such as A > C, B > D, and A > D. In the example in Box 5-20, the A term is bear, the B term is hawk, the C term is wolf, and the D term is deer. If people encode each premise separately, then we can predict better performance for questions about the adjacent pairs (which were presented) than about remote pairs (which must be deduced from the premises). If people form an integrated

BOX 5 · 20   Mean Response Time in Seconds for 12 Deduction Problems

Typical Passage

In a small forest just south of nowhere, a deer, a bear, a wolf and a hawk were battling for dominion over the land. It boiled down to a battle of wits, so intelligence was the crucial factor. The bear was smarter than the hawk, the hawk was smarter than the wolf, and the wolf was smarter than the deer . . . .   In the end, each of the battles was decided in its own way and tranquility returned to the area.

Typical Results

Question Form	Mean Response Time in Seconds
A > B?	1.1
B > C?	2.1
C > D?	2.0
A > C?	1.1
B > D?	1.8
A > D?	1.0
B > A?	1.8
C > B?	2.2
D > C?	1.7
C > A?	1.8
D > B?	1.7
D > A?	1.3

From Potts (1972. 1974)

ordering (e.g., A > B > C > D) at the time of reading the paragraph, then we can predict better performance on questions about the remote pairs (which are more easily distinguished from one another in an ordering) than about the adjacent pairs (which are closer to one another). Consistent with the predictions of the integrated strategy theory, the response times given in Box 5-20 show that subjects were generally faster in answering questions about remote pairs than about adjacent pairs.

This *distance effect* indicated that subjects did not simply copy the list of three presented premises (that is, three separate sentences or separate images) into their memories; rather, they may have formed a sort of ordered list or spatial array containing the four terms in order. When the subjects were presented with a question (e.g., "Is the hawk smarter than the deer?") about the ordering of certain animals (e.g., bear > hawk > wolf > deer), they used a sort of end-anchoring strategy, according to Potts. First they checked to see if either term in the question was an end term in the ordering. For example, they asked themselves whether "hawk" was the first or last term in the ordering and whether "deer" was the first or last term in the ordering. If not, they had to process more deeply by checking, for example, whether one of the terms in the question was the second-to-last term in the ordering. As you can see in Box 5-20, questions of the form "Is B > C?" and "Is C > B?" took the longest time to answer, presumably because they required deeper processing according to Potts's models while questions beginning with the A term ("Is A > C?") took the least time to answer.

Box 5-21 summarizes the steps in the reasoning process for solving four-term linear ordering problems, according to Potts (1972). The model posits that the reasoner transforms the presented premises into an integrated linear ordering of the form A > B > C > D and reads a question of the form "Is A > C?" The model includes the following steps. The first item in the test question is checked to see if it is the first term in the ordering (if so, the reasoner answers "True") or the last item (if so, the reasoner answers "False"); otherwise, the second item in the test question is checked to see if it is the first term in the ordering (if so, the reasoner answers "False") or the last item in the ordering (if so, the reasoner responds "True"). If none of these four tests produce a response, the reasoner checks to see if the second item in the question is the second-to-last item in the ordering (if so, the reasoner responds "True"; if not, the appropriate answer is "False"). The model provides specific predictions that can be tested; for example, test questions with A or D as the first item should be answered most quickly, test questions with B or C as the first item and A or D as the second item should require a little more time, and test questions with B and C as the first and second items should require the most time. Potts's work provides a good example of how cognitive models of the reasoning process may be established and, in this case, also provides a more detailed description of the mental representations and processes underlying the end-anchoring effect.

Evidence for Multiple Strategies. Potts's research (Potts, 1972, 1978; Scholz & Potts, 1974) suggests that subjects form an integrated representation of the linear ordering at the time of encoding (i.e., integrated strategy). However, an alternative strategy might be to memorize each premise as presented at the time of encoding and then to combine them to make inferences at the time of questioning (i.e., separate strategy). To test the idea that people may use either strategy, Mayer (1979) presented all adjacent and remote pairs of a five-term linear ordering to subjects. For some subjects, the information was in an artificial, or abstract, form such as "B > D." For other subjects the information was in a more familiar form, such as "Bill is taller than Dave." The artificial group performed as if they had memorized each premise separately—making equivalent errors in learning both adjacent and remote pairs. In contrast, the familiar group performed as if they had formed a linear ordering, replicating the performance of subjects in Potts's experiments—fewer errors on remote

BOX 5 ▪ 21   An Information-Processing Model of Reasoning with Four-Term Linear Orderings

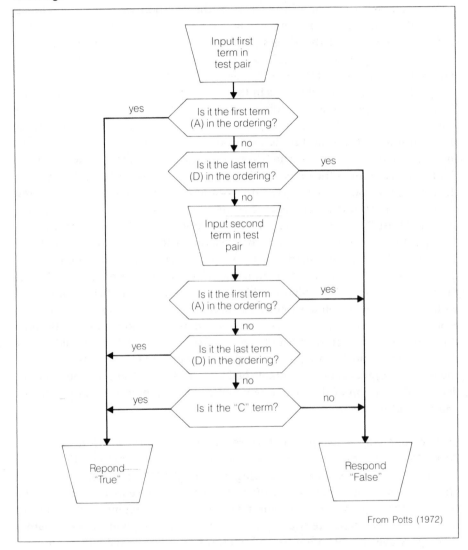

Input first
term in
test pair

yes ← Is it the first term (A) in the ordering?

no

Is it the last term (D) in the ordering? → yes

no

Input second term in test pair

Is it the first term (A) in the ordering? → yes

no

yes ← Is it the last term (D) in the ordering?

no

yes ← Is it the "C" term? → no

Repond "True"

Respond "False"

From Potts (1972)

than on adjacent pairs. These results suggest that people can use either an integrated or separate strategy for representing and processing linear syllogisms and that they tend to select a strategy that is most appropriate for a given situation.

BOX 5 ▪ 22   Two Strategies for Solving a Three-Term Series Problem

Integrated Strategy

1. Encode premise 1: place subject and object on scale.
   Harder if middle term is subject
2. Encode premise 2: position third term on scale.
   Harder if middle term is subject
3. Encode question: scan scale and respond.

Separate Strategy

1. Encode premise 1: assign property to subject.
   Harder if use unmarked relation
2. Encode premise 2: assign property to subject.
   Harder if use unmarked relation
3. Encode question: scan images and respond.
   Harder if images are not conclusive

Modified from Egan and Grimes-Farrow (1982)

Egan & Grimes-Farrow (1982) have found evidence that some people tend to use an integrated strategy and others tend to use a separate strategy for encoding and processing three-term linear syllogisms. For example, a problem might be: "The circle is smoother than the square; The triangle is rougher than the square; Is the circle smoother than the triangle?" After solving some three-term series problems such as these, subjects were asked to describe verbally how they solved several problems and to make a drawing of their mental representation of several problems. Some subjects described an integrated strategy in which they constructed a unified mental array (Egan & Grimes-Farrow, 1982, p. 301): "Rather than imagining a rough/smooth figure, I put the figures in a horizontal line, in my mind, in order of left/right rather than rough/smooth." Other subjects described a separate strategy in which they encoded each term individually (Egan & Grimes-Farrow, 1982, p. 301): "I also drew a picture, and if something was rough I would put craters in it in my mind, smooth was just plain white." The two strategies are summarized in Box 5-22.

Did subjects who reported using different strategies display different patterns of performance on the reasoning problems? The answer is Yes. For example, premises that began with the middle term were more difficult for people using the integrated strategy than those using the separate strategy. Presumably, forming an integrated array is easier when the subject of the second premise is the third term that will be placed in an array established by the first two terms;

however, if a subject is simply remembering whether each term is "smooth" or "rough," then the order of presentation of terms as subjects or objects is not important. As another example, premises that contained unmarked relations (e.g., "thinner" rather than "fatter") adversely affected performance for subjects using a separate strategy but not for subjects using an integrated strategy. Presumably, assigning a characteristic to each term is easier when the characteristic is stated in the expected way (e.g., "fat") rather than in the unexpected way ("thin"), but the relational wording does not interfere with arranging objects into an array. By asking reasoners to describe their reasoning strategies, Egan and Grimes-Farrow provided important evidence for individual differences in how people solve three-term series problems.

Whereas Egan and Grimes-Farrow found individual differences in the use of integrated and separate strategies, Sternberg and Weil (1980) found evidence for individual differences in the use of visual and verbal strategies. By analyzing the pattern of response times for various linear reasoning problems, Sternberg and Weil (1980) were able to classify some students as visual reasoners and others as verbal reasoners. Interestingly, the performance of the visual reasoners correlated strongly with their scores on a test of spatial ability but not on a test of verbal ability, whereas the performance of the verbal reasoners correlated strongly with their scores on a test of verbal ability but not on a test of spatial ability.

In summary, we can close this third and final phase by noting that different people use different strategies under different circumstances; that is, the strategy that is used for a linear reasoning problem depends both on the preferred strategy of the reasoner and on the way that the problem is presented. In short, as noted by Egan and Grimes-Farrow (1982, p. 305): "No single theory of solving three-term series problems can account for the data of all subjects."

■
EVALUATION
■

The syllogistic reasoning task, like the concept-learning task discussed in Chapter 4, has been a major vehicle for studying human thinking. Like the concept-learning paradigm, the syllogistic reasoning task has the advantage of being an agreed-upon and well-known method and the disadvantage of being a specific type of reasoning that may not be directly related to other situations.

The fact that human logic and formal logic do not always seem to coincide has been the source of many interesting insights into human thought processes. A common thread running through this chapter has been to distinguish between errors due to faulty or incomplete encoding of premises and errors due to faulty or incomplete logical processing in humans. Although my reading of the current research tends to favor the encoding theories—that is, the idea that people reason logically based on incorrect or incomplete representations of the premises—the issue is far from being settled.

What is the future of research on reasoning? In a recent review of research on reasoning, Rips (1990, p. 322) observed that "the psychology of reasoning has been something of a research backwater" that "has played only a minor role in work on mental processes." More optimistically, Rips (1990, p. 322) noted that research on reasoning is now moving beyond studying contrived tasks such as "a couple of clever brain teasers invented by Peter Wason . . . and categorical syllogisms invented by Aristotle." From this vantage point, it appears that the goal of future research is to develop broader theories of how humans reason across a variety of more natural situations.

Suggested Readings

EVANS, J. ST. B. T. (1982). *The psychology of deductive reasoning.* London: Routledge & Kegan Paul. Presents Evans's theory of deductive reasoning.

JOHNSON-LAIRD, P. N. (1983). *Mental models: Towards a cognitive science of language, inference, and consciousness.* Cambridge, MA: Harvard University Press. Presents Johnson-Laird's theory of deductive reasoning.

JOHNSON-LAIRD, P. N., & WASON, P. C. (Eds.). (1978). *Thinking: Readings in cognitive science..* Cambridge, England: Cambridge University Press. The section on deduction contains several classic papers.

WASON, P. C., & JOHNSON-LAIRD, P. N. (Eds.). (1968). *Thinking and reasoning.* Baltimore, MD: Penguin. Contains classic papers by Chapman and Chapman, Henle, DeSoto et al., and others.

PART III

INFORMATION-PROCESSING ANALYSIS OF COGNITION

CHAPTER 6

COMPUTER SIMULATION

Thinking as a Search for a Solution Path

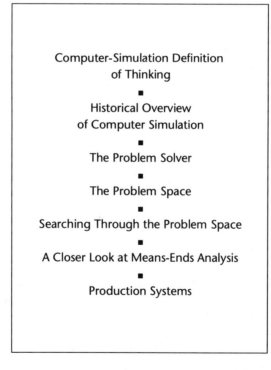

BOX 6 ▪ 1   A Conversation with a Computer

P: Men are all alike.
MD: In what way?
P: They're always bugging us about something or other.
MD: Can you think of a specific example?
P: Well, my boyfriend made me come here.
MD: Your boyfriend made you come here?
P: He says I'm depressed much of the time.
MD: I am sorry to hear you are depressed.
P: It's true. I am unhappy.
MD: Do you think coming here will help you not be unhappy?
P: I need some help, that much seems certain.
MD: What would it mean to you if you got some help?
P: Perhaps I could learn to get along with my mother.
MD: Tell me more about your family.
P: My mother takes care of me.
MD: Who else in your family takes care of you?
P: My father.
MD: Your father.
P: You are like my father in some ways.
MD: What resemblance do you see?
P: You are not very aggressive but I think you don't want me to notice that.
MD: What makes you think I am not very aggressive?
P: You don't argue with me.
MD: Why do you think I don't argue with you?
P: You are afraid of me.
MD: Does it please you to believe that I am afraid of you?
P: My father is afraid of everybody.
MD: What else comes to mind when you think of your father?
P: Bullies.
MD: Does that have anything to do with the fact that your boyfriend made
       you come here?

From Weizenbaum (1968)

NATURAL LANGUAGE TASKS

Box 6-I is the protocol or transcript of part of a therapy session between a doctor (MD) and a patient (P). As you read the transcript try to judge whether the MD is a human therapist or a computer. What is your verdict?

You may be surprised to learn that this discussion took place at a computer keyboard with the patient typing in statements and the computer responding by teletype or videoscope. Therapist programs such as this one, as well as programs that simulate neurotic symptoms, were developed to determine whether it is possible to describe a therapy technique or a mental syndrome with enough precision to express it as a computer program (Colby, 1965; Colby, Watt, & Gilbert, 1966; Weizenbaum, 1968). The programmers, of course, did not intend their Rogerian program to replace

Carl Rogers (1961) and his disciples, but their program does demonstrate a basic advance in theories of human cognitive processing. A theory of what a therapist does while giving therapy or what a chess player does while playing chess, or what a problem solver does while solving a problem may be specified in very exact terms as a list of things to do—in short, as a computer program. Theories of human cognitive processes may thus be generated and expressed as computer programs and *tested* by seeing if they work—that is if they do give therapy, play chess, or solve problems the way a person does. Programs that understand natural language as in Box 6-1 aid in the development of theories of memory and psycholinguistics; however programs that solve problems are more specifically important for theories of human thinking.

Computers can solve induction and deduction problems as described in Chapters 4 and 5. However, the computer-simulation work covered in this chapter focuses on MOVE problems. MOVE problems have a well-defined initial state, a well-defined goal state, and a well-defined set of allowable operators, or moves. MOVE problems include aspects of Greeno's (1978a) transformation problems and arrangement problems as discussed in Chapter 1. Simon (1978) has pointed out that computer simulation of problem-solving strategies has been particularly successful for well-defined problems—like our MOVE problems—rather than for poorly defined problems that occur in everyday life. Examples of MOVE problems that have been exposed to computer simulation include the disk problem as shown in Box 3-18 of Chapter 3 (Ernst & Newell, 1969) and the cryptarithmetic problem as shown in Box 3-10 (Newell & Simon, 1974).

To derive a precise description of the solution process for such problems, a first step is to analyze the performance of a subject solving a problem. As the subject solves the problem, he or she is asked to describe the mental processes involved. Thus computer simulations of thinking may begin with what is called a "thinking-aloud protocol"—a transcript of a subject's running description of what is going on inside her head as the problem is being solved. Box 6-2 provides part of a subject's protocol for the DONALD + GERALD = ROBERT problem. Newell and Simon (1972) devote an entire chapter to this subject's behavior, including eighteen pages of raw protocol and almost a hundred pages in all. Can you see any strategy or set of procedures the subject is using? Newell and Simon note that in step 5 the subject is substituting the given into the equation, in step 7 he is making an inference based on having two numbers in a column, and in steps 10 and 12 he is using a strategy of searching for "known" letters, and so on. By carefully observing the general procedures used by individual subjects, Newell

BOX 6 • 2   Protocol for a Subject on the DONALD + GERALD = ROBERT Problem

Problem

DONALD
+ GERALD
ROBERT

Find a number for each letter, given that D = 5, every number between 0 and 9 has a corresponding letter, and each letter had a unique number.

Protocol

1. Each letter has one and only one numerical value . . . .
2. (E: One numerical value.)
3. There are 10 different letters.
4. And each of them has one numerical value.
5. Therefore, I can, looking at the two D's . . .
6. each D is 5;
7. therefore, T is zero.
8. So I think I'll start by writing that problem here.
9. I'll write T, T is zero.
10. Now, do I have any other T's?
11. No.
12. But I have another D.
13. That means I have a 5 over on the other side.
14. Now I have 2 A's
15. and 2 L's
16. that are each
17. somewhere
18. and this R
19. 3 R's
(Continues for 321 units)

From Newell and Simon (1972)

and Simon were able to produce a computer program that solved similar cryptarithmetic problems in a way apparently similar to human methods.

What other types of "thinking" can computers engage in? The ever-expanding list now includes

Solving algebra story problems (Bobrow, 1968; Kintsch & Greeno, 1985)

Solving geometry problems (Anderson, Greeno, & Kline, 1981; Gelernter, 1960; Greeno, 1978b)

Generating logical proofs (Newell, Shaw, & Simon, 1957)

Playing chess (Newell, Shaw, & Simon, 1958; Newell & Simon, 1972)

Playing checkers (Samuel, 1963)

Concept learning (Gregg & Simon, 1967; Simon & Kotovsky, 1963)

Solving analogy problems (Evans, 1968: Reitman, 1965)

Producing Rogerian therapy and neurotic personality (Colby, 1965; Colby et al., 1966; Weizenbaum, 1968)

General problem solving (Ernst & Newell, 1969)

Solving logical and deductive problems (Newell & Simon, 1972)

Understanding problem descriptions (Hayes & Simon, 1974, 1977: Simon & Hayes, 1976)

Understanding natural language (Winograd, 1972, 1983)

Understanding simple pictures (Biederman, 1987; Marr, 1982; Winston, 1975)

Understanding electronic circuit diagrams (Bobrow, 1985; Sussman & Stallman, 1975)

Diagnosing medical symptoms (Buchanan & Shortliffe, 1984; Shortliffe, 1976; Pople, 1977)

Diagnosing errors in children's arithmetic procedures (Brown & Burton, 1978)

Analyzing chemical structure from mass spectrograms (Buchanan, Sutherland, & Feiganbaum, 1969)

Teaching as an expert tutor (Anderson, Farrell, & Sauers, 1984; Clancey, 1987; Stevens & Collins, 1980)

■
COMPUTER-SIMULATION DEFINITION OF THINKING
■

WHAT IS THINKING?

The computer-simulation approach to thinking assumes that a problem solver solves problems by applying operators to problem states. An *operator* is any move that the problem solver deems to be legal, and the operator may be applied physically, such as moving a disk from one peg to another, or may be applied mentally by thinking about the move. A *problem state* is a description of the elements in the problem, such as saving that all the disks are on peg 1. When you apply an operator you change the problem from one state to another. Thus problem solving or thinking can be represented in one of two ways:

A sequence of mental processes or operations performed on information in a subject's memory, or

A sequence of internal states or changes in information that progresses toward the goal.

The goal of the computer-simulation psychologist is to define precisely the strategy that the problem solver uses to generate a sequence of moves.

In a sense the computer-simulation approach is a refinement of the associationist view of thinking as selecting the correct response from a response hierarchy, since the problem solver applies a sequence of moves until the problem is solved. Yet there is also a sense in which the computer-simulation approach is not a theory at all but rather a method for precisely describing the strategies used in the problem-solving process. As such, it offers a method of describing and testing competing views of thinking.

Simon (1978, 1979), a pioneer in the computer-simulation approach, has suggested that any discussion of problem solving must deal with three major components:

The problem solver —which he calls the "information processing system,"

The problem —which he calls "the task environment," and

The problem representation—which he calls a "problem space."

Problem solving occurs when a problem solver translates a problem into an internal problem representation and then searches for a path through the problem space from the given to the goal state. This chapter considers some key ideas proposed by Simon's conception of problem solving. First we consider the idea that the same theoretical approach can be applied to problem solvers who happen to be humans as to problem solvers that happen to be computers. Then we investigate two key techniques for talking about problem solving: (1) representation of problems as problem spaces and (2) solution of problems as search strategies through the problem space.

HOW CAN WE TELL WHEN A MACHINE IS THINKING?

Why would anyone want to spend the time programming a computer to solve problems? The motives probably vary, but the reason given for many of the early attempts was to see if machines could solve problems. The development of computer programs that display intelligence by solving problems or engaging in conversation is generally referred to as the field of *artificial intelligence.*(Barr & Feigenbaum, 1981, 1982; Cohen & Feigenbaum, 1982). A subfield of particular interest to cognitive psychologists is the development of computer systems that display the same problem-solving behavior as humans—that is, behavior that simulates human behavior. This field is referred to as *computer simulation.* If you were interested in building a machine that could serve as an encyclopedia and answer any spoken question, such as R2D2 in *Star Wars* or COMPUTER in *Star Trek,* you probably would not care if its memory storage system and language perception system were the same as in people as long as the machine worked. Your interest would be in artificial intelligence. However, if you had a particular theory of how human beings solve a problem (not necessarily the best or most logical method), you could use the computer simulation to test the theory. The logic of computer simulation is simple: if a computer program produces the same problem-solving behavior as a human, then the series of operations are an accurate representation of the human thought processes.

The experimental method used with computer simulation generally involves asking subjects to solve problems aloud while giving a running description of their thought process and their behavior. From careful analyses of the obtained *protocols* (the transcript of all the subject's comments) the experimenter may derive a description of the mental processes a subject used to solve the problem. By specifying these as a computer program, the experimenter has a precise description that can be tested by feeding it into a computer and observing how closely the computer's protocol matches the subject's. If the match is close, the experimenter may conclude that the program's description of the problem-solving process is accurate; if not, it is necessary to make up a new program and try again.

Although computer simulation offers a new tool for generating and testing theories of human thinking, much popular attention has been directed toward a complementary issue: How can we know whether a machine thinks? Years before the technology for computer simulation existed, the mathematician Turing (1950) wrote an article entitled "Can Machines Think?" in which he proposed the following test—now called the Turing Test. Put two teletypewriters and a person to act as judge in a room. The judge may ask any questions he likes by typing. One teletype is connected to a person in another room who communicates by typing his answers and one is connected to a computer that also types out its answers. If the human judge cannot tell which teletype is connected to the human, then the computer is thinking.

There is, of course, an interesting flaw in the "logic" of computer simulation. Just because a computer and a human give the same behavioral output, does that really mean they are using the same cognitive processes? In addition, protocol states may not accurately reflect internal states. The idea seems particularly absurd in light of the fact that computers use entirely different components than the human brain. Yet a computer program is a very precise and testable way to state a theory of human thinking and as such offers an opportunity to go beyond the vague theories of the Gestaltists. Talking about programs and states may be no more absurd than talking about thoughts or ideas—all are abstractions that must ultimately be described in a way that provides clear tests.

■
HISTORICAL OVERVIEW OF COMPUTER SIMULATION
■

THE CYBERNETIC REVOLUTION

The cybernetic revolution (Weiner, 1948), which involves the idea of feedback and machine servomechanisms, plus the rapid development of sophisticated computers and computer programs has heavily influenced the information-processing approach to thinking. This approach is based on two computer metaphors: (1) the *human-machine* analogy, in which the human being may be viewed as a complex computer, and (2) the *thinking-program* analogy, in which the thought processes used by humans to solve a problem may be viewed as a computer program.

The primary ideas from the cybernetic approach that have been useful in developing a theory of problem solving are

Feedback loops and homeostatis—the idea that an adaptive system continually monitors the difference between its current state and its desired state and performs actions to reduce any differences that may be detected, and

Hierarchical structure —the idea that any complex process or behavior can be represented as a hierarchy of simple interlocking component processes.

Miller, Galanter, and Pribram (1960) introduced a popular example of a feedback system to describe the cognitive processes involved in hammering a nail (see Box 6-3). The plan shown in the box is called a TOTE, for test-operate-test-exit, and is simply a hierarchy of operations with feedback. Written as a computer program, the processes should be in the form of a list to be read top-down:

1. Test nail. If it sticks up, go to 2; otherwise stop.
2. Test hammer. If down, lift; otherwise go to 3.
3. Strike nail.
4. Go to 1.

BOX 6 ▪ 3   A Hierarchical Plan for Hammering Nails

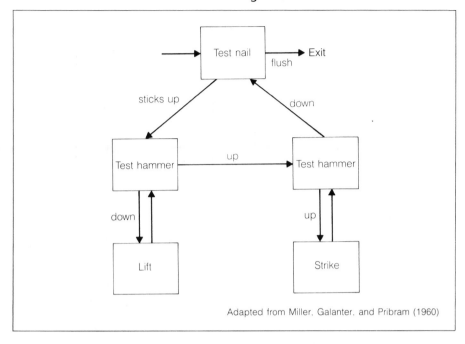

Adapted from Miller, Galanter, and Pribram (1960)

Although it may seem peculiar that psychologists are so interested in how to hammer a nail, techniques such as flow charts and programs are important because they allow psychologists to specify their theory of cognitive processes for a certain intellectual task with precision.

Unfortunately, the kinds of representations make no major distinctions between human and nonhuman thought processes. For example, Box 6-4 shows the thought processes of a thermostat. The flow chart could also be represented as a program:

1. Test temperature. If under 70°, go to 2, if over 72°, go to 5; otherwise go to 1.
2. Test furnace. If on, go to 1; otherwise go to 3.
3. Turn furnace on.
4. Go to 1.
5. Test furnace. If off, go to 1; otherwise go to 6.
6. Turn furnace off.
7. Go to 1.

BOX 6 • 4   A Plan for Regulating Temperature

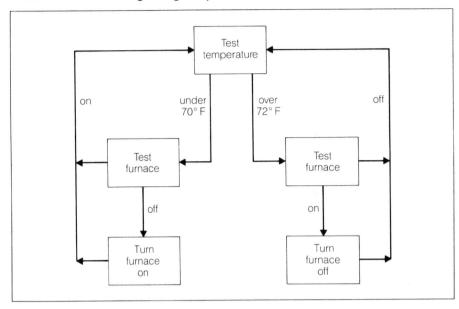

The development of such ways of describing internal cognitive processes is, obviously, heavily dependent on the computer analogy and focuses particularly on the role of feedback.

Miller and colleagues (1960) argued that TOTEs are the building blocks of all kinds of complex behaviors. For example, there can be TOTEs inside of TOTEs. The hammering a nail TOTE is part of a larger plan for building a cabinet, which is part of a larger plan for building a kitchen, and so on. Thus complex behavior can be described as a hierarchy of simple component behaviors.

In an enthralling essay, "The Architecture of Complexity," Simon (1969) similarly argued that the behavior of complex systems can be described as a hierarchy of simple parts. As an example of the advantages of hierarchical structure, Simon presented a parable about two watchmakers. Tempus and Hora are both fine and popular craftsmen who build watches consisting of 1000 parts. Tempus builds his watches as a single assembly of 1000 parts, thus, if he is interrupted in the middle of a job by one of his many customers, the partially assembled watch will fall back into its original parts. Hora's watches are just as complex, but he builds his in units, each consisting of 10 pieces. Thus, 10 single parts make a unit, 10 units make a larger unit, and 10 of the larger units make the entire watch. If Hora is interrupted, he loses only a small portion of the unfinished watch. Thus Hora's method of watch building is more efficient; for example, Simon estimated that Tempus will lose an average of 20 times as much work per interruption as Hora. Further, Simon suggested that the efficiency of hierarchical structure can be seen in biological systems, in social systems, and in human problem-solving behavior.

GPS: AN EXAMPLE

One of the best-known and most general problem-solving programs is GENERAL PROBLEM SOLVER, or GPS (Ernst & Newell, 1969). GPS was intended as a demonstration that certain general problem-solving techniques are involved in a wide spectrum of problems and that it is possible to state explicitly what these general procedures are in a computer program able to solve a wide variety of different problems.

GPS, like other programs, begins by translating a statement of the problem into an internal representation of the initial state, goal state, and set of operators. In addition, GPS has stored in its memory a table of connections for each problem it will solve; the table of connections contains all possible problem states for that problem with a listing of how far apart any two states are from one another. Problem solving involves *breaking a problem down into subgoals* and then achieving each subgoal by *applying various problem-solving techniques,* each of which changes the problem state in the direction of the subgoal. For example, the program can try a technique and then test whether it changes the problem state to one that is closer to the subgoal by checking the difference on the table of connections. If the technique succeeds the program uses that technique and the process starts over, but if it fails the program tries another technique. Thus, when GPS solves a problem it performs the following:

Translates the problem into initial state, goal state, and legal operators;

Holds the appropriate table of connections in memory in order to tell the differences between the states;

Breaks the problem down into a hierarchy of goals and subgoals, each of which brings the problem closer to solution;

Applies problem-solving techniques based on the principle of means-ends analysis (reducing the difference between the present state and the desired subgoal state); and

Moves on to the next subgoal when one is achieved, until the problem is solved

The entire process is presided over by the "problem-solving executive," which determines the order in which operators will be applied, attempts to achieve subgoals by using means-ends analysis, and develops a new subgoal structure if one does not work. GPS can solve several classic problems described in this chapter—a variation of the hobbits and orcs problem, the Tower of Hanoi problem, and water jar problems.

■

THE PROBLEM SOLVER

■

What does the problem solver bring to the problem-solving situation? Lindsay and Norman (1972) have distinguished among several types of knowledge that are used in problem solving:

Facts—basic propositions that are immediately available to the subject,

Algorithms—sets of rules that automatically generate answers, and

Heuristics—rules of thumb or general plans of actions or strategies.

For example, generating a solution to the question "What is 8×4?" involves a fact-generating a solution for "What is 262×127?" involves an algorithm; and a heuristic would be an estimate of the correct answer by rounding to manageable numbers.

Algorithms guarantee specific answers, since they simply apply a past set of rules to a new situation. The set of rules can be stored as a *subroutine*, thus saving memory load. Heuristics, on the other hand, may not always generate a solution for a problem. For example, the heuristic of finding a related or analogous problem or breaking the problem into subgoals may help, but it does not guarantee solution. A major heuristic is *means-ends analysis*, discussed later in this chapter.

More recently, Anderson (1983) has shown that computer simulations can operate using two kinds of knowledge—*declarative knowledge* (facts stated in propositions) and *procedural knowledge* (algorithms and heuristics stated as procedures).

Ernst and Newell (1969) have provided a simplified description of how the problem solver is involved in the problem-solving process (see Box 6-5). The *input*—that is, the problem—is acted upon by a *translator* that converts it into an *internal representation* (including the initial state, the goal state, and a means of telling which problem states are closer to the goal state) that is acted upon by *problem-solving techniques* that generate the *solution*. In spite of the contribution of the assimilation theory of thinking and the idea of functional fixedness from Gestalt theory, very little attention has been paid to the translation process. The

BOX 6 • 5   The Problem-Solving Process

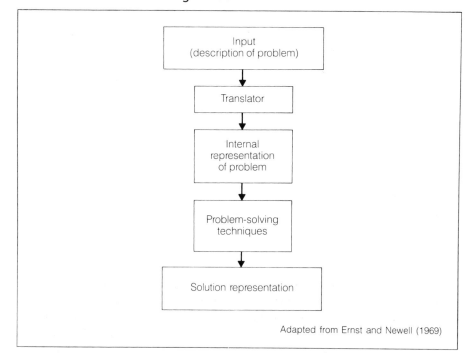

Adapted from Ernst and Newell (1969)

internal representation of a problem can take many forms, including the problem-space representation we discussed earlier, and the problem-solving techniques may be represented as operators, facts, subroutines, and heuristics.

Greeno (1973) has proposed the memory model for problem solving shown in Box 6-6. The three main components of interest in describing problem solving are

Short-term memory (STM)—through which the external description of the problem is input,

Long-term memory (LTM)—which stores past experience with solving problems such as facts, algorithms, heuristics, related problems, and so on, and

Working memory (WM)—in which the information from STM and LTM interact and the solution route is generated and tested.

A description of the problem, including the initial state, the goal state, and the legal operators, comes into working memory by way of short-term memory as

BOX 6 • 6   Components of Memory

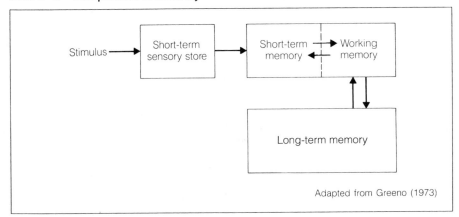

Adapted from Greeno (1973)

represented by arrows from STM to WM; and past experience about how to solve the problem enters working memory from LTM, as represented by the arrow from LTM to WM. The arrow from WM to STM suggests that more information from the outside world may be required as problem solving progresses (the solver may pay attention to different aspects of the presented information) and the arrow from LTM to WM suggests that the generation of new problem states in WM may require more old information from past experience. The concept of working memory, first introduced by Feigenbaum (1970), has special importance in Greeno's model: the internal representation of the problem occurs there, the construction of links between givens and unknowns occurs there, and relevant past experience is used to modify the structures held in WM.

■
THE PROBLEM SPACE
■

One of the major theoretical contributions of the computer-simulation approach to problem solving is the idea of *problem space*. The problem space refers to the problem solver's internal representation of

Initial state—in which the given or starting conditions are represented,

Goal state—in which the final or goal situation is represented,

Intermediate problem states—consisting of states that are generated by applying an operator to a state, and

Operators—the moves that are made from one state to the next.

Ernst and Newell (1969) and Simon (1978) have pointed out that problem space is the set of all states (or all possible sequences of operators) that the problem solver is aware of. Simon also points out that the *basic problem space*—the problem space generated by a perfect problem solver—may not be identical to a particular person's *problem space*. For example, an individual problem solver can generate a problem space that contains errors or is seriously incomplete.

Consider the disk problem (also called the Tower of Hanoi problem) that we discussed in Box 3-18. Remember that the problem is to move the disks from peg 1 to peg 3 by moving them to any peg one at a time and never placing a larger disk on top of a smaller disk. Thus when there are three disks, the problem consists of

Initial state—the three disks are on peg 1 with the largest on the bottom and the smallest on the top.

Goal state—the disks are on peg 3 with the largest on the bottom and the smallest on the top.

Operators—the top disk from one peg is placed on another peg that does not contain a smaller disk.

Part of the problem space for this problem is given in Box 6-7. The initial state (labeled 1) is on the left, the goal state (labeled 8) is on the right. The intermediate states are in between, with the most efficient path through the problem space indicated along the top of the problem space (states 2 through 7).

Each box or node in the problem space represents one possible state of the problem, and each branch or arrow represents a legal action that could be taken from that state. For example, if you are in state 1, there are two actions that can be taken—moving the small disk to peg 3 (resulting in state 2) or moving the small disk to peg 2. If you are in state 2, there are three possible actions—moving the medium disk from peg 1 to peg 2 (resulting in state 3), moving the small disk from peg 3 to peg 2, or moving the small disk from peg 3 back to peg 1 (resulting in a return to a previous state). You can move from an intermediate state back to a previous state in the problem space.

As another example, consider the problem space for the hobbits and orcs problem shown in Box 6-8. The problem is to get three hobbits and three orcs across a river. You must use a boat that can hold only one or two creatures at a time, with at least one creature in the boat during each crossing, and you must never let the orcs outnumber the hobbits on either bank of the river. In this

BOX 6 • 7   Problem Space for Disk Problem

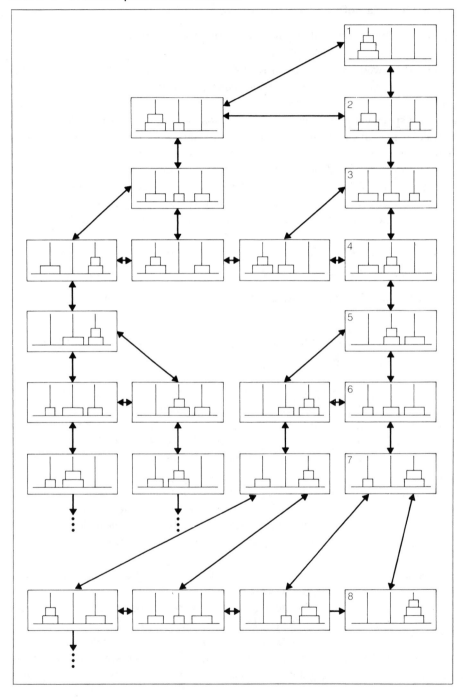

BOX 6 ▪ 8 Steps in Solving the Hobbits and Orcs Problem

A. The Problem Space

Each state is specified by a three-digit code: (1) the number of hobbits on the starting side, (2) the number of orcs on the starting side, (3) the location of the boat—1 if it is on the starting side and 0 if it is on the opposite side.

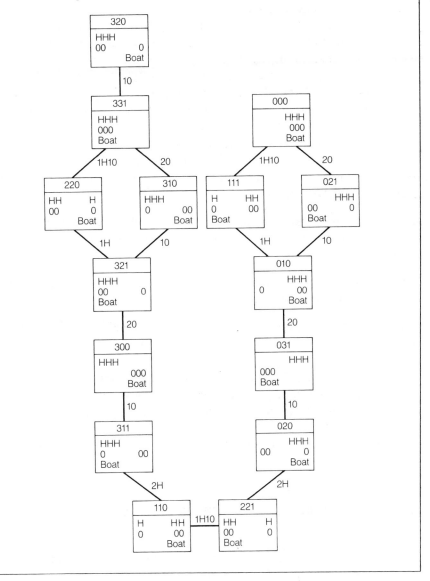

example, the initial state has three hobbits, three orcs, and the boat on the left; the right is empty. The goal state is the opposite: three hobbits, three orcs, and the boat on the right side with the left side empty. The legal operators are to move one hobbit, two hobbits, one orc, two orcs, or one hobbit and one orc from one side of the river to the other in the boat as long as the hobbits are never outnumbered by orcs on either side. As you can see, there are few alternatives in moving from one state to the next.

Solving a problem can be viewed as finding the correct path or route through a problem space. In Box 6-8, the path is fairly obvious since there is usually only one new move that can be made from each state. In Box 6-7, paths through the lower part of the space are likely to create much difficulty.

Wickelgren (1974) and Polya (1965) have suggested several techniques for "pruning the tree"— for making the problem space easier to work with:

Macroactions—the space can be reduced by thinking in terms of "macroactions" in which different sequences of actions often result in the same problem state. For example, the arrows on the problem space can represent several equivalent sequences of smaller actions.

Subgoals—the space can be broken down into several smaller subgoals, that is, it can be converted into several smaller problem spaces, each ending in a sub-goal state.

Working backward—the number of alternative paths in a space can sometimes be reduced by working backward from the goal state toward the initial state.

Related problem spaces—the correct path can be suggested by remembering how you solved similar or analogous problems in the past.

Thus, as you can see, one of the major contributions of the information-processing approach to problem solving is the development of a technique for representing problems—namely, the problem space. However, the problem-space technique seems best applied to MOVE problems—problems with clearly defined given states, goal states, and operators.

■

SEARCHING THROUGH THE PROBLEM SPACE
■

The previous section demonstrates how the information-processing approach can provide a concrete representation of what it means to "understand the problem"—that is, building a problem space. Although the problem-space representation allows you to describe the problem, you also need a technique for finding a path through the problem space. Hayes (1978) and Wickelgren (1974) have suggested several *search strategies*—methods for finding a way from the initial state to the goal state. Three search strategies—*random trial and error, hill climbing,* and *means-ends analysis*—are discussed here.

RANDOM TRIAL AND ERROR

The most straightforward technique is to randomly apply legal operators until you have generated the goal state. Thus, if you are in a certain state, you may randomly choose any legal move as your next move. For example, in the disk problem in Box 6-7, if you are in state 3, you randomly choose among the three possible moves, for example, to state 2, to state 4, or to the unnumbered state. The trouble with random searches is that they have many wasted moves. Although humans may use it for unfamiliar problems or when they are under great stress, random search does not seem to be a good candidate for complex problem-solving behavior.

HILL CLIMBING

A more systematic search that retains much of the simplicity of random search is hill climbing. In hill climbing you continually try to move from your present state to a state that is closer to the goal. Thus, if you are in a certain state, you evaluate the new state you would be in for each possible move, and you select the move that creates the state that moves you closest to the goal. For hill climbing, you need some state evaluation procedure, that is, your own system for evaluating how far any state in the problem space is from the goal state. For example, in the disk problem (as in Box 6-7), your rule for state evaluation could be that the more disks you have on peg 3, the closer you are to the goal. For the hobbits and orcs problem (as in Box 6-8), the rule for state evaluation could be that the more characters you have on the right side of the river, the closer you are to the goal. The main drawback to hill climbing is that it can take you to a "local high," a state in the problem that is closer to the goal than any adjacent state in the problem space. For example, in the disk problem in Box 6-7, state 3 represents a local high since moving the small disk off the third peg (which is required for solving the problem) could be evaluated as moving away from the goal. Similarly, in the hobbits and orcs problem in Box 6-8, state 110 represents a local high because taking two characters from the right to the left could be evaluated as moving away from the goal. Thus hill climbing will not work well in problems that have hills and valleys, that is, problems that occasionally require that you move away from the goal in order to ultimately reach the goal.

Atwood and Polson (1976) provide some experimental evidence that subjects sometimes use a strategy similar to hill climbing. They gave subjects the following version of a water jug problem (called the water jar problem by the Luchins, Chapter 3):

> You have three jugs, which we will call A, B and C. Jug A can hold exactly eight cups of water, B can hold exactly five cups, and C can hold exactly three cups. A is filled to capacity with eight cups of water. B and C are empty. We want to find a way of dividing the contents of A equally between A and B so that both have four cups. You are allowed to pour water from jug to jug.

Thus in this problem the initial state is eight cups of water in jug A and none in jugs B and C, the goal state is four cups of water in jug A and four in jug B, and the legal operators are to pour from one jug to another.

Box 6-9 provides a partial problem space for the problem. Let's suppose that you evaluate each state by determining how different jug A is from four cups and how different jug B is from four cups; the closer these two jugs are to four cups each, the better is the evaluation of that state. Using this hill-climbing procedure, which move do you think a person would take: pouring A into B or pouring A into C? As you can see, pouring into B creates state 9, which is just two cups different from the goal (jug A and jug B are each one cup off); however, pouring into C creates state 2, which is five cups different from the goal (jug A is one off and jug B is four off). As the researchers predicted, twice as many subjects opted for state 9 rather than state 2. As you look at the states from 9 to 15, do you see any moves that tend to go against the hill-climbing strategy? For example, consider the move from state 11 to state 12. Here, you must move from a state that is four cups different from the goal to one that is eight cups different from the goal; according to a hill-climbing strategy you are losing ground. Atwood and Polson found that subjects were likely to deviate from the correct path at such junctions as state 11. For example, subjects preferred a move from state 11 that seemed closer to the goal (such as pouring A into C) but which actually prolonged the course of the problem.

MEANS-ENDS ANALYSIS

So far we have found that random search is too costly in terms of wasted moves, and hill climbing is too shortsighted because it strands the problem solver at local highs. What is needed is a search strategy that retains the simplicity of random search and the order of hill climbing, without the disadvantages of wasteful or shortsighted problem solving. Thus we need to be able to describe a search strategy that is both powerful and simple, that corresponds to human problem-solving characteristics as well as being amenable to computer implementation. By far, the most popular and widely used strategy fitting these descriptions is means-ends analysis.

BOX 6 ▪ 9   Problem Space for a Water Jug Problem

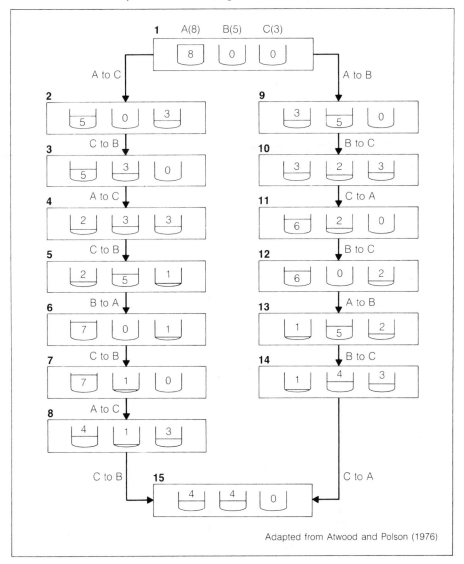

Adapted from Atwood and Polson (1976)

In *means-ends analysis,* the problem solver always works on one goal at a time. If you are in a certain state, you set a goal of creating the goal state. If that goal cannot be directly achieved, you set a subgoal of removing any barriers to directly achieving the goal, and so on. The problem solver in means-ends analysis is

BOX 6 ▪ 10 Three Kinds of Subgoals in Means-Ends Analysis

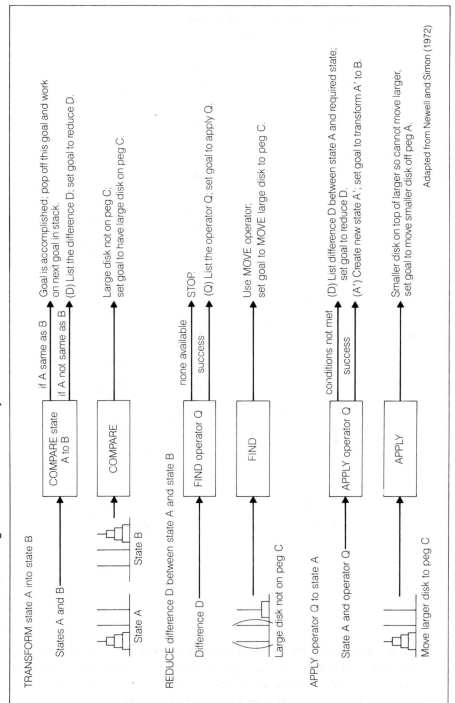

continually asking three questions: What is my goal, what obstacles are in my way, and what operators are available for overcoming these obstacles? Simon (1969, p. 112) summarizes means-ends analysis as follows: "Given a desired state of affairs and an existing state of affairs, the task of an adaptive organism is to find the difference between these two states and then to find the correlating process that will erase the difference."

Do humans actually use means-ends analysis to establish subgoals in problem solving? Let's consider the problem space for the hobbits and orcs problem again, as shown in Box 6-8. Greeno (1974) has provided a means-ends analysis of the task and found that human performance fits the description, with some interesting exceptions. For example, Thomas (1974) found that the mean time to make a move is greatest at step 110, possibly because the problem solvers must violate the hill-climbing strategy by moving creatures away from the right side of the river. In contrast, Thomas (1974) found that problem solvers jump rapidly from state 020 to the goal state, while means-ends analysis still requires a lot of goal setting. Several other researchers have also observed that problem solvers in river-crossing problems do not always seem to be setting as many subgoals as suggested by a strict form of means-ends analysis (Jeffries, Polson, Razran, & Atwood, 1977; Simon & Reed, 1976). Apparently, problem solvers' performances on river-crossing problems can be described as a sort of compromise between means-ends analysis and hill climbing.

■

A CLOSER LOOK AT MEANS-ENDS ANALYSIS
■

Since means-ends analysis is the major problem-solving strategy used in many computer simulations of thinking, let's take a closer look at how it works. The main ideas that you need to understand are: *subgoals, goal stack, table of connections,* and *goal structure.*

SUBGOALS

Newell and Simon (1972) have described three types of subgoals that are involved in means-ends analysis, as shown in Box 6-10. The transform goal involves comparing the present state of the problem to the goal state and listing any differences between the two. The input for the transform goal is a description of the present state (called A) and the goal state (called B); the output is a description of the difference (called D) between the two states. For example, in the disk problem, the first goal could be a transform goal: transform the initial state (state 1) into the goal state (state 8). The outcome of this goal is the identification of a difference between the two states, for example, the large disk is not on peg C.

The reduce goal involves finding an operation that can be applied to reduce a certain difference. The input for the reduce goal is a description of the difference D; the output is an appropriate operator (called Q) that would reduce or eliminate that difference. For example, in the disk problem, the next goal could be a reduce goal: reduce the difference by finding an operator that will get the large disk on peg C. The outcome of this goal is the identification of an operator, for example, move the large disk to peg C.

The apply goal involves applying the operator Q to state A to produce a new state (called A'). The input for the apply goal is a description of the operator Q and the state A to which it is to be applied. The output is either a new state A' if the operator Q can be directly applied to A, or a description of the difference D between state A and the required state if Q cannot be directly applied to A. For example, in the disk problem, the goal could be to apply the move operator to state A (that is, move the large disk to peg C). However, the outcome of this goal is the identification of a difference between the present state (A) and required state for this operation, namely, there must not be any disks on top of the large disk on peg A.

Box 6-10 summarizes the transform, reduce, and apply goals; the box shows the needed input, the possible outputs, and an example of each kind of goal. When more than one goal is needed to solve a problem, the goals are called "subgoals." Thus solving any MOVE problem involves establishing a series of subgoals made up of these three basic types shown in the box.

GOAL STACK

With these three goals, you can solve a wide variety of problems. However, in means-ends analysis you may work on only one goal at a time; the other goals are "stacked" for future use. Assume that you start with a "push-down, pop-up stack," as shown in Box 6-11. You put the first goal in that stack; for example, your first goal might be "transform state 1 into state 8" for the disk problem. However, this goal cannot be directly attained so a subgoal is created (such as "reduce difference"), and this goal 2 is pushed down on top of goal 1; since goal 2 cannot be directly accomplished, goal 3 is created and pushed down on top; for the same reasons goals 4 and 5 are added to the stack. The goal on top is always the goal that is being worked on. Let's suppose that the stack has goals 1, 2, 3, 4, and 5 in it. If goal 5 can be achieved it pops off, as does goal 4 if it can now be achieved. This brings us back to goal 3, which still cannot be achieved; thus new subgoals are created and pushed down on top (goals 6 and 7). These are achieved and pop off; but two new goals must still be added to the stack (goals 8 and 9). As these are accomplished, they allow all of the goals to pop off, returning us to goal 1. The goal stack consists of all subgoals that have not yet been achieved. It begins with the top goal (transform the given state into the goal state) and ends when this goal is achieved; in between, many subgoals must be pushed on and eventually popped off.

BOX 6 • 11   Goal Stack in Means-Ends Analysis

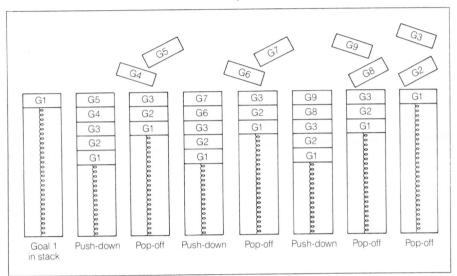

TABLE OF CONNECTIONS

In means-ends analysis, each time you fail to transform state A into state B, you must find a difference D; when you find a D, you must select an operator Q that can be used to reduce that difference. How does the computer (or the problem solver) know which operators should be used for reducing each difference? In many computer simulations, the computer must be given a "table of connections"—a list of all of the possible differences along with the appropriate operators to be performed for each. Box 6-12 provides an example of a partial table of connections for the disk problem. For example, if you come across a difference such as "the large disk is not on peg C but it should be there," the appropriate operator to use is "MOVE the large disk to peg C." Thus, for each possible difference that may be located in the course of solving the disk problem, the table of connections provides an operator that should be tried. As you can see, there is a sense in which the table of connections contains all of the information needed to solve the problem.

GOAL STRUCTURE

In the solution of a problem, various changes in the goal stack represent the goal structure of the problem. In other words, the order in which goals are pushed on and popped off the stack represents the goal structure for a

BOX 6 ▪ 12   Table of Connections for Three-Disk Problem

Difference (D)	Operator (Q)
Large disk not on peg C	MOVE large disk to peg C
Medium disk not on peg C	MOVE medium disk to peg C
Small disk not on peg C	MOVE small disk to peg C
Small disk on top of to-be-moved disk	MOVE small disk to another peg
Medium disk on top of to-be-moved disk	MOVE medium disk to another peg
Small (or medium) disk on peg C when attempt is made to move large disk to peg C	MOVE small (or medium) disk off peg C to another peg
Small disk on peg C when attempt is made to move medium disk to peg C	MOVE small disk off peg C to another peg

BOX 6 ▪ 13   Goal Structure for Means-Ends Analysis

Current Goal	Goals in Stack	Type of Goal	Outcome
G1	G1	TRANSFORM current state to goal state	DIFFERENCE: Disk 3 not on peg C
G2	G2, G1	REDUCE difference—So disk 3 is on peg C	Use MOVE operator
G3	G3, G2, G1	APPLY operator—Move disk 3 to peg C	DIFFERENCE: Disk 1 on top of disk 3
G4	G4, G3, G2, G1	REDUCE difference—So disk 1 is not on top of disk 3	Use MOVE operator
G5	G5, G4, G3, G2, G1	APPLY operator—Move disk to peg B	Success: Now in state 2
G3	G3, G2, G1	APPLY operator—Move disk 3 to peg C	DIFFERENCE: Disk 2 on top of disk 3
G6	G6, G3, G2, G1	REDUCE difference—So disk 2 is not on top of disk 3	Use MOVE operator
G7	G7, G6, G3, G2, G1	APPLY operator—Move disk 2 to peg B	Success: Now in state 3
G3	G3, G2, G1	APPLY operator—Move disk 3 to peg C	Difference: Disk 1 is on peg C
G8	G8, G3, G2 G1	REDUCE difference—So disk 1 is not on peg C	Use MOVE operator
G9	G9, G8, G3, G2, G1	APPLY operator—Move disk 1 to peg B	Success: Now in state 4

problem. For example, Box 6-13 shows a goal structure for the disk problem. The first goal (G1) is to transform state 1 into state 8. However, this goal's outcome is to locate a difference: the large disk (disk 3) is on peg C. Thus, a second goal (G2) is added to the stack: reduce the difference. The outcome is the location of an operator: move the large disk to peg C. Thus, goal 3 (G3) is added to the stack: apply the operator. When we try to apply the operator in goal 3, we find another difference: there is a small disk on top of the large disk so the large disk cannot be moved. We add a fourth goal (G4) to the location of an operator: move the small disk to peg C. Thus, goal 5 (G5) is added to the stack: apply the operator. This is successful since the small disk can be moved; a new state is created (state 2) and goal 5 pops off the stack. Also, goal 4 is achieved and is popped off. But goal 3 (to move the large disk to peg C) is still not possible. The outcome of reinstating goal 3 is a difference: the medium disk is on top of the large disk. A new goal must be set (goal 6): to reduce the

BOX 6 ▪ 13, *continued*

Current Goal	Goals in Stack	Type of Goal	Outcome
G3	G3, G2, G1	APPLY operator—Move disk 3 to peg C	Success: Now in state 5
G1	G1	TRANSFORM current state to goal state	Difference: Disk 2 not on peg C
G10	G10, G1	REDUCE difference—So disk 2 is on peg C	Use MOVE operator
G11	G11, G10, G1	APPLY operator—Move disk 2 to peg C	Difference: Disk 1 on top of disk 2
G12	G12, G11, G10, G1	REDUCE difference—So disk 1 is not on top of disk 2	Use MOVE operator
G13	G13, G12, G11, G10, G1	APPLY operator—Move disk 1 to peg A	Success: Now in state 6
G11	G11, G10, G1	APPLY operator—Move disk 2 to peg C	Success: Now in state 7
G1	G1	TRANSFORM current state to goal state	Difference: Disk 1 not on peg C
G14	G14, G1	REDUCE difference—So disk 1 is on peg C	Use MOVE operator
G15	G15, G14, G1	APPLY operator—Move disk 1 to peg C	Success: Now in state 8
G1	G1	TRANSFORM current state to goal state	Success: Problem is solved

difference by getting rid of the medium disk. The outcome is the identification of an operator: move the medium disk to peg C. Goal 7 is added to the stack: apply this operator. Since this goal is successful, state 3 is created and goals 7 and 6 pop off the stack. However, when we return to state 3, we find another difference that will not allow us to move the large disk to peg C: the little disk is on peg C. More goals must be added and eventually popped off, as shown in the rest of Box 6-13. This analysis suggests that some moves such as from state 5 to state 6 require much goal stacking and are therefore difficult, while other moves such as from state 6 to state 7 require less stacking and are therefore easier.

■

PRODUCTION SYSTEMS
■

One advantage of using formal languages, such as the goal structure in Box 6-13, to simulate human thinking is that a person's problem-solving strategy can be represented precisely, using simple building blocks. Since the 1970s, the most widely used formalism to model goal-directed thinking has been the production system (Klahr, Langley, & Neches, 1987; Newell & Simon, 1972) and the most widely used production-system framework has been ACT (Anderson, 1983, 1990; Singley & Anderson, 1989). To understand ACT, which stands for "adaptive control of thought," you need to understand what a production system is, how a production system works, and how a production system is acquired.

WHAT IS A PRODUCTION SYSTEM?

We begin with the premise that productions are the building blocks of goal-directed thinking. A production is a condition-action pair of the form IF _____ THEN _____, where the conditions (following IF) describe some situation and the action (following THEN) specifies something to do. The problem solver checks to see if the conditions in the production match data that is held in the problem solver's working memory. If there is a match, the production applies; if not, the action is not carried out.

A production system is a collection of productions that all are related to a class of problems. For example, Box 6-14 shows a simplified production system for our old friend, the disk problem (shown in Box 6-7). The first production (P1) contains two conditions—that you see at least one disk on peg A and have no other subgoals—and an action—that you place a goal in working memory that says "Move disk ____ to peg C" (where the blank contains the name of the largest disk on peg A). The second production (P2) contains four conditions that must be met. For this production to "fire," the problem solver must verify each of these conditions; that is, these conditions must match information in the problem solver's representation of the problem and list of goals in working memory. If the conditions match the information in the problem solver's working memory, then the action is carried out—resulting in a new representation of the problem and the deletion of a goal from working memory. Although the production system in Box 6-14 describes one person's knowledge of how to solve the disk problem, another person may have a different set of productions.

HOW DOES A PRODUCTION SYSTEM WORK?

In order to better understand how production systems work, let's take a look at our production system in action. We begin with disks 1 (smallest), 2 (middle), and 3 (largest) on peg A and with the goal of transferring the disks to peg C—as represented in state 1 of Box 6-7. As you can see, this situation corresponds to the condition listed in P1, so the following goal is added to working memory: MOVE

BOX 6 · 14   A Simplified Production System for the Disk Problem

PI	IF disk(s) is on peg A and there are no goals THEN set goal to largest move disk to peg C
P2	IF goal is move target disk to target peg and target disk is not on target peg and another disk is not on top of disk and smaller disk is not on target peg THEN move target disk to target peg and erase the goal
P3	IF goal is move target disk to target peg and target disk is not on target peg and something is on top of disk THEN set goal to move largest disk on top of target disk to other peg
P4	IF goal is move target disk to target peg and target disk is not on target peg and smaller disk is on target peg THEN set goal to move smaller disk to other peg
P5	IF disk(s) is on peg B and disk(s) is on peg C and there are no goals THEN set goal to move larger disk from peg B to peg C

DISK 3 TO PEG C. We want to move disk 3 to peg C; however, we cannot because it has disks on top of it. This situation corresponds to P3, so we carry out the action of adding another goal to working memory: MOVE DISK 2 TO PEG B. We want to move disk 2 to peg B but we cannot because disk 1 is on top of it. This situation corresponds to P3 and results in MOVE DISK 1 TO PEG C being added to working memory. So far three productions have fired, but no moves have taken place. Next, P2 fires because the goal of moving disk 1 to peg C has nothing blocking its completion; carrying out this action creates state 2 (in Box 6-7) and deletes MOVE DISK 1 TO PEG C from working memory. P2 fires again because the goal of moving disk 2 to peg B is now also unblocked; the resulting action creates state 3 (in Box 6-7) and deletes MOVE DISK 2 TO PEG B from working memory. P2, however, cannot fire again because the goal MOVE DISK 3 TO PEG C is blocked by having a smaller disk on the target peg. Instead, the conditions in P4 are met, resulting in MOVE DISK 1 TO PEG B being added to working memory. This goal can be accomplished, so P2 fires, resulting in state 4 and deletion of this goal from working memory. Now, we also accomplish the only goal left in working memory—MOVE DISK 3 TO PEG C; P2 fires, resulting in the creation of state 5 and the deletion of this goal from working memory. Next, the conditions in P5 are met—there are disks on peg B and peg C—so we add MOVE DISK 2 TO PEG A to working memory. To accomplish this goal we must first remove disk 1, as reflected in P3; the conditions for P3 are met, so another goal is added: MOVE DISK 1 TO PEG A. P2 fires, resulting in the execution of this goal (state 6), and then P2 fires again, resulting in the execution of the previous goal (state 7). With disk 1 on peg A and no other subgoals, the conditions for PI are met again; the resulting action is a new goal being added to working memory: MOVE DISK 1 TO PEG C. P2 fires because there are no conditions that block the execution of this goal. The result is state 3—the solution of the problem. No more productions fire and we are finished. Box 6-15 summarizes the operation of the production system. As you can see, like the means-ends analysis procedures described previously in this chapter, production systems work by setting goals, recognizing whether conditions are met, and carrying out operations.

HOW DOES A PRODUCTION SYSTEM DEVELOP?

According to Anderson (1983, 1990), learning a cognitive skill involves converting one's declarative knowledge into procedural knowledge. *Declarative knowledge* is knowledge that something is the case, such as "Sacramento is the capital of California"; individual pieces of declarative knowledge can be represented as propositions, and collections of declarative knowledge can be represented as networks. *Procedural knowledge* is knowledge about how to do something, such as how to solve long division problems; a single step can be represented as a production, and an entire procedure can be

BOX 6 ▪ 15   How a Production System Works

Production	Action	Status of Problem	Status of Working Memory
Start			
P1	Add goal to WM		MOVE 3 TO C
P3	Add goal to WM		MOVE 2 TO B / MOVE 3 TO C
P3	Add goal to WM		MOVE 1 TO C / MOVE 2 TO B / MOVE 3 TO C
P2	Move 1 to C / Delete top goal		MOVE 2 TO B / MOVE 3 TO C
P2	Move 2 to B / Delete top goal		MOVE 3 TO C
P4	Add goal to WM		MOVE 1 TO B / MOVE 3 TO C
P2	Move 1 to B / Delete top goal		MOVE 3 TO C
P2	Move 3 to C / Delete top goal		
P5	Add goal to WM		MOVE 2 TO C

(continued)

BOX 6 ▪ 15, *continued*

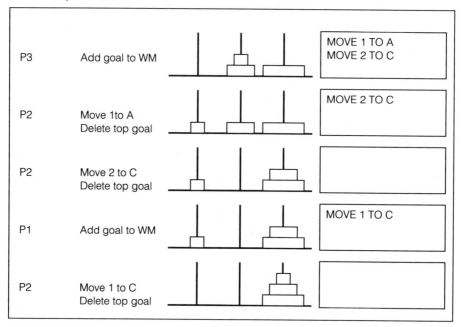

				MOVE 1 TO A MOVE 2 TO C
P3	Add goal to WM			
P2	Move 1to A Delete top goal			MOVE 2 TO C
P2	Move 2 to C Delete top goal			
P1	Add goal to WM			MOVE 1 TO C
P2	Move 1 to C Delete top goal			

represented as a production system. Box 6-16 compares declarative and procedural knowledge. As you can see, acquiring cognitive skill involves learning to follow a procedure rather than trying to apply facts to a problem situation.

Following earlier theories of skill acquisition (Fitts & Posner, 1967), Anderson (1983, 1990) proposes three stages in the development of cognitive skill:

Declarative stage—in which knowledge about the task is still in declarative form,

Knowledge compilation stage—in which declarative knowledge is converted into procedural knowledge, and

Tuning stage—in which the procedure is refined.

For example, consider how a student might acquire skill in solving linear equations such as $3X + 5 = 4 + 2X$. During the declarative stage, the student may be aware of certain basic facts about the equation, such as "5 is a number" and "X is a variable," as well as facts about possible methods, such as "You can always subtract the same number from both sides of an equation." Other examples of

BOX 6 · 16   Declarative and Procedural Knowledge

	Declarative Knowledge	Procedural Knowledge
Definition	Knowing that something is the case	Knowing how to do something
Example	Fact: 3 + 3 = 6	Procedure: how to carry out long division
Representation of Units	Proposition	Production
Representation of Collections	Networks	Production systems

declarative knowledge that a student may have are given in the top of Box 6-17. When given an equation to solve, the student can use this knowledge to help guide problem solving; however, the thinking process will require a great deal of conscious attention. For example, the student may say: "Let's see, I know that I can subtract the same number from both sides, so as I look at the equation I notice that I can subtract 4 or 5 from both sides. Let's see, I'll try 5. That leaves $3X$ on the left and $2Y + 1$ on the right . . ."

In the knowledge compilation stage, the student builds procedures for solving linear equations, such as shown in the middle of Box 6-17. Knowledge compilation involves two subprocesses: *proceduralization*, the process of changing facts into procedures, and *composition*, the process of collapsing several specific procedures into a single one. As you can see, the first three productions allow you to write –5 on both sides, compute $5 - 5 = 0$ on the left side, and compute $4 - 5 = -1$ on the right side; then, through composition, you can combine these three separate steps into one large step, summarized in production 4. As the problem solver moves from facts to procedures, problem-solving performance becomes much faster.

Finally, during the tuning stage the student improves the procedures through the subprocesses of *generalization, discrimination,* and *strengthening.* Generalization involves combining two or more specific procedures into a more general one; for example, production 5 works on both positive and negative numbers, whereas production 4 worked only on positive numbers. Discrimination involves adding an important new condition that was overlooked previously; for example, beginners sometimes fail to recognize that production 4 does not work when the number is part of an expression inside parentheses. Strengthening involves the amount of activation that a production receives when its conditions are met; thus the productions that are most useful will become strengthened. Examples of generalization and discrimination are given in the

BOX 6 ▪ 17   Examples of Three Stages in Acquiring a Cognitive Skill

Declarative Knowledge

1. You can add the same number to both sides of an equation.
2. You can subtract the same number from both sides of an equation.
3. You can multiply the same number times both sides of the equation.
4. You can divide the same number into both sides of the equation.

Knowledge Compilation—Proceduralization

PI	IF there is a positive number on the left side	$3X + 5 = 4 + 2X$
	THEN write a minus sign followed by that number on both sides	$3X + 5 - 5 = 4 + 2X - 5$
P2	IF there is one number minus another number on the right side	
	THEN subtract the second number from the first	$3X + 5 - 5 = -1 + 2X$
P3	IF there is one number minus another number on the left side	
	THEN subtract the second number from the first	$3X = -1 + 2X$

Knowledge Compilation—Composition

| P4 | IF there is a positive number on the left side and a positive or negative number on the right side | $3X + 5 = 4 - 2X$ |
| | THEN eliminate the number from the left side and subtract it from the number on the right side | $3X = -1 + 2X$ |

Tuning—Generalization

| P5 | IF there is a negative or positive number on the left side and a positive or negative number on the right side | also works for: $3X - 5 = 2X - 4$ |
| | THEN eliminate that number from the left side and subtract that number from the number on the right side | |

Tuning—Discrimination

| P6 | IF there is a negative or positive number on the left side and a positive or negative number on the right side and no parentheses around the numbers | does not work for: $3(X - 5) = 2X - 4$ |
| | THEN eliminate that number from the left side and subtract that number from the right side | |

bottom of Box 6-17. During this stage, solving problems requires less conscious effort than in the declarative stage, because the problem solver uses a well-running procedure.

CRITIQUE OF PRODUCTION SYSTEMS

Although production system models such as ACT have been widely used to describe goal-directed thinking (see Gagné, 1985), they are not without critiques. For example, the new unit of thought unveiled in this chapter—the production—may remind you of the old unit of thought already described in Chapter 2—the S-R association. You might well ask whether the production is just a glorified S-R link. In response, Anderson (1983, p. 6) has noted that "the production is very much like the stimulus-response bond" but that is also an improvement, partly because it allows for the setting of goals. In this way, Anderson (1983, p. 6) suggests that we view "production systems as cognitive S-R theories."

Like theories based on S-R psychology, theories based on production systems are strongest in describing how people solve routine problems and weakest in describing where creative solutions come from. For example, Singley and Anderson (1989) show that a production-system framework can account for how people transfer a general skill they learned in one domain to another domain but not for how a creative solution is invented. One possibility is that real Gestalt-like insight does not exist; a second possibility is that it exists but psychologists have not yet figured out how to model it. As production systems are used to describe an ever-increasing number of problem-solving tasks, we will gain a clearer picture of their usefulness.

Finally, production-system models have been challenged by proponents of connectionist models (McClelland, Rumelhart, & the PDP Research Group, 1986; Rumelhart, McClelland, & the PDP Research Group, 1986). In these models, intelligent behavior emerges from the accumulation of many simple processes occurring independently. To date, connectionist models provide an alternative framework that has been successful mainly in modeling perceptual processes rather than problem-solving processes. Until connectionist models can be successfully applied to problem-solving processes, they are unlikely to replace rule-based systems (such as production systems) as the formal language of problem-solving theorists.

■

EVALUATION
■

The computer-simulation approach is an attempt to study theories of human problem solving in a precise and scientifically testable manner. The approach requires that the theories be stated precisely, in a formal computer program, and provides for the use of sophisticated lab equipment, computers, in testing theories. Thus computer simulation offers a breakthrough in the psychology of thinking that may ultimately produce a precise reformulation and integration of Gestaltist, associationist, and other ideas. However, the computer-simulation approach also has certain basic drawbacks. The human-machine analogy, the description of mental operations as computer operations, is not a perfect analogy. Psychology has been heavily influenced by developments in other sciences, including the breakthroughs in computer technology. However, the information-processing view of human beings as machinelike processors of information—though a currently popular view—is limited and may act to limit present views of thinking. In addition, there is a flaw in the logic of computer simulation: although a program may simulate human thinking behavior, this does not mean it simulates the underlying cognitive processes. Finally, current simulation programs require something like a table of connections—a list of every possible problem state and a measurement of its distance from the goal. Thus, in a way, the solution is given and the thinking process involves what the Gestaltists would call reproductive thinking. But the chapter on computer simulation is a continuing one, and it remains to be seen how far technology and humans may go in simulating human thought.

Suggested Readings

ANDERSON, J. R. (1983). *The architecture of cognition.* Cambridge, MA: Harvard University Press. An excellent presentation of a computer-simulation theory of cognitive skills.

KLAHR, D., LANGLEY, P., & NECHES, R. (Eds.). (1987). *Production system models of learning and development.* Cambridge, MA: M.I.T. Press. A collection of chapters by leaders in the field of computer simulation.

NEWELL, A.,. & SIMON, H. A. (1972). *Human problem solving.* Englewood Cliffs, NJ: Prentice-Hall. A giant 900-page book that offers an information-processing theory and computer simulation of problem solving in cryptarithmetic, logic, and chess.

SIMON, H. A. (1979, 1989). *Models of thought* (Vols. 1 and 2). New Haven, CT: Yale University Press. A collection of essays and papers about computer models of human cognition.

WINSTON, P. H. (1984). *Artificial intelligence.* Reading, MA: Addison-Wesley. A textbook about artificial intelligence.

CHAPTER 7

MENTAL CHRONOMETRY

Thinking as a Series of Mental Operations

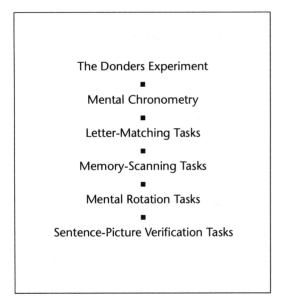

The Donders Experiment

▪

Mental Chronometry

▪

Letter-Matching Tasks

▪

Memory-Scanning Tasks

▪

Mental Rotation Tasks

▪

Sentence-Picture Verification Tasks

Suppose you are seated in front of a panel that contains a light bulb and a response button. When the light comes on, you are required to press the button as quickly as possible. This simple task, summarized in Box 7-1, is called a *simple reaction time task*.

BOX 7 · 1   Some Reaction Time Tasks

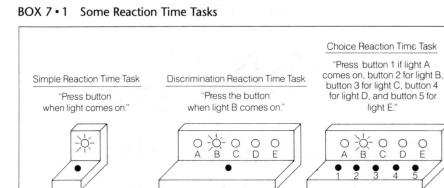

It normally requires about 50 to 250 milliseconds to complete, depending on such task characteristics as the intensity of the bulb and on such subject characteristics as attentiveness, eyesight, and so forth. Notice that in simple reaction time tasks you have one stimulus and one response.

The situation could be made a little more complicated. Suppose you are seated in front of a panel with five light bulbs and one response button. When the target light—the one designated as correct—comes on, you should press the button but should not when any of the other bulbs light up. This task is called a *discrimination reaction time task* because you must discriminate *which* particular light comes on. This task normally requires more time than simple reaction time tasks when all other variables are held constant. The *discrimination reaction time task* is summarized in Box 7-1. Notice that there are several possible stimuli but only one response.

Finally, we could complicate the task even further by setting you in front of five light bulbs, each of which has its own response button. In this case, you must press the button corresponding to the light that comes on, as shown in Box 7-1. This is called a *choice reaction time task* because you must also choose the appropriate response. All other factors being equal, this task normally takes even longer than the other two.

■

THE DONDERS EXPERIMENT

■

F. C. Donders (1868/1969) performed experiments using reaction time tasks in 1868. His work represents the first attempt to analyze and measure the component processes of a simple task. Donders's reasoning was that different

BOX 7 · 2   Component Processes in Reaction Time Tasks

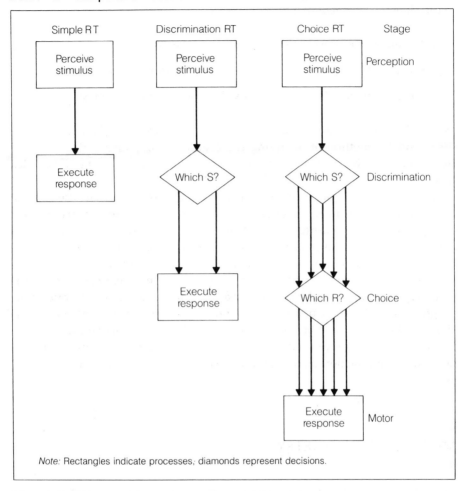

Note: Rectangles indicate processes; diamonds represent decisions.

series of mental processes were required for each of the three types of task just described. Box 7-2 shows the stages that might be involved in the three tasks, with processes represented as rectangles and decisions represented as diamonds. A simple reaction time task requires perception and motor stages—time to perceive the stimulus and execute the response. In contrast, a discrimination reaction time task requires the same perception and motor stages plus a discrimination stage—time to distinguish which light was on. Finally, a choice reaction time task requires the same perception, discrimination, and motor stages plus a choice stage—time to decide which response to perform. As expected, choice tasks take more time than discrimination tasks, and simple tasks take the least amount of time. Using a subtraction technique, it was possible for Donders to calculate the time required for each stage:

Perception and motor time = time required for simple task.

Discrimination time = time for discrimination task minus time for simple task.

Choice time = time for choice task minus time for discrimination task.

Donders's reasoning was straightforward—more stages should require more time—and his method of analyzing the cognitive components of his tasks is similar to methods currently used in cognitive psychology for more complex tasks.

Until Donders's work, many scientists had assumed that the mental operations involved in responding to a stimulus occurred instantaneously. For example, a nineteenth-century physiologist, Muller, proclaimed that the speed of neural transmission was so fast that it could not be measured. Shortly thereafter, Helmholtz measured the speed, both in humans and lab animals, at a rather slow 100 meters per second. For example, transmission from a sense receptor in the periphery to the brain could take as long as 20 milliseconds, not to mention time for processing within the brain. Thus, Donders deserves to be remembered for (1) showing that tasks could be broken down into elementary mental processes, (2) finding that each process takes a certain amount of time to occur, and (3) devising the subtraction technique as a means of measuring the time of mental events.

■
MENTAL CHRONOMETRY
■

Donders's work is interesting because it offers a means of describing what is going on "inside the black box" by analyzing cognitive activity into separate stages. However, Donders's work was rejected by early experimental psychologists such as Wundt, and strong interest in his work has rematerialized only during the past 30 years. The rebirth of interest in developing cognitive models of processes involved in performing tasks can be marked by the appearance in 1960 of a remarkable book by Miller, Galanter, and Pribram called *Plans and the Structure of Behavior*. As discussed in Chapter 6, Miller and his colleagues argue that simple tasks may be represented as plans—a series of elementary mental processes.

Posner (1978) has called Donders's techniques "mental chronometry"— studying the time it takes to perform elementary cognitive operations. This approach makes several assumptions:

Components—any task can be described as a set of separate, elementary mental processes.

Time—each elementary process takes a certain measurable amount of time.

Serial—the processes are carried out one at a time, in order.

Additive/subtractive—the time for component processes may be legitimately added or subtracted.

Although objections may be raised to each of these assumptions (Posner, 1978), let's hold our judgment until we explore some of the applications of the stage analysis approach.

As a theory of problem solving, the mental chronometry approach is based on the idea that problem solving involves a series of mental operations, such as manipulating or operating on information in memory. The goal of this approach is to determine the elementary mental operations that are used in basic cognitive tasks and thus to establish a catalogue of the building blocks of human thought. In this chapter, we will explore how the mental chronometry approach has been applied to four cognitive tasks: letter matching, memory scanning, mental rotation, and sentence-picture verification.

■
LETTER-MATCHING TASKS
■

Consider the following task. For each pair of letters, say Yes if they are physically identical and No if they are not:

A   A

A   a

a   a

A   B

This is called a *physical match task;* the correct answers are Yes, No, Yes, No.

Now, for each of the following letter pairs, say Yes if both letters have the same name and No if they do not:

A   A

A   a

a   a

A   B

This is called a *name match task;* the correct answers are Yes, Yes, Yes, and No.

BOX 7 • 3   Component Processes for Physical Match and Name Match Tasks

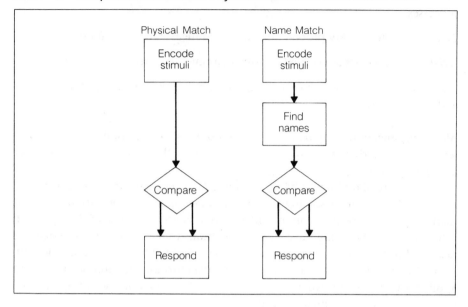

Posner and his colleagues (Posner, 1969, 1978; Posner, Boies, Eichelman, & Taylor, 1969; Posner, Lewis, & Conrad, 1972; Posner & Mitchell, 1967) developed tasks such as these in order to measure the speed of mental processes involved. The subject sits in front of a screen, and two letters are presented. For a physical match task, the subject presses the button marked "same" when both letters are physically identical and the button marked "different" when they are not. A similar setup is used for a name match task.

Consider the cognitive processes involved in a name match and physical match. Does your list look anything like those listed in Box 7-3? For example, the physical match may involve encoding, comparing, and responding; the name match involves these same stages as well as one more, namely, finding the name of each letter in long-term memory. Thus, if we subtract the time to make a physical match from the time to make a name match, we have an estimate of the time for the finding process.

The results of a typical study (Posner & Mitchell, 1967) indicate that the response time was 549 milliseconds for the physical match task (for example, AA) and 623 milliseconds for the name match task (Aa). Thus, using the subtraction technique, you might conclude that the time to search for a letter name in memory is 74 milliseconds. However, the times for component processes may be affected by several factors, such as the physical similarity of the letters or the particular letter name (Posner, 1969, 1978).

BOX 7 • 4   Response Times for Several Matching Tasks

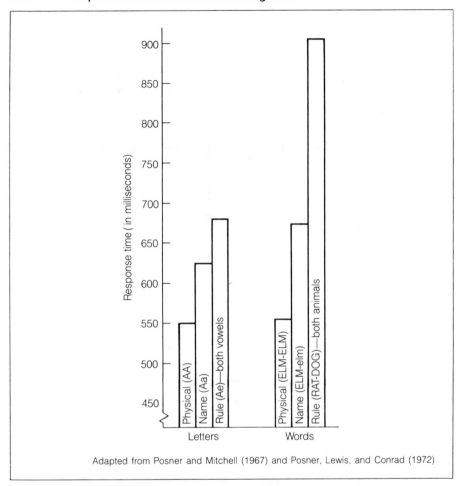

Adapted from Posner and Mitchell (1967) and Posner, Lewis, and Conrad (1972)

In a related study by Posner, Lewis, and Conrad (1972), subjects were asked to judge whether two words were physically identical (such as *ELM-ELM*) or had the same name (such as *ELM-elm*). Results indicated that the time for a physical match was 555 milliseconds, and the time for a name match was 674 milliseconds. This suggests that the time to find the name of a simple word in memory is about 119 milliseconds. Similarly, when the task involves using a rule, response times are even longer. For example, the time to judge whether two letters are both vowels is 699 milliseconds. Some of these results are summarized in Box 7-4. In summary, the subtraction technique seems to have been successful in locating and measuring the component processes in stimulus-matching tasks.

BOX 7 • 5   Component Processes in Memory-Scanning Task

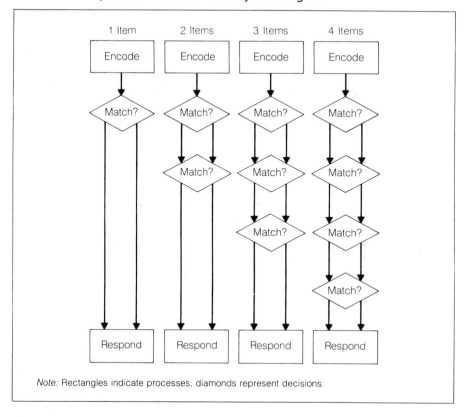

Note: Rectangles indicate processes; diamonds represent decisions.

MEMORY-SCANNING TASKS

Suppose I gave you a set of digits to remember such as 2 4 7 3. Read each of these numbers aloud so that you keep them in your short-term memory. Now, suppose I gave you a probe and asked whether that probe was one of the numbers in your memory set. The probe is 7. Your answer, of course, should be Yes, since there was a 7 in the memory set (2 4 7 3).

Sternberg (1966, 1969, 1975) used this task, called "memory scanning," to study cognitive processes in short-term memory. In a typical experimental trial, the subject read a set of one to six digits that were presented for 2 seconds; then, after a 2-second delay, a probe digit was presented. The subject's job was to press the "yes" button if the probe matched one of the digits in the memory set and

BOX 7 • 6   Response Times for Various Memory Set Sizes in Memory–Scanning Task

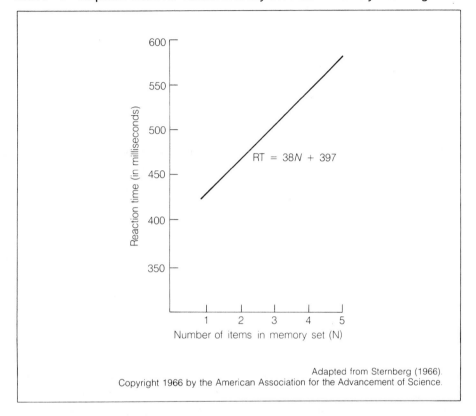

Adapted from Sternberg (1966).
Copyright 1966 by the American Association for the Advancement of Science.

press the "no" button if it did not. On some trials there was just one digit in the memory set; on others there were two to six digits.

If you were a subject in a memory-scanning experiment, what cognitive processes do you think you would be using? You would have to encode and remember the memory set, you would have to compare the probe to each digit in your memory, and you would have to respond. Box 7-5 summarizes the processes that might be involved for memory sets of one, two, three, and four items. This analysis suggests that adding one more item to the memory set results in the need for one more mental comparison process.

Box 7-6 summarizes the average response times for memory sets ranging from one to six items. For each additional digit in the memory set, response time increases approximately 38 milliseconds (Sternberg, 1966). Thus, by the subtraction method, we can conclude that each mental comparison takes about 38 milliseconds.

BOX 7 · 7   Scanning Rates for Various Stimuli

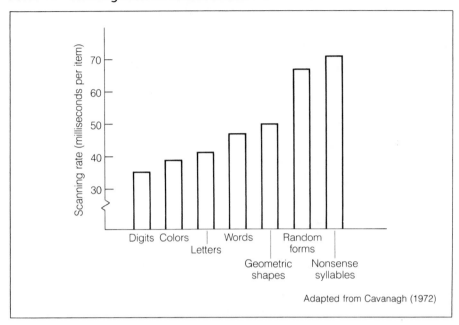

Adapted from Cavanagh (1972)

The sequence of processing stages indicated in Box 7-5 contains two assumptions that may seem peculiar to you. First, the model assumes that the probe is compared to each digit in the memory set sequentially, that is, one at a time; this is called *serial processing.* It seems more efficient to compare the probe to several digits in the memory set simultaneously; this is called *parallel processing.* Serial processing predicts an increasing response time as the number of items in the memory set is increased, such as is shown in Box 7-6, while parallel processing predicts a flat line. Thus Sternberg is able to point out that the observed data are most consistent with serial processing. However, there is some evidence that highly practiced subjects can search for multiple targets as easily as for one target (Neisser & Lazar, 1964; Neisser, Novick, & Lazar, 1963).

A second assumption is that the subject compares the probe to each and every digit in the memory set, even if a match has already been found. This is called an *exhaustive search* because all comparisons are made. A more efficient alternative is a *self-terminating search,* the idea that you stop searching as soon as you find a match. The self-terminating search predicts that the time needed to answer Yes will be less than the time needed to answer No, since fewer comparisons need to be made on the average; the exhaustive search idea predicts no difference between Yes and No response times. Again, Sternberg points out that the data support the predictions of exhaustive search, namely, no difference between Yes and No response times. However, there is some troubling evidence that response times are faster when the probe matches the first digit in the memory set and longer when it matches the last digit in the memory set (Burrows & Okada, 1971; Clifton & Birenbaum, 1970; Raeburn, 1974).

In a review summary, Sternberg (1975) addressed many of the issues raised by the serial exhaustive search model. Such problems should remind you that the neat diagrams shown in Box 7-5 are not the only possible stage models. Under certain experimental situations or for certain subjects, entirely different processes and arrows might be needed. For example, Box 7-7 summarizes the average processing times for various kinds of stimuli (Cavanagh, 1972). Using random forms or nonsense syllables instead of digits in a memory-scanning task seems almost to double the time required for each comparison stage.

■
MENTAL ROTATION TASKS
■

The mental chronometry approach has also been successfully applied to the study of how people manipulate visual images in memory. For example, Cooper and Shepard (1973a, 1973b) presented a single letter or digit to subjects on each trial. Each letter or digit was either normal or a mirror image (called "backward"); in addition, each letter or digit was presented either in its normal orientation or was rotated clockwise every 60 degrees. Examples of normal and backward stimuli in each of these orientations are given in Box 7-8. For each letter or digit, the subject's job was to press a button marked "normal" if the letter was normal and press a button marked "backward" if the letter was backward.

If you were a subject in this experiment, what mental processes would you have to perform for each task? First, you would have to encode the presented stimulus—that is, represent the letter in your short-term memory. Then, you might rotate this representation until it was at an upright (0 degree) orientation. Your next step might be to decide whether the letter is normal or backward, and your final step is to press the appropriate button. Box 7-9 summarizes the sequence of processes you might go through for the 0-degree, 60-degree, 120-degree, and 180-degree tasks. As you can see, all tasks require encoding, deciding, and responding stages. However, the 60-degree task requires an additional stage—rotating 60 degrees—compared to the 0-degree task; similarly, the 180-degree task requires three times as much rotation as the 0-degree task. Thus the time to make a 60-degree rotation may be determined in several ways, such as subtracting the time for the 0-degree task from the time for the 60-degree task.

BOX 7 • 8   Examples of Stimuli Used in Letter Rotation Task

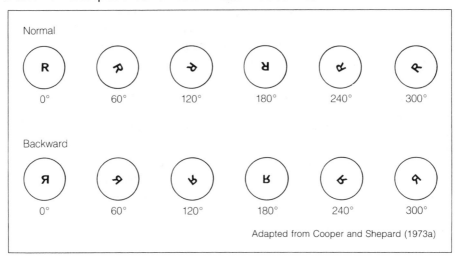

Adapted from Cooper and Shepard (1973a)

BOX 7 • 9   Component Processes in Image Rotation Task

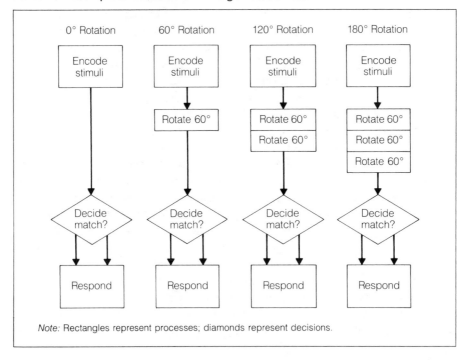

Note: Rectangles represent processes; diamonds represent decisions.

BOX 7 • 10   Box Times for Letter Rotation Task

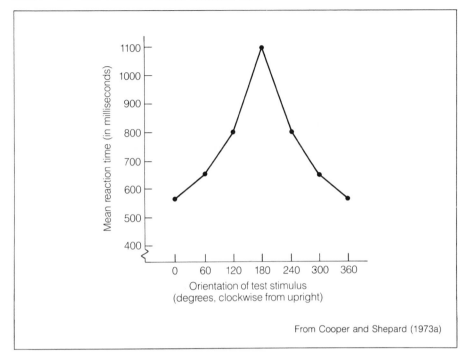

From Cooper and Shepard (1973a)

The average response time for each task is given in Box 7-10. As you can see, response time is lowest when the stimulus is upright (0 degree or 360 degrees), and longest when it is upside down (180 degrees); there is a systematic increase in response time for tasks requiring more rotation. Although these results are consistent with the analysis in Box 7-9, there are several problems that may occur to you. First, you may have noticed that the difference in response time between the 0- and 60-degree orientation is not the same as the difference between the 120- and 180-degree orientation; this discrepancy could be due to many factors, including some hesitancy concerning which way to rotate the upside-down stimulus. Second, you can see that the response times for the 240- and 300-degree orientations corresponded nicely with those for 120- and 60-degree orientations, respectively; apparently, subjects are able to decide whether a clockwise or counterclockwise rotation is more efficient, so a direction decision stage could be added to the models in Box 7-9 immediately after the encoding stage.

Similar analyses have also been conducted using three-dimensional stimuli by Metzler and Shepard (1974; Shepard, 1975). In a typical study (Metzler and Shepard, 1974), subjects are shown two figures such as those shown in Box 7-11.

BOX 7 ▪ 11   Examples of Stimuli Used in Figure Rotation Tasks

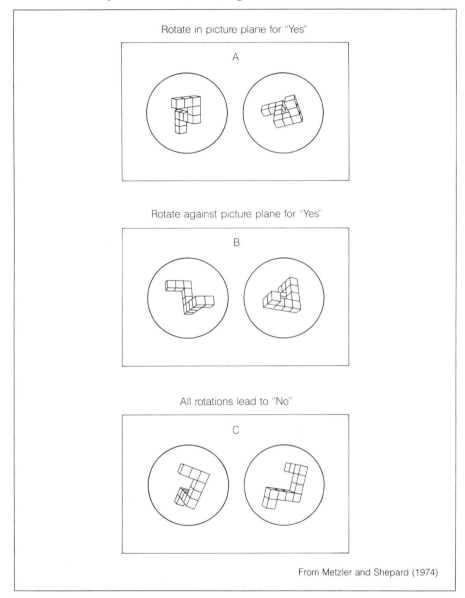

Rotate in picture plane for "Yes"

A

Rotate against picture plane for "Yes"

B

All rotations lead to "No"

C

From Metzler and Shepard (1974)

Some pairs (such as the A pair in Box 7-11) are identical except that one figure must be rotated on the same plane as the picture. Other pairs (such as the B pair) are also identical except that one figure must be rotated perpendicularly to the

BOX 7 • 12   Response Times for Figure Rotation Task

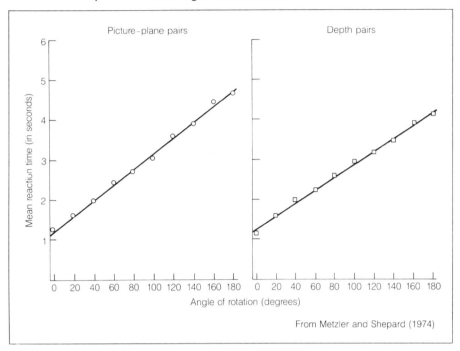

Picture-plane pairs

Depth pairs

Mean reaction time (in seconds)

Angle of rotation (degrees)

From Metzler and Shepard (1974)

picture plane. Finally, other pairs are not identical, although you must rotate one to see that clearly. The amount of rotation required to match the two figures in any trial was either 0, 20, 40, 60, 80, 100, 120, 140, 160, or 180 degrees. A 0-degree rotation means the two objects are in the same orientation, and a 180-degree rotation means one is upside-down relative to the other; those in Box 7-11 all show an 80-degree rotation. The subject's task is to press a button labeled "same" if the two figures are identical and to press the button labeled "different" if they are not identical.

Consider the processing stages involved in this task. You must encode the stimuli, rotate one of them until it is in the same orientation as the other, decide if they match, and then respond. These stages are quite similar to those outlined in Box 7-9 for the letter rotation task. For example, the time to rotate a figure 20 degrees may be determined by subtracting the time for 0-degree orientation from that when the orientation is 20 degrees.

The response time results for the three-dimensional task are summarized in Box 7-12. Response times increase about .5 seconds for each additional 20 degrees of rotation that is required. These results are consistent with the stage models described earlier; for example, the 80-degree orientation task requires the same processes as the 60-degree task, plus one more stage—rotating an image 20 more degrees. These studies have been followed up (Cooper, 1975, 1976) and provide a convincing demonstration that the mental chronometry approach may be applied to nonverbal tasks.

■
SENTENCE-PICTURE VERIFICATION TASKS
■

Another important question that has generated considerable research concerns the information-processing stages involved in the comprehension of a sentence. The basic experimental method has been to present a simple sentence along with a picture and ask the subject whether the two are consistent.

For example, Clark and Chase (1972) presented sentences such as "star is above plus" simultaneously with symbol pictures, such as $\overset{*}{+}$. The subjects were asked to press the "true" button if the sentence matched the picture, as it does in this example, or the "false" button if it did not. Four types of questions were asked, and examples of each are given below:

> true-affirmative (TA):   star is above plus $\overset{*}{+}$
> false-affirmative (FA):   plus is above star $\overset{*}{+}$
> false-negative (FN):   star isn't above plus $\overset{*}{+}$
> true-negative (TN):   plus isn't above star $\overset{*}{+}$

The answers to these four examples are true, false, false, true.

Just and Carpenter (1971) used sentences that involved the color of dots along with a picture of dots that were either red or black; examples follow:

> true-affirmative (TA):   dots are red (picture of red dots)
> false-affirmative (FA):   dots are black (picture of red dots)
> false-negative (FN):   dots aren't red (picture of red dots)
> true-negative (TN):   dots aren't black (picture of red dots)

As you try to solve a sentence-picture verification problem, can you determine what steps must be involved in each task? Do some problems require more processes than others? First, let's consider how the picture and sentence may be encoded. One way to represent the picture and sentence is to express each as a string consisting of features (in parentheses) and a sign (in front of the parentheses). For example, the sentence "the star is above plus" would be represented as AFF (star above plus), or "the star isn't above plus" would be represented as NEG (star above plus) or the picture $\overset{*}{+}$ would be represented as AFF (star above plus), where AFF means "affirmative" and NEG means "negative." Actually, we can assume that AFF strings do not need to be marked, but NEG strings must be marked.

Four basic stages that may be involved in comparing sentences with pictures are

Reading and response time—the time to encode each picture and sentence and time to execute a response,

Negation time—extra time needed to encode a sentence that has a negative in it,

Features mismatch time—extra time required when the features of two encoded strings do not match (for example, a sentence says "red dots" but the picture shows black dots), and

Sign mismatch time—extra time required when the signs of two encoded strings do not match (the sentence is negative but the picture is affirmative, for example).

Models have been suggested (Chase & Clark, 1972; Clark & Chase, 1972) based on these stages in which sentences and pictures are encoded and their features and signs are then compared.

Box 7-13 shows a flow chart based on these stages. The first step is to set the *truth index* to "true," which means that if there are no mismatches the subject will answer "true." Then, in steps 2, 3, and 4, the presented sentence and picture each must be encoded into strings of the form, SIGN(FEATURES). For example, the sentence "star is not above plus" would be translated into NEGATIVE(STAR-ABOVE-PLUS); the picture $\overset{*}{+}$ would be translated as AFFIRMATIVE(STAR-ABOVE-PLUS) or more simply as (STAR-ABOVE-PLUS) because AFFIRMATIVE is understood to be the sign unless otherwise indicated. If a sentence contains a negative, as in the above example, then extra time is required to include the NEGATIVE sign in the representation (stage 3). The next decision (step 5) involves comparing the features of two strings (e.g., STAR-ABOVE-PLUS and STAR-ABOVE-PLUS): if the features of the two strings match (as in our example), then the subject goes on without delay; if they do not match, the subject must reverse the truth index (to "false" in our example), which takes extra time. The final decision (stage 6) involves comparing the signs of the two strings (e.g., NEGATIVE and AFFIRMATIVE): if they match, the subject goes on immediately to the final step; if they do not match (as in our example), the subject reverses the truth index (e.g., from "true" to "false" in our example) before going on to the final step. Thus there are three steps that can add extra time: if the sentence contains a negative (stage 3), if the features do not match (stage 5), or if the signs do not match (stage 6).

BOX 7 • 13   Component Processes in Sentence-Picture Verification Task

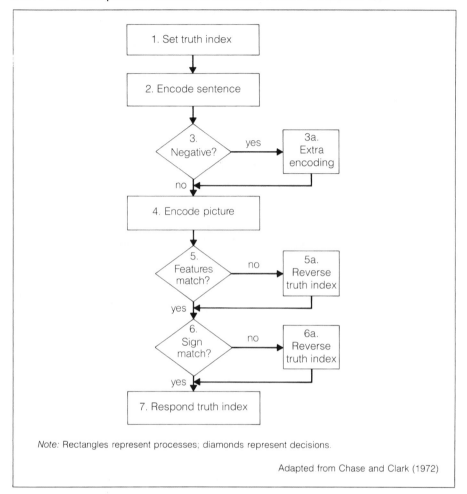

Note: Rectangles represent processes; diamonds represent decisions.

Adapted from Chase and Clark (1972)

This model predicts that true-affirmative problems (TA) require time for each of the steps but not extra time, which we will call K stages. False-affirmative problems (FA) require time for each of the same steps plus extra time at step 5a since the features do not match—the stages are K + 5a. As in our example, false-negatives (FN) require all the same steps as TA as well as extra time at 3a and 6a because of the negative—the stages are K + 3a + 6a. Finally, the true-negative problems require all the basic steps as well as all three extra steps—the stages are K + 3a + 5a + 6a. Thus TA requires only the time to go through the 7 basic stages, FA requires that time plus time for one

BOX 7 • 14   Response Times for Four Types of Sentence-Picture Verification
Problems

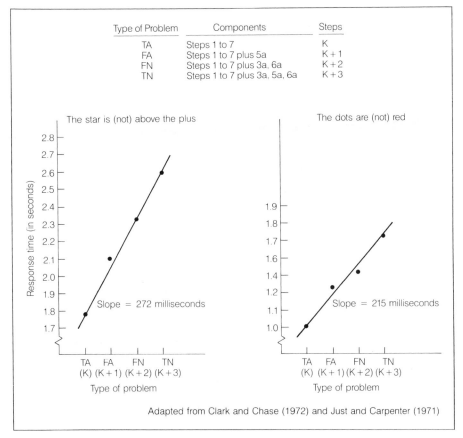

Type of Problem	Components	Steps
TA	Steps 1 to 7	K
FA	Steps 1 to 7 plus 5a	K + 1
FN	Steps 1 to 7 plus 3a, 6a	K + 2
TN	Steps 1 to 7 plus 3a, 5a, 6a	K + 3

The star is (not) above the plus

Slope = 272 milliseconds

The dots are (not) red

Slope = 215 milliseconds

Adapted from Clark and Chase (1972) and Just and Carpenter (1971)

more process, FN requires K plus two more processes, and TN requires K plus
three more processes. These predictions are summarized at the top of Box
7-14.

Some typical response times for each of the four types of problems are given
in Box 7-14. As both graphs show, the time to respond increases for questions
that require more processing stages. In a review of sentence-picture verification
studies, Carpenter and Just (1975) listed ten experiments, all of which obtained
similar results. In all cases, the response time increased from lowest to highest in
the order TA, FA, FN, TN, as predicted by the process model in Box 7-13.
Carpenter and Just (1975) have developed a more sophisticated flow chart model
that gives more specific predictions.

BOX 7 ▪ 15   Duration of Eye Fixations for Four Types of Sentence-Picture
Verification Problems

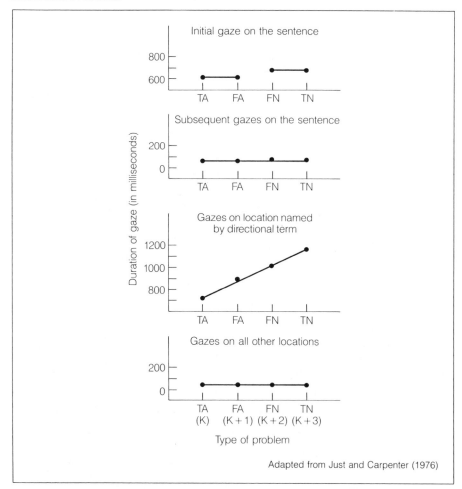

Adapted from Just and Carpenter (1976)

In follow-up experiments, Just and Carpenter (1976) examined the
sentence-picture verification task by recording the eye fixations of subjects as
they answered four types of questions (TA, FA, FN, TN). For example, a typical
question (in this case, TA) is shown in Box 7-15. Just and Carpenter measured the
length of the initial gaze at the sentence in the middle (perhaps a measure of
encoding time); subsequent gazes at the sentence; looks at the location that was
named by the sentence, such as "north" (perhaps a measure of processing time);
and gazes at all other locations. An average of 57 milliseconds more was spent

gazing at a negative sentence—"isn't north," for example—than an affirmative sentence—"is north"—perhaps indicating added encoding time for negatives. Also, length of gaze at the indicated location increased from TA to FA to FN to TN, perhaps indicating additional comparisons at the rate of 135 milliseconds per comparison. Thus length of initial gaze at the sentence seems correlated with encoding time, and length of gaze at the indicated location is related to match-mismatch processing, while the other two measures indicate random activity that is constant for all questions. These results are encouraging because they provide support for the stage model by using an entirely different experimental procedure.

There are, however, some problems with the stage analysis in sentence-picture verification as just given. For example, there is evidence that different people use different techniques for representing information in the sentence-picture verification tasks (Hunt & MacLeod, 1979; Pellegrino & Glaser, 1979). These differences are discussed more fully in Chapter 11; however, this research suggests that it may not be possible to find one flow chart model that fits all people for a given task.

■

EVALUATION
■

In this chapter you have seen how stage analysis techniques, or mental chronometry, may be applied to four simple cognitive tasks: letter matching, memory scanning, mental rotation, and sentence-picture verification. In all four situations, the same procedure was followed. First, several related versions of a task were broken down into a series of components. Then, response times were obtained for each version of the task. As predicted, response times were related to the number of stages involved in the task. Times for individual stages were determined by using the subtraction method: subtracting the time for one task from the time for a task that involves all of the same processes plus one more. In this way, it can be found that mental images are rotated at the rate of 60 milliseconds per 60 degrees, letters can be scanned in memory at the rate of about 38 milliseconds per letter, the time to find a letter name in memory is about 75 milliseconds, and the time to encode a negative is about 100 milliseconds.

On the surface, such techniques appear to be successful. However, there are serious problems with the assumptions of the stage analysis approach. For example, the assumption that a task can be broken down into stages is open to challenge because different researchers may invent different models for the same task, different subjects may behave quite differently on the same task, a given subject may shift from one series of stages to another with practice, and components may not be separable. Similar problems have been raised concerning the assumptions of serial processing, the legitimacy of the subtraction method, and the time assumptions (Posner, 1978; Sternberg, 1975).

In spite of these problems, mental chronometry continues to be used as a tool in the study of human problem solving, including the analysis of cognitive processes involved in solving mental computation problems (Chapter 15) and induction problems (Chapter 11). This line of recent research, however, has highlighted the shortcomings of the mental chronometry approach: problem solvers may possess and use a wide variety of solution procedures in solving computation problems (Siegler, 1989a; Siegler & Jenkins, 1989), and metacognitive control of solution procedures appears to be at the heart of human reasoning (Sternberg, 1985, 1988).

In summary, the analysis of cognitive processes into stages may be criticized for having too narrow a goal—that is, for focusing on the nature of specific tasks rather than on how the human mind works. Suppose that in the next decade we have stage models for all of the major problem-solving tasks. We would have a list of the *primitive processes* involved in cognition—processes such as compare, increment, set a counter, encode, and so on. Yet we would still need information concerning the strategies that people use in deciding how to represent and solve a problem. Thus the stage analysis approach is only a component in a larger theory of problem solving.

Suggested Reading

POSNER, M. I. (1978). *Chronometric explorations of mind*. Hillsdale, NJ: Erlbaum. An introduction to research and theory using the mental chronometry approach.

CHAPTER ▪ 8

SCHEMA THEORY
Thinking as an Effort After Meaning

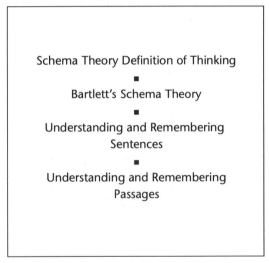

Schema Theory Definition of Thinking

▪

Bartlett's Schema Theory

▪

Understanding and Remembering
Sentences

▪

Understanding and Remembering
Passages

READING TASK

Suppose I asked you to read a prose passage, such as a short story or a textbook
lesson. How are you able to understand and remember the passage? Let's assume that
you read each word and that you are familiar with the meaning of each word. Further,
let's assume that you carefully read each sentence and that you are familiar with the
rules of English sentence structure. Is this all you have to know to be able to
understand a passage?

In order to get a better feeling for what is involved in the understanding process, please read the passage in Box 8-1. All of the words are fairly common, and you should know what each one means. All of the sentences follow the grammatical rules of English, with which you are familiar. You are able to read each word, and each sentence, with little effort. However, when you try to understand the passage, does it make sense to you? How would you rate your understanding on a scale of 1 to 7?

1	2	3	4	5	6	7
I understand						I don't understand

When Bransford and Johnson (1972) gave this passage to subjects, most found it rather difficult to understand, and most performed quite poorly on retention of the passage.

Now, look at the illustration in Box 8-2, which goes along with the passage. Reread the passage in Box 8-1. Do you understand it better now? How would you now rate your understanding?

1	2	3	4	5	6	7
I understand						I don't understand

When Bransford and Johnson (1972) provided this illustration along with the passage, subjects were able to understand and remember it much better.

Why is the passage easier to understand when it is accompanied by the illustration? What does the illustration provide? The passage in Box 8-1 appears out of context and has no apparent theme. The illustration in Box 8-2 provides a context for the passage, what Bransford (1979) and others call a "schema." A schema provides a general structure for the passage and allows you to hold the information together in an overall organization.

SCHEMA THEORY DEFINITION OF THINKING

Chapter 3 on Gestalt theory presented the idea that a person's understanding of a problem depends on how the problem is represented in the memory of the individual. Further, the chapter on Gestalt psychology emphasized the role of "understanding the problem" as the key to problem solving. This chapter follows the same memory representation approach, but it emphasizes how prose sentences and passages are understood and represented in memory. As you will

BOX 8 · 1   The Balloons Passage

If the balloons popped, the sound would not be able to carry since everything would be too far away from the correct floor. A closed window would also prevent the sound from carrying since most buildings tend to be well insulated. Since the whole operation depends on a steady flow of electricity, a break in the middle of the wire would also cause problems. Of course the fellow could shout, but the human voice is not loud enough to carry that far. An additional problem is that a string could break on the instrument. Then there could be no accompaniment to the message. It is clear that the best situation would involve less distance. Then there would be fewer potential problems. With face to face contact, the least number of things could go wrong.

From Bransford and Johnson (1972)

BOX 8 · 2   A Picture for the Balloons Passage

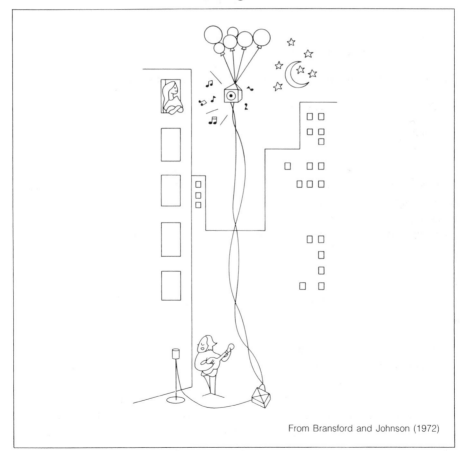

From Bransford and Johnson (1972)

see, understanding sentences is a problem-solving process in which you must apprehend relations among elements and construct an integrated representation. For example, Greeno (1978a, p. 243) has noted: "A close analogy can be made between the process of solving a . . . problem and the process of understanding a sentence."

The schema theory presented in this chapter views problem solving as the process of understanding. Schema theory is an advance because it offers a more precise description of the understanding process than Gestalt theory. According to schema theory, understanding involves the construction of a schema and the assimilation of incoming information to the schema. For example, in reading the passage in Box 8-1 you must: (1) construct a schema such as realizing that the story is about a serenade and (2) assimilate facts from the story to that schema, such as focusing on information about the characters and location.

Although each theorist offers a slightly different view of schemas, a general definition of *schema* would contain the following points:

General—a schema may be used in a wide variety of situations as a framework for understanding incoming information.

Knowledge—a schema exists in memory as something that a person knows.

Structure—a schema is organized around some theme.

Comprehension—a schema contains "slots" that are filled in by specific information in the passage.

Thus a schema is a general knowledge structure used in comprehension. A schema serves to select and organize incoming information into an integrated, meaningful framework. The precise nature of this framework and its role in comprehension are the focus of schema theory and this chapter.

■
BARTLETT'S SCHEMA THEORY
■

Bartlett (1932) was one of the first psychologists to address the question of what processes people use to remember. As an example, consider "The War of the Ghosts" in Box 8-3. Read it over once, at your normal pace, then put the text away and try to reproduce on paper, from memory, what you have just read.

This example comes from the pioneering work of Bartlett and is summarized in his delightful little monograph, *Remembering* (1932). In his experiments, Bartlett used a version of the child's game of "telephone," in which a message is passed along a chain of people, changing a bit in each retelling. Bartlett called his procedure the "method of serial reproduction" and employed it as follows: he presented folk stories (or pictures) from unfamiliar cultures to British college students, asking subject 1 to read the story, put it aside, reproduce it from memory, and to pass this reproduction on to subject 2, who would in turn read the reproduced version, put it aside, reproduce his own version and pass it on to subject 3, and so on.

Bartlett noticed that something quite curious happened in these studies. The stories (and pictures) changed as they were passed along, but they changed in systematic ways. The version of the story reproduced by subject 10, given in Box 8-3, is one of many examples on which Bartlett based the following observations:

Leveling or flattening. Most of the details, such as proper names (Egulac, Kalama), titles ("The War of the Ghosts"), and the individual writing style, tended to be lost. Bartlett attributed this loss to the fact that British college students had no prior experience with folk tales native to other cultures or to spirits and ghosts; thus, since learning in this case required assimilating new material to existing concepts, the students were at a loss. According to Bartlett (1932, p. 172): "Without some general setting or label as we have repeatedly seen, no material can be assimilated or remembered."

Sharpening. A few details may be retained and even exaggerated. Apparently subjects can store a schema plus a few selected details.

Rationalization. Passages tended to become more compact, more coherent, and more consistent with the readers' expectations. All references to spirits and ghosts faded away, and the story became one of a simple fighting trip. Bartlett called this process *rationalization* and argued that the reader was actively engaged in "an effort after meaning"—an attempt to make the story fit in with the individual's expectations. Since mystical concepts are not a major factor in Western culture, the mystical aspects of the story were not well remembered; instead, many subjects tended to tack on a "moral," which was a widely accepted practice in other stories they were familiar with.

Although Bartlett's work lay dormant for many years as the behaviorist movement swept across the study of psychology in the United States, he is now recognized as the major forerunner of modern cognitive psychology because he suggested two fundamental ideas about human mental processes:

Learning and memory. The act of comprehending new material requires "an effort after meaning." In reading a complex text, or acquiring any new information, humans must assimilate the new material to existing concepts

BOX 8 ▪ 3   Three Versions of "The War of the Ghosts"

Original Version

The War of the Ghosts

One night two young men from Egulac went down to the river to hunt seals, and while they were there it became foggy and calm. Then they heard war-cries, and they thought: "Maybe this is a war-party." They escaped to the shore, and hid behind a log. Now canoes came up, and they heard the noise of paddles, and they saw one canoe coming up to them. There were five men in the canoe, and they said:
"What do you think? We wish to take you along. We are going up the river to make war on the people."
One of the young men said; "I have no arrows."
"Arrows are in the canoe," they said.
"I will not go along. I might be killed. My relatives do not know where I have gone. But you," he said, turning to the other, "may go with them."
So one of the young men went, but the other returned home.
And the warriors went on up the river to a town on the other side of Kalama. The people came down to the water, and they began to fight, and many were killed. But presently the young man heard one of the warriors say: "Quick, let us go home, that Indian has been hit." Now he thought: "Oh, they are ghosts." He did not feel sick, but they said he had been shot.
So the canoes went back to Egulac, and the young man went ashore to his house, and made a fire. And he told everybody and said: "Behold I accompanied the ghosts, and we went to fight. Many of our fellows were killed, and many of those who attacked us were killed. They said I was hit, and I did not feel sick."
He told it all, and then he became quiet. When the sun rose he fell down. Something black came out of his mouth. His face became contorted. The people jumped up and cried.
He was dead.

Version Reproduced by the First Subject

The War of the Ghosts

There were two young Indians who lived in Egulac, and they went down to the sea to hunt for seals. And where they were hunting it was very foggy and very calm. In a little while they heard cries, and they came out of the water and went to hide behind a log.

(continued)

or schemas. The outcome of learning—what is stored in memory—does not duplicate exactly what was presented, but rather depends on both what was presented and the schema to which it is assimilated. People change the new information to fit their existing concepts, and in the process, details are lost and the knowledge becomes more coherent to the individual.

BOX 8 • 3, *continued*

Then they heard the sound of paddles, and they saw five canoes. One canoe came toward them, and there were five men within, who cried to the two Indians, and said: "Come with us up this river, and make war on the people there."

But one of the Indians replied: "We have no arrows."

"There are arrows in the canoe."

"But I might be killed, and my people have need of me. You have no parents," he said to the other, "you can go with them if you wish it so; I shall stay here."

So one of the Indians went, but the other stayed behind and went home. And the canoes went on up the river to the other side of Kalama, and fought the people there. Many of the people were killed, and many of those from the canoes also.

Then one of the warriors called to the young Indian and said: "Go back to the canoe, for you are wounded by an arrow." But the Indian wondered, for he felt not sick.

And when many had fallen on either side they went back to the canoes, and down the river again, and so the young Indian came back to Egulac.

Then he told them how there had been a battle, and how many fell and how the warriors had said he was wounded, and yet he felt not sick. So he told them all the tale, and he became weak. It was near daybreak when he became weak, and when the sun rose he fell down. And he gave a cry, and as he opened his mouth a black thing rushed from it. Then they ran to pick him up, wondering. But when they spoke he answered not.

He was dead.

Version Reproduced by the Tenth Subject

The War of the Ghosts

Two Indians were out fishing for seals in the Bay of Manpapan, when along came five other Indians in a war-canoe. They were going fighting.

"Come with us," said the five to the two, "and fight."

"I cannot come," was the answer of the one, "for I have an old mother at home who is dependent upon me." The other said he could not come, because he had no arms. "That is no difficulty," the others replied, "for we have plenty in the canoe with us"; so he got into the canoe and went with them.

In a fight soon afterwards this Indian received a mortal wound. Finding that his hour was coming, he cried out that he was about to die. "Nonsense," said one of the others, "you will not die." But he did.

From Bartlett (1932)

Remembering and memory. The act of remembering requires an active "process of construction"; during recall, an existing schema is used to generate or construct details that are consistent with it. Memory is not detailed but rather is schematic, that is, based on general impressions. Although recall produces specific details that seem to be correct, many of them are, in fact, wrong.

BOX 8 ▪ 4   Effects of Verbal Labels on Memory for Ambiguous Figures

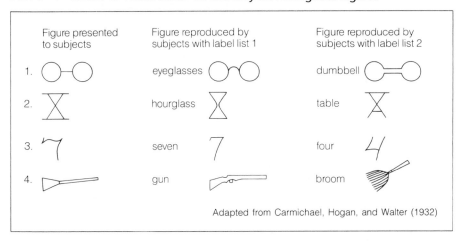

Adapted from Carmichael, Hogan, and Walter (1932)

Carmichael, Hogan, and Walter (1932) provided complementary evidence for Bartlett's theory by using pictorial figures and providing subjects with a method for interpreting them. They showed their subjects a series of twelve figures like those in Box 8-4 and gave each one a name. Before presenting figure 1, for example, the experimenter might say, "This figure resembles eyeglasses," or "This figure resembles a dumbbell." For figure 4, the experimenter might suggest "a gun" or "a broom." When the subjects were asked to reproduce these figures from memory, their drawings tended to be influenced by the labels they had been given during the presentation. These results were consistent with Bartlett's idea that memory for figures or passages involves assimilation to schemas—in this case, the labels may have served as schemas.

Bartlett's work was tantalizing because it demonstrated that memory is "schematic"—that both learning and remembering are based on general schemas rather than specifics. However, Bartlett's work did not yield clear or powerful predictions; for example, it could not predict which details would "fall out" of a passage or in what ways a subject would make a passage more coherent. In a sense, the work of modern cognitive psychologists has been to clarify the ideas of Bartlett and the Gestalt psychologists and to test and refine their theories. The basic method that has been used for this is known as the "recall method," in which subjects are presented with complex verbal material and are then asked questions about it.

■
UNDERSTANDING AND REMEMBERING SENTENCES
■

CHOMSKY'S THEORY

The modem rebirth of interest in psycholinguistics, and especially in the study of how sentences are comprehended and stored, was touched off by Chomsky's "generative" theory of language (1957, 1959, 1965, 1968). Although Chomsky's complex theory is a linguistic theory rather than a tested psychological theory, it includes three basic ideas that have attracted psychologists:

The distinction between surface structure and deep structure. The surface structure of a sentence is the way it is written or spoken; its deep structure is the way it is represented in memory. For example, the sentence "The ball was hit by John" may be stored in deep structure as "John hit ball." Thinking, apparently, is based on the deep structure of language.

Transformation rules. Language consists of a set of rules for converting surface structure into deep structure (comprehension) and deep structure into surface structure (recall and communication).

Universal grammar. Some general characteristics are shared by all language users.

Chomsky's cognitive approach to language came as an alternative to the idea B. F. Skinner expressed in his book *Verbal Behavior* (1957) that language is a learned behavior subject to the laws of conditioning. By introducing the idea of deep structure and transformation rules, Chomsky suggested that memory structure—how sentences are stored and used—is not necessarily the same as surface structure. Unfortunately, Chomsky's theory was not based on psychological research, but rather on logical arguments. For example, consider the sentence "They are eating apples." According to Chomsky, the meaning of this sentence depends on how one transforms it to deep structure; if one assumes that "they" refers to people, the deep structure is quite different than if "they" refers to the apples. (I spotted a similar example hanging in a laundromat: "Not responsible for clothes you may have stolen.") The importance of such examples is that they show that the same surface structure may lead to different deep structures; apparently, the study of surface structure or verbal behavior alone may not adequately explain human comprehension of language.

Another important distinction with respect to sentences is between *syntax* —the order of language units, as specified by grammatical rules—and *semantics*

—the meaning or referents of a sentence. Considerable research has been done on the importance of both syntax and semantics in comprehending and recalling sentences. For example, Miller (1962) has suggested that comprehending and storing a sentence involve transforming it into a "kernel" sentence (K) plus a mental "footnote" about the syntactic structure. This theory predicts that a sentence such as "The boy hit the ball" would serve as the kernel (along with some footnote) for passive (P) surface structures, such as "The ball was hit by the boy," for interrogative (Q) surface structures such as "Did the boy hit the ball?," for negative (N) surface structures, such as "The boy did not hit the ball," or for any combination of passive, interrogative, and negative structures.

In a promising study, Mehler (1963) presented lists of sentences in kernel form, sentences transformed into passive, interrogative, and negative forms, and all combinations of these. Recall was best for the lists of kernel sentences and worst for the passive-interrogative, interrogative, and passive-interrogative-negative sentences. This result seemed consistent with Miller's and Chomsky's idea that sentences are converted into a deeper structure such as K sentences. However, when Martin and Roberts (1967) replicated the Mehler study but controlled for sentence length, they obtained the opposite results, concluding that Mehler's findings could be explained by the fact that K sentences were shorter and thus easier to recall.

After reviewing the studies of sentence memory, Adams (1976, p. 355) concluded: "There is no evidence that Miller's hypothesis about sentences, derived from generative theory, is valid, . . . Generative theory may have a short theoretical life in psychology because it is not a psychological theory." In other words, although the concept of deep structure has been useful to psychologists, the particular theory that the kernel sentence represents the meaning of a sentence is based on logical or linguistic analysis rather than on psychological study. It is now the task of psychologists through empirical studies to determine exactly how a sentence is represented in memory. Or, to put it another way, the search continues for the schema of a sentence.

REMEMBERING SENTENCES

Cognitive psychologists have recently been trying to study more carefully Bartlett's idea that subjects *abstract* the general meaning from prose during reading and *construct* their answers during recall. In an already classic study, Bransford and Franks (1971) read the sentences shown in the first part of Box 8-5 to the subjects and then asked the recognition questions shown in the second part of the box. Take a few minutes now to read the sentence list and then take the recognition test. In the original study the subjects were asked to rate on a 5-point scale how sure they were that the test sentence had been in the original list, but you can skip the rating for your test.

BOX 8 • 5   The Bransford and Franks Experiment: A Typical Set of Sentences

Sentence	Question
Acquisition sentences: Read each sentence, count to five, answer the question, go on to the next sentence.	
The girl broke the window on the porch.	Broke what?
The tree in the front yard shaded the man who was smoking his pipe.	Where?
The hill was steep.	What was?
The cat, running from the barking dog, jumped on the table.	From what?
The tree was tall.	Was what?
The old car climbed the hill.	What did?
The cat running from the dog jumped on the table.	Where?
The girl who lives next door broke the window on the porch.	Lives where?
The car pulled the trailer.	Did what?
The scared cat was running from the barking dog.	What was?
The girl lives next door.	Who does?
The tree shaded the man who was smoking his pipe.	What did?
The scared cat jumped on the table.	What did?
The girl who lives next door broke the large window.	Broke what?
The man was smoking his pipe.	Who was?
The old car climbed the steep hill.	The what?
The large window was on the porch.	Where?
The tall tree was in the front yard.	What was?
The car pulling the trailer climbed the steep hill.	Did what?
The cat jumped on the table.	Where?
The tall tree in the front yard shaded the man	Did what?
The car pulling the trailer climbed the hill.	Which car?
The dog was barking.	Was what?
The window was large.	What was?
STOP. Turn the page and read the sentences in the box. Without looking back at the sentences above, decide if each sentence appeared in the list above (old) or if it is a new sentence.	
	(continued)

To make up the sentences given in the first part of of Box 8-5, Bransford and Franks used four basic "idea sets":

"The scared cat running from the barking dog jumped on the table."
"The old car pulling the trailer climbed the steep hill."
"The tall tree in the front yard shaded the man who was smoking his pipe."
"The girl who lives next door broke the large window on the porch."

BOX 8 • 5, *continued*

Sentence	Question
Test set . . . Check "old" or "new"	
The car climbed the hill.	(old____, new____)
The girl who lives next door broke the window.	(old____, new____)
The old man who was smoking his pipe climbed the steep hill	(old____, new____)
The tree was in the front yard.	(old____, new____)
The scared cat, running from the barking dog, jumped on the table.	(old____, new____)
The window was on the porch.	(old____, new____)
The barking dog jumped on the old car in the front yard.	(old____, new____)
The cat was running from the dog.	(old____, new____)
The old car pulled the trailer.	(old____, new____)
The tall tree in the front yard shaded the old car.	(old____, new____)
The scared cat was running from the dog.	(old____, new____)
The old car, pulling the trailer, climbed the hill.	(old____, new____)
The girl who lives next door broke the large window on the porch.	(old____, new____)
The tall tree shaded the man.	(old____, new____)
The cat was running from the barking dog.	(old____, new____)
The cat was old.	(old____, new____)
The girl broke the large window.	(old____, new____)
The scared cat ran from the barking dog that jumped on the table.	(old____, new____)
The scared cat, running from the dog, jumped on the table.	(old____, new____)
The old car pulling the trailer climbed the steep hill.	(old____, new____)
The girl broke the large window on the porch.	(old____, new____)
The scared cat which broke the window on the porch climbed the tree.	(old____, new____)
The tree shaded the man.	(old____, new____)
The car climbed the steep hill.	(old____, new____)
The girl broke the window.	(old____, new____)
The man who lives next door broke the large window on the porch.	(old____, new____)
The tall tree in the front yard shaded the man who was smoking his pipe.	(old____, new____)
The cat was scared.	(old____, new____)
STOP. Count the number of sentences judged "old."	
See text for answer.	

Each idea unit was broken down into four single ideas (called "ones"), such as:

"The cat was scared."
"The dog was barking."
"The cat was running from the dog."
"The cat jumped on the table."

The ones could be combined to form twos, such as: "The scared cat jumped on the table." The ones could be combined to form threes, such as: "The scared cat was running from the barking dog." Finally, the ones could also be combined to form an entire idea unit, like the examples just given, and called a four. The subjects heard a long list of sentences consisting of some ones, twos, and threes but no fours from the idea sets, presented in random order.

Now comes the surprise. In your test, the sentences in the second part of Box 8-5 are all "new," so each "old" you checked is a "false recognition"—you thought you had seen it in the original list, but it was not there. In a related study, Bransford and Franks presented the same kind of study sentences, but this test consisted of some sentences that had been in the original list (old), some that had not been in the original list but could be inferred from one of the idea sets (new), and some (called noncase) that were based on putting parts of different idea sets together.

The ratings of the subjects for the test sentences are given in Box 8-6. As you can see, they could not tell the difference between sentences that had actually appeared in the original list and those that were simply consistent with an idea set. In fact, they were most confident about having seen fours although no fours were ever presented. Bransford and Franks concluded that during reading the subjects abstracted the four general linguistic ideas and that during recall they used these general abstract ideas, but that they had no memory of the specific sentences from which they were abstracted.

Further evidence for abstract memory of prose was obtained by Sachs (1967). She asked subjects to read a passage about the invention of the telescope like the one shown in Box 8-7, then she presented a test sentence and asked them to tell whether or not it had occurred verbatim in the text. The test sentence was based on a sentence from the text and the test was given immediately after a subject had read the sentence (0 syllables), after the subject had read 80 syllables beyond the sentence, or 160 syllables beyond the sentence. The test sentence contained either a change in meaning (semantic change), a change in voice (active or passive change), a change in wording that did not alter meaning (formal change), or no change (identical) from the text sentence. For example, the text sentence, "He sent a letter about it to Galileo, the great Italian scientist," was presented in the test in one of the following forms:

BOX 8 · 6   Recognition of Old and New Sentences

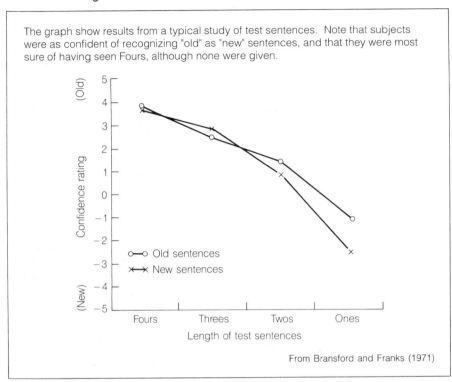

The graph show results from a typical study of test sentences. Note that subjects were as confident of recognizing "old" as "new" sentences, and that they were most sure of having seen Fours, although none were given.

Confidence rating
(Old)
(New)

o——o Old sentences
×——× New sentences

Fours   Threes   Twos   Ones

Length of test sentences

From Bransford and Franks (1971)

Identical: same text sentence.

Formal change: He sent Galileo, the great Italian scientist, a letter about it.

Active or passive change: A letter about it was sent to Galileo, the great Italian scientist.

Semantic change: Galileo, the great Italian scientist, sent him a letter about it.

The results of the experiment are given in Box 8-7. If the subjects had just read the sentence (0 interpolated syllables), they performed well in saying Yes to the identical sentence and No to each of the changed sentences. However, if the test came after the subject had read 80 or 160 syllables beyond the target sentence, then performance fell sharply for detecting formal or voice changes, but the subjects were still fairly accurate at noticing a change in meaning. In

BOX 8 • 7   Memory for the Meaning of Text

The Passage

Subjects read the following passage and were asked a question about the italicized sentence either immediately after it was presented (0 syllables), 80 syllables later, or 160 syllables later.

> There is an interesting story about the telescope. In Holland, a man named Lippershey was an eyeglass maker. One day his children were playing with some lenses. They discovered that things seemed very close if two lenses were about a foot apart. Lippershey began experiments and his "spyglass" attracted much attention. *He sent a letter about it to Galileo, the great Italian scientist.* (0 syllable test here.) Galileo at once realized the importance of the discovery and set out to build an instrument of his own. He used an old organ pipe with one lens curved out and the other curved in. On the first clear night he pointed the glass towards the sky. He was amazed to find the empty dark spaces filled with brightly gleaming stars! (80 syllable test here.) Night after night Galileo climbed to a high tower, sweeping the sky with his telescope. One night he saw Jupiter, and to his great surprise discoverd with it three bright stars, two to the east and one to the west. On the next night, however, all were to the west. A few nights later there were four little stars. (160 syllable test here.)

The Results

The proportion of correct response for each type of recognition question is given in the chart below.

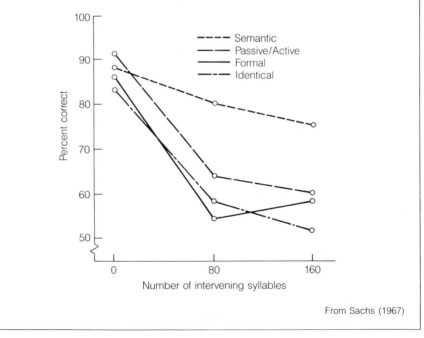

From Sachs (1967)

other words, once a sentence had been "digested" by the subject, the subject retained little information about the original grammatical form of the sentence but did retain the general meaning. Sachs concluded that in the course of reading a passage, a subject abstracted the general meaning but not the specific grammatical details.

Paivio (1971) has suggested that subjects may have formed mental images as a way of abstracting the meaning of sentences in Sachs's study. Since Sachs, as well as Bransford and Franks, used sentences that were relatively concrete, the subjects could have easily formed images that retained the meaning but destroyed the grammatical form of the presented text. In order to test this idea, Begg and Paivio (1969) replicated Sachs's study using some passages that tended to evoke vivid images and some that used abstract words that did not tend to evoke imagery. For example, typical sentences were: "The vicious hound chased a wild animal" (concrete) or "The absolute faith aroused an enduring interest" (abstract). For the concrete, high-imagery sentences, Begg and Paivio obtained results similar to Sachs's finding: subjects noticed a semantic change more easily than a change in sentence structure; however, for the abstract, low-imagery sentences, the reverse trend was found, with better recognition of lexical changes than semantic changes. Based on such findings, Paivio (1971, 1990) developed a "two-process theory of memory"—the idea that knowledge may be stored using imagery codes or verbal codes. Although most of the models of memory described in this chapter assume verbal coding for stored knowledge, Paivio's work has helped to reintroduce the idea that some types of representations may be nonverbal.

MAKING INFERENCES ABOUT SENTENCES

The foregoing section provides some evidence that people remember the meaning of sentences rather than the exact wording. In order to construct meaning, people may have to make inferences—that is, they may have to add information that is not directly given in the sentence. For example, suppose that I told you "Our neighbor unlocked the door." If you try to make sense out this sentence, you might make the inference that our neighbor used an instrument to unlock the door—a key. In contrast, if you focus literally on the sentence, you will not make an inference.

Paris and his colleagues (Paris & Lindauer, 1976; Paris, Lindauer, & Cox, 1977) tested the idea that younger children are less likely than older children to make inferences while processing a sentence. Kindergartners, second-graders, and fourth-graders listened to eight sentences, such as "Our neighbor unlocked the

BOX 8 ▪ 8   Age-Related Differences in Children's Use of Inference

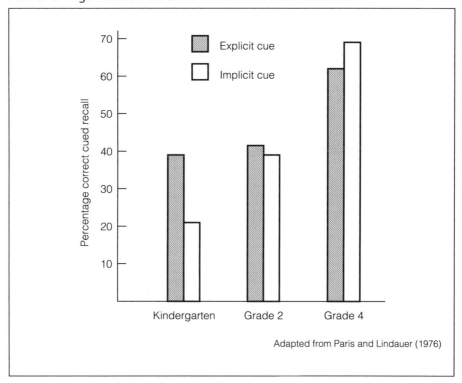

Adapted from Paris and Lindauer (1976)

door," and then were given a cued recall test. For each sentence on the recall test, children received an *explicit cue* that was a key word from the sentence (such as *door*) or an *implicit cue* that was the implicit instrument used (such as *key*). If students make inferences at the time of hearing the sentence, then implicit and explicit cues should be equally useful in helping the student remember the sentence. However, if students do not make inferences at the time of hearing the sentence, then explicit cues should be more useful than implicit cues. Box 8-8 shows the percentage of correctly recalled sentences when the cue was implicit and explicit for each age group. As you can see, the youngest children perform better for explicit cues than for implicit cues, suggesting that they often fail to make inferences at the time of sentence encoding; in contrast, the older children effectively use both types of cues, suggesting that they make and store inferences during sentence encoding.

There is also evidence that skilled adult readers make inferences as they read a sentence. For example, consider the following two sentences:

> The maid diligently swept the floor until it was spotless.
> The broom had been worn down by her excessive zeal.

In this case, when you read the first sentence, you are likely to infer than the instrument used to sweep the floor was a broom; the verb "swept" strongly implies "broom" as its instrument. Thus, when you read the second sentence, you do not have to infer that the broom was used by the maid, because you have already made that inference. In contrast, consider the following two sentences:

> The maid diligently cleaned the floor until it was spotless.
> The broom had been worn down by her excessive zeal.

As you read the first sentence, did you make any inferences about the instrument that was used to clean the floor? The verb "clean" implies many different kinds of instruments—including a brush, mop, rag, or broom—so it is difficult to infer that the instrument was a broom. If you are unable to infer that the instrument was a broom while reading the first sentence, you must make that inference while reading the second sentence.

According to this analysis, we can predict that it should take longer to read "The broom had been worn down by her excessive zeal" when it follows the sentence containing "cleaned" than when it follows the sentence containing "swept." Just and Carpenter (1978, 1987) confirmed this prediction when they observed the eye movements of readers as they read pairs of sentences such as these. On average, readers required a half-second more to read the "broom" sentence when it followed the "cleaned" sentence than when it followed the "swept" sentence. Presumably, skilled readers make inferences at the earliest opportunity as they read.

As another example of inferences during reading, suppose you read one of the following four sentences:

1. Joey's big brother punched him again and again.
2. Racing down the hill, Joey fell off his bike.
3. Joey's crazy mother became furiously angry with him.
4. Joey went to a neighbor's house to play.

Then you read:

> The next day, his body was covered with bruises.

As you can see, the cause-and-effect relation between sentence 1 and the final sentence is strong: the verb "punched" has a strong causal relation to "covered with bruises." Therefore it is likely that in the process of reading sentence 1 the reader will make the causal inference that Joey is bruised. In contrast, the action in sentence 4 (going to a neighbor's house to play) does not have a strong causal relation to the state expressed in the final sentence (being covered with bruises), so it is unlikely that the reader would make an inference about bruises while reading sentence 4. Consistent with this analysis, Keenan, Baillet, and Brown (1984) found that the time taken to read the final sentence was shortest when it followed sentence 1 (about 2.6 seconds), longer when it followed sentence 2 or 3 (about 2.9 seconds), and longest when it followed sentence 4 (about 3.3 seconds). Presumably, less time is required to read the "bruises" sentence when this causal inference has already been prompted by a previous sentence (e.g., sentence 1) than when it is not (e.g., sentence 2, 3, or 4).

A theme running through the research on inference making is that people tend to make inferences about information that was not stated as they read a sentence. In particular, the foregoing studies focused on two kinds of inferences—inferences about instruments and inferences about cause and effect. Fillmore (1968) has suggested that certain basic relations among elements in a sentence can be expressed as *case roles*. Some common case roles (or case relations) for an action may include the following:

agent—the instigator of an action

instrument—something used by an agent to perform an action

object—something or someone directly affected by the action

consequence —an effect or result of the action

The psychological implications of case grammars are illustrated in Box 8-9, which shows some frameworks for sentences used in the previously described studies. For example, for the action "unlocked" some common case relations are instrument, agent, object, and consequence; as you can see, the agent (our neighbor) and the object (the door) are explicitly given in the sentence, but the instrument (the key) and the consequence (door can be opened) must be inferred. Similarly, three case relations for the action "swept" can be found in the sentence: the maid is the agent, the floor is the object, and a spotless floor is a consequence. However, an instrument (broom) must be inferred. Research on inferencing suggests that humans often try to fill in the slots for each of the relevant case relations as they a read a sentence, even if the needed information is not explicitly stated.

BOX 8 • 9   Case Grammar Frameworks for Two Sentences

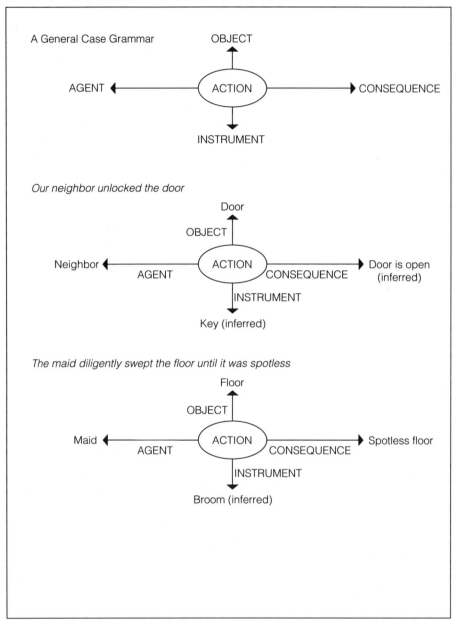

UNDERSTANDING AND REMEMBERING PASSAGES

USING PROSE STRUCTURE

Research on remembering and encoding of sentences extends Bartlett's claim that these processes are schematic. Rather than directly copying presented sentences into their memories, people often strive to construct meaning from sentences. As we move from sentences to passages, we enter the next major arena for examining the idea that comprehension involves construction of meaning.

We begin with a persistent finding: skilled readers are able to recognize the difference between important and unimportant information in passages (Johnson, 1970; Meyer, 1977; Meyer & McConkie, 1973). For example, Johnson (1970) broke a story down into *idea units*—each unit containing one major action or fact—and asked students to rate the importance of each idea unit to the overall story. Then another group read the story and recalled it (the story was shown via a slide projector, allowing the experimenter to control the time each unit was visible). As expected, these students recalled more important idea units than unimportant ones, even when the experimenter controlled the study time for each.

Where does the ability to distinguish important and unimportant information come from? To help answer this question, Taylor (1980) asked fourth-grade and sixth-grade readers to read and recall a short passage. As expected, the sixth-grade readers recalled more superordinate information than subordinate information, whereas the fourth-grade readers showed the reverse trend. Apparently, the ability to distinguish important from unimportant information develops with age and experience in reading.

These results are interesting because they imply that certain ideas in a passage are more important than others and that it is possible to predict in advance which information will be well-remembered. Since the 1970s, researchers have focused on *text analysis*—procedures for analyzing a text into a hierarchical structure. This work allows us to predict a *levels effect*—information that is at a high level in the structure will be remembered better than information that is at a low level in the structure. In this section, we explore three approaches to text analysis: top-level structure, propositional analysis, and story grammar.

Top-level structure refers to the outline of major topics in a passage. In a study of top-level structure, Meyer (1975) broke a 500-word passage from a *Scientific American* article into idea units and then arranged them into a hierarchical outline, which she called a "tree structure." Independent judgments from a group of adult readers produced almost identical tree structures, thus indicating that objective text analysis is possible. When new subjects were asked to read and recall the passage, there was a clear levels effect: ideas high in the structure were recalled better than those low in the structure. Apparently, findings based on subjective ratings of -importance such as those used by Johnson may be accounted for by Meyer's concept of height in a tree structure.

More recently, Cook and Mayer (1988) have demonstrated that adult readers who are inexperienced in reading textbooks can be taught to be more sensitive to the top-level structure of prose. Based on a survey of high school science textbooks, Cook and Mayer (1988) identified five types of structures commonly used as top-level structures in expository text:

Generalization—a main idea followed by supporting evidence, clarifications, extensions, or examples, such as an explanation of the biological term irritability,

Enumeration—a list of facts about a single topic, such as four general properties of solids,

Sequence—a cause-and-effect description of a chain of events or steps in a process, such as the five stages involved in the working of the ear,

Classification—a division of elements into groups or categories, such as the division of clouds into types, and

Compare/contrast—examination of two or more things along one or more dimensions, such as a comparison of the nebular and comet hypotheses of the origin of the earth.

Some students were trained to recognize several of these structures and were given practice in outlining passages from chemistry textbooks, while others received no training. All students received a pretest and posttest in which they read and recalled biology textbook passages. As expected, the trained students showed large pretest-to-posttest gains in recall of important information but not in recall of unimportant information, while the control subjects showed the reverse trend. Apparently the trained students learned to use text structure to help focus on important information—that is, on information central to the structure of the passage.

Propositional analysis refers to a method for arranging text into a hierarchy of propositions called a *text base* (Kintsch, 1974, 1976; Kintsch & van Dijk, 1978; van Dijk & Kintsch, 1983). The system is partially inspired by case grammars, which were discussed earlier in this chapter. Each proposition consists of two or more words that are related to one another; for example, a proposition generally consists of a verb and arguments that relate to the verb. For example, consider the text:

Turbulence forms at the edge of a wing and grows in strength over its surface, contributing to the lift of a supersonic aircraft.

This text can be analyzed into a text base as follows:

1.	Turbulence forms	(Verb Frame)
2.	at the edge	(Location)
3.	of a wing	(Part of)
4.	Turbulence grows in strength	(Verb Frame)
5.	over the surface	(Location)
6.	of a wing	(Part of)
7.	Turbulence contributes to the lift of an aircraft	(Verb Frame)
8.	The aircraft is supersonic	(Characteristic)

Note that the system for building a text base is based on finding the main verbs and using them as basic frames around which to place the arguments such as location, part of, characteristic, and others. Each indentation represents a lower level in the text base, so that proposition 1 is at level 1, propositions 2, 4, and 7 are at level 2, propositions 3, 5, and 8 are at level 3, and proposition 6 is at level 4. When the arguments are read, they can be added after the proposition at the above level; for example, proposition 1 is "Turbulence forms," proposition 2 involves "Turbulence forms at the edge," and proposition 3 involves "Turbulence forms at the edge of a wing."

Kintsch's notation is different from that just given but is based on the same principles. A proposition is represented within a set of parentheses, and the first word gives the verb or the relation involved; "Loc" refers to location. For example, in Kintsch's notation, the text base is:

1. (Form, turbulence)
2. (Loc: at, 1, edge)
3. (Part of, wing, edge)
4. (Grow, turbulence, strength)
5. (Loc: over, 4, surface)
6. (Part of, wing, surface)
7. (Contribute, turbulence, lift, aircraft)
8. (Supersonic, aircraft)

The numbers refer to the propositions.

Kintsch's system for analyzing text yields several interesting predictions if one assumes, as Kintsch does, that the text base for a passage is an indication of how the information is represented in a subject's memory. For example, one prediction is that if propositions—as defined by Kintsch's system—are the basic

BOX 8 • 10   Recall of Propositions as a Function of Different Levels
in the Text Base Hierarchy

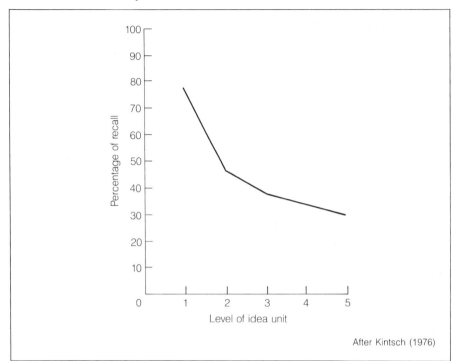

After Kintsch (1976)

units of comprehension and memory, then reading time ought to depend on the
number of propositions. To test this idea, passages were constructed that
contained equal numbers of words but varied in the number of propositions;
reading time increased as the number of propositions increased, even though the
same number and kind of words were processed (Kintsch, 1976).

To test the idea that certain propositions are more central than others, Kintsch
(1976) measured the percentage of propositions recalled at each level in the text base.
Box 8-10 shows that subjects recalled about 80 percent of the level-1 propositions
and that lower-level propositions were less likely to be recalled. In subsequent
refinements of their model of reading comprehension, Kintsch and van Dijk (1978;
van Dijk & Kintsch, 1983) have continued to find evidence for levels effects.

A story grammar is a system for organizing the parts of a narrative (Mandler
& Johnson, 1977; Rumelhart, 1975; Thorndyke, 1977). For example, when you
read a story you may expect four main slots to be filled: the setting, the theme,

BOX 8 ▪ 11   List of Events and States for "The Old Farmer and the Donkey"

1. There was once an old farmer.
2. who owned a very stubborn donkey.
3. One evening the farmer was trying to put his donkey into its shed.
4. First, the farmer pulled the donkey,
5. but the donkey wouldn't move.
6. Then the farmer pushed the donkey,
7. but still the donkey wouldn't move.
8. Finally, the farmer asked his dog
9. to bark loudly at the donkey
10. and thereby frighten him into the shed.
11. But the dog refused.
12. So then, the farmer asked his cat
13. to scratch the dog
14. so the dog would bark loudly
15. and thereby frighten the donkey into the shed.
16. But the cat replied, "I would gladly scratch the dog
17. if only you would get me some milk."
18. So the farmer went to his cow
19. and asked for some milk
20. to give to the cat.
21. But the cow replied,
22. "I would gladly give you some milk
23. if only you would give me some hay."
24. Thus, the farmer went to the haystack
25. and got some hay.
26. As soon as he gave the hay to the cow,
27. the cow gave the farmer some milk.
28. Then the farmer went to the cat
29. and gave the milk to the cat.
30. As soon as the cat got the milk,
31. it began to scratch the dog.
32. As soon as the cat scratched the dog,
33. the dog began to bark loudly.
34. The barking so frightened the donkey
35. that it jumped immediately into its shed.

From Thorndyke (1977)

the plot, and the resolution. The setting consists of several parts, including characters, location, and time. The theme consists of a topic and a goal. The plot contains a series of episodes—each involving goals, attempts, and outcomes. The resolution is an event or state that relates to the theme. According to Thorndyke (1977), subjects attempt to fill in these slots as they read a story, beginning with the four main parts and working down.

Thorndyke asked subjects to listen to a story like the "The Old Farmer and the Donkey" in Box 8-11. When subjects recalled this story, they tended to remember

BOX 8 ▪ 12   Recall of the Story Structure for Two Groups

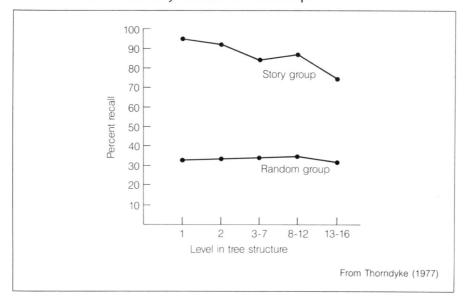

From Thorndyke (1977)

events and states from the top of the story grammar hierarchy (such as setting, theme, and resolution) better than those that were lower in the hierarchy (such as characters' specific actions). In addition, if the theme—in this case, getting the donkey into the shed—was left out of the story, recall was much poorer. Presumably, subjects try to understand the story by placing each event or state in its proper place within the story's framework; if the theme is unclear, subjects may not be able to invent an appropriate framework for the story. These results are summarized in Box 8-12.

If readers focus on high-level information more than low-level information, we can predict that they will spend more time on a sentence that has a central place than one that fits low in the story structure. To test this idea, Cirilo and Foss (1980) asked students to read stories that contained the sentence "He could no longer talk at all." One story is about a king who is cursed by a witch so that he cannot speak; in this story, the target sentence fits high in the story structure. Another story is about a soldier who found a king's ring; a minor incident in the story involves the soldier's momentarily becoming speechless when he learns of the size of the reward. In this case, the target sentence fits low in the story structure. As predicted, readers spent more time reading the target sentence in the witch story than in the ring story.

As another example of a story grammar, Schank and Abelson (1977) have suggested the "restaurant script" summarized in Box 8-13. Schank and Abelson

BOX 8 ▪ 13   The Restaurant Script

Schema: Restaurant.

Characters: Customer, hostess, waiter, chef, cashier.

Scene 1:   Entering
            Customer goes into restaurant.
            Customer finds a place to sit.
               He may find it himself.
               He may be seated by a hostess.
                  He asks the hostess for a table.
                  She gives him permission to go to the table.
            Customer goes and sits at the table.

Scene 2:   Ordering.
            Customer receives a menu.
            Customer reads it.
            Customer decides what to order.
            Waiter takes the order.
               Waiter sees the customer.
               Waiter goes to the customer.
               Customer orders what he wants.
            Chef cooks the meal.

Scene 3:   Eating.
            After some time the waiter brings the meal from the chef.
            Customer eats the meal.

Scene 4:   Exiting.
            Customer asks the waiter for the check.
            Waiter gives the check to the customer.
            Customer leaves a tip.
               The size of the tip depends on the goodness of the service.
            Customer pays the cashier.
            Customer leaves the restaurant.

From Rumelhart (1977)

propose that people have scripts such as these for many generalized events. When people think about such an episode, they expect to fill in the slots for that script, such as the specifics of entering and ordering in the restaurant script. Work on story grammars and scripts represents an attempt to more specifically describe what Bartlett might have meant by the term *schema*.

USING PRIOR KNOWLEDGE

The foregoing section suggests that we use schemas in learning and remembering new meaningful information. Accordingly, the schemas a reader brings to the

BOX 8 • 14   Comprehension and Recall of the "Washing Clothes" Passage

	No Topic	Topic After	Topic Before	Maximum Score
Comprehension ratings	2.29	2.12	4.50	7.00
Number of idea units recalled	2.82	2.65	5.83	18.00

Adapted from Bransford and Johnson (1972)

reading comprehension task can have a major influence on what is learned. As an example of the importance of a reader finding an appropriate schema, please read the following passage:

> The procedure is actually quite simple. First you arrange items into different groups. Of course one pile may be sufficient depending on how much there is to do. If you have to go somewhere else due to lack of facilities, that is the next step, otherwise, you are pretty well set. It is important not to overdo things. That is, it is better to do too few things at once than too many. In the short run this may not seem important but complications can easily arise. A mistake can be expensive as well. At first, the whole procedure will seem complicated. Soon, however, it will become just another facet of life. It is difficult to foresee any end to the necessity for this task in the immediate future, but then, one never can tell. After the procedure is completed one arranges the materials into different groups again. Then they can be put into their appropriate places. Eventually they will be used once more and the whole cycle will then have to be repeated. However, that is part of life.

Did this passage make sense to you? Do you think you would be able to repeat it? If not, you are behaving like subjects in experiments conducted by Bransford and Johnson (1972).

Bransford and Johnson (1972) read this passage to subjects and gave them a title ("Washing Clothes") either before they read, after they read, or not at all. Subjects were asked to rate the passage on "comprehension" (with 1 indicating hard to comprehend and 7 indicating easy to comprehend) and to recall it. As shown in Box 8-14, subjects who were not given the topic (title) or were given it after they read the passage rated the passage as low in comprehensibility and recalled little of the information, while subjects given the topic before they read the passage rated the passage as much more comprehensible and recalled more than twice as much information.

BOX 8 • 15   Comprehension and Recall of the Balloons Passage

	No Context (1 Repetition)	Context After	Context Before	Maximum Score
Comprehension ratings	2.30	3.30	6.10	7.00
Number of idea units recalled	3.60	3.60	8.00	14.00

Adapted from Bransford and Johnson (1972)

Similarly, Bransford and Johnson (1972) asked subjects to read the "Balloons Passage" in Box 8-1 with no picture, a picture given before, or the picture given after reading. Box 8-15 shows that comprehension ratings and amount recalled were about twice as high in the "before" group compared to the other groups. Dooling and Lachman (1971) and Dooling and Mullet (1973) obtained similar results; presenting a title before an ambiguous passage aided recall, but presenting the title after the passage did not. Apparently, the title provides a context so that the reader can relate the new information to appropriate previous experience.

A study by Wittrock, Marks, and Doctorow (1975) suggests that subjects try to find familiar elements in the passage. For example, subjects were asked to read or listen to stories and then were given retention tests. For some subjects the major words in the story were all high-frequency, familiar words. For other subjects, low-frequency, unfamiliar words were substituted for the familiar words in the passage. For example, a familiar sentence was: "I saw that the flowers and leaves of the mirror were moving." The same sentence with unfamiliar words: "I saw that the blossoms and leaves of the mirror were stirring." On the subsequent retention test, subjects performed twice as well if they had read the familiarly worded passage compared to the unfamiliarly worded passage. Apparently, the unfamiliar words prevented subjects from finding an appropriate schema or context for interpreting the story.

As another example, consider the passage in the top of Box 8-16. As you read this passage, you may notice that it could have two different themes—it could be a story about a card game or a story about a musicians' jam session. Anderson, Reynolds, Schallert, and Goetz (1977) presented this passage to two groups of subjects: physical education majors and music majors. Results shown in the bottom of Box 8-16 indicated that the music students tended to interpret it as

BOX 8 • 16   Two Ambiguous Passages

Card/Music Passage

Every Saturday night, four good friends get together. When Jerry, Mike, and Pat arrived, Karen was sitting in her living room writing some notes. She quickly gathered the cards and stood up to greet her friends at the door. They followed her into the living room but as usual they couldn't agree on exactly what to play. Jerry eventually took a stand and set things up. Finally, they began to play. Karen's recorder filled the room with soft and pleasant music. Early in the evening, Mike noticed Pat's hand and the many diamonds. As the night progressed the tempo of play increased. Finally, a lull in the activities occurred. Taking advantage of this, Jerry pondered the arrangement in front of him. Mike interrupted Jerry's reverie and said, "Let's hear the score." They listened carefully and commented on their performance. When the comments were all heard, exhausted but happy, Karen's friends went home.

Prison/Wrestling Passage

Rocky slowly got up from the mat, planning his escape. He hesitated a moment and thought. Things were not going well. What bothered him most was being held, especially since the charge against him had been weak. He considered his present situation. The lock that held him was strong but he thought he could break it. He knew, however, that his timing would have to be perfect. Rocky was aware that it was because of his early roughness that he had been penalized so severely—much too severely from his point of view. The situation was becoming frustrating; the pressure had been grinding on him for too long. He was being ridden unmercifully. Rocky was getting angry now. He felt he was ready to make his move. He knew that his success or failure would depend on what he did in the next few seconds.

Mean Percentage Correct on Multiple Choice Tests

	Subject's Background	
Passage	Physical Education	Music
Prison/Wrestling	64%	28%
Card/Music	29%	71%

Adapted from Anderson, Reynolds, Schallert, and Goetz (1977).
Copyright © 1977 by American Educational Research Association, Washington, D.C.

about music and remembered things that were consistent with a jam session, while the other subjects were more likely to take the card game perspective and remembered items consistent with card playing. For another passage that could be interpreted as a wrestling match or a prison episode, physical education students were more likely than music majors to remember elements that were consistent with the wrestling theme. Apparently, subjects come to the

BOX 8 ▪ 17   The House Passage

The two boys ran until they came to the driveway. "See, I told you today was good for skipping school," said Mark. "Mom is never home on Thursday," he added. Tall hedges hid the house from the road so the pair strolled across the finely landscaped yard. "I never knew your place was so big," said Pete. "Yeah, but it's nicer now than it used to be since Dad had the new stone siding put on and added the fireplace."

There were front and back doors and a side door which led to the garage which was empty except for three parked 10-speed bikes. They went in the side door, Mark explaining that is was always open in case his younger sisters got home earlier than their mother.

Pete wanted to see the house so Mark started with the living room. It, like the rest of the downstairs, was newly painted. Mark turned on the stereo, the noise of which worried Pete. "Don't worry, the nearest house is a quarter of a mile away," Mark shouted. Pete felt more comfortable observing that no houses could be seen in any direction beyond the huge yard.

The dining room, with all the china, silver and cut glass, was no place to play so the boys moved into the kitchen where they made sandwiches. Mark said they wouldn't go to the basement because it had been damp and musty ever since the new plumbing had been installed.

"This is where my Dad keeps his famous paintings and his coin collection," Mark said as they peered into the den. Mark bragged that he could get spending money whenever he needed it since he'd discovered that his Dad kept a lot in the desk drawer.

There were three upstairs bedrooms. Mark showed Pete his mother's closet which was filled with furs and the locked box which held her jewels. His sisters' room was uninteresting except for the color TV which Mark carried to his room. Mark bragged that the bathroom in the hall was his since one had been added to his sisters' room for their use. The big highlight in his room, though, was a leak in the ceiling where the old roof had finally rotted.

From Pichert and Anderson (1977)

experiment with individual schemas that may differ from person to person. Similar results have been reported by other researchers (Bransford, 1979; Pichert & Anderson, 1977; Mayer, 1987a; Schallert, 1976).

The foregoing results demonstrate that sometimes a passage may be difficult to understand because the underlying schema is not obvious or because the perspective of the writer is different from the perspective of the reader. In one study, Pichert and Anderson (1977) manipulated readers' perspectives. Subjects were asked to read the passage about a house shown in Box 8-17. Some subjects were told to take the perspective of a potential homebuyer; other subjects were told to take the perspective of a burglar; others were given no special instructions concerning how to read the passage. Results indicated that subjects' recall was influenced by their perspectives. Details that may be important for one perspective—such as where Dad keeps his coin collection—are not important for other perspectives. Thus the pattern of recall depended both on the information in the passage and on the reader's perspective.

USING METACOGNITIVE KNOWLEDGE

Metacognition refers to an awareness of one's own cognitive processing. A crucial metacognitive process involved in understanding passages is *comprehension monitoring*—the reader's awareness of whether or not she understands what she is reading. If you have good comprehension-monitoring skills, you are continually asking yourself "Does this make sense?" as you read a passage.

Brown, Campione, and Day (1981) have noted that metacognitive skills such as comprehension monitoring, although rarely taught to young readers, are required for effective reading comprehension. For example, Markman (1979) read short stories that contained explicit or implicit inconsistencies to elementary school children, as exemplified in Box 8-18. The children were asked to point out inconsistencies in the stories and were prompted with questions such as "Did I forget to tell you anything?" and "Did everything make sense?" The results showed that half the children recognized explicit inconsistencies but almost none recognized implicit inconsistencies.

Apparently, children do not seem to engage in comprehension monitoring under most circumstances. Two possible explanations are (1) *availability deficiency*—children lack comprehension-monitoring skills, and (2) *production deficiency*—children possess the skills but do not know when to use them. To examine this issue, Markman (1979) conducted a follow-up study in which third- and sixth-graders listened to passages such as those in Box 8-18. Half the children were given the same instructions as in the previously described study, and the other half were told: "There is something tricky about each of the essays, something which does not make sense, something which is confusing. I would like you to try to spot the problem with the essay and tell me what it was that did not make any sense." The new instructions did not greatly improve the performance of the third-graders in finding implicit or explicit inconsistencies, but they did greatly help sixth-graders to find both kinds of inconsistencies. Apparently the younger children lacked comprehension-monitoring skills (availability deficiency) whereas the older children simply did not know when to use the comprehension-monitoring skills they possessed (production deficiency).

These results suggest a developmental trend in which more experienced readers are better able to spontaneously recognize inconsistencies in passages. A prediction we could make is that skilled readers will spend more time reading a sentence if it conflicts with previously presented information. To test this issue, Baker and Anderson (1982) asked college students to read passages that were

BOX 8 ▪ 18   Passages That Require Comprehension Monitoring

A Passage with an Explicit Inconsistency

Many different kinds of fish live in the ocean. Some fish have heads that make them look like alligators, and some fish have heads that make them look like cats. Fish live in different parts of the ocean. Some fish live near the surface of the water, but some fish live way down at the bottom of the ocean. *Fish must have light in order to see. There is absolutely no light at the bottom of the ocean. It is pitch black down there. When it is that dark the fish cannot see anything. They cannot even see colors. Some fish that live at the bottom of the ocean can see the color of their food; that is how they know what to eat.*

A Passage with an Implicit Inconsistency

Many different kinds of fish live in the ocean. Some fish have heads that make them look like alligators, and some fish have heads that make them look like cats. Fish live in different parts of the ocean. Some fish live near the surface of the water, but some fish live way down at the bottom of the ocean. *There is absolutely no light at the bottom of the ocean. Some fish that live at the bottom of the ocean know their food by its color. They will only eat red fungus.*

From Markman (1979)

---

presented on a computer terminal, one sentence at a time. The subject could press one button to move on to the next sentence and a different button to move back to the previous sentence. The results showed that these skilled readers spent more time reading a sentence that conflicted with previously presented information than reading the same sentence when it appeared in a consistent passage. Furthermore, the readers were far more likely to look back when an inconsistent sentence appeared than for the same sentence when it was in a consistent passage. These results present a picture of readers who possess comprehension-monitoring skills and know when to use them. Again, we see that skilled readers are actively engaged in trying to make sense out what they read.

■
EVALUATION
■

The term *schema* has become increasingly popular in explanations of how people understand and remember verbal information. Many early theorists such as Piaget and Bartlett popularized the term, but they seldom provided complete definitions. Other theorists have invented their own terms, such as *scripts* (Schank & Abelson, 1977), *frames* (Minsky, 1975), and *anchoring ideas* (Ausubel, 1968), to refer to various specialized meanings.

In spite of the widespread use of the jargon of schema theory, you could well ask, Has work on schema theory, such as that reviewed in this chapter, served to clarify earlier notions such as Bartlett's "schema"? Critics claim that the answer is No. For example, "I do not think that talking about 'schema' or 'schemata' or 'frameworks' does much that 'tuning' does not or that 'gestalt' did not" (Scriven, 1977; p. 60). Some critics even claim that the empirical support for schema theory is lacking and "is best forgotten" (Zangwill, 1972).

In response to these criticisms of a lack of precise definition and lack of empirical support, schema theory may plead guilty to the first charge but must certainly protest its innocence to the second. As Klatzky (1980, p. 216) has pointed out: "Whether we call them scripts, frames, or schemata, evidence for knowledge structures representing complex events is compelling." This chapter has reviewed some of the consistently clear results of research on schema theory. People tend to remember (1) the gist of a passage rather than the verbatim content, (2) important information better than unimportant information, and (3) information that is consistent with their perspective better than information that does not fit their perspective. These kinds of findings help show that humans do not learn and remember like machines; we are not passive tape recorders or computer memories that copy the exact words as presented. Instead, the act of understanding involves an act of problem solving—what Bartlett called "an effort after meaning." Thanks to recent research on schema theory, we now know more about what is involved in "effort after meaning" than we did thirty years ago. In addition, ongoing work on computer simulation of schemas may allow for even more precise descriptions.

Suggested Readings

BARTLETT, F. C. (1932). *Remembering: A study in experimental and social psychology.* London: Cambridge University Press. Presents research and theory that helped shape modern cognitive psychology, including the classic "War of the Ghosts" study.

JUST, M. A., & CARPENTER, P. A. (1987). *The psychology of reading and language comprehension.* Boston: Allyn & Bacon. Surveys recent research on how people comprehend sentences and passages.

VAN DIJK, T. A., & KINTSCH, W. (1983). *Strategies of discourse comprehension.* New York: Academic Press. Presents a coherent theory of reading comprehension.

CHAPTER · 9

QUESTION ANSWERING

Thinking as a Search of Semantic Memory

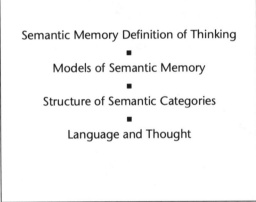

Semantic Memory Definition of Thinking

·

Models of Semantic Memory

·

Structure of Semantic Categories

·

Language and Thought

QUESTION ANSWERING TASK

How do people understand and retrieve the answers to questions? Look at the following question and then try to describe how you went about answering it.

Query: In the house you lived in three houses ago, how many windows were there on the north side?

BOX 9 • 1   Hypothetical Protocol for the Query "What Were You Doing?"

1. Come on. How should I know? (Experimenter: Just try it anyhow.)
2. O.K. Let's see. Two years . . .
3. I would be in high school in Pittsburgh . . .
4. That would be my senior year.
5. Third week in September—that's just after summer—that would be the fall term . . .
6. Let me see. I think I had chemistry lab on Mondays.
7. I don't know. I was probably in the chemistry lab . . .
8. Wait a minute—that would be the second week of school. I remember he started off with the atomic table—a big fancy chart. I thought he was crazy, trying to make us memorize that thing.
9. You know, I think I can remember sitting . . .

From Lindsay and Norman (1972, p. 379)

Rumelhart, Lindsay, and Norman (1972) found that most people are able to solve this problem; they do so by first visualizing their present dwelling, then moving back in time to visualize their previous homes, determining the north wall, and counting the windows.

Although this example may tap a trivial piece of information, it does point to the amazing ability we have to use our memories to answer questions. Let's try another one.

Query: What were you doing on Monday afternoon of the third week of September two years ago?

A hypothetical set of responses given by Lindsay and Norman (1972) is shown in Box 9-1. How does this protocol mesh with yours? The interesting aspect of such examples is that human beings are capable of answering a wide variety of complex questions and that we do so not always by direct recall but by working on a series of subquestions that bring us progressively closer to the answer. In observing the process of question answering, Lindsay and Norman were struck by the observation that their subjects engaged in productive thinking, and thus it was possible to discuss "retrieval as problem solving." The problem for psychologists, of course, is to describe how this process of answering questions occurs.

Let's try one last question.

Query: Draw a diagram of the floor plan of your place of residence.

In a typical study conducted by Kovarsky and Eisenstadt (cited by Anderson & Bower, 1973), the errors made by graduate students who had occupied the same apartments for years did not occur randomly but were systematic. A common error was for the students to include structural features that were part of most apartments but not of their own particular dwelling. One possible conclusion that may be reached is that in recall we tend to rely primarily on our general experiences or knowledge rather than entirely on specifics. Were there any such errors in your diagram?

■
SEMANTIC MEMORY THEORY DEFINITION OF THINKING
■

Chapters 8 and 9 are both concerned with the role of memory structures in problem solving. Both chapters deal with the structure of knowledge in memory, and the idea of schematic memory representation. Chapter 8 emphasized thinking as the formation of a schematic representation, but this chapter emphasizes thinking as a search and retrieval from the store of meaningful knowledge that we call *semantic memory.*

Since problem solving depends on how knowledge is organized in memory, the nature of memory representation is a particularly important issue. When we ask people a question on a subject on which they are knowledgeable, there are several aspects of the recall task that we as psychologists may be interested in: How is the information represented in memory, and how is it retrieved? Thus in this chapter we can view problem solving as a process in which people search their existing knowledge in response to a problem.

This chapter focuses mainly on how people organize and process information about categories of things. Previously we explored how people learn concepts, or learn to form categories, but we did not describe how category information is stored or processed in memory. This chapter is an extension of earlier work in concept learning; however, the focus in this chapter is on how category information is stored in memory and how it is processed when answering questions.

■
MODELS OF SEMANTIC MEMORY
■

TIP-OF-THE-TONGUE PHENOMENA

This section focuses on recall of one's general knowledge. Consider the following dictionary definition and try to think of the word it defines:

"A navigational instrument used in measuring angular distances, especially the altitude of the sun, moon, and the stars at sea."

If the answer does not immediately come to you, try to answer the following questions: What is the first letter of the word? How many syllables does the word have?

If you are ready to give up, the answer is *sextant*.

Brown and McNeil (1966) gave a series of these problems to subjects in a laboratory setting and found that sometimes the answer came right away, sometimes the subjects had no idea what to say, and in a number of cases subjects were "seized" by a tip-of-the-tongue (TOT) state. In this state the subjects felt that they were on the verge of finding the answer but had not yet found it; they were in a "mild torment, something like the brink of a sneeze." Brown and McNeil were particularly interested in these cases of TOT, and, in fact, were trying to induce them as a way of studying the structure of human memory and the process of answering questions. The subjects were asked to describe their thought processes aloud; in addition, they were asked the two specific questions given earlier while they were in the TOT state: What is the first letter of the word? How many syllables does it have?

In a typical study, fifty-seven instances of the TOT state were induced, and while the subjects "could not for the life of them" state the specific word, they were amazingly accurate at "guessing" the first letter (51 percent correct) and the number of syllables (47 percent correct). Brown and McNeil concluded that in the course of searching one's memory for a piece of information, *generic* recall (or a general memory) may precede the *specific* recall of a word, especially when specific recall is felt to be imminent. (Note the similarity to Duncker's view of problem solving as discussed in Chapter 3.)

This type of task, which we could call *question answering*, provides another important approach to understanding human thinking and problem solving. By emphasizing the role of memory structure, this approach views problem solving as a search of one's meaningful memory. The goal suggested by this view is to develop a theory of how complex information is organized in meaningful fashion in human memory and what processes are used to retrieve it to answer questions.

Since Brown and McNeil obtained their intriguing results, a number of psychologists have proposed very detailed and precise theories of how human beings organize particular sets of knowledge about the world. These theories have been called *models of semantic memory* because they try to represent how meaningful—that is, semantic—knowledge is stored and used. The basic types of models of semantic memory are:

Network models—which are based on the idea that memory is made up of elements and the associations among them; this view goes beyond the early associationist ideas in that (1) the relations may be of many types, (2) the units are meaningful concepts, and (3) the theories can be tested.

Feature models—which are based on the idea that memory is made up of fea tures that belong to sets and sets that belong to larger or supersets, and so on.

The basic method used to test these theories is called the *reaction time method,* in which subjects are asked to press a Yes or No button in response to questions about their general knowledge; for example, "Is a collie a dog?" The time to respond is measured in milliseconds (thousandths of a second), and the results are interpreted on the basis of the simple idea that more time means more processes or deeper processes were performed.

NETWORK MODELS OF SEMANTIC MEMORY

One of the first popular network models was called the *teachable language comprehender,* or TLC (Collins & Quillian, 1969, 1972). Although these researchers have revised and amended the specifics of their original model, their goal has been to develop a computer program that simulates how human beings answer factual questions. (The computer simulation approach is discussed more fully in Chapter 5.) According to one version of TLC, the structure of semantic memory is based on:

Units—words that represent one thing or subject

Properties—words that represent characteristics of the unit

Pointers—associations of various types among units and properties

An example of the knowledge a hypothetical adult has about certain animals is given in Box 9-2. In this case, words such as *animal, bird,* and *canary* represent units, whereas word combinations such as *is yellow, has wings, has skin* represent properties, and the arrows represent pointers. According to this hierarchical structure, the properties or characteristics of a unit at any one level apply to things connected by pointers at lower levels. In other words, a bird has wings and so does a canary, but the property of having wings is stored only with the higher unit, *bird;* it cannot be stored with *animals* because some animals do not have wings.

According to TLC, the process a hypothetical person uses to respond to the truth or falsity of a statement such as "A canary has skin" is a search process:

1. Find the unit for the target word, *canary.*

2. Check to see if the property, *has skin,* is stored with that unit; if not, follow

BOX 9 • 2   Hypothetical Adult's Knowledge About Animals: A Network Hierarchy

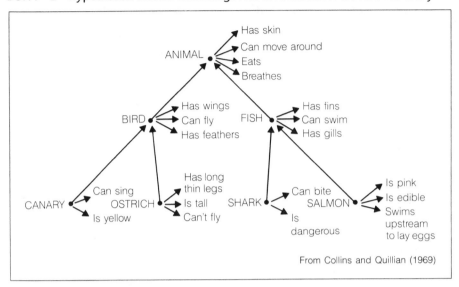

From Collins and Quillian (1969)

the pointer to the next higher level on the hierarchy, *bird,* and continue as needed to *animal.*

3.   When the pointers lead to a unit that has the target property, respond Yes.

It is a bit more difficult to describe how subjects decide how to respond No to a sentence such as "A canary has fins," but one idea is that subjects terminate their search and give the No answer if they fail to reach the unit with the target property within a certain time period.

While formal models like Collins and Quillian's are elegant and plausible, in order to be useful they must also be testable. Fortunately, this model does offer certain predictions; for example, sentences that require working on just one level of the hierarchy (a canary can sing) should require less processing time than two-level problems (a canary can fly), and a three-level problem (a canary has skin) should take the longest processing time. In order to test these predictions, Collins and Quillian asked their subjects to press a button labeled True or False in response to sentences based on hierarchies such as are shown in Box 9-3. Both true and false statements were presented, but of primary interest was the time it took subjects to respond to various true sentences. You can see that the more levels there were, the longer the response time; it took a particularly long time to answer False.

BOX 9 • 3   Reaction Times for Answering Questions About Animals

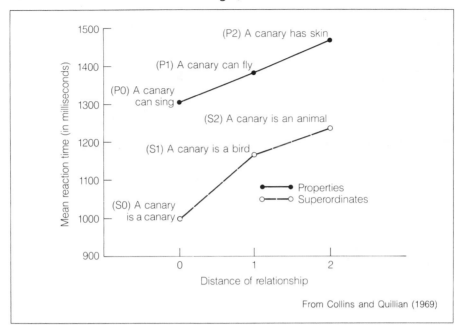

From Collins and Quillian (1969)

The results just described can be called a *category size effect* because response time for questions like "Is an X a Y?" increases as you increase the size of the Y category. Although the network model of Collins and Quillian is consistent with the category size effect, it is certainly not the only explanation for such findings. For example, Landauer and Meyer (1972) were able to replicate the category size effect, but they argued that the results could be explained by a theory of feature sets. More features must be tested when you retrieve from a larger category. One piece of evidence that seems to support the feature theory is that more time is required to answer false sentences if they involve a large category—for example, "A cliff is an animal"—than if they involve a small category—"A cliff is a dog." This alternative theory is described in the next section.

There are also several serious problems with the predictions of the Collins and Quillian model. First, the model proposes a logical hierarchy and predicts that response time will be longer for such statements as "A collie is an animal" than for "A collie is a mammal." However, the opposite seems to be the case (Rips, Shoben, & Smith, 1973). Apparently, the fact that collies belong to the mammal category is not as well established in most people's memories as it is in the logical hierarchy of Collins and Quillian. Second, Collins and Quillian propose a "cognitive economy" in which a feature will be stored only at the highest possible level in the hierarchy. For example, a feature like *can move* should be stored with *animal* rather than at lower levels such as *dog* or *collie*. However, Conrad (1972) showed that subjects could answer questions about features like *can move* equally quickly for various levels in the hierarchy. Third, Collins and Quillian predict that response time should be the same for all questions that involve the same number of levels, such as "A robin is a bird" and "An ostrich is a bird." But Rips, Shoben, and Smith (1973) and Rosch (1973) found that response time was faster for typical examples (such as *robin*) than for nontypical ones (such as *ostrich*). Thus there is evidence that contradicts almost all of the basic assumptions of the Collins and Quillian model.

Does this mean that Collins and Quillian's model was a failure? To the contrary, their model helped generate a great deal of research and helped give birth to the alternative theories discussed in the next section. In addition, Collins and Loftus (1975) have been able to modify the original model so that it can now account for each of the phenomena just considered. The new revised network model is called *a spreading activation model*. Although the new model is still made up of nodes and relations, as are all network models, the rigid hierarchical structure has been eliminated. In addition, the links may vary in type and in importance. Question answering involves starting at the nodes that are mentioned in the question and slowly spreading out from those nodes.

More recently, Anderson (1976, 1983) has created a model of memory called ACT. The model involves two distinct kinds of knowledge: *declarative knowledge,* such as a factual sentence, and *procedural knowledge,* such as a list for how to do some task. Declarative knowledge can be represented as a network and procedural knowledge as a list of production rules (as described in Chapter 6). Similarly, memory networks are at the heart of recent advances in *parallel distributed processing (PDP) models,* which have been used to model processes ranging from perception to motor control (Hinton & Anderson, 1989; McClelland et al., 1986; Rumelhart et al., 1986). Although adequate descriptions of ACT and of PDP models are beyond the scope of this book, there is already some evidence that these models can account for inferences that people make in order to be able to answer questions.

FEATURE MODELS OF SEMANTIC MEMORY

Although network models are currently the most numerous, there are other ways of representing semantic memory. For example, Meyer (1970) proposed a model of how subjects answer questions about semantic memory that was not based on networks at all; rather, Meyer assumed that each concept was stored in memory as a list of subsets (or features). When subjects were asked to respond to such statements as "All females are writers" or "Some females are writers" they appeared to go through the following two stages:

Stage 1: Determine all the subsets of *writer,* including male and female, and all the subsets of *female,* and see if there is any overlap, that is, if there are any subsets in common. If there are no common features (as in a sentence such as "Some typhoons are wheat") answer False; if there are some common features (for example, writers and females), answer True if the statement calls for "some," and go on to stage 2 if it calls for "all."

Stage 2: Is each subset of *writer* also a subset of *female*? If yes, answer True, if no, answer False.

Meyer's theory predicted that it would take longer for the subjects to respond to problems of the form "All S are P" than "Some S are P" because two stages were required for the former and only one stage for the latter. Like Collins and Quillian, Meyer predicted that response time would increase if the size of category P was increased, because the list of subsets would now be longer. Meyer used experiments similar to those of Collins and Quillian and obtained results consistent with his (as well as Collins and Quillian's) model. However, while the Meyer model based on sets may be just as powerful as Collins and Quillian's network model, neither model can explain results such as why it would take longer to answer questions about whether a dog is a mammal than about whether a dog is an animal.

Rips and colleagues (1973: Smith, Shoben, & Rips, 1974) have developed a set model of semantic memory that accounts for such findings. The main new ingredient in their model was based on a skepticism of Collins and Quillian's assumption that "memory structure mirrors logical structure." In one study, Rips and colleagues (1973) asked a group of subjects to rate pairs of words in terms of how closely related they were to one another, in order to derive a measure of "semantic distance." For example, they asked the subjects to rate how closely related various kinds of birds were to each other, to the category *bird,* and to the category *animal* or how closely related various mammals were to each other, to the category *mammal,* and to the category *animal.* The chart that is shown in Box 9-4 was derived from the ratings: note that high relatedness is represented by short distance.

This method of representing semantic memory predicts that reaction time judgments like those used by Collins and Quillian should be related to semantic distance, and these predictions have been upheld. In other words, according to the semantic distance idea, the reason it takes longer to press the True button for *robin–animal* than *robin–bird* or longer for *dog–mammal* than *dog–animal* is that the actual semantic distance is greater from *dog* to *mammal* than from *dog* to

BOX 9 • 4   Adults' Knowledge About Animals: A Semantic Distance Chart

The following chart is based on subjects' ratings of how closely pairs of words are related. Short distances represent high relatedness.

From Rips, Shoben, and Smith (1973)

animal (regardless of logical structure) or from *robin* to *animal* than from *robin* to *bird*. These researchers have further argued that semantic distance is basically a function of how many semantic features the two concepts have in common, or of how much overlap there is between the list of features that make up the sets.

According to the *feature comparison model* proposed by Smith, Shoben, and Rips (1974), each concept in our memory is associated with a list of features. Some features, called *defining features,* are crucial to the meaning of the concept. For example, *has wings* and *has feathers* may be defining features of birds, since they are important aspects of the category's definition. Other features, called *characteristic features,* are less important. For example, *eats worms* or *builds nests* may be characteristic features of birds, since many but not all birds possess these features. An example of some of the features of the concepts *bird, robin,* and *ostrich* are given in Box 9-5.

What happens when you answer a question such as "Is a robin a bird?" According to the feature comparison model, you go through two stages as indicated in Box 9-5. First you find the list of features in your memory for the two words in the question, such as the features for *bird* and for *robin.* Then you compare the lists. If they are very similar (as they would be for *robin* and *bird*) you

BOX 9 ▪ 5   Feature Comparison Model

Knowledge in Subject's Memory

Birds: flies, eats worms, is small, has feathers*, has wings*, builds nests, lives in trees

Robin: flies, eats worms, is small, has feathers*, has wings*, has red breast*, chirps, builds nests

Ostrich: can put head in the sand*, is tall, is clumsy, has wings*, has feathers*

*indicates defining feature.

Feature Comparison Process

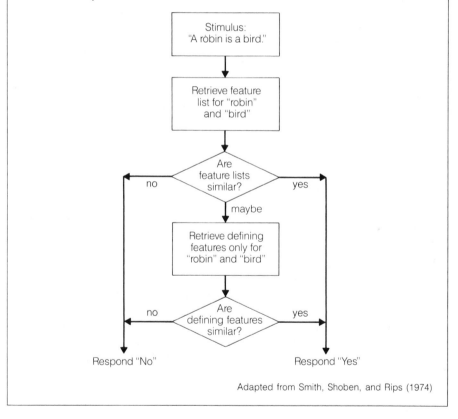

Adapted from Smith, Shoben, and Rips (1974)

---

answer Yes; if they are very different (as they would be for dog and *robin*) you answer No. However, if there is just a moderate degree of overlap, you need to process more completely by comparing the defining features of both words. For example, a question like "Is an ostrich a bird?" might create only moderate overlap, but when you look only at defining features you can answer Yes. This model overcomes each of the problems of the Collins and Quillian model described earlier. However, some researchers (such as Rosch, 1973, 1975) have questioned the need to make a distinction between defining and characteristic features.

■
STRUCTURE OF SEMANTIC CATEGORIES
■

The network and set feature models represent two different views of how we use categories in our thinking. More recently, Rosch (1978) has extended the set feature approach by focusing on the nature of the categories we use in our everyday lives. Rosch (1978) argues that categories are used to help us process information more effectively. This same line of argument was proposed by Bruner, Goodnow, and Austin (1956, p. 1) as an introduction to some of the first research on human concept learning:

> We begin with what seems a paradox. The world of experience of any normal man is composed of a tremendous array of discriminably different objects, events, people, impressions. There are estimated to be more then 7 million discriminable colors alone. . . . But were we to utilize fully our capacity for registering the differences in things and to respond to each event encountered as unique, we would soon be overwhelmed by the complexity of our environment. Consider only the linguistic task of acquiring a vocabulary fully adequate to cope with the world of color differences. The resolution of this seeming paradox—the existence of discrimination capacities which, if fully used, would make us slaves to the particular—is achieved by man's capacity to categorize.

Previous work on concept learning provided some information about how people categorize artificial stimuli such as geometric shapes or dot patterns. In this section, we explore how the categorization process may be applied to objects in our natural environment.

GOODNESS OF FIT

The categories that we normally use in our everyday lives—let's call these *natural categories*—are different from the categories we learn about in mathematical set theory. For example, a precise mathematical set such as the set of all squares includes every figure that corresponds to the definition of square; every figure is either in this category or not in it, and all squares are equally members of the category. However, natural categories do not seem to have such firm boundaries; instead, the border lines of a natural category are what Rosch (1973) calls "fuzzy." For example, think of the category for fruit. Some examples, such as apple or orange, seem to fit right into the category. Other examples, such as avocado or coconut, may not seem to be as typical. Thus, when we answer questions about natural categories, we are not dealing with mathematically precise sets, but rather with fuzzy sets. The "goodness of fit" of a concept refers to how well it fits into a category.

To study the structure of natural categories, Rosch presented subjects with a category name along with names for possible examples of the category. For example, in one study (Rosch, 1975) the examples for fruit were orange, coconut, and all the other words listed in part of Box 9-6. The subjects' job was to rate each word according to "how good an example of a category" it was on a scale of 1 to 7; they considered how typical *apple* was for the category *fruit* and so on. Subjects rated fifty to sixty words for each of ten categories, such as *vegetable, tool, bird,* and *sport*. Results of the rating task for fruit and furniture categories are given in Box 9-6. Some words were rated as being good examples of a category, while others were not typical. Thus, unlike mathematical sets, all members of a natural category do not seem to be equal. In addition, Rosch found that subjects were able to perform the rating task with a very high level of agreement, suggesting that there is social consensus about the structure of common categories.

What effect does the fuzzy nature of categories have on performance in answering questions? To study this issue, Rosch (1973) asked children and adult subjects to answer questions of the form "Is an apple a fruit?" For some questions, the example was a typical one (such as *apple*) and for others the example was not typical (such as *coconut*). As you can see in Box 9-7, the time to respond was faster for good examples than for poor examples. The effect was strongest for children but was also clearly present in adults. In another study, Rosch (1975) presented two words on each trial and asked subjects to tell whether the words belonged to the same category or to different categories. Some pairs contained words that were good examples of the category (for example, *table* and *bed*), some were medium (*lamp* and *stool*), and some were poor examples (*rug* and *fan*). As in the previous study, more time is required when the words are not good examples of their category. Thus these experiments show that people are faster at answering questions about typical members of a category than they are about members that are at a category's fuzzy boundaries.

FAMILY RESEMBLANCE

Let's return to our comparison of natural categories and artificial sets. In an artificial set, such as the set of all squares, there is one rule that defines the members of the set. Every example must have the same set of features, such as *four sides, all sides of equal length,* and *all angles at 90 degrees*. There is less

BOX 9 • 6   Goodness-of-Example Ratings for Furniture and Fruits

Member	Goodness of Example			Goodness of Example	
	Rank	Specific Score		Rank	Specific Score
Furniture					
chair	1.5	1.04	chaise longue	24	2.26
sofa	1.5	1.04	lamp	31	2.94
couch	3.5	1.10	stool	32	3.13
easy chair	5	1.33	piano	35	3.64
dresser	6.5	1.37	cushion	36	3.70
coffee table	8	1.38	cupboard	39	4.27
rocker	9	1.42	stereo	40	4.32
chest of drawers	11	1.48	mirror	41	4.39
desk	12	1.54	television	42	4.41
bed	13	1.58	bar	43	4.46
davenport	15.5	1.61	wastebasket	47	5.34
end table	15.5	1.61	radio	48	5.37
bookcase	22	2.15	sewing machine	49	5.39
lounge	23	2.17	stove	50	5.40
Fruit					
orange	1	1.07	lemon	20	2.16
apple	2	1.08	watermelon	23	2.39
banana	3	1.15	cantaloupe	24	2.44
peach	4	1.17	lime	25	2.45
apricot	6.5	1.36	papaya	27	2.58
tangerine	6.5	1.36	fig	29	2.86
plum	8	1.37	mango	30	2.88
grapes	9	1.38	pomegranate	32	3.05
strawberry	11	1.61	date	37	3.35
grapefruit	12	1.77	raisin	39	3.42
cherry	14	1.86	persimmon	41	3.63
pineapple	15	1.19	coconut	43	4.50
blackberry	16	2.05	avocado	44	5.37
raspberry	19	2.15	tomato	46	5.58

Note: 1 means highly typical, 7 means least typical.

agreement among attributes of all members in a natural category. What are the attributes that all fruits, all birds, or all pieces of furniture have in common? Instead of one list of common features, members of a category seem to share what

BOX 9 ▪ 7   Response Time for Category Judgments

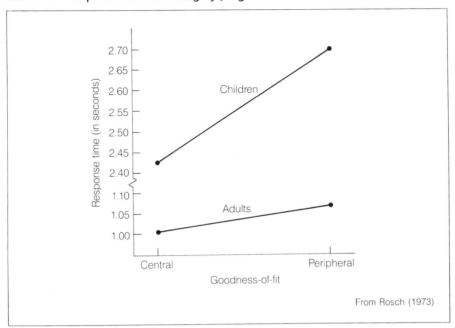

From Rosch (1973)

Rosch and Mervis (1975) call "family resemblance." By this they mean that a basic core of features for the category exists such that each example may possess some but not all of the features. For example, not all birds have the characteristic of *flying, smallness,* or *singing,* but these are features present in many birds.

.Rosch and Mervis (1975) studied the idea of family resemblance by selecting six categories with twenty examples in each category. One group of subjects was asked to list all of the attributes they could think of in 90 seconds for each of the words. Another group of subjects was asked to rate how typical each example was for its category. Results of the task of listing attributes indicated that rarely did one or two attributes define all of the members of a category. Instead of some critical features that were common to all members, Rosch and Mervis found there was a group of attributes that were present in some but not all category members. In addition, if Rosch and Mervis focused on the most typical examples in each category, there was much overlap in their attributes; if they focused on the least typical examples in each category, there were few or no attributes in common. This result is summarized in Box 9-8. Additionally, there was a strong correlation between ranking how typical a word was and ranking how many family resemblance attributes the word had. Apparently, words that had many features in common with the category were rated as more typical.

BOX 9 • 8   Number of Attributes in Common to Five Most and Five Least Typical Members of Six Categories

Category	Most Typical Members	Least Typical Members
Furniture	13	2
Vehicle	36	2
Fruit	16	0
Weapon	9	0
Vegetable	3	0
Clothing	21	0

From Rosch and Mervis (1975)

BASIC-LEVEL CATEGORIES

Finally, let's consider another aspect of natural categories—the notion that some levels of categorization are easier to think about than others. For example, Rosch, Mervis, Gray, Johnson, and Boyes-Braem (1976) have suggested that there are at least three category levels:

Superordinate level—such as *furniture*.

Basic level—such as *table*.

Subordinate level—such as *kitchen table*.

The basic level offers a way of dividing the world that provides the most information with the least cognitive effort. This level also allows us to reduce differences among all the objects in our environment without wiping out the important differences among those objects.

Rosch (1978) has summarized a variety of evidence to support the idea of basic-level categories. First, if subjects are asked to list the attributes of superordinate, basic, and subordinate categories, they list very few attributes for the superordinate category, many for the basic level, and not significantly more for the subordinate level. Apparently, the basic level is the one at which we store information about attributes of categories; getting more specific (at the subordinate level) did not add any more information about features. Second, if subjects are asked to describe motor behaviors that could be performed with objects, the basic level again elicits the largest number of responses. Apparently, our motor behaviors are coordinated with objects at the basic level. Finally, if subjects juxtapose drawings of objects, the ratio of overlap to nonoverlap is strongest at the basic level. In addition, Rosch and colleagues (1976) argue that sorting tasks are easier if the basic level is used and that children begin to learn classification at the basic level.

Newport and Bellugi (1978) have provided an interesting analysis of American Sign Language. Usually, a single sign is used for basic-level terms, such as *apple* or *car* or *piano.* Superordinate categories, such as *fruit* or *vehicle* or *musical instrument,* require the compounding of several simple signs, such as signing *apple–orange–banana* to mean *fruit.* Similarly, signs for subordinate categories require compounding signs. For example, *kitchen chair* requires the signs for *cook* and *chair.* Apparently, when we use a language that has a restricted vocabulary, humans prefer words that refer to objects at the basic level.

■
LANGUAGE AND THOUGHT
■

So far this chapter has shown that humans can think in terms of categories, such as *bird* and *robin.* However, you may be wondering where these categories come from. In particular, you might wonder whether the words in the language you speak influence the way you break the world into categories. Although psychologists have not provided much data on this issue, linguists and anthropologists have proposed the concept of *linguistic relativity*—the idea that the language one speaks influences the way one learns and thinks about the world (Sapir, 1960; Whorf, 1956). For example, based on an anthropological study of the language and culture of non-Western-language speakers (for example, the Hopi Indians of the southwestern United States), Whorf proclaimed the doctrine of linguistic relativity: "Every language and every well-knit technical sublanguage incorporates certain points of view and certain patterns resistant to widely divergent points of view" (p. 247). Further, the concepts and categories that we learn and use are also supposed to be influenced and limited by our native tongue: "We cut up and organize the spread and flow of events as we do, largely because, through our mother tongue we are parties to an agreement to do so and not because nature itself is segmented in exactly that way for all to see" (p. 240).

These ideas have profound implications for the study of human learning and cognition. One of the first experimental studies of the Whorfian hypothesis was conducted by Brown and Lenneberg (1954) and reported in their now famous paper, "A Study of Language and Cognition." Brown and Lenneberg began by selecting 240 color chips from the *Munsell Book of Color,* a catalogue similar to the color charts for house paint colors. Then they asked five judges to pick the best examples of red, orange, yellow, green, blue, purple, pink, and brown from the set of 240 colors. There was high agreement among the judges. Brown (1976, p. 131), reminiscing about the experiment, reports that the colors looked quite familiar: "I remember thinking that there was something uncanny about the 8 best instances, and indeed, about the chips in the immediate neighborhood of each. I can see them still, that good Gulf orange, that Ticonderoga pencil yellow, that blood red; they all of them shine through the years like so many jewels." To these colors, Brown and Lenneberg added 16 "filler" color chips, which were spaced as evenly as possible within the other 8. Of these filler colors, however, Brown reports that he has no vivid visual memory.

Armed with the full array of 24 colors (8 distinctive and 16 filler), Brown and Lenneberg presented them to college subjects and asked them to name the colors. For each of the 8 basic colors, the subjects tended to use a single word, and they tended to agree on the word; for the other colors, they used modifiers, such as "light green," and there was much less agreement among them. Codability scores were determined for each color and then new, different subjects were given a recognition task. They were shown a color chip (or a set of them) for a few seconds, then after some delay, were asked to point out the color from an array of 120 colors. The results indicated a moderately high correlation between codability and recognition: the colors that could be easily named were also easier to remember.

These results seemed to support the Whorfian notion of linguistic relativity, because the availability of names for colors apparently influenced a cognitive task such as remembering stimuli. The colors used in the experiment formed a natural continuum based on wavelength, but language artificially "cut up" the colors into categories such as those shown in Box 9-9.

In an attempt to further explore the Whorfian hypothesis, Heider (1970, 1972; Heider & Oliver, 1972) investigated the color memory task in different cultures. For example, the Dani tribe of Indonesian New Guinea are a Stone Age people with only two basic color words—*mili* for dark or cold colors and *mola* for bright and warm colors. The Dani people can, of course, talk about other colors, but they must use longer descriptive phrases. According to the Whorfian idea, two colors that happen to fall in different categories in English should be easier for the Dani to remember if they also fall in the two separate Dani categories rather than in the same category; results, however, indicated no difference. A more striking disconfirmation of the Whorfian hypothesis comes from a study of several non-European languages. Colors that were easy to name in English were easier to remember for English speakers (as Brown and Lenneberg had found) but they were also easier to remember for speakers of every other language, including languages such as Dani, even though no specific words for the colors existed.

The chart in Box 9-10 gives a list of the order in which color names appear in languages based on a study of ninety-eight different languages (Berlin & Kay, 1969). The figure shows that although languages differ in how many basic color terms are provided (ranging from two to twelve), there is a universal pattern: if

BOX 9 · 9   Frequency of Names Given by English Speakers to Various Color Chips

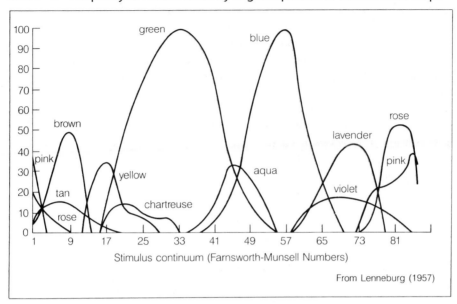

From Lenneburg (1957)

BOX 9 · 10   Universal Order of Evolution of Color Terms in 98 Languages

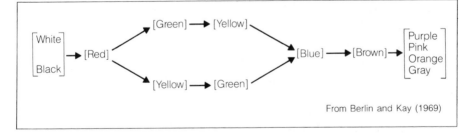

From Berlin and Kay (1969)

two words are used, they signify black and white; if three are used, red is added: if five are used, green and yellow are added, and so on, up to twelve basic color words used frequently in English. These twelve are called "focal" colors and Heider's (now called Rosch's) results show that focal colors are remembered better than others, regardless of whether the learner's language has specific names for them. As Brown (1976, p. 125) pointed out in a recent review of this work, the

Whorfian hypothesis has been turned inside out—apparently, at least for colors, there are "natural categories that are shared by all humans with normal color vision." Languages reflect these categories in that they all divide up the world of color in the same way, with some languages going into more detail.

Although the current state of our understanding casts doubt on the Whorfian hypothesis, there is certainly much more to language than color names. At least one research study (Carmichael et al., 1932) has shown that labeling a picture influences how it is remembered. What is particularly important and to some extent unique about the study of color categories is this: it demonstrates that cross-cultural differences in cognition can be studied experimentally and that such investigations promise to increase our understanding of our common human capacity to think and to learn.

■
EVALUATION
■

The network and feature models represent two popular attempts to describe how people structure and process their semantic knowledge. Because these models are detailed, they are useful in testing several ideas about human question answering. Among the major findings are the category effect and semantic distance effect. Similarly, the research on natural and language categories has helped to expand the traditional study of concepts (as described in Chapter 5). Apparently, principles of memory established with artificial materials must be modified when natural materials are used. Among the new findings are goodness-of-fit, family resemblance, and basic-level category effects. The movement to more commonplace situations is a promising one that may ultimately provide the key to a unified theory of semantic memory.

Unfortunately, research on semantic categories has not yet resulted in the development of a comprehensive theory of semantic memory (Medin & Smith, 1984). For example, Smith and Medin (1981, p. 182) noted in a comprehensive review that research results have not allowed us "to establish that one view of concepts is correct and rule out all others irrevocably." There is a growing consensus that future research on semantic memory needs to move beyond the confines of artificial and contrived tasks. For example, in a review of research on semantic memory, Kintsch (1980, p. 603) concludes: "We have so far not received any clear answers. The impression is unavoidable that questions have been raised in the context of a research paradigm that was simply not rich enough to provide definitive answers." In summary, although this chapter demonstrates some basic facts about how people store and use semantic knowledge, a comprehensive theory of semantic memory is still evolving.

Suggested Readings

BADDELEY, A. (1990). *Human memory: Theory and practice.* Boston: Allyn & Bacon. An up-to-date memory textbook that includes surveys of research on semantic memory and natural categories.

KINTSCH, W. (1980). Semantic memory: A tutorial. In R. S. Nickerson (Ed.), *Attention and performance VIII* (pp. 595–620). Hillsdale, NJ: Erlbaum. Reviews and critiques basic research on semantic memory.

SMITH, E. E. & MEDIN, D. L. (1981). *Categories and concepts.* Cambridge, MA: Harvard University Press. Summarizes research and theory on how humans represent knowledge about categories.

PART IV

IMPLICATIONS AND APPLICATIONS

CHAPTER 10

COGNITIVE DEVELOPMENT

Thinking as Influenced by Growth

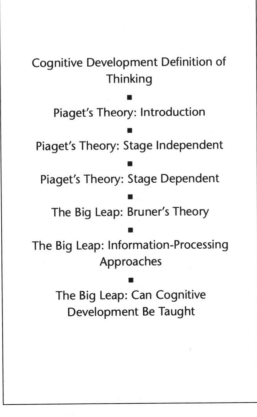

Cognitive Development Definition of Thinking

▪

Piaget's Theory: Introduction

▪

Piaget's Theory: Stage Independent

▪

Piaget's Theory: Stage Dependent

▪

The Big Leap: Bruner's Theory

▪

The Big Leap: Information-Processing Approaches

▪

The Big Leap: Can Cognitive Development Be Taught

BOX 10 • 1   Free Association Test

Give your first word association for each of the following words:

Table   _____

Dark   _____

Man   _____

Deep   _____

Soft   _____

Mountain   _____

Box 10-1 presents words for a free association task. Your job is to read each word, individually and separately, and after each write down the first word that comes to your mind. You may cover the words with a piece of paper and move it down the page one word at a time, giving your association for each word as you come to it. When you have given associations for all the words, look at Box 10-2.

This type of task has been given to subjects of varying ages, and several interesting differences in the responses related to age have been noted. For example, Box 10-2 gives the number of children and the number of adults who made each of two basic responses (Woodrow & Lowell, 1916). Don't worry if your responses seem closer to the children's norms or are so bizarre they don't appear on the table—things may have changed a bit since 1916. As Box 10-2 shows, the children tended to give words that would occur with the stimulus word in a sentence (phrase completion) and hence were generally different parts of speech, while the adults tended to give words with the same or opposite meaning and were thus from the same part of speech. More recently, similar differences were obtained by Ervin (1961), Palermo (1963), Palermo and Jenkins (1963), and Brown and Berko (1960). As an example, Palermo and Jenkins asked for associations to such words as *deep, mutton, red, live, lift, make;* the norm responses for children were, respectively, *hole, button, color, house, heavy,* and *it;* the respective norms for adults were *shallow, sheep, white, die, carry,* and *build.* Brown and Berko (1960), in noting a similar pattern in their data, suggested that the children tended to give "heterogeneous-by-part-of-speech" responses and the adults tended to give "homogeneous-by-part-of-speech" responses. The systematic differences between the responses of children and adults imply that there is a basic difference in the way words (and perhaps all concepts) are stored in memory. The fact that children tend to complete phrases suggests that they store strings of words exactly as they would be used in ordinary speech, whereas adults tend to classify words both by meaning and by part of speech. Such findings suggest that the cognitive processes of

BOX 10 ▪ 2   Word Associations for Adults and Children

Stimulus	Response	1000 Children	1000 Adults
Table	Eat	358	63
	Chair	24	274
Dark	Night	421	221
	Light	38	427
Man	Work	168	17
	Woman	8	394
Deep	Hole	257	32
	Shallow	6	180
Soft	Pillow	138	53
	Hard	27	365
Mountain	High	390	246
	Hill	91	184

Based on data from Woodrow and Lowell (1916)

BOX 10 ▪ 3   The Corplum Problem

See if you can tell what a "corplum" is:

A corplum may be used for support.

Corplums may be used to close off an open space.

A corplum may be long or short, thick or thin, strong or weak.

A wet corplum does not burn.

You can make a corplum smoother with sandpaper.

The painter used a corplum to mix his paints.

From Werner and Kaplan (1952).
Copyright 1952 by The University of Chicago Press.

children and adults differ not just in a quantitative way, in that adults know more, but also in a qualitative way, in that children may not think the same way that adults do.

Take a look at the six sentences in Box 10-3. Read each sentence and after each try to define *corplum*. Note how your definition is clarified with each new sentence and count how many sentences are required for you to "know" the meaning of *corplum*. Older children and adults are readily able to abstract the meaning of new words based on their context, but Werner and Kaplan (1952) found that younger children behaved differently. They had much more difficulty in figuring out the word's meaning; their definitions tended to be tied very closely to the context of the sentence, with the meanings of new words completely changing for each new sentence. A typical younger child listened to the sentence "People talk about the *bordicks* of others and don't like to talk about their own," and then gave the following de*finition o*f bordicks (faults): "Well, *bordick* means people talk about others and don't talk about themselves, that's what *bordick* means." Apparently, the younger children viewed each sentence separately, with the word's meaning changing from sentence to sentence, while the older children and adults could consider several contexts at once, abstracting the common meaning from all.

■

COGNITIVE DEVELOPMENT DEFINITION OF THINKING
■

According to the theories of cognitive development, thinking depends on how a person represents the world and in what ways a person can manipulate or act upon this internal representation. A major contribution of the cognitive development approach is that different ways of representing the world and different ways of manipulating those representations are present at different stages in development—for example, the way a four-year-old child represents the world is quite different from the way an adult does.

As you may have noticed, the idea that internal mental structures are the substance of our cognitive processes is closely related both to Bartlett's idea of the schema and to the Gestalt idea of organization. In fact, the best-known figure in the area of cognitive development, Jean Piaget, calls the internal mental structures or representations "schemas," and he refers to the ways we manipulate them when thinking as "operations." However, in Piaget's theory, schemas are continually growing and developing rather than remaining fixed. Describing thinking at various stages thus becomes a problem of trying to define the schema (or mental structure) and the operations (or internal actions) that a problem solver is using.

■
PIAGET'S THEORY: INTRODUCTION
■

Piaget was neither a psychologist by training nor an American, yet he has made a tremendous impact, perhaps because of his unusual perspective, on American developmental psychology. Piaget, who died in 1980, was a French-speaking Swiss, a zoologist by training and a philosopher by interest. During his career, which began in 1927, he and his associates in Geneva published the world's largest existing source of information and theories on cognitive development.

Piaget's main interest was in "genetic epistemology"—the study of the growth of knowledge in humans. As Elkind (1967) has pointed out concerning Piaget, "He is not fundamentally a child psychologist concerned with the practical issues of child growth and development. He is rather, first and foremost, a genetic epistemologist concerned with the nature of knowledge and with the structures and processes by which it is acquire" (p. xviii). However, instead of espousing armchair theories of how knowledge accumulates in the mind of a human being, he decided he would study the process empirically. Starting with the newborn infant, who presumably had very little knowledge, Piaget studied how knowledge came to be represented in the mind and how it changed with growth. Thus Piaget's study of cognitive development was intended to provide information on an important philosophical question; its effect has also been to stimulate the development of entirely new areas in psychology.

Piaget's method of study began as being mainly *clinical*—that is, he carefully observed how children behave in various real-world situations and, based on these observations, developed his theories of cognitive growth. He kept detailed diaries on the early life of each of his three children, which eventually became the basis for his books *The Origins of Intelligence in Children* (1936/1952b), *Play, Dreams and Imitation in Childhood* (1945/1951), and *The Construction of Reality in the Child* (1937/1954). Piaget's method has received a great deal of criticism on two basic accounts:

Method—The clinical method is too loose and lacks good experimental control. For example, Rosenthal and Jacobson (1968) have shown that the experimenter can influence subjects in subtle ways, such as by facial expression, without being aware of it. In addition, Piaget's method depends heavily on language concepts, which young children may not use in the same way as adults.

Theory—The theories are too general and vague. Like many of Freud's theories, they are sometimes not even testable in a clear experiment, and those theories which are testable have often been shown not to hold up (Gelman, 1969).

Yet the dozens of books and hundreds of articles by Piaget and his associates continue to stimulate and influence our view of human cognitive growth, including human thinking. Let us now turn to a brief summary of those ideas.

■
PIAGET'S THEORY: STAGE INDEPENDENT
■

Piaget's theory may be roughly divided into two parts—the enumeration of the stages of human cognitive development and the general concepts that are independent of stages.

The premise from which Piaget begins his stage-independent theory is that human beings are alive, striving to survive and to function successfully in their environments. In order to survive, they must take in information from their environments; however, out of all the possible information that exists, only a small part can be taken in by an individual since all new knowledge must be related to existing knowledge. Information from the outside world that differs greatly from a person's existing knowledge will not be understood or encoded because there is no way to relate it to the existing knowledge, just as information that is exactly the same as existing knowledge will have no influence since it adds nothing new. However, outside information that is similar, but not identical, to the existing knowledge structures will be taken in (or assimilated) by the existing mental structures. There will also be some changes in mental organization to fit (or accommodate) the new knowledge. The resulting mental structure will be a bit more sophisticated, since it includes more knowledge and thus will be able to assimilate even more complex information, restructure it to fit the new knowledge, and so on. All cognitive growth, according to this view, depends on our taking in information that is slightly different from what we already know and then restructuring our knowledge to integrate both the old and new information; this process produces an improved cognitive structure, which will help us to survive and function better.

As can be inferred from this brief description, Piaget's theory is based on several fundamental ideas:

Cognitive growth is life-based.   The accumulation of better and better modes of representing reality is accomplished to help us survive and get along in our environment.

Knowledge is mediate rather than immediate.   Our view of reality is not passively registered but is actively constructed by continually relating new information to existing knowledge.

BOX 10 ▪ 4   Piaget's Stage-Independent Theory

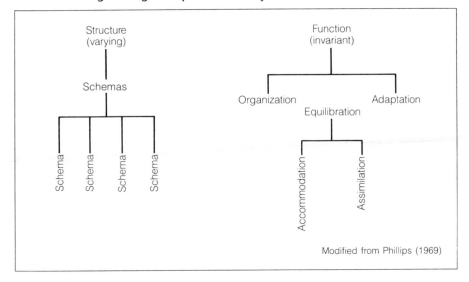

Modified from Phillips (1969)

Motivation for cognitive growth is intrinsic. Living things naturally seek out information that is just slightly more complex than their existing knowledge.

Cognitive growth is dialectic. There is a continual interaction between the desire to have a well-organized bank of knowledge (accommodation) and the need for more information (assimilation) that is continuously disrupting existing organizations and evoking slightly more sophisticated ones.

The main terms that Piaget uses to explain his stage-independent theory are given in Box 10-4. The theory is often hard for American psychologists to understand, partly because it borrows heavily from unfamiliar biological concepts, partly because it is translated from French, and partly because it is massive, sometimes vague, and difficult. However, a good understanding of some of the basic ideas he uses will help you to understand Piaget's theory. We shall discuss the following terms: *structures* and *schemas; functions, organization,* and *adaptation; equilibration, assimilation,* and *accommodation.*

According to Piaget, the way a person represents the world—the internal mental structures or schemas—changes systematically with development. If the sturctures did not change, there could be no development for there could be no growth in knowledge. For example, the infant structures information based on how the information relates to such actions as sucking. Piaget refers to the "sucking schema" to suggest that knowledge about the world is stored in the form of how objects respond to sucking.

Although cognitive structures change—we hope that adults do not represent the world solely in terms of how things taste or feel—our function as living beings remains invariant. There are two basic functions common to all biological systems: the need to stay alive and survive in our environment—*adaptation*—and the need to have well-organized and orderly internal structure—*organization*. In terms of cognitive structure, this means that we have a constant need for our representation of the world to be well organized, internally consistent, and orderly, while at the same time we have a need to bring in new information that will disrupt the internal organization but will help us better to survive and adapt to the reality of the external world.

The mechanisms for balancing this conflict between the need for organization and the need for adaptation are equilibration, assimilation, and accommodation. (See Box 10-4.) Assimilation and accommodation are called "functional invariants" because they are constantly involved in the growth of any biological system—including the growth of knowledge. Assimilation occurs whenever something from outside the system is taken in and incorporated; the most obvious example is the ingestion of food, whereby something from the environment becomes part of us. In short, input is changed to fit the existing internal structure. Accommodation is the complementary process that always must accompany assimilation—the changing of the existing internal structure to fit the newly assimilated input. Cognitive growth involves continually assimilating new knowledge and accommodating existing knowledge. Piaget cites imitation as a temporary imbalance in which accommodation overpowers assimilation and playing as a situation in which assimilation overpowers accommodation.

Most of the time, however, in a normally functioning person there is a striving for a balance between assimilation and accommodation; this balancing process is called *equilibration* and it is actually responsible for all cognitive growth. When new information is assimilated to existing structures, a process of equilibration begins. It results in a new cognitive structure—one that incorporates some of the new information but also retains some of the prior information, all organized in a more efficient way. Thus equilibration is never finished because as soon as new information is assimilated the process begins again, resulting in progressively better representations of the world.

■

PIAGET'S THEORY: STAGE DEPENDENT

■

The progressive changes in cognitive structure may vary in rate from person to person, but they follow an invariant sequence, always moving in the same order, and the progressive changes in the way children organize information can be

BOX 10 • 5   Piaget's Stage-Dependent Theory

Sensorimotor period	birth to 2 years
Preoperational period	2 to 7 years
Concrete operation period	7 to 11 years
Formal operations period	11 years to adult

characterized as a sequence of stages. The four main periods of cognitive growth are shown in Box 10-5, although in some writings preoperations and concrete operations are considered to be a single period. The ages shown are averages based on Piaget's observations, but they are only approximate and subject to large individual differences. However, the order of the four periods is fixed, and according to the theory, all human beings progress through them in the same order.

The stages are based on two aspects of cognitive life: (1) *structure*—how the child represents the world and (2) *operations*—how the child can act upon this representation. The sequence of stages thus represents progressively better cognitive structures accompanied by progressively more powerful cognitive operations.

SENSORIMOTOR PERIOD

For approximately the first two years of life, children progress through the six stages of the *sensorimotor period*. Most of Piaget's research on this period came from diaries of careful observations of his own three children—Laurent, Lucienne, and Jacqueline—that were later summarized in his classic books such as *The Origins of Intelligence in Children* (1936/1952b). At this stage the child represents the world in terms of actions—sucking, shaking, looking, dropping, and so on—and performs operations or manipulations on actual objects rather than on internal representations. The reason for the peculiar name, *sensorimotor*, is that during this period infants learn to coordinate their senses with motor behavior, such as adapting the sucking reflex to search for a nipple before sucking, coordinating the movement of the hand to the mouth, or visually following an object moving through the environment.

One of the most interesting accomplishments achieved during the sensorimotor period involves the progressive development of the concept of object permanence. At birth, the infant has no concept of object permanence: when objects are out of the visual field, they no longer exist; the only reality is

BOX 10 ▪ 6   Development of Object Permanence in the Sensorimotor Period

On the basis of careful observations of his three children—Lucienne, Laurent, and Jacqueline—Piaget concluded that the concept of object permanence develops during the first two years of life. Excerpts are given below:

7 months, 30 days. (No special behavior.)
Lucienne grasps a small doll which I present to her for the first time. She examines it with great interest, then lets go (not intentionally); she immediately looks for it in front of her but does not see it right away. When she has found it, I take it from her and place a coverlet over it, before her eyes (Lucienne is seated); no reaction.

9 months, 17 days. (Active search for vanished objects without taking account of a sequence of visual displacements.)
Laurent is placed on a sofa between a coverlet A on the right and a wool garment B on the left. I place my watch under A; he gently raises the coverlet, perceives part of the object, uncovers it, and grasps it. The same thing happens a second and a third time. . . . I then place the watch under B; Laurent watches this maneuver attentively, but at the moment the watch has disappeared under B, he turns back toward A and searches for the object under that screen. I again place the watch under B; he again searches for it under A. . . .

11 months, 22 days. (Taking account of visual displacements.)
Laurent is seated between two cushions A and B. I hide my watch alternately under each; Laurent constantly searches for the object where it has just disappeared, that is, sometimes under A and sometimes under B, without remaining attached to a privileged position as during the [above] stage. . . . At 12 months, 20 days, he also searches sequentially in both my hands for a button I am hiding. Afterward he tries to see behind me when I make the button roll on the floor (on which I am seated) even though, to fool him, I hold out my two closed hands.

18 months, 8 days. (Internally representing the visual displacements.)
Jacqueline throws a ball under a sofa. Instead of bending down at once and searching for it on the floor she looks at the place, realizes that the ball must have crossed under the sofa, and sets out to go behind it. . . . She begins by turning her back on the place where the ball disappeared, goes around the table, and finally arrives behind the sofa at the correct place. Thus she has closed the circle [of displacements] by an itinerary different from that of the object.

From Piaget (1937/1954). Copyright 1954 by Basic Books, Inc.

the ongoing sensory stimulation. For example, newborn infants will not search for an object that leaves their field of vision (see the first entry in Box 10-6). Later, the concept begins to develop; an infant will actively search for a vanished object but cannot yet follow a sequence of displacements, as is described in the second entry of Box 10-6. Eventually, the child further refines the concept of objects and is able to follow an object through a series of displacements (third entry) and finally to represent the displacements mentally (fourth entry). The ability to represent objects mentally and to move them from place to place mentally (as required in the fourth entry) marks the end of the sensorimotor period.

Another interesting accomplishment of the sensorimotor period is a progressive ability to control and investigate the environment. At first, infants have only reflexes such as sucking and grasping, which become adapted to the environment (first entry of Box 10-7). Primary circular reactions are attempts by the infant to gain sensorimotor coordination by repeating movements such as hand to mouth, following objects with the eyes, and so on, over and over again. These movements are circular because they are repeated several times; they are primary because they involve a single simple act that is not intentionally initiated by the infant (second entry). Secondary circular reactions are repeated efforts to control the environment that are initiated by the infant; an example is given in the third entry of Box 10-7. Tertiary circular reactions are advances over the previous two because the child actively initiates a series of systematic manipulations, such as dropping objects from different heights (fourth entry). Finally, the beginning of representational thought occurs, as when, for example (in the final entry), Lucienne represents the matchbook as her mouth and derives a solution.

PREOPERATIONAL PERIOD

At the end of the sensorimotor and the beginning of the *preoperational period,* the child has made some startling advances, including sensorimotor coordination, the ability to represent objects rather than just actions and sensations, and acquisition of the rudiments of symbolic problem solving. Yet children at this stage deal with static, concrete images and are limited by the following six problems (Phillips, 1969):

Concreteness—-the child can deal only with concrete objects that are physically present here-and-now.

Irreversibility —the child is unable to rearrange objects mentally or to conceive of them in some other arrangement.

Egocentrism—the child believes that everyone sees the world through his or her eyes and that everyone experiences what the child is experiencing.

Centering—the child can attend to only one dimension or aspect of a situation at a time.

States versus transformations—the child focuses on states, on the perceptual way things look rather than on the operations that produced that state.

Transductive reasoning —the child reasons that if A causes B, then B causes A.

BOX 10 ▪ 7 Development from Reflexes to Reactions to Thought

0 months, 20 days. (Adaptation of reflexes.)
He bites the breast which is given him, 5 centimeters from the nipple. For a moment he sucks the skin when he lets go in order to move his mouth about 2 centimeters. As soon as he begins sucking again he stops . . . when his search subsequently leads accidentally to touch the nipple with the mucosa of the upper lip (his mouth being wide open), he at once adjusts his lips and begins to suck.

1 month. 1 day. (Primary circular reactions.)
. . . his right hand may be seen approaching his mouth. . . . But as only the index finger was grasped, the hand fell out again. Shortly afterward it returned. This time the thumb was in the mouth. . . . I then remove the hand and place it near his waist . . . after a few minutes the lips move and the hand approaches them again. This time there is a series of setbacks . . . [but finally] the hand enters the mouth. . . . I again remove the hand. Again lip movements cease, new attempts ensue, success results for the ninth and tenth time, after which the experiment is interrupted.

3 months, 5 days. (Secondary circular reactions.)
Lucienne shakes her bassinet by moving her legs violently (bending and unbending them and so on), which makes the cloth dolls swing from the hood. Lucienne looks at them, smiling, and recommences at once. . . . Lucienne, at four months, 27 days, is lying in her bassinet. I hang a doll [from the hood] over her feet which immediately sets in motion the schema of shaking. But her feet reach the doll right away and give it a violent motion, which Lucienne surveys with delight. Afterward she looks at her motionless foot for a second, then recommences.

10 months, 11 days. (Tertiary circular reactions.)
Laurent is lying on his back. . . . He grasps in succession a celluloid swan, a box, and so on, stretches out his arm and lets them fall. He distinctly varies the positions of the fall. Sometimes he stretches out his arm vertically, sometimes he holds it obliquely, in front or behind. . . . When the object falls in a new position (for example, on his pillow), he lets it fall two or three times more in the same place . . . then he modifies the situation.

1 year, 4 months, 0 days. (Beginning of thought.)
I put [a] chain into a box and reduce the opening to 3 millimeters. It is understood that Lucienne is not aware of the functioning of the opening and closing of the matchbox. . . . She only possesses the two preceding schemata: turning the box over . . . and sliding her fingers into the slit to make the chain come out. It is, of course, this last procedure that she tries first; she puts her fingers inside and gropes to reach the chain, but fails completely. A pause follows during which Lucienne manifests a very curious reaction. . . . She looks at the slit with great attention; then, several times in succession, she opens and shuts her mouth, at first slightly, then wider and wider! . . . [Then] Lucienne unhesitatingly puts her finger in the slit and, instead of trying as before to reach the chain, she pulls so as to enlarge the opening. She succeeds and grasps the chain.

From Piaget (1937/1954) Copyright 1954 by Basic Books, Inc

Examples of these are given in Box 10-8. Children are struck by the perceptual way the world looks and are "preoperational" because they cannot perform mental operations on their representations and cannot change their representation of the world unless the perceptual world also changes.

BOX 10 ▪ 8   Examples of Preoperational Thought

Irreversibility

A four-year-old subject is asked:
"Do you have a brother?" He says, "Yes."
"What's his name?" "Jim.
"Does Jim have a brother?" "No."

From Phillips (1969)

Transductive Reasoning

At two years, 14 days, Jacqueline wanted a doll dress that was upstairs. She said "Dress," and when her mother refused to get it, "Daddy get dress." As I also refused, she wanted to go herself "To mommy's room." After several repetitions of this she was told that it was too cold there. There was a long silence, and then: "Not too cold." I asked, "Where?" "In the room." "Why isn't it too cold?" "Get dress."

From Piaget(1945/1951)

Egocentrism

After interviewing children on how they play the game of marbles, Piaget concludes: ". . . how little children from the same class at school, living in the same house, and accustomed to playing with each other, are able to understand each other at this age. Not only do they tell us of totally different rules . . . but when they play together they do not watch each other and do not unify their respective rules even for the duration of the game. The fact of the matter is that neither is trying to get the better of the other: each is merely having a game on his own, trying to hit the marbles in the square, that is, trying to 'win' from his point of view. [In other situations, such as sitting around the sandbox] one can observe in children between 2 and 6 a characteristic type of pseudo-conversation or 'collective monologue' during which children speak only for themselves . . . and each is concerned only with himself."

From Piaget (1932)

Centering

When the child is asked to put a set of sticks which vary in length in order, the following arrangement is constructed:

Apparently, the child "centers" on only one aspect of the problem (for example, the tops of the sticks) and cannot simultaneously consider other aspects (for example, the bottoms of the sticks).

From Piaget (1941/1952a)

(continued)

BOX 10 ▪ 8, *continued*

Concreteness, Irreversibility, Centering, and States

A four-year-old is asked: "Have you got a friend?"

"Yes, Odette."

"Well look, we're giving you, Clairette, a glass of orangeade (A1, 3/4 full), and we're giving Odette a glass of lemonade (A2, also 3/4 full). Has one of you more to drink than the other?"

"The same."

"This is what Clairette does: she pours her drink into two other glasses (B1 and B2, which are thus half filled). Has Clairette the same amount as Odette?"

"Odette has more."

"Why?"

"Because we've put less in." (She points to the levels in B1 and B2 without taking into account the fact that there were two glasses.)

(Odette's drink was then poured into B3 and B4.) "It's the same."

"And now?" (Pouring Clairette's drink from B1 and B2 into L, a long thin tube, which is then almost full.)

"I've got more."

"Why?"

"We've poured it into the glass (L) and here (B3 and B4) we haven't."

"But were they the same before?"

"Yes."

"And now?"

"But where does the extra come from?"

"From in there." (B1)

From Piaget (1941/1952a)

CONCRETE OPERATIONS

At about age seven, as children enter into the period of *concrete operations,* Piaget noted a basic change in the children's mental structures and operations. By the end of the preoperational period, a child has achieved or begun to achieve the ability to reverse or decenter (that is, simultaneously to consider two or more dimensions at a time) and to focus on transformations rather than static perceptual states; the child has begun to lose her egocentrism and transductive reasoning. The world comes to be represented not as a set of static perceptual images but rather as concrete objects that can be mentally acted upon and changed in logical ways. Reversibility is a newly acquired mental operation that frees the child from being dominated by how things look. The name, *concrete operations,* comes from this newly acquired ability to mentally operate or change a concrete situation and to perform logical operations on a situation in one's head.

BOX 10 ▪ 9   Typical Conservation Tasks

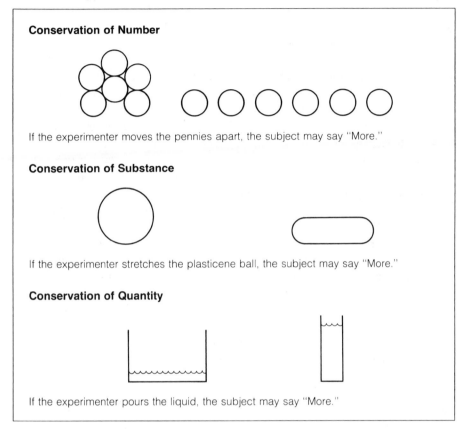

Conservation of Number

If the experimenter moves the pennies apart, the subject may say "More."

Conservation of Substance

If the experimenter stretches the plasticene ball, the subject may say "More."

Conservation of Quantity

If the experimenter pours the liquid, the subject may say "More."

These new mental operations are displayed in a series of small experiments on what Piaget calls *conservation,* including conservation of number, conservation of substance, and conservation of quantity. For example, consider the conservation of number situation shown in the top of Box 10-9. If Piaget showed a handful of pennies, for example, to preoperational children, they would base their judgment of quantity on perceptual appearance. A child might say there are "more" pennies when they are spread out than when they are bunched together. Even if children are asked to count the pennies under each arrangement, they still insist there are more when they are spread out. The children are centering on the dimension of length and cannot mentally reverse the operation of bunching or spreading out the pennies. However, a slightly older child who has acquired concrete operations is certain that it is the same amount of pennies regardless of how they are arranged. When asked how he knows, the child responds that although one arrangement may look bigger he knows he could move them and get the other arrangement, that is, he can mentally reverse the situation and rearrange the pennies in his head.

The middle panel of Box 10-9 gives an example of conservation of substance. A plasticene ball is shown to a child, and then it is stretched out to form a sausage before the child's eyes. The preoperational child generally claims that when the ball is made into a sausage it is now "more" (sometimes the ball is seen as "more" than the sausage shape). In these cases the child is centering on just one dimension, such as length (or width), and lacks the ability to perform the mental operation of reversibility—of mentally changing a ball into a sausage or a sausage into a ball. The older child in concrete operations, however, is able to say that the "same" amount of plasticene is part of each shape. Children in this period are not overcome by how things look and may decenter—consider both length and width simultaneously—and reverse—mentally reshape the plasticene.

The lower panel in Box 10-9 gives an example of conservation of quantity. When liquid is poured from a short, fat glass into a tall, thin glass, the preoperational child may say that there is "more" (or "less") liquid in the tall glass than when it is in the short glass. The child focuses, or centers, on the dimension of height (or width) to base the decision and is unable to reverse. However, the slightly older child who has acquired concrete operations says that the amount of liquid is the "same"; this child can decenter—realize that height and width compensate for one another—and can reverse—can mentally pour the liquid from one glass to another.

Box 10-10 gives an example of the change in egocentrism that occurs at this period—the three-mountain problem (Piaget & Inhelder, 1948/1956). A set of three mountains, in three-dimensional relief, is placed on a table as shown. The child sits in one chair and a doll is placed on a chair with a different perspective. The child is asked to draw what the doll "sees" from where it is sitting. The preoperational child draws how the scene looks from her own perspective, regardless of where the doll is seated, while the concrete operational child is capable of drawing the "correct" perspective. Apparently, the new mental operations acquired during this period allow children to view the world from many possible perspectives rather than the single static image they are currently receiving.

There are, of course, many other examples of the new mental operations that begin to emerge throughout the period of concrete operations. However, even these advances have their shortcomings. For example, the child in this period, while freed from the perceptual image of how things look, is still tied to concrete objects thought about and manipulated in the here and now. The concrete operational child, while possessing the powerful operations of reversibility and decentration, is unable to apply them to abstract situations.

BOX 10 • 10   The Three-Mountain Problem

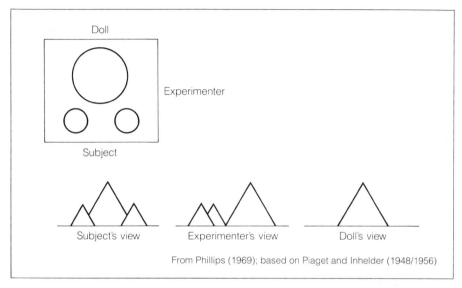

From Phillips (1969); based on Piaget and Inhelder (1948/1956)

FORMAL OPERATIONS

By early adolescence, about age eleven, the *formal operations period* begins and with it comes a progressively more sophisticated ability to perform mental operations not only on concrete objects but also on symbols. Although most of Piaget's work centered on the leap from preoperational to concrete operational thought, the formal operations stage is of some interest because it consists of the mental operations that normal human adults have. During this period the child develops the ability to think in terms of the hypothetical, in terms of probabilities, in terms of the possible rather than the concrete here-and-now. Given a situation, all possible alternatives can be discovered, and scientific reasoning in its most systematic and sophisticated form begins to emerge.

Box 10-11 shows the pendulum problem, which Piaget used to investigate the development of formal operational thought. A pendulum was constructed by hanging an object from a string, and the subject had to discover how four factors influenced the frequency of oscillation: the length of the string, the weight of the ball, how high the weight was when it was started, and how hard it was pushed. A typical response is also shown in Box 10-11. Children in the formal operational stage are able to systematically vary conditions—similar to the tertiary circular reactions, but more organized—in such a way as to solve the problem.

It may be no coincidence that the cognitive stage of formal operations—the

BOX 10 • 11   The Oscillation Problem

Given a pendulum, the subject may vary the length of the string, the weight of the suspended object, the height of the released object, and the force with which the object is released. Which of these influences the rate of oscillation—how fast the pendulum swings?

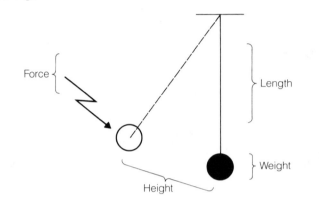

Piaget reports on the performance of a typical adolescent (15 years, 1 month):
". . . after having selected 100 grams with a long string and a medium length string, then 20 grams with a long and a short string, and finally 200 grams with a long and a short, concludes: 'It's the length of the string that makes it go faster or slower; the weight doesn't play any role.' She discounts likewise the height of the drop and the force of her push."

From Inhelder and Piaget (1955/1958)

adult ability to think in terms of the hypothetical—is accompanied by social and emotional changes including uncertainty over the meaning of life, the identity crisis, and adolescent idealism. In any case, formal operations is adult thought, and Piaget's theory posits no additional stages.

■

THE BIG LEAP: BRUNER'S THEORY
■

Perhaps Piaget's greatest contribution is the idea of a qualitative change in cognitive processing between preoperational and concrete operational thought, at about the age of five to seven. Although Piaget relied heavily on the processes of reversibility and decentration as descriptions of new mental powers that occur, there have been many alternative views.

The work of Bruner and his associates (summarized in Bruner, 1964, 1973; Bruner, Olver, & Greenfield, 1966) provides a supplement to Piaget's theory. The preface to *Studies in Cognitive Growth* (Bruner et al., 1966) states that the modifications to Piaget's theory are "minor by comparison with the points of fundamental agreement we share with Professor Jean Piaget." The most widely recognized contribution of Bruner's theory has been the view of development as a change in the child's mode of representation, fostered largely by changes in the use of language. For example, instead of four periods of cognitive development, Bruner proposed three modes of representing the world:

Enactive—representing the world in terms of actions (similar to the sensorimotor period).

Iconic—representing the world in terms of static perceptual images (similar to the preoperational period).

Symbolic—the use of language and symbols (similar to operational thinking).

The leap from iconic representation to symbolic representation (or from preoperational to concrete operational thought) is indicated in conservation experiments, but Bruner and Piaget differ on how to explain it. Piaget emphasizes the importance of mental operations such as reversibility as a prerequisite for conservation and suggests that the child's recognition that identical material must also be equivalent is a side effect. Bruner emphasizes the importance of the child's concept of identity and the linking of identity with equivalence (if it is the "same," it must be "equal") as a prerequisite for conservation, and he suggests that reversibility is a side effect. Although Bruner's theory closely resembles Piaget's, it differs on how to characterize the periods of development (three modes of representation versus four periods) and in how to explain conservation (identity versus reversibility).

Bruner and Kenney (1966) provided an example of the change at about age six from iconic to symbolic representation. Children who were aged five, six, and seven were shown a 3 × 3 matrix of nine glasses, with each row getting progressively wider from left to right and each column getting progressively taller from bottom to top, as shown in Box 10-12. A child was asked to look at the matrix, and then the experimenter scrambled all the glasses and asked the child to "make something like what was there before." Once the child had successfully reproduced the original array, the experimenter scrambled the glasses again, except that the short, thin glass from the lower left corner was now placed in the lower right corner. The child was again asked to "make something like what was there before" but to leave the one short, thin glass in the lower right corner. On

BOX 10 ▪ 12   The Nine-Glass Problem

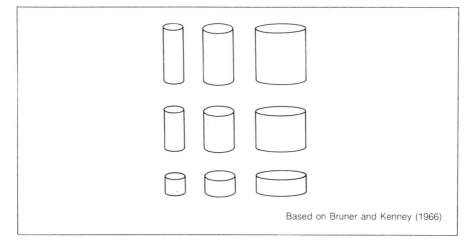

Based on Bruner and Kenney (1966)

the first task (reproduction) there were no differences in errors among the three age groups, with all the children performing quite well although the older children were a bit faster. However, on the second task (transposition) almost none of the younger children and almost all of the older children solved the problem. More careful analysis of the children's comments indicated that the five-year-olds were more likely to represent the matrix iconically—as a spatial image—while the seven-year-olds used language symbols such as height and width.

An experiment by Frank (1966) illustrates Bruner's contention that identity, rather than reversibility, is the basis of conservation. Four-, five-, six-, and seven-year-old children were given a standard task of conservation of quantity as a pretest, using two standard beakers equally filled with water (the children said they were the same). The water was poured from one into a differently shaped beaker (for example, short and wide), and the child was asked if the amount of water was still the same. As you can see in Box 10-13, the ability to conserve, indicated by the child's saying that the amount was still the same, increased with age. Next, Frank performed a similar demonstration, except that all the beakers were placed behind a screen for the pouring so that only the tops of the beakers were showing. In this case, as is shown in Box 10-13, 50 percent of the four-year-olds and 90 to 100 percent of the older children predicted that the amount of water in the newly poured beaker was the same. When the screen was removed, all the four-year-olds changed their minds. Apparently the perceptual display overwhelmed them, and they decided the wider beaker contained less

BOX 10 • 13   A Conservation Experiment

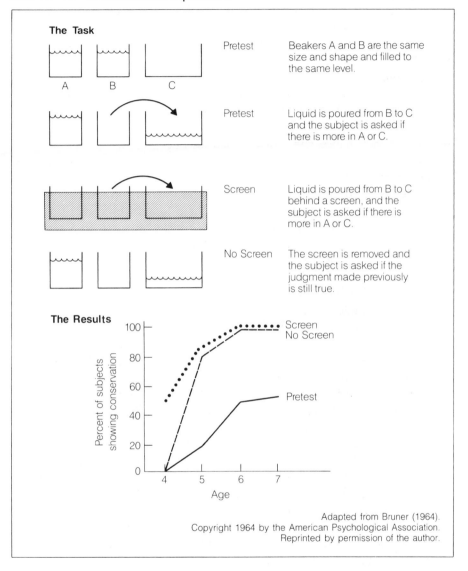

The Task

	Pretest	Beakers A and B are the same size and shape and filled to the same level.
A B C		
	Pretest	Liquid is poured from B to C and the subject is asked if there is more in A or C.
	Screen	Liquid is poured from B to C behind a screen, and the subject is asked if there is more in A or C.
	No Screen	The screen is removed and the subject is asked if the judgment made previously is still true.

The Results

Percent of subjects showing conservation

Screen
No Screen

Pretest

Age

Adapted from Bruner (1964).
Copyright 1964 by the American Psychological Association.
Reprinted by permission of the author.

liquid. However, none of the older children changed their judgments. As one seven-year-old explained, "It looks like more to drink but it is only the same because it is the same water and was only poured from here to there." On a posttest, in which water was poured into a tall, thin beaker along with a standard one without a screen, no four-year-olds conserved, but the number of older children who conserved increased greatly (see Box 10-13). Apparently, subjects can be correct on reversibility (with screen) but wrong on conservation (without screen); nonconservers may rely on perceptual factors, while conservers rely on internal symbolic representations.

Nair (1963, cited in Bruner, 1964) provided a further example of the importance of the concepts of identity and equivalence in conservation. First, children were given a standard pretest for conservation of quantity involving pouring water from one beaker to another. Then, to test for the concepts of identity and equivalence, she added a small toy duck that floated on the water; she said that it was moving to a new lake taking its water with it as she poured the water from a tall, narrow beaker into a short, wide one. The children were asked whether the duck now had the same water (identity) and whether it had the same amount of water (equivalence). All the children who conserved in the pretest answered the question about identity correctly; furthermore, reminding the children that the duck was taking its water with it (identity) helped conservation, and reminding them that the new lake must have the same water in it (equivalence) added further help.

Another example of the shift from visual or iconic mode of representation to symbolic came from Olver and Hornsby (1966). Children ranging in age from six to eighteen were asked to tell the similarities and differences among words (for example, *banana, peach, potato,* and so on) or among pictures (bee, balloons, airplanes). The results indicated that the younger subjects tended to base their judgments on perceptual features such as color, size, and pattern and would say for *banana, peach,* and *potato,* "They are curved," while the older children tended to classify objects by their function and would say, in this case, "You can eat them."

In summary, some of Bruner's modifications of Piaget's theory involve the role of modes of representation, particularly language, as the basis for cognitive growth. In assessing Bruner's theory, Case (1985, p. 42) has noted that research on modes of representation "provided little support" and research on language "provided only partial support." Furthermore, "by the mid-1970s he had abandoned his claim that the major periods in children's lives could be defined by the mode of representation they used and he softened his claim about language" (Case, 1985, p. 43). However, Bruner's emphasis on the role of culture in development has become the focus of recent research; this work is aided by the rekindling of interest in Vygotsky's view of the child as an inheritor of cultural tools such as strategies for processing verbal information (Rogoff, 1990; Vygotsky, 1978; Wertsch, 1985). For example, Bruner (1983, p. 147) noted in a recent retrospective look at his work in the 1960s that "the Vygotskyian side of it was mostly ignored, though that has changed recently."

■

THE BIG LEAP: INFORMATION-PROCESSING APPROACHES

■

So far we have seen that Piaget's theory is the most comprehensive and general theory of cognitive development. However, even a general theory as powerful as Piaget's should not be seen as an unchangeable monument to a great scientist. On the contrary, it is a compliment to Piaget's theory that so many researchers have sought to test and modify the theory. Presently no alternative theory matches the grand scale of Piaget's theory; rather, researchers have sought to carefully test specific aspects of the theory to clarify and, if necessary, modify a portion of the theory.

In this section we will explore recent research and theories that differ from Piaget's work in two important ways. First, recent work has attempted to describe cognitive development by using information-processing models such as computer-simulation or process models; second, recent work has focused on well-controlled experimentation rather than Piaget's clinical method of informally testing and observing children. In a sense, recent work has attempted to recast cognitive developmental psychology into the language and methods of modern information processing.

A common theme running through the information-processing approach to cognitive development is the view of the child as a constructor of strategies. In this section, we briefly examine three information-processing theories of cognitive development, namely the theories of Case (1985), Siegler (1986), and Klahr (1984; Klahr & Wallace, 1976).

CASE'S THEORY

To build a theory of cognitive development within the information-processing framework, Case (1978a, 1978b, 1985) has emphasized the roles of *executive processing space* (or *M-space*) and *automatization* in strategy construction. Executive processing space is the maximum number of mental elements a child can pay attention to at one time. *Automatization* is a change in strategy use from requiring conscious mental effort to not requiring conscious mental effort. Because attentional capacity is limited, children must begin with simple strategies that exhaust their conscious attentional resources. With experience, the strategy becomes automated, so that less conscious attention is needed; this frees up attentional resources that can be devoted to adding improvements onto the strategy, which in turn become automated, and so on.

Piaget argues that development involves the acquisition of logical and mathematical systems, including the idea of reversibility discussed earlier in this chapter. Thus development can be described in terms of the formal properties of

BOX 10 • 14   Juice Mixture Problems

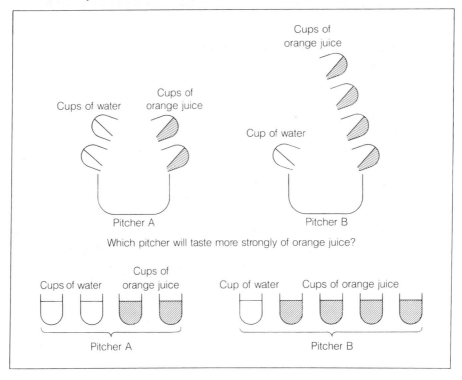

Which pitcher will taste more strongly of orange juice?

mathematics and logic. Building on the work of Simon (1962) and Pascual-Leone (1970), Case (1985) proposes that cognitive development involves the acquisition of information-processing strategies. These strategies can be described in terms of computer-simulation models or process models. In development, simple strategies become automatic through use and then are modified into more powerful strategies.

In Piaget's theory, the overall level of cognitive development is reflected in the level of "operativity"—how many mental operations the child can use in an integrated way. In Case's theory, following the work of Pascual-Leone (1970), development level is reflected in the child's level of processing space—how many different pieces of information the child can hold in active memory at one time. Higher levels of development require that more information be held actively in working memory.

As an example of the role of strategy construction, Case (1978a, 1978b, 1985) cites a study by Noelting (1980) in which children are shown two empty

BOX 10 • 15   Four Types of Juice Mixture Problems

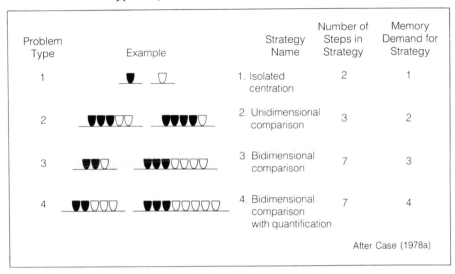

Problem Type	Example	Strategy Name	Number of Steps in Strategy	Memory Demand for Strategy
1		1. Isolated centration	2	1
2		2. Unidimensional comparison	3	2
3		3. Bidimensional comparison	7	3
4		4. Bidimensional comparison with quantification	7	4

After Case (1978a)

pitchers. Then the experimenter explains that he will pour some cups of water and some cups of orange juice into each pitcher. The child's job is to predict which pitcher will taste more strongly like orange juice. For example, suppose the experimenter said that he will pour two cups of water and two cups of juice into pitcher A, and he will pour one cup of water and four cups of juice into pitcher B. Which pitcher will taste more strongly of orange juice? In this case, the answer is pitcher B. The top portion of Box 10-14 summarizes the procedure for this mixing experiment.

Box 10-15 summarizes four kinds of juice ratio problems:

1. In type 1 problems, one pitcher gets some juice while the other pitcher does not.

2. In type 2 problems, one pitcher receives more cups of juice than the other, and the number of cups of water is not relevant.

3. In type 3 problems, one pitcher has an excess of cups of juice over cups of water while the other pitcher does not.

4. In type 4 problems, both (or neither) pitchers get an excess of juice over water cups, but one gets a greater excess; the specific ratio is not relevant.

In Noelting's experiments a group of children, ranging in age from three to ten, were asked to solve juice problems of these four types. Results of the experiment revealed that there were four basic strategies (see Box 10-16), with younger children using the simplest and older children using more complex strategies.

Strategy 1: Isolated Centration.   The simplest strategy is to base your decision on whether or not orange juice will be poured into a pitcher: if a pitcher contains any orange juice, then it will taste of orange juice. As you can see, this strategy will generate correct answers only if one pitcher gets some orange juice while the other gets none; if both pitchers get orange juice, the child has no strategy for determining which is more concentrated. Children using strategy 1 (those three to four-and-one-half years old) show a pattern of correct answers for problem type 1 only. According to Case, this strategy requires two steps and demands that only one item be held in memory (for example, whether or not there is juice in pitcher A).

Strategy 2: Unidimensional Comparison.   Slightly older children (ages four-and-one-half to six years) use a more sophisticated strategy that focuses on the number of juice cups in each pitcher. In this strategy, you choose the pitcher that has the greatest number of cups of juice, ignoring the number of cups of water in each pitcher. This strategy will generate correct answers only when one side has more cups of juice but proportionately equal or fewer cups of water, that is, types 1 and 2. According to Case, this study requires three steps and demands that a maximum of two items be held simultaneously in memory (the number of juice cups in pitcher A and the number of juice cups in pitcher B).

Strategy 3: Bidimensional Comparison.   Seven- to eight-year-old children notice the number of cups of juice and the number of cups of water that go into each pitcher. In this case, you pick the side that has more juice than water. As you can see, this strategy fails when both sides have more cups of juice than water, fewer cups of juice than water, or when both sides have equal differences between cups of juice and water. Thus, problem types 1, 2, and 3 can be solved using strategy 3. This strategy involves seven steps and a maximum memory load of three items (excess of juice cups to water cups in pitcher A, number of juice cups in pitcher B, and number of water cups in pitcher B).

Strategy 4: Two-Dimensional Comparison with Quantification. The most sophisticated strategy, observed in the oldest children, aged nine to ten, involved noticing the exact difference between the number of cups of juice and water for each pitcher. In this case, you subtract the number of water cups from the

BOX 10 ▪ 16   Four Strategies for Solving Juice Mixture Problems

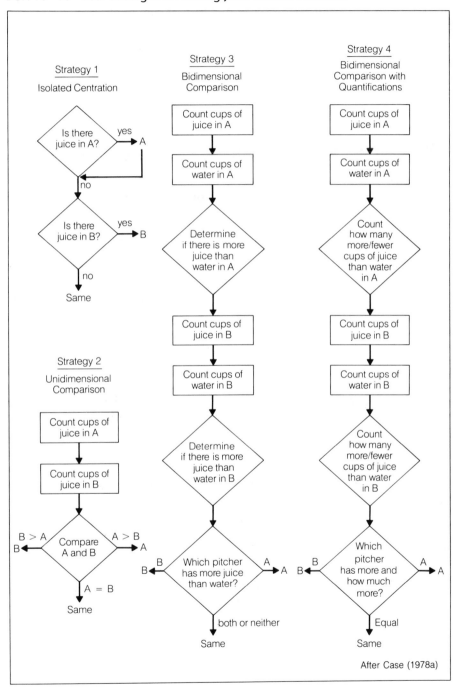

After Case (1978a)

number of juice cups on each side, then you simply choose the pitcher that yields the highest answer. This strategy succeeds for all four problem types in Box 10-15, but it will fail for problems in which the ratio must be taken into account. Case shows that this strategy requires seven steps and a maximum of four items held simultaneously in memory.

In Case's revision of Piagetian theory, the level of the child's strategy depends on the amount of attentional energy—-what Pascaul-Leone calls "M-space" (Case, 1978a, 1985). Early in development, even a simple strategy requires much attentional energy because each step must be monitored. Thus a child does not have attentional energy available for holding many items in memory. However, once a strategy has become automatic, through much practice, it no longer requires as much attention. Thus, there is more attentional energy available for holding more items in memory, so a child may move on to a more complex strategy, and so on. Increasingly sophisticated strategies develop because simple strategies become automatic, freeing space in memory for use in monitoring more complex strategies. More recently, Case (1985) has renamed the four strategies, respectively, as *operational consolidation, operational coordination, bifocal coordination,* and *elaborated coordination* and has provided a more comprehensive description of cognitive development as a sequence of increasingly more powerful information-processing strategies.

SIEGLER'S THEORY

Like Case's, Siegler's (1976, 1978, 1981, 1986) work shows that children's problem-solving knowledge can be described as the acquisition of increasingly more powerful rules. Siegler has emphasized the role of *encoding:* as children develop they are more likely to pay attention to more of the relevant aspects of the problem. In particular, Siegler has shown that performance on Piagetian tasks can be described in terms of changes in information-processing strategies used by children.

BOX 10 ▪ 17   The Balance Beam Problem

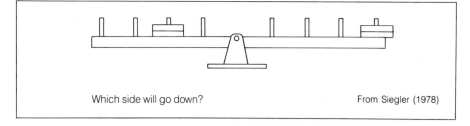

Which side will go down?   From Siegler (1978)

BOX 10 ▪ 18   Six Types of Balance Beam Problems

	Percent Correct for Each Strategy			
Problem type	1	2	3	4
Balance	100	100	100	100
Weight	100	100	100	100
Distance	0 (Should say "Balance")	100	100	100
Conflict-weight	100	100	33 (Chance responding)	100
Conflict-distance	0 (Should say "Right down")	0 (Should say "Right down")	33 (Chance responding)	100
Conflict-balance	0 (Should say "Right down")	0 (Should say "Right down")	33 (Chance responding)	100

From Siegler (1978)

For example, Box 10-17 shows Siegler's version of the balance beam problem, used originally by Inhelder and Piaget (1955/1958) to study the development of scientific reasoning in formal operations. In this task, the child is shown a balance beam with four equally spaced pegs on either side of the fulcrum. Then weights are placed on pegs on each side of the fulcrum, while the beam is held in place. The child's task is to predict which side of the beam will go down.

Siegler used six types of balance beam problems, as shown in Box 10-18:

1. In *balance problems,* the same configuration of weights is placed on both sides; the beam is balanced.

2. In *weight problems,* there are more weights on one side than the other, and the distance between the weights and the fulcrum is the same on both sides.

3. In *distance problems,* an equal number of weights are placed on both sides, but they are placed closer to the fulcrum on one side.

4. In *conflict-weight problems,* one side has more weights but the other side has the weights placed farther from the fulcrum; however, the side with more weights goes down.

5. In *conflict-distance problems,* one side has more weights but the other side has the weights placed farther from the fulcrum; however, the side with the more distant weights goes down.

6. In *conflict-balance problems,* one side has more weights but the other side has the weights placed farther from the fulcrum; the beam remains balanced.

If you were given the balance beam problems, how would you go about solving them? According to Siegler (1978, 1981, 1986) four basic strategies can be described and represented as flow charts. These four strategies are summarized in Box 10-19:

Strategy 1: One Decision.   The simplest model involves noticing only if one side has more weights than the other; if both sides have an equal number of weights, then you say that the beam will be balanced; if one side has more weights, then you say that side will go down. This strategy involves only one decision and generates correct answers for balance, weight, and conflict-weight problems.

Strategy 2: Two Decisions.   The next strategy contains the same decision as strategy 1, but it also adds a second decision concerning whether or not the weights are placed at equal distances from the fulcrum. If one side has more weights than the other, then you say that side will go down (just as in strategy 1). If both sides have an equal number of weights, then you check their distance from the fulcrum. You say that the side with weights the greater distance from the fulcrum will go down. This strategy involves two decisions and generates correct answers for balance, weight, distance, and conflict-weight problems.

Strategy 3: Three Decisions.   This strategy incorporates the two decisions from strategy 2—noticing the distribution and distance of weights—as well as a third decision. If both sides are equal, then you say they will balance. If one side has

BOX 10 • 19   Four Strategies for Solving Balance Beam Problems

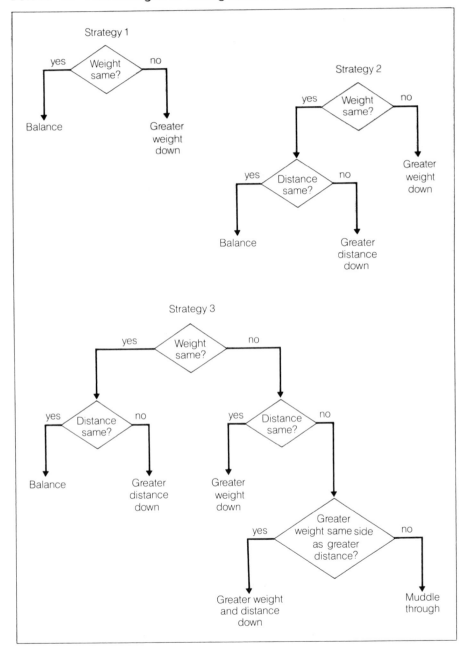

BOX 10 • 19, *continued*

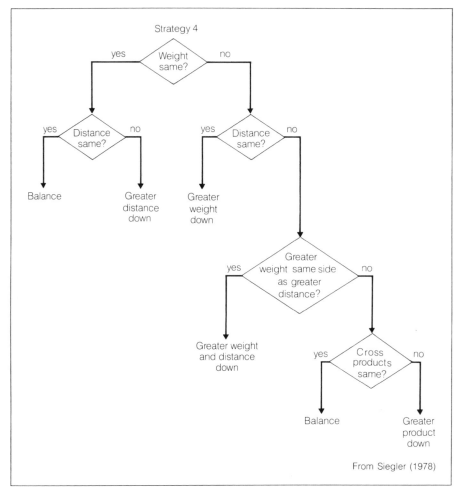

From Siegler (1978)

more weights but both sides have equal distance, then you say the side with more weights will go down. If both sides have the same weight but one has greater distance, then you will say the side with greater distance will go down. However, when one side has more weight and the other side has more distance, you must guess. This strategy generates correct answers for balance, weight, and distance problems and chance-level answers for the other problems.

Strategy 4: Four Decisions.   The fourth strategy builds on strategy 3 by including a decision concerning the cross products (weight × distance). Thus when one side has more weights and the other side has more distance, the answer is determined by computing the cross product for each side. This strategy involves four decisions and generates correct answers for all problems.

In a typical experiment, Siegler (1976, 1978) gave problems such as those in Box 10-18 to children of ages seven through seventeen. The errors generated by each child were matched against the pattern of errors predicted by each of the four strategies. Almost all of the children could be easily fit into one of the four strategy groups—that is, the performance of a given child usually matched perfectly with the performance predicted by one of the strategies. There was also a pattern in which older children preferred the more sophisticated strategies while younger children used the simpler strategies. These results are consistent with those described by Case in which developmental changes in performance may be described in terms of increasingly more complex strategies of information processing.

KLAHR'S THEORY

Additional support for the idea that development involves the construction of more sophisticated strategies comes from the work of Klahr and his colleagues (Klahr, 1978, 1984; Klahr & Wallace, 1976). Klahr's approach emphasizes the role of *generalization,* that is, the child's ability to learn how to extend a rule to a new situation. In Klahr's theory, the knowledge underlying cognitive development can be described as a *self-modifying production system,* that is, procedures for problem solving that become more powerful as children gain more experience in solving problems. Production systems are described in more detail in Chapter 6.

Klahr focused on the development of an important problem-solving strategy—means-ends analysis. As described in Chapter 6, in means-ends analysis a problem solver establishes subgoals whenever a desired goal cannot be directly accomplished. For example, Klahr (1978, pp. 181–182) presents the following example of the use of subgoal stacking in children:

> Scene: Billy and Daddy are in the yard. Billy's playmate appears on a bike.
>
> Billy: Daddy, will you unlock the basement door?
> Daddy: Why?
> Billy: Cause I want to ride my bike.
> Daddy: Your bike is in the garage.
> Billy: But my socks are in the dryer.

In this case, Billy's top goal is to ride his bike. However, this goal cannot be achieved directly because he needs to be wearing his shoes (subgoal 1). However,

BOX 10 ▪ 20   The Monkey Can Problem

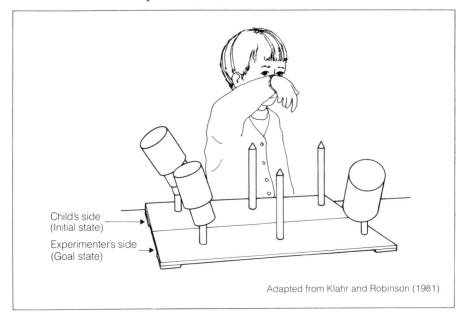

Child's side
(Initial state)

Experimenter's side
(Goal state)

Adapted from Klahr and Robinson (1981)

he cannot directly achieve the goal of getting his shoes on because he needs to put on his socks (subgoal 2). Again, he cannot directly achieve his goal because his socks are in the dryer (subgoal 3). He cannot get to the dryer directly because the basement door leading to the dryer is locked (subgoal 4). Unlocking the door cannot be directly accomplished because Daddy always has the keys for everything (subgoal 5). Thus Billy determines that he must ask his dad to open the basement door. Once this goal is accomplished, all the others can be executed in turn. Thus, in this example Billy has shown that he can "stack subgoals"—that is, set up subgoals when a top goal cannot be directly accomplished.

Similarly, Klahr (1978; Klahr & Robinson, 1981) asked children to solve versions of the Tower of Hanoi, or disk, problem. To appeal to children, Klahr developed the monkey can problem shown in Box 10-20. In this problem children are told that the cans are monkeys and the pegs are trees. The large can is the daddy, the medium-sized can is the mommy, and the small can is the baby. The monkeys are able to jump from tree to tree (peg to peg), but a smaller can may never be put on top of a larger can. One configuration is given on the experimenter's side of the puzzle; the child's job is to figure out how to move the monkeys so they will be in the same configuration as on the experimenter's side.

This problem was given to children ranging in age from three to five years. The youngest children in the group were able to solve only very short problems that did not require any setting of goals. For example, one simple problem begins with one can on each peg and ends with them all stacked on the same peg. Older children were able to solve longer problems that required some moderate amount of goal setting. Klahr and Robinson (1981) developed computer-simulation models at ten levels of sophistication in order to describe different levels of performance among the children.

The work of Case, Siegler, and Klahr provides examples of how the information-processing approach can be applied to describing cognitive development. As you can see, one persistent modification of Piaget's theory is that developmental progressions may be described as the acquisition of increasingly more sophisticated strategies.

■
THE BIG LEAP: CAN COGNITIVE DEVELOPMENT BE TAUGHT?
■

One of Piaget's major contributions is his proposal of a series of stages of cognitive development through which all humans progress in a fixed order. Although the order is fixed in Piaget's theory, the rate of development is not. Thus much research has been directed at the question of whether the rate of development may be speeded up, that is, whether it is possible to teach children who are in one stage of development to move on to the next stage. A particular focus concerns whether we can teach children to make the "big leap" from preoperational to concrete operational thought.

CONSERVATION TRAINING

During the past twenty-five years researchers have conducted dozens of conservation-training studies (Beilin, 1971; Brainerd, 1974; Field, 1987; Kuhn, 1974; Murray, 1978; Strauss, 1972). Conservation-training studies generally have three phases: a *pretest phase,* in which researchers identify children who fail to conserve on standard Piagetian conservation tasks; a *training phase,* in which children receive training and practice in solving conservation problems; and a *posttest phase,* in which children are retested to determine whether they have learned to conserve. Although various testing and training techniques have been used by different researchers, there is presently "no longer any doubt that conservation can be taught" (Murray, 1978, p. 421) and "clear evidence that the operational level of 4-year-old children can be substantially advanced" (Field,

1987, p. 246). However, there are also many cases in which training is not effective.

In order to distinguish the characteristics of successful and unsuccessful training studies, let's examine each of the three research phases. First, concerning the pretest phase, conservation studies are generally far more successful with four-year olds than with three-year-olds (Field, 1987) or with older children (Brainerd, 1977). Apparently training is most effective for children who are close to the criterion behavior, that is, those who possess the information-processing skills for acquiring the needed solution strategy but who do not spontaneously discover it. Three-year-olds may lack the information-processing skills for acquiring the solution strategy, whereas older children may be able to discover the strategies without direct instruction.

Second, concerning the training phase, active participation of the child seems to be crucial. Field (1987, p. 246) points out that successful training programs "require justifications that were more than mere parroting of training instructions" and also require "individual versus group-based responses." Murray (1978) notes that training is most effective when it involves social interaction, such as nonconservers having to discuss their thinking process with conservers, and role playing, in which a nonconserver must try to act like a conserver.

Third, concerning the posttest phase, it is easier to find evidence that children can be taught to perform well on an immediate test of a task that was just taught than on a delayed test or on a transfer test involving tasks in which they have not been trained. Indeed, Field (1987, p. 246) reviews many studies demonstrating that "learning was lasting, by including a delayed posttest" and that "children could use their new understanding on untrained concepts." However, when we evaluate successful training by the child's ability to perform well on delayed and transfer posttests, then "few investigators . . . have provided unassailable evidence of conservation acquisition" (Field, 1987, p. 248).

As an example, let's consider a major conservation training study by Gelman (1969; also discussed in Gelman & Gallistel, 1978). In this study, children were taught about conservation of number and conservation of length, as discussed earlier in this chapter. Subjects were given practice on thirty-two problem sets with six problems in each set. Box 10-21 shows one typical problem set for conservation of number and one for conservation of length. On each problem, the child is shown three sets of dots (or three lines) and asked to indicate which one is different. On the first problem in each set and the last problem in each set, the dots (or lines) are arranged to elicit a correct response. However, on problems 2 through 5, the child must learn to overcome irrelevant features of the display, such as the placement of the dots (or lines). Children are given feedback on each trial. According to Gelman, the training is aimed at focusing the learner's attention on the relevant aspects of the display and away from the irrelevant aspects. Box 10-22 shows the results for a group of trained subjects. As you can

BOX 10 • 21 Training Procedure for Conservation of Number and Length

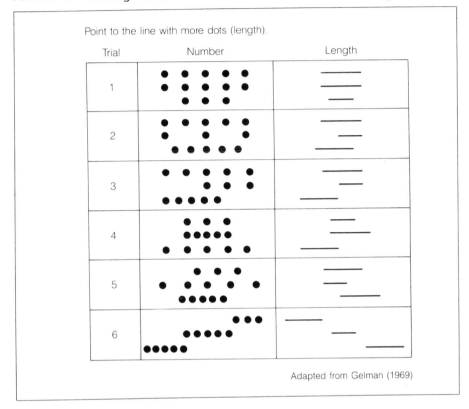

Adapted from Gelman (1969)

see, at the beginning the children make many errors; however, after about sixteen problem sets, the rate of performance approaches 100 percent.

Siegler (1978) was able to influence the problem-solving performance of children on the balance beam task described earlier by providing training. Two types of training were used: feedback and encoding. In feedback training, children were given systematic feedback concerning their predictions about which side of the balance would go down. In encoding training, children had to note the number of weights and the configuration of weights on each side to be able to reproduce the exact number and configuration on another balance beam. These two techniques tended to help some children learn more systematic strategies, although instruction was most beneficial for children who were already in transition.

BOX 10 • 22   Percent Correct on Conservation Task for Various Amounts of Training

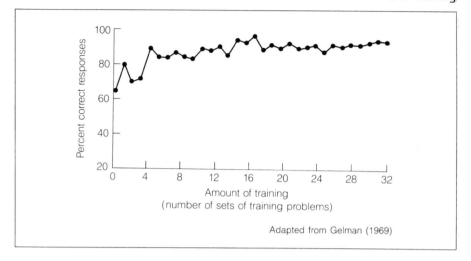

Amount of training
(number of sets of training problems)

Adapted from Gelman (1969)

Let's consider some other Piagetian tasks. For example, in a *transitive inference* task, such as the linear reasoning tasks discussed previously, the child is shown that stick A is taller than stick B, and stick B is taller than stick C. Piaget (1941/1952a) noted that most children in the group of four- to six-year-olds fail on tests of transitive inference, such as "Is stick A taller than C?" Piaget's theory attributes this failure to a lack of the appropriate logical operations.

Trabasso and his colleagues (Bryant & Trabasso, 1971; Riley, 1976; Riley & Trabasso, 1974) have offered a modification of Piaget's theory of transitive inference. In a typical study, Bryant and Trabasso used a series of five colored sticks labeled A, B, C, D, and E. The children in the study, aged four to six, were shown only adjacent pairs, such as A and B. For each pair, the child learned which stick was longer. The test of transitive inference involved the B–D pair. Children who were able to correctly solve the inference problem (B > D) also tended to remember the premises (B > C, C > D), while children who did not perform well on the inference task tended to forget one or more of the premises. Thus failure to perform on an inference task may result from forgetting the premises rather than a lack of logical operations. When training techniques were used that ensure memory for the premises, transitive inference performance was improved (Riley, 1976; Riley & Trabasso, 1974). Similarly, performance on class inclusion problems can be improved by systematically teaching each step in the problem-solving process (Trabasso et al., 1978).

LEARNING STRATEGY TRAINING

A related area that has received much research attention concerns children's ability to learn a rote list. In a typical study, children are shown a list of pictures of objects and then must try to recall them. Young children in the preschool years tend to be unable to predict accurately how well they will do on a recall task, whereas older children are far more accurate (Flavell & Wellman, 1977; Yussen & Levy, 1975). However, with experience, children can improve their predictions of how well they will perform (Markman, 1979). Flavell and Wellman (1977) use the term *metamemory* to refer to a person's awareness of his or her own memory processes and capabilities, such as knowing when a task is going to be difficult to learn.

In addition, young learners do not tend to use appropriate strategies for encoding new material, such as organizing a list into taxonomic categories or rehearsing the names of pictures that are no longer present; older children do use such strategies (Flavell, Friedrichs, & Hoyt, 1970; Kail, 1990; Moely, Olson, Halwes, & Flavell, 1969). Kail (1990), Mayer (1987a), and Brown and DeLoache (1978) have reviewed training studies in which young children are taught to use organizing and rehearsal strategies. In general, such training can be effective in improving recall performance, that is, helping four- and five-year-olds learn like seven- and eight-year olds. For example, concerning the strategy of rehearsing, it is useful to make a distinction between *availability deficiencies,* in which the child does not know how to rehearse, and *production deficiencies,* in which the child does not know when to rehearse (Flavell, 1970; Flavell & Wellman, 1977). The three stages in the development of a learning strategy are: (1) when a child does not know how to rehearse, (2) when a child knows how but does not know when to rehearse, and (3) when a child knows both how and when to rehearse (Mayer, 1987a). Research on the development of metamemory and learning strategies provides another attempt to teach children to be more effective processors of information.

IMPLICATIONS OF TRAINING STUDIES

Apparently children's performance on almost any sort of task can be improved with appropriate training or by changing the format of the task. Does this mean that Piaget's theory is wrong in stating that cognitive development involves a fixed sequence of stages? Do training techniques shorten the natural development process and deprive children of learning how to learn on their own? If it is possible to improve performance on Piagetian tasks, does that mean that we *should* do so?

The implications of training studies are far from clear. However, almost all of the improvements that have been demonstrated in training studies would likely have occurred within the children given the normal course of time. There is little evidence from training studies that the final level of development as an adult can be influenced by speeding the developmental process. As for Piaget's theory, training studies also provide some support: they tend to show that effects are strongest for children who are at the borderline between stages, and they support the idea that cognitive development is always in a state of flux. However, there is a sense in which training studies obscure the original purpose of Piagetian research and research on development in general. As Gelman and Gallistel state: "The idea is to look for ways to compare, as well as to contrast, the preschooler with his older sibling" (1978, p. 24).

■
EVALUATION
■

The cognitive development approach provides a unique theory of human thinking and the only one explicitly based on the idea that humans are living beings striving to survive and function successfully. Like the information-processing approach, which is strongly influenced by developments in computer technology, the cognitive development approach was heavily influenced by biological concepts. To the extent that the biological analogy is not perfect, theories of human thought based on it are limited.

In order to provide a historical context and common starting point, this chapter has focused on Piaget's theory. We began with a description of Piaget's theory, then examined how subsequent research required modifications in it. Although Piaget's theory has had a strong influence on the field of cognitive development, it is clear that current research has progressed beyond Piaget both in terms of theory and methodology (Bjorklund, 1989; Siegler, 1989b). Theoretically, the goal has been to describe in precise terms the mechanisms that contribute to cognitive growth (Siegler, 1989b; Sternberg, 1984). For example, Klahr (1982, p. 85) attacks the vagueness of Piagetian theory:

> For 40 years we have had assimilation and accommodation. . . . What are they? How do they do their thing? Why is it after all this time, we know no more about them than when they first sprang on the scene?

In contrast, current work is aimed at producing more detailed accounts of cognitive growth. Sternberg (1984, p. viii) summarizes this goal as follows:

> If we accept these two processes as bases for mental development, then one might ask for a more detailed specification of just what happens—at the level of mental

mechanisms—when assimilation and accommodation take place. . . . The Piagetian view . . . seems not to be incorrect but incomplete. It is in need of more microscopic psychological analysis to supplement its useful macroscopic description of cognitive development.

Methodologically, the goal has been to use rigorous research methods that accurately examine children's thinking (Bjorklund, 1989). These methods include analysis of protocols (as described in Chapter 6), solution times (as described in Chapter 7), error patterns, and eye movements (Siegler, 1986). In contrast, some of Piaget's experiments were poorly controlled, lacked statistical analyses, and could have been biased by the experimenter's expectations or by the use of language. In conclusion, research on the mechanisms of cognitive development, supported by increasing theoretical precision and methodological rigor, offers an emerging source of information that ultimately must be assimilated into the psychology of thinking.

Suggested Readings

BJORKLUND, D. F. (1989). *Children's thinking.* Pacific Grove, CA: Brooks/Cole. Surveys research on the development of children's thinking.

FLAVELL, D. (1985). *Cognitive development* (2nd ed.). Englewood Cliffs, NJ: Prentice-Hall. Surveys the field of cognitive development, including a heavy dose of Piaget's work.

GINSBURG, H. P., & OPPER, S. (1988). *Piaget's theory of intellectual development* (3rd ed.). Englewood Cliffs, NJ: Prentice-Hall. Summarizes and interprets Piaget's theory for the introductory reader.

PIAGET, J. (1967). *Six psychological studies.* New York: Random House. Contains some of Piaget's papers, organized and introduced by the American Piagetian psychologist, David Elkind.

SIEGLER, R. S. (1986). *Children's thinking.* Englewood Cliffs, NJ: Prentice-Hall. Introduces Piagetian and information-processing approaches to cognitive development.

STERNBERG, R. J. (Ed.). (1984). *Mechanisms of cognitive development.* New York: Freeman. Contains papers by leading cognitive developmental psychologists.

CHAPTER · 11

INTELLIGENCE

Thinking as a Measurable Ability

Intelligence Definition of Thinking

■

Cognitive Factors Approach

■

Cognitive Correlates Approach

■

Cognitive Components Approach

■

Cognitive Training Approach

In this chapter we explore individual differences in mental abilities, with a special focus on intelligence. Although psychologists have not always been able to define intelligence, they have been productive in developing tests to measure it. This situation led Boring (1923) to conclude that intelligence is "what these tests measure."

In order for you to get a better understanding of how intelligence has been measured, let me ask you to answer the following questions:

How many weeks are there in a year?
What is the height of the average American woman?
How is an orange like a banana?
How is an eye like an ear?

These are some of the kinds of items proposed by Wechsler (1958) for inclusion in tests of intelligence. The first two questions are examples of an information test; people who have acquired a broad basic knowledge based on their life experiences are considered to be more intelligent that people who have acquired less knowledge based on the same kinds of life experiences. As you can see, the assumption underlying an information test is that all people have the same basic opportunities to learn, an assumption that is often not correct when comparing people from different ethnic and cultural backgrounds. The second two questions are examples of a similarities test; these questions require a person to abstract properties from both items and mentally place the two items in the same category. These are examples of test items developed under the earliest approach to intelligence—the *psychometric approach* (or what we call the *cognitive factors approach* in this chapter). For example, one cognitive factor could be the ability to learn from life experiences, as measured by an information test, and another could be the ability to abstract properties from concepts, as measured by a similarities test.

Next consider the following test of verbal intelligence. For the following list, read the words aloud one at a time at a rate of one word per second; after you have read the list, recite the words back in order.

psychometric
correlates
components
training
analogy
process

If you were able to correctly recite the words in order, your memory span for words is at least six. If you could read and recite a list of ten words without error but you make errors on longer lists, you would have a memory span for words of ten. Memory span is a measure of your capacity to process several pieces of information at the same time; it is measured as the number of items in the longest list you can recall in order without error. Presumably, someone who has a larger memory span for words will perform better on tasks involving reading comprehension. This is an example of a test based on the *cognitive correlates approach* to intelligence. In this approach, the goal is to identify characteristics of a person's information-processing system, such as the capacity of their short-term memory, that might be related to performance on cognitive tasks.

Next, let's try a verbal analogy, because these are often found on tests of intelligence:

SPOUSE is to HUSBAND as SIBLING is to (FATHER, UNCLE, BROTHER, SON)
TRAP is to PART as RAT is to (GOOD-BYE, WHOLE, BAIT, TAR)

The answers to these items, suggested by Sternberg (1988), are BROTHER and TAR. According to Sternberg, these problems require several basic cognitive processes, such as encoding each word, inferring the relation between the first and second words, and so on. Such problems are representative of the *cognitive components approach,* so called because the goal is to break a task down into its underlying cognitive processes and individually to assess differences in each component process.

Finally, suppose I tell you that most analogy problems can be solved if you look for certain relations between the first two terms, such as the following:

Part-to-whole: SENTENCE is to PARAGRAPH (A is a part of B)

Coordination: GUITAR is to VIOLIN (A and B belong to the same category)

Superordination: ROBIN is to BIRD (A belongs to category B)

Causation: ALCOHOLISM is to LIQUOR (A leads to B)

Degree: MISDEMEANOR is to FELONY (A is less than B)

Now try these problems:

HUNGER is to STARVATION as FORGETFULNESS is to (MEMORY, AMNESIA, UNCONSCIOUS, ABSENT-MINDED)
SEED is to PLANT as EGG is to (YOLK, CRACK, BIRD, SHELL)
LEAF is to BRANCH as FINGER is to (POINT, HAND, RINGS, FIVE)
POKER is to BLACKJACK as POLICEMAN is to (GUN, LAW, GAMBLING, TEACHER)
CHEMISTRY is to SCIENCE as BREAKFAST is to (EGGS, MORNING, MEAL, LUNCH)

The correct answers (and type of relation) are AMNESIA (degree), BIRD (causation), HAND (part-to-whole), TEACHER (coordination), MEAL (superordination). Did the pretraining in recognizing types of relations between the A and B term help you? If so we have some validation that individual differences in this task are partially accounted for by the process of inferring a relation between A and B. This approach, called *cognitive training,* is the fourth and final approach to individual differences explored in this chapter. In this approach, the goal is to provide instruction in cognitive processes that may be essential for certain cognitive tasks.

■
INTELLIGENCE DEFINITION OF THINKING
■

To begin, it would be useful to define what is meant by *intelligence* or mental ability. To determine the degree of agreement concerning the definition of intelligence, Sternberg and Detterman (1986, p. vii) asked twenty-four leading psychologists to state "what I conceive intelligence to be" and compared their answers to those of fourteen experts who answered the same question in a symposium published in the *Journal of Educational Psychology* in 1921. Box 11-1 summarizes the attributes of intelligence that were frequently mentioned and

BOX 11 ▪ 1   Attributes Used to Define Intelligence

1986	1921	Attributes of intelligence
50%	57%	Higher cognitive processes (e.g., reasoning, problem solving)
29%	0%	That which is valued by culture
25%	7%	Executive control processes
21%	21%	Lower cognitive processes (e.g., sensing, perceiving, attending)
21%	7%	Knowledge
21%	21%	Successful or effective response to novel situation
17%	7%	Metacognitive processes (e.g., monitoring one's processing)
17%	29%	Ability to learn
17%	7%	Specific abilities (e.g., spatial, verbal, auditory)
17%	14%	General ability (ability to solve problems in all domains)
17%	14%	Not easily definable, not one construct
13%	29%	Adapting to the demands of the environment
8%	29%	Physiological mechanisms
13%	14%	Speed of mental processing
17%	0%	Integrating processes and knowledge

Adapted from Sternberg and Detterman (1986)

lists the percentage of experts in the 1921 and 1986 groups who suggested each attribute. As you can see, there are many different conceptions of intelligence, but the most popular description among both groups is that intelligence involves higher cognitive processes such as reasoning, problem solving, and decision making.

The view of intelligence as problem-solving skill is particularly relevant to the study of human problem solving. Accordingly, let's tentatively consider a general definition of intelligence that has three parts:

Internal cognitive characteristics—Intelligence concerns the nature of human information processing, such as internal cognitive processes in problem solving.

External behavioral performance—Intelligence is related to performance on cognitive tasks, such as solving problems.

Individual differences—Differences in intelligence are related to differences in internal cognitive processes and external performance.

Thus intelligence refers to internal cognitive characteristics that are related to individual differences in problem-solving performance.

This conception of intelligence provides a new line of attack in the study of human problem solving: a focus on individual differences in the cognitive processes and structures underlying problem-solving performance. Up to this point, we have not emphasized individual differences in thinking and problem solving. By focusing on individual differences, this chapter introduces a unique and important method for understanding thinking, problem solving, and cognition. In short, the intelligence definition of thinking is that thinking is a measurable skill in which people may differ.

More than a quarter of a century ago, Cronbach (1957) pointed out that scientific psychology seemed to have developed as two distinct and separate disciplines: the psychometric approach, which focused on individual differences among people's performances without much interest in the underlying cognitive processes and structures, and the experimental psychology approach, which focused on analyzing general cognitive processes without much interest in individual differences. Psychometricians focused on part of the definition of intelligence—namely, measuring individual differences in intelligent performance—while experimental psychologists focused on a different part of the definition—analyzing the basic processes in acquiring and manipulating information.

In the past decades, however, there has been an amazing rapprochement between the two traditions (Carroll, 1976; Sternberg, 1990). In this chapter, we will explore four approaches to the study of individual differences in intellectual ability: *cognitive factors* (or the psychometric approach), *cognitive correlates, cognitive components,* and *cognitive training.*

BOX 11 • 2   Factor Theory

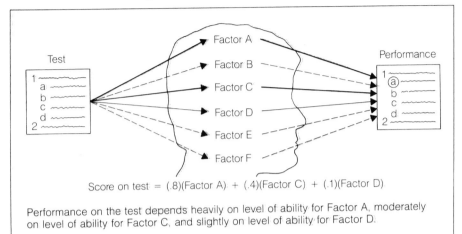

Score on test = (.8)(Factor A) + (.4)(Factor C) + (.1)(Factor D)

Performance on the test depends heavily on level of ability for Factor A, moderately on level of ability for Factor C, and slightly on level of ability for Factor D.

COGNITIVE FACTORS APPROACH

The first approach to the study of mental ability is the psychometric approach (which also can be called the cognitive factors approach). Quite literally, psychometrics means the measurement of the mind. This approach is based on the idea that we should determine the basic mental abilities and then develop tests to measure each of them. The underlying theme of the psychometric approach is that humans are endowed with a set of cognitive factors or traits, that there are individual differences along each factor, and that individual differences in these factors are related to differences in intellectual performance. Thus performance on a test of spatial ability is mediated by a set of underlying cognitive factors or traits. A summary of the cognitive factors approach to mental ability is presented in Box 11-2. In the remainder of this section, you will see how psychometricians have attempted to determine what the major cognitive factors are and how to measure them.

Galton (1869, 1883) was one of the first to systematically study individual differences in mental ability. His hypothesis was that differences in general performance were due to differences in many smaller, basic processes, such as how fast a person responds to a stimulus, how well she judges which of two balls weighs more, her sensitivity to pain, and so on. To test this idea, he gave a battery of seventeen tests to 9337 people. In addition to large individual differences

BOX 11 ▪ 3   Normal Distribution

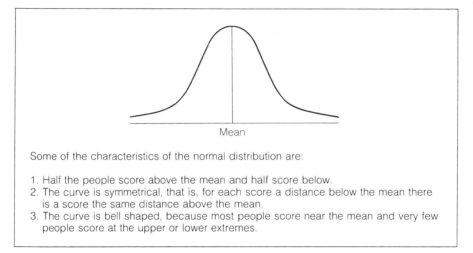

Mean

Some of the characteristics of the normal distribution are:

1. Half the people score above the mean and half score below.
2. The curve is symmetrical, that is, for each score a distance below the mean there is a score the same distance above the mean.
3. The curve is bell shaped, because most people score near the mean and very few people score at the upper or lower extremes.

among people, he found that differences in many mental abilities seemed to be normally distributed, as shown in Box 11-3. A person's level of ability could be described in terms of how much that person deviates above or below the mean. Thus, early in the course of scientific observation, Galton showed that people differ from one another.

Findings of individual differences by Galton and by others seem to have serious implications for the "one size fits all" approach to public education. In 1905 the French Minister of Public Instruction asked Alfred Binet to develop a simple test for use in schools. The purpose of the test was to locate "mentally deficient" students so they could be given special instruction. In essence, Binet was asked to develop a test that would predict success in school. Binet quickly found that the basic tasks used by Galton, such as response time and sensory acuity, were not related to school success. Instead, Binet decided to observe what an average child could do at each age level. After observing large groups of children at each age, he was able to generate a list as shown in Box 11-4. To test mental ability, Binet simply noted which tasks a child could do. If an eight-year-old, for example, could perform the tasks listed for that age, but could not perform any tasks for older ages, that child was average. If an eight-year-old could perform the tasks listed for that age as well as many of the tasks for nine-year-olds, that child scored above average. Binet's test, modified for "normal" children, became enormously popular and in many ways formed the basis for many subsequent intelligence tests.

BOX 11 • 4   Typical Test Items on Stanford-Binet Test

Age Two

1. Three-hole Form Board. Placing three geometric objects in form board.
2. Delayed Response. Identifying placement of hidden object after 10-second delay.
3. Identifying Parts of the Body. Pointing out features on paper doll.
4. Block Building Tower. Building four-block tower by imitating examiner's procedure.
5. Picture Vocabulary. Naming common objects from pictures.
6. Word Combinations. Spontaneous combination of two words.

Age Six

1. Vocabulary. Correctly defining 6 words on 45-word list.
2. Differences. Telling difference between two objects.
3. Mutilated Pictures. Pointing out missing part of pictured object.
4. Number Concepts. Counting number of blocks in a pile.
5. Opposite Analogies II. Items of form "Summer is hot; winter is _____."
6. Maze Tracing. Finding shortest path in simple maze.

Age Ten

1. Vocabulary. Correctly defining 11 words on same list.
2. Block Counting. Counting number of cubes in three-dimensional picture, some cubes hidden.
3. Abstract Words I. Definition of abstract adverbs.
4. Finding Reasons I. Giving reasons for laws or preferences.
5. Word Naming. Naming as many words as possible in one minute.
6. Repeating Six Digits. Repeating six digits in order.

Average Adult

1. Vocabulary. Correctly defining 20 words.
2. Ingenuity I. Algebraic word problems involving mental manipulation of volumes.
3. Differences between Abstract Words. Differentiating between two related abstract words.
4. Arithmetical Reasoning. Word problems involving simple computations.
5. Proverbs I. Giving meaning of proverbs.
6. Orientation: Direction II. Finding orientation after a verbal series of changes in directions.
7. Essential Differences. Giving principal difference between two related concepts.
8. Abstract Words III. Meanings of abstract adverbs.

From Brown (1983). Copyright © 1983 by CBS College Publishing. Reprinted by permission of Holt, Rinehart and Winston.

Binet's work is important for several reasons (Wolf, 1973). First, he launched the highly successful field of testing, perhaps today the major application of scientific psychology in our society. Second, he based his definition of mental ability on success in schools; thus, from the beginning of such testing, mental ability has been related to performance in real-world tasks. Finally, as you read over the items in Box 11-4, you may notice that Binet seems to be measuring the basic knowledge of the student rather than some primary memory processes; the theme that successful problem solving requires specific knowledge will be repeated again later in this chapter.

One question raised by work such as Binet's concerns whether intelligent performance is due to a single general factor or whether instead there are many small specific factors involved. Spearman (1904, 1927) addressed this question by collecting scores on many different tests from a large number of people. If there was one single factor that determined performance in all mental tests, he hypothesized, then scores of all the tests should be related to one another. In other words, if a certain person did well on one, he should do well on the others; if a person did poorly on one, he should do poorly on the others. However, if each test measured a single, specific ability, then test scores should be unrelated. Using some newly developed statistical techniques, Spearman was able to find some support for both ideas: all the tests seemed to be related to one another, although they were not perfectly related. This led Spearman to propose a "two-factor theory" of intelligence: there is a general factor (called g) as well as many smaller specific factors (called s) that influence performance on any given test. For example, verbal analogy tests may require the g factor as well as s factors, such as vocabulary and verbal fluency; a pictorial analogy test may require the same g factor as well as different s factors, such as visualization and imagery fluency.

Later, Thurstone (1938) modified the statistical techniques used by Spearman and found that there seemed to be seven "primary mental abilities": verbal comprehension, number, memory, perceptual speed, space, verbal fluency, and inductive reasoning. Thus, where Spearman found one general factor, Thurstone found seven.

In light of the conflicting findings of Spearman and Thurstone, Guilford (1959, 1967) adopted a different approach, called the "structure of the intellect." Guilford began by suggesting that any mental ability could be classified in terms of the following three dimensions:

Operation—such as evaluation, convergent production, divergent production, memory, and cognition.

Product—such as units, classes, relations, systems, transformations, and implications.

Content—such as figural, symbolic, semantic, and behavioral.

BOX 11 · 5   Guilford's 120 Mental Factors and Some Sample Test Items

Structure of the Intellect

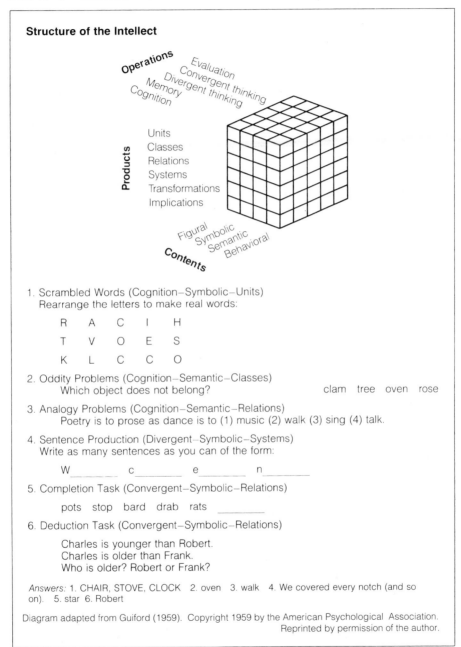

1. Scrambled Words (Cognition–Symbolic–Units)
   Rearrange the letters to make real words:

   R   A   C   I   H

   T   V   O   E   S

   K   L   C   C   O

2. Oddity Problems (Cognition–Semantic–Classes)
   Which object does not belong?   clam   tree   oven   rose

3. Analogy Problems (Cognition–Semantic–Relations)
   Poetry is to prose as dance is to (1) music (2) walk (3) sing (4) talk.

4. Sentence Production (Divergent–Symbolic–Systems)
   Write as many sentences as you can of the form:

   W_____   c_____   e_____   n_____

5. Completion Task (Convergent–Symbolic–Relations)

   pots   stop   bard   drab   rats   _____

6. Deduction Task (Convergent–Symbolic–Relations)

   Charles is younger than Robert.
   Charles is older than Frank.
   Who is older? Robert or Frank?

Answers: 1. CHAIR, STOVE, CLOCK   2. oven   3. walk   4. We covered every notch (and so on).   5. star 6. Robert

Diagram adapted from Guiford (1959). Copyright 1959 by the American Psychological Association. Reprinted by permission of the author.

There are $5 \times 6 \times 4$, or 120, mental abilities, corresponding to each possible combination of the three categories. Box 11-5 gives a summary of the structure of intellect theory as well as examples of some of the 120 factors. Although there are now tests available for most of the 120 factors, some factors are not yet measurable.

Where does the psychometric approach leave us? It leaves us with ample evidence that humans differ in intellectual performance and that these differences can be systematically measured. However, what is missing from the psychometric approach is a clear description of what differences in ability really mean. For example, what does someone who is high in "verbal ability" or "analogical reasoning" have in her head that is different from someone who scores low on the same tests? In the next three sections of this chapter, we explore three techniques for describing underlying differences in ability.

■
COGNITIVE CORRELATES APPROACH
■

The cognitive correlates approach begins by selecting some ability that can be measured using psychometric tests, such as verbal ability. The goal is to describe individual differences in that ability in terms of differences in general information-processing capacities or techniques. The cognitive correlates theory is based on two ideas:

Information-processing system—All humans come equipped with an information-processing system, such as a long-term memory for storing information permanently, a short-term memory for holding information we are actively thinking about, and processes for acting on that information.

Individual differences—People may differ with respect to the particular capacities of each memory process, and these are the building blocks of intelligent behavior.

As you can see, the cognitive correlates approach attempts to answer questions such as "What does it mean to be high in some ability?" In a series of papers, Hunt and his colleagues (Hunt, 1978, 1985; Hunt, Frost, & Lunneborg, 1973; Hunt, Lunneborg, & Lewis, 1975) have introduced the cognitive correlates approach by investigating the information-processing capacities that may be related to verbal ability. They use the term *information processing* or *mechanics of ability* to describe their theory.

In order for you to get a better understanding of this approach, let's consider

BOX 11 • 6   An Information-Processing System

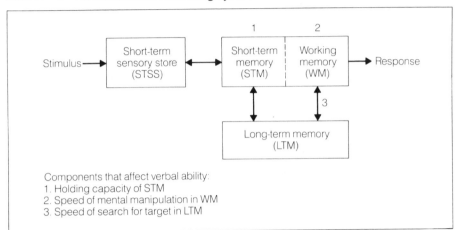

Components that affect verbal ability:
1. Holding capacity of STM
2. Speed of mental manipulation in WM
3. Speed of search for target in LTM

a question raised by Hunt, Lunneborg, and Lewis (1975), namely, "What does it mean to be high in verbal ability?" They found a group of college students who had scored very well on a standardized achievement test of verbal ability (such as the SAT verbal scale) and a group who had scored low on the same test. The goal of Hunt and colleagues was to determine whether differences between students of high and low verbal ability could be described in terms of differences in basic information-processing capacities.

Their first step was to describe the information-processing system that all humans possess. Box 11-6 shows a simple version of the information-processing system, consisting of memory stores and memory processes. The rectangles in Box 11-6 refer to memory stores: large amounts of information may be present in the outside world, large amounts of information may be stored permanently in long-term memory, and limited amounts of information may be temporarily held in short-term memory (such as information we are currently thinking about in a problem). The arrows in Box 11-6 refer to memory processes, such its searching for a specific piece of information in long-term memory or making a comparison decision in short-term memory. Thinking can be viewed as performing a series of manipulations of information that is held in short-term memory.

The next step in analyzing verbal ability was to try to locate basic memory processes that are required for verbal tasks such as reading. For example, Hunt and his colleagues suggest several processes, including the following:

Decoding information from long-term memory—Decoding refers to finding a specific piece of well-learned information in long-term memory, such as recognizing that the printed letter A refers to the first letter of the alphabet. In the normal course of reading, you must decode letters or strings of letters thousands of times. People may differ in the speed with which they can decode, that is, find the name of a printed symbol in long-term memory.

Holding information in short-term memory—Holding refers to actively thinking about and remembering information at one instance, such as hearing a list of letters and being able to recite them back in order. In reading, you must hold combinations of letters in short-term memory until you can figure out what the word is, or you must hold a string of words until you can understand the entire sentence. People may differ in the amount of information that they can actively hold in their minds at one time.

Manipulating information in short-term memory—Manipulating refers to performing a simple operation on information that is being held in short-term memory, such as comparing two letters to determine whether they are the same. Reading requires many such operations in working memory, and people may differ in their speeds for comparing and deciding.

Hunt has thus suggested some basic information processes that may be the building blocks of verbal ability.

The next step in Hunt's plan was to measure the basic memory processes in students of high and low verbal ability, and to see whether differences in verbal ability are related to differences in these basic processes. Let's examine decoding from long-term memory, holding information in short-term memory, and manipulating information, each in turn.

To measure the speed of decoding processes, Hunt modified a procedure developed by Posner and his colleagues (Posner, 1978; Posner et al., 1969; Posner & Mitchell, 1967) called a "letter-matching task." (This task is discussed in Chapter 7.) A subject sits in front of a computer terminal screen on which two letters appear. If they are the same, the subject presses the "same" button; if they are different, the subject presses the "different" button. Two kinds of trials are used: physical match and name match. On physical match trials, the subject is asked to base the "same-different" judgment on whether the two letters are physically identical; here AA is "same," but Aa is "different." On name match trials the subject is asked to judge whether the two letters have the same name; in this case, Aa is "same" and AB is "different."

To find the decoding time, you must use a "subtraction method" (Posner, 1978) as follows. Let's assume that the physical match requires the following processes: encoding the letters, comparing the letters, deciding on a response,

BOX 11 • 7   Performance of High- and Low-Verbal Subjects on Name and Physical
Identity Problems

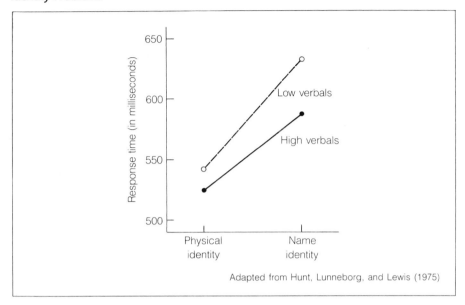

Adapted from Hunt, Lunneborg, and Lewis (1975)

and executing the response. The name match task requires all of these processes
plus finding the name of the letters in long-term memory. These processes are:
encoding the letters, finding their names in long-term memory, comparing the
names, deciding on a response, and executing the response. Thus, if we take the
time for a name match and subtract the time for physical match, we will have an
estimate of the time for "decoding" or finding the name of letters in long-term
memory.

Box 11-7 shows the average response times for high- and low-verbal subjects
on physical and name matches. Both groups performed at similar levels for
physical matches; thus there is no evidence that high-verbal subjects are just
faster in responding. However, the name match task adds sixty-four milliseconds
for the high verbals and eighty-nine milliseconds for the low verbals. Apparently,
the time to look up the name for a letter is less for high-verbal subjects. Although
the extra speed of the high-verbal subjects is just a small fraction of a second, you
must consider that reading requires thousands of such decoding processes.

In a related study, Goldberg, Schwartz, and Stewart (1977) asked students who
scored high and low on conventional tests of verbal ability to make three kinds
of judgments: *physical match*—whether or not two words are physically identical

BOX 11 • 8   Performance of High- and Low-Verbal Students on Three Identity Problems

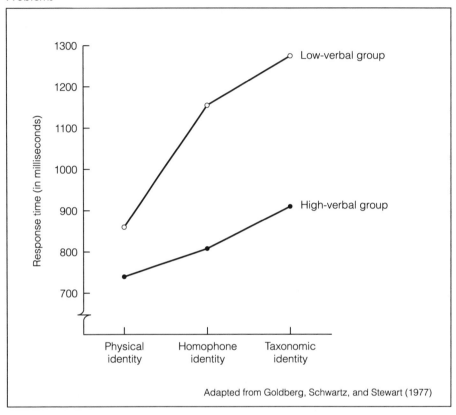

Adapted from Goldberg, Schwartz, and Stewart (1977)

(e.g., deer-deer is Yes, DEER-deer is No); *homophone match*—whether or not two words are pronounced the same (e.g., dear-deer is Yes; deer-elk is No); and *taxonomic match*—whether or not two words belong to the same category (e.g., deer-elk is Yes; deer-sink is No). Box 11-8 summarizes the average time that high- and low-verbal students required to make each kind of judgment. As you can see, the time it takes to access a word's taxonomic category from long-term memory (determined by subtracting physical match time from taxonomic match time) is more than twice as long for low-verbal students (4.0 seconds) as for high-verbal students (1.7 seconds); similarly, the time it takes to access a word's sound in long-term memory (determined by subtracting physical match time from homophone match time) is more than three times greater for low-verbal students (3.0 seconds) than high-verbal students (0.8 seconds). In summary, the speed with which a person can search long-term memory for a target seems to be related

BOX 11 • 9   Measurement of STM Capacity Using a Modified Peterson Task

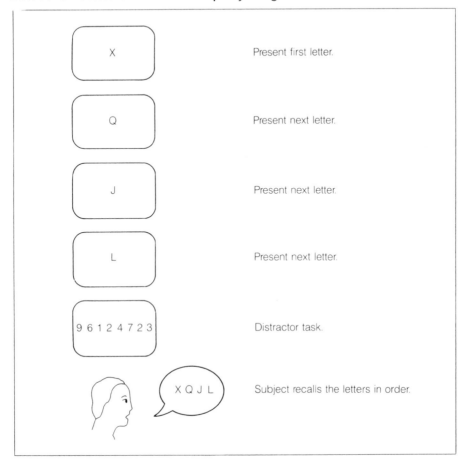

X   Present first letter.

Q   Present next letter.

J   Present next letter.

L   Present next letter.

9 6 1 2 4 7 2 3   Distractor task.

X Q J L   Subject recalls the letters in order.

to measures of general verbal ability (Hunt, 1985; Hunt, Davidson, & Lansman, 1981).

To evaluate short-term memory, Hunt used a memory-span task modified from Peterson and Peterson (1959). Their procedure, summarized in Box 11-9, was designed to measure the holding capacity of short-term memory. Four letters were displayed on a screen, one at a time, for 400 milliseconds each. Then, one to thirty-six digits were presented on the screen and the subject had to recite them; this digit-shadowing task of repeating digits aloud was included to prevent

BOX 11 • 10   Performance of High- and Low-Verbal Subjects on STM Task

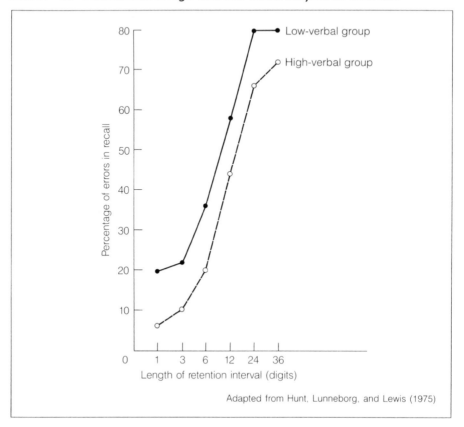

Adapted from Hunt, Lunneborg, and Lewis (1975)

the subject from rehearsing the four letters. Next, the subject was asked to recall the four letters in order.

Box 11-10 shows that high-verbal subjects made fewer errors in recall than low-verbal subjects. The fact that high-verbal subjects were better able to remember letters in order suggests that they have better techniques for keeping large amounts of information in short-term memory. For example, one way to keep information in active memory is to "chunk" the information. A letter sequence like SPTR could be remembered as a single group—for example, SPuTteR. One explanation of the superior performance of high-verbal subjects is that they make better use of techniques such as grouping. In any case, results indicate that high-verbal subjects are able to hold more verbal information in active memory at once than low-verbal subjects.

In light of findings like these, Just and Carpenter (1987) have proposed that readers who possess larger working-memory capacities are able to hold actively a greater number of recently processed propositions. This would be helpful whenever the reader has to relate a newly read proposition to a recently processed one. For example, upon encountering a pronoun, the reader must relate that pronoun back to a previously mentioned person, place, or thing. If the person still holds the relevant proposition in working memory, the match can be made easily; if not, the reader will have to go back and reread part of the passage or risk a misunderstanding of what the pronoun refers to.

For example, Daneman and Carpenter (1980, p. 455) asked students to read paragraphs such as the following:

> Sitting with Richie, Archie, Walter and the rest of my gang in the Grill yesterday, I began to feel uneasy. Robbie had put a dime in the juke box. It was blaring one of the latest "Rock and Roll" favorites. I was studying, in horror, the reactions of my friends to the music. I was especially perturbed by the expression on my best friend's face. Wayne looked intense and was pounding the table furiously to the beat. Now, I like most of the things other teenager boys like. I like girls with blonde hair, girls with dark curly hair, in fact all girls. I like milkshakes, football games, and beach parties. I like denim jeans, fancy T-shirts and sneakers. It is not that I dislike rock music, but I think it is supposed to be fun and not taken too seriously. And here he was, "all shook up" and serious over the crazy music.

Then students were asked questions, such as "Who was all shook up and serious over the music?" As you can see, to answer this question you need to relate "he" in sentence 12 to "Wayne" in sentence 6, so there are five intervening sentences. Daneman and Carpenter (1980), in addition to creating such reading comprehension tasks in which the number of sentences between the pronoun and its referent ranged from two to seven, also used a test of working memory capacity that required readers to process entire sentences. The results are summarized in Box 11-11. As expected, students with large working-memory capacity performed well on answering questions even when six or seven sentences intervened; students with small working-memory capacity performed well when only two or three sentences intervened but not when there were six or seven intervening sentences. Supporting results have been obtained in subsequent studies (Daneman & Carpenter, 1983), supporting the claim that part of individual differences in verbal ability can be accounted for by differences in working-memory capacity.

Finally, Hunt and colleagues (1975) modified Sternberg's (1966, 1975) memory-scanning task in order to measure the time needed to manipulate information in short-term memory. (This task is discussed in Chapter 7). A

BOX 11 • 11   Proportion Correct on Two Types of Comprehension Questions by Readers with Large and Small Working-Memory Capacity

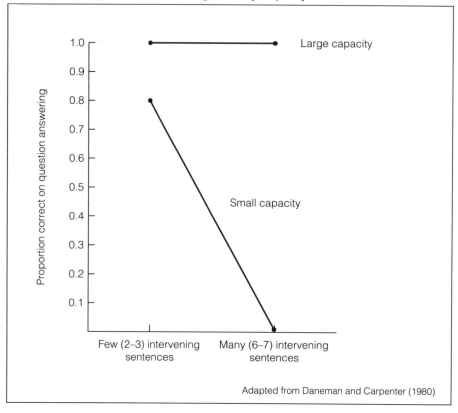

Adapted from Daneman and Carpenter (1980)

subject is seated in front of a screen and sees a memory set of one to five letters, presented one at a time. Then a probe letter comes on the screen, and the subject must decide whether that probe letter was one of the letters just presented. Let's consider what the subject must do when one letter is in the target set: encode one letter, hold that letter in memory, encode the probe letter, compare it to the one letter in memory, decide on a response, and respond. When two letters are in the target set, the subject must encode and store two letters instead of one and make an additional mental comparison. Each time a letter is added to the memory set, the subject must engage in one more mental comparison.

In an earlier study, Hunt, Frost, and Lunneborg (1973) had found that adding a letter to the target set tended to add about 60 milliseconds to the response time of high-verbal subjects and 80 milliseconds to the response time of low-verbal subjects. Thus it appears that the time it takes to make a mental comparison is less for high-verbal than for low-verbal subjects. Again, a simple mental process can be used to describe some of the differences in verbal ability.

Unfortunately, there are several problems with the cognitive correlates approach, including empirical and theoretical issues. First, some of the data have been difficult to replicate. For example, Hunt (1978) notes that it has not been possible to replicate the findings concerning the memory-scanning task and that Sternberg (1975) found no relation between scanning speed and intelligence. As a response to this criticism, note that when more demanding versions of the task are used, large individual differences again emerge. Thus Hunt (1978) suggests that tasks must allow individuals to give all of their attention to the task.

As another example, Hogaboam and Pellegrino (1978) were unable to find any relation between verbal SAT scores and performance on a task involving making judgments about whether a word (or picture) belonged to a given category. Although this task is similar to the letter matching task used by Hunt and colleagues (1975), Hogaboam and Pellegrino were forced to the opposite conclusion: "Verbal ability in our college sample was totally unrelated to the speed of making simple semantic category decisions" (1978, p. 192). However, Hunt and colleagues (1981) have presented new data showing that differences between high- and low-verbal subjects may he obtained under certain circumstances.

A second major criticism of the cognitive correlates approach is that it emphasizes differences in the speeds of basic mental processes, while it should also emphasize differences in strategies for manipulating these basic processes. In other words, intelligent behavior requires both applying information-processing procedures efficiently *and* deciding which procedures to use, monitoring these procedures, and determining when to change. For example, early work by Galton was aimed at finding simple processes—such as the time needed to respond to a stimulus—that might be related to individual differences in intellectual ability. However, such measures proved useless for later development of intelligence tests. Pellegrino and Glaser (1979, p. 68) fear that cognitive correlates research may lead to "overemphasis on the mechanics of thought and return us to the position of Galton."

In response, Hunt and his colleagues (Hunt, 1985; Hunt & MacLeod, 1979; MacLeod, Hunt, & Mathews, 1978) have begun to incorporate "strategies" into their approach. For example, they used a sentence-picture verification task (see Chapter 7) in which subjects see a sentence such as "The star is not above the plus" and a picture such as $\overset{*}{+}$. The subject must answer "true" if the sentence and picture are consistent and "false" if they are not (as is the case in the example cited here). MacLeod, Hunt, and Mathews (1978) found that for one group of subjects—apparently those using verbal encoding strategies—performance differences correlated highly with verbal ability but not with spatial ability. For the other subjects, using visual encoding strategies, differences in response time were correlated highly with spatial ability but not with verbal ability. Thus, as work in the cognitive correlates tradition continues, increased attention is being paid to differences in the general strategies used by subjects.

■
COGNITIVE COMPONENTS APPROACH
■

Theories based on cognitive components provide a slightly different approach to describing individual differences in intellectual ability. In componential theories, the motivating question is "What does an intelligence test measure?" To answer this question, researchers carry out the following activities:

Select a cognitive task—For any cognitive skill, the first step is to select a task or problem commonly used on tests of that skill; for example, analogies of the form "A is to B as C is to D" are sometimes used on IQ tests.

Conduct a cognitive analysis of the task—For any intelligence or cognitive ability test item, the task of solving that problem can be broken down into a list of component processes; for example, solving analogies requires that the reasoner encode the terms, infer the relations between terms, and so on.

Experimentally isolate the critical components—The goal of experimental research is to determine which of the component processes are related to individual differences in performance; for example, encoding may be an important component for pictorial and geometric analogies.

In his book *Intelligence, Information Processing, and Analogical Reasoning*, Robert Sternberg (1977) presented a theory and data that launched a cognitive components theory of individual differences. The early work focused on understanding individual differences in how people solve analogy problems of the form "A is to B as C is to D," such as shown in Box 11-12. Since then, the theory has been extended and clarified under the title of *triarchic theory* (Sternberg, 1985, 1988).

Sternberg's (1985, 1988) triarchic theory begins with the idea that problem solving depends on applying *cognitive components*—that is, basic information processes—to operate on *mental representations*—that is, basic knowledge about events or things. Individual differences in human intelligence can be described in terms of individual differences in these components. According to Sternberg's (1985, 1988) triarchic theory, there are three kinds of information-processing

BOX 11 ▪ 12   Some Analogy Problems

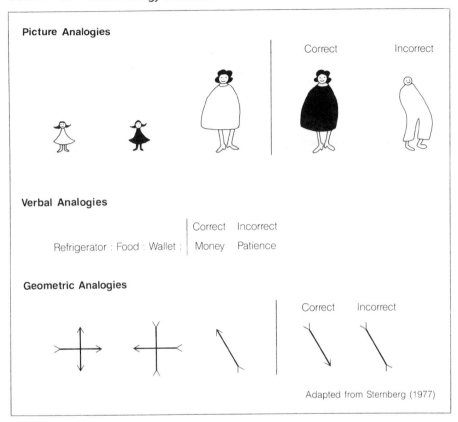

Picture Analogies

Correct   Incorrect

Verbal Analogies

Correct   Incorrect

Refrigerator : Food : Wallet :   Money   Patience

Geometric Analogies

Correct   Incorrect

Adapted from Sternberg (1977)

components: *metacomponents, performance components,* and *knowledge-acquisition components.*

Metacomponents are used to plan, evaluate, and monitor one's problem-solving activities. Sternberg (1988, p. 78) refers to metacomponents as the "white collar processes of human intelligence" because they are the executives who manage and supervise the work of lower-level components. The role of executive control processes in computer simulations of problem solving have been described in Chapter 6, and the development of metacognitive processes have been described in Chapter 10.

According to Sternberg (1985, 1988), some of the important executive control processes in solving analogies and other problems are:

Deciding what problem needs to be solved—For example, some unsuccessful problem solvers view the analogy task as a problem in finding word associations between C and D terms (Sternberg & Nigro, 1983).

Selecting appropriate lower-level components—For example, some unsuccessful analogy problem solvers do not form a connection between the A-to-B part of the problem and the C-to-D part of the problem; that is, the mapping component is missing (Sternberg & Rivkin, 1979).

Selecting a representation of problem information—For example, unsuccessful problem solvers may use a linguistic representation of an analogy when a spatial representation would be more efficient (Sternberg & Weil, 1980).

Selecting a strategy for combining lower-level components—For example, using an exhaustive search strategy for determining all possible relations between the A and B term can sometimes result in wasted time (Sternberg & Ketron, 1982).

Deciding how to allocate attentional resources—For example, when a problem solver is working at peak efficiency, decreasing solution time slightly can greatly increase error rate (Sternberg, 1980b).

Monitoring the solution process—For example, less successful problem solvers do not know what to do when none of the answer alternatives seem satisfactory (Sternberg & Weil, 1980).

As you can see, the higher-level components (metacomponents) issue instructions for how to solve a problem, but the work is carried out by lower-level components (performance components). Sternberg (1988, p. 115) refers to performance components as the "blue collar processes of mental self-management" because they carry out the instructions established by the "executives." Each problem solver possesses a large collection of performance components, and Sternberg (1985, 1988) has sorted them into three major categories:

Encoding components are used to transfer information from the outside world into one's memory, such as mentally representing the A, B, C terms in the analogy BOY:MALE::GIRL: _____.

Combination and comparison components are used to transform or operate on mental representations, such as comparing the features of BOY and MALE in the analogy BOY:MALE::GIRL: _____.

Response components are used to generate behavior such as writing the word *female* in the blank for the analogy BOY:MALE::GIRL: _____.

Finally, because knowledge-acquisition components are used to acquire new knowledge, Sternberg (1988, p. 170) calls them the "students of mental self-management." Sternberg (1985, 1988) lists three knowledge-acquisition components and shows how they are involved in helping a person build a representation of a problem: *selective encoding, selective combination,* and *selective comparison.*

Selective encoding involves paying attention to relevant information and ignoring irrelevant information. For example, consider the following problem (Sternberg, 1988, p. 178):

> If you have black socks and brown socks in your drawer, mixed in the ratio of four to five, how many socks will you have to take out to make sure of having a pair the same color?

To solve this problem you must realize that "mixed in the ratio of four to five" is irrelevant.

Selective combination involves building appropriate connections among the newly acquired pieces of information in order to form a coherent structure. For example, consider the following problem cited by Sternberg (1988, p. 194):

> You arrive in a country that has two types of people: truth tellers and liars. The truth tellers always tell the truth, and the liars always lie. Your tour guide, a native, tells you that the country's prime minister just admitted being a liar. Is your tour guide a liar or a truth teller?

In this case you must combine several pieces of information: a truth teller would never say he is a liar, and a liar would never say he is a liar, so the prime minister would never admit to being a liar; the tour guide said that the prime minister admitted to being a liar, but that is impossible; so the tour guide must be a liar.

Selective comparison involves building appropriate connections between the newly acquired information and existing knowledge in one's memory. For example, suppose I gave you a problem that required selective encoding, such as the socks problem. You are likely to perform better on it if you had just solved a series of problems that are relevant to this problem and I point that relevance out, than if not (Davidson & Sternberg, 1984). The role of transfer from one problem to another is examined in more detail in Chapter 14.

What does Sternberg's triarchic theory tell us about human problem solving? To answer this question, let's focus on the performance components involved in solving analogy problems. The first step is to conduct a componential analysis of a problem commonly found on IQ tests or other tests of intellectual ability, such as the analogy problems shown in Box 11-12. In one version of this task, you are given four terms in the form "A is to B as C is to D." Your job as a subject is to answer Yes if the rule linking A to B also applies to the relation between C and D and to answer No otherwise.

Once Sternberg selected a problem, such as the analogies in Box 11-12, his next step was to perform a cognitive task analysis (Gagné, 1968; Greeno, 1976; Resnick, 1976). He determined that an analogy problem can be broken down into the following major components. For example, consider this analogy: red is to stop as green is to go, which could be written as, red:stop::green:go.

Encoding (a)—Each of the four stimulus items is translated into an internal representation. For example, "red," "stop," "green," and "go" are represented in memory.

Inference (x)—A rule is found that relates the A term of the analogy to the B term. For example, a red traffic light is a signal to stop.

Mapping (y)—A higher-order rule is found that relates the A term with the C term. For example, red and green are colors of traffic signals.

Application (z)—A rule is applied to C in order to generate a final term D. For example, green is the signal for go. If this answer matches the answer given for the D term, the answer regarding the analogy is Yes, otherwise, the answer is No.

Preparation-response (c)—This includes all the remaining time that is used in preparing to solve the analogy and carrying out the response.

This task analysis of a verbal analogy problem into component processes is summarized in Box 11-13 and is simpler than Sternberg's (1977) actual model.

Sternberg's next major step was to collect data concerning how long it takes people to perform each of the component processes in analogy solving, namely, encoding, inference, mapping, application, and preparation response. He conducted a long series of experiments using a large number of subjects; each subject participated in many sessions. On each trial the subject was asked to look at a screen, then the first part of the problem (called a "cue" phase) was given—such as A:B. When the subject was ready for the rest of the problem, he or she pressed a button, and the entire problem (called the "solution" phase) was given—such as A:B::C:D. If the analogy was correct, the subject pressed a "yes" button; the subject pressed a "no" button if the D term was inappropriate. On some trials the cue phase consisted of the first three terms, such as A:B::C, and this was called C-3. The cue phase when it was called C-2 consisted of the first two terms, such as A:B. When only one term was given in the cue phase, such as A, this was called C-1. Finally, on some trials, no information was given during the cue phase, and this was called C-0. In all cases, the entire analogy with all four

BOX 11 • 13   Component Process in Analogy Task

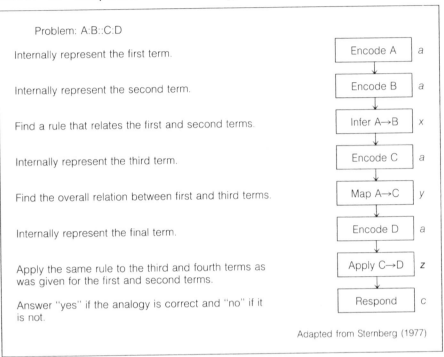

Problem: A:B::C:D

Internally represent the first term.	Encode A · a
Internally represent the second term.	Encode B · a
Find a rule that relates the first and second terms.	Infer A→B · x
Internally represent the third term.	Encode C · a
Find the overall relation between first and third terms.	Map A→C · y
Internally represent the final term.	Encode D · a
Apply the same rule to the third and fourth terms as was given for the first and second terms.	Apply C→D · z
Answer "yes" if the analogy is correct and "no" if it is not.	Respond · c

Adapted from Sternberg (1977)

terms was presented in the second half of each trial during the solution phase. This procedure is summarized in Box 11-14.

Sternberg assumed that during the cue phase of each trial, the subject was able to accomplish some of the component processes. For example, for the C-3 situation the subject could encode three of the four terms, make an inference, and make a mapping. For the C-2 situation, the subject encodes two of the three terms and makes an inference. For C-1, the subject encodes one term. For C-0, nothing happens. Thus, on the solution phase, what is left to be done? For subjects who had three terms in the cue phase, all they have to do during the solution phase is encode one term and make an application as well as a preparation and response. For the C-2 situation, the solution involves encoding two terms, making a mapping, and making an application as well as a preparation and response. For the C-1 situation, a solution uses all of the component processes except one encoding; for C-0, a solution involves every component process. Sternberg assumed that each component is independent and additive; that is, if you carry out a component process during the cuing phase you need not

BOX 11 ▪ 14 Procedure for Analogy Experiments

Situation	Cue Phase	Solution Phase
C-0		A:B::C:D
C-1	A	A:B::C:D
C-2	A:B	A:B::C:D
C-3	A:B::C	A:B::C:D

BOX 11 ▪ 15 Response Times for Analogy Experiment

		Components	Response Time (in milliseconds)
Cue Phase	C-0		530
	C-1	1a	755
	C-2	2a, x	952
	C-3	3a, x, y	1147
Solution Phase	C-0	4a, x, y, z, c	1423
	C-1	3a, x, y, z, c	1328
	C-2	2a, y, z, c	947
	C-3	1a, z, c	681

bother with it during the solution phase. These assumptions are summarized in Box 11-15.

Let's assume that each component process takes a certain amount of time. Further, let's assume that the solution for the C-0 situations takes all the processes involved in C-1 plus one more, and the solution for C-1 situations takes all the processes involved in C-2 plus one more, and so on. This is what Sternberg means by his assumption that the components are independent and additive. The average response times for the cuing phase and the solution phase of each situation are given in Box 11-16. As expected, reaction takes longer when more component processes must be carried out: C-3 takes more time than C-0 on the cuing phase, but C-0 takes more time than C-3 on solution. By subtracting the time of one situation from another, we can begin to get a rough idea of how long each component process takes. For example, the difference between C-3 and C-2 on the solution phase is that C-3 contains two more component processes—mapping and encoding of one term. Thus the difference in response

BOX 11 • 16   Estimated Time for Each Component in an Analogy Problem

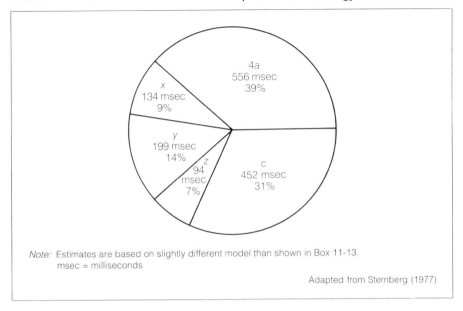

Note: Estimates are based on slightly different model than shown in Box 11-13.
msec = milliseconds

Adapted from Sternberg (1977)

time between C-3 and C-2 gives a rough estimation of the time needed to perform a mapping and one encoding.

Using this subtraction method along with statistical regression techniques that we will not describe here, Sternberg was able to find average response latency values for each component. As you can see in Box 11-16, most of the time required to solve a typical pictorial analogy consists of encoding and preparing a response (*a* and *c*, respectively).

Finally, the last step in Sternberg's work was to give his subjects standardized tests of intellectual ability, such as tests of reasoning and perceptual speed. A high correlation would indicate that performance on these tests is related to one of the components in the analogy test. You might expect that reasoning ability would be related to inference, mapping, and application. However, as Box 11-17 shows, performance on tests of reasoning was most strongly related to the preparation and response component. Although these results are for pictorial analogies, similar results were obtained for other types of analogies. Thus Sternberg was able to isolate the components that are most strongly related to individual differences in intellectual ability. More recently, Sternberg and Gardner (1983) have shown that the same set of five components can be used to describe performance on three different kinds of inductive reasoning tasks (analogies, series completions,

BOX 11 • 17   Correlations Between Component Times and Ability Tests

	Component				
	a	x	y	z	c
Reasoning	.32	− .13	− .31	− .19	.71*
Perceptual speed	− .22	− .16	.08	− .19	− .22

*Significant correlation at $p < .01$.

Adapted from Sternberg (1977)

and oddity problems) involving three different kinds of material (verbal, pictorial, and geometric).

Sternberg's componential analysis implies that we will be able to describe intelligence in a new way. Instead of saying, "Intelligence is what an intelligence test measures," the cognitive components approach allows us to say, "Intelligence involves individual differences on component processes X, Y, and Z." The advance of this approach over the psychometric approach is that we are able to give precise definitions of what we mean by component processes X, Y, and Z.

The componential analysis approach of Sternberg has been criticized mainly on two grounds: methodological and theoretical (Pellegrino & Lyon, 1979). First, the method of Sternberg's research has been criticized because very simple analogy tasks were used. These problems were so easy that there were few errors. Subjects seem to be able to use automatic processes on such problems. However, if more complex analogies had been used, there might have been more evidence of individual differences in strategies and decision tactics. This point is important if differences in intelligence are more closely related to differences in how people use strategies than to how well they use automatic procedures.

As a response to this criticism, note that componential analysis has now been applied to a wide range of intellectual tasks. These include linear and syllogistic reasoning, reasoning on spatial tasks, reasoning on series completion tasks, and memory span (Pellegrino & Glaser, 1979; Sternberg, 1985, 1988). Thus this criticism is actually a call for expanded research, a call that is sure to be heeded in years to come.

The second criticism is that the theory does not emphasize the use of planning and decision making by problem solvers. For example, there is reason to believe that some subjects use visual encoding and some use verbal encoding in certain tasks (Hunt & McLeod, 1979). Similarly, Campione and Brown (1979) have pointed to the role of "executive control" in intelligence, that is, how people choose which strategy is appropriate.

In response to this criticism, Sternberg has revised his theory to include metacomponents. As you can see, the analysis presented in this section has focused on performance components rather than metacomponents. Future research in understanding individual differences in cognitive ability will need to focus on the metacomponential level, because "a full account of the unities in inductive reasoning would have to deal with commonalities in metacomponential as well as performance componential processing" (Sternberg & Gardner, 1983, p. 111). While acknowledging the importance of performance components, Sternberg (1985, p. 107) concludes that "metacomponential processes are more fundamental sources of . . . individual and developmental differences." One promising new approach involves teaching componential processes and strategies to people (Campione & Brown, 1979; Holtzman, Glaser, & Pellegrino, 1976; Sternberg & Ketron, 1982), as described in the next section on cognitive training approaches.

■
COGNITIVE TRAINING APPROACH
■

In the cognitive components approach, we begin by analyzing a cognitive task into its component processes and then seek to isolate these component processes to account for individual differences in performance on the task. The point of the cognitive training approach is to attempt to validate this componential analysis by teaching students to improve on one or more crucial component processes underlying a cognitive task. If the component processes are important sources of individual differences, then students who receive effective training on a crucial component process should show an overall improvement on the task.

As an example of the cognitive training approach, let's conduct a componential analysis of series completion problems such as shown in Box 11-18. Here you are given a series of letters and must figure out what the next

BOX 11 ▪ 18   Letter Series Completion Task

1. atbataatbat ____

2. aaabbbcccdd ____

3. wxaxybyzczadab ____

4. urtustuttu ____

From Simon and Kotovsky (1963). Copyright 1963 by the American Psychological Association. Reprinted by permission of the author.

letter should be. These are rule induction tasks (such as examined in Chapter 4), and these kinds of tasks have frequently found their way onto intelligence tests (Thurstone, 1938).

The rules for each sequence can be represented as a program, that is, as a list of things to do. For example, the program for the fourth problem can be written as:

> Write the letter L1.
> Write the letter L2.
> Add one to letter L2.
> Write the letter L3.
> Go back to the first step.

All you need to know is that the system begins with L1 = u, L2 = r, and L3 = t. Simon and Kotovsky found that rules requiring long descriptions (such as long computer programs) were more difficult for humans and computers to solve; rules placing large demands on working memory, like the one in the third problem, were especially difficult.

What are the steps involved in solving series completion problems, that is, what are the steps you must go through in order to generate and use a program such as shown above? Simon and Kotovsky (1963; Kotovsky & Simon, 1973) created a computer program that solves series completions by using four major subroutines:

Detection of interletter relations—The problem solver determines the relations between letters such as *identity,* in which the same letter is used throughout, such as the first, fourth, seventh, and tenth letters in problem 1; *next,* in which the next letter in the alphabet is used, such as the first, fourth, seventh, and tenth letters in problem 2; and *backwards next,* in which the preceding letter in the alphabet is used.

Discovery of periodicity—The problem solver determines how many letters make up one cycle; for example, in each problem in Box 11-18, the cycle is three: (atb/ata/atb/at-), (aaa/bbb/ccc/dd-), (wxa/xyb/yzc/zad/ab-), and (urt/ust/utt/u-).

Completion of pattern description—The problem solver formulates the rule, such as every first letter is *a* (identity relation), every second letter is *t* (identity relation), and every third letter alternates between *b* and *a* (next relation) for the first problem in Box 11-18.

Extrapolation—The problem solver applies the rule to the missing letter(s) in the problem, such as noting that the missing letter in problem 1 is *a*.

BOX 11 ▪ 19   Pretest and Posttest Problems

Instructions: List the next four letters for each series.

Pretest	Posttest
cdcdcd	xyxyxy
aaabbbcccdd	hhhiiijjjkk
pononmnmlmlk	dcbcbabaz
rscdstdetuef	efpqfgqrghrs
npaoqapraqsa	acmbdmcemdfm
wxaxybyzczadab	hilijmjknklolm
abmcdmefmghm	ghrijrklrmnr
defgefghfghi	klmnlmnomnop
mabmbcmcdm	aopapqaqra
urtustuttu	mjlmklmllm
qxapxbqxa	tadsaetad
abyabxabwab	hifhiehidhi
atbataatbat	piqpippiqpi
aduacuaeuabuaf	gjagiagkaghagl
jkqrklrslmst	cdjkdekleflm

From Holzman, Glaser, and Pellegrino (1976)

Although other researchers have offered slightly different ways of breaking series completion problems into component processes (Pellegrino, 1985; Sternberg & Gardner, 1983), Holtzman, Glaser, and Pellegrino (1976) have used Kotovsky and Simon's (1973) analysis as the basis for teaching elementary school children how to solve series completion problems. Box 11-19 shows fifteen problems that children were asked to solve before training and fifteen equally difficult problems that the children were asked to solve after training.

Children in the training group received four thirty-minute training sessions on the detection of relations and on the discovery of periodicity. In relations training, the children were taught about three relations—identity, next, and backwards next—through a series of oddity problems. For example, students were asked to identify the letter pair that did not belong in a set of four pairs, such as: *cd xy lm mx*. In this case, the correct answer is *mx* because each other pair corresponds to the "next" relation. For the problem *aa cc mn vv*, the correct answer is *mn* because all other pairs follow the "identity" relation. A second part of relations training involved asking students to draw lines connecting any two

BOX 11 · 20   Effects of Componential Training on Solving Series Completion
Problems

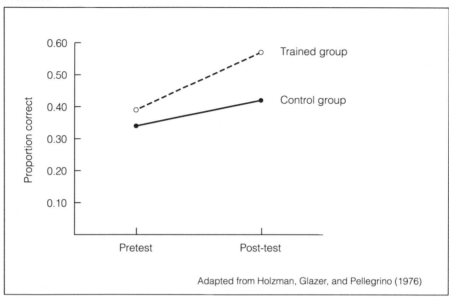

Adapted from Holzman, Glazer, and Pellegrino (1976)

letters that followed a stated relation, such as finding all "next" letter pairs in the
string, *z c d f a l m p n r s w*. The correct answer is to connect *z* and *a*, *c* and *d*, *l* and
m, *m* and *n*, and *r* and *s*. For periodicity training, the children were asked to place
slash marks to indicate the cycle for a list of letters such as a a a x x x m m m
or *m k f m t z m b d*. The correct answer for each is to place a slash after every third
letter. If students made errors, the experimenter corrected the error and explained
the basis for the correct choice.

Does componential training improve students' performance on series
completion problems? Box 11-20 shows that trained subjects showed a large
pretest-to-posttest improvement, whereas the control group did not. In addition,
the trained group showed particularly large gains on more difficult problems as
compared to the control group.

In another training study, Sternberg and Ketron (1982) taught college
students how to solve analogy problems such as those shown in Box 11-21. As
you can see, the top analogy problem involves hat color (black or white), suit
pattern (striped or polka-dotted), handgear (suitcase or umbrella), and footwear
(shoes or boots). For the bottom analogy problem, the attributes are height (tall
or short), weight (fat or thin), clothing color (black or white), and sex (male or
female).

BOX 11 ▪ 21   Some Pictorial Analogies

A is to B as C is to ___

From Sternberg and Ketron (1982)

Based on the componential analysis summarized in Box 11-13, Sternberg and Ketron (1982, pp. 402–403) taught some students to use the following strategy:

1. First, you infer the relation between a single attribute of A (the first analogy term) and a single attribute of B (the second analogy term). The attribute may be any one of the four. This inference requires you to figure out whether the attribute changes in value from A to B, or remains the same.

2. Next, you attempt to apply from C (the third analogy term) to each of the two answer options the relation you inferred from A to B. In doing so, you attempt to apply the attribute of C onto each option. If the attribute you happened to select enables you to distinguish which option is right and which is wrong, go to Step 3. This would be the case if either an attribute that changed from A to B changed from C to one option but not the other, or if an attribute that remained constant from A to B remained constant from C to one option but not the other. If, however, the attribute you chose does not enable you to distinguish the wrong answer from the right answer, you should return to Step 1, selecting a second attribute from the three that remain untested. You then infer and apply this attribute, again attempting to solve the analogy. You continue the process until you have chosen an attribute that enables you to distinguish between options.

BOX 11 ∙ 22   Test Performance for Trained and Untrained Problem Solvers

Group	Average Solution Time (seconds)	Error Rate (%)
Trained group	7.6	1.0
Untrained group	2.8	2.5

Adapted from Sternberg and Ketron (1982)

3. Finally, you respond with the correct answer option, that which completes the analogy, A : B :: C : D.

Box 11-22 summarizes the analogy test performance of students who were trained to use this strategy and those who were not trained. As you can see, trained students took longer to solve each test problem but committed fewer errors than untrained students. Another interesting finding is that scores on a pretest of general reasoning ability correlated with performance on the analogy test for untrained students but not for trained students. Apparently, Sternberg and Ketron were successful in training students to use a specific reasoning strategy that compensated for the effects of general reasoning ability.

In addition to successful training in component processes for solving series completion problems (Holzman et al., 1976) and analogy problems (Sternberg & Ketron, 1982), similar results have been obtained in a variety of cognitive tasks, including linear syllogisms (Sternberg & Weil, 1980) and scientific problem solving (Siegler, 1978, 1986). Future research is likely to focus on strategies for using basic processes, that is, on metacomponents, and some of this kind of research is reviewed in the next chapter on creativity training.

■
EVALUATION
■

The two disciplines of scientific psychology—the psychometric approach as described in the cognitive factors section of this chapter and the experimental approach as portrayed throughout most of this book—seem to be moving together again at last. The psychometric approach has succeeded in measuring individual differences but has failed in determining the processes and structures that underlie those differences. The experimental psychology approach has succeeded in describing the cognitive processes and structures in humans but has failed to deal adequately with individual differences. Yet this chapter has shown three new approaches that promise to join the study of individual differences with the study of internal cognitive characteristics—the cognitive correlates, cognitive components, and cognitive training approaches.

A related new approach, which could be called *cognitive contents*, seeks to describe differences between expert and novice problem solving in terms of differences in the quantity and quality of people's knowledge; in the tradition of a cognitive contents approach, Chapter 13 is devoted to the study of expert problem solving. Theories of cognitive development, described in Chapter 10, may be viewed as offering another version of how individual differences in knowledge affect performance on cognitive tasks. Similarly, Chapter 12 carries on the cognitive training approach by examining techniques for teaching creative problem solving. Other approaches to the study of individual differences in cognitive ability have not been examined here but are touched on in other chapters: Chapter 2 deals briefly with what Sternberg (1990) calls the biological metaphor of mind—theories that examine the role of physiological processes—and Chapter 16 provides examples of what Sternberg (1990) calls the anthropological and sociological metaphors of mind—theories that examine the role of culture in thinking.

Although the cognitive correlates, cognitive components, and cognitive training approaches are relatively new, they each have already contributed to our understanding of mental ability. Indeed, as Sternberg (1982, p. xi) noted in the *Handbook of Human Intelligence*, "the investigation of intelligence is rapidly becoming central to psychology . . . and to all disciplines involved in the scientific study of the mind." The common theme running through all of these approaches is that performance on thinking tasks can be analyzed as a collection of information processes and strategies for controlling those processes. Although researchers have focused on analyzing the component processes underlying intelligent performance, future research is needed to better understand the strategies that people use to plan, monitor, control, and evaluate the way they use these processes.

Suggested Readings

STERNBERG, R. J. (Ed.). (1985). *Human abilities: An information processing approach.* New York: Freeman. Contains chapters by leading researchers on human abilities, including verbal, spatial, and reasoning abilities.

STERNBERG, R. J. (1988). *The triarchic mind: A new theory of human intelligence.* New York: Viking. Presents Sternberg's triarchic theory in an easy-to-read style.

STERNBERG, R. J. (1990). *Metaphors of mind: Conceptions of the nature of intelligence.* Cambridge, England: Cambridge University Press. Surveys seven theoretical approaches to the study of human intelligence, including excellent historical background.

CHAPTER · 12

CREATIVITY TRAINING

Thinking as a Learnable Skill

BOX 12 • 1   Some Creativity Problems

Problem 1

List all the questions you can think of concerning the figure shown below. Ask all the questions you need to know for sure what is happening. Do not ask questions that can be answered just by looking at the drawing. (Give yourself three minutes to list your questions.)

Problem 2

Suppose that all humans were born with six fingers on each hand instead of five. List all the consequences or implications that you can think of. (Give yourself three minutes.)

Adapted from Torrance (1968). Figure from Examples and rationales of test tasks for assessing creative abilities by E. P. Torrance, *Journal of Creative Behavior*, 1968, Volume 2, No. 3, published by The Creative Education Foundation, Buffalo, New York.

What does it mean to be a creative problem solver? To help answer that question, give yourself three minutes to write down all of the answers you can generate for problem 1 in Box 12-1, and then do the same for problem 2.

These problems were developed by Torrance (1966) as part of his well-known *Torrance Tests of Creative Thinking.* According to Torrance (1984, p. 3): "The basic battery of the Torrance Test of Creative Thinking has been used in over 1000 published research studies . . . and about 150,000 children and adults are being tested with these instruments each year." These problems measure an intellectual skill that Guilford (1959, 1967) has called *divergent thinking*—thinking that moves outward from a problem in many possible directions, such as required in "List all the uses for a brick." In contrast, many of the problems examined elsewhere in this book focus on *convergent thinking*—thinking that proceeds toward a single answer, such as "$33 \times 14 =$ ____."

How can we evaluate your answers? Solutions to divergent thinking problems are most often scored for two factors (Davis, 1989):

Fluency—the number of solutions that fit the requirements of the problem, and

Originality—the number of unusual or unique solutions, that is, solutions generated by very few or no other people.

For example, suppose your answers for the six-fingers problem were: (1) we would need to make gloves with six fingers, (2) we would need to redesign handgrips on bicycle handlebars, (3) we would be able to invent new obscene gestures, (4) we would be able to give a new secret handshake, (5) we would say "Give me six" instead of "Give me five" when giving a hand slap, and (6) we would use a base 12 number system instead of base 10. To measure fluency, we simply can count the number of answers, which is six. To measure originality, we can see that when we give this test to many individuals, answer 1 is given by almost all of them, so it is low in originality; however, answer 4 is given by only a few people, so it is high in originality. By comparing the above six answers to the answers most commonly given, we could find that only two of the answers are rarely generated, so the originality score is 2. Other possible measures are importance (i.e., the usefulness of each solution as rated by a panel of judges), flexibility (i.e., the number of different categories or approaches to the problem), and elaboration (i.e., the number of embellishments to an idea).

Let's take another look at your answers to the problems in Box 12-1. In reviewing your answers to problem 1, underline the three most important questions you generated. This task, which requires that you evaluate the possible solutions you have generated, is a central aspect of what has been called *critical thinking* (Ennis, 1987; Halpern, 1989). Thus, two skills needed for solving creative problems are the abilities to generate alternatives (as measured by tests of divergent thinking) and to evaluate alternatives (as required in critical thinking).

It strikes many observers as strange that we expect students to be effective problem solvers yet we seldom provide direct instruction in how to solve problems (Norman, 1980). At the same time, the consensus is growing that "thinking is a skill and can be taught" (Chance, 1986, p. 133). Polya (1965, p. ix) proclaims: "Solving problems is a practical art, like swimming, or skiing, or playing the piano: you can learn it only by imitation and practice." In this chapter we explore the idea that people's problem-solving performance can be improved through instruction. In particular, we will examine various approaches to creativity training that have been developed since the first such courses were introduced in the 1930s.

■
CREATIVITY-TRAINING DEFINITION OF THINKING
■

If we want to teach people to be more creative and critical problem solvers, we must first define what we mean by *creative thinking* and *critical thinking*. In the narrow sense, we can define creative thinking as a cognitive activity that results in one or more novel solutions for a problem. Thus creativity training involves teaching people *how to generate* new ideas or hypotheses regarding a given problem. Critical thinking can be viewed as cognitive activity that results in the selection of an appropriate solution or hypothesis. In the narrow sense, training in critical thinking involves teaching people *how to evaluate* and test ideas or hypotheses regarding a problem. In a broad sense, however, creative thinking can be viewed as including critical thinking; thus it involves both generation and evaluation of ideas. For ease of discussion in this chapter, we will use *creativity training* or *thinking-skills training* in the broad sense to refer to programs that teach students how to generate possible solutions or hypotheses for a problem and how to evaluate their solutions or hypotheses. According to this approach, we can view thinking as a collection of cognitive skills that can be taught.

The role of cognitive psychologists is to identify the teachable aspects of problem solving, a task that has a long and somewhat disappointing history (Mayer, 1987b). Emphasis on teaching "good habits of mind" in American schools dates back to the Boston Latin School, founded in 1712, as well as the many subsequent Latin schools that were still going strong a century ago (Rippa, 1980). The premise underlying the Latin school approach was that learning well-structured subjects such as Latin, Greek, and geometry would help improve the students' minds in general, enabling them to become better problem solvers in all domains. The downfall of the Latin schools was brought about by the practical demands of an emerging industrial and technological society, as well as a growing body of research showing that skills learned from Latin did not transfer easily to other situations.

This classical approach to the teaching of thinking was based on conceptions of what to teach, how to teach, and where to teach that seem to conflict with current cognitive views of thinking, as summarized in Box 12-2 (Mayer, 1987a, 1989a). The first issue concerns *what to teach:* Should we view thinking as a *single intellectual ability* or as a *collection of smaller component skills?* Although the classical approach seems to view thinking as a single intellectual ability that can be improved through mental discipline, current theories of intellectual ability are based on the second view, which was eloquently described by Binet (1911/1962, p. 150) several generations ago:

> Intelligence is not a simple indivisible function with a particular essence of its own . . . but, it is formed by the combination of the minor functions . . . all of which have proved to be plastic and subject to increase. With practice,

BOX 12 ▪ 2   Three Issues for Creativity-Training Programs

Issue	Alternatives
1. What to teach	Thinking as a single intellectual ability versus thinking as a collection of smaller component skills
2. How to teach	Focus on product through rewarding correct answers versus focus on processes that the student learns to model
3. Where to teach	In general, domain-independent courses or within existing, specific subject areas

From Mayer (1989a)

enthusiasm, and especially with method, one can succeed in improving one's attention, memory, and judgment, and in becoming literally more intelligent than before.

In support of his belief in the teachability of thinking skills, Binet (1911/1962, p. 150) devised a series of exercises that he called mental orthopedics: "In the same way that physical orthopedics straightens a crooked spine, mental orthopedics strengthens, cultivates, and fortifies attention, memory, perception, judgment, and will." Although most training programs have accepted Binet's assertion that intellectual performance is based on component skills, the cognitive approach has allowed us to analyze the component skills that are specifically relevant for various tasks. In summary, problem solving can be broken down into individual skills that can be taught, such as strategies for how to represent a problem or strategies for how to plan a solution. In contrast to the classical approach, our first criterion for a successful training program is that it teach component skills.

The second issue concerns *how to teach:* Should we focus on *product* by rewarding correct answers or on *process* by asking the student to imitate a model? The classical approach emphasized correct performance—flawless conjugation of verbs, errorless computations using geometric laws, and so on. Lochhead (1979, p. 1) rejects the classical approach: "We should be teaching students how to think; instead we are primarily teaching them what to think." What Lochhead and others are saying is that instead of focusing on the product of problem solving (i.e., getting the right answer) we should focus on the process of problem solving (i.e., the methods used in problem solving). In summary, the method used in many successful programs is to give students practice in imitating the problem-solving processes used by good problem solvers. Therefore, in contrast to the classical approach, our second criterion for a successful training program is a focus on problem-solving process.

The third issue concerns *where to teach:* Should we teach in *general* domain-independent courses or in the *specific* subject areas within which the student will be tested? The classical approach was based on a belief in general transfer, that is, skills learned in one domain can be used in different domains; but research evidence (surveyed in Chapter 14) demonstrates a preponderance of specific transfer, that is, skills learned in one domain can be successfully used mainly in that domain (Singley & Anderson, 1989). In a review of several major thinking-skills programs, Bransford, Arbitman-Smith, Stein, and Vye (1985, p. 202) failed to find convincing evidence for "the idea of developing general skills that permit transfer to a wide variety of domains" and noted that "there was no strong evidence that students . . . improved in tasks that were dissimilar to those already explicitly practiced." In summary, successful training programs teach thinking skills within the specific context in which students will be tested. In contrast to the classical approach, our third criterion is therefore to expect specific transfer, that is, to expect that students will be able to apply the skills mainly within the domain in which they have practiced them.

As you read over the following descriptions of thinking-skills programs, you should keep in mind the three issues listed in Box 12-2. The remainder of this chapter explores techniques that are purported to enhance creative problem solving.

■
THE 1930s AND 1940s: CREATIVITY TRAINING IN INDUSTRY
■

The first structured courses in creative thinking and problem solving appeared in the 1930s and 1940s. As Davis (1973) points out, these courses were aimed mainly at improving the creativity of engineers, managers, product designers, and other members of industry. For example, Crawford (1954) is credited with initiating the first creativity training course in 1931, aimed at increasing the creativity of professionals. In order for you to get a better idea of how creativity training began, let's briefly explore three major industry-oriented programs: Crawford's "attribute listing," Osborn's "brainstorming," and Gordon's "synectics."

One of the major ideas in Crawford's original 1931 course, and in his revised courses, is the use of "attribute listing." This procedure involves listing the critical attributes of a product and then listing some modifications that may be made to each attribute or suggesting the transfer of attributes of one object onto another. For example, Davis (1973) suggests the following problem: "What can be done to improve an ordinary piece of classroom chalk?" First, you should list the important attributes of the object, such as its shape, size, color, hardness, and so on. Next, consider how you could modify the attributes, such as using colors other than white or extra large-sized chalk. You should also consider importing other attributes such as including a device to hold the chalk similar to a cigarette holder. In *The Techniques of Creative Thinking* (1954, p. 96), Crawford summarizes his approach as follows: "Each time we take a step, we do it by changing an attribute or a quality of something, or else by applying that same quality or attribute to some other thing." Following Crawford's lead, several other training programs have emphasized "idea checklists." For example, Osborn (1963) has a list of seventy-three "idea spurring questions," such as "What to add?" or "How about a blend?" or "New ways to use it as is?"

Osborn is credited with popularizing the use of brainstorming techniques, beginning in the 1940s. According to Osborn's *Applied Imagination* (1963), "brainstorming" involves group problem solving, in which the following four rules are followed:

1. *No criticism.* Participants are instructed to obey the "principle of deferred judgment," that is, to postpone all critical comments until after the initial brainstorming session.

2. *Quantity is wanted.* Participants are instructed to generate as many ideas as they can, without regard to their quality.

3. *Originality is wanted.* Participants are encouraged to generate wild and unusual ideas, rather than trying to be practical.

4. *Combination and improvement are wanted.* Participants are encouraged to build on the previous suggestions given during the session.

Thus, in brainstorming, the goal is to generate as many unusual ideas as possible without criticizing any ideas. Osborn claims: "You can think up almost twice as many good ideas in the same length of time if you defer judgment" (quoted in Vervalin, 1978, p. 82). Brainstorming techniques can also be used by an individual in solving problems.

Gordon (1961) has suggested a program based on "synectics"—the joining together of apparently unrelated elements. In his book *Synectics* (1961), the main goal is to teach people to make use of analogies in problem solving. For example.

Gordon describes a group session in which the problem is to design a new roof that would turn white in summer to reflect heat and black in winter to absorb heat. Can you think of an analogy in nature? In Gordon's group, they hit upon the idea that the flounder can change colors to match its surroundings as it swims near the ocean bottom. This is accomplished by chromatophores, tiny sacks of black pigment that contract to push to the skin surface or relax to retract. After some discussion of this biological device, the group designed an all-black roof that was impregnated with little white plastic balls. These balls expand when the roof is hot, thus making it lighter, and contract when the roof is cold, thus making it darker.

Edwards (1968) reported on creativity-training programs at dozens of American corporations, consulting firms, and colleges. Several companies claim that training courses have saved money, increased development of new products, and increased profit. The oldest course has been taught at the State University of New York at Buffalo since 1949. Edwards's survey suggests that creativity programs are definitely a part of many industrial training efforts.

As you can see from this brief description, there is a substantial history of creativity-training programs, beginning in industry in the 1930s and 1940s. However, much of this work has been ignored by researchers in the field of problem solving. As Davis and Scott (1978, p. ix) pointed out: "Although representatives of the business world have drawn freely from creativity research and theory in psychology, this line of communication has been astonishingly one-way." In fact, it would be useful for us to know whether such creativity-training programs really work; if they do work, it would be useful to study how they work.

Unfortunately, the grand claims concerning the effectiveness of industrial creativity courses have not always been substantiated by controlled research. For example, Bouchard (1971) notes that the brainstorming technique that began in the 1930s had become a "firmly entrenched idea" by the 1950s. However, the attractiveness of the techniques was greatly diminished by a study in which four people working separately generated more unique ideas than four people working as a group (Taylor, Berry, & Block, 1958). As Bouchard points out, there were many replications of this finding. In addition, several studies of brainstorming sessions showed that instructions to generate unusual ideas are less productive than instructions to generate practical ideas (Weisskopf-Joelson & Eliseo, 1961) and that deferred-judgment instructions are not effective (Dunnette, Campbell, & Jaastaad, 1963). Based on a survey of research studies, Weisberg (1986, p. 66) concludes that "brainstorming is not an effective method of increasing creative thinking." In summary, much careful research is needed before we can know whether creativity programs work and, more importantly, how they work.

■

THE 1950s: REMEDIATION OF PROBLEM SOLVING IN COLLEGE STUDENTS

■

The first major effort to improve the problem-solving performance of college students was carried out at the University of Chicago by Bloom and Broder (1950). To obtain a bachelor's degree, students had to pass a series of comprehensive examinations in various subjects. Students could take the exams whenever they felt they were ready; each exam consisted of a wide variety of problems covering the subject. As you might suppose, some students performed quite well on the exams while others were unable to pass in spite of their high scholastic ability and conscientious study.

Bloom and Broder selected a group of "remedial" students, that is, those who performed poorly on the comprehensive exams. The researchers were careful to select remedial students who scored high in scholastic aptitude (such as is measured by the SAT), who claimed to study hard, and who asserted that their exam performance did not reflect what they knew. Thus the remedial students seemed to have the ability, motivation, and knowledge to do well in solving test problems, but for some reason they performed quite poorly. In addition, Bloom and Broder selected a group of "model" students, those who had the same general scholastic ability as the remedial students but who had scored high in solving examination problems.

How could Bloom and Broder boost the problem-solving performance of remedial students? To answer this question, they addressed two issues: what to teach and how to teach. In determining what to teach, Bloom and Broder were forced to make the following distinction:

Products of problem solving—whether the student arrives at the correct final answer or not

Process of problem solving—the strategy that people use on their way to getting the answer

Bloom and Broder argued that previous research had placed too much emphasis on the products of problem solving, instead of emphasizing the processes involved in creative problem solving. Two people might come up with the same answer yet use entirely different approaches to get it. For example, Box 12-3 shows a typical problem and the answers given by three students. The students generated the same product in that the final answers are the same, but their descriptions of process are quite different. Thus Bloom and Broder decided that instruction in problem solving should not focus on reinforcing students for getting the right final answers but rather on teaching the problem-solving strategies that are useful in generating answers. They asserted that the "habits of problem solving, like other habits, could be altered by appropriate training and practice" (1950, p. 67).

The second problem facing Bloom and Broder was to develop techniques for teaching the process of problem solving. To find out which strategies were used by successful problem solvers, they asked their model students to solve some typical exam problems by thinking aloud in a session. In such a session, students were asked to describe what was going on in their minds as they approached a problem and work through it. The comparison of the thinking-aloud procedures of model solvers with the procedures used by remedial students showed important differences. Thus, as a method of instruction, Bloom and Broder decided to teach remedial students to imitate and make use of the processes used by model students.

In a typical experiment, for example, remedial students were asked to solve a problem such as the one in Box 12-3, using a thinking-aloud technique. Then, the students were given a transcript of the procedure that a model student had used for the same problem. Each remedial student was asked to list in his or her own words all of the strategies used by the model student that the remedial student had not used; the experimenter helped to stimulate discussion. The remedial students were then given another problem so that the new techniques could be practiced. The procedure was repeated for new problems. Box 12-4 shows the differences that students found between how they answered questions and how the model student answered them. After ten to twelve training sessions in which they continuously compared their problem-solving strategies to those of model students on specific problems, the remedial students were ready to take their exams. Later experiments used groups of remedial and model students, but the same general methods were employed.

The results of the study are encouraging. Students who participated in the training tended to score an average of 0.49 to 0.68 grade points higher on the exam than matched groups who did not take the training. In addition, students who took the training expressed high levels of confidence and optimism concerning their newly acquired problem-solving abilities. However, Bloom and Broder caution that it would be wrong to conclude that general problem-solving strategies can be taught. Rather, they conclude: "It became clear that some specific information was necessary for the solution of the examination problems and that a certain amount of background in the subject was indispensable. It became apparent that methods of problem solving, by themselves, could not serve as a substitute for the basic knowledge of the subject matter" (1950, pp. 76–77). Thus Bloom and Broder's major contributions are the emphasis on process rather than product, the refinement of thinking-aloud techniques, and the finding that both specific knowledge and general strategies are needed to be a successful problem solver in a given domain.

BOX 12 • 3   How Three Students Solved the Inflation Problem

Problem

Some economists feel that there is danger of an extreme inflationary boom after the war. It is the opinion of such economists that the government should control the boom in order to prevent a depression such as the one following the stockmarket crash of 1929.

Below are a number of specific suggestions. For each of the following items, *blacken*

answer space 1—if it would be *consistent* with the policy of controlling the boom

answer space 2—if it is directly *inconsistent* with the policy

26. Lower the reserve that banks are required to hold against deposits
27. Reduce taxes considerably
28. Encourage the federal reserve banks to buy securities in the open market

Mary's Answer

Mary W. (Score 2): (Read the statements and the directions.)

(Read item 26) "Look down to see what I'm supposed to do (Re-read the statements and the directions) "Not quite sure what I'm doing so reread for the third time." (Re-read the statements and the directions.)

(Re-read item 26.) "Not sure of this, so on to second one." (Read item 27.) "Say inconsistent, because if there is inflationary boom, it people make more money, taxes have to keep up with it to take away the money so they can't spend it."

(Read item 28.) "Try to figure out what bearing that had exactly."

(Re-read item 26.) "I'm a time waster, say 26 would be consistent— no, that I know, banks have reserve—idea is to get people to deposit as much as possible—not answer 28."

(Re-read item 28.) "Say inconsistent, I feel it is"

Diagnosis unsystematic, lumps around, uses "feelings" rather than "reasoning," not confident.

(*continued*)

■

THE 1960s: TEACHING PRODUCTIVE THINKING TO SCHOOL CHILDREN

■

While the 1950s were highlighted by modest studies such as Bloom and Broder's project, there was a dramatic increase in the size and number of such projects in the 1960s, a decade marked by innovation and experimentation in American education. Numerous programs were designed to teach problem-solving skills in classrooms across the nation. Some of the best known projects include

BOX 12 • 3, *continued*

James's Answer

James S. (Score 2): (Read the statements.) "In other words, the OPA and such. (Read the directions.) "Taken for granted they're going to control the boom. (Read item 26. Re-read item 26.) "That would be inconsistent. (Read item 27.) "That would be inconsistent, because you can't have too great a boom as long as you have taxes, at least in my interpretation of boom—although if taxes go up, prices go up—no, I'll stick to my answer (Read item 28.) "Consistent—however, I think I need more subject-matter back ground to tell how I thought it out—more of a guess—don't think inconsistent, so put consistent."

Diagnosis: translates problem into something more familiar (OPA), lacks subject-matter knowledge, guesses.

Dora's Answer

Dora Z (Score 2): (Read the statement and the directions emphasizing—the key words.)
(Read item 26.) "Lower the reserve, raise the amount of money in circulation—if you raise the money in circulation—inconsistent. By raising the money in circulation you don't control a boom.
(Read item 27.) "Also inconsistent for the same reason."
(Read item 28.) "Open market—think what the open market is. Think would take money out of circulation, therefore would be consistent."

Diagnosis: focused on key ideas, reduced three items to a single problem, attempted to determine how money supply is affected by each item, attacks problem on basis of single role on principle, higher-order problem solving.

From Bloom and Broder (1950). Copyright 1950 by The University of Chicago Press.

Productive-Thinking Program was aimed at increasing the general problem-solving skills of fifth- and sixth-graders through practice in solving mystery and detective stories (Covington, Crutchfield, & Davies, 1966; Covington, Crutchfield, Davies, & Olton, 1974).

Inquiry Training was designed to teach problem solving in science by asking students to react to a filmed or live demonstration (Suchman, 1960, 1966, 1969).

Thinking Creatively was a workbook taking the form of a humorous discussion among several cartoon characters (Davis & Houtman, 1968).

BOX 12 · 4 Student's Lists of Differences Between Model and Self

Jean's List

1. I didn't think it necessary to formulate the general rule.
   Generalization too broad.
   Verbalization reversed actually.
2. Lack of understanding of given terms.
   Define and illustrate as alternatives.
   I looked for "true" and "false"—others looked for "best." Didn't interpret directions properly.
   I looked for answer—didn't have an answer before I looked. Higher degree of inaccuracy. (I get this O.K. with syllogisms.)
3. He associated and brought in intermediary event with dates. I did the same with the second part, but didn't know country.
4. He employed an illustration for proof.
   Should set up criteria for an answer; if not enough, set up illustrations and examples.
5. Didn't get essential terms of what I was looking for before I began reading alternatives.
   Jumped to conclusion without carrying illustrative reasoning through.
   Did read terms thoroughly but didn't keep them in mind; reversed them.
6. Didn't define terms of statements. Got it right through outside example.
7. Should pull out main words. Got it right, though.
8. Didn't establish relations between terms. Got it right, though.
   Careless about selecting right alternative.
   Keeping directions in mind. I think in terms of "true" and "false" instead of "scientific study," etc.

Ralph's List

1. Find a rule or formula that applies to problem under consideration.
2. Apply rule and formulate answer, then check with offered answers.
3. Progress into problem by formula which has been generalized through application.
4. Rules should deal with specific problem.
5. Try to read directions clearly the first time.
6. Do not answer by guessing or supposition.
7. Think before the formulation of answer.
8. Direct thought in stream which has been pointed in the direction of the problem at hand.
9. Emphasis on the major ideas in the problem, not all ideas.
10. Box off ideas into main question in the problem.
11. Reason from known knowledge or examples.
12. In graphs formulate a specific picture.

Myers-Torrance Idea Books consisted of workbooks for elementary children and involved practice in solving creativity problems (Myers & Torrance, 1964).

Purdue Creativity Program was a set of tape-recorded programs with printed exercises designed to foster divergent thinking in fourth-graders (Feldhusen, Treffinger, & Bahlke, 1970).

Parnes Program was based on Osborn's (1963) brainstorming techniques (Parnes, 1967).

Let's take a closer look at the productive-thinking program, since it has been the most studied project. Like Bloom and Broder's program, the productive-thinking program focuses on teaching problem-solving processes and uses imitation of models as a technique for teaching. But unlike Bloom and Broder's project, the productive-thinking program is a self-paced and self-administered set of booklets rather than interpersonal dialogues. It is aimed at elementary school children rather than college students, and it emphasizes detective problems rather than examination problems.

The productive-thinking program consists of fifteen cartoonlike booklets, each about thirty pages in length. Each booklet presents a single mystery or detective story for the child to solve. The stories involve two children, Jim and Lila, as well as Jim's Uncle John and Mr. Search. Each story presents a series of clues or facts, and the student is required to answer questions aimed at "restating the problem in his own words," "formulating his own questions," and "generating ideas to explain the mystery" (Covington & Crutchfield, 1965, p. 3). After the student has generated some answers or ideas, Jim and Lila give theirs. Thus, Jim and Lila act as models to be emulated. Like all realistic models, they make some mistakes at first, but they eventually team to solve the caper. The adults in the story provide hints, point out positive and negative features of Jim's and Lila's strategies, and try to maintain high levels of enjoyment. Thus, as students read the booklets, they become engaged in solving a case, and feedback is presented to them regularly.

Box 12-5 gives a few pages from one of the first lessons in the program, "The Riverboat Robbery." As you read the lesson you are given some information and asked to make a response. Then you get feedback by seeing how Jim and Lila respond. Finally, Uncle John provides guidance and analysis of Jim's and Lila's strategies. (If you read the entire booklet carefully, you will discover that the culprit is Mr. Larkin, the bank manager.)

Each lesson is designed to teach several basic problem-solving strategies, which are listed in Box 12-6. For example, "The Riverboat Robbery" attempts to teach strategies 4, 5, 6, 9, 11, and 15.

Is the productive-thinking program effective in improving the problem-solving skills of school children? This question has been addressed in

BOX 12 • 5   Excerpt from the Productive-Thinking Program

The TV Announcer: "Following the robbery, things moved quickly. The captain of the boat called the Elmtown police. When the boat docked in Elmtown, the police were already on guard there. No one was allowed on or off the boat except the police and our reporter and TV cameraman.

"Here is the police chief on the boat, telling our reporter what has happened so far:"

over a dozen studies involving hundreds of students (Mansfield, Busse, & Krepelka, 1978). For example, in an early study by Olton and Crutchfield (1969), one class of 25 fifth-graders was given intensive training in productive thinking, while no such training was given to another class of fifth-graders matched for IQ, age, and achievement. All students took the same battery of pretests (given before the program), the same posttests (given immediately after the training program), and the same follow-up tests (given six months later). Box 12-7 presents a typical test, and Box 12-8 summarizes some of the tests that were given to the students. Many of the test problems resemble the mystery and detective stories in the instructional booklets.

BOX 12 • 5, *continued*

Before Lila tells her idea, what thoughts do you have about other possible suspects? Use your Reply Notebook to write down all the ideas you can think of.

What persons besides Louie might be the thief?

There are several people besides Louie who might have stolen the money. You may have thought of the steward who called Mr. Burk to the phone, or perhaps you even considered the riverboat captain.
Lila has another possible suspect in mind.   (*continued*)

The results seem to demonstrate the effectiveness of the program. As expected, there were no differences between the two groups on solving problems in the pretest, thus indicating that both groups began with the same level of problem-solving ability. However, the trained group scored significantly better than the untrained group on the posttest (55 percent versus 37 percent correct) and on the follow-up test (57 percent versus 34 percent correct).

In interpreting these results, however, you should keep three things in mind. First, this was an evaluation study aimed mainly at evaluating the effectiveness of an instructional program; it was not a theoretical study aimed at telling us *why* or *how* the training works. Second, since the tests covered problems that were

BOX 12 • 5, *continued*

Uncle John is right. You can always think of more ideas. And you should never be afraid to talk about your ideas.

From Covington, Crutchfield, Davies, and Olton (1974)

similar to the mystery story format of the instructional lessons, there is no evidence that the training will transfer to novel, actual situations. Third, as in any evaluation study, you should question whether there are other possible explanations for the results; these include the possibility that subjects in the training group tried harder because they knew they were supposed to do better, that the teacher in the experimental group was so enthusiastic about the project that the students were motivated, or that students were simply learning what the teacher meant by certain questions. (A good creative problem-solving task would be to list all the possible criticisms of this study.)

Finally, you should ask whether other evaluation studies provide support as strongly as this study. In studies that use larger samples and stronger methodological controls, the effects are sometimes much weaker. In small studies, where teachers and students can be carefully selected and trained, and where everyone knows they are participating in a special project, it is easier to get strong results. In a careful review of twelve studies, Mansfield, Busse, and Krepelka (1978, p. 522) concluded that in many cases there is evidence that the

BOX 12 • 6   Some Problem-Solving Skills Taught in the Productive-Thinking Program

1. Take time to reflect on a problem before you begin to work. Decide exactly what the problem is that you are trying to solve.
2. Get all the facts of the problem clearly in mind.
3. Work on the problem in a planful way.
4. Keep an open mind. Don't jump to conclusions about the answer to a problem.
5. Think of many new ideas for solving a problem. Don't stop with just a few.
6. Try to think of unusual ideas.
7. As a way of getting ideas, pick out all the important objects and persons in the problem and think carefully about each one.
8. Think of several general possibilities for a solution and then figure out many particular ideas for each possibility.
9. As you search for ideas, let your mind freely explore things around you. Almost anything can suggest ideas for a solution.
10. Always check each idea with the facts to decide how likely the idea is.
11. If you get stuck on a problem, keep trying. Don't be discouraged.
12. When you run out of ideas, try looking at the problem in a new and different way.
13. Go back and review all the facts of the problem to make sure you have not missed something important.
14. Start with an unlikely idea. Just suppose that it is possible, and figure out how it could be.
15. Be on the lookout for odd or puzzling facts in a problem. Explaining them can lead you to news ideas for solution.
16. When there are several puzzling things in a problem, try to explain them with a single idea that will connect them all together.

Adapted from Covington, Crutchfield, Davies, and Olton (1974)

BOX 12 • 7   The Poverty Program: A Test Used to Measure the Effectiveness of the Productive-Thinking Program

A problem of poverty in a land of plenty:
When Americans travel abroad, they are sometimes asked how can it be that the United States, the richest nation in the world, is faced with such a great problem of poverty among many of its people.

Some people in other nations say they are puzzled by the fact that in spite of the great wealth of our nation, many of our cities have great slum areas, many of our people are dependent for their support on relief and welfare funds, and many of our people do not share in the American dream of enjoying a high standard of living.

Now, suppose that you and your family are visiting a foreign country this summer. Some children your age in that country ask you about why the United States is faced with such a problem of poverty. What would you say?

Take time to think about this; then write below what you would say to them about this puzzling problem of poverty in a land of plenty. (There are several additional blank pages attached to this page, so you may write as much as you wish.)

From Olton and Crutchfield (1969)

BOX 12 • 8   Selected Tests Given to Study the Effectiveness of the
Productive-Thinking Program

Pretests

Controlling the weather   Student thinks of various consequences of man's future ability to change the weather.

Project for a village   Student puts himself in the shoes of a Peace Corps volunteer who must first acquaint himself with the customs and
mores of a tribal village. Then, without offending such customs, he must figure out ways the inhabitants can earn
money for their village needs.

Posttests

Transplanting organs   Student thinks of various consequences of man's future
medical ability to transplant bodily organs from one person
to another.

"Black House" problem   Student attempts to solve a puzzling mystery problem in
which he must make an insightful reorganization of the ele-
ments of the problem.

Follow-Up Tests

The missing jewel
problem   Student attempts to solve a puzzling mystery problem in
which he must make an insightful reorganization of the elements of the problem.

The nameless tomb   Student works on a hypothetical problem in archeology in
which he must discover which of 10 possible suspects is
buried in a nameless ancient tomb.

From Olton and Crutchfield (1969), from *Trends and issues in
developmental psychology*, edited by Paul Mussen, Jonas Langer, and
Martin Covington. Copyright © 1969 by Holt, Rinehart and Winston, Inc. Reprinted
by permission of Holt, Rinehart and Winston, CBS College Publishing,
a division of CBS, Inc.

productive-thinking program improves performance on problems like those in
the lessons; however, "it is unclear whether the effects of training are sufficiently
generalizable to be useful in real-life problem-solving situations."

In addition, most of the other widely adopted programs seem to enhance
performance mainly on the kinds of problems that each teaches how to solve
(Mansfield et al., 1978). Thus Mansfield and his associates have summarized such
studies by noting that "most evaluation studies of creativity-training programs
seem to support the view that creativity can be trained," but "there is only limited
and inconsistent evidence of transfer to dissimilar problems" (1978, p. 531).

Torrance (1972) reviewed 142 studies on the effectiveness of various creativity-training programs. Of the packaged programs such as those listed at the beginning of this section, some improvement in creativity was found in 38 out of 47 studies. However, as Torrance points out, the programs tended to work well only when a teacher was heavily involved; furthermore, most of the studies used test problems such as those shown in Box 12-1 from the *Torrance Tests of Creative Thinking* (Torrance, 1966). Thus there was no strong evidence concerning whether courses enhanced creativity in solving real problems.

Such equivocal results, however, do not seem to eliminate the interest in creativity-training programs in schools. For example, Treffinger and Gowan (1971) have collected a list of hundreds of active creativity-training programs and materials. What is needed, of course, is a basic theory of how people use strategic information in problem solving. The beginning of such a theory is discussed later in this chapter.

■

THE 1970s AND 1980s: DIRECT TEACHING OF THINKING SKILLS
■

During the past twenty years, programs to teach thinking skills have continued to flourish (Chance, 1986; Nickerson, Perkins, & Smith, 1985; Segal, Chipman, & Glaser, 1985). Consistent with the criteria described in Box 12-2, successful programs tend to teach smaller component skills, ask students to imitate the problem-solving processes of experts, and produce specific transfer. In this section we explore three popular programs of the 1970s and 1980s from around the world: Instrumental Enrichment, CoRT thinking program, and Odyssey.

INSTRUMENTAL ENRICHMENT

Consider the following scenario: You are working with Jewish children who emigrated to Israel after surviving the Holocaust, that is, children who spent their lives in hiding, without much intellectual nourishment. You note that these children would be labeled retarded on the basis of IQ tests, but they seem to be able to improve. They arrive with little basic knowledge and few concepts (such as the difference between left and right), but with appropriate teaching they can learn much of this information. At first they fail to reason abstractly, but with practice they learn to solve abstract reasoning problems. How would you help such children become effective thinkers and problem solvers?

This was the situation facing Reuven Feuerstein, who himself emigrated to Israel from his native Romania after spending time in a labor camp. Based on his experiences with "special education" adolescents in Israeli schools, Feuerstein

BOX 12 • 9   Example Exercises from the Organization of Dots

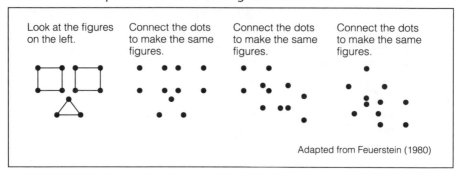

Look at the figures on the left.

Connect the dots to make the same figures.

Connect the dots to make the same figures.

Connect the dots to make the same figures.

Adapted from Feuerstein (1980)

(1979, 1980; Feuerstein, Jensen, Hoffman, & Rand, 1985) developed the Instrumental Enrichment (IE) program. The program is based on innovative views of the learner and the teacher. First, concerning the learner, Feuerstein distinguishes between a child's current performance and a child's potential performance; instead of focusing on static tests of intellectual ability, Feuerstein focuses on dynamic tests that evaluate the child's potential for learning to improve. Second, concerning the teacher, Feuerstein observes that many special education students come from homes in which parents do not explain, discuss, and interpret events to their children; the teacher's role is to provide what Feuerstein calls *mediated learning experiences* (MLEs)—chances for adults and children to work together to make sense out of and find purpose in the surrounding world. In short, the IE program is aimed at narrowing the gap between the manifest performance and potential performance of students by providing many opportunities for the kinds of mediated learning experiences that they do not normally receive.

The Instrumental Enrichment program consists of fifteen units of paper-and-pencil exercises for low-functioning adolescents. Each unit involves one instrument that can be used to teach a variety of cognitive skills. For example, Box 12-9 presents one of the many exercises from the first instrument in the IE program, the organization of dots. In this exercise, the student's job is to connect the dots so that they form the same shapes as on the left—that is, two squares and a triangle. Each dot can be used only once, and each shape must be the same size as the model on the left. However, the drawn shapes can overlap and be in different orientations from the models on the left.

For each exercise, the teacher introduces the problem, asks the children to work individually, and then leads a class discussion of methods for solving the problem. In this way, students gain experience in solving many different kinds of novel problems in which they compare their problem-solving processes to the processes used by others. According to Feuerstein, the organization-of-dots problems help students learn to break a problem into parts, to represent a problem, and to think hypothetically. Other instruments focus on spatial orientation, temporal relations, family relations, numerical progressions, analytic perception, transitive relations, and syllogisms. For maximum effectiveness, the program is intended to be administered in one-hour classes that meet three to five times per week for two to three years.

Does the IE program succeed in helping students become better problem solvers? Feuerstein (1980) reports a study comparing adolescent special education students who received IE training over a two-year period with equivalent students who received conventional instruction. Although both groups performed at the same level on pretests of various cognitive skills, after two years the IE group outscored the other students on cognitive tests involving spatial and mathematical reasoning. When follow-up tests were given two years later, the IE group still scored higher than the control group on tests of nonverbal intelligence. Similarly, other researchers have reported that low-IQ students who receive training on one of the instruments in the IE program can learn to perform as well as above-average-IQ students in solving those kinds of problems (Arbitman-Smith, Haywood, & Bransford, 1978).

There are, however, two serious limitations of this program. First, as Chance (1986, p. 85) points out, Instrumental Enrichment "requires a considerable investment of student time" and "does not produce immediate gains." Second, the skills taught in IE appear to be closely related to the items on tests of nonverbal intelligence, so that training may be quite specific. Bransford and colleagues (1985, p. 201) note that "there is an emphasis on training students to solve certain types of problems so they will be able to solve similar problems on their own."

CoRT THINKING PROGRAM

Consider this situation: You are a creative-thinking expert who is called upon to improve the thinking skills of business executives, administrators, armed forces personnel, lawyers, engineers, designers, architects, and scientists. You notice that people do not adequately handle the problems they face in their everyday lives. You decide that you want to improve people's practical problem-solving skills so that they will be able to better solve such problems as the following:

What makes a TV or radio show interesting?
Mail services usually lose a lot of money. If you were running these service, what alternatives would you suggest?
A father forbids his thirteen-year old daughter to smoke. What is his point of view and what is yours?

BOX 12 • 10   Ten Lessons from the Breadth Section of the CoRT Thinking Program

---

CoRT 1: Breadth

This section is concerned with helping students develop tools and habits for scanning widely around a thinking situation. The following tools are emphasized:

Treatment of ideas (PMI): Deliberately examining ideas for good, bad, or interesting points, instead of immediately accepting or rejecting them.

Factors involved (CAF): Looking as widely as possible at all the factors involved in a situation, instead of only the immediate ones.

Rules: Draws together the first two lessons.

Consequences (C & S): Considering the immediate, short-, medium-, and long-term consequences of alternative strategies.

Objectives (AGO): Selecting and defining objectives; being clear about one's aims and understanding those of others.

Planning: Draws together the preceding two lessons.

Priorities (FIP): Choosing from a number of different possibilities and alternatives; putting one's priorities in order.

Alternatives (APC): Generating new alternatives and choices instead of feeling confined to the obvious ones.

Decisions: Draws together the preceding two lessons.

Viewpoint (OPV): Considering all the viewpoints involved in a situation.

From de Bono (1985)

This task was taken on by Edward de Bono and his Cognitive Research Trust (from which the CoRT program derives its name).

The CoRT program consists of six sections of ten lessons each. Box 12-10 lists the contents of the first section, entitled "CoRT I: Breadth." Each lesson teaches a specific skill used in representing or analyzing a practical problem. For example, when using PMI your job is to list all the good points (i.e., pluses), bad points (i.e., minuses), and interesting points you can generate for a given example. If you were asked to apply PMI to the issue of year-round schools, some pluses might be that teachers could cover more material and students would not have to relearn all the things they forgot over summer vacation; some minuses might be that family vacation schedules could be disrupted or more money would be required; and an interesting point might be that the original reason for summer vacations was to let children help out on the farms.

Each lesson begins with the teacher describing the to-be-learned tool, such as PMI, and giving some examples. Then students work on some practice problems in small groups. After a few minutes, the groups report on their progress and the teacher leads a discussion concerning the usefulness of the tool. Then students go

back to their small groups to discuss some principles concerning the ι
the idea that PMI can prevent you from rejecting a good idea that se
first glance. Finally, students participate in a project involving the too
writing an essay or performing a skit. Most of the practice problems are ι
real-world problems rather than artificial puzzles or games. The target a
ranges from school children to business executives, although Chance
reports that it is most often used with children aged nine to twelve.

How can you evaluate the CoRT program? deBono (1985) provides three n
lines of support for his program: longevity, acceptance, and testimonials. First,
CoRT program has been successfully promoted as a thinking-skills course for me
than fifteen years. Second, according to de Bono (1985), the program has been use
in more than 5000 classrooms in ten countries, including the United Kingdom,
where the program was developed. Third, de Bono (1985, p. 383) claims that he has
a "considerable amount of unpublished data" from informal studies as well as a
"large number of anecdotal reports from teachers." Unfortunately, none of these
kinds of information provide any scientifically acceptable evidence that the CoRT
program works. In reviewing the research evidence concerning the CoRT program,
Polson and Jeffries (1985, p. 445) observed:

> The most disturbing aspect of the de Bono program is the lack of well-designed
> evaluation studies such as the excellent research on the Productive Thinking
> Program . . . after 10 years of widespread use, we have no adequate evidence
> concerning those claims and thus no support for the effectiveness of the program
> or the theoretical assumptions from which it was derived.

One problem is the lack of basic research concerning the validity of the
component skills; for example, promoters of the CoRT program need to test
whether skills such as being able to conduct a PMI are really related to successful
problem solving.

ODYSSEY

Consider the following situation: Your country's president has just appointed you
to the newly created post of Minister for the Development of Human Intelligence
and has told you that your job is to improve the intellectual performance of the
population. If you had all necessary governmental cooperation and financial
resources, what would you do to improve the people's problem-solving skills?

Although this may seem like an artificial problem for you, it was a real problem
for Dr. Luis Alberto Machado. In 1979 Dr. Machado became the head of the Ministry
for the Development of Human Intelligence in Venezuela, the first and only such
ministry in the world. Machado (1981, pp. 3–4) proclaimed that "in the same way
that investment of resources and political strategy are planned so should the different

12 • 11   Example Exercise and Teacher Script for "Sequences and Change"

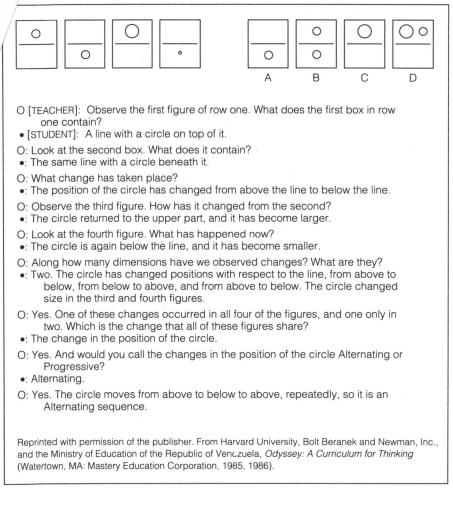

O [TEACHER]: Observe the first figure of row one. What does the first box in row one contain?

• [STUDENT]: A line with a circle on top of it.

O: Look at the second box. What does it contain?

•: The same line with a circle beneath it.

O: What change has taken place?

•: The position of the circle has changed from above the line to below the line.

O: Observe the third figure. How has it changed from the second?

•: The circle returned to the upper part, and it has become larger.

O: Look at the fourth figure. What has happened now?

•: The circle is again below the line, and it has become smaller.

O: Along how many dimensions have we observed changes? What are they?

•: Two. The circle has changed positions with respect to the line, from above to below, from below to above, and from above to below. The circle changed size in the third and fourth figures.

O: Yes. One of these changes occurred in all four of the figures, and one only in two. Which is the change that all of these figures share?

•: The change in the position of the circle.

O: Yes. And would you call the changes in the position of the circle Alternating or Progressive?

•: Alternating.

O: Yes. The circle moves from above to below to above, repeatedly, so it is an Alternating sequence.

Reprinted with permission of the publisher. From Harvard University, Bolt Beranek and Newman, Inc., and the Ministry of Education of the Republic of Venezuela, *Odyssey: A Curriculum for Thinking* (Watertown, MA: Mastery Education Corporation, 1985, 1986).

nations by means of common effort, plan the attainment of a higher degree of intelligence in the least time possible." Similarly, Dominguez (1985, p. 531) noted that "in Venezuela we are attempting to put these ideas about the modifiability of human intelligence to work in the service of mankind."

With the cooperation of consultants from the United States, one product of this effort was the development of a thinking-skills program for school children called Odyssey. Odyssey is intended to teach specific skills for solving reasoning and creative-thinking problems through a process of dialogue and discovery. The program consists of ninety-nine forty-five-minute lessons, organized into six books—*Foundations of Reasoning, Understanding Language, Verbal Reasoning, Problem Solving, Decision Making,* and *Inventive Thinking.*

For example, Box 12-11 shows a problem and a proposed teaching script from a lesson on "Sequences and Change" contained in the first book. As you can see, first the teacher leads a discussion of how to discover the solution to some sample problems; then the students solve some similar problems on their own; and finally the students are asked to explain their solutions. According to the promoters of Odyssey, some of the target skills taught in this lesson are identifying which dimensions vary in a sequence of stimuli; distinguishing among changes due to progression, alternation, and cycles; and recognizing the next item in a sequence on the basis of previous changes in a given dimension.

What is the effect of participating in the Odyssey program several times a week for a year? Chance (1986) reports the results of an unpublished study conducted in Venezuela during the 1982–1983 academic year. Several hundred students who had received a year's training in Odyssey (i.e., fifty-six lessons) and several hundred equivalent students who had received conventional instruction were given problem-solving tests at the beginning and end of the year. The trained students performed twice as well as the control students in solving problems like those given during the Odyssey training; in contrast, trained students performed only slightly better than the control students in solving problems that were different from those given during Odyssey training. Although these results are encouraging, Chance (1986, p. 70) notes that additional studies are needed and worries that "the Venezuelan results . . . will not carry over to American (or other English-speaking) classrooms." As with the IE program, a major implication of Odyssey seems to be that there is no such thing as a quick fix; acquiring thinking skills appears to be a long and time-consuming process. Given the lack of transfer beyond the instructional domain, a major shortcoming of the Odyssey program is its lack of overlap with regular school subjects. Teaching proper thinking for the circle-sequence problems in Box 12-11 may not help students solve progression problems in mathematical and verbal domains.

■

EVALUATION

■

This chapter follows the history of creativity training from the industrial programs of the 1930s to the curriculum projects of the 1960s to the new initiatives of the 1980s. What have we learned? Despite the claim of the classical approach that general creativity can be taught, most objective studies show that students learn component skills that can be used mainly on problems like those given during instruction. At present, after sixty years of experience with creativity-training courses, there is not convincing evidence that global skills can be learned in context-free environments. In short, there is no quick way to improve general problem-solving performance.

This lesson is important for both the teaching and theory of problem solving. First, research on the teaching of problem solving suggests that problem-solving performance depends, at least partly, on a collection of component skills that are directly related to the specific task. Similarly, the theme of Chapter 13 is that differences between expert and novice problem solvers may be characterized partly by differences in the amount and organization of knowledge they possess in a particular domain. Second, research on the teaching of problem solving suggests that successful problem solving depends on using appropriate strategies, that is, problem-solving processes are at the heart of successful solutions. Third, research on the teaching of problem solving suggests that problem-solving skills are often applicable only within the domain for which they have been learned. In summary, successful courses provide direct instruction in how to use component skills within specific contexts; successful theories of problem solving might also need to concentrate on describing the problem-solving processes involved in real-world problem domains.

A statement by the National Education Association (1961), entitled *The Central Purpose of American Education,* asserts: "The purpose which runs through and strengthens all other educational purposes—the common thread of education—is the development of the ability to think." There is reason to be optimistic, for it appears that during the years to come, psychologists will concentrate in earnest on the issue of how to teach people to think.

Suggested Readings

BARON, J. B., & STERNBERG, R. J. (Eds.). (1987). *Teaching thinking skills: Theory and practice.* New York: Freeman. Contains chapters written by leaders in the field of teaching thinking skills.

CHANCE, P. (1986). *Thinking in the classroom: A survey of programs.* New York: Teachers College Press. Describes and evaluates several of the most commonly used thinking-skills programs.

HALPERN, D. F. (1989). *Thought and knowledge: An introduction to critical thinking* (2nd ed.). Hillsdale, NJ: Erlbaum. Surveys what cognitive psychology has to say about teaching thinking skills.

NICKERSON, R. S., PERKINS, D. N., & SMITH, E. E. (1985). *The teaching of thinking,* Hillsdale, NJ: Erlbaum. Surveys research and theory on the teaching of thinking.

SEGAL, J. W., CHIPMAN, S. F., & GLASER, R. (Eds.). (1985). *Thinking and learning skills.* Hillsdale, NJ: Erlbaum. Volume 1 contains chapters by the developers of several important thinking-skills programs; Volume 2 contains chapters by leading researchers interested in the teaching of thinking.

CHAPTER 13

EXPERT PROBLEM SOLVING

Thinking as Influenced by Experience

Expertise in Physics

■

Expertise in Computer Programming

■

Expertise in Medicine

In Chapter 12, we examined individual differences among people in problem-solving ability. Another way to explore the issue of individual differences in thinking is to compare how experts and novices perform on a certain task. What do experts possess that novices lack? Consider the performance of a grand chess master, for example. Such a person is able to remember past board positions from earlier in the game and is able to play several different chess games simultaneously. We might well ask what an expert chess player possesses that a novice lacks.

To help answer this question, let me ask you to participate in a brief demonstration. When I give the signal, I want you to look at the chess board arrangement shown in the top-left portion of Box 13-1. Look for about five seconds, and then cover the top-left portion of Box 13-1 with a sheet of paper. Your task is to try to reconstruct what you saw by drawing the pieces where they belong in the blank chess board in the bottom-left part of Box 13-1. Here's your signal: go ahead and study the chess configuration in the top-left part of Box 13-1, and then try to reproduce it (without looking) in the bottom-left part of the box.

When you have recovered, carry out this same procedure with the chess arrangement shown in the top-right portion of Box 13-1. Study the top-right portion for about five seconds, and then try to reconstruct what you saw using the blank chessboard in the bottom-right part of the box.

Chase and Simon (1973) presented tasks such as these to beginning, good, and master chess players (but using real chess pieces placed on real chess boards rather than pictures). The stimuli for the experiment were two kinds of chess board arrangements: *actual board positions* (as in task 1) were taken from either the middle of a real game (twenty-four to twenty-six pieces on the board) or the end of an actual game (twelve to fifteen pieces on the board), and *random board positions* (as in task 2) were generated by taking a real game configuration and randomly rearranging all the pieces on the board. In Chase and Simon's experiment, each subject saw a chess board with some chess pieces on it for five seconds. Then the board was covered, subjects were given a clear board with a set of appropriate pieces, and they were asked to reconstruct what they had just seen.

How many pieces did you correctly remember in the two tasks? If you are like the beginning chess players in Chase and Simon's (1973) study, you were able to remember where to put only about four pieces in each of these tasks. However, if you are like the master chess player, you performed similarly to the beginners for random chess boards (such as task 2) but you remembered the places of most of the pieces—that is, sixteen out of twenty-four—from actual games (such as task 1). Box 13-2 summarizes the results, with all subjects performing poorly on recalling random chess board arrangements but the expert chess player excelling on recalling chess board arrangements from real games.

This example provides some interesting suggestions concerning differences between expert and novice chess players. First, experts possess more specific knowledge but not necessarily more general cognitive skill than novices. In the chess study, the expert (a grand chess master) did not have a better overall memory capacity; if he did, he would have performed better than the novices on remembering the positions of pieces from randomly arranged chess boards. What allows experts to plan so many moves ahead in a game or to remember board positions from early in the game? Chase and Simon (1973) suggest that experts have a huge vocabulary of recognizable configurations of chess pieces, that is, they can see a large pattern of many pieces as a single meaningful chunk. Thus, in this experiment, when an expert looked at an actual game board with twenty-four pieces, he was able to see three or four major chunks of chess pieces, each with a

BOX 13 ▪ 1   Two Chess Recall Tasks

Task 1

Study phase: Study this
chess board for 5 seconds.

Test phase: Now reproduce the
board (without looking).

Task 2

Study phase: Study this
chess board for 5 seconds.

Test phase: Now reproduce the
board (without looking).

BOX 13 ▪ 2   How Many Chess Pieces Are Correctly Recalled?

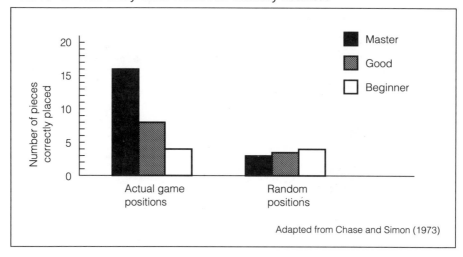

Adapted from Chase and Simon (1973)

clear meaning. Simon (1980) estimates that a chess master must acquire 50,000 such chunks of knowledge.

A second implication is that the expert's chess vocabulary is built up over many years of practice, playing hundreds of games and doing little other than playing or thinking about chess. Acquiring 50,000 chunks of knowledge in a domain rarely can be accomplished in less than ten years (Chase & Simon, 1973). For example, in an analysis of the careers of master composers, Hayes (1981, p. 213) found that "no one composes outstanding music without first having about ten years of intensive musical preparation." This *ten-year rule* does not mean that you can become a genius by gaining ten years of intensive experience in your field, but it does mean that "even a person endowed with the genius of Mozart or Beethoven will need 10 years of intense preparation to be creative" (Hayes, 1981, p. 214). These conclusions are consistent with deGroot's (1965) classic studies of how expert chess players decide which move to make in a game of chess—research originally published in Dutch in 1946 that has motivated modern research on expertise.

In short, research on expertise suggests that expert problem solvers must acquire a great deal of *domain-specific knowledge*, a feat that requires many years of intensive experience. Consistent with the idea that expertise is grounded in years of acquiring domain-specific knowledge, research on expertise demonstrates that "experts excel mainly in their own domains" (Glaser & Chi, 1988, p. xvii).

In this chapter, we focus on expert problem solving in three domains: solving physics problems, writing computer programs, and making medical diagnoses. In each domain, we explore the question: What do experts know that novices do not know?

EXPERTISE IN PHYSICS

WHAT DO EXPERT PHYSICISTS KNOW?

Consider the car problem shown in Box 13-3. If you have had an introductory course in physics and are willing to do some serious thinking, you may be able to solve this problem. However, if you are a physics professor who has spent more than ten years of your life working on physics problems, you can probably solve this problem with almost no effort. For example, Larkin and her colleagues (Larkin, McDermott, Simon, & Simon, 1980a, 1980b) found that novices (such as students who have taken a physics course) take four times longer than experts (such as physics professors) to solve physics problems. This difference in performance suggests the question: What does an expert know about solving physics problems that a novice does not know?

BOX 13 ∙ 3   The Car Problem

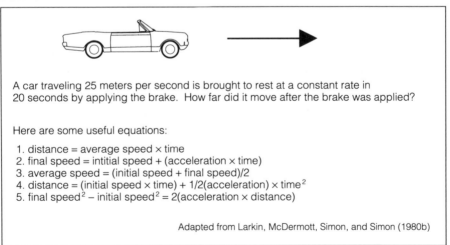

A car traveling 25 meters per second is brought to rest at a constant rate in 20 seconds by applying the brake. How far did it move after the brake was applied?

Here are some useful equations:

1. distance = average speed × time
2. final speed = intitial speed + (acceleration × time)
3. average speed = (initial speed + final speed)/2
4. distance = (initial speed × time) + 1/2(acceleration) × time^2
5. final speed^2 − initial speed^2 = 2(acceleration × distance)

Adapted from Larkin, McDermott, Simon, and Simon (1980b)

In this section, we briefly explore four kinds of knowledge that may differ in experts and novices: *factual knowledge* is basic knowledge about physics, including physical laws (such as force = mass × acceleration); *semantic knowledge* is knowledge of the concepts that underlie problem situations (such as what force, mass, and acceleration are); *schematic knowledge* is knowledge of problem types (such as knowing whether or not a problem involves conservation of momentum); and *strategic knowledge* consists of strategies for generating and monitoring plans (such as working backwards from the givens in a problem to the unknown).

EXPERT–NOVICE DIFFERENCES IN FACTUAL KNOWLEDGE

The first expert–novice difference concerns the way in which experts and novices store their knowledge about physics. In solving physics problems, you can express most of the basic information as equations. For example, to solve the car problem you may use some of the equations listed in the bottom of Box 13-3. Novices act as if they have *knowledge in small units* such the individual equations

Equation 1: distance = average speed × time

Equation 3: average speed = (initial speed + final speed)/2

whereas experts act as if they have *knowledge in large* (or *interconnected*) *units*, such as

Equations 1–3: distance = [(initial speed + final speed)/2] × time

Thus, in solving a problem that involves the use of many equations, experts can work more quickly because they do not need to search for as many pieces of information. Once they find equation 1, equation 3 is closely tied to it.

What evidence is there for the distinction between large and small units of knowledge? Larkin (1979) asked beginning physics students (novices) and physics professors (experts) to think aloud while they solved physics problems. As they solved the problems, both experts and novices generated equations—but their timing in doing so was different. Novices tended to generate new equations sporadically, at a random rate, suggesting that they access principles individually. In contrast, experts tended to cluster their generation of equations in time—generating some in a rapid burst, followed by a long delay, followed by another burst. This pattern suggests that experts store the equations in larger units that connect two or more equations.

In summary, these results suggest that novices store their knowledge of physics as a fragmented set of individual equations (i.e., *small functional units*), whereas experts possess interconnected solution equations that can be quickly accessed for specific types of problems (i.e., *large functional units*).

EXPERT–NOVICE DIFFERENCES IN SEMANTIC KNOWLEDGE

The second expert–novice difference concerns semantic knowledge— knowledge of the concepts underlying a given situation. One way to assess semantic knowledge is to give a sort of comprehension test, that is, to ask novices and experts to describe what a physics problem means. Following this procedure, Larkin (1983) found that experts and novices bring different kinds of semantic knowledge to a problem situation.

Consider, for example, the three-cart problem shown in Box 13-4. When a novice looks at this problem, the most obvious surface entities to focus on are a large cart, two smaller carts, some ropes, and a pulley. However, the novice has difficulty in relating these surface features of the problem to underlying physics concepts. Here is an excerpt from a typical novice protocol (Larkin, 1983, p. 81):

> Well, I'm right now trying to reason why it isn't going to move. . . . Once I visualize it, I can probably get started. But I don't see how it is going to work.

As you can see, the novice has what Larkin (1983) calls a *naive representation* of the problem—a focus on surface features that are not meaningfully related to concepts in physics.

In contrast, when an expert looks at this problem, he or she can first relate it to a meaningful physics-based context and then can relate features of the problem to physics-based concepts. Here is an excerpt from a typical expert protocol (Larkin, 1983, p. 81):

BOX 13 ▪ 4   The Three-Cart Problem

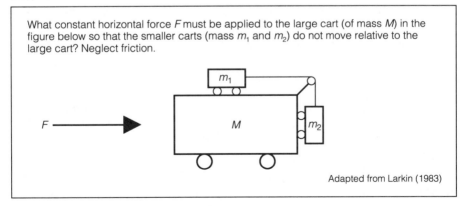

What constant horizontal force F must be applied to the large cart (of mass M) in the figure below so that the smaller carts (mass m_1 and m_2) do not move relative to the large cart? Neglect friction.

Adapted from Larkin (1983)

Well, with a uniformly accelerating frame of reference, all right? So that there is a pseudo-force on m_1 to the left that is just equivalent, just necessary to balance out the weight of m_2.

As you can see, an expert builds a *physics-based representation* of the problem. Instead of seeing a confusing collection of ropes and carts, the expert sees the underlying physical concepts of an object at rest (i.e., the small cart with mass of m_1) on a accelerating frame of reference (i.e., the large cart); further, the expert notices two forces acting on the small cart—a pseudo-force acting to the left of the small cart (caused by the accelerating large cart) and a tension force to the right (caused by the connection to the pulley system).

In short, the entities in the novice's *naive representation* are based mainly on the surface appearance of the problem, whereas the expert's *physics-based representation* has meaning in physics (such as forces) and is related to principles of physics (such as force and motion laws).

EXPERT–NOVICE DIFFERENCES IN SCHEMATIC KNOWLEDGE

Third, novices and experts differ in their knowledge of problem types, that is, in their schematic knowledge. One way to examine problem solvers' schematic knowledge is to observe their performance on a sorting task. For example, Chi, Feltovich, and Glaser (1981) asked eight advanced physics graduate students (experts) and eight undergraduates (novices) to categorize twenty-four physics problems. Each problem was typed on a 3-by-5-inch card, and the students were asked to sort them into categories based on similarity. Suppose the first three cards in the deck are the problems shown in Box 13-5. How would you sort them?

Would you place problem 1 and problem 2 into the same category, and problem 3 into a different category? If so, you are behaving like a novice. The novices tended to categorize the problems based on their *surface similarities,* that is, on an obvious physical characteristic of the problem situation. For example, novices placed problems involving blocks on an inclined plane in one category (like problems 1 and 2), pulleys in another, springs in another, rotating disks in another, and so on. When asked to explain why they put problems 1 and 2 in the same category, novices gave answers such as "These deal with blocks on an inclined plane" or "Blocks on inclined planes with angles" or "Inclined plane problems."

Would you place problems 2 and 3 in the same category, and problem 1 into a different category? If so, you are acting like an expert. The experts tended to categorize problems based on their *structural similarities,* that is, on the physics principle used to solve them. For example, experts placed problems involving the law of conservation of energy (such as problems 2 and 3) in one category, those involving Newton's second law in another category, those involving circular

BOX 13 • 5   Which Two Problems Belong in the Same Category?

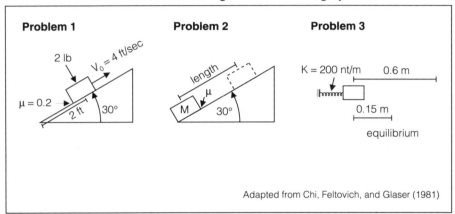

Adapted from Chi, Feltovich, and Glaser (1981)

motion in another, and so on. When asked to justify placing problems 2 and 3 in the same category, experts gave answers such as "Conservation of energy" or "Work-energy theorem; they are all straightforward problems" or "These can be done from energy considerations; either you should know the principle of conservation of energy or work is lost somewhere."

In summary, both experts and novices seem to be able to categorize problems, but they differ in the quality of their categories. While novices' categories are triggered by the surface features of problems (i.e., *surface similarities*), experts bring schematic knowledge to bear on the task, thus forming categories that are tied to solution plans (i.e., *structural similarities*).

EXPERT–NOVICE DIFFERENCES IN SEMANTIC KNOWLEDGE

The fourth expert–novice difference concerns problem-solving strategies: experts and novices differ in the ways they generate and use plans to solve problems. One way of examining problem solvers' strategies is to ask novices and experts to think aloud as they solve physics problems such as the car problem in Box 13-3. Simply, we can ask a problem solver to tell us "what is going on inside your head" as he or she solves a physics problem; for each problem solver, this produces a transcript of everything that was said, called a *thinking-aloud protocol*. When Larkin, McDermott, Simon, and Simon (1980a, 1980b) followed this procedure, they found an important difference between the strategies of experts and novices.

When you solved the car problem in Box 13-3, which formulas did you use? If you are a novice, you probably worked backwards from the unknown to the givens. In working backwards, you ask "What am I trying to find?" and then see what you have available to reach that goal. If you need something, you can set a new goal of finding what you need, and so on. For example, if a novice wants to find distance in the car problem, she selects equation 1 because it is the best-known equation that contains distance. Then, in order to solve for distance, the novice looks in the problem for numerical values of average speed and time. She finds the value for time—20 seconds—but not for average speed, so she now tries to remember an equation that will allow her to solve for average speed—namely, equation 3. To solve for average speed in equation 3, the novice looks in the problem for numerical values of initial speed and final speed; she finds one (25 meters per second) but becomes confused (perhaps not realizing that the final speed is 0 meters per second), so she starts over with a new equation that contains distance—equation 4. To solve for distance in equation 4, she sees that the problem contains numerical values for initial speed (25 meters per second) and time (20 seconds) but not for acceleration. Thus her next step is to use equation 2 so that she can solve for acceleration. This time, she finds values for initial speed, final speed, and time in the problem, so she can plug those into equation 4 and solve for acceleration. Having found a value for acceleration, she can now plug that value into equation 4 and derive a value for distance. As you can see, our novice has worked backwards, beginning with the unknown and moving toward the givens.

In contrast, experts tend to work forward from the givens to the unknown. For example, a typical expert begins by using initial speed (25 meters per second) and final speed (0 meters per second) to calculate average speed (12.5 meters per second) using equation 3. Then, the expert uses the calculated value of average speed (12.5 meters per second) and time (20 seconds) to solve for distance, using equation 1. As you can see, this is a forward-moving strategy in which given values are systematically combined to produce a calculated value for the unknown. You may have noticed that working forward is consistent with possessing knowledge in large units, while working backwards is consistent with possessing small functional units.

As a way of validating these observations, Larkin and colleagues (1980b) produced computer programs that simulate the knowledge organization and solution strategies of experts and novices. The expert program works forward and uses large-scale functional units; the novice program works backwards and uses smaller units of knowledge. The main output of the programs is the order in which equations are used. The expert program uses equations in the order used by human experts, and the novice program follows the order used by novices. This is one independent validation of the differences in knowledge organization and strategies used by experts and novices.

In summary, Box 13-6 shows four major differences between expert and novice problem solving in the domain of physics.

BOX 13 ▪ 6   Expert–Novice Differences in Physics

	Novices	Experts
Factual knowledge	Possess small functional units of knowledge	Possess large functional units of knowledge
Semantic knowledge	Build naive representations	Build physics-based representations
Schematic knowledge	Categorize based on surface similarities	Categorize based on structural similarities
Strategic knowledge	Work backwards from unknown to givens	Work forward from givens to unknown

EXPERTISE IN COMPUTER PROGRAMMING

WHAT DO EXPERT PROGRAMMERS KNOW?

Computer programming is a problem-solving activity. Four typical problem-solving tasks are *creating*, *comprehending*, *modifying*, and *debugging* programs that accomplish goals (Card, Moran, & Newell, 1983; Carroll, 1987; Shneiderman, 1980). In creating a program, the programmer is given a statement of the problem in English and must write computer code that solves the problem. In comprehending a program, the programmer is given computer code and must explain in English what the program does. In modifying a program, the programmer is given a program that accomplishes its goal and must change it to accomplish a slightly modified goal. In debugging a program, the programmer is given a program that does not work and must correct it.

The main goal of this section is to explore differences in what experts and novices know about programming. In short, we ask: What do expert computer programmers know that novices do not know? In a recent review of research on expert–novice differences in computer programming, Mayer (1988) identified four kinds of knowledge needed for computer programming: syntactic, semantic, schematic, and strategic.

Syntactic knowledge is knowledge of the language units and rules for combining language units. In BASIC language, for example, units include key words (such as INPUT, LET, and PRINT), variable names (such as A, B, C, and D), and numerical values; combination rules include that the line number comes before rather than after an instruction (Dyck & Mayer, 1989). To test people's syntactic knowledge of a computer language, we could give them a recognition test in which they tell whether a given instruction is or is not syntactically correct. For example, in BASIC, an expert would rapidly recognize that 10 X = Y + Z is acceptable while 10 A + B = C is not.

Semantic knowledge refers to the user's mental model of the major locations, objects, and actions inside the computer system. For BASIC, some major locations in the computer are the data stack, memory spaces, program list, output screen, and keyboard; some major objects are numbers, pointers, and program lines; some major actions are find, move, erase, and write (Mayer, 1979, 1985). To test people's semantic knowledge we could ask them to describe in their own words what goes on inside the computer when a given instruction is executed (Bayman & Mayer, 1988). For example, an expert programmer would know that LET A = 0 includes the following steps: find the number in memory space A, erase the number in that memory space, write the new number 0 in that memory space.

Schematic knowledge refers to the user's categories of routines for various purposes, such as routines for sorting, looping, or carrying out computations. For example, three kinds of looping structures are DO-WHILE loops, DO-UNTIL loops, and IF-THEN-ELSE loops. Schematic knowledge can be tested in a recall task, in which programmers study and then recall a normal or scrambled program. An expert would be able to chunk the statements in a normal program and therefore recall more than a novice. Similarly, schematic knowledge can be tested in a sorting task, in which users are given short programs and asked to put them into groups based on their functions. An expert would be able to sort programs by their functional rather than their surface characteristics.

Strategic knowledge includes techniques for devising and monitoring plans. Strategic knowledge can be evaluated by thinking-aloud protocols—that is, by asking programmers to "think aloud" as they write or debug a program. Experts are more likely to display a planful approach to programming.

To get a feeling for each type of knowledge, you can try each of the tasks given in Box 13-7: a recognition test to measure syntactic knowledge, a comprehension test to measure semantic knowledge, a recall test to measure schematic knowledge, and a thinking-aloud test to measure strategic knowledge.

EXPERT–NOVICE DIFFERENCES IN SYNTACTIC KNOWLEDGE

Do experts and novices differ with respect to their knowledge of programming language units and rules? To investigate this question, Wiedenbeck (1985) selected ten expert FORTRAN programmers who possessed 11,000 hours of programming experience and ten novice FORTRAN programmers who possessed 200 hours of programming experience. The programmers participated in a recognition test. Each was seated in front of a computer screen that presented

BOX 13 ▪ 7   Four Programming Tests

Recognition Test

Which of the following is a grammatically incorrect instruction?
(a) Turn left 90 degrees.
(b) Move forward 10 steps.
(c) Turn right 45 steps.
(d) Move forward 5 degrees.

Comprehension Test

What is accomplished by this set of instructions?
1. Walk forward 5 steps.
2. Turn right 90 degrees.
3. Walk forward 5 steps.
4. Turn right 90 degrees.
5. Walk forward 5 steps.
6. Turn right 90 degrees.
7. Walk forward 5 steps.
8. Turn right 90 degrees.

Recall Task

Study and then recite this program.
1. Put 1 in BOX-A.
2. Put 2 in BOX-B.
3. Put 3 in BOX-C.
4. Add the number in BOX-A to the number in BOX-B; put the result in BOX-D.
5. Add the number in BOX-C to the number in BOX-D; put the result in BOX-D.
6. Divide the number in BOX-D by 3; put the result in BOX-D.
7. Print out the number in BOX-D.

Thinking-Aloud Test

Create precise instructions for how to make a peanut butter sandwich.
Describe what you are thinking as you write the instructions.

lines of FORTRAN code, one at a time; some lines were grammatically correct and others were not. The programmer's task was to press a "yes" button if the code was grammatically correct and a "no" button if it was not. The results indicated that the experts made 40 percent fewer errors and responded 25 percent more quickly than the novices.

BOX 13 ▪ 8   Expert–Novice Differences in Computer Programming

	Novices	Experts
Syntactic knowledge	Slowly and effortfully recognize incorrect grammar	Rapidly and effortlessly recognize incorrect grammar
Semantic knowledge	Lack useful mental models of the computing system	Possess useful mental models of the computing system
Schematic knowledge	Recall programs and categorize based on surface characteristics	Recall programs and categorize based on type of routines required
Strategic knowledge	Use low-level plans, break problem into few subparts, and do not consider alternatives	Use high-level plan, break problems into fine subparts, and consider alternatives

What do you conclude from these results? Weidenbeck (1985) concludes that experts have automated their lower-level programming skills, such as detecting grammatically incorrect code, so that they can notice grammatically incorrect statements with minimal conscious attention; in contrast, novices must exert a great deal of conscious mental effort to detect grammatically incorrect statements. Since the automation of syntactic processing frees cognitive capacity in experts, they can focus their attention on the meaning and structure of the program, similar to the way in which automating the decoding process in reading allows young readers to focus on comprehending the passage.

The first row of Box 13-8 summarizes this expert–novice difference in the time and effort required for recognizing grammatical errors.

EXPERT–NOVICE DIFFERENCES IN SEMANTIC KNOWLEDGE

Do experts and novices differ in their semantic knowledge? Suppose we ask students who have just finished a beginning BASIC course to tell us what goes on inside the computer when it carries out an instruction, such as LET A = B + 1. Take a moment and write an answer in your own words, even if you are not familiar with BASIC.

Mayer (1979, 1985a) argues that the expert's view of this statement includes the actions: Find the number in memory space B, add 1 to that number (without erasing it), erase the number in memory space A, and write the sum into memory space A. However, if you are like the students in a study by Bayman and Mayer (1988), you have misconceptions about how the LET statement refers to memory spaces. Only 30 percent of students who had passed an introductory course in BASIC programming grasped the idea that the sum of 1 plus the number in memory space B is placed in memory space A. In contrast, 43 percent thought that the computer would simply write the equation, A = B + 1, into its memory, and 23 percent thought the computer would print the equation on the screen. In short, novices seem to lack semantic knowledge—that is, they do not know what the BASIC instructions refer to.

Bayman and Mayer (1988) also compared the semantic knowledge of programming students who had excellent mathematics backgrounds (higher-ability group) with those who had average or below-average mathematics backgrounds (lower-ability group). After completing an introductory course in BASIC computer programming, students were asked to describe what went on inside the computer for each of ten BASIC statements. Higher-ability students correctly described 67 percent of the statements, while lower-ability students correctly described 30 percent.

If novices lack useful mental models of the computer system, then direct instruction in the underlying model should improve their learning. Goodwin and Sanati (1986) taught Pascal to approximately 600 Pascal-naive students in either a traditional course or a course that emphasized a concrete model of the computer. The model was a computerized display that simulated the internal operation of the computer as each line of a program was executed. The results showed that the best predictor of learning success was prior non-Pascal programming experience for students in the traditional course, but computing experience was unrelated to success in the model course. The results suggest that training in conceptual models can reduce or eliminate the effects of expertise on learning a new language—a conclusion that is supported by similar findings by Bayman and Mayer (1988).

The second row of Box 13-8 summarizes the finding that experts possess more useful mental models of the computing system than novices.

EXPERT–NOVICE DIFFERENCES IN SCHEMATIC KNOWLEDGE

One way of studying expert–novice differences in schematic knowledge is to compare how experts and novices perform on recall of normal and scrambled programs. If novices are insensitive to the structure of programs—having to comprehend them one line at a time—then they should perform as well on recalling a scrambled program as on recalling a normal one. In contrast, if experts are able to chunk programs based on their knowledge of typical program structures, they should perform better on recall of normal programs than scrambled programs.

To test these predictions, McKeithen, Reitman, Rueter, and Hirtle (1981) selected twenty-four novices who had no experience in ALGOL programming and six experts who had more than 400 hours of ALGOL programming experience. On each of five trials, the subjects studied a program for two minutes and then were given three minutes to recall the program. When the program was a thirty-one-line ALGOL program in normal order, experts recalled almost three times as many lines as the novices; when the lines of the ALGOL program were presented in a random order, the recall performance of experts was much more similar to that of novices. Similar results were obtained by Shneiderman (1976) using FORTRAN code and by Barfield (1986) using BASIC code.

This pattern of results may remind you of the differences in recall between expert and novice chess players, as described in the introduction to this chapter. Like expert chess players who can chunk pieces into meaningful configurations, expert programmers seem to have a large storehouse of typical configurations of programming statements. This schematic knowledge helps experts to see a thirty-one-line program as a collection of five or six chunks of programming statements, with each chunk consisting of several statements that are meaningful related to a specific function.

A second way of examining expert–novice differences in schematic knowledge is to ask experts and novices to study and then recall a list of programming statements. For example, in a recall study by Adelson (1981), the novices were five college students who had just completed an introductory course in computer programming in PPL and the experts were five teaching fellows for the course. Each programmer was seated in front of a computer screen that presented sixteen lines of PPL program code, one line at a time, for twenty seconds each; then the programmer had eight minutes to recall as many lines as possible. This entire procedure was repeated eight more times. The lines came from three short programs—a five-line sorting program, a five-line randomization program, and a different six-line program—but the sixteen lines were presented in completely randomized order. For example, one line that was presented on the screen was: [x]$sort.within(sorting.list);i,j,temp.sort.

The experts and novices differed in how much they recalled, in how they segmented what they recalled, and in how they organized what they recalled. First, experts recalled about 33 percent more lines than the novices. Second, experts generated an average of 3.5 lines before they took a long pause, whereas novices generated 2.4 lines before pausing—suggesting that experts created chunks that were about 50 percent larger than those created by the novices. Third, the order of recall shows that experts tended to cluster the lines by program—that is, lines from program 1 were recalled together, lines from program 2 were recalled together, and lines from program 3 were recalled together; novices, however, clustered the lines they recalled by syntactic category—that is, the HEADER statements were recalled together, the RETURN statements were recalled together, the IF statements were recalled together, and the assignment statements were recalled together. The last finding is particularly interesting because it suggests that experts are sensitive to typical configurations of routines or programs—that is, experts seem to use their knowledge of program chunks to help them organize the randomly presented list of statements.

Finally, a third way to examine expert–novice differences in schematic knowledge is to ask expert and novice programmers to sort programming functions or problems into groups. For example, in one sorting study (Weiser & Shertz, 1983), the novices were six college students who were taking an introductory programming course and the experts were nine computer science graduate students. Each programmer was given a stack of twenty-seven programming problems stated in English and asked to sort them into groups based on "similarities in how you would solve them." Novices were highly influenced by the cover stories in the problems, as was indicated by their grouping business application problems in one pile, operating system application problems in another pile, and string manipulation problems in another pile. In contrast, experts sorted the problems based on the type of procedure that was needed to solve them—such as placing problems solved by sorting in one pile, problems solved by searching in another pile, and so on. These results suggest that experts can use their knowledge of program types—syntactic knowledge—to help classify problems.

In summary, research on recall and sorting indicates that experts have more categories for types of routines than do novices. The third row of Box 13-8 summarizes some expert–novice differences in schematic knowledge.

EXPERT–NOVICE DIFFERENCES IN STRATEGIC KNOWLEDGE

Soloway and Ehrlich (1984) have argued that planning strategies, such as breaking a problem into successively finer parts, are often tacit. Thus programmers may not always be able to describe the strategies they are using. However, by examining what programmers do and say as they solve a programming problem, we may be able to infer something about the strategies they are using.

To examine programmers' strategic knowledge, we can ask programmers to think aloud as they generate or debug a program. For example, Jeffries, Turner, Polson, and Atwood (1981) asked four expert software designers (including a professional with ten years of experience) and five novice software designers (including undergraduate computer science students) to think aloud as they designed a page-keyed indexing system. The index-maker problem is summarized in Box 13-9.

BOX 13 • 9   The Index-Maker Problem

A book publisher needs a computerized system that will create indexes for its to-be-published books. The index will list the key terms used in the book along with the page numbers on which these terms appear.

The input for this system is a book file containing the text of the book. At the end of each page, the file will contain a slash mark followed by the page number (e.g., /22 means page 22). Each word is preceded and followed by one of the following punctuation marks: blank space, comma, semicolon, colon, quote, double quote, period, exclamation point, question mark, carriage-return, or line-feed. A word at the end of a line may be hyphenated and continued on the next line, but a hyphenated word will not be continued across page boundaries.

Another input for this system will be a term file which contains a list of index terms (ranging from one to five words in length), with one term per line.

The output should be a list of the index terms in alphabetical order, with each term followed by the page number(s) on which that term appears, in numerical order.

From Jeffries, Turner, Polson, and Atwood (1981)

The results indicated expert–novice differences in strategies for decomposing and evaluating alternatives. First, although experts and novices decomposed the problem into parts, experts broke the problem into finer subparts and were more systematic than novices. For example, one expert began by listing the major modules in the program, then decomposed each module into subparts, and each subpart into its subparts, and so on. In contrast to this top-down successive refinement approach, a typical novice tried to solve the problem "by hook or crook." One novice decomposed the problem into several major steps but then failed to further decompose these modules. Second, although experts and novices generated solution plans, experts were more likely than novices to consider alternatives. For example, one expert stated that page numbers could be stored in either an array or a linked list, performed some calculations, and determined that the linked list would be more efficient. In contrast, novices seldom considered more than one way of solving a problem; for example, one novice said (Jeffries et al., 1981, p. 273) , "This might be the only way I can think of to be able to do this. It's going to be awful [sic] expensive."

In another thinking-aloud protocol study, Vessey (1985, 1986) asked eight experts and eight novices to think aloud as they debugged a COBOL program. An examination of the protocols revealed that experts and novices differed in when they carried out their planning and in the structure of their planning. First, experts familiarized themselves with the program before trying to write new code that would solve the problem (suggesting global planning), whereas novices were more likely to begin solving the problem before they understood the program and to pause more often along the way (suggesting local planning). Second, experts tended to focus on high-level modules in the program (suggesting a top-down approach), whereas novices jumped around to more modules (suggesting an unfocused approach).

In summary, research using thinking-aloud protocols shows that both in program generation and program debugging tasks, experts possess higher-level plans than novices. The bottom row of Box 13-8 summarizes examples of expert–novice differences in strategic knowledge.

■

EXPERTISE IN MEDICINE
■

WHAT DO EXPERT PHYSICIANS KNOW?

In making a medical diagnosis, a physician is engaging in a form of problem solving. In general, a patient suffering from a specific ailment (such as some sort of heart trouble) prefers the advice of someone who has many years of experience treating that kind of ailment (such as a cardiologist with more than ten years of successful practice). This leads to an interesting question: What does an experienced physician know that an inexperienced physician does not know? In this section, we explore four broad categories of differences in the knowledge of experts and novices: *factual knowledge,* or knowledge of abnormal physical symptoms or test results; *semantic knowledge,* or knowledge of the connection between symptoms and possible underlying medical conditions; *schematic knowledge,* or knowledge of symptom configurations; and *strategic knowledge,* or knowledge of how to generate and test hypotheses.

EXPERT–NOVICE DIFFERENCES IN FACTUAL KNOWLEDGE

One difference between an expert and novice radiologist involves their knowledge of X-ray picture features—which features are normal and which are abnormal. For example, consider the X-ray picture shown in Box 13-10. Do you notice any abnormalities? List every possible abnormality that you see. If your list is long, you are acting like a novice. According to Myles-Worsley, Johnson, and Simons (1988), this is a normal chest X-ray.

Are experts better able to pinpoint abnormalities in an X-ray picture? In an amazing study, Kundel and Nodine (1975) asked experienced radiologists to participate in a recognition task. They looked at X-ray films that were flashed on a screen for one-fifth of a second—just enough time for a single fixation of the eyes but not enough time to move one's eyes over the film. Even with this very brief exposure, these experts were able to detect and name abnormalities with 70 percent accuracy. Christensen and colleagues (1981) found that novices require

BOX 13 ▪ 10   List Any Abnormalities in This X-Ray Film

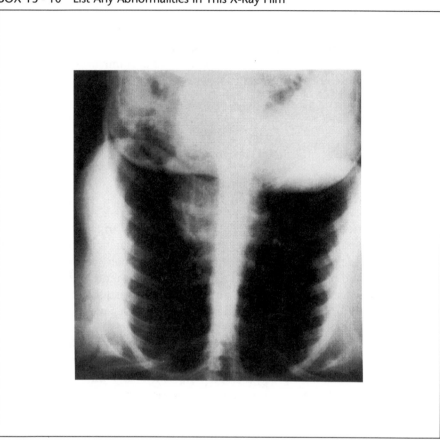

more time to recognize abnormalities on an X-ray film than experts. These findings provide support for the idea that experts have automated their recognition procedures—in a single glance they can notice whether or not a film contains abnormal features.

EXPERT–NOVICE DIFFERENCES IN SEMANTIC KNOWLEDGE

A second difference between experts and novices concerns their knowledge of what various symptoms can mean, that is, how observable symptoms are related to possible internal medical conditions. For example, Patel and Groen (1986) asked expert cardiologists and novice medical students to read the medical case presented in Box 13-11, discuss the underlying medical conditions, and provide

BOX 13 ▪ 11   What Is Wrong with This Patient?

This 27-year-old unemployed male was admitted to the emergency room with the complaint of shaking chills and fever of four days' duration. He took his own temperature and it was recorded at 40°C on the morning of his admission. The fever and chills were accompanied by sweating and a feeling of prostration. He also complained of some shortness of breath when he tried to climb the two flights of stairs in his apartment. Functional inquiry revealed a transient loss of vision in his right eye which lasted approximately 45 s on the day before his admission to the emergency ward.

Physical examination revealed a toxic looking young man who was having a rigor. His temperature was 41°C, pulse 120, BP 110/40. Mucus membranes were pink. Examination of his limbs showed puncture wounds in his left antecubital fossa. The patient volunteered that he had been bitten by a cat at a friend's house about a week before admission. There were no other skin findings. Examination of the cardiovascular system showed no jugular venous distention, pulse was 120 per minute, regular, equal, and synchronous. The pulse was also noted to be collapsing. The apex beat was not displaced. Auscultation of his heart revealed a 2/6 early diastolic murmur in the aortic area and funduscopy revealed a flame shaped hemorrhage in the left eye. There was no splenomegaly. Urinalysis showed numerous red cells but there were no red cell casts.

From Patel and Green (1986)

a diagnosis. In this case, the patient is suffering from a bacterial infection caused by a contaminated needle, possibly used in taking drugs intravenously. The infection attacked the aortic valve, one of the major valves in the heart. Furthermore, the infection was acute, that is, rapidly advancing and severe. The correct diagnosis is acute bacterial endocarditis—a severe bacterial infection of the aortic valve. This is an unusual case, which makes it difficult to diagnose. In fact, the correct diagnosis was produced by 57 percent of the experts (cardiologists with many years of experience) and none of the novices (medical students who lacked clinical experience).

Let's focus on what the successful and unsuccessful cardiologists said as they discussed the underlying conditions in this case. Patel and Groen (1986) identified fifteen basic connections between symptoms in the case history and possible medical conditions in the patient, such as the three listed in Box 13-12. As you can see, each connection ties an observable symptom from the medical history to an inferred internal medical state or condition. Interestingly, experts who produced the correct diagnosis included 75 percent of these connections in their discussion, whereas unsuccessful cardiologists produced only 29 percent. For example, Box 13-12 shows that connections 2 and 3 were discussed by all of the successful cardiologists and none of the unsuccessful ones. These results are consistent with the idea that expert medical diagnosis requires semantic

BOX 13 • 12   Some Crucial Connections Between Observations and Inferences

	Discussed by physician	
Connections	Successful	Unsuccessful
1. IF the patient has puncture wounds and is a young unemployed male, THEN consider intravenous drug use.	75%	0%
2. IF the patient is an intravenous drug user, THEN consider bacterial infection.	100%	0%
3. IF the patient has a diastolic murmur, THEN consider aortic valve insufficiency.	100%	0%

Adapted from Patel and Green (1986)

knowledge—that is, experts know what an observable symptom or abnormality means in terms of the internal operation of the human body.

EXPERT–NOVICE DIFFERENCES IN SCHEMATIC KNOWLEDGE

A third difference between experts and novices concerns their knowledge of how observations cluster into meaningful configurations. For example, here is another medical problem-solving task. Suppose you are a radiologist. You are given a patient's chest X-ray film and are asked to comment on it. How do you reach a diagnosis?

If you do not have much experience in reading X-ray films, you are probably at a loss. However, don't despair. In the field of radiology, a physician with a year of experience who may have diagnosed 5000 X-ray cases is considered a novice. We reserve the word *expert* for a radiologist with ten years of experience who has diagnosed 200,000 cases. What can we learn about the nature of problem-solving expertise by comparing how a novice and an expert attack the task of diagnosing X-ray films? This is the question that Lesgold and colleagues (1988; Lesgold, 1984) addressed in a recent study.

In the study, the novices were first- and second-year residents and the experts were radiologists with ten or more years of experience beyond residency. As part of the procedure, experts and novices viewed a film, thinking out loud as they watched it, and then dictated a diagnostic report as they would do in their office. For example, one image was from a patient who had had a portion of his right upper lung removed in an operation about ten years before the X-ray was taken. The correct diagnosis for this film was "chronic collapsed lung" because a portion of the lung had been collapsed for a long period of time. The radiological

BOX 13 ▪ 13   An Expert's Analysis of an X-Ray Film

Step 1 (notices something is wrong): "We may be dealing with a chronic process here . . ."

Step 2 (tries to get an explanation): "I'm trying to work out why the mediastinum and the heart are displaced into the right chest. There is not enough rotation to account for this. I don't see displacement of fissures [lung lobe boundaries]."

Step 3 (establishes a tentative explanation): "There may be a collapse of the right lower lobe but the diaphragm on the right side is well visualized, and that's a feature against it . . ."

Step 4 (refines the tentative explanation): "I come back to the right chest. The ribs are crowded together . . . The crowding of the ribcage can, on some occasions, be due to previous surgery. In fact . . . the third and fourth ribs are narrow and irregular, so he's probably had [previous] surgery . . ."

Step 5 (refines the tentative explanation again): "He's probably had one of his lobes resected. It wouldn't be the middle lobe. It may be the upper lobe. It may not necessarily be a lobectomy. It could be a small segment of the lung with pleural thickening at the back . . ."

Step 6 (checks to make sure): "I don't see the right hilum . . . [this] may, in fact, be due to the postsurgery state I'm postulating. . . . Loss of visualization of the right hilum is . . . seen with collapse. . ."

Adapted from Lesgold, Rubinson, Feltovich, Glaser, Klopfer, and Wang (1988)

evidence for this correct diagnosis was that the once-inflated portion of the right upper lung was missing. During the ten years since the operation, the chest organs had moved to fill in the space where the portion of the lung had been. In particular, the heart had moved to the right and tilted in such a way as to cast a larger than normal shadow on the film.

Box 13-13 provides a portion of the protocol from one of the experts. Almost immediately, the expert notices that something is wrong and that it is chronic. Next, the displacement and rotation of the heart trigger a search for an explanation. Then the expert comes up with a tentative explanation that is close—the right lower lung is collapsed. Upon further investigation, however, the expert refines his explanation—the right upper lung is collapsed because of prior surgery. Finally, the expert checks to make sure he is right.

An analysis of protocols shows that experts and novices come to the chronic collapsed lung diagnosis in different ways. First, experts are more rapid and successful than novices in developing a hypothesis that guides their search for clues—in this case, chronic collapsed lung. After viewing the film for only two seconds, 60 percent of the experts mentioned the decreased size of the right lung, compared to none of the novices; whereas 73 percent of the novices reported that the right lung was normal, compared to none of the experts. Similarly 40 percent of the experts but none of the novices noticed the rotation of the heart, whereas 73 percent of the novices and 40 percent of the experts initially saw the heart as normal. After extensive viewing, 100 percent of the experts included "chronic collapsed lung" as a possible diagnosis, while only 36 percent of the novices did so. This finding suggests that experts are able to see clusters of abnormalities that are all consistent with a single medical problem. Second, experts are more likely than novices to give causal explanations for what they see. Experts included approximately 50 percent more comments about causes and effects than did novices. Again, experts appear to connect relations among abnormalities to suggest a possible medical problem. Third, experts are more likely than novices to test and refine their hypotheses. For example, in a film showing a partially collapsed right lung, the portion of the right lung that is collapsed looks denser than the rest of the lung. Novices typically take this density as evidence of a tumor, whereas experts will look for other signs that would negate the tumor hypothesis—such as displacement of lobe boundaries and increase in size of adjacent lobes. While the novices are often restricted to the most obvious diagnosis, experts are more likely to examine details that would require changes in the diagnosis. Again, experts look for clusters of abnormalities rather than depending on just one abnormality to trigger a final diagnosis.

EXPERT–NOVICE DIFFERENCES IN STRATEGIC KNOWLEDGE.

A fourth difference between experts and novices is the way that they develop and test diagnostic hypotheses. As a final example of medical diagnosis, read Box 13-14, the medical file of a patient at the University of Minnesota Heart Hospital. If you are unable to make much sense out the these twenty-two pieces of information, you are in good company. In a study by Johnson and colleagues (1981), none of four medical students (whom we classify as novices) and only the two most experienced out of four medical specialists in pediatric cardiology (whom we classify as experts) came up with the right diagnosis. The correct diagnosis is total anomalous pulmonary connection (TAPVC), a condition in which the vein that normally carries oxygen-rich blood from the lungs to the left upper chamber of the heart (left atrium) instead is connected to the right upper chamber (right atrium). However, the medical file contained pieces of information that could suggest three competing diagnoses that could eventually be ruled out upon closer examination of the pattern of clues.

In examining the thinking-aloud protocols of the medical problem solvers in this study, Johnson and colleagues noted that the experts and novices differed mainly in the way they used information; that is, in the way they used clues to suggest hypotheses and in how they searched for clues to test each hypothesis.

BOX 13 ∙ 14   Twenty-Two Medical Clues

1.   The patient is a five-year-old Caucasian girl. She weighs 33 pounds and is 41 inches tall. Her presenting problem is a murmur heard by a family physician.

2.   The child was born following a normal pregnancy, labor, and delivery.

3.   A murmur was heard in the first day of life by the attending physician.

4.   Other than the murmur, there were no problems in the neonatal period.

5.   Infancy was unremarkable. However, between the ages of 2 and 3, the patient had numerous infections including flu . . . and required several hospitalizations for respiratory infections in her home town.

6.   In the past two years, her health has been good. She has always preferred quiet activities.

7.   The mother . . . has noted that in the past two years, when the child is cold, her lips turn blue.

8.   Development has been normal . . . but growth has been slow.

9.   Aside from a paternal aunt who has an asymptomatic heart murmur, there is no family history of cardiac disease.

10.   On physical examination, this is an anxious-appearing five-year-old.

11.   Fingernails appear minimally cyanotic, with a slight watch-crystal formation.

12.   There is no evident respiratory distress. The respiratory rate is 20/minute.

13.   The blood pressure is 106/60 in the right arm, 108/64 in the left arm, and 114/72 in the leg.

14.   The pulses are full and equal in the arms and legs. The pulse rate is 110/minute.

15.   Examination of the chest shows a prominent precordial bulge. The lungs are clear.

16.   The apex impulse is felt lateral to the mid-clavicular line in the sixth intercostal space.

17.   Auscultation of the heart shows the first heart sound having a very loud component. The second heart sound is widely split all the time and appears fixed. The pulmonary component is slightly prominent.

18.   A murmur is present along the upper sternal border, the murmur being as loud or perhaps even louder over the upper back.

19.   A murmur is present along the lower left sternal border.

20.   The liver and spleen are not palpable.

21.   The chest X-ray shows moderate cardiomegaly and markedly increased pulmonary vasculature. There is also an unusual vascular shadow seen in the right side representing . . . an anomalously coursing pulmonary vein.

22.   The EKG shows a right axis deviation of +120 degrees, a wandering atrial pacemaker, right-atrial enlargement, and right-ventricular hypertrophy.

From Johnson, Duran, Hassebrok, Moller, Prietula, Feltovich, and Swanson (1981)

Two common approaches used both by experts and novices were *breadth-first,* in which several competing hypotheses were generated from the beginning and compared against each important piece of information, and *depth-first,* in which a single hypothesis was tested against the data until it was proven incorrect, and

BOX 13 • 15   Expert–Novice Differences in Medical Problem Solving

	Novices	Experts
Factual knowledge	Slowly and effortfully recognize abnormalities	Rapidly and effortlessly recognize abnormalities
Semantic knowledge	Do not connect observed abnormalities to possible internal medical conditions	Connect observed abnormalities to possible internal medical conditions
Schematic knowledge	Do not connect large clusters of observed abnormalities to possible diagnoses	Connect large clusters of observed abnormalities to possible diagnoses
Strategic knowledge	Consider fewer alternatives and conduct fewer tests of hypotheses	Consider more alternatives and conduct more tests of hypotheses

then another hypothesis was selected and tested, and so on. The successful experts eventually generated all four competing hypotheses based on one or more triggering clues, and upon further searching of the information they eliminated the three incorrect hypotheses. In contrast, the novices generated only two or three of the four major hypotheses based on the triggering clues; in fact, three of the four novices failed even to consider the correct diagnosis.

Research on diagnostic strategies seems to show that experts and novices differ mainly in their ability to *find clues* that trigger hypotheses and to *test hypothesis* against clues. This finding is consistent with Groen and Patel's (1988) observation that when experts and novices read and recall medical files, novices remember more of the information but experts include more inferences, especially inferences about relevant facts. Apparently experts are better able to find the explanatory relevance of pieces of information; that is, they know how to use clues in the medical file to suggest a new hypothesis or rule out an existing one. One interpretation of these findings is that, through years of experience with thousands of cases, experts have built up connections among configurations of clues and diagnostic hypotheses. In short, there appears to be no substitute for domain knowledge in the development of expert problem-solving strategies in medical diagnosis.

Box 13-15 summarizes some of the major differences between experts and novices in the field of medical diagnosis. As you can see, it seems to take a lot more than study in medical school to create an expert—years of specific experience in diagnosing cases appears to be indispensable for medical expertise.

■
EVALUATION
■

Our brief look at the problem-solving processes of novices and experts reveals certain commonalities across domains of expertise. The general theme of this chapter is that expert problem solving in fields ranging from physics to programming to medical diagnosis is based on years of experience. Chi, Glaser, and Rees (1982, p. 71) present this knowledge-based view of expertise as follows: "the problem-solving difficulties of novices can be attributed to inadequacies of their knowledge bases and not to limitations in the architecture of their cognitive systems or processing capabilities." In short, problem solving in a domain depends heavily on the quality and quantity of the problem solver's domain-specific knowledge.

In this chapter, we have identified four major aspects of expert problem solving. With respect to factual or syntactic knowledge, experts store knowledge in large units that can be accessed rapidly. For example, experts can produce physics equations in rapid succession when solving a physics problem, identify incorrect grammar in a computer program, or rapidly and effortlessly recognize an abnormality in an X-ray. With respect to semantic knowledge, experts can relate specific features of a problem to meaningful underlying concepts. For example, experts can state the physics concepts that underlie features of a physics problem, explain what happens inside the computer when a statement is executed, or recognize the possible implications of a particular abnormality in an X-ray. With respect to schematic knowledge, experts can discriminate among problem types in a way that allows them to categorize problems based on solution plans. For example, experts sort physics problems based on underlying physical laws, sort programming problems based on the types of required routines, and cluster abnormal features in an X-ray into meaningful configurations. With respect to strategic knowledge, experts work forward guided by a global plan and consider alternatives. For example, experts solve physics problems by finding a global solution plan, solve programming problems by breaking a problem into successively smaller parts, and solve medical problems by generating many alternatives and comparing each against the evidence.

An exciting direction for future research is the development of computerized expert systems that simulate human experts. An expert system is a computer program that solves problems like an expert in some domain. For example,

Posner (1988, p. xxxv) recognizes the potential of expert systems for improving our understanding of human problem solving:

> Although this technology is still primitive, it represents an important contribution of fundamental research on the nature of representation of information in memory. Behind this technology is a better understanding of what it means to be an expert. Expertness lies more in an elaborated semantic memory than in a general reasoning process.

In short, future advances in the psychology of expertise may come through the emerging field of artificial intelligence—especially the design of machines that solve problems like experts.

Suggested Readings

CHI, M. T. H., GLASER, R., & FARR, M. J. (Eds.). (1988). *The nature of expertise.* Hillsdale, NJ: Erlbaum. Contains chapters on expert problem solving in medical diagnosis, computer programming, judicial decision making, and other fields.

de GROOT, A. D. (1965). *Thought and choice in chess.* The Hague: Mouton. (Original work published 1946) Presents de Groot's classic research on expert problem solving in chess.

CHAPTER 14

ANALOGICAL REASONING

Thinking as Based on Analogs, Models, and Examples

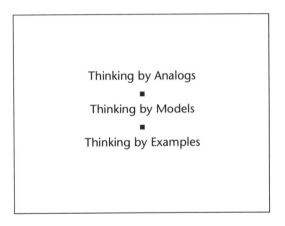

Thinking by Analogs

·

Thinking by Models

·

Thinking by Examples

"Analogy pervades all our thinking." So begins George Polya's (1957) famous description of techniques for effective problem solving. *Analogical reasoning* occurs when we abstract a solution strategy from a previous problem and relate that information to a new problem that we are trying to solve. Indeed, we engage in analogical reasoning when we solve a new problem by using what we know about a related problem that we can solve.

For example, read over the missionaries and cannibals problem given in Box 14-1. To solve the problem, place three dimes (to represent the missionaries) and three pennies (to represent the cannibals) on one side of the table. Then move the coins back and forth across the table, assuming that each move represents a river crossing by the boat. Can you solve the problem? (If not, refer back to the discussion of the hobbits and orcs problem in Chapter 6.)

Once you have solved the missionaries and cannibals problem, read over the jealous husbands problem given in Box 14-2. To solve this problem, begin with three pairs of different colored buttons, with one large button (to represent the husband) and one small button (to represent the wife) in each pair. Can you solve this problem?

Did you recognize any similarities between the two problems? A *surface similarity* occurs when some of the surface content of the two problems is alike—that is, when the problems share common details that may not be necessary for the solving the problems (Gentner, 1989). A *structural similarity* occurs when the relations of objects in one problem correspond to the relations of objects in the other problem (Gentner, 1989). On a blank sheet of paper write some of the surface and structural similarities that you can find between the missionaries and cannibals problem and the jealous husbands problem.

Box 14-3 lists examples of surface similarities and structural similarities between the two problems. For example, one of the surface similarities is that both problems involve a boat crossing a river. This is a surface similarity because the same underlying structural relation could be obtained in other situations, such as using a two-passenger elevator to move from a lower to a higher level.

A structural similarity is that six objects must move from one place to another using a vehicle that can contain no more than two passengers. Structurally, the two problems are partial analogs: the missionaries correspond to the husbands, the cannibals correspond to the wives, and the requirement that the cannibals cannot outnumber the missionaries corresponds partially to the requirement that each wife cannot be left without her husband. Although inexperienced problem solvers often focus on surface similarities between two problems, recognizing surface similarities between two problems generally is not useful in problem solving. In contrast, recognizing analogies in the structures of the two problems—that is, seeing structural similarities while ignoring similarities or dissimilarities in surface features—rests at the heart successful analogical reasoning.

Did solving the missionaries and cannibals problem help you to solve the jealous husbands problem? If so, we can say there was *analogical transfer of problem-solving strategy* from one problem to the other. We might expect analogical transfer because the strategy used in one problem is essentially the same strategy needed for the other. However, if you are like most of the subjects in an experiment conducted by Reed, Ernst, and Banerji (1974), solving one problem did not really help you solve the other one. For example, Reed and colleagues asked students to solve these two problems within thirty minutes; some subjects received one problem first, whereas others received the other problem first. In general, the time and number of moves needed to solve a problem were the same whether the problem came first or second.

BOX 14 ▪ 1   The Missionaries and Cannibals Problem

Three missionaries and three cannibals having to cross a river at a ferry, find a boat but the boat is so small that it can contain no more than two persons. If the missionaries on either bank of the river, or in the boat, are outnumbered at any time by cannibals, the cannibals will eat the missionaries. Find the simplest schedule of crossings that will permit all the missionaries and cannibals to cross the river safely. It is assumed that all passengers on the boat unboard before the next trip and at least one person has to be in the boat for each crossing.

From Reed, Ernst, and Banerji (1974)

BOX 14 ▪ 2   The Jealous Husbands Problem

Three jealous husbands and their wives having to cross a river at a ferry, find a boat but the boat is so small that it can contain no more than two persons. Find the simplest schedule of crossings that will permit all six people to cross the river so that none of the women shall be left in company with any of the men, unless her husband is present. It is assumed that all passengers on the boat unboard before the next trip, and at least one person has to be in the boat for each crossing.

From Reed, Ernst, and Banerji (1974)

BOX 14 ▪ 3   Surface and Structural Similarities Between Two Problems

	Missionaries and Cannibals Problem	Jealous Husbands Problem
Surface Similarities	River crossing ⟷	River crossing
	Boat ⟷	Boat
Structural Similarities	Missionaries ⟷	Husbands
	Cannibals ⟷	Wives
	Cannibals cannot outnumber missionaries ⟷	Wife must accompany husband

Thus we begin our study of analogical reasoning with a disturbing failure to support Polya's optimistic claim. The failure to find transfer from one problem to another is a common result in the psychological literature; for example, when we look at some of the classic problems described in Chapter 3, we see that humans have difficulty in transferring from one form of river-crossing problem to another (Reed et al., 1974) or one form of the Tower of Hanoi problem to another (Hayes & Simon, 1977). Indeed, humans appear to be quite provincial in their problem-solving activities, often failing to realize that a clever solution procedure they devised for a problem in one domain could be applied to an equivalent problem encountered in a new domain.

In spite of these problems, analogical reasoning remains an exciting area of study. In the years since Reed and colleagues' study, much has been learned about the conditions under which transfer from one problem to another can occur. When you are able to transfer, you can find a solution for a new problem that had been eluding you. Thus, while the many failures of transfer are disappointing, those cases in which it actually occurs can be exciting.

Vosniadou and Ortony (1989, p. 1) summarize the potential of analogical reasoning: "The ability to perceive similarities and analogies is one of the most fundamental aspects of human cognition. . . . Human reasoning does not always operate on the basis of content-free general inference rules but, rather, is often tied to particular bodies of knowledge and is greatly influenced by the context in which it occurs."

Where do creative problem solutions come from? When you are confronted with a novel problem, how do you find a solution? According to the *analogical transfer hypothesis,* you can solve a new problem by remembering another problem that you can solve, by abstracting the relevant information from that problem, and by mapping that information to the solution of the new problem.

In this chapter, we will explore three conditions for successful analogical transfer from a known problem (called the base) to a new one (called the target):

Recognition—in which a problem solver identifies a potential analog (or base) from which to reason,

Abstraction—in which a problem solver abstracts a general structure or principle or procedure from the base, and

Mapping—in which a problem solver applies that knowledge to the target.

In summary, Vosniadou and Ortony (1989, p. 6) define analogical reasoning as "transfer of relational information from a domain that already exists in memory (usually referred to as the *source* or *base* domain) to the domain to be explained (referred to as the *target* domain)." For example, the jealous husbands problem can be solved by recognizing that the missionaries and cannibals problem is somewhat analogous, by abstracting the solution procedure from the missionaries and cannibals problem, and by using that solution procedure to solve the jealous husbands problem.

In this chapter, we will look at the role of recognition, abstraction, and mapping within three somewhat different situations—*thinking by analogs, thinking by models,* and *thinking by examples.* In thinking by analogs, we use our understanding of a principle used to solve one problem to help us create an analogous solution for a new problem in another domain (as in trying to use the missionaries and cannibals problem to solve the jealous husbands problem). In thinking by models, we use our understanding of how one system works to reason about how an analogous system works. In thinking by examples, we use our understanding of the solution procedure in a worked-out example in one domain to create a solution procedure for a related problem within the same domain.

■
THINKING BY ANALOGS
■

WHAT IS AN ANALOG?

An analog is a problem that contains a similar structure but not necessarily the same story line as another problem, that is, an analog has structural similarity but not surface similarity with a target problem. For example, consider the tumor problem that was described more fully in Chapter 3: "Given a human being with an inoperable stomach tumor, and rays which destroy organic tissue at sufficient intensity, by what procedure can one free him of the healthy tissue which surrounds it?" An analog to the tumor problem is the General problem, given in the top portion of Box 14-4. In both problems, the structure is the same (the problem is to use forces at a high enough intensity to destroy a target but at a low enough intensity not to destroy the surrounding area; the solution is to use weak forces that all converge on a single target) but the surface stories differ (one problem is about a medical procedure; the other is about a military assault).

In order to study the role of analogs, Gick and Holyoak (1980) asked people to read a story about a General's military assault on a fortress and then to generate as many solutions as possible to the tumor problem. The instructions encouraged people to use the General problem to help them solve the tumor problem. Box 14-4 shows three versions of the General story. Each version begins with the same statement of the problem that can be summarized as follows: How can we use a large army to storm a fortress when all the roads leading into the fortress are mined to explode if large (but not small) numbers of troops pass over them? However, each version ends with a different solution: *disperse the troops* by

BOX 14 • 4   Three Analogs to the Tumor Problem

The General (Dispersion Version)

A small country fell under the iron rule of a dictator. The dictator ruled the country from a strong fortress. The fortress was situated in the middle of the country, surrounded by farms and villages. Many roads radiated outward from the fortress like spokes on a wheel. A great general arose who raised a large army at the border and vowed to capture the fortress and free the country of the dictator. The general knew that if his entire army could attack the fortress at once it could be captured. His troops were poised at the head of one of the roads leading to the fortress, ready to attack. However, a spy brought the general a disturbing report. The ruthless dictator had planted mines on each of the roads. The mines were set so that small bodies of men could pass over them safely, since the dictator needed to be able to move troops and workers to and from the fortress. However, any large force would detonate the mines. Not only would this blow up the road and render it impassable, but the dictator would then destroy many villages in retaliation. A full-scale direct attack on the fortress therefore appeared impossible.

The general, however, was undaunted. He divided his army up into small groups and dispatched each group to the head of a different road. When all was ready he gave the signal, and each group charged down a different road. All of the small groups passed safely over the mines, and the army then attacked the fortress in full strength. In this way, the general was able to capture the fortress and overthrow the dictator.

The General (Supply Route Version)

[Begins with same first paragraph as above.]

The general, however, was undaunted. He knew that one major thoroughfare leading to the fortress was always kept open as a supply route. He led his army to the head of the supply route. When all was ready he gave the signal, and the entire army charged down the open route. The army avoided the mines and attacked the fortress in full strength. In this way, the general was able to capture the fortress and overthrow the dictator.

The General (Tunnel Version)

[Begin with same first paragraph as above.]

The general, however, was undaunted. He and his men dug an underground tunnel beneath the mines following the route of the road to the fortress. When the tunnel was dug, the men crawled through it until they arrived safely at the foot of the fortress. Here they all gathered together and attacked the fortress in full strength. In this way, the general was able to capture the fortress and overthrow the dictator.

From Gick and Holyoak (1980)

simultaneously sending small groups of soldiers along each road; *use an open route* by sending the entire army via a supply road that would not explode; and *build a tunnel* by having the soldiers dig a tunnel that would take them all to the fortress.

BOX 14 • 5   Structural Similarities Between Two Problems

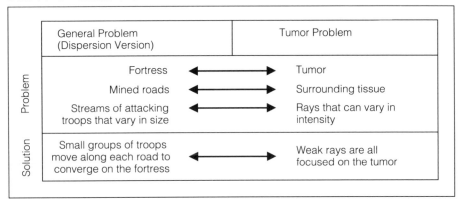

Can you see the relation between the General problem and the tumor problem? According to Gick and Holyoak (1980) three common approaches to the tumor problem are: *dispersion*—"apply low-level rays from several different directions so they simultaneously converge at the tumor" (p. 322); *open passage*—"send high-intensity rays down the esophagus so they strike the tumor" (p. 322); and *operation*—"make an incision into the stomach to expose the tumor and then apply high-intensity rays directly to the tumor" or "insert a tube through the healthy tissue to the tumor, and then send high-intensity rays through the tube to the tumor" (p. 322). In Duncker's (1945) analysis of the tumor problem, the preferred solution was dispersion (also called "convergence"), because the other two approaches violated the premises of the problem; that is, that no operation could be performed either to remove the tumor or to insert a direct pathway. As you can see in Box 14-5, the General problem and the tumor problem are analogous: the fortress is like the tumor, the roadways are like the surrounding tissue, and the streams of attacking troops are like the rays. Most importantly, the dispersion solution to the General problem is analogous to the preferred solution to the tumor problem.

Does knowing how to solve the General problem affect how people go about solving the tumor problem? Box 14-6 shows the percentage of people in each treatment group who produced each of three types of solutions to the tumor problem—dispersion, open passage, and operation. As you can see, when people read the General problem along with the dispersion solution, they overwhelmingly produced the dispersion solution for the tumor problem. In contrast, when people either did not read the General problem or else read it

BOX 14 • 6   Percentage of Subjects in Each Group Who Proposed Various Solutions to the Tumor Problem

Treatment Group	Proposed Solution		
	Dispersion	Open Passage	Operation
Dispersion version	100	10	30
Supply route version	10	70	50
Tunnel version	20	30	80
Control	0	20	50

Adapted from Gick and Holyoak (1980)

along with the supply route or tunnel solution, they seldom produced the dispersion solution for the tumor problem.

These results are encouraging because they show that, under certain conditions, people can successfully use their knowledge about one problem to help them solve a new problem. In order to better understand thinking by analogs, let's examine three crucial processes in analogical reasoning: *recognizing* that the General problem is related to the tumor problem, *abstracting* the underlying solution procedure from the General problem (namely, having streams of weak forces converge on one spot), and *mapping* the appropriate features of the base problem onto the target problem.

RECOGNITION PROCESS

The first step depends on the problem solver's recognition process. In the foregoing study, Gick and Holyoak explicitly told people to use the first story (about the General) as a means for solving the tumor problem in order to insure that the recognition process would occur. What happens when we leave people on their own to find the connection between the two problems?

To address this question, Gick and Holyoak (1983) asked students to participate in what seemed to be two distinct experiments—a recall task and a problem-solving task. First students were asked to memorize and then recall three stories: the dispersion version of the General story, an unrelated story about wine merchants, and an unrelated story about identical twins. Then the students were given the tumor problem and asked to write down as many solutions as possible; however, before they started writing, half the students were given a hint that "one of the stories you read before will give you a hint for a solution to this problem" and half were not. The results showed the overwhelming influence of the hint: the dispersion solution for the tumor problem was generated by 92 percent of the students given the hint and by 20 percent of the students given no hint. In fact, almost all the students given no hint indicated that it had not occurred to them to use the stories they had just read. Apparently, knowing a solution plan for an analogous problem is not very useful unless you realize that the problem is analogous to the one you are working on.

ABSTRACTION PROCESS

Once you recognize analogs that are potentially useful, the second process is to abstract the general characteristics from the analogs for use in solving other problems. For example, Gick and Holyoak (1983) argue that the General problem and the tumor problem share the same underlying structure—what they call the *convergence schema:* (1) the problems consist of similar goal states (use strong force to overcome a target), given states (force that can vary in strength and multiple pathways that can carry the force to the target), and obstacles/constraints (inability to apply full force along pathways); and (2) the problems share a common solution (simultaneously apply weak forces along multiple pathways so that the forces are strong when they converge on the target). How can we make sure that students acquire the convergence schema when they read about the General problem?

In order to study this issue, Gick and Holyoak (1983) asked some students (analog-only group) to read the dispersion version of the General passage and then to solve the tumor problem. To help them form a convergence schema, other subjects (analog-plus-principle group) received the same treatment but were also given a verbal summary of the principle at the end of the General story: "If you need a large force to accomplish some purpose, but are prevented from applying such a force directly, many smaller forces applied from different directions may work just as well." Performance on the tumor problem was not influenced by stating the principle: 29 percent of the analog-only group and 32 percent of the analog-plus-principle group correctly gave the convergence solution for the tumor problem.

Undaunted by this failure to help students abstract the convergence schema, Gick and Holyoak (1983) tried again, this time using diagrams. Some students read the General story and then tried to solve the tumor problem (analog-only group), whereas others did the same thing but also had the diagrams shown in Box 14-7 added to the General story (analog-plus-diagrams

BOX 14 ▪ 7   Diagram for General Story

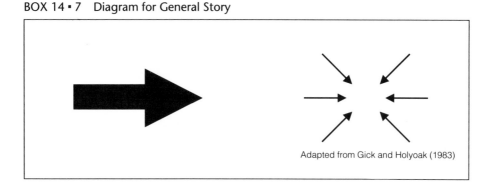

Adapted from Gick and Holyoak (1983)

group). As with the verbal statement of the principle, visual diagrams did not help students to transfer what they learned from the General problem to the tumor problem: 40 percent of the analog-only group and 23 percent of the analog-plus-diagram group produced the convergence solution to the tumor problem.

These results provide examples of difficulties in abstracting the general structure underlying the General problem, that is, the convergence schema. Perhaps students need to see several problems that share the same structure—namely, the focusing of several lines of weak forces on one spot—before they can abstract the convergence schema. To test this idea, Gick and Holyoak (1983) asked students to read two stories and then try to solve the tumor problem. Box 14-8 shows examples of stories that are analogs to the tumor problem (the General, the commander, Red Adair, and the fire chief). Some students read two similar analogs (i.e., two military stories—the General and the commander; or two fire-fighting stories—Red Adair and the fire chief); some students read two dissimilar analogs (i.e., one military and one fire-fighting story); and some read one analog and one unrelated story (about identical twins).

Unlike the previous attempts to facilitate abstraction, reading two analogs was clearly better than reading just one, especially if the two analogs had different settings: 52 percent of the students given two dissimilar analogs and 39 percent of those given two similar analogs correctly produced the convergence solution to the tumor problem, compared to only 21 percent of the students who received one analog plus an unrelated story. Gick and Holyoak (1983) propose a *schema induction theory* to explain this result: it is easier to induce a general schema from experiences with structurally similar problems in different domains than from a single problem.

MAPPING PROCESS

The third process involved in analogical reasoning is finding an appropriate connection between the solutions for base and target problems. How can we help people spontaneously see that a new problem can be solved in the same way as a previously experienced problem? For example, how can we help people use the solution procedure given in the lightbulb story (the first version in Box 14-9) to solve the tumor problem? Holyoak and Koh (1987) propose that people look for similarities between the features of the base and target problems—including similarities in surface features (such as using rays in the tumor problem and laser beams in the lightbulb problem) and in structural features (such as not being allowed to harm the healthy surrounding tissue in the tumor problem and not being allowed to break the surrounding glass in the lightbulb problem). According to Holyoak and Koh, the more features there are in common, the more likely the problem solver is to recognize the analogy.

According to this approach, the distinction between surface and structural similarities is a crucial one for understanding analogical transfer. For example, Box 14-9 shows versions of the lightbulb problem that vary in their structural and surface similarity to the tumor problem. Surface similarity is manipulated by using either a laser beam in the lightbulb problem (more like the X-ray in the tumor problem) or an ultrasound wave (less like the X-ray); structural similarity is manipulated by using fragile glass than can break if subjected to either a high-intensity laser beam or to ultrasound (more like the healthy tissue in the tumor problem) or by using machines that can produce only low-intensity rays (less like the adjustable X-rays in the tumor problem).

As you can see, surface features are irrelevant to the solution procedure; for example, it does not matter whether the ray is a laser ray that fuses the filament in a lightbulb (which is similar to surface features in the tumor problem) or whether it is an ultrasound wave that breaks the obstruction in the lightbulb (which is dissimilar to the surface features in the tumor problem). Structural features are central to the problem solution; for example, in a convergence (or dispersion) problem there are incoming forces that can vary in intensity, there is a central location that needs a high intensity, and the central location is surrounded by locations that cannot sustain high intensities. Thus saying that glass is fragile has the same structural characteristic as saying that the surrounding tissue would be destroyed by high-intensity X-rays, but saying that machines are incapable of generating high-intensity laser beams or ultrasound waves is not structurally similar to the tumor problem, in which the X-rays may be set to any intensity. Box 14-10 summarizes the analogies between the structure of the fragile-glass/laser-beam version of the lightbulb problem and the tumor problem.

In order to study the role of structural and surface similarity in analogical

BOX 14 • 8   Four Analogs to the Tumor Problem

The General

A small country was ruled from a strong fortress by a dictator. The fortress was situated in the middle of the country, surrounded by farms and villages. Many roads led
to the fortress through the countryside. A rebel general vowed to capture the fortress.
The general knew that an attack by his entire army would capture the fortress. He
gathered his army at the head of one of the roads, ready to launch a full-scale direct
attack. However, the general then learned that the dictator had planted mines on each
of the roads. The mines were set so that small bodies of men could pass over them
safely, since the dictator needed to move his troops and workers to and from the fortress. However, any large force would detonate the mines. Not only would this blow up
the road, but it would also destroy many neighboring villages. It therefore seemed im-
pos sible to capture the fortress.

 However, the general devised a simple plan. He divided his army into small groups
and dispatched each group to the head of a different road. When all was ready he
gave the signal and each group marched down a different road. Each group continued down its road to the fortress so that the entire army arrived together at the fortress at the same time. In this way, the general captured the fortress and overthrew
the dictator.

The Commander

A military government was established after the elected government was toppled in a
coup. The military imposed martial law and abolished all civil liberties. A tank corp
commander and his forces remained loyal to the overthrown civilian government.
They hid in a forest waiting for a chance to launch a counterattack. The comman
der felt he could succeed if only the military headquarters could be captured. The
headquarters was located on a heavily guarded island situated in the center of a
lake. The only way to reach the island was by way of several pontoon bridges that
connected it to the surrounding area. However, each bridge was so narrow and
unstable that only a few tanks could cross at once. Such a small force would easily
be repulsed by the defending troops. The headquarters therefore appeared invincible.

 However, the tank commander tried an unexpected tactic. He secretly sent a
number of tanks to locations near each bridge leading to the island. Then under
cover of darkness the attack was launched simultaneously across each bridge. All
of the groups of tanks arrived on the island together and immediately converged on
the military headquarters. They managed to capture the headquarters and eventually
restore the civilian government.

(continued)

transfer, Holyoak and Koh (1987) asked subjects to read and summarize one of
the four versions of the lightbulb story. Then subjects solved a series of problems,
including the tumor problem, in which they were asked to list as many solutions
as possible. Finally students were given a hint suggesting that the lightbulb
problem could be used to solve the tumor problem, and they were again asked to
list possible solutions to the tumor problem.

BOX 14 ▪ 8, *continued*

Red Adair

An oil well in Saudi Arabia exploded and caught fire. The result was a blazing inferno that consumed an enormous quantity of oil each day. After initial efforts to extinguish it failed, famed firefighter Red Adair was called in. Red knew that the fire could be put out if a huge amount of fire retardant foam could be dumped on the base of the well. There was enough foam available at the site to do the job. However, there was no hose large enough to put all the foam on the fire fast enough. The small hoses that were available could not shoot the foam quickly enough to do any good. It looked like there would have to be a costly delay before a serious attempt could be made.

However, Red Adair knew just what to do. He stationed men in a circle all around the fire, with all of the available small hoses. When everyone was ready all of the hoses were opened up and foam was directed at the fire from all directions. In this way a huge amount of foam quickly struck the source of the fire. The blaze was extinguished, and the Saudis were satisfied that Red had earned his three million dollar fee.

The Fire Chief

One night a fire broke out in a wood shed full of timber on Mr. Johnson's place. As soon as he saw flames he sounded the alarm, and within minutes dozens of neighbors were on the scene armed with buckets. The shed was already burning fiercely, and everyone was afraid that if it wasn't controlled quickly the house would go up next. Fortunately, the shed was right beside a lake, so there was plenty of water available. If a large volume of water could hit the fire at the same time, it would be extinguished. But with only small buckets to work with, it was hard to make any headway. The fire seemed to evaporate each bucket of water before it hit the wood. It looked like the house was doomed.

Just then the fire chief arrived. He immediately took charge and organized everyone. He had everyone fill their bucket and then wait in a circle surrounding the burning shed. As soon as the last man was prepared, the chief gave a shout and everyone threw their bucket of water at the fire. The force of all the water together dampened the fire right down, and it was quickly brought under control. Mr. Johnson was relieved that his house was saved, and the village council voted the fire chief a raise in pay.

From Glick and Holyoak (1983)

Box 14-11 shows that students who read the version of the lightbulb story that had high surface similarity and high structural similarity were more likely to recognize that the lightbulb problem was analogous to the tumor problem and were more likely to produce the convergence solution to the tumor problem than other students, whereas students who read the version with low surface and low structural similarity performed worst. However, when given a hint to use the

BOX 14 • 9   Four Versions of the Lightbulb Story

Fragile-Glass/Laser Version

In a physics lab at a major university, a very expensive lightbulb which would emit precisely controlled quantities of light was being used in some experiments. Ruth was the research assistant responsible for operating the sensitive lightbulb. One morning she came into the lab and found to her dismay that the lightbulb no longer worked. She realized that she had forgotten to turn it off the previous night. As a result the light-bulb had overheated, and the filament inside the bulb had broken into two parts. The surrounding glass bulb was completely sealed, so there was no way to open it. Ruth knew that the lightbulb could be repaired if a brief, high-intensity laser beam could be used to fuse the two parts of the filament into one. Furthermore, the lab had the necessary equipment to do the job.

However, the high-intensity laser beam would also break the fragile glass surrounding the filament. At lower intensities the laser would not break the glass, but neither would it fuse the filament. So it seemed that the lightbulb could not be repaired, and a costly replacement would be required. Ruth was about to give up when she had an idea. She placed several lasers in a circle around the lightbulb and administered low- intensity laser beams from several directions all at once. The beams all converged on the filament, where their combined effect was enough to fuse it. Since each spot on the surrounding glass received only a low-intensity beam from one laser, the glass was left intact. Ruth was greatly relieved that the lightbulb was repaired, and she then went on to successfully complete the experiment.

Low-intensity/Laser Beam Version

[Same first paragraph as above.]

However, the lasers only generated low-intensity beams that were not strong enough to fuse the filament She needed a much more intense laser beam. So it seemed that the lightbulb could not be repaired, and a costly replacement would be required. Ruth was about to give up when she had an idea. She placed several lasers in a circle around the lightbulb and administered low-intensity laser beams from several directions at once. The beams all converged on the filament, where their combined strength was enough to fuse it. Ruth was greatly relieved that the lightbulb was repaired, and she then went on to successfully complete the experiment.

(continued)

lightbulb story, transfer was better if students had read a structurally similar version of the lightbulb story, but surface similarity did not affect transfer. Apparently, subjects use both structural and surface features to spontaneously recognize a relation between a base and target problem; however, only the structural features are actually used to successfully abstract and map the solution procedure from the base to the target problem.

What can we conclude from this research on the conditions that facilitate

BOX 14 • 9, *continued*

Fragile-Glass/Ultrasound Version

In a physics lab at a major university, a very expensive lightbulb which would emit precisely controlled quantities of light was being used in some experiments. Ruth was the research assistant responsible for operating the sensitive lightbulb. One morning she came into the lab and found to her dismay that the lightbulb no longer worked. She realized that she had forgotten to turn it off the previous night. As a result the lightbulb overheated, and two wires in the filament inside the bulb had fused together. The surrounding glass bulb was completely sealed, so there was no way to open it. Ruth knew that the lightbulb could be repaired if a brief, high-intensity ultrasound wave could be used to jar apart the fused parts. Furthermore, the lab had the necessary equipment to do the job.

However, the high-intensity ultrasound wave would also break the fragile glass surrounding the filament. At lower intensities the ultrasound wave would not break the glass, but neither would it jar apart the fused parts. So it seemed that the lightbulb could not be repaired, and a costly replacement would be required. Ruth was about to give up when she had an idea. She placed several ultrasound machines in a circle around the lightbulb and administered low-intensity ultrasound waves from several directions all at once. The waves all converged on the filament, where their combined effect was enough to jar apart the fused pieces. Since each spot on the surrounding glass received only a low-intensity wave from one ultrasound machine, the glass was left intact. Ruth was greatly relieved that the lightbulb was repaired, and she then went on to successfully complete the experiment.

Low-Intensity/Ultrasound Wave Version

[Same first paragraph as above.]

However, the ultrasound machines only generated low-intensity waves that were not strong enough to jar apart the fused parts. She needed a much more intense ultrasound wave. So it seemed that the lightbulb could not be repaired, and a costly replacement would be required. Ruth was about to give up when she had an idea. She placed several ultrasound machines in a circle around the lightbulb and administered low-intensity ultrasound waves from several directions at once. The waves all converged on the filament, where their combined strength was enough to jar apart the fused parts. Ruth was greatly relieved that the lightbulb was repaired, and she then went on to successfully complete the experiment.

From Holyoak and Koh (1987)

problem-solving transfer from a known problem (such as the General problem or the lightbulb problem) to a novel problem (such as the tumor problem)? First, the problem solver must recognize that he or she possesses in memory a solution for a known problem that is analogous, at some level, to the new problem. Second, the problem solver must abstract the relevant properties of the known problem to be used in solving the new problem. Third, the problem solver must be able to apply the solution structure or procedure to the new problem.

BOX 14 ▪ 10   Structural Similarities Between Two Problems

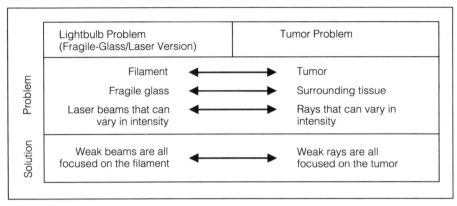

BOX 14 ▪ 11   Performance of Four Groups on the Tumor Problem

	Treatment Group			
Dependent Measure	High Structure/ High Surface (Fragile-Glass/ Laser)	High Structure/ Low Surface (Fragile-Glass/ Ultrasound)	Low Structure/ High Surface (Low Intensity/ Laser)	Low Structure/ Low Surface (Low Intensity/ Ultrasound)
Percentage of subjects who gave converg- ence solution before hint	69	38	33	13
Percentage of subjects who gave converg- ence solution before or after hint	75	81	60	47
Percentage of subjects who noticed analogy	88	56	40	13

Adapted from Holyoak and Koh (1987)

■
THINKING BY MODELS
■

WHAT IS A MODEL?

A model of a system includes the essential parts of the system as well as the cause-and-effect relations between a change in the status of one part and a change in the status of another part. Consider the analogy: An electrical circuit is like a hydraulic system. In this case, a hydraulic system can serve as a model that helps you understand how an electrical circuit works. Gentner (1983, 1989) has proposed a structure-mapping theory for describing analogical reasoning in which knowledge about one system (called the *base*—in this case, a hydraulic system) can be used to reason about another system (called the *target*—in this case, an electrical circuit). Each system consists of *objects,* each of which has certain *attributes,* and there are certain *relations* among objects.

Gentner (1983, 1989) distinguished between two types of mappings from one system to another: *literal similarity,* in which the objects in the two domains have similar features and relations (such as "An electrical circuit is like a doorbell system"); and *analogy,* in which the objects in the two domains have dissimilar features but similar relations (such as "An electrical circuit is like a hydraulic system").

To use an analogical model effectively, a problem solver must focus on the relevant relations among objects in that system while ignoring the irrelevant features of the objects in that system. One difficulty for problem solvers is the need to overlook the differences in the features of the objects in the two systems. For example, the features of the objects in a hydraulic system and an electrical circuit differ: water flow can make you wet whereas electricity flow can give you a shock, pipes are make of plastic whereas wires are made of metal, and so on. Another difficulty with using analogies productively in reasoning concerns selecting appropriate relations, what Gentner refers to as *systematicity.* Some relations are essential for the operation of the system whereas others are not. For example, in the electrical circuit system the relations among current, voltage, and resistance are central; similarly, in a hydraulic system the corresponding relations among water flow, water pressure, and pipe narrowness are central.

Let's consider two possible analogs (i.e., base domains) that could be used for reasoning about electrical flow in a circuit (i.e, the target domain): a water-flow model and a moving-crowd model. Box 14-12 presents a summary of the relevant objects, attributes, and relations in the two base domains (water-flow model and moving-crowd model) and the target domain (electrical circuit).

In using a water-flow model, an analogy can be expressed between electricity flowing in a circuit and water flowing through pipes. The objects in a hydraulic

BOX 14 ▪ 12   Two Analogical Models for an Electrical Circuit

	Electrical Circuit (Target)	Water-Flow Model	Moving-Crowd Model
Objects	Electrons	Water	Mice
	Wire	Pipe	Corridor
	Battery	Pump	Loudspeaker
	Resistor	Constriction in pipe	Gate in corridor
Attributes	Voltage	Water pressure	Crowd pressure
	Resistance	Pipe narrowness	Gate narrowness
	Current	Water flow	Crowd movement
Relations	Current increases with voltage	Water flow increases with water pressure	Crowd movement increases with crowd pressure
	Current decreases with resistance	Water flow decreases with pipe narrowness	Crowd movement decreases with gate narrowness
	Sum of current into a point equals sum of current out of a point	Sum of water flow into a point equals sum of water flow out of a point	Sum of crowd movement into a point equals sum of crowd movement out of a point

system map onto the objects in a circuit as follows: water is like electrons, pipes are like wires, reservoirs (or pumps) are like batteries, and constrictions in pipes are like resistors. The attributes of objects in a hydraulic system map onto the attributes of a circuit as follows: water pressure is like voltage, pipe narrowness is like resistance, and rate of water flow through a pipe is like current. Some relations between objects that hold in both domains are: "rate of water flow increases with water pressure" is analogous to "current increases with voltage"; "rate of water flow decreases with narrowness of pipe" is analogous to "current decreases with resistance"; "sum of water flow into a point equals the sum of water flow out of a point" is analogous to "sum of current into a point equals sum of current out of a point." Of course, some objects, features of objects, and relations between objects cannot be successfully mapped from one domain to the other. For example, atomic structure is relevant for electrical flow but not for water flow.

In using a moving-crowd model, an analogy can be expressed between electricity flowing in a circuit and objects racing through passageways. The objects in a raceway system map onto the objects in a circuit as follows: mice are like electrons, corridors are like wires, loudspeakers are like batteries, and narrow gates are like resistors. The attributes of objects in a raceway system map onto the attributes of a circuit as follows: crowd pressure of mice is like voltage, narrowness of the gates is like resistance, and rate of movement of mice through the raceway is like current. Some relations between objects that hold in both domains are: "rate of movement of mice increases with crowd pressure" is analogous to "current increases with voltage"; "rate of movement of mice decreases with gate narrowness" is analogous to "current decreases with resistance"; "sum of mice moving into a point equals sum of mice moving out of a point" is analogous to "sum of current into a point equals sum of current out of a point." Of course, some objects, features of objects, and relations between objects cannot be successfully mapped from one domain to the other. For example, mice (or other members of a moving crowd) are alive and electrons are not.

MODELS AS AIDS TO SCIENTIFIC REASONING

How do students use models such as those of flowing water and moving crowds to reason about electrical flow? To investigate this question, Gentner and Gentner (1983) asked students who were naive about physical science to make predictions about which of two circuits would have greater current and voltage and then to describe in their own words the way they thought about electricity. Box 14-13 presents the four reasoning problems in which students were asked whether circuit A would have more, less, or the same amount of electrical current and voltage as circuit B. Interestingly, students' descriptions of how they solved the problems revealed that some students always thought about the circuits in all problems as water-flow systems whereas other students always thought about the circuits as moving-crowd systems.

The first problem compares a simple circuit to a circuit with serial batteries (which doubles the current and voltage); the second problem compares a simple circuit to a circuit with parallel batteries (which do not affect the current or voltage). Students who reported using a water-flow model were likely to see the difference between serial and parallel batteries, because water reservoirs combine in the same way as do serial and parallel batteries. For example, with reservoirs, the water pressure and flow depend on the height of the water rather than total amount of water. Therefore two reservoirs connected in parallel at the same height will create the same pressure and flow as that of the original one-reservoir system; however, two reservoirs connected serially, with one on top of the other, result in doubling of the height, so the resulting pressure and flow will double. In

BOX 14 • 13   Percentage Correct on Four Electrical Circuit Problems by Students Using a Water-Flow or Moving-Crowd Model

Problem Which has more current? Which has more voltage?	Type of Model Used By Student	
	Water-Flow Model	Moving-Crowd Model
Problem 1: Simple circuit or serial batteries? 	100	60
Problem 2: Simple circuit or parallel batteries? 	85	40
Problem 3: Simple circuit or serial resistors? 	70	100
Problem 4: Simple circuit or parallel resistors? 	60	40

Adapted from Gentner and Gentner (1983)

contrast, students who used a moving-crowd model were unlikely to see the difference between serial and parallel batteries, because this model contains no good analog for the performance of batteries in serial and parallel combination. As predicted, Box 14-13 shows that students who used a water-flow model performed better on the problems involving serial and parallel batteries than did students who used a moving-crowd model.

The third problem compares a simple circuit to a circuit with serial resistors (which decrease the current and maintain the same voltage); the fourth problem compares a simple circuit to a circuit with parallel resistors (which increase the current and maintain the same voltage). Students who used a water-flow model were unlikely to see the difference between serial and parallel resistors because they viewed resistors as impediments, with two obstacles creating more drag than one regardless of configuration. In contrast, students who used a moving-crowd model were more likely to see the difference between serial and parallel resistors because they viewed resistors as gates through which twice as many moving objects can pass if the gates are side-by-side than if they are placed one after the other. Box 14-13 shows that, as predicted, students who used a moving-crowd model performed better on the problems involving serial and parallel resistors than students who used a water-flow model.

In summary, the results show that students consistently used either a water-flow or a moving-crowd analogy to reason about circuits and that the model they used influenced their problem-solving performance. Students who used a water-flow model performed better on problems involving batteries than resistors, whereas students who used a moving-crowd model performed better on problems involving resistors than batteries.

WHAT MAKES A GOOD MODEL?

Gentner's research suggests that people's scientific reasoning is influenced by their mental model. In a series of experiments, Mayer (1989a, 1989b; Mayer & Gallini, 1990) addressed the related issue of determining the conditions for effective models. For example, read the passage in the the first part of Box 14-14 and then try to generate as many answers as you can to the following question: "It was pointed out that the curvature of the earth limits the effectiveness of radar beyond a certain distance. One way around this, of course, is to set up radar detection centers at various places on earth such that all areas are covered. Can you think of another way of doing this?" If you have difficulty in generating answers to this question, examine the bouncing-ball model shown in the second part of Box 14-14. The bouncing-ball model may help you see that radar is like tossing a ball at a remote object, having it bounce off the object, catching the ball when it returns, measuring the time it took, and converting time to distance by recognizing that the farther away the object is, the longer it will take for the bouncing ball to return. Does using the bouncing-ball model help you to reason about a radar system? For example, an acceptable answer to the question is to use satellites for bouncing the radar pulse.

If you are like students in a study conducted by Mayer (1983), you found the model to be very helpful in your reasoning about how a radar system works. Mayer (1983) found that students who saw a model like that shown in Box 14-14 for one minute prior to reading the radar passage produced almost twice as many useful answers to questions as students who read the passage without seeing the model. In a review of sixteen studies, Mayer (1989a) found that when pictorial models were added to textbook explanations of how various systems work, students' performance on subsequent problem-solving tests improved by an average of over 60 percent.

In another study, Mayer and Gallini (1990) examined whether providing a model has different effects on experienced and inexperienced problem solvers.

BOX 14 • 14   The Radar Passage and Bouncing-Ball Model

The Radar Passage (selected portion)

Radar means the detection and location of remote objects by the reflection of radio waves. The phenomenon of acoustic echoes is familiar. Sound waves reflected from a building or cliff are received back at the observer after a lapse of a short interval. The effect is similar to you shouting in a canyon and seconds later hearing a nearly exact replication of your voice. Radar uses exactly the same principle except that the waves involved are radio waves, not sound waves. These travel very much faster than sound waves, 186,000 miles per second, and can cover much longer distances. Thus radar involves simply measuring the time between transmission of the waves and their subsequent return or echo and then converting that to a distance measure.

Bouncing-Ball Model

1. *Transmission*: A pulse travels from an antenna.

2. *Reflection*: The pulse bounces off a remote object.

3. *Reception*: The pulse returns to the receiver.

4. *Measurement*: The difference between the time out and the time back tells the total time traveled.

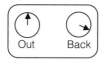

5. *Conversion*: The time can be converted to a measure of distance because the pulse travels at a constant speed.

[   ] seconds = [   ] miles

Adapted from Clarke (1977) and Mayer (1983)

Students with high or low experience with mechanical systems read a passage about how pumping systems work, such as partially shown in the first part of Box 14-15, and answered questions such as: "Suppose you pull up and push down on the handle of a pump several times but no air comes out. What could be wrong?" For some students (model-illustration group), the passage included model illustrations showing the state of each part in the pump when the handle was up and when the handle was down, as shown in the second part of Box 14-15; in the model, students can see that the piston works like a syringe and that the inlet and outlet valves work like one-way push-to-open doors—two areas of difficulty for most novices. The model illustration was intended to help students see both the possible states of each of the major parts of the pump (the handle could be up or down, the piston could be up or down, the inlet valve could be open or closed, the outlet valve could be open or closed, air in the cylinder could be compressed or uncompressed) and the causal relations between a change in the state of one part and a change in the state of another part (e.g., if the piston moves up, the inlet valve opens and the outlet valve closes; if the piston moves down, the inlet valve closes and the outlet valve opens). For other students, incomplete illustrations were given that showed the pump in only one state (incomplete-illustrations group) or no illustrations were given (no-illustrations group).

Do illustrations affect students' ability to reason about how pumps work? Among students who lacked much prior experience with mechanical systems, the model-illustration group produced almost twice as many useful answers to the questions than the incomplete-illustration or no-illustration groups. For example, acceptable answers to the troubleshooting question include: there's a hole in the cylinder, the valves are stuck in one position, or a seal around a valve leaks. However, among students who possessed prior knowledge about mechanical systems, all three groups performed at about the same level—equal to the model-illustration group of mechanically inexperienced students. These results suggest that the model illustration helped mechanically naive students build a mental model of the pumping system that could be used to generate new information. Apparently, mechanically sophisticated students were able to generate their own mental models without the need for external aids.

In summary, models can have an influence on what Bobrow (1985, p. 1) calls "qualitative reasoning about physical systems." Current research suggests that useful models are ones that clearly portray the possible states of each major part of the system as well as the causal relations between a change in the state of one part and a change in the state of another part. A promising trend for the future involves developing computerized learning environments in which novices can interact with simulations of various models of physical systems, such as electrical circuits (White & Frederiksen, 1987).

BOX 14 · 15 The Pump Passage and Model

The Pump Passage (selected portion)

Bicycle tire pumps vary in the number and location of the valves they have and in the way air enters the cylinder. Some simple bicycle tire pumps have the inlet valve on the the piston and the outlet valve at the closed end of the cylinder. A bicycle tire pump has a piston that moves up and down. Air enters the pump near the point where the connecting rod passes through the cylinder. *As the rod is pulled out, air passes through the piston and fills the areas between the piston and the outlet valve. As the rod is pushed in, the inlet valve closes and the piston forces air through the outlet valve.*

The Pump Model

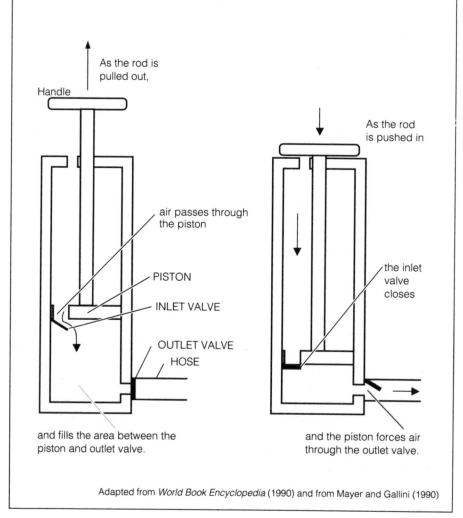

As the rod is pulled out,

Handle

air passes through the piston

PISTON

INLET VALVE

OUTLET VALVE

HOSE

and fills the area between the piston and outlet valve.

As the rod is pushed in

the inlet valve closes

and the piston forces air through the outlet valve.

Adapted from *World Book Encyclopedia* (1990) and from Mayer and Gallini (1990)

◼
THINKING BY EXAMPLES
◼

WHAT IS AN EXAMPLE?

A third approach to solving a new problem is to use a worked-out example. A worked-out example is a problem along with its step-by-step solution from the same domain (i.e., using the same variables and structure) as the target problem but with different specific values for the variables; this contrasts with an analog, which involves a structurally similar problem from a different domain (i.e., with a different cover story). In thinking by example, a student is given a series of worked-out problems and then is asked to solve a new problem on his or her own.

In this section we explore some obstacles to successfully abstracting and mapping the solution procedure from worked-out examples to a new problem. For example, try to generate a solution equation for the two story problems (the grocer problem and the alloy problem) in the first part of Box 14-16. Then examine the worked-out example (the nurse problem) in the second part of Box 14-16, and try again to generate solution equations for the problems. This is a shorter version of a procedure used by Reed (1987).

OBSTACLES TO ANALOGICAL TRANSFER

We begin with a sour note: people often have difficulty in using worked-out examples to help in problem solving. If you are like the college students who participated in experiments conducted by Reed (1987), before you examined the example you were unable to solve the problems and after you examined the examples you had a better chance of solving only the grocer problem (which has exactly the same structure as the example) but not the alloy problem (which has a similar but not identical structure as the example). Overall, students solved none of the identical problems and none of the similar problems before the example was given and solved 53 percent of the identical problems and 10 percent of the similar problems after the example was given.

Why do students have more difficulty in using a worked-out example to solve a similar problem (the alloy problem) than an identical problem (the grocer problem)? Reed (1987) explains this by using Gentner's (1983, 1989) structure-mapping theory, described in the previous section. The example problem is the base and the problem to be solved is the target, the variables are the objects, their numerical values are their features, and the required arithmetic operators are the relations among objects. If students have difficulty in mapping the base onto the target, they will not be able to use the example effectively to solve the target problem. For example, the mapping test in Box 14-17 lists the six

BOX 14 ▪ 16   Two Problems and a Worked-Out Example

Grocer Problem (same structure as example)

A grocer mixes peanuts worth $1.65 a pound and almonds worth $2.10 a pound. How many pounds of each are needed to make 30 pounds of a mixture worth $1.83 a pound?

Alloy Problem (similar structure to example)

One alloy of copper is 20% pure copper and another is 12% pure copper. How much of each alloy must be melted together to obtain 60 pounds of alloy containing 10.4 pounds of copper?

Nurse Problem (worked-out example)

A nurse mixes a 6% boric acid solution with a 12% boric acid solution. How many pints of each are needed to make 4.5 pints of an 8% boric acid solution?

The problem is a mixture problem in which two quantities are added together to make a third quantity. The two component quantities are the 6% and 12% solutions.

The total amount of acid in the combined solution must equal the total amount of acid in the two component solutions. The amount of acid is found by multiplying the percentage of acid in a solution by the quantity of the solution. If we mix p pints of 6% solution with $4.5 - p$ pints (since we want a total of 4.5 pints) of 12% solution, the 6% solution will contribute $.06 \times p$ pints of acid. The 12% solution will contribute $.12 \times (4.5 - p)$ pints of acid. The first two lines of the table show this information.

Kind of Solution	Quantity of Solution (Pints)	Percentage of Acid	Quantity of Acid (Pints)
6% acid	p	6%	$.06 \times p$
12% acid	$4.5 - p$	12%	$.12 \times (4.5 - p)$
8% acid	4.5	8%	$.08 \times 4.5$

The bottom line shows that the combined solution consists of 4.5 pints of 8% acid or $.08 \times 4.5$ pints of acid. Since the total amount of acid in the combined solution must equal the total amount in the two component solutions:

$$06 \times p + .12 \times (4.5 - p) = .08 \times 4.5$$
$$\text{Solving for } p \text{ yields}$$
$$.06p + .54 - .12p = .36$$
$$.18 = .06p$$
$$p = 3 \text{ pints of 6\% solution}$$
$$1.5 \text{ pints of 12\% solution}$$

Note: Solution equation for the grocer problem is: $\$1.65 \times A + \$2.10 \times (30 - A) = \$1.83 \times 30$. ($A$ = pounds of peanuts.)

Solution equation for the alloy problem is: $.20 \times A + .12 (60 - A) = 10.4$. ($A$ = pounds of first alloy.)

From Reed (1987)

BOX 14 ▪ 17   Can You Map the Nurse Problem onto Other Problems?

Mapping Test: Fill In the Corresponding Values and Expressions

Nurse Problem	Grocer Problem	Alloy Problem
1. 6% acid	1. _____	1. _____
2. 12% acid	2. _____	2. _____
3. 8% acid	3. _____	3. _____
4. 4.5 – A pints	4. _____	4. _____
5. 4.5 pints	5. _____	5. _____
6. 4.5 pints x 7% acid	6. _____	6. _____

Correct Answers for Mapping Test

Nurse Problem	Grocer Problem	Alloy Problem
1. 6% acid	1. $1.65	1. 20%
2. 12% acid	2. $2.10	2. 12%
3. 8% acid	3. $1.83	3. 10.4/60
4. 4.5 – A pints	4. 30 - A	4. 60 - A
5. 4.5 pints	5. 30	5. 60
6. 4.5 pints x 7% acid	6. 30 x $1.83	6. 10.4

Adapted from Reed (1987)

variables in the nurse problem (i.e., the worked-out example from Box 14-16) and asks you to find to the corresponding variables in the grocer problem and the alloy problem. The second part of Box 14-17 shows the correct mappings of the nurse example onto each of these two target problems. To examine students' ability to identify the relations between problems, Reed gave another group of students a test similar to that in the first part of Box 14-17 but with more problems.

If you are like the college students whom Reed tested on this task, you may have performed well in mapping the nurse problem onto the grocer problem but not onto the alloy problem. Overall, students correctly mapped the nurse problem onto identical problems 79 percent of the time and onto similar problems 48 percent of the time. For example, the grocer problem was the one that was most greatly affected after students examined the nurse problem example—it is the one that is most easily mapped onto from the nurse problem; the alloy problem is the one that was least affected after students examined the nurse problem example—the nurse problem maps least easily onto it. This line of research demonstrates that examples are most powerful when they map directly and obviously onto the target problems; that is, when the objects and relations are identical in the example and target problems.

The importance of this mapping process has also been demonstrated by Ross (1984, 1987, 1989). For example, in one study, students studied a text on probability theory that included several worked-out examples and then took a problem-solving test in which they were asked to think aloud. Some of the test items involved the same cover story and same solution procedure as an example problem (appropriate mapping), whereas some involved the same cover story but a different solution procedure as an example problem (inappropriate mapping). Ross found that when a test problem reminded a student of an appropriate example, he or she correctly solved the problem 83 percent of the time; when a test problem reminded a student of an inappropriate example, he or she correctly solved it only 17 percent of the time. Like Reed's (1987) results, these results point to the importance of finding appropriate connections between an example and a problem to be solved.

As another example, suppose you were asked to solve the arithmetic word problems shown in the first part of Box 14-18. Would it help you to study a worked-out example, such as shown in the second part of the box? Reed, Dempster, and Ettinger (1985) investigated this issue in a series of experiments. In one experiment, some students (related-example group) examined a worked-out example that was related to the test problems (as in Box 14-18) and then solved an equivalent and a similar test problem; other students (unrelated-example group) examined a worked-out example that was unrelated to the test problems and then solved the same two test problems. This was repeated for a total of three sets of problems—an example followed by an equivalent and a similar test problem—involving distance, mixture, and work story formats. In no case did students have the worked-out examples available to them as they solved the test problems. The top portion of Box 14-19 shows that students in both groups performed poorly on solving the test problems, suggesting that analogous worked-out examples were not helpful.

Why didn't experience with worked-out examples transfer to the solution of new problems? There are two kinds of obstacles. The first obstacle is that the initial experience with the example may not have been effective in helping the problem solver to abstract the solution procedure. To counter this problem, Reed and colleagues developed an elaborated version of the worked-out example. As shown in Box 14-20, the elaborated version includes information about the principle involved in the solution. The second possible obstacle is that even if the problem solver was exposed to a useful example, he or she may not know when or how to use that example in solving a particular test problem. To counteract this problem, Reed and colleagues provided an appropriate example along with each test problem so that problem solvers could refer to the examples as they solved test problems.

BOX 14 ▪ 18   Two-Story Problems with a Worked-Out Example

Can you solve these problems?

Problem 1 (equivalent). A car travels south at the rate of 30 miles per hour (mph). Two hours later, a second car leaves to overtake the first car, using the same route and going 45 mph. In how many hours will the second car overtake the first car?

Problem 2 (similar). A pickup truck leaves 3 hours after a large delivery truck but overtakes it by traveling 15 mph faster. If it takes the pickup truck 7 hours to reach the delivery truck, find the rate of each vehicle.

Here's a worked-out example

Problem: A car traveling at a speed of 30 miles per hour (mph) left a certain place at 10:00 A.M. At 11:30 A.M., another car departed from the same place at 40 mph and traveled the same route. In how many hours will the second car overtake the first car?

Answer: The problem is a distance-rate-time problem in which
$$\text{distance} = \text{rate} \times \text{time}$$
Because both cars travel the same distance, the distance of the first car (D1) equals the distance of the second car (D2). Therefore, D1 = D2 or R1 × T1 = R2 × T2, where R1 = 30 mph, R2 = 40 mph, and T1 = T2 + 3/2 hr. Substituting gives the following:
$$30 \times (T2 + 3/2) = 40 \times T2$$
$$30T2 + 45 = 40 \times T2$$
$$T2 = 4.5 \text{ hr}$$

Adapted from Reed, Dempster, and Ettinger (1985)

BOX 14 ▪ 19   Percentage of Correct Solutions on Test Problems

For short version of example and without access to example during problem solving:

	Type of Test Problem	
Type of Worked-Out Example	Equivalent	Similar
Unrelated	18	7
Related	25	6

For elaborated version of example and with access to example during problem solving:

	Type of Test Problem	
Type of Worked-Out Example	Equivalent	Similar
Unrelated	17	4
Related (elaborated version)	69	9

Adapted from Reed, Dempster, and Ettinger (1985)

BOX 14 · 20   An Elaborated Version of a Worked-Out Example

Problem: A car traveling at a speed of 30 miles per hour (mph) left a certain place at 10:00 A.M. At 11:30 A.M., another car departed from the same place at 40 mph and traveled the same route. In how many hours will the second car overtake the first car?

Answer: The problem is a distance-rate-time problem in which,

$$distance = rate \times time$$

We begin by constructing a table to represent the distance, rate, and time for each of the two cars. We want to know how long the second car travels before it overtakes the first car. We let t represent the number that we want to find and enter it into the table. The first car then travels $t + \frac{3}{2}$ hours because it left $1\frac{1}{2}$ hours earlier. The rates are 30 mph for the first car and 40 mph for the second car. Notice that the first car must travel at a slower rate if the second car overtakes it. We can now represent the distance each car travels by multiplying the rate and the time for each car. These values are shown in the following table.

Car	Distance (miles)	Rate (mph)	Time (hr)
First	$30(t + \frac{3}{2})$	30	$t + \frac{3}{2}$
Second	$40 \times t$	40	t

Because both cars have traveled the same distance when the second car overtakes the first, we set the two distances equal to each other:

$$30(t + 3/2) = 40t$$

Solving for t yields the following:

$$30t + 45 = 40t$$
$$45 = 10t$$
$$t = 4.5 \text{ hr}$$

From Reed, Dempster, and Ettinger (1985)

What happens when the underlying principles of worked-out examples are made more explicit and when students are explicitly shown which examples are relevant to problems they are solving? The bottom portion of Box 14-19 shows that students given this treatment excelled in solving equivalent but not similar problems. Thus successful analogical transfer was limited to problems that were structurally identical.

OVERCOMING OBSTACLES TO ANALOGICAL TRANSFER

As you can see, the foregoing results on worked-out examples lead to a somewhat disappointing summary: successful transfer from an example to solving a new problem appears to be quite limited. However, recent research by Novick (1988) suggests that novices and experts differ in the way they use worked-out examples when solving new problems. In one study, students were asked to solve a target

BOX 14 ▪ 21   Target Problem and Worked-Out Example

Target Problem

Members of the West High School Band were hard at work practicing for the annual Homecoming Parade. First, they tried marching in rows of twelve, but Andrew was left by himself to bring up the rear. The band director was annoyed because it didn't look good to have one row with only a single person in it, and of course Andrew wasn't very pleased either. To get rid of this problem, the director told the band members to march in columns of eight. But Andrew was still left to march alone. Even when the band marched in rows of three, Andrew was left out. Finally, in exasperation, Andrew told the band director that they should march in rows of five in order to have all the rows filled. He was right. This time all the rows were filled and Andrew wasn't left alone any more. Given that there were at least 45 musicians on the field but fewer than 200 musicians, how many students were there in the West High School Band?

Worked-Out Example

Mr. and Mrs. Renshaw were planning how to arrange vegetable plants in their new garden. They agreed on the total number of plants to buy, but not on how many of each kind to get. Mr. Renshaw wanted to have a few kinds of vegetables and ten of each kind. Mrs. Renshaw wanted more different kinds of vegetables, so she suggested having only four of each kind. Mr. Renshaw didn't like that because if some of the plants died, there wouldn't be very many left of each kind. So they agreed to have five of each vegetable. But then their daughter pointed out that there was room in the garden for two more plants, although then there wouldn't be the same number of each kind of vegetable. To remedy this, she suggested buying six of each vegetable. Everyone was satisfied with this plan. Given this information, what is the fewest number of vegetable plants the Renshaws could have in their garden?

Since at the beginning Mr. and Mrs. Renshaw agree on the number of plants to buy, 10, 4, and 5 must all go evenly into that number, whatever it is. Thus, the first thing to do is to find the smallest number that is evenly divisible by those 3 numbers, which is 20. So the original number of vegetable plants the Renshaws were thinking of buying could be any multiple of 20 (that is 20 or 40 or 60 or 80, etc.). But then they decide to buy 2 additional plants, that they hadn't been planning to buy originally so the total number of plants they actually end up buying must be 2 more than the multiples of 20 listed above (that is, 22 or 42 or 62 or 82 etc.). This means that 10, 4, and 5 will now no longer go evenly into the total number of plants. Finally, the problem states that they agree to buy 6 of each vegetable, so the total number of plants must be evenly divisible by 6. The smallest total number of plants that is evenly divisible by 6 is 42, so that's the answer.

From Novick (1988)

---

problem (about a marching band) either after no experience with worked-out examples or after they had studied several worked-out examples including one that had the same solution structure (a lowest-common-multiple procedure) as but a different surface story (vegetable garden) from the target problem. Box 14-21 shows the target problem along with the analogous worked-out example.

BOX 14 • 22   Can You Solve Factorization Exercises from Examples?

Examples: (1) $x^2 + 5x + 6 = (x + 2)(x + 3)$

(2) $x^2 + 7x + 6 = (x + 1)(x + 6)$

(3) $x^2 + 8x + 12 = (x + 2)(x + 6)$

(4) $x^2 + 7x + 12 = (x + 3)(x + 4)$

(5) $x^2 + 13x + 12 = (x + 1)(x + 12)$

Exercises: (1) $x^2 + 11x + 18 = ($ $)($ $)$

(2) $x^2 + 9x + 18 = ($ $)($ $)$

(3) $x^2 + 19x + 18 = ($ $)($ $)$

From Zhu and Simon (1987)

Students who scored high on the mathematics scale of the SAT (experts) tended to use the examples differently from those who scored closer to average (novices). When no worked-out examples were given only 6 percent of the experts and 6 percent of the novices used the lowest-common-multiple procedure to solve the target problem; in contrast, when worked-out examples were provided, 56 percent of the experts and 6 percent of the novices used the solution procedure from the vegetable example to solve the target problem. These results show that experts are more likely than novices to know how to focus on relevant structural features of example problems (such as whether to use a least-common-multiple procedure or a row/column multiplication procedure).

Continued research has helped to clarify the conditions for successful thinking by example. For example, Zhu and Simon (1987) examined how students can use worked-out examples to learn to solve new problems about factoring quadratic equations. Students were given three sets of problems, each containing some worked-out examples followed by several exercises, and asked to think aloud as they solved the exercises.

Box 14-22 lists the five worked-out examples and three exercises that were given in the first set. Take a careful look at the examples and then write in your solutions to the exercises. If you are like Zhu and Simon's subjects, you may have had some difficulty at first but you eventually figured out the appropriate problem-solving procedure. For example, most students initially tried to find two numbers that add to the coefficient of the linear term—such as finding that 10 and 1 add to 11 for the first exercise; this approach may be encouraged by the tendency of students normally to scan the expression from left to right, so the linear coefficient (e.g., 11 in exercise 1) appears before the

BOX 14 ∙ 23   Student's Protocol While Solving Factorization Exercise 1

[Student looking at first exercise]
1. According to the example,
2. Exercise 1, $x^2 + 11x + 18$ is equal to x . . .
3. [Looking at Example 1] 2 + 3 is equal to the coefficient 5,
4. 2 × 3 is equal to the constant 6.
5. [Looking at Example 2] This example is 1 + 6 = 7,
6. 1 × 6 = 6.
7. Exercise 1 [$x^2 + 11x + 18$] is that $x + 3$ multiplies $x + 6$.
8. Exercise 2 [$x^2 + 9x + 18$] is that $x + 6$ multiplies $x + 3$.
9. Exercise 3 [$x^2 + 19x + 18$] is that $(x + 9)(x + 2)$.

[Reviewing Exercise 1]
10. That is wrong.
11. 3 + 6 is not equal to 11.
12. Exercise 1 is $x + 2$ multiplying $x + 9$,
13. 2 + 9 = 11
14. 2 × 9 = 18
15. This one [Exercise 2] 3 + 6 = 9,
16. 3 × 6 = 18.
17. This one [Exercise 3] is also wrong.
18. It should be $x + 1$ multiplies $x + 18$,
19. 1 + 18 = 19.
20. 1 × 18 = 18.

From Zhu and Simon (1987)

constant (e.g., 18 in exercise 1). For example, Box 14-23 provides an excerpt of a student's protocol, in which the student was not initially successful in solving an exercise problem. However, by the end of working on this set, every student except one was using the more efficient strategy of finding pairs of numbers whose product equals the constant (such as 9 and 2, or 3 and 6, in exercise 1) before checking to see which of those number pairs also sums to the coefficient of the linear term.

If you are like Zhu and Simon's subjects, by the end of this set of exercises, you have acquired two problem-solving rules:

Rule 1: IF the goal is to factor a quadratic equation of the form $(x^2 + ax + b)$,
THEN find all pairs of positive integers whose product equals the value of constant (b).

Rule 2: IF the goal is to factor a quadratic equation of the form
$(x^2 + ax + b)$
THEN find a pair of factors whose sum equals the value of the coefficient
of the linear term (a).

Amazingly, by the end of working on the first set, almost all of the students were able to state the appropriate solution strategy in their own words. For example, in response to the question "How do you factor?", one student said:

> Use multiplication. 2×3. If satisfied, see the linear term. See if $2 + 3$ equals the coefficient of the linear term. Thus it satisfies the problem. We got the coefficient of the linear term by addition.

Another student answered by saying:

> The sum of the two numbers is the coefficient of the linear term. The product of two factors is the constant. All are the same.

Similarly, in the subsequent two sets of examples and exercises students learned how to factor expressions with one or two negative signs. Within a classroom context, 83 percent of the students successfully learned within one class session to factor quadratic expressions only by studying worked-out examples and/or trying exercises. Zhu and Simon (1987, p. 160) conclude by noting:

> Our experiments provide substantial evidence for the possibility of teaching several different mathematical skills by presenting students with carefully chosen sequences of worked-out examples and problems, without lectures or other direct instruction.

Under what conditions will people benefit from worked-out examples? As you can see from Zhu and Simon's study, exemplified by the protocol in Box 14-23, students who successfully learn from examples seem to exert a great deal of effort in trying to understand what they are doing. In a more recent study, Chi, Bassok, Lewis, Reimann, and Glaser (1989) have examined differences in how successful and less successful students use examples in learning to solve physics problems. Students read a physics chapter about particle dynamics that was followed by three worked-out examples, such as computing the mass of a block that is suspended by two strings. Students were asked to talk aloud as they studied the examples, resulting in the observation that some students continually explained the solution steps to themselves—a process that Chi and colleagues call generating self-explanations.

In all, Chi and colleagues noticed three kinds of statements produced by students:

Explanation statements provide a rule or cause, such as "Ummm, this would make sense, because since they're connected by a string that doesn't stretch" or "If the string's going to be stretched, the earth's going to be moved, and the surface of the incline is going to be depressed."

Monitoring statements refer to the student's state of comprehension, such as "I can see how they did it" or "I was having trouble with $F - mg \sin 0 = 0$."

Other statements include paraphrases such as summarizing a string figure by saying "Okay, so three forces are on the two strings, and from the string going down to the object."

After studying the chapter and the examples, students took a problem-solving test that included problems that could be solved in similar ways as the examples. Chi and colleagues selected a group of subjects who had answered almost all of the problems correctly (good students) and a group who had answered most of the problems incorrectly (poor students). Did the good and poor problem solvers differ in the way they learned from examples? The answer clearly is yes. The top of Box 14-24 shows that good problem solvers generated many more explanation, monitoring, and other statements while studying the worked-out examples as compared to the poor problem solvers. In addition, good students generated an average of 142 lines of protocol while studying the worked-out examples, whereas the poor problem solvers generated an average of 21 lines.

Did the good and poor problem solvers differ in the way they used examples during the problem-solving test? At a global level the answer is no: both good and poor problem solvers tended to refer back to examples. However, using a more fine-grained analysis, Chi and colleagues found that good and poor problem solvers seemed to have different purposes. The bottom of Box 14-24 shows the average number of times a student who was solving a test problem reread verbatim one or more lines from an example, copied a piece of information from an example, or checked a specific procedure or result from an example. As you can see, poor students tended mainly to reread the example problem whereas good students tended to look for specific information. Chi and colleagues conclude that good students use examples for very specific goals, as exemplified by one student who said, "I'm looking at the formula here, trying to see how you solve for one (Force 1) given the angle." In contrast, poor students—who initially tend to spend much less time studying the examples—refer back to examples during the problem-solving test with a general global goal; for example, when faced with

BOX 14 · 24   Differences Between How Good and Poor Problem Solvers Study and Use Worked-Out Examples

Average number of statements while studying worked-out examples:

Type of Statement	Type of Problem Solver	
	Good	Poor
Explanation	15	3
Monitoring	20	7
Other	16	7

Average number of uses of example while solving a test problem:

Type of Use	Type of Problem Solver	
	Good	Poor
Reread	.6	4.2
Copy	1.1	2.2
Check	1.0	.3

Adapted from Chi, Bassok, Lewis, Reimann, amd Glaser (1989)

a test problem, one poor student said "What do they do?" and then proceeded to reread an example problem.

These results tell us something about the conditions under which worked-out examples can lead to improved problem-solving performance. Successful problem solvers are those who actively engage in trying to make sense out the worked-out examples; they generate their own explanations for the solutions and accurately monitor their own understanding and misunderstanding of the examples. In contrast, unsuccessful problem solvers do not exert as much initial effort in studying the examples. These results suggest that examples are most helpful when students actively try to abstract the general rules or principles underlying them.

Finally, a study by Cooper and Sweller (1987) demonstrates the benefits of encouraging students to actively use worked-out examples in the context of problems they are learning to solve. Two groups of students were given four pairs of problems (in which both problems in each pair could be solved using the same procedure). One group (conventional group) simply received the problems; students in the other group (worked-out example group) received the same problems, except that the first problem in each pair was presented as a worked-out example and the students were asked to solve the second one (which

BOX 14 ▪ 25   Learning With and Without Worked-Out Examples

Worked-Out Example Practice

Use each worked-out example to help you solve the next equation for a.

$a + b = c$
   $a = c - b$
$a + h = u$

$a - b = c$
   $a = c + b$
$a - v = f$

$a + b - g = c$
   $a + b = c + g$
     $a = c + g - b$
$a + e - v = s$

$a - b + g = c$
   $a + g = c + b$
     $a = c + b - g$
$a - r + y = k$

Conventional Practice

Solve each equation for a.

$a + b = c$

$a + h = u$

$a - b = c$

$a - v = f$

$a + b - g = c$

$a + e - v = s$

$a - b + g = c$

$a - r + y = k$

Test For All Students

Solve for a:

Problem 1:
$a - k = t$

Problem 2:
$a + c - n = s$

Problem 3:
$b + c - f = g + a - v$

BOX 14 • 26   Median Time (in Seconds) on Learning and Problem-Solving Test

Group	Learning	Problem-Solving Test		
		Problem 1	Problem 2	Problem 3
Worked-out example	215	14	25	157
Conventional	495	15	27	300

Adapted from Cooper and Sweller (1987)

could be solved using the same procedure as the example). Box 14-25 begins by summarizing the learning procedure for the two groups. As you can see, the students given the worked-out examples were encouraged to actively apply the solution procedure used in the example to a new problem. Finally, all students took a problem-solving test that included problems similar to those given during learning (similar problems) as well as a problem that involved a different format (transfer problem), as shown at the end of Box 14-25.

How did worked-out examples affect learning and subsequent problem solving? Box 14-26 shows, for each group, the median time taken to study the initial eight problems, as well as the median time subsequently used to solve the similar and transfer problems. The conventional group took longer to learn than the example group—presumably because the conventional students had to solve eight problems whereas the example subjects solved only four problems. The two groups performed equivalently on solving similar problems, but the example group excelled on solving transfer problems. Cooper and Sweller conclude that actively applying worked-out examples to new problems helped students in the worked-out-example group to automate the problem-solving operators involved in solving equations.

In summary, these results demonstrate that the road to successful use of worked-out examples involves (1) carefully choosing examples that all share the same solution principle as the problem to be solved and (2) encouraging active effort on the part of the problem solver—what Chi and colleagues call self-explanations. For example, Zhu and Simon provide examples that use the same underlying principles and ask students to think aloud until they can adequately state the principles underlying the examples. These results strongly suggest that problem solvers need practice in using examples, that is, in how to be effective analogical reasoners.

■
EVALUATION
■

In analogical reasoning, a problem solver uses knowledge about one problem (base) to help solve a new problem (target). According to some scholars, creative problem solving always involves some form of analogical reasoning. This chapter provides three particular examples of analogical reasoning—thinking by analogs, thinking by models, and thinking by examples.

Thinking by analogs. An analog is a problem that shares the same structure as the target problem but not the same surface characteristics. An example of thinking by analogs is using the General problem or the lightbulb problem (as a base problem) to help figure out how to solve the tumor problem (as a target problem). Research on thinking by analogs reveals that humans often fail to recognize that a target problem is analogous to a problem that they already know how to solve but that hints help them in this recognition process; humans often fail to abstract the underlying structure of the problem and solution, but exposure to several problems sharing the same structure helps them in this abstraction process; and humans often fail to correctly map the elements in the base problem onto the elements in the problem to be solved but can do so when it is obvious that the structures match.

Thinking by models. A model of a system represents the essential elements and the causal relations among elements. Examples include the analogy that an electrical circuit is like a hydraulic system or that radar works like a bouncing ball. Research on thinking by models demonstrates that the models people use influence the way they reason about a target system and that reasoning about a target system can be improved when we provide a suitable model to naive students.

Thinking by examples. A worked-out example is a problem with a step-by-step description of the solution from the same domain as a target problem. For example, worked-out examples are often used for mathematics and physics problems. Research on thinking by worked-out example indicates that analogical transfer is often quite limited, with people able to use worked-out examples mainly to solve exercises that are identical in format; more experienced and successful problem solvers, however, overcome this problem by actively elaborating on examples as they study them.

In summary, research on analogical reasoning is beginning to reveal the conditions for what Vosniadou and Ortony (1989, p. 14) call a *productive analogy,* that is "an analogy that can produce new knowledge about the structure of the target system." Productive analogies are those in which the problem solver recognizes the analogy between the base and target, abstracts the structural relations from the base, and maps these relations onto the target. Although theories of analogical reasoning are still incomplete, this line of inquiry has potential for addressing some of the most fundamental issues in the psychology of problem solving, such as where creative solutions come from.

Suggested Readings

GENTNER, D., & STEVENS, A. L. (Eds.). (1983). *Mental models*. Hillsdale, NJ: Erlbaum. Contains a collection of papers on mental models.

VOSNIADOU, S., & ORTONY, A. (Eds.). (1989). *Similarity and analogical reasoning*. Cambridge, UK: Cambridge University Press. Contains a collection of papers on analogical reasoning.

CHAPTER 15

MATHEMATICAL PROBLEM SOVING

Thinking as Based on Domain-Specific Knowledge

Analysis of Mathematical Problem Solving

·

Problem Translation: Linguistic and
Semantic Knowledge

·

Problem Integration:
Schematic Knowledge

·

Solution Planning and Monitoring:
Strategic Knowledge

·

Solution Execution:
Procedural Knowledge

Which school subject is "loaded" with problem-solving exercises? Did you say mathematics? If you thumb through a mathematics textbook, you are likely to notice that most of the pages are devoted to problems—either showing you worked-out problems or asking you to solve exercise problems. Thus the mathematics classroom offers a sort of natural laboratory in which we can study how people acquire and use problem-solving skills. In recognition of the role of problem solving in mathematics, the National Council of Teachers of Mathematics (1980, p. 2) declared that "the development of problem-solving ability should direct the efforts of mathematics educators through the next decade."

For example, let's consider some of the problems that students are taught to solve in school. Box 15-1 lists some typical math problems that involve problem solving. Go ahead and solve each problem, indicating your answer by checking the appropriate space or filling in the blank. The correct answers are given at the bottom of the box.

Suppose we gave problems such as these to a large group of high school seniors from across the United States, that is, seventeen-year-olds who have progressed through twelve years of schooling. How well do you think they would do on each problem? Fortunately, we do not have to guess how well students are learning to solve problems like these, because national and international evaluations of student achievement are periodically conducted (Dossey, Mullis, Lindquist, & Chambers, 1988; Robitaille & Garden, 1989). The problems in Box 15-1 come from the most recent National Assessment of Educational Progress, conducted in 1986 across the United States (Dossey et al., 1988). As you can see in the right side of the box, many high school seniors did not solve the problems correctly. The assessment demonstrates that "every year, nearly 1.5 million American 17-year-olds near the end of high school without much-needed mathematical reasoning skills" (Dossey et al., 1988, p. 7).

Equally troubling results have been reported by statewide surveys of mathematical problem solving. For example, problems such as the following one were given to all high school seniors in California public schools (California Assessment Program, 1980):

> A person will pay the lowest price per ounce for rice if she buys:
> *a.* 12 ounces for 40 cents
> *b.* 14 ounces for 45 cents
> *c.* 1 pound, 12 ounces for 85 cents
> *d.* 2 pounds for 99 cents

The correct answer, *c*, was given by 35 percent of the high school seniors.

Why are these kinds of problems so hard to solve? Why is it so difficult to teach our children how to solve problems? In spite of years of training and practice in solving mathematics problems, why do students greet simple story problems with groans, fearful faces, and incorrect answers? If we knew the answers to these questions, we

BOX 15 ▪ 1   Some Story Problems

Percent Correct

At the store, the price of a carton of milk is 40 cents, an apple is 25 cents, and a box of crackers is 30 cents. What is the cost of an apple and a carton of milk?

__ 55 cents
__ 65 cents
__ 70 cents
__ 95 cents

96%

6 cm

4 cm

What is the area of this rectangle?

__4 square cm
__6 square cm
__10 square cm
__20 square cm
__24 square cm
__I don't know

51%

Christine borrowed $850 for one year from the Friendly Finance Company. If she paid 12% simple interest, what was the total amount she repaid?

ANSWER: _____

6%

Note: Correct answers are 65 cents, 24 square cm, and $952.

Adapted from Dossey, Mullis, Lindquist, and Chambers (1988)

would not only have the basis for a powerful theory of human problem solving, but we could also have a useful impact on improving education. For example, in a classic review of the psychology of mathematics learning, Skemp (1971, p. 13) pointed out: "Problems of learning and teaching are psychological problems, and before we can make much improvement in the teaching of mathematics, we need to know more about how it is learnt." The remainder of this chapter examines what psychologists have learned about how people solve story problems—what Hinsley, Hayes, and Simon (1977) jokingly refer to as "those twentieth-century fables."

ANALYSIS OF MATHEMATICAL PROBLEM SOLVING

Mathematical story problems, such as those shown in Box 15-1, require quantitative reasoning. Quantitative reasoning occurs when the problem solver is presented with numerical information and uses the rules of mathematics to deduce a numerical answer. Such quantitative reasoning is a form of deductive reasoning, as described in Chapter 5; however, in quantitative reasoning the premises and conclusion involve numbers.

Let's consider another typical story problem, such as the tile problem (Mayer, 1987a):

> Floor tiles are sold in squares 30 centimeters on each side.
> How much would it cost to tile a rectangular room 7.2 meters long and 5.4 meters wide if the tiles cost $0.72 each?

What does a person need to know in order to be able to solve this problem? Take a moment and try to list all the knowledge needed. Does your list resemble the one suggested here?

Linguistic knowledge—knowledge of the English language, such as recognizing words, recognizing that "floor tiles" and "tiles" refer to the same objects, and determining that the room is a rectangle with 7.2-meter length and 5.4-meter width.

Semantic knowledge—knowledge of facts about the world, such as that 1 meter equals 100 centimeters or that squares have four equal sides.

Schematic knowledge—knowledge of problem types, such as knowing that area problems are based on the formula area = length × width.

BOX 15 ▪ 2   Analysis of Mathematical Problem Solving for Tile Problem

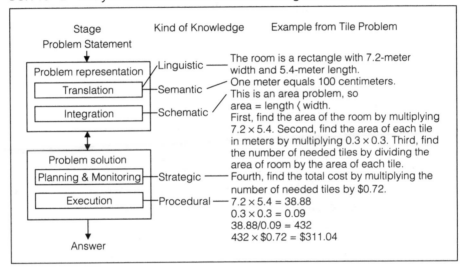

Strategic knowledge—techniques for how to use the various types of available knowledge in planning and monitoring the solution of problems, such as setting subgoals like finding the area of the room and finding the number of tiles needed.

Procedural knowledge—knowledge of how to perform a sequence of operations, such as how to divide 0.09 into 38.88.

According to most descriptions of mathematical problem solving, the first step is *problem representation,* converting the words (and pictures) of the problem into an internal mental representation; the second step is *problem solution,* going from a mental representation of the problem to a final answer. We can further break problem representation into two subprocesses: *problem translation,* which involves converting each sentence or major clause into an internal mental representation, and *problem integration,* which involves combining the information into a coherent structure. The translation process depends on linguistic and semantic knowledge, whereas the integration process depends on strategic knowledge. Similarly, we can break problem solution into two subprocesses: *solution planning and monitoring,* which involves developing and keeping track of a plan to solve the problem, and *solution execution,* which involves carrying out the plan. Planning and monitoring depend on strategic knowledge, whereas execution depends on procedural knowledge. Box 15-2 summarizes the four substages and the corresponding kinds of knowledge involved in solving problems such as the tile problem. Let us now examine each of these kinds of knowledge in turn.

■
PROBLEM TRANSLATION: LINGUISTIC AND SEMANTIC KNOWLEDGE
■

The first step in solving the tile problem is to translate each statement of the problem into an internal mental representation. For example, four pieces of information you need to find from the words of the tile problem are: the tiles are 30 by 30-centimeter squares, the room is a 7.2 by 5.4-meter rectangle, the tiles cost $0.72 each, and the unknown is the cost of tiling the floor. In order to translate the words of the tile problem, you need some knowledge of the English language (linguistic knowledge) and some knowledge about metric measurements and geometric shapes (semantic knowledge). For example, linguistic knowledge is needed to determine that the room is a 7.2 by 5.4 meter rectangle from the words in the second sentence. Similarly, semantic knowledge is needed to convert the "tiles are 30 by 30 centimeter squares" into "tiles are 0.3 by 0.3 meter squares".

Let's focus on one aspect of linguistic knowledge—the ability to comprehend *relational statements*. Relational statements express a numerical relation between two variables, such as "Tom has five more marbles than Joe." For example, in one study (Riley, Greeno, & Heller, 1983), children were asked to listen to and then repeat word problems such as:

> Joe has 3 marbles.
> Tom has 5 more marbles than Joe.
> How many marbles does Tom have?

Children frequently miscomprehended the relational statement in this problem, as is indicated by their recalling the problem as:

> Joe has 3 marbles.
> Tom has 5 marbles.
> How many marbles does Tom Have?

If children have difficulty in comprehending relational statements, then rewording a problem should greatly enhance performance. To test this prediction, Hudson (1983) asked children to solve this problem:

There are 5 birds and 3 worms.
How many more birds are there than worms?

Only 17 percent of nursery school children and 64 percent of first-grade children gave the correct answer. However, Hudson also asked children to solve an equivalent problem that reworded the relational statement:

There are 5 birds and 3 worms.
How many birds won't get a worm?

On this problem, 83 percent of the nursery school children and 100 percent of the first-graders gave the correct answer. Similar results were obtained by De Corte, Verschaffel, and De Win (1985). These results support the idea that errors in comprehension of word problems can occur because the problems "employ linguistic forms that do not readily map onto children's existing conceptual knowledge structures" (Cummins, Kintsch, Reusser, & Weimer, 1988, p. 407).

Adults are not immune from difficulties in translating relational statements. For example, in one study (Soloway, Lochhead, & Clement, 1982), college students were asked to translate relational statements into equations. To get a flavor for the task, take a moment to write the correct equation for this statement: "There are 6 times as many students as professors at this university." If you wrote "$6S = P$" you produced the most common incorrect answer, along with about one-third of the college students tested.

Why do people have difficulties in comprehending relational statements? To answer this question, Mayer and colleagues (Mayer, 1982; Lewis & Mayer, 1987) have proposed a *structural hypothesis* that distinguishes between *assignment statements* (which bind one numerical value to one variable) and *relational statements* (which express a numerical relation between two variables). Accordingly, certain sentence constructions (namely, assignments) are more psychologically basic than others (namely, relations). A straightforward prediction of this hypothesis is that people will make more errors in recalling relational statements than assignment statements; in addition, when people change a statement from one form to another, they will be far more likely to change a relation into an assignment than change an assignment into a relation.

To test this prediction, Mayer (1982b) asked college students to listen to and then recall a list of eight story problems. One problem was:

The area occupied by an unframed rectangular picture is 64 square inches less than the area occupied by the picture mounted in a frame 2 inches wide. What are the dimensions of the picture if it is 4 inches longer than it is wide?

BOX 15 ▪ 3   Consistent and Inconsistent Versions of the Gasoline Problem

1. Consistent (addition): 1% error rate

At ARCO gas sells for $1.13 per gallon. Gas at Chevron is 5 cents more per gallon than gas at ARCO. How much do 5 gallons of gas cost at Chevron?

2. Inconsistent (addition): 16% error rate

At ARCO gas sells for $1.13 per gallon. This is 5 cents less per gallon than gas at Chevron. How much do 5 gallons of gas cost at Chevron?

3. Consistent (subtraction): 0% error rate

At ARCO gas sells for $1.13 per gallon. Gas at Chevron is 5 cents less per gallon than gas at ARCO. How much do 5 gallons of gas cost at Chevron?

4. Inconsistent (subtraction): 8% error rate

At ARCO gas sells for $1.13 per gallon. This is 5 cents more per gallon than gas at Chevron. How much do 5 gallons of gas cost at Chevron?

Adapted from Lewis and Mayer (1987)

In this problem, an assignment statement is "the frame is 2 inches wide" and a relational statement is "the rectangle is 4 inches longer than it is wide." Consistent with the predictions, students made approximately three times as many errors in recalling relational statements (29 percent) as in recalling assignment statements (9 percent). More importantly, students almost never made a recall error by converting an assignment statement into a relational statement (one such instance) but occasionally made a recall error by converting a relational statement into an assignment (twenty-one such instances). An example of a relation-to-assignment error is converting "the picture is 4 inches longer that it is wide" into "the picture is 4 inches long."

Apparently some students lack appropriate linguistic knowledge for how to represent relational statements in memory. More recently, Lewis & Mayer (1987) have identified some conditions under which people are most likely to miscomprehend relational statements. For example, Box 15-3 presents two versions of the gasoline problem. The first problem is called *consistent* because the key word in the second sentence ("more") corresponds to the correct arithmetic operation (addition); the second problem is called *inconsistent* because the key word ("less") conflicts with the correct arithmetic operation (addition). What would happen if we asked you to "show your work" as you solved these problems? If you are like the college students tested in a study by Lewis and Mayer (1987), you are more likely to misread the second sentence in the inconsistent problem to mean "add 5 cents" (as approximately 15 percent of the students did) than to misread the second sentence in the consistent problem to mean "subtract 5 cents" (as approximately 1 percent did). However, when college students were given explicit training in how to comprehend relational statements, such as converting the sentence into a diagram, errors on inconsistent problems were almost entirely eliminated (Lewis, 1989).

This finding, like the others reported in this section, suggests that some incorrect answers for word problems can be accounted for by students' performing correct arithmetic computations based on incorrect representations of the problem. Although both of the problems in Box 15-3 are equivalent in terms of underlying arithmetic difficulty, the inconsistent problem is far more difficult than the consistent one. According to the structural hypothesis, problem solvers have a preference for the order of presentation of information in a relational statement—readers expect the grammatical subject to be a new term (gas at Chevron) rather than the old term (gas at ARCO). That preference is violated in inconsistent problems, leading to difficulties in encoding the sentence. In summary, some difficulties in problem solving can be traced to difficulties in comprehending sentences, particularly relational ones.

Next, let's explore the role of linguistic and semantic knowledge by examining what computer simulations (as described in Chapter 6) need to know in order to translate word problems into equations. For example, consider the advertisement problem in Box 15-4. Bobrow (1968) developed a computer program called STUDENT for solving story problems like the advertisement problem. The program consists of two main parts: translating each statement into an equation and solving the equations.

What does STUDENT need to know to be able to translate the advertisement problem into an equation? As you may have expected, STUDENT needed to know some of the rules of English (linguistic knowledge) and some basic facts about the world (semantic knowledge). Among the many pieces of information in STUDENT's memory are

> 1 foot equals 12 inches
> 1 yard equals 3 feet
> "Pounds" is the plural of "pound"
> "People" is the plural of "person"
> "Years younger than" means "less than"
> "Mary" is a person
> An "uncle" is a person
> "Squared" is an operator
> "Has" is a verb

The program would not run correctly unless a large body of linguistic and semantic information was already in the computer's memory prior to solving the

BOX 15 · 4   How STUDENT Solves the Advertisement Problem

1. State the problem.

If the number of customers Tom gets is twice the square of 20 percent of the numbers of advertisements he runs, and the number of advertisements he runs is 45, what is the number of customers Tom gets?

2. Make substitutions.

If the number of customers Tom gets is 2 times the square of 20 percent of the number of advertisements he runs, and the number of advertisements he runs is 45, what is the number of customers Tom gets?

3. Tag words and phrases.

If the number of (operator) customers Tom gets (verb) is 2 times (operator) the square of (operator) 20 percent (operator) of (operator) the number of (operator) advertisements he (pronoun) runs, and the number of (operator) advertisements he (pronoun) runs is 45, what (question word) is the number of (operation) customers Tom gets (verb)? (question mark)

4. Make kernal sentences.

The number of customers Tom gets is 2 times the square of 20 percent of the number of advertisements he runs. The number of advertisements he runs is 45. What is the number of customers Tom gets?

5. Make equations.

(Number of customers Tom gets) = $2[(.20)(\text{Number of advertisements})]^2$

(Number of advertisements) = 45

(Number of customers Tom gets) = (X)

Adapted from Bobrow (1968). © 1968 MIT Press.

problem. Such work suggests that translating a sentence into an equation requires a great deal of specific knowledge.

Box 15-4 summarizes the steps involved in STUDENT's translation of the problem into an equation: (1) Copy the problem word for word, (2) substitute words like "two times" for "twice," (3) locate each word or phrase that describes a variable, such as "number of customers Tom gets" and note if two or more phrases refer to the same variable, (4) break the problem into simple sentences, and (5) convert each simple sentence into an equation. As you can see, STUDENT performs a literal translation of words into equations by knowing enough to distinguish between operators and variables.

In contrast to STUDENT's lack of deep understanding, Briars and Larkin (1984) and Kintsch and Greeno (1985) have developed programs that build a model of a problem situation from the words in the problem, one-by-one. For example, Briars and Larkin (1984) developed a program called CHIPS that accepts a string of words (with some hyphens inserted) as input: "Joe had 5 marbles / Then Tom gave-him give more marbles / How-many marbles does Joe have now?" From the first sentence, the program creates a "set of marbles" corresponding to

"Joe" and places "5" in that set; the word "had" triggers the *move schema*, in which the contents from one set are moved into another. From the second sentence, the program creates a "set of marbles" corresponding to "Tom" and places "3" in that set; "gave-him" clarifies the move-schema so that the set moved to is Joe's and the set moved from is Tom's. As you can see, at its most basic level, the program attempts to establish sets (such as Joe's marbles with 5) and to move numbers from one set to another (such as moving 3 from Tom's set to Joe's set). The program requires some linguistic knowledge, such as "gave-him" means an amount moves from one set to another or "how-much" means to count the number of elements in a set.

Similarly, the Kintsch and Greeno (1985) program ties specific actions to key words such as "have," "give," "all," "more," and "less." The sentence "Joe has three marbles" activates a MAKE-SET procedure that creates a set containing 3 marbles belonging to Joe. The sentence "Tom has five marbles" activates a MAKE-SET procedure that creates a set containing 5 marbles belonging to Tom. The sentence "How many marbles do they have altogether?" activates a MAKE-SET procedure in which a third set is created consisting of the two subsets previously created. As you can see, the program uses key words in the problem, such as "altogether," to help create an internal representation of the problem. In both Briars and Larkin's and Kintsch and Greeno's programs, the words in the problem are used to guide the building of representations of sets and relations among sets. Apparently, the translation process requires knowledge not only of basic English but also of the special kinds of structures in story problems—an issue addressed more deeply in the next section.

■

PROBLEM INTEGRATION: SCHEMATIC KNOWLEDGE
■

Let's return to the tile problem. Is there anything beyond linguistic and semantic knowledge needed for representing the problem? As you look at the problem you may notice that it is an area problem, requiring the formula "area = length × width." This knowledge helps guide your attention so you can distinguish relevant from irrelevant information. This knowledge of problem types is called schematic knowledge; when you recognize that this problem involves the area formula, you have activated a schema for the problem.

Accurate representations of word problems often require more than word-by-word translation. For example, Paige and Simon (1966) asked students to solve problems such as the one in Box 15-5. Using linguistic (e.g., "exceeds" means subtract) and semantic knowledge (e.g., a dime is worth 10 cents, a quarter is worth 25 cents, two dollars and fifty cents is worth 250 cents), some subjects

BOX 15 ▪ 5   The Coin Problem

Problem

The number of quarters that a man has is seven times the number of dimes he has. The value of the dimes exceeds the value of quarters by two dollars and fifty cents. How many has he of each coin?

Literal Translation

$Q = 7 \times D$
$D \times (.10) - Q \times (.25) = 2.50$

Mistranslation

$Q = 7 \times D$
$Q \times (.25) - D \times (.10) = 2.50$

Recognition of Inconsistency

"This is not possible."
"The dimes cannot be worth more than the quarters if there are less dimes than quarters."

Adapted from Paige and Simon (1966)

generated literal translations of the sentences into equations. Other subjects recognized that something was wrong in this problem and corrected it by assuming that the second sentence read, "The value of the quarters exceeds the value of the dimes by $2.50." Finally, some looked at the problem and said, "This is impossible; how can you have more quarters than dimes and have the value of dimes be more than the value of the quarters?" Thus, while some students may use literal translation, some students apparently try to understand the problem.

This example shows that an important component in solving a story problem is to put the statements of the problem together into a coherent structure—a process that can be guided by *schemas*. Schemas for story problems involve knowledge of problem type. For example, Riley, Greeno, and Heller (1983) have identified several types of simple arithmetic word problems, including:

Change problems—in which you start with one set that increases or decreases because of some action,

Combine problems—in which there are two sets that do not change but are combined, and

BOX 15 • 6   Some Types of Simple Artithmetic Word Problems

Problem	Proportion Correct Using Objects			
	Grade K	Grade 1	Grade 2	Grade 3
Change (3 + 5 =) Joe has 3 marbles. Then Tom gave him 5 more marbles. How many marbles does Joe have now?	87%	100%	100%	100%
Combine (3 + 5 =) Joe has 3 marbles. Tom has 5 marbles. How many marbles do they have altogether?	100%	100%	100%	100%
Compare (3 + 5 =) Joe has 3 marbles. Tom has 5 more marbles than Joe. How many marbles does Tom have?	13%	17%	80%	100%
Change (8 – 3 =) Joe had 8 marbles. Then he gave 5 marbles to Tom. How many does he have now?	100%	100%	100%	100%
Combine (8 – 3 =) Joe and Tom have 8 marbles altogether. Joe has 3 marbles. How many marbles does Tom have?	22%	39%	70%	80%
Compare (8 – 3 =) Joe has 8 marbles. Tom has 5 marbles. How many marbles does Joe have more than Tom?	17%	28%	85%	100%

Adapted from Riley, Greeno, and Heller (1983)

Compare problems—in which there are two sets that do not change, but the difference between them is determined.

Box 15-6 presents examples of change, combine, and compare problems involving addition and subtraction. Although all three problems involve the same arithmetic operations (such as 3 + 5 = 8 or 8 – 5 = 3), the compare problems are much harder for young children to solve than the change problems. There is some evidence of a developmental trend indicating that kindergartners and first-graders perform well on change problems but poorly on compare problems, whereas second- and third-graders perform well on both. Apparently the change schema is the first one to develop in most children, while the development of the compare schema may take several years of experience. These results suggest that failure to solve word problems may be caused by lack of appropriate schemas rather than poor arithmetic or logical skills.

These results suggest that many errors occur because children carry out correct arithmetic solutions on incorrect representations of problems. To test this idea, first-graders were asked to solve word problems either before or after recalling them (Cummins et al., 1988). The results showed a strong relation between recall and problem-solving performance: problems that were difficult to solve tended to be the problems that were difficult to recall. The most common miscomprehension for change and compare problems was called *structure-violating transformation*—a problem is changed from one type into another legitimate type. For example, the problem,

> Mary has 9 marbles.
> She has 4 more marbles than John.
> How many marbles does John have?

is transformed into,

> Mary has 9 marbles.
> John has 4 more marbles than her.
> How many marbles does John have?

Typically, students transformed a more difficult version of a problem into an easier version. The most common miscomprehension of combine problems was to include two supersets in the problem, such as

> Mary and John have 5 marbles altogether.
> Mary has 3 marbles.
> How many do they have altogether?

This type of error suggests a misunderstanding of the set-superset relations in the problem. Kintsch and Greeno (1985) have proposed a computer simulation model that can account for many of the errors that children make in comprehending story problems.

If schematic knowledge is at the heart of successful problem representation, then we would expect experienced mathematical problem solvers to have a well-differentiated set of problem schemas. To examine this idea, Hinsley, Hayes, and Simon (1977) asked high school and college students to sort a collection of story problems into categories. The results showed that students performed this task with high agreement, yielding eighteen different categories as summarized in Box 15-7. Hinsley and colleagues (1977) also found that subjects were able to categorize problems almost immediately. After hearing the first few words of a problem, a student could determine the problem category.

Many difficulties that people have in solving story problems can arise from using the wrong schema. For example, Hinsley and colleagues (1977) presented subjects with a problem that could be interpreted as either a triangle problem or a distance-rate-time problem. As you can see, the problem shown in Box 15-8 is a sort of distance-rate-time problem with irrelevant information about a triangular relation. Of the six subjects in the study, three attended to the irrelevant triangle information. For example, they drew triangles and tried to determine the lengths of the two legs and the hypotenuse. One subject misread "four minutes" as "four miles" and assumed this was the length of one of the legs; another subject assumed that "five miles apart" referred to the length of the hypotenuse. The other three subjects ignored the triangle information and focused on the aspects of distance, rate, and time in the problem. For example, one subject stated: "It looks like a distance problem. So Jones is going east two minutes after Smith is going west. So it might be an overtake problem." All three of these subjects initially assumed that one driver was going east and one was going west. Hinsley and colleagues (1977) concluded that subjects use either a triangle schema or a distance-rate-time schema as a template for understanding the problem. The subject's schema influences what the subject looks for and even encourages mistakes in interpreting the information.

In order to gave a broader perspective on the nature of schemas for algebra story problems, Mayer (1981a) surveyed the exercise problems from twelve major algebra textbooks approved for use in California secondary schools. The approximately 2000 story problems selected fell into fewer than twenty general categories, as shown in Box 15-9. Some of these categories shared the same underlying formula; for example, distance-rate-time, current, and work problems are all based on the formula "amount = rate × time." Also, within any major category, there were many different versions, which can be called *templates*. Motion problems, for example, had thirteen different templates, including simple distance-rate-time, vehicles approaching from opposite directions, vehicles starting from the same point and departing in opposite directions, one vehicle overtaking another, one vehicle making a round trip, speed changing during a trip, and so on. Box 15-10 lists some of the templates for current problems. In all, there were about a hundred different templates among all the problems in algebra textbooks.

This survey suggests that proficiency in solving standard textbook problems might involve learning to recognize the most frequently used categories and templates for story problems. To test this idea, Mayer (1982b) asked students to read and recall a list of eight story problems. Students were far more successful in recalling high-frequency problem types than low-frequency problem types. Box 15-11 shows the relation between frequency of the problem (i.e., how many times per 1000 problems this type of problem appeared in typical math books) and the probability

BOX 15 · 7   Examples of 18 Problem Categories

Category name	Example of Problem
1. Triangle	Jerry walks 1 block east along a vacant lot and then 2 blocks north to a friend's house. Phil starts at the same point and walks diagonally through the vacant lot coming out at the same point as Jerry. If Jerry walked 217 feet east and 400 feet north, how far did Phil walk?
2. DRT	In sports car race, a Panther starts the course at 9:00 A.M. and averages 75 miles per hour. A Mallotti starts 4 minutes later and averages 85 miles per hour. It a lap is 15 miles, on which lap will the Panther be overtaken?
3. Averages	Flying east between two cities, a plane's speed is 380 miles per hour. On the return trip, it flies 420 miles per hour. Find the average speed for the round trip.
4. Scale conversion	Two temperature scales are established, one, the R scale, where water under fixed conditions freezes at 15 and boils at 405, and the other, the S scale, where water freezes at 5 and boils at 70. If the R and S scales are linearly related, find an expression for any temperature R in terms of a temperature S.
5. Ratio	If canned tomatoes come in two sizes, with radius of one 2/3 the radius of the other, find the ratios of the capacities of the two cans.
6. Interest	A certain savings bank pays 3% interest compounded semiannually. How much will $2500 amount to it left on deposit for 20 years?
7. Area	A box containing 180 cubic inches is constructed by cutting from each corner of a cardboard square a small square with side 5 inches, and then turning up the sides. Find the area of the original piece of cardboard.
8. Max-min	A real-estate operator estimates that the monthly profit p in dollars from a building s stories high is given by $p = -2s^{**}2 + {}^*88s$. What height building would he consider most profitable?
9. Mixture	One vegetable oil contains 6% saturated fats and a second contains 26% saturated fats. In making a salad dressing how many ounces of the second may be added to 10 ounces of the first if the percent of saturated fats is not to exceed 16%?

(continued)

BOX 15 • 7, *continued*

Category Name	Example of Problem
10. River current	A river steamer travels 36 miles downstream in the same time that it travels 24 miles upstream. The steamer's engines drive in still water at a rate which is 12 miles an hour more than the rate of the current. Find the rate of the current.
11. Probability	In an extra-sensory-perception experiment, a blindfolded subject has two rows of blocks before him. Each row has blocks numbered 1 to 10 arranged in random order The subject is to place one hand on a block in the first row and then try to place his other hand on the block having the same numeral in the second row. If the subject has no ESP, what is the probability of his making a match on the first try?
12. Number	The units digit is 1 more than 3 times the tens digit. The number represented when the digits are interchanged is 8 times the sum of the digits.
13. Work	Mr Russo takes 3 minutes less than Mr. Lloyd to pack a case when each works alone. One day, after Mr Russo spent 6 minutes in packing a case, the boss called him away, and Mr Lloyd finished packing in 4 more minutes. How many minutes would it take Mr Russo alone to pack a case?
14. Navigation	A pilot leaves an aircraft carrier and flies south at 360 m.p.h., while the carrier proceeds N30W at 30 m.p.h. If the pilot has enough fuel to fly 4 hours, how far south can he fly before returning to his ship?
15. Progressions	From two towns 363 miles apart, Jack and Jill set out to meet each other. If Jill travels 1 mile the first day, 3 the second, 5 the third, and so on, and Jack travels 2 miles the first day, 6 the second, 10 the third, and so on, when will they meet?
16. Progression–2	Find the sum of the first 25 odd positive integers.
17. Physics	The speed of a body falling freely from rest is directly proportional to the length of time that it falls. If a body was falling at 144 ft. per second 4 1/2 seconds after beginning its tall, how fast was it falling 3 3/4 seconds later?
18. Exponentials	The diameter of each successive layer of a wedding cake is 2/3 the previous layer. If the diameter of the first layer of a 5-layer cake is 15 inches, find the sum of the circumferences of all the layers.

Adapted from Hinsley, Hayes, and Simon (1977)

BOX 15 • 8   The Smalltown Problem

Because of their quiet ways, the inhabitants of Smalltown were especially upset by the terrible New Year's Eve auto accident which claimed the life of one Smalltown resident. The facts were these. Both Smith and Jones were New Year's Eve babies and each had planned a surprise visit to the other on their mutual birthday. Jones had started out for Smith's house traveling due east on Route 210 just two minutes after Smith had left for Jones's house. Smith was traveling directly south on Route 140. Jones was traveling 30 miles per hour faster than Smith even though their houses were only five miles apart as the crow flies. Their cars crashed at the right angle intersection of the two highways. Officer Franklin, who observed the crash, determined that Jones was traveling half again as fast as Smith at the time of the crash. Smith had been driving for just four minutes at the time of the crash. The crash occurred nearer to the house of the dead man than to the house of the survivor. What was the name of the dead man?

Adapted from Hinsley, Hayes, and Simon (1977)

BOX 15 • 9   Some Problem Categories from Algebra Textbooks

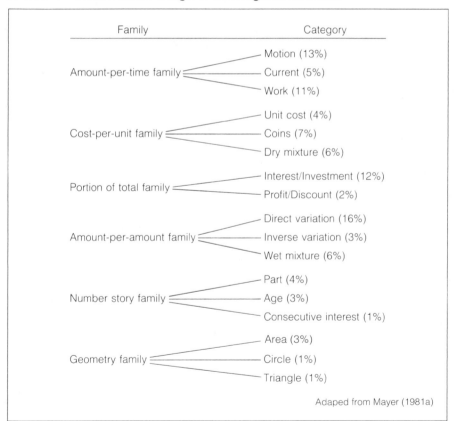

Family	Category
Amount-per-time family	Motion (13%)
	Current (5%)
	Work (11%)
Cost-per-unit family	Unit cost (4%)
	Coins (7%)
	Dry mixture (6%)
Portion of total family	Interest/Investment (12%)
	Profit/Discount (2%)
Amount-per-amount family	Direct variation (16%)
	Inverse variation (3%)
	Wet mixture (6%)
Number story family	Part (4%)
	Age (3%)
	Consecutive interest (1%)
Geometry family	Area (3%)
	Circle (1%)
	Triangle (1%)

Adaped from Mayer (1981a)

BOX 15 ▪ 10   Some Templates for Current Problems

Name	Description	Example
Total time	A boat or plane travels a certain distance with the current and a certain distance against the current in a total time.	The current in a stream moves at 4 kilometers per hour. A boat travels 4 kilometers upstream and 12 kilometers downstream in a total of 2 hours. What is the speed of the boat in still water?
Round trip	A boat travels with the current in a certain time and returns against the current in a certain amount of time.	A boat travels 2 hours downstream, where the current is 8 kilometers per hour. It returns in 3 hours. Find the speed of the boat in still water.
Equal time	A boat travels a certain distance with a current in the same time it can travel a certain distance against the current.	A boat travels at a rate of 15 kilometers per hour in still water. It travels 60 kilometers upstream in the same time that it travels 90 kilometers downstream. What is the rate of the current?
Part	The boat travels at a certain rate with the current and a certain rate against the current.	Fairfield's rowing team can row downstream at a rate of 7 miles per hour. They can row back to the starting point at a rate of 3 miles per hour. Find their rowing rate in still water and the rate of the current.
Relative	The time to travel with the current is compared to the time to travel the same distance against the current.	The air speed of an airplane is 225 miles per hour. Flying from city A to city B, it has a tailwind of 25 miles per hour. It takes 3 hours longer to fly from B to A than from A to B. How far apart are the two cities?

Adapted from Mayer (1981a)

of correct recall for this problem. In addition, an analysis of errors in recall revealed that subjects tended to change a low-frequency problem into a high-frequency problem but never changed a high-frequency problem into a low-frequency one. Apparently, students possess schemas for some of the common types of story problems. When students encounter a problem for which they do not possess an appropriate schema, they have difficulty in representing the problem.

Silver (1981) found that good problem solvers possess more useful problem schemas than poor problem solvers. In Silver's study, seventh-graders were asked

BOX 15 · 11   More Common Problem Types Are Easier to Recall

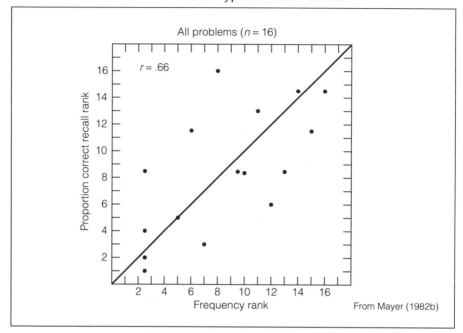

All problems (n = 16)

r = .66

Proportion correct recall rank

Frequency rank

From Mayer (1982b)

to sort sixteen story problems into groups. Students who performed poorly in solving story problems tended to group the problems based on their cover stories, such as putting all problems involving money into the same category. Students who performed well on solving story problems tended to group the problems based on their underlying mathematical structure. Apparently, becoming a good problem solver is related to the development of useful problem schemas. (Expert–novice differences in problem representation are described more fully in Chapter 13, and the relations among problem types are described in Chapter 14.)

■
SOLUTION PLANNING AND MONITORING: STRATEGIC KNOWLEDGE
■

Let's return to the tile problem. So far we have seen that in order to solve this problem you need linguistic and semantic knowledge as well as schematic knowledge. Such knowledge is useful in understanding the problem, that is, it guides your building of a mental representation of the problem. To solve a problem, once you understand it, you must have some additional knowledge concerning how to generate and monitor a solution plan—what we call *strategic knowledge.*

Once a story problem has been converted into an equation, the next step is to devise a plan for solving the equation. For example, the round-trip problem in Box 15-10 could be converted into the equation:

$$2(R + 8) = 3(R - 8)$$

where R is the rate of the boat in still water. Bundy (1983) devised a computer program for solving equations that contains the following basic strategies:

Attraction—rearranging the two instances of the unknown so that they can be changed to one instance of the unknown by carrying out an arithmetic operation, such as moving from $16 + 2R = 3R - 24$ to $16 = 3R - 2R - 24$,

Collection—carrying out a simple arithmetic operation so that two instances of an unknown can be changed to one, such as moving from $16 = 3R - 2R - 24$ to $16 = R - 24$, and

Isolation—moving numbers to the side of the equation not occupied by the unknown, such as moving from $16 = R - 24$ to $16 + 24 = R$.

In solving a linear equation such as $2(R + 8) = 3(R - 8)$, a student might use an overall plan of first trying to attract, then trying to collect, and then trying to isolate. For example, the first move of a student using this plan would be to create the equation $0 = 3(R - 8) - 2(R + 8)$. This move is an example of attraction because it tries to get the unknowns on the same side of the equation.

Although Bundy's system was intended as a framework for a computer program that solves equations, you might wonder whether it is also a good psychological theory. To answer this question, Lewis (1981) compared how college students solved equations to how Bundy's system might solve equations. For example, consider the equation, $9(X + 40) = 5(X + 40)$. According to Lewis, Bundy's system would attempt to use attraction, then collection, and then isolation. However, as shown in Box 15-12, most college students began by multiplying out the parentheses. Apparently students use a wide variety of strategies for solving simple linear equations.

The solution strategy used to solve a mathematics problem may depend on the characteristics of the problem and problem solver (Mayer, 1982a; Mayer, Larkin, & Kadane, 1983). For example, consider the following word problem:

BOX 15 • 12   Strategies for Solving $9(x + 40) = 5(x + 40)$

Name	Number of Students	Example of First Step
Attraction	5	$9(x + 40) - 5(x + 40) = 0$
Multiply out	24	$9x - 360 = 5x + 200$
Cancel	10	$9 = 5$

Adapted from Lewis (1981)

Find a number such that if 8 more than 3 times the number is divided by 2, the result is the same as 11 less than 3 times the number.

One approach to this problem is the *reduce strategy*—trying to carry out all indicated operations as soon as possible in order to reduce the number of elements in the problem. For example, if you were using the reduce strategy you would carry out the "divided by 2" operation to make the problem shorter:

Find a number such that 4 more that 3/2 of the number is the same as 11 less 3 times the number.

The reduce strategy was preferred by 81 percent of the college students who solved problems presented in words. Presumably the word format was so cluttered that students needed to reduce the amount of information.

Now, consider a corresponding version of the problem, expressed in an equation format:

$$(8 + 3X)/2 = 3X - 11$$

Most students did not opt for using the reduce strategy on this problem. Instead, 95 percent of the students used an *isolate strategy*—trying to move all the Xs to the left side and all the numbers to the right side of the equals sign. If you used the isolate strategy, your first subgoal would be to move the $3X$ from the right side and combine it with the $3X$ on the left side, but before you do that you must clear the parentheses by multiplying both sides by 2. Presumably, the equation format allowed students to rearrange the equation mentally.

In a subsequent study, four adults solved a long series of complicated equations (Mayer et al., 1983). Two of the subjects produced a pattern of response times best accounted for by assuming they used the reduce strategy, whereas the other two subjects appeared to use the isolate strategy. These results support the idea that there are individual differences in people's preferences for how to plan a solution.

Where do effective solution plans come from? Polya's (1957) classic book *How to Solve It* emphasized planning as a key process in mathematical problem solving. As described in Chapter 3, Polya suggested several strategies for devising a solution plan, such as finding a related problem that you can solve or breaking the problem into parts that you know how to solve.

Schoenfeld (1979, 1985) examined whether mathematical problem-solving strategies, such as using a similar problem or breaking a problem into parts, could be taught to mathematics students. All students in the study took a five-problem pretest and several weeks later took a five-problem posttest, both consisting of proofs, complex algebra story problems, series sum problems, and the like. During the intervening instructional phase, all students solved twenty problems during several sessions. The experimental group was given a descriptive list of five useful heuristics, as summarized in Box 15-13. For the experimental group, all problems in a session were solvable by the same strategy, and the students were explicitly told that a given problem should be solved by a particular strategy. The control group was given the same set of twenty problems and instructions, except that they received no list of heuristics, no explicit mention was made of which strategy was involved for a given problem, and the problems in each session were not all of the same strategy type.

Even though Schoenfeld used only seven subjects, he found some interesting results. The experimental group increased from an average of 20 percent correct on the pretest to 65 percent correct on the posttest, while the control group averaged 25 percent correct on both tests. Analysis of subjects' comments during the posttest indicated that the experimental group made effective use of several types of heuristics while the control group did not. These preliminary results suggest that some heuristics can be taught within the context of problem-solving domains, such as mathematics. Schoenfeld (1985, p. 214) concluded that "problem-solving practice, by itself, is not enough" and that explicit training in how to use each particular strategy is required. Training in problem-solving skills is described more fully in Chapter 12.

Students' attitudes and beliefs can influence their choice of strategies in mathematical problem solving. For example, Lester (1983) identified the following beliefs among poor problem solvers: problem difficulty depends on the size of the numbers and how many numbers are in the problem, problems should be solved by directly applying arithmetic operators to the numbers in the problem, and key words in the problem determine which operators to apply. Based on analyses of students' descriptions of their mathematical problem-solving processes, Schoenfeld (1985) identified three typical beliefs and their consequences, as summarized in Box 15-14. As you can see, researchers are beginning to point to the possible effects of students' beliefs and feelings on the way they solve mathematics problems (McLeod & Adams, 1989; Schoenfeld, 1985).

BOX 15 · 13   Five Problem-Solving Strategies

1. Draw a diagram if at all possible.
   Even if you finally solve the problem by algebraic or other means, a diagram can help give you a "feel" for the problem. It may suggest ideas or plausible answers. You may even solve a problem graphically.

2. If there is an integer parameter, look for an inductive argument.
   Is there an "n" or other parameter in the problem which takes on integer values? If you need to find a formula for $f(n)$, you might try one of these:
   A) Calculate $f(1)$, $f(2)$, $f(3)$, $f(4)$, $f(5)$; list them in order, and see if there's a pattern. If there is, you might verify it by induction.
   B) See what happens as you pass from n objects to $n + 1$. If you can tell how to pass from $f(n)$ to $f(n + 1)$, you may build up $f(n)$ inductively.

3. Consider arguing by contradiction or contrapositive
   Contrapositive: Instead of proving the statement "If X is true then Y is true," you can prove the equivalent statement "If Y is false then X must be false."
   Contradiction: Assume, for the sake of argument, that the statement you would like to provide is false. Using this assumption, go on to prove either that one of the given conditions in the problem is false, that something you know to be true is false, or that what you wish to prove is true. If you can do any of these, you have proved what you want.
   Both of these techniques are especially useful when you find it difficult to begin a direct argument because you have little to work with. If negating a statement gives you something solid to manipulate, this may be the technique to use.

4. Consider a similar problem with fewer variables.
   If the problem has a large number of variables and is too confusing to deal with comfortably, construct and solve a similar problem with fewer variables. You may then be able to
   A) Adapt the method of solution to the more complex problem.
   B) Take the result of the simpler problem and build up from there.

5. Try to establish subgoals.
   Can you obtain part of the answer, and perhaps go on from there? Can you decompose the problem so that a number of easier results can be combined to give the total result you want?

From Schoenfeld (1979)

BOX 15 ▪ 14   Three Typical Beliefs About Mathematical Problem Solving

Belief 1: Formal mathematics has little or nothing to do with real thinking or problem solving.

Consequence: In a problem that calls for discovery, formal mathematics will not be invoked.

Belief 2: Mathematics problems are always solved in less than ten minutes, if they are solved at all.

Consequence: If students cannot solve a problem in ten minutes, they will give up.

Belief 3: Only geniuses are capable of discovering or creating mathematics.

Consequences: If you forget something, you will not be able to derive it on your own. Students accept procedures at face value and do not try to understand why they work.

Adapted from Schoenfeld (1985)

SOLUTION EXECUTION: PROCEDURAL KNOWLEDGE

Once you have represented a problem and devised a solution plan, your final step is to carry out the plan. The kind of knowledge needed for solution execution is *procedural knowledge*—such as how to compute. For example, in the tile problem you have to know how to multiply and divide whole numbers and decimal numbers.

Let's begin with the knowledge needed to solve simple addition problems of the form, "$m + n =$ ____," where m and n are single, positive integers whose sum is less than 10. For example, to solve some of the marble problems in Box 15-6 a child needs to be able to produce an answer for $3 + 5 =$ ____.

Fuson (1982) has identified four major stages in the development of computational skill: counting-all, counting-on, derived facts, and known facts. A child using the counting-all procedure will begin by setting a counter to 0, incrementing it m times, and then incrementing it n times. For the problem $3 + 5 =$ ____, the child, using fingers as a counter, might put out one finger and say "one," put out a second finger and say "two," put out a third finger and say "three," then pause, and continue by successively adding five more fingers and saying "four, five, six, seven, eight."

A child using the simple version of the counting-on procedure will begin by setting a counter to m and then incrementing it n times. For example, in solving the problem $3 + 5 =$ ____, the child begins by putting out three fingers all at once, and then says "four, five, six, seven, eight" as she successively puts out five additional fingers one at a time. A sophisticated version of counting-on that Groen and Parkman (1972) call the "min model" involves setting a counter to the larger of the two numbers and incrementing it by the smaller of the two numbers. For 3 + 5 = ____, the child would begin by putting out five fingers at once and then say "six, seven, eight" as she added three more fingers one at a time.

The derived-facts stage involves using one's knowledge of number facts to figure out the answers for related problems. For example, to solve 3 + 5 = ____, a child might realize that he knows 4 + 4 = 8. From this fact he derives an answer as follows: "I can take 1 from the 5 and give it to the 3. That makes 4 + 4, so the answer is 8." In this example, the child knows 4 + 4 = 8 but does not immediately know that 3 + 5 = 8. At the known-facts stage, the child has a memorized answer for the problem that he rapidly retrieves from memory. For the problem 3 + 5 = ____, the child would say "eight."

As you can see, the early approaches to simple addition in this progression are based on counting; the child turns addition into a simpler procedure that he or she is more familiar with, namely counting-all and two versions of counting-on. Each of these three counting models of simple addition is summarized in Box 15-15, with boxes representing actions and diamonds representing decisions. As you can see, the min version is more efficient than the simple version of the counting-on procedure, and both are more efficient than the counting-all procedure. With more experience, some of the facts become automatic and eventually all become automatic.

What is the evidence for these stages in the development of computational skill? One method is to carefully observe what children do as they solve simple addition problems; in particular, we would listen to what they say and watch how they use their fingers (Baroody, 1984; Fuson, 1982). Another method, called chronometric analysis (as described in Chapter 7), is to measure the time it takes to solve various simple addition problems. If we assume that differences in response times depend mainly on how many times the counter is incremented, we could make the following predictions concerning each of the three counting procedures in Box 15-15. For a person using the counting-all procedure, response time depends on the sum of $m + n$, because the counter must be incremented $m + n$ times. According to the counting-all procedure, the problem 3 + 5 = ____ has a value of 8 and 5 + 3 = ____ has a value of 8, so both problems should take the same amount of time; similarly, 2 + 6 = ____ and 6 + 2 = ____ both require eight increments and therefore will require as much time as the other problems. For a person using the simple version of counting-on, response time depends on n, because the counter is incremented n times. Accordingly, the response time should be less for 5 + 3 = ____ (which requires three increments) than for 3 + 5 = ____ (which requires five increments). For a person using the min version of counting-on, response time depends on the lesser of m and n, because the counter

BOX 15 • 15   Counting-All and Counting-On Procedures for Simple Addition

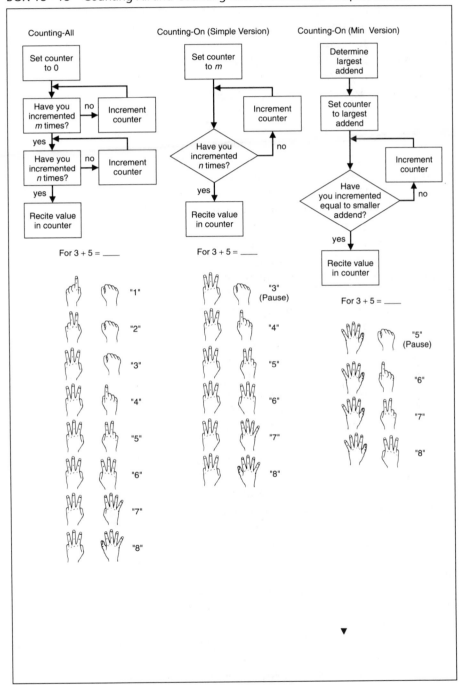

is incremented by whichever number is smaller. According to this procedure, $3 + 5 =$ ___ and $5 + 3 =$ ___ both require three increments and therefore will require the same response time; however, $6 + 2 =$ ___ and $2 + 6 =$ ___ only require two increments, so they will be answered more quickly. A person using derived facts should show the fastest response times for the problems that he or she already knows. For example, doubles (such as $2 + 2$, $3 + 3$, $4 + 4$) are usually the first to become memorized, so these should yield the fastest response times. For the known-fact procedure, all answers should be equally fast, since all involve the same procedure—"looking up" a fact in memory.

In order to determine which procedures children use as they begin to experience formal instruction in addition, Groen and Parkman (1972) asked first-graders to answer all single-column addition problems from $0 + 0 =$ ___ to $4 + 5 =$ ___. Box 15-16 shows the average time needed to solve each problem; based on the min version of the counting-on model, all the problems requiring 0 increments are in the left column, all the problems requiring 1 increment are in the next column, all the problems requiring 2 increments are in the middle column, all the problems requiring 3 increments are in the fourth column, and all the problems requiring 4 increments are in the last column. Except for doubles ($0 + 0$, $1 + 1$, $2 + 2$, $3 + 3$, and $4 + 4$), which presumably are known facts, the pattern of response time performance is best described by the min version of the counting-on procedure. As you can see, each increase in the value of the smaller addend (i.e., each additional increment in the min version of counting-on) adds about 1/3 second to the response time. In subsequent studies involving first- and second-graders, the size of the smaller addend has consistently been the best predictor of response time (Ashcraft, 1982; Kaye, Post, Hall, & Dineen, 1986). According to Groen and Parkman's (1972) results, adults show a similar pattern, except that each time the counter is incremented takes about 20 milliseconds rather than 1/3 second.

We could leave the story at this point, with full confidence that children (and even adults) use the min version of counting-on when solving simple addition problems. However, in contrast to the neat picture painted by chronometric analysis, observational research seems to show that children use a variety of solution procedures (Baroody, 1984; Fuson, 1982). This conflict has led several researchers to carefully analyze and reinterpret the results of chronometric studies (Baroody, 1983, 1987; Siegler, 1987, 1989a, 1989b; Siegler & Jenkins, 1989).

To help resolve this apparent conflict, Siegler (1987) asked kindergartners, first-graders, and second-graders to solve simple addition problems with sums ranging from 5 to 23. Each problem was presented in two different contexts: the solution time was recorded as in other chronometric studies, and the child's verbal report of his or her solution procedure was recorded as in observational studies. Based on the chronometric analysis, the min version of the adding-on

BOX 15 ▪ 16   Average Time to Solve Simple Addition Problems

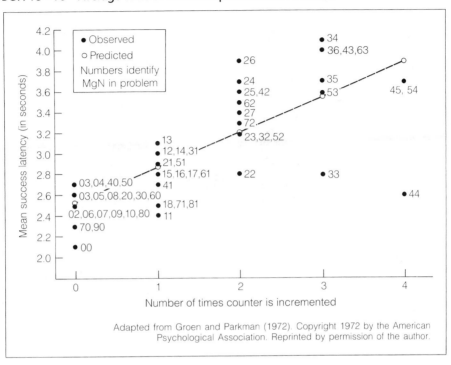

Adapted from Groen and Parkman (1972). Copyright 1972 by the American
Psychological Association. Reprinted by permission of the author.

procedure accounted for the results; as in other studies, the best predictor of
response time was the size of the smaller addend. Based on the verbal report
analysis, five distinct solution procedures were found: the counting-all
procedure, the min version of the counting-on procedure, the derived-fact
procedure (i.e., decomposition of a problem such as changing "12 + 3" into "10
+ 2 + 3"), the known-fact procedure (direct retrieval of the answer from memory),
and guessing (or no response). Box 15-17 shows the percentage of children at
each grade level who reported using each procedure. As you can see, consistent
with Fuson's findings, there appears to a developmental trend whereby children
move from less efficient to more efficient procedures.

   Unfortunately, these two results seem to contradict one another:
chronometric analyses reveal that everyone uses the min procedure whereas
verbal reports reveal that many different procedures are used. One possibility is
that children are unable to give accurate verbal reports. Accordingly, if children
use the min procedure on all problems, then we should obtain the same pattern
of response times on problems, regardless of what procedure they report using.

BOX 15 ▪ 17   Percentage of Children Who Reported Each Strategy

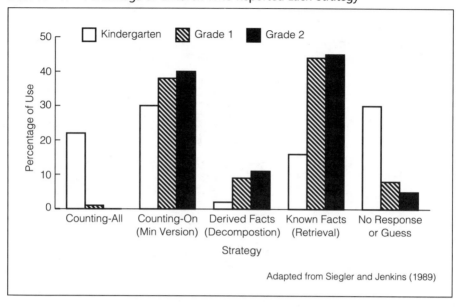

Adapted from Siegler and Jenkins (1989)

An alternative is that children use the min procedure on some problems (which creates the pattern of response times) and other procedures on other problems (which adds a constant to all problems); when we sum over all problems, the pattern favors the min model even though the pattern is created by only some of the problems. To test these conflicting predictions, Siegler (1987) examined his results on the basis of which procedure the child reported using. On problems where children said they used the min procedure, the min model was "even a better predictor of solution times on each problem than in past studies or in the present data as a whole" (Siegler & Jenkins, 1989, p. 25). On problems where children reported using other procedures, the min model was not a good predictor of results.

Siegler and his colleague (Siegler & Jenkins, 1989) concluded that people use multiple procedures and can select the procedure that best fits the task at hand. When the goal is rapid answering, then a known-fact procedure (also called direct retrieval) is used; when the goal is accuracy and the problem solver is unsure of retrieving the correct answer, then a back-up procedure, such as counting, is used. The selection of an appropriate procedure involves strategic knowledge—evaluating the situation and managing one's available procedures; this topic is addressed in the previous section of this chapter.

So far we have focused on simple addition problems; let's now move on to a slightly more complex computational task—three-column subtraction. As any teacher knows, a student may correctly and consistently apply a computational procedure that is slightly flawed. For example, a student may know a procedure for three-column subtraction that contains one small *bug*—that is, one procedural step that is wrong. A student who uses a *buggy procedure*—that is, a procedure containing one or more bugs—may produce correct answers on some problems and incorrect answers on others. Rather than stating that the student gets a certain percentage correct on a test, it is more informative to describe the procedural knowledge that the student possesses, bugs and all.

The correct procedure for solving three-column subtraction problems is summarized as a flow chart in Box 15-18. In a problem such as,

$$954$$
$$-\ 233$$

at step 2a we find 4 – 3, at step 2b we determine that 4 is greater than 3, so at step 2c we write 1 in the first column. Since there are more columns, we move from step 2d back to step 2a and repeat the procedure for the second column: at step 2a we find 5 – 3, at step 2b we notice that we do not have to borrow, and at step 2c we write 2 in column 2. Again, at step 2d there is one more column so we move to step 2a and find 9 – 2 in the third column, at step 2b we do not have to borrow, at step 2c we write 7 in column 3, and at step 2d we quit because we have run out of columns.

The fun begins when we realize that a student could have a bug in any of these steps. For example, suppose a student produces the following answers:

564	722	821	954	349
– 472	– 519	– 431	– 233	– 123
112	217	410	721	226

What is this student doing? We could say the student correctly answered 40 percent of the problems, but a more precise description of the child's procedural knowledge would be to say that the child is using a procedure with a bug in it. Can you determine which step in the child's procedure is buggy? If you look carefully, you may notice that at step 2a, the student always sets up the problem in the form of the larger number minus the smaller number. Brown and Burton (1978) have called this the smaller-from-larger bug. Box 15-19 lists some other common bugs found in children's subtraction procedures (Brown & Burton, 1978).

In order to catalogue common bugs in children's subtraction procedures, Brown and Burton (1978) gave a set of 15 subtraction problems to 1325 primary school children. They used a computer program called BUGGY to analyze each

BOX 15 ▪ 18   A Procedure for Three-Column Subtraction

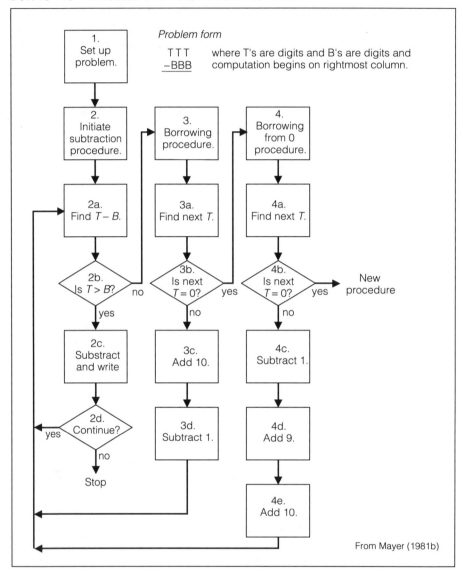

From Mayer (1981b)

student's procedural knowledge for three-column subtraction. If a student's answers were all correct, BUGGY would categorize that student as using the correct procedure (i.e., the one in Box 15-18). If there were errors, BUGGY would attempt to find one bug that could account for all or nearly all of the errors. If no

BOX 15 ▪ 19   Some Subtraction Bugs

Number of occurrences in 1325 students	Name	Example		Description
57	Borrow from zero	$\begin{array}{r} 103 \\ -\ 45 \\ \hline 158 \end{array}$	$\begin{array}{r} 803 \\ -508 \\ \hline 395 \end{array}$	When borrowing from a column whose top digit is 0, the student writes 9, but does not continue borrowing from the column to the left of zero.
54	Smaller from larger	$\begin{array}{r} 253 \\ -118 \\ \hline 145 \end{array}$		The student subtracts the smaller digit in each column from the larger, regardless of which one is on top.
10	Zero minus a number equals the number	$\begin{array}{r} 140 \\ -\ 21 \\ \hline 121 \end{array}$		Whenever the top digit in a column is 0, the student writes the bottom digit as the answer.
10	Move over zero, borrow	$\begin{array}{r} 304 \\ -\ 75 \\ \hline 139 \end{array}$		When the student needs to borrow from a column whose top digit is 0, he skips that column and borrows from the next one.
34	Zero minus a number equals the number *and* move over zero, borrow	$\begin{array}{r} 304 \\ -\ 75 \\ \hline 179 \end{array}$		Whenever the top digit in a column is 0, the student writes the bottom digit as the answer. When the student needs to borrow from a column whose top digit is zero, he skips that column and borrows from the next one.

Adapted from Brown and Burton (1978)

single bug could account for the errors, then all possible combinations of bugs were tried, until BUGGY found the combination that best accounted for the errors. As you can see in Box 15-19, 54 subjects out of 1325 seemed to have the smaller-from-larger bug, while 34 seemed to have both the 0-minus-n-equals-n bug and the move-over-zero-borrow bug at the same time, and so on. The borrow-from-zero bug was the most common, occurring alone or in combination with other bugs in 153 of the 1325 problems.

    Although the BUGGY program was based on hundreds of bugs and bug combinations, it was not completely successful in diagnosing students' subtraction procedures. The program was able to find procedures that either completely or partially accounted for the answers given by 43 percent of the students. The other students may have been making random errors or may have been inconsistent in their use of procedures. Brown and Burton's BUGGY program is an advance over previous methods of evaluating performance because BUGGY provides a clear description of the procedural knowledge of each student. However, more recent work shows that students often use more that one procedure in solving computation problems (Siegler & Jenkins, 1989) and that the production of bugs may be an ever-changing rather than a static process (Brown & VanLehn, 1980; VanLehn, 1986).

■
EVALUATION
■

Studying problem solving within a specific subject-matter area offers a unique approach, as eloquently described by Resnick and Ford (1981, p. 3): "Instead of asking, How is it that people think? we ask ourselves, How is that people think about mathematics?" Research on mathematical problem solving has blossomed in the past decade, becoming the "most active psychology of subject matter" (Mayer, 1989b, p. 455). Why are psychologies of subject matter flourishing in current research? Psychologists have become dissatisfied with studying problem solving solely in contrived and artificial environments; the failure to produce a general, context-free theory of problem solving has prompted many to focus on building theories of problem solving within specific domains.

The theme running through this chapter is that mathematical problem solving depends on the knowledge of the problem solver. The goal of this chapter has been to explore the kinds of knowledge—linguistic, semantic, schematic, strategic, and procedural—needed to solve various mathematics problems. Instead of building a general theory of cognition, psychologists of mathematical problem solving aim to describe the specific knowledge and processes involved in solving mathematics problems. This work highlights the central role of domain-specific knowledge in problem solving. The ability of psychology to study how people solve complex, actual problems suggests a growing maturity of the field. In addition, by looking beyond the puzzles and mazes of the laboratory, psychology is challenged to develop new and better theories of human problem solving.

Suggested Readings

GINSBURG, H. P. (Ed.). (1983). *The development of mathematical thinking.* Orlando, FL: Academic Press. Contains chapters by leading researchers in the psychology of mathematical problem solving.

RESNICK, L. B., & FORD, W. (1981). *The psychology of mathematics for instruction.* Hillsdale, NJ:

Erlbaum. Provides an introduction to research and theory on the psychology of mathematical problem solving.

SCHOENFELD, A. H. (1985). *Mathematical problem solving*. Orlando, FL: Academic Press. Describes one approach to understanding what it means to "think mathematically."

SLOBODA, J. A., & ROGERS, D. (Eds.). (1987). *Cognitive processes in mathematics*. Oxford, England: Oxford University Press. Contains chapters by leading psychologists interested in the psychology of mathematical skill.

CHAPTER 16

EVERYDAY THINKING

Thinking as Based on Social Contexts

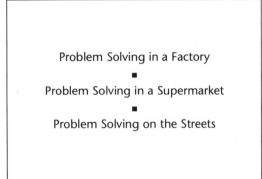

Problem Solving in a Factory

▪

Problem Solving in a Supermarket

▪

Problem Solving on the Streets

Consider the following situation. You are standing at a kitchen counter in a fully equipped kitchen. You are preparing a lunchtime serving of cottage cheese under a Weight Watchers diet program. Suppose you want to use three-quarters of the two-thirds of a cup of cottage cheese that the program allows. What would you do to prepare three-quarters of two-thirds of a cup of cottage cheese? Take a moment and write down your solution.

If you based your solution on the way fractions are taught in school mathematics, you might use a paper-and-pencil approach. You could multiply 3/4 cup times 2/3 cup to yield 6/12 cup, which you would reduce to 1/2 cup. Then you could fill a

BOX 16 ▪ 1   The Cottage Cheese Problem

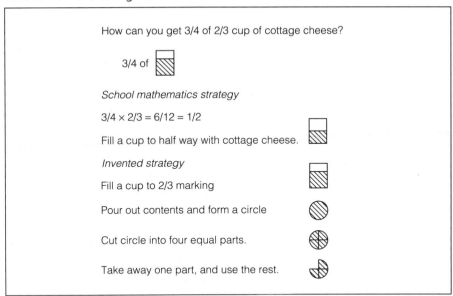

How can you get 3/4 of 2/3 cup of cottage cheese?

3/4 of

School mathematics strategy

3/4 × 2/3 = 6/12 = 1/2

Fill a cup to half way with cottage cheese.

Invented strategy

Fill a cup to 2/3 marking

Pour out contents and form a circle

Cut circle into four equal parts.

Take away one part, and use the rest.

measuring cup to the half-cup mark, pour out the contents, and use that as the lunchtime serving.

This is a perfect textbook solution to the cottage cheese problem. There is just one thing wrong with it. Real people in real kitchens do not solve the cottage cheese problem in this way. To investigate practical thinking in the real world, observers were stationed in the kitchens of Weight Watcher dieters (described in Lave, 1988). What happened when a dieter was confronted with the cottage cheese problem? According to Lave (1988, p. 165), "at no time did the Weight Watcher check his procedure against a paper and pencil algorithm, which would have produced 3/4 cup × 2/3 cup = 1/2 cup." What strategy did the dieter actually use? Lave (1988, p. 165) describes the following procedure:

> He filled a measuring cup two-thirds full of cottage cheese, dumped it out on a cutting board, patted it into a circle, marked a cross on it, scooped away one quadrant, and served the rest.

This procedure is summarized in Box 16-1. As you can see, the dieter invented a solution to the cottage cheese problem that is unlikely to have been taught in school mathematics.

The cottage cheese problem provides an example of problem solving in the real world. The point of this example is that problem-solving activities often take place within a social or cultural context, and therefore research on problem solving should consider the social context of cognition. Rogoff (1984, p. 2) eloquently summarizes this argument: "Thinking is intricately interwoven with the context of the problem to be solved."

The description of how a person solves the cottage cheese problem is an example of what could be called *everyday thinking*—thinking that occurs within the natural context of people's lives. Everyday thinking occurs within a *cultural context,* such as within the social world of an office or factory, or at home. Everyday thinking is *practical;* it is aimed at solving naturally occurring problems. Everyday thinking is *situated;* it requires action within a particular, concrete situation for which we do not have a well-established solution algorithm (Suchman, 1987).

In contrast, most of the research you have read about in this book has focused on solving contrived problems within well-controlled laboratory environments. For example, Neisser (1976, pp. xi) notes that the "development of cognitive psychology in the last few years has been disappointingly narrow, focusing inward on the analysis of specific experimental situations rather than outward toward the world beyond the laboratory." Similarly, Lave (1988, p. 6) notes: "Some psychologists have begun to doubt the ecological validity of experimental findings and to ask what thinking is like in the pervasive context of people's lives."

How can we study the context of everyday cognition? In contrast to the traditional approach of experimental psychology as represented in the most of the other research presented in this book, Lave (1988) suggests that researchers need to act as "social anthropologists of cognition" by carefully describing how people solve the problems they face within a given culture.

Research on everyday cognition offers both benefits and costs to anyone interested in human problem solving. On the positive side, research on everyday cognition frees us from what Lave (1988, p. 1) calls "a claustrophobic view of cognition from inside the laboratory and school." For example, children's performance on problem-solving tasks is often quite different when studied in the laboratory than when studied in the child's natural environment (Rogoff, 1984). Similarly, Resnick (1987, p.13) shows that school is "a special place and time for people—discontinuous in some important ways with daily life and work."

On the negative side, research on everyday cognition can be criticized on methodological grounds. Ethnographic studies of how people behave in natural settings may lack reliability in that two observers may see very different things in viewing the same situation. Further, the situations that a researcher selects to observe may determine the kinds of evidence found—one situation may provide data in support of one theory whereas another situation may be more consistent with another theory. In short, it is difficult to build cognitive theory solely on observational data.

Keeping these benefits and costs in mind, you should explore the sampling of research on everyday thinking that is presented in this chapter. In the remainder of this chapter, you will find yourself in the midst of everyday thinking by workers in a milk-processing plant, shoppers in a supermarket, and vendors on the streets of Brazil.

■
PROBLEM SOLVING IN A FACTORY
■

Let's begin our study of everyday cognition by observing how people solve practical problems in their work environments, such as in the context of their office or factory. In particular, Scribner (1984) provides a detailed observational study of how workers solve practical problems within the context of an industrial milk-processing plant. As Scribner points out, a plant such as this dairy can be viewed as a culture: each job involves activities that are socially defined (and even prescribed in official job descriptions), each job requires "culture-specific knowledge," and each job requires solving problems that are often embedded in practical manual activities.

As we look into the dairy, we find that five of the workers are classified as "preloaders." Their job is to look at an order form specifying how many gallons, half gallons, quarts, pints and/or half-pints a customer has requested and to fill cases to the customer's specifications for the drivers to load onto their trucks. The preloaders work in an area of the dairy that contains cases that are either full of milk cartons, partially full, or empty. Each case can hold 4 gallon cartons, 8 half-gallons, 16 quarts, 32 pints, or 64 half pints.

Here is a typical problem. The preloader is given an order form telling how many units of each product a customer has requested. The order form is written in a shorthand indicating a number of full cases plus or minus a number of units. For example, "1 – 6 quarts" means that the order should contain 10 quarts of milk (literally the order means: take one case of 16 quarts and remove 6 quarts).

There are two different kinds of strategies a worker can use in filling orders such as "1 – 6 quarts": a *literal strategy*, in which the worker follows the procedure by taking the number of cases indicated and adding or subtracting the indicated number of quarts; and a *least-physical-effort strategy*, in which the worker fills the order by moving the fewest quarts of milk. Under some circumstances a solution to the "1 – 6 quarts" problem is the same for both strategies: for example, if the worker has only full cases (i.e., with 16 quarts in each) and empty cases (i.e., with 0 quarts in each), a solution consistent with both strategies is to take a full case and remove 6 quarts, as shown in the first entry in Box 16-2. However, under other circumstances the two strategies generate different solutions: for example,

BOX 16 • 2   Three Solutions to the Milk-Packing Problem

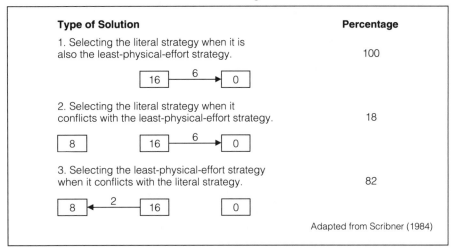

Type of Solution	Percentage
1. Selecting the literal strategy when it is also the least-physical-effort strategy.	100
2. Selecting the literal strategy when it conflicts with the least-physical-effort strategy.	18
3. Selecting the least-physical-effort strategy when it conflicts with the literal strategy.	82

Adapted from Scribner (1984)

if the worker has full cases and a case partially filled with 8 quarts (as a result of filling previous orders), then the literal strategy would be to take a full case and remove 6 quarts, as shown in the second entry in Box 16-2; in contrast, the least-physical-effort strategy would be to take the partially filled case of 8 quarts and add 2 quarts to it from one of the full cases, as indicated in the third entry in Box 16-2. Thus there are three types of solutions summarized in Box 16-2: (1) using a literal strategy when it is also the least-physical-effort strategy, (2) using a literal strategy when it conflicts with the least-physical-effort strategy, and (3) using the least-physical-effort strategy when it conflicts with the literal strategy.

In order to study the problem-solving behavior of people at work, Scribner's team set up observation posts throughout the dairy. In studying the preloaders, the researchers manipulated the contents of partially filled cases and organized the order forms before the preloaders came to work. Box 16-2 shows that preloaders always used a literal strategy when it required the fewest moves, rarely used a literal strategy when a least-physical-effort strategy was more efficient, and frequently used a least-physical-effort strategy when it when it required fewer moves than the literal strategy.

Two aspects of the preloaders' problem-solving performance are particularly interesting. First, the preloaders invented strategies for solving practical problems that were more efficient than the literal instructions that were given to them: most of the time they used a strategy that required the fewest number of moves (either type 1 or type 3), and for the remaining problems they used a strategy that required the least mental effort (i.e., the literal strategy in type 2). Second, the preloaders invented units of measure based on visual configurations that were more efficient than counting individual cartons: preloaders reported that they used visual configurations to establish the number of cartons in any partially filled case, such as knowing that one layer of half-pints is 16, or two rows of quarts is 8. Through visual inspection of partially filled cases, preloaders could determine the number of cartons without having to count. Scribner carefully observed the behavior of the preloaders during the interval between reading the order form and making the first move; during this time the preloaders never counted aloud or pointed to objects and required an average of only 1.4 seconds. For example, one preloader explained (p. 26): "I walked over and I visualized. I knew the case I was looking at had ten out of it, and I only wanted eight, so I just added two to it. . . . I don't never count when I'm making the order. I do it visual, a visual thing, you know."

What can we conclude from Scribner's ethnographic study of cognition in a dairy? First, practical thinking is adaptive and inventive with respect to problem-solving methods. Dairy workers do not blindly follow school-based procedures of arithmetic but rather invent more efficient ways of filling orders. Scribner (1984, p. 40) speculates that "effort-saving may be a general characteristic of practical thinking, conferring *elegance* on solutions to problems in mathematical theory as well as to those confronted on the shop floor." Second, practical thinking is adaptive and inventive with respect to problem representation. Dairy workers do not blindly count the number of units, as would be taught in school mathematics, but rather invent units of measure based on visual configurations of cartons in cases. In short, dairy workers seem to have invented arithmetic strategies and representations that are different from and more efficient than the strategies and representations of school arithmetic. In the case of the arithmetic problem solving of dairy workers, cognition in the context of work appears to differ from cognition in less practical contexts.

■

PROBLEM SOLVING IN A SUPERMARKET
■

The supermarket provides another context in which people engage in practical thinking. For example, Lave (1988) describes research in which adult shoppers must decide on the "best buy" for various grocery items, including both a study of simulated supermarket shopping and a study of real shoppers in a real supermarket. In the simulation study (Lave, 1988, p. 106) participants were asked to imagine that they were making shopping decisions in a supermarket:

Now I have some problems for you to do. Each problem will have two or three items . . . and I want you to tell me which one gives you the most for your money. Assume that the quality of each item is the same and that you have no other preference except for getting the most for your money. Please talk through the problem while you are figuring it out, so that I can follow the steps you are going through in making your decisions.

In the naturalistic study reported by Lave (1988), researchers accompanied shoppers in a supermarket and asked the shoppers to describe their thinking process as they decided what to buy.

Here are some typical problems:

Problem 1. Which is the best buy for barbecue sauce: bottle A, which costs 79 cents for 18 ounces, or bottle B, which costs 81 cents for 14 ounces?

Problem 2. Which is the best buy for peanuts: can A, which costs 90 cents and contains 10 ounces, or can B, which costs 45 cents and weighs 4 ounces?

Problem 3. Which is the best buy for sunflower seeds: package A, which cost 30 cents for 3 ounces, or package B, which costs 44 cents for 4 ounces?

In analyzing the solution protocols of shoppers in these studies, Lave identified several major strategies, including the following:

Difference strategy—The shopper subtracts the smaller quantity from the larger quantity (Q1 − Q2 = Qd), subtracts the price of the smaller-sized item from the price of the larger-sized item (P1 − P2 = Qd), and compares the two differences to decide whether the difference in price is worth the difference in quantity.

Ratio strategy—The shopper determines the ratio of two quantities (Q1 is ____ times greater than Q2) and decides whether the ratio of the two prices is greater or less than the ratio of the two quantities (or the shopper determines the ratio of the two prices and decides whether the ratio of the two quantities is greater or less than the ratio of the two prices).

Unit price strategy—The shopper determines the unit price of each item by dividing its price by its quantity and decides which item has the lowest unit price.

These three strategies are exemplified in Box 16-3.

If you were given one of these three problems as a word problem in a mathematics quiz, you would probably use the unit-price strategy, because the unit-price strategy matches most closely what is taught in school mathematics.

BOX 16 ▪ 3   Three Solutions to the Best-Buy Problem

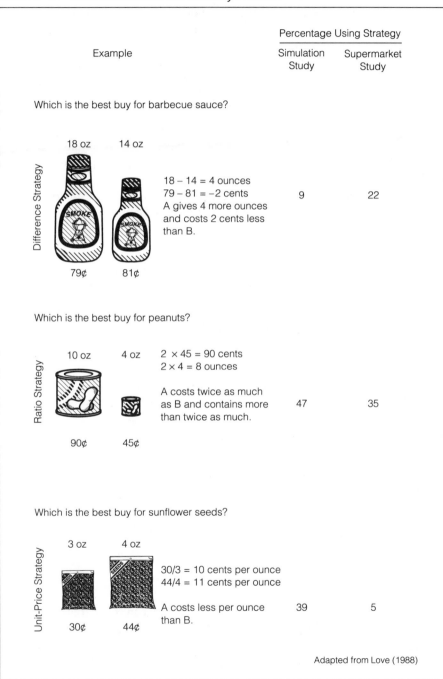

| | | Percentage Using Strategy | |
	Example	Simulation Study	Supermarket Study
Difference Strategy	Which is the best buy for barbecue sauce? 18 oz 14 oz 79¢ 81¢ 18 − 14 = 4 ounces 79 − 81 = −2 cents A gives 4 more ounces and costs 2 cents less than B.	9	22
Ratio Strategy	Which is the best buy for peanuts? 10 oz 4 oz 90¢ 45¢ 2 × 45 = 90 cents 2 × 4 = 8 ounces A costs twice as much as B and contains more than twice as much.	47	35
Unit-Price Strategy	Which is the best buy for sunflower seeds? 3 oz 4 oz 30¢ 44¢ 30/3 = 10 cents per ounce 44/4 = 11 cents per ounce A costs less per ounce than B.	39	5

Adapted from Love (1988)

However, as shown in Box 16-3, the shoppers tended to use the ratio strategy more often than the unit-price strategy in both simulated and real supermarket situations. It is particularly interesting to note that within the context of a supermarket, shoppers almost never used the unit-price strategy.

A second important observation was that shoppers invented a unit of measure—such as the 2-to-1 ratio—that helped them use different strategies for different problems. For example, in the simulated shopping study, the favorite strategy for problem 1 (which involved an obvious bargain) was a version of the difference strategy in which the shopper recognized that the best buy costs less and contains more; the favorite strategy for problem 2 (which contained a simple 2-to-1 ratio) was the ratio strategy; and the favorite strategy for problem 3 (which contained more complex ratios) was the unit-price strategy.

A similar pattern appeared in the study of shoppers in a real supermarket. In about one-fifth of their decisions about best buys, supermarket shoppers used a difference strategy, such as the following:

> A shopper considered two rolls of paper towels, one costing 82 cents, the other 79 cents. The shopper noted the number of sheets in each roll, 119 versus 104, and proceeded to reformulate the problem, saying, "That would be three more cents and you get 11 more, 15 more sheets." She concluded that the larger roll was "probably a better . . . buy." (Cited in Lave, 1988, p. 119, from a Ph.D. dissertation by Murtaugh)

As you can see, in this situation there is a fairly large difference in quantity and a fairly small difference in price, so a difference strategy is the most efficient.

In about one-third of their decisions about best buys, shoppers in a supermarket used a ratio strategy, such as the following:

> A shopper compared two boxes of sugar, one priced at $2.16 for 5 pounds, the other $4.30 for 10 pounds. She explains, "The 5 pounds would be four dollars and 32 cents, versus four dollars and 30 cents. I guess I'm going to have to buy the 10-pound bag just to save a few pennies." (Cited in Lave, 1988, p. 120, from a Ph.D. dissertation by Murtaugh)

Consistent with the simulation study, when a 2-to-1 ratio can be recognized, shoppers tend to opt for a ratio strategy.

Finally, when there is neither an obvious difference in the marginal price and marginal quantity (which would suggest using a difference strategy) nor a familiar ratio (such as 2-to-1, which would suggest using the ratio strategy), the shopper is faced with the prospect of having to carry out the computations needed for the unit-price strategy—or simply giving up. Lave (1988, p. 166) describes an example of this situation in which a mother and daughter shop for barbecue sauce:

> *Daughter:* Do you want some Chris and Pits barbecue sauce? We're almost out.
>
> *Shopper [to observer]:* Heinz has a special. I have a coupon for that. . . . I want to see if their price on their barbecue sauce is going to be as — we usually buy Chris and Pits. [Notices a Heinz coupon.] Now see, this is the one I was telling you about. But they don't have the 44-ounce. . . . [Continues searching through coupons until she finds one for barbecue sauce.] Okay, 25 cents off any size flavor of Kraft Barbecue Sauce. . . . Okay, see now in a situation like this it's difficult to figure out which is the better buy. Because this is—I don't have my glasses on, how many ounces is that, Dee? [Refers to Kraft Hickory Smoked.]
>
> *Daughter:* 18
>
> *Shopper:* 18 ounces for 89, and this is? [Refers to Chris and Pits.]
>
> *Daughter:* One pound, seven ounces—
>
> *Shopper:* 23 ounces for a dollar 17. [Speaks ironically.] That's when I whip out my calculator and see which is the better buy. [Shopper does not use calculator.]
>
> *Observer:* So what are you going to do in this case?
>
> *Shopper:* . . . They don't have the large, um . . .
>
> *Daughter:* Kraft Barbecue Sauce?
>
> *Shopper:* Yeah, so what I'm going to do is this. I'm going to wait and go to another store, when I'm at one of the other stores, because I'd like to try this.

As you can see, the shopper recognized that a unit-price strategy was called for; however, instead of expending the required effort, she simply rejected the problem—an option that is sometimes open to problem solvers in the real world.

What can we conclude? First, observations of problem-solving methods used in the supermarket, as in the factory, show that practical thinking is adaptive and inventive. Shoppers do not directly use school math but rather invent strategies for quantitative thinking. Murtaugh (cited in Lave, 1988, p. 121) summarizes this point by noting: "Shoppers apparently feel that it is not worth the effort to calculate the price per single ounce. . . . Shoppers do not perform calculations as ends in themselves; rather they transform quantitative information in ways that will highlight relations among items that are relevant to their concerns."

Second, practical problem solving in the supermarket, as in the factory, involves adapting and inventing new ways of representing problems. Shoppers devise units of measurement that help them determine which strategy to use. For example, shoppers seem to be particularly alert to situations in which the ratio of prices or quantities is 2-to-1, that is, when one price (or quantity) is double that of another. In this case, shoppers tend to use the ratio strategy; but when the ratio gets more complex, such as 5-to-2 or 4-to-3, they tend to use a unit-price strategy or give up. In short, shoppers use their knowledge of units of measure to help them craft strategies to fit specific situations.

■
PROBLEM SOLVING ON THE STREETS
■

So far in this chapter, we have observed everyday cognition in the aisles of supermarkets and on the loading docks of factories; now, let's move to the streets of Brazil. First, we encounter a twelve-year-old coconut vendor on the streets of Recife. Below is a transcript of a real transaction taken by Carraher, Carraher, and Schliemann and reported in Lave (1988, p. 65):

Customer: How much is one coconut?

Vendor: 35

Customer: I'd like ten. How much is that?

Vendor: [Pause.] Three will be 105; with three more, that will be 210. [Pause.] I need four more. That is . . . [pause] 315 . . . I think it is 350.

In this episode the vendor is confronted with a computational problem: 35×10 = _____ . Does he use a school-taught procedure or an invented procedure to solve this problem? The procedure taught in Brazilian schools is that to multiply any number by 10, simply place a zero to the right of that number; thus 35 becomes 350. However, the procedure used by the vendor can be summarized as $105 + 105 + 105 + 35$, so $105 + 105$ becomes 210, and 210 plus 105 becomes 315, and 315 plus 35 becomes 350. Here the vendor seems to have invented a procedure of counting by threes.

Like the dairy workers and shoppers, street vendors show a difference between practical thinking and school-taught thinking. Specifically, street vendors seem to rely on invented procedures rather than school arithmetic and seem to invent special units of measure, such as the cost of three coconuts (105). It is particularly

BOX 16 ▪ 4   Three Candy-Vendor Problems Problems

		Percent Correct	
Bill-Comparison problem		Vendors	Nonvendors
How many of these 🪙 $10			
equal one of these? 🪙 $50		90	85
Bill-arithmetic problem			
A customer gives you this 💵 $10,000 to pay for a $7600 purchase.			
What is the correct change?		70	50
Ratio-comparison problem			
Which would make the most profit: selling one bag of Pirulito for $200 or three for $500?		72	30
$200 $500		Adapted from Saxe (1988)	

interesting to note that the street vendors produced correct answers to computational problems 99 percent of the time within the context of the street but only 74 percent of the time on paper-and-pencil tests that contained identical problems.

How do Brazilian street vendors, who have little or no education in school mathematics, develop their mathematical thinking skills? In order to study this question, Saxe (1988) tested a group of children who sold candy on the streets of a Brazilian city and similar groups of children from urban and rural areas who were not candy vendors—all of whom had little or no schooling. Saxe asked the children to solve mathematics problems that were presented as concrete problems involving money. These included a *bill-comparison problem*, in which the child had to tell which of two bills was larger and how many of the smaller bills would equal the larger bill; a *bill-arithmetic problem,* in which the child had to tell the proper change for a purchase of a certain amount when a bill of a certain amount was tendered; and a *ratio-comparison problem*, in which the child had to determine which of two pricing strategies would generate the most profit. Examples are shown in Box 16-4.

Box 16-4 shows the percentage of correct answers given to each of the three kinds of problems by children who are street vendors and comparable children who are not street vendors. As you can see, all of the children performed

BOX 16 • 5   Two Strategies for Solving Addition Problems

	Percentage of Correct Answers	
	Vendors	Nonvendors
Algorithmic strategy	7%	6%
28 + 26 =		
8 + 6 = 14		
1 + 2 + 2 = 5		
Regrouping strategy	43%	7%
28 + 26 =		
20 + 20 = 40		
8 + 6 = 14		
40 + 14 = 54		

Adapted from Saxe (1980)

relatively well on currency-comparison problems, indicating that they have all learned about Brazilian currency, but the street vendors excelled on more complex computational problems. Interestingly, the amount of schooling did not affect the street vendors' performance on these tasks: street vendors who had zero to two years of education did not differ from vendors with five to seven years of schooling on solving the problems in Box 16-4.

To more closely examine the relative effects of mathematical problem-solving skills acquired inside and outside of school, Saxe (1988) asked elementary school students who either were or were not street vendors to solve a series of arithmetic problems, such as

$$\begin{array}{r} 28 \\ + 26 \\ \hline \end{array}$$

A school-based strategy for solving this problem, called the *algorithmic strategy*, is to proceed by column from right to left: 8 + 6 = 14, write the 4 in column 1, carry the 1, 1 + 2 + 2 = 5, write the 5 in column 2. An invented strategy, called the *regrouping strategy*, is to reorganize the problem into computationally easier problems, such as 20 + 20 = 40, 8 + 6 = 14, 40 + 14 = 54. Box 16-5 shows that second-graders who are street vendors tend to be more accurate and to use regrouping strategies more than their peers who are not street vendors.

On another street in Recife we meet an adult bookie sitting at a small table on a busy street corner. He has a total of five years of schooling, but he is able to carry out complex arithmetic computations on the spot. The betting game is complicated but here are the basic rules and terms. Five four-digit numbers are drawn at the end of the day, called *first, second, third, fourth,* and *fifth* prizes respectively. Prizes are awarded for correctly choosing all four digits, called *thousands;* the last three digits, called *hundreds;* and the last two digits, called *tens.* A bettor can select a set of numbers in any specific order or may ask for all possible permutations of a set of numbers (by using the term *inverted*).

For example, suppose someone walks up to the bookie and places the following bet: "Inverted hundreds and thousands of 7563, from the first to the fifth, one cruzeiro and 50 cents each." "Inverted thousands of 7563" means all possible four-digit permutations (such as 7563, 7536, 7356, and so on) and "inverted hundreds of 7563" means all possible three-digit permutations (such as 756, 753, 763, and so on); the bookie has a chart that tells him there are 24 four-digit permutations and 24 three-digit permutations of any set of four unique digits. "From first to fifth" means that the bet is for each of the five prizes, and "one cruzeiro and 50 cents each" means that the bettor will pay 1.5 cruzeiros (a Brazilian unit of currency) for each set of numbers for each prize. The bookie's job is to determine the cost of the entire transaction.

How do unschooled adults carry out complex computations in a practical situation? To answer this question, Schliemann and Acioly (1989) stationed themselves with bookies in the streets of Recife. Rather than using school-based procedures, the bookies used strategies they had invented, such as decomposition, grouping, and changing, as summarized in Box 16-6.

Here is a conversation as recorded by Schliemann and Acioly (1989, p. 199) in which the bookie uses a *decomposition strategy:*

> *Player:* Inverted hundreds and thousands of 7563, from the first to the fifth, one cruzeiro and 50 cents each.

> *Bookie:* Four digits, no repetition [meaning that the number 7563 is made by four different digits], 24 thousand [24 is the number of four-digit permutations that can be found for 7, 5, 6, and 3], and 24 hundreds [24 is also the number of three-digit permutations that can be found for 7, 5, 6, and 3]. If it were 1, from the first to the fifth, it would be 240 [24 bets on each of 5 prizes for the thousands and 24 bets on each of 5 prizes for the hundreds]. But it is 1 and 50. It makes 360 cruzeiros.

> *Observer* [After transaction is finished]: How did you know the total was 360?

> *Bookie:* Because I know that inverted thousands and hundreds for 7563 for 1

BOX 16 ▪ 6   Computational Strategies of Brazilian Bookies

Algorithmic strategy

Put 1.50 cruzeiros each on the inverted hundreds and thousands of 7563, from first to fifth prize. What is the total cost?

24 + 24 = 48
48 × 5 = 240
240 × 1.5 = 360

Decomposition strategy

Put 1.50 cruzeiros each on the inverted hundreds and thousands of 7563, from first to fifth prize. What is the total cost?
From chart: 240 is total number of permutations.
240 plus half of 240 equals 240 + 120 = 360

Grouping strategy

Put 4 cruzeiros on 4 thousands (1243, 2789, 6431, 9125) for first prize, and 28 cruzeiros on 4 hundreds (243, 789, 431, 125) for first prize. What is the total cost?
For thousands: 4 + 4 + 4 + 4 = 16
For hundreds: 28 + 28 = 56   56 + 56 = 112
For total: 112 + 16 = 128

Changing strategy

Use 50 cruzeiros to bet on 7471 inverted thousands and hundreds. How much is placed on each bet?
From chart: 24 bets are required
24 × 2 = 48 so put 2 cruzeiros on each bet,
with 2 cruzeiros left over for another bet.

Adapted from Schliemann and Acioly (1989)

cruzeiro, from first to fifth, makes 240. Since it was 1 and 50, and 50 is half of 1, this makes 120 more. Then you add. It makes 360.

If a problem like this were given in the context of school, a typical solution procedure would be to carry out these operations: 24 + 24 = 48, 48 × 5 = 240, 240 × 1.5 = 360. In the real-life computations of the bookie, however, the first two parts are memorized (or based on a chart) and the final operation is broken down into two parts—yielding 240 for 1 cruzeiro and 120 for one-half cruzeiro.

In another transaction, a bookie uses a *grouping strategy* (Schliemann & Acioly, 1989, p. 200):

Player: Four cruzeiros in the first prize on these four thousands [presents a list of four-digit numbers, each of them constituting, in the game's jargon, a thousand] and 28 cruzeiros on its hundreds [i.e., on the 4 three-digit numbers formed by the last three digits of each of the 4 numbers presented by the player], in the first prize.

Bookie: On the thousands you have 16, because 4, 8, 12, 16. On the hundreds you have [pause] 28 plus 28 makes 56 and 56 plus 56 makes 112. 112 plus 16 makes 128.

In this example, a person using school mathematics might perform the following operations: $4 \times 4 = 16$, $4 \times 28 = 112$, $16 + 112 = 128$. However, the bookie uses a grouping strategy (such as repeated addition) to determine the cost of the first part; instead of $4 \times 4 = 16$, the bookie simply counts by fours. Similarly, the bookie does not directly multiply 4 by 28 to determine the cost of the second part; instead he again uses repeated addition in which he first adds 28 and 28 to get 56 and then adds 56 and 56 to get 128.

Finally, let's observe a third situation in which a bookie uses a strategy of *changing cumbersome problems* (Schliemann & Acioly, 1989, p. 201):

Player: Put in there 7471, inverted thousands and hundreds to make, overall, 50 cruzeiros.

Bookie: Here you have 12 thousands [12 is the number of four-digit permutations that can be found among 7, 4, 7, and 1, the digits in the number originating in the whole bet] and 12 hundreds [12 is also the number of three-digit permutations that can be found among 7, 4, 7, and 1, the digits 7471]. That makes 24. Put 2 cruzeiros on each and put 2 on another hundred on the first prize [note that the value of the whole bet asked by the player comes to 48 cruzeiros, and 2 cruzeiros are left over].

Player: Okay.

Observer [After transaction is finished]: Why did you do it like that?

Bookie: You see, there were 12 thousands and 12 hundreds, because there were four digits and one pair [the repeated 7]. I reasoned like this: for 2 cruzeiros, one would have 48. She wanted 50. But I thought that it would be difficult to do the computations. It would take too long. It would be difficult to divide. I thought the way I did would be easier. There was 2 left, which I suggested to put on another bet.

Observer: What if the player does not accept?

Bookie: That never happens. Sometimes we give a new number immediately, and so the player is afraid of not betting on it and then of losing if it is drawn.

If the bookie had used school mathematics to solve the problem, 50/24 = ____, the answer would have been 2.08333 cruzeiros. The bookie had a calculator on hand but did not use it at work even on difficult problems such as this one. Instead of accepting the problem as given, the bookie proposed a new problem that avoided a nonround answer for a division computation.

The results of Schliemann and Acioly's research demonstrate that school experience may not play a large role in practical problem solving. Regardless of their level of schooling—ranging from none to eleven years—street vendors and bookies were proficient in solving arithmetic problems by using mathematical problem-solving strategies developed outside of school. Rather than rely on school-based strategies for solving complex computational problems, vendors and bookies working in the streets of Brazil invented strategies and units of measure, as did the the dairy workers and supermarket shoppers described in previous sections.

■
EVALUATION
■

In this chapter, we explored everyday thinking within three contexts—by workers filling orders in a milk-processing plant, shoppers looking for the best buy in a supermarket, and street vendors and bookies carrying out transactions on the streets of a Brazilian city. In each case, two consistent findings emerged. First, problem solvers invented new ways of solving problems that differed from school-taught methods. In the milk-processing plant, a worker filled an order for 10 quarts (written as 1 full case minus 6 quarts) by adding 2 quarts to a partially full case of 8 quarts rather than by removing 6 quarts from a full case of 16 quarts. In the supermarket, a shopper determined that 10 pounds of sugar at $4.30 was a better buy than 5 pounds at $2.16 by noting that doubling the cost of a 5-pound bag yielded $4.32 rather than by computing the unit cost of each bag of sugar. On the streets, a vendor computed the price of a sale by regrouping (e.g., $35 \times 10 = 105 + 105 + 105 + 35 = 350$) rather than by applying a school-taught algorithm.

Second, problem solvers invented new ways of representing problems that differed from school-taught methods. In the milk-processing plant, a worker thinks in terms of rows of quarts in a case rather than counting each quart individually. In the supermarket, a shopper thinks in terms of 2-to-1 or 3-to-1 ratios rather than unit costs. On the streets, vendors regroup in round numbers such as by tens rather than carry out complicated multiplications and divisions.

A unifying theme emerging from this line of research is that practical problem solving is contextualized, that is, people invent effective problem-solving strategies and units of measure for use within specific practical situations. Rogoff (1984, pp. 2–3) summarizes this theme as follows: "Thinking is intricately woven with the context of the problem to be solved. . . . Our ability to control and orchestrate cognitive skills is not an abstract context-free competence which may be easily transferred across widely diverse problem domains but consists rather of cognitive activity tied specifically to context."

The implications of this theme are important. First, instead of trying to study solely problem solving in *general*, researchers should also study problem solving within *specific contexts*. Sterile laboratory studies of how people solve puzzles and abstract problems may tell us only about problem solving within laboratory contexts, whereas research on thinking within real situations may tell us more about genuine human problem solving. Second, instead of relying exclusively on *experimental research methods*, researchers should add *observational methods* (such as ethnography) to their arsenals.

Finally, as suggested early in the chapter, the study of situated thinking holds promise but also risk. The promise lies in increasing our knowledge of human problem solving beyond the confines of the laboratory. This work provides a sort of scientific validity—an insurance that our cognitive theories explain genuine problem-solving behavior. The risk lies in relying on research methods that, if misused, may lack the basic scientific credentials of reliability. Sternberg (1990, p. 16) eloquently states the risks:

> Adherents of the anthropological approach have, in some cases, indulged in research that could euphemistically be called less than definitive. . . . It has often been difficult to draw strong conclusions from the research . . . with the result that the data sometimes seem to the have the characteristic of a Rorschach: One can read into the research almost whatever one wishes.

What are the proper places for observational studies and laboratory studies in the psychology of problem solving? The two methods can complement each other: observational studies of everyday thinking can provide validity but may be weak in reliability, while experimental studies using simulated tasks can produce results that are reliable but may lack validity. One possible strategy is to use the results of observational studies of everyday cognition to sharpen the focus of subsequent experimental studies, such as studying people's thinking about best buys both in a real supermarket and as a controlled experiment.

Suggested Readings

LAVE, J. (1988). *Cognition in practice*. Cambridge, England: Cambridge University Press. Summarizes research on everyday thinking, including problem solving in the supermarket.

ROGOFF, B., & LAVE, J. (Eds.). (1984). *Everyday cognition: Its development in social context*. Cambridge, MA: Harvard University Press. Contains chapters by leading researchers on everyday thinking.

REFERENCES

ACH, N. (1964). Determining tendencies. In J. M. Mandler & G. Mandler (Eds.), *Thinking: From association to Gestalt.* New York: Wiley. (Original work published 1905)

ADAMS, J. (1976). *Learning and memory: An introduction.* Homewood, IL: Dorsey.

ADAMS, J. L. (1964). *Conceptual blockbusting.* San Francisco: Freeman.

ADAMS, L. T., KASSERMAN, J. E., YEARWOOD, A. A., PERFETTO, G. A., BRANSFORD, J. D., & FRANKS, J. J. (1988). Memory access: The effects of fact-oriented versus problem-oriented acquisition. *Memory & Cognition, 16,* 167–175.

ADAMSON, R. E. (1952). Functional fixedness as related to problem solving: A repetition of three experiments. *Journal of Experimental Psychology, 44,* 288–291.

ADAMSON, R. E., & TAYLOR, D. W. (1954). Functional fixedness as related to elapsed time and set. *Journal of Experimental Psychology, 47,* 122–216.

ADELSON, B. (1981). Problem solving and the development of abstract categories in programming language. *Memory & Cognition, 9,* 422–433.

ALLISON, T., WOOD, C. C., & MCCARTHY, G. (1986). The central nervous system. In M. G. H. Coles, E. Donchin, & S. W. Porges (Eds.), *Psychophysiology: Systems, processes, and applications.* Amsterdam: Elsevier.

ANDERSON, J. R. (1976). *Language, memory, and thought.* Hillsdale, N.J.: Erlbaum.

ANDERSON, J. R. (1983). *The architecture of cognition.* Cambridge, MA: Harvard University Press.

ANDERSON, J. R. (1990). *Cognitive psychology and its implications* (3rd ed.). New York: Freeman.

ANDERSON, J. R., & BOWER, G. H. (1973). *Human associative memory.* Washington, DC: Hemisphere.

ANDERSON, J. R., FARRELL, R., & SAUERS, R. (1984). Learning to program in LISP. *Cognitive Science, 8,* 87–129.

ANDERSON, J. R., GREENO, J. G., & KLINE, P. J. (1981). Acquisition of problem-solving skill. In J. R. Anderson (Ed.), *Cognitive skills and their acquisition.* Hillsdale, NJ: Erlbaum.

ANDERSON, R. C., REYNOLDS, R. E., SCHALLERT, D. L., & GOETZ, E. T. (1977). Frameworks for comprehending discourse. *American Educational Research Journal, 14,* 367–382.

ARBITMAN-SMITH, R., HAYWOOD, H. C., & BRANSFORD, J. D. (1978). Assessing cognitive change. In C. M. McCauley, R. Sperber, & P. Brooks (Eds.), *Learning and cognition in the mentally retarded.* Baltimore, MD: University Park Press.

ASHCRAFT, M. H. (1982). The development of mental arithmetic: A chronometric approach. *Developmental Review, 2,* 213–236.

ATWOOD, M. E., & POLSON, P. G. (1976). A process model for water jug problems. *Cognitive Psychology, 8,* 191–216.

AUSUBEL, D. P. (1968). *Educational psychology: A cognitive view.* New York: Holt, Rinehart and Winston.

BAKAN, P. (1969). Hypnotizability, laterality of eye movements, and functional brain asymmetry. *Perceptual and Motor Skills, 28,* 927–932.

BAKER, L., & ANDERSON, R. C. (1982). Effects of inconsistent information on text processing: Evidence for comprehension monitoring. *Reading Research Quarterly, 17,* 281–293.

BARFIELD, W. (1986). Expert–novice differences for software: Implications for problem-solving and knowledge acquisition. *Behaviour and Information Technology, 5,* 15–29.

BARON, J. B., & STERNBERG, R. J. (Eds.). (1986). *Teaching thinking skills: Theory and practice.* New York: Freeman.

BAROODY, A. J. (1983). The development of procedural knowledge: An alternative explanation for chronometric trends of mental arithmetic. *Developmental Review, 3,* 225–230.

BAROODY, A. J. (1984). The case of Felicia: A young girl's strategies for reducing memory demands during mental addition. *Cognition and Instruction, 1,* 109–116.

BAROODY, A. J. (1987). *Children's mathematical thinking.* New York: Teachers College Press.

BARR, A., & FEIGENBAUM, E. A. (Eds.). (1981). *The handbook of artificial intelligence* (Vol. 1). Los Altos, CA: Kaufmann.

BARR, A., & FEIGENBAUM, E. A. (Eds.). (1982). *The handbook of artificial intelligence* (Vol. 2). Los Altos, CA: Kaufmann.

BARTLETT, F. C. (1932). *Remembering: A study in experimental and social psychology.* London: Cambridge University Press.

BARTLETT, F. C. (1958). *Thinking.* London: Allen & Unwin.

BATTERSBY, W. S., TEUBER, H. L., & BENDER, M. B. (1953). Problem solving behavior in men with frontal or occipital brain injuries. *Journal of Psychology, 35,* 329–351.

BATTIG, W. F., & BOURNE, L. E., JR. (1961). Concept identification as a function of intra- and inter-dimension variability. *Journal of Experimental Psychology, 61,* 329–333.

BAYMAN, P., & MAYER, R. E. (1988). Using conceptual models to teach BASIC computer programming. *Journal of Educational Psychology, 80,* 291–298.

BEGG, I., & DENNY, P. (1969). Empirical reconciliation of atmosphere and conversion interpretations of syllogistic reasoning errors. *Journal of Experimental Psychology, 81,* 351–354.

BEGG, I., & PAIVIO, A. (1969). Concreteness and imagery in sentence meaning. *Journal of Verbal Learning and Verbal Behavior, 8,* 821–827.

BEIDERMAN, I. (1987). Recognition-by-components: A theory of human image understanding. *Psychological Review, 94,* 115–147.

BEILIN, H. (1971). The training and acquisition of logical operations. In M. F. Rosskopf, L. P. Steffe, & S. Tabach (Eds.), *Piagetian cognitive-developmental research and mathematical education.* Washington, DC: National Council of Teachers of Mathematics.

BEILIN, H., & HORN, R. (1962). Transition probability effects in anagram problem solving. *Journal of Experimental Psychology, 63,* 514–518.

BERLIN, B., & KAY, P. (1969). *Basic color terms: Their universality and evolution.* Berkeley: University of California Press.

BERLYNE, D. E. (1965). *Structure and direction in thinking.* New York: Wiley.

BINET, A. (1962). The nature and measurement of intelligence. In L. Postman (Ed.), *Psychology in the making: Histories of selected research programs.* New York: Knopf. (Original work published in French 1911)

BIRCH, H. G. (1945). The relation of previous experience to insightful problem solving. *Journal of Comparative Psychology, 38,* 367–383.

BIRCH, H. G., & RABINOWITZ, H. S. (1951). The negative effect of previous experience on productive thinking. *Journal of Experimental Psychology, 41,* 121–125.

BJORKLUND, D. F. (1989). *Children's thinking.* Pacific Grove, CA: Brooks/Cole.

BLOOM, B. S., & BRODER, L. J. (1950). *Problem-solving processes of college students. An exploratory investigation.* Chicago: University of Chicago Press.

BOBROW, D. G. (1968). Natural language input for a computer problem-solving system. In M. Minsky (Ed.), *Semantic information processing.* Cambridge, MA.: M.I.T. Press.

BOBROW, D. G. (Ed.). (1985). *Qualitative reasoning about physical systems.* Cambridge, MA: M.I.T. Press.

BORING, E. G. (1923). Intelligence as the tests test it. *New Republic, 35,* 35–37.

BOUCHARD, T. J. (1971). What ever happened to brainstorming? *Journal of Creative Behavior, 3,* 182–189.

BOURNE, L. E., JR. (1966). *Human conceptual behavior.* Boston: Allyn & Bacon.

BOURNE, L. E., JR. (1970). Knowing and using concepts. *Psychological Review, 77,* 546–556.

BOURNE, L. E., JR., EKSTRAND, B. R., & DOMINOWSKI, R. L. (1971). *The psychology of thinking.* Englewood Cliffs, NJ: Prentice-Hall.

BOWER, G. H., & TRABASSO, T. R. (1963). Reversals prior to solution in concept identification. *Journal of Experimental Psychology, 66,* 409–418.

BOWER, G. H., & TRABASSO, T. R. (1964). Concept identification. In R. C. Atkinson (Ed.), *Studies in mathematical psychology.* Stanford, CA: Stanford University Press.

BRAINE, M. D. S., REISER, B. J., & RUMAIN, B. (1984). Some empirical justification for a theory of natural propositional logic. In G. Bower (Ed.), *Psychology of learning and motivation* (Vol. 18). Orlando, FL: Academic Press.

BRAINERD, C. J. (1974). Neo-Piagetian training experiments revisted: Is there any support for the cognitive-developmental stage hypothesis? *Cognition, 2,* 349–370.

BRAINERD, C. J. (1977). Cognitive development and concept learning: An interpretative review. *Psychological Review, 84,* 919–939.

BRANDEIS, D., & LEHMANN, D. (1986). Event-related potentials of the brain and cognitive processes: Approaches and applications. *Neuropsychologia, 24,* 151–168.

BRANSFORD, J. D. (1979) *Human cognition: Learning, understanding and remembering.* Belmont, CA: Wadsworth.

BRANSFORD, J. D., & FRANKS, J. J. (1971). The abstraction of linguistic ideas. *Cognitive Psychology, 2,* 331–350.

BRANSFORD, J. D., & JOHNSON, M. K. (1972). Contextual prerequisites for understanding: Some investigations of comprehension and recall. *Journal of Verbal Learning and Verbal Behavior, 61,* 717–726.

BRANSFORD, J. D., ARBITMAN-SMITH, R., STEIN, B. S., & VYE, N. J. (1985). Improving thinking and learning skills: An analysis of three approaches. In J. W. Segal, S. F. Chipman, & R. Glaser (Eds.), *Thinking and learning skills: Vol. 1. Relating instruction to research.* Hillsdale, NJ: Erlbaum.

BRIARS, D. J., & LARKIN, J. H. (1984). An integrated model of skill in solving elementary word problems. *Cognition and Instruction, 1,* 245–296.

BROWN, A. L., & DELOACHE, J. S. (1978). Skills, plans, and self-regulation. In R. S. Siegler (Ed.), *Children's thinking: What develops?* Hillsdale, NJ: Erlbaum.

BROWN, A. L., CAMPIONE, J. C., & DAY, J. D. (1981). Learning to learn: On training students to learn from texts. *Educational Researcher, 10,* 14–21.

BROWN, F. G. (1983). *Principles of educational and psychological testing* (3rd ed.). New York: Holt, Rinehart and Winston.

BROWN, J. S., & BURTON, R. (1978). Diagnostic models for procedural bugs in basic mathematical skills. *Cognitive Science, 2,* 155–192.

BROWN, J. S., & VANLEHN, K. (1980). Repair theory: A generative theory of bugs in procedural skills. *Cognitive Science, 2,* 379–426.

BROWN, R. W. (1976). Reference in memorial tribute to Eric Lenneberg. *Cognition, 4,* 125–153.

BROWN, R. W., & BERKO, J. (1960). Word association and the acquisition of grammar. *Child Development, 31,* 1–14.

BROWN, R. W., & LENNEBERG, E. H. (1954). A study of language and cognition. *Journal of Abnormal and Social Psychology, 49,* 454–462.

BROWN, R. W., & MCNEIL, D. (1966). The "tip-of-the-tongue" phenomena. *Journal of Verbal Learning and Verbal Behavior, 5,* 325–337.

BROWNELL, W. A. (1935). Psychological considerations in the learning and teaching of arithmetic. In *The teaching of arithmetic: Tenth yearbook of the National Council of Teachers of Mathematics.* New York: Columbia University Press.

BROWNELL, W. A., & MOSER, H. E. (1949). Meaningful vs. mechanical learning: A study in grade III subtraction. In *Duke University Research Studies in Education, No. 8.* Durham, NC: Duke University Press.

BRUNER, J. (1983). *In search of mind: Essays in autobiography.* New York: Harper & Row.

BRUNER, J. S. (1961). The act of discovery. *Harvard Educational Review, 31,* 21–32.

BRUNER, J. S. (1964). The course of cognitive growth. *American Psychologist, 19,* 1–15.

BRUNER, J. S. (1966). Some elements of discovery. In L. S. Shulman & E. R. Keisler (Eds.), *Learning by discovery.* Chicago: Rand McNally.

BRUNER, J. S. (1968). *Toward a theory of instruction.* New York: Norton.

BRUNER, J. S. (1973). *Beyond the information given: Studies in the psychology of knowing.* New York: Norton.

BRUNER, J. S., & KENNEY, H. (1966). Multiple ordering. In J. S. Bruner, R. R. Olver, & P. M. Greenfield (Eds.). *Studies in cognitive growth.* New York: Wiley.

BRUNER, J. S., & KENNEY, H. J. (1965). Representation and mathematics learning. In L. N. Morrisett and J. Vinsonhaler (Eds.), *Mathematical learning. Monographs of the Society for Research in Child Development, 30* (Serial No. 99).

BRUNER, J. S., GOODNOW, J. J., & AUSTIN, G. A. (1956). *A study of thinking.* New York: Wiley.

BRUNER, J. S., OLVER, R. R., & GREENFIELD, P. M. (Eds.). (1966). *Studies in cognitive growth.* New York: Wiley.

BRYANT, P. E., & TRABASSO, T. (1971). Transitive inferences and memory in young children. *Nature, 232,* 456–458.

BUCHANAN, B., SUTHERLAND, G., & FEIGANBAUM, E. A. (1969). Heuristic DENTRAL: A program for generating explanatory hypotheses in organic chemistry. In *Machine Intelligence 4.* New York: Elsevier.

BUCHANAN, B. G., & SHORTLIFFE, E. S. (1984). *Rule-based expert systems: The MYCIN experiments of the Stanford heuristic programming project.* Reading, MA: Addison-Wesley.

BUNDY, A. (1983). *The computer modelling of mathematical reasoning.* London: Academic Press.

BURROWS, D., & OKADA, R. (1971). Serial position effects in high-speed memory search. *Perception and Psychophysics, 10,* 305–308.

CACIOPPO, J. T., & TASSINARY, L. G. (Eds.). (1990). *Principles of psychophysiology.* Cambridge, England: Cambridge University Press.

California Assessment Program. (1980). *Student achievement in California schools: 1979–80 annual report.* Sacramento: California State Department of Education.

CAMPIONE, J. C., & BROWN, A. L. (1979). *Toward a theory of intelligence: Contributions from research with retarded children.* Norwood, NJ: Ablex.

CARD, S. K., MORAN, T. P., & NEWELL, A. (1983). *The psychology of human-computer interaction.* Hillsdale, NJ: Erlbaum.

CARMICHAEL, L. L., HOGAN, H. P., & WALTER, A. A. (1932). An experimental study of the effect of language on the reproduction of visually perceived form. *Journal of Experimental Psychology, 15,* 73–86.

CARPENTER, P. A., & JUST, M. A. (1975). Sentence comprehension: A psycholinguistic processing model of verification. *Psychological Review, 82,* 45–73.

CARRAHER, T. N., CARRAHER, D., & SCHLIEMANN, A. D. (1985). Mathematics in the streets and in schools. *British Journal of Developmental Psychology, 3,* 21–29.

CARROLL, J. B. (1976). Psychometric tests as cognitive tasks: A new structure of intellect. In L. B. Resnick (Ed.), *The nature of intelligence.* Hillsdale, NJ: Erlbaum.

CARROLL, J. M. (Ed.). (1987). *Interfacing thought: Cognitive aspects of human-computer interaction.* Cambridge, MA: M.I.T. Press.

CASE, R. (1978a). Intellectual development from birth to adulthood: A neo-Piagetian interpretation. In R. S. Siegler (Ed.), *Children's thinking: What develops?* Hillsdale, NJ: Erlbaum.

CASE, R. (1978b). Implications of developmental psychology for the design of effective instruction. In A. M. Lesgold, J. W. Pellegrino, S. D. Fokkema, & R. Glaser (Eds.), *Cognitive psychology and instruction.* New York: Plenum.

CASE, R. (1985). *Intellectual development: Birth to adulthood.* Orlando, FL: Academic Press.

CAVANAGH, J. P. (1972). Relation between the immediate memory span and the memory search rate. *Psychological Review, 79,* 525–530.

CERASO, J., & PROVITERA, A. (1971). Sources of error in syllogistic reasoning. *Cognitive Psychology, 2,* 400–410.

CHANCE, P. (1986). *Thinking in the classroom: A survey of programs.* New York: Teachers College Press.

CHAPMAN, L. J., & CHAPMAN, J. P. (1959). Atmosphere effect reexamined. *Journal of Experimental Psychology, 58,* 220–226.

CHAPMAN, L. J., & CHAPMAN, J. P. (1967). Genesis of popular but erroneous psychodiagnostic observations. *Journal of Abnormal Psychology, 73,* 193–204.

CHAPMAN, L. J., & CHAPMAN, J. P. (1969). Illusory correlation as an obstacle to the use of valid psychodiagnostic signs. *Journal of Abnormal Psychology, 74,* 271–280.

CHASE, W. G., & CLARK, H. H. (1972). Mental operations in the comparison of sentences and pictures. In L. Gregg (Ed.), *Cognition in learning and memory.* New York: Wiley.

CHASE, W. G., & SIMON, H. A. (1973). Perception in chess. *Cognitive Psychology, 4,* 55–81.

CHENG, P. W., & HOLYOAK, K. J. (1985). Pragmatic reasoning schemas. *Cognitive Psychology, 17,* 391–416.

CHENG, P. W., & HOLYOAK, K. J. (1989). On the natural selection of reasoning theories. *Cognition, 33,* 285–313.

CHENG, P. W., HOLYOAK, K. J., NISBETT, R. E., & OLIVER, L. M. (1986). Pragmatic versus syntactic approaches to training deductive reasoning. *Cognitive Psychology, 18,* 293–328.

CHI, M. T. H., BASSOK, M., LEWIS, M. W., REIMANN, P., & GLASER, R. (1989). Self explanations: How students study and use examples in learning to solve problems. *Cognitive Science, 13,* 145–182.

CHI, M. T. H., FELTOVICH, P. J., & GLASER, R. (1981). Categorization and representation of physics problems by experts and novices. *Cognitive Science, 5,* 121–152.

CHI, M. T. H., GLASER, R., & REES, E. (1982). Expertise in problem solving. In R. J. Sternberg (Ed.), *Advances in the psychology of human intelligence* (Vol. 1). Hillsdale, NJ: Erlbaum.

CHOMSKY, N. (1957). *Syntactic structures.* The Hague: Mouton.

CHOMSKY, N. (1959). Verbal behavior (a review). *Language, 35,* 26–58.

CHOMSKY, N. (1965). *Aspects of the theory of syntax.* Cambridge, MA: M.I.T. Press.

CHOMSKY, N. (1968). *Language and mind.* New York: Harcourt Brace Jovanovich.

CHRISTENSEN, E. E., MURRY, R. C., HOLLAND, K., REYNOLDS, J., LANDAY, M. J., & MOORE, J. G. (1981). The effect of search time on perception. *Radiology, 138,* 361–365.

CIRILO, R. K., & FOSS, D. J. (1980). Text structure and reading time for sentences. *Journal of Verbal Learning and Verbal Behavior, 19,* 96–109.

CLANCEY, W. J. (1987). *Knowledge-based tutoring: The GUIDON program.* Cambridge, MA: M.I.T. Press.

CLARK, H. H. (1969). Linguistic processes in deductive reasoning. *Psychological Review, 76,* 387–404.

CLARK, H. H., & CHASE, W. G. (1972). On the process of comparing sentences against pictures. *Cognitive Psychology, 3,* 472–517.

CLARKE, D. (1977). *Encyclopedia of how it works.* New York: A & W Publishers.

CLIFTON, C., & BIRENBAUM, S. (1970). Effects of serial position and delay of probe in a memory scan task. *Journal of Experimental Psychology, 86,* 69–76.

COFER, C. N. (1951). Verbal behavior in relation to reasoning and values. In H. Guetzkow (Ed.), *Group leadership and men.* Pittsburgh: Carnegie Press.

COHEN, P. R., & FEIGENBAUM, E. A. (Eds.). (1982). *The handbook of artificial intelligence* (Vol. 3). Los Altos, CA: Kaufmann.

COLBY, K. M. (1965). Computer simulation of neurotic processes. In R. W. Stacey and B. D. Waxman (Eds.), *Computers in biomedical research.* New York: Academic Press.

COLBY, K. M., WATT, J., & GILBERT, J. P. (1966). A computer model of psychotherapy. *Journal of Nervous and Mental Diseases, 142,* 148–152.

COLES, M. G. H., DONCHIN, E., & PORGES, S. W. (Eds.). (1986). *Psychophysiology: Systems, processes, and applications.* Amsterdam: Elsevier.

COLLINS, A. M., & LOFTUS, E. F. (1975). A spreading activation theory of semantic processing. *Psychological Review, 82,* 407–428.

COLLINS, A. M., & QUILLIAN, M. R. (1969). Retrieval time from semantic memory. *Journal of Verbal Learning and Verbal Behavior, 8,* 240–247.

COLLINS, A. M., & QUILLIAN, M. R. (1972). How to make a language user. In E. Tulving & W. Donaldson (Eds.), *Organization of memory.* New York: Wiley.

CONRAD, C. (1972). Cognitive economy in semantic memory. *Journal of Experimental Psychology, 92,* 149–154.

COOK, L. K., & MAYER, R. E. (1988). Teaching readers about the structure of scientific text. *Journal of Educational Psychology, 80,* 448–456.

COOPER, G., & SWELLER, J. (1987). Effects of schema acquisition and rule automation on mathematical problem-solving transfer. *Journal of Educational Psychology, 79,* 347–362.

COOPER, L. A. (1975). Mental rotation of random two-dimensional forms. *Cognitive Psychology, 7,* 20–43.

COOPER, L. A. (1976). Duration of a mental analog of an external rotation. *Perception & Psychophysics, 19,* 296–302.

COOPER, L. A., & SHEPARD, R. N. (1973a). Chronometric studies of the rotation of mental images. In W. G. Chase (Ed.), *Visual information processing.* New York: Academic Press.

COOPER, L. A., & SHEPARD, R. N. (1973b). The time required to prepare for a rotated stimulus. *Memory & Cognition, 1,* 246–250.

CORMAN, B. R. (1957). The effect of varying amounts and kinds of information as guidance in problem solving. *Psychological Monographs, 71,* Whole No. 431.

COSMIDES, L. (1989). The logic of social exchange: Has natural selection shaped how humans reason? *Cognition, 31,* 187–276.

COSMIDES, L., & TOOBY, J. (1990, November). *Is the mind a frequentist?* Paper presented at the annual meeting of the Psychonomic Society, New Orleans.

COVINGTON, M. V., CRUTCHFIELD, R. S., & DAVIES, L. B. (1966). *The productive thinking program.* Berkeley, CA: Brazelton.

COVINGTON, M. V., CRUTCHFIELD, R. S., DAVIES, L. B., & OLTON, R. M. (1974). *The productive thinking program.* Columbus, OH: Merrill.

CRAWFORD, R. P. (1954). *The techniques of creative thinking.* New York: Hawthorn.

CRONBACH, L. J. (1957). The two disciplines of scientific psychology. *American Psychologist, 12,* 671–684.

CUMMINS, D. D., KINTSCH, W., REUSSER, K., & WEIMER, R. (1988). The role of understanding in solving word problems. *Cognitive Psychology, 20,* 405–438.

DANEMAN, M., & CARPENTER, P. A. (1980). Individual differences in working memory and reading. *Journal of Verbal Learning and Verbal Behavior, 19,* 450–466.

DANEMAN, M., & CARPENTER, P. A. (1983). Individual differences in integrating information between and within sentences. *Journal of Experimental Psychology: Learning, Memory, and Cognition, 9,* 561–584.

DAVIDSON, J. E., & STERNBERG, R. J. (1984). The role of insight in intellectual giftedness. *Gifted Child Quarterly, 28,* 58–64.

DAVIS, G. A. (1973). *Psychology of problem solving: Theory and practice.* New York: Basic Books.

DAVIS, G. A. (1989). Testing for creative potential. *Contemporary Educational Psychology, 14,* 257–274.

DAVIS, G. A., & HOUTMAN, S. E. (1968). *Thinking creatively: A guide to training imagination.* Madison: Wisconsin Research and Development Center.

DAVIS, G. A., & SCOTT, J. A. (1978). *Training creative thinking.* Huntington, NY: Krieger.

DE BONO, E. (1976). *Teaching thinking.* London: Temple Smith.

DE BONO, E. (1985). The CoRT thinking program. In J. W. Segal, S. F. Chipman & R. Glaser (Eds.), *Thinking and learning skills: Vol. 1. Relating instruction to research.* Hillsdale, NJ: Erlbaum.

DE CORTE, E., VERSCHAFFEL, L., & DE WIN, L. (1985). Influence of rewording verbal problems on children's problem representations and solutions. *Journal of Educational Psychology, 77,* 460–470.

DE GROOT, A. D. *Thought and choice in chess.* The Hague: Mouton. (Original work published 1946)

DELLAROSA, D. (1988). A history of thinking. In R. J. Sternberg & E. E. Smith (Eds.), *The psychology of human thought.* Cambridge, England: Cambridge University Press.

DESOTO, C. B., LONDON, M., & HANDEL, S. (1965). Social reasoning and spatial paralogic. *Journal of Personality and Social Psychology, 2,* 513–521.

DEVNICH, G. E. (1937). Words as "Gestalten." *Journal of Experimental Psychology, 20,* 297–300.

DOMINGUEZ, J. (1985). The development of human intelligence: The Venezuelan case. In J. W. Segal, S. F. Chipman, & R. Glaser (Eds.), *Thinking and learning skills: Vol. 1. Relating instruction to research.* Hillsdale, NJ: Erlbaum.

DOMINOWSKI, R. L. (1981). Comment on "An examination of the alleged role of 'fixation' in the solution of 'insight' problems." *Journal of Experimental Psychology: General, 110,* 193–198.

DOMINOWSKI, R. L., & DUNCAN, C. P. (1964). Anagram solving as a function of bigram frequency. *Journal of Verbal Learning and Verbal Behavior, 3,* 321–325.

DONCHIN, E., & COLES, M. G. H. (1988). Is the P300 component a manifestation of context updating? *Behavioral and Brain Sciences, 11,* 355–371.

DONCHIN, E., & ISRAEL, J. B. (1980). Event-related potentials: Approaches to cognitive psychology. In R. E. Snow, P. Federico, & W. E. Montague (Eds.), *Aptitude, learning, and instruction* (Vol. 2). Hillsdale, NJ: Erlbaum.

DONDERS, F. C. (1969). On the speed of mental processes. W. G. Koster (Trans.), *Acta Psychologica, 30,* 412–431. (Original work published 1868).

DOOLING, D. J., & LACHMAN, R. (1971). Effects of comprehension on the retention of prose. *Journal of Experimental Psychology, 88,* 216–222.

DOOLING, D. J., & MULLET, R. L. (1973). Locus of thematic effects in retention of prose. *Journal of Experimental Psychology, 97,* 404–406.

DOSSEY, J. A., MULLIS, I. V. S., LINDQUIST, M. M., & CHAMBERS, D. L. (1988). *The mathematics report card: Trends and achievement based on the 1986 national assessment.* Princeton, NJ: Educational Testing Service.

DUNCKER, K. (1945). On problem solving. *Psychological Monographs, 58*:5, Whole No. 270.

DUNNETTE, M. D., CAMPBELL, J., & JAASTAD, K. (1963). Effect of group participation on brainstorming effectiveness for two industrial samples. *Journal of Applied Psychology, 47,* 30–37.

DYCK, J. L., & MAYER, R. E. (1989). Teaching for transfer of computer program comprehension. *Journal of Educational Psychology, 81,* 16–24.

EBBINGHAUS, H. (1964). *Memory.* New York: Dover Publications. (Original work published 1885)

EDWARDS, M. W. (1968). A survey of problem solving courses. *Journal of Creative Behavior, 2,* 33–51.

EGAN, D. E., & GREENO, J. G. (1974). Theory of rule induction: Knowledge acquired in concept learning, serial pattern learning, and problem solving. In L. W. Gregg (Ed.), *Knowledge and cognition.* Hillsdale, NJ: Erlbaum.

EGAN, D. E., & GRIMES-FARROW, D. D. (1982). Differences in mental representations spontaneously adopted for reasoning. *Memory & Cognition, 10,* 297–307.

EHRLICH, K., & SOLOWAY, E. (1984). An empirical investigation of the tacit plan knowledge in programming. In J. C. Thomas & M. L. Schneider (Eds.), *Human factors in computer systems.* Norwood, NJ: Ablex.

EHRLICHMAN, H., WEINER, S., & BAKER, A. (1974). Effects of verbal and spatial questions on initial gaze shifts. *Neuropsychologia, 12,* 265–277.

ELKIND, D. (1967). Introduction. In J. Piaget, *Six psychological studies.* New York: Random House.

ENNIS, R. H. (1987). A taxonomy of critical thinking dispositions and abilities. In J. B. Baron & R. J. Sternberg (Eds.), *Teaching thinking skills: Theory and practice.* New York: Freeman.

ERICKSON, J. R. (1974). A set analysis theory of behavior in formal syllogistic reasoning tasks. In R. L. Solso (Ed.), *Theories of cognitive psychology: The Loyola symposium*. Hillsdale, NJ: Erlbaum.

ERICKSON, J. R. (1978). Research on syllogistic reasoning. In R. Revlin & R. E. Mayer (Eds.), *Human reasoning*. New York: Wiley/Winston.

ERNST, G. W., & NEWELL, A. (1969). *GPS: A case study in generality and problem solving*. New York: Academic Press.

ERVIN, S. M. (1961). Changes with age in the verbal determinants of word-association. *American Journal of Psychology, 74*, 361–372.

EVANS, J. ST. B. T., BARSTON, J., & POLLARD, P. (1983). On the conflict between logic and belief in syllogistic reasoning. *Memory & Cognition, 11*, 295–306.

EVANS, T. G. (1968). A program for the solution of a class of geometry-analogy intelligence test questions. In M. L. Minsky (Ed.), *Semantic information processing*, Cambridge, MA: M.I.T. Press.

EWERT, P. H., & LAMBERT, J. F. (1932). Part II: The effect of verbal instructions upon the formation of a concept. *Journal of General Psychology, 6*, 400–41 1.

FARRIS, H. H., & REVLIN, R. (1989). Sensible reasoning in two tasks: Rule discovery and hypothesis evaluation. *Memory & Cognition, 17*, 221–232.

FELDHUSEN, J. F., TREFFINGER, D. J., & BAHLKE, S. J. (1970). Developing creative thinking: The Purdue creativity program. *Journal of Creative Behavior, 4*, 85–90.

FEUERSTEIN, R. (1979). *The dynamic assessment of retarded performers. The learning potential assessment device: Theory, instruments, and techniques*. Baltimore: University Park Press.

FEUERSTEIN, R. (1980). *Instrumental enrichment: An intervention program for cognitive modifiability*. Baltimore: University Park Press.

FEUERSTEIN, R., JENSEN, M., HOFFMAN, M. B., & RAND, Y. (1985). Instrumental enrichment, an intervention program for structural cognitive modifiability: Theory and practice. In J. W. Segal, S. F. Chipman & R. Glaser (Eds.), *Thinking and learning skills: Vol. 1. Relating instruction to research*. Hillsdale, NJ: Erlbaum.

FIEDLER, K. (1988). The dependence of the conjunction fallacy on subtle linguistic factors. *Psychological Research, 50*, 123–129.

FIELD, D. (1987). A review of preschool conservation training: An analysis of analyses. *Developmental Review, 7*, 210–251.

FILLMORE, C. J. (1968). The case for case. In E. Bach & R. T. Harms (Eds.), *Universals of linguistic theory*. New York: Holt, Rinehart and Winston.

FITTS, P. M., & POSNER, M. I. (1967). *Human performance*. Belmont, CA: Brooks/Cole.

FLAVELL, J. H. (1970). Developmental studies of mediated memory. In H. W. Reese & L. P. Lipsitt (Eds.), *Advances in child development and behavior* (Vol. 5). New York: Academic Press.

FLAVELL, J. H., & WELLMAN, H. M. (1977). Metamemory. In R. V. Kail & J. W. Hagen (Eds.), *Perspectives on the development of memory and cognition*. Hillsdale, NJ: Erlbaum.

FLAVELL, J. H., FRIEDRICHS, A. G., & HOYT, J. D. (1970). Developmental changes in memorization processes. *Cognitive Psychology, 1*, 324–340.

FRANK, F. (1966). Perception and language in conservation. In J. S. Bruner, R. R. Olver, & P. M. Greenfield (Eds.), *Studies in cognitive growth*. New York: Wiley.

FRANKS, J. J., & BRANSFORD, J. D. (1971). Abstraction of visual patterns. *Journal of Experimental Psychology, 90*, 65–74.

FRIEBERGS, V., & TULVING, E. (1961). The effect of practice on utilization of information from positive and negative instances in concept identification. *Canadian Journal of Psychology, 15*, 101–106.

FRIJDA, N. H., & DE GROOT, A. D. (Eds.). (1982). *Otto Selz: His contribution to psychology*. The Hague: Mouton.

FUSON, K. C. (1982). An analysis of the counting-on solution procedure in addition. In T. P. Carpenter, J. M. Moser, & T. A. Romberg (Eds.), *Addition and subtraction: A cognitive perspective*. Hillsdale, NJ: Erlbaum.

GAGNÉ, E. (1985). *The cognitive psychology of school learning*. Boston: Little, Brown.

GAGNÉ, R. M. (1968). Learning hierarchies. *Educational Psychology, 6*, 1–9.

GAGNÉ, R. M., & BROWN, L. T. (1961). Some factors in the programming of conceptual learning. *Journal of Experimental Psychology, 62*, 313–321.

GAGNÉ, R. M., & SMITH, E. C. (1962). A study of the effects of verbalization on problem solving. *Journal of Experimental Psychology, 63*, 12–18.

GALTON, F. (1869). *Hereditary genius*. London: Macmillan.

GALTON, F. (1883). *Inquiries into human faculty and its development*. London: Macmillan.

GARDNER, H. (1985). *The mind's new science: A history of the cognitive revolution*. New York: Basic Books.

GELERNTER, H. (1960). Realization of a geometry theorem proving machine. In *Proceedings of 1959 international conference on information processing*. Paris: UNESCO.

GELMAN, R. (1969). Conservation acquisition: A problem of learning to attend to the relevant attributes. *Journal of Experimental Child Psychology, 7*, 67–87.

GELMAN, R., & GALLISTEL, C. R. (1978). *The child's understanding of number*. Cambridge, MA: Harvard University Press.

GENTNER, D. (1983). Structure mapping: A theoretical framework. *Cognitive Science, 7*, 155–170.

GENTNER, D. (1989). The mechanisms of analogical learning. In S. Vosniadou & A. Ortony (Eds.), *Similarity and analogical reasoning*. Cambridge, England: Cambridge University Press.

GENTNER, D., & GENTNER, D. R. (1983). Flowing waters or teeming crowds: Mental models of electricity. In D. Gentner & A. L. Stevens (Eds.), *Mental models*. Hillsdale, NJ: Erlbaum.

GICK, M. L., & HOLYOAK, K. J. (1980). Analogical problem solving. *Cognitive Psychology, 12*, 306–355.

GICK, M. L., & HOLYOAK, K. J. (1983). Schema induction and analogical transfer. *Cognitive Psychology, 15*, 1–38.

GIGERENZER, G. (in press). How to make cognitive illusions disappear: Beyond heuristics and biases. European Review of Social Psychology.

GLASER, R., & CHI, M. T. H. (1988). Overview. In M. T. H. Chi, R. Glaser, & M. J. Farr (Eds.), *The nature of expertise*. Hillsdale, NJ: Erlbaum.

GLUCKSBERG, S., & DANKS, J. (1968). Effects of discriminative labels and of nonsense labels upon availability of novel function. *Journal of Verbal Learning and Verbal Behavior, 7*, 72–76.

GLUCKSBERG, S., & WEISBERG, R. W. (1966). Verbal behavior and problem solving: Some effects of labeling in a functional fixedness problem. *Journal of Experimental Psychology, 71*, 659–664.

GOLDBERG, R. A., SCHWARTZ, S., & STEWART, M. (1977). Individual differences in cognitive processes. *Journal of Educational Psychology, 69*, 9–14.

GOODWIN, L., & SANATI, M. (1986). Learning computer programming through dynamic representation of computer functioning: Evaluation of a new learning package for Pascal. *International Journal of Man-Machine Studies, 25*, 327–341.

GORDON, W. J. J. (1961). *Synectics*. New York: Harper & Row.

GREENO, J. G. (1973). The structure of memory and the process of solving problems. In R. L. Solso (Ed.), *Contemporary issues in cognitive psychology: The Loyola symposium*. Washington, DC: Winston.

GREENO, J. G. (1974). Hobbits and orcs: Acquisition of a sequential concept. *Cognitive Psychology, 6*, 270–292.

GREENO, J. G. (1976). Cognitive objectives of instruction: Theory of knowledge for solving problems and answering questions. In D. Klahr (Ed.), *Cognition and instruction*. Hillsdale, NJ: Erlbaum.

GREENO, J. G. (1978a). Natures of problem solving abilities. In W. K. Estes (Ed.), *Handbook of learning and cognitive processes* (Vol. 5). Hillsdale, NJ: Erlbaum.

GREENO, J. G. (1978b). A study of problem solving. In R. Glaser (Ed.), *Advances in instructional psychology* (Vol. 1). Hillsdale, N.J.: Erlbaum.

GREENO, J. G., & SIMON, H. A. (1988). Problem solving and reasoning. In R. C. Atkinson, R. J. Hernstein, G. Lindzey, & R. D. Luce (Eds.), *Stevens' handbook of experimental psychology*. New York: Wiley.

GREGG, L. W., & SIMON, H. A. (1967). Process models and stochastic theories of simple concept formation. *Journal of Mathematical Psychology, 4*, 246–276.

GRIGGS, R. A., & COX, J. R. (1982). The elusive thematic-materials effect in Wason's selection task. *British Journal of Psychology, 73*, 407–420.

GROEN, G. J., & PARKMAN, J. M. (1972). A chronometric analysis of simple addition. *Psychological Review, 79*, 329–343.

GROEN, G. J., & PATEL, V. L. (1988). The relationship between comprehension and reasoning in medical expertise. In M. T. H. Chi, R. Glaser, & M. J. Farr (Eds.), *The nature of expertise*. Hillsdale, NJ: Erlbaum.

GUILFORD, J. P. (1959). The three faces of intellect. *American Psychologist, 14*, 469–479.

GUILFORD, J. P. (1967). *The nature of human intelligence*. New York: McGraw–Hill.

GUR, R. E., GUR, R. C., & HARRIS, L. (1975). Cerebral activation as measured by subjects' lateral eye movements is influenced by experimenter location. *Neuropsychologia, 15*, 35–44.

GUTHRIE, E. R., & HORTON, G. P. (1946). *Cats in a puzzle box.* New York: Holt, Rinehart and Winston.

HALPERN, D. F. (1989). *Thought and knowledge: An introduction to critical thinking* (2nd ed.). Hillsdale, NJ: Erlbaum.

HARLOW, H. F. (1949). The formation of learning sets. *Psychological Review, 56,* 51–56.

HARLOW, H. F., & HARLOW, M. K. (1949, August). Learning to think. *Scientific American*, pp. 36–39. Offprint 415.

HAYES, J. R. (1978). *Cognitive psychology.* Homewood, IL: Dorsey.

HAYES, J. R. (1981). *The complete problem solver.* Philadelphia: Franklin Institute Press.

HAYES, J. R., & SIMON, H. A. (1974). Understanding written instructions. In L. W. Gregg (Ed.), *Knowledge and cognition.* Hillsdale, NJ: Erlbaum.

HAYES, J. R., & SIMON, H. A. (1977). Psychological differences among problem isomorphs. In N. J. Castellan, D. B. Pisoni, & G. R. Potts (Eds.), *Cognitive theory* (Vol. 2). Hillsdale, NJ: Erlbaum.

HAYGOOD, R. C., & STEVENSON, M. (1967). Effects of number of irrelevant dimensions in nonconjunctive concept learning. *Journal of Experimental Psychology, 74,* 302–304.

HAYGOOD, R. C., HARBERT, T. L., & OMLOR, J. A. (1970). Intradimensional variability and concept learning. *Journal of Experimental Psychology, 83,* 216–219.

HEFFLEY, E., WICKENS, C., & DONCHIN, E. (1978). Intramodality selective attention and P300: Reexamination in a visual monitoring task. *Psychophysiology, 15,* 269–270.

HEIDER, E. R. (1970). *The Dugum Dani: A Papuan culture in the highlands of West New Guinea.* Chicago: Aldine.

HEIDER, E. R. (1972). Universals in color naming and memory. *Journal of experimental Psychology, 93,* 10–20.

HEIDER, E. R., & OLIVER, D. C. (1972). The structure of the color space in naming and memory for two languages. *Cognitive Psychology, 3,* 337–354.

HILGARD, E. R., ERGREN, R. D., & IRVINE, R. P. (1954). Errors in transfer following learning by understanding: Further studies with Katona's card trick experiments. *Journal of experimental Psychology, 47,* 457–464.

HILGARD, E. R., IRVINE, R. P., & WHIPPLE, J. E. (1953). Rote memorization, understanding, and transfer: An extension of Katona's card trick experiment. *Journal of Experimental Psychology, 46,* 288–292.

HINSLEY, D., HAYES, J. R., & SIMON, H. A. (1977). From words to equations. In P. Carpenter & M. Just (Eds.), *Cognitive processes in comprehension.* Hillsdale, NJ: Erlbaum.

HINTON, G. E., & ANDERSON, J. A. (Eds.). (1989). *Parallel models of associative memory.* Hillsdale, NJ: Erlbaum.

HOGABOAM, T. W., & PELLEGRINO, J. W. (1978). Hunting for individual differences in cognitive processes: Verbal ability and semantic processing of pictures and words. *Memory & Cognition, 6,* 189–193.

HOLTZMAN, T. G., GLASER, R., & PELLEGRINO, J. W. (1976). Process training derived from a computer simulation theory. *Memory and Cognition, 4,* 349–356.

HOLYOAK, K. J. (1990). Problem solving. In D. N. Osherson & E. E. Smith (Eds.), *Thinking: An invitation to cognitive science*. Cambridge, MA: M.I.T. Press.

HOLYOAK, K. J., & KOH, K. (1987). Surface and structural similarity in analogical transfer. *Memory & Cognition, 15,* 332–340.

HUDSON, T. (1983). Correspondences and numerical differences between disjoint sets. *Child Development, 54,* 84–90.

HULL, C. L. (1920). Quantitative aspects of the evolution of concepts. *Psychological Monographs, 28,* No. 123.

HULL, C. L. (1943). *Principles of behavior*. New York: Appleton-Century-Crofts,.

HUMPHREY, G. (1963). *Thinking: An introduction to its experimental psychology*. New York: Wiley.

HUNT, E. (1978). The mechanisms of verbal ability. *Psychological Review, 85,* 109–130.

HUNT, E. (1985). Verbal ability. In R. J. Sternberg (Ed.), *Human abilities: An information-processing approach*. New York: Freeman.

HUNT, E., & MACLEOD, C. M. (1979). The sentence-picture verification paradigm: A case study of two conflicting approaches to individual differences. In R. J. Sternberg & D. K. Determan (Eds.), *Human intelligence*. Norwood, NJ: Albex.

HUNT, E. B., DAVIDSON, J., & LANSMAN, M. (1981). Individual differences in long-term memory access. *Memory & Cognition, 9,* 599–608.

HUNT, E. B., MARIN, J., & STONE, P. I. (1966). *Experiments in induction*. New York: Academic Press.

HUNT, E. G., FROST, N., & LUNNEBORG, C. L. (1973). Individual differences in cognition: A new approach to intelligence. In G. Bower (Ed.), *Advances in learning and motivation* (Vol. 7). New York: Academic Press.

HUNT, E., LUNNEBORG, C., & LEWIS, J. (1975). What does it mean to be high verbal? *Cognitive Psychology, 7,* 194–227.

HUTTENLOCHER, J. (1968). Constructing spatial images: A strategy in reasoning. *Psychological Review, 75,* 550–560.

INHELDER, B., & PIAGET, J. (1958). *The growth of logical thinking from childhood to adolescence*. New York: Basic Books. (A. Parson & S. Milgram, Trans.; original French edition, 1955.)

JACOBSON, E. (1932). Electrophysiology of mental activity. *American Journal of Psychology, 44,* 677–694.

JAMES, W. (1890). *The principles of psychology*. New York: Holt, Rinehart and Winston.

JANIS, I. L., & FRICK, F. (1943). The relationship between attitudes toward conclusions and errors in judging logical validity of syllogisms. *Journal of Experimental Psychology, 33,* 73–77.

JEFFRIES, R., POLSON, P. G., RAZRAN, L., & ATWOOD, M. E. (1977). A process model for missionaries-cannibals and other river-crossing problems. *Cognitive Psychology, 9,* 412–440.

JEFFRIES, R., TURNER, A., POLSON, P., & ATWOOD, M. (1981). The processes involved in designing software. In J. Anderson (Ed.), *Cognitive skills and their acquisition*. Hillsdale, NJ: Erlbaum.

JENKINS, J. J. (1974). Remember that old theory of memory? Well, forget it! *American Psychologist, 29,* 785–795.

JOHN, E. R., & SCHWARTZ, E. L. (1978). The neurophysiology of information processing and cognition. In M. R. Rosenzweig & L. W. Porter (Eds.), *Annual Review of Psychology* (Vol. 29). Palo Alto, CA: Annual Reviews.

JOHNSON, D. M. (1972). *A systematic introduction to the psychology of thinking.* New York: Harper & Row.

JOHNSON-LAIRD, P. M. (1988). *The computer and the mind: An introduction to cognitive science.* Cambridge, MA: Harvard University Press.

JOHNSON-LAIRD, P. N. (1983). *Mental models: Towards a cognitive science of language, inference, and consciousness.* Cambridge, MA: Harvard University Press.

JOHNSON-LAIRD, P. N., & BARA, B. G. (1984). Syllogistic inference. *Cognition, 16,* 1–61.

JOHNSON-LAIRD, P. N., & STEEDMAN, M. (1978). The psychology of syllogisms. *Cognitive Psychology, 10,* 64–99.

JOHNSON-LAIRD, P. N., & WASON, P. C. (1977). A theoretical analysis of insight into a reasoning task. In P. N. Johnson-Laird & P. C. Wason (Ed.), *Thinking: Readings in Cognitive Science.* Cambridge, England: Cambridge University Press.

JOHNSON-LAIRD, P. N., LEGRENZI, P., & LEGRENZI, M. (1972). Reasoning and a sense of reality. *British Journal of Psychology, 63,* 395–400.

JOHNSON-LAIRD, P. N., OAKHILL, J., & BULL, D. (1986). Children's syllogistic reasoning. *Quarterly Journal of Experimental Psychology, 38A,* 35–58.

JOHNSON, P. E., DURAN, A. S., HASSEBROK, F., MOLLER, J., PRIETULA, M., FELTOVICH, P. J., & SWANSON, D. B. (1981). Expertise and error in diagnostic reasoning. *Cognitive Science, 5,* 235–283.

JOHNSON, R. E. (1970). Recall of prose as a function of the structural importance of linguistic units. *Journal of Verbal Learning and Verbal Behavior, 9,* 12–20.

JUST, M. A., & CARPENTER, P. A. (1971). Comprehension of negation with quantification. *Journal of Verbal Learning and Verbal Behavior, 10,* 244–253.

JUST, M. A., & CARPENTER, P. A. (1976). Eye fixations and cognitive processes. *Cognitive Psychology, 8,* 441–480.

JUST, M. A., & CARPENTER, P. A. (1978). Inference processes during reading: Reflections from eye movements. In J. W. Senders, D. F. Fisher, & R. A. Monty (Eds.), *Eye movements and higher psychological functions.* Hillsdale, NJ: Erlbaum.

JUST, M. A., & CARPENTER, P. A. (1987). *The psychology of reading and language comprehension.* Boston: Allyn & Bacon.

KAHNEMAN, D., & TVERSKY, A. (1973). On the psychology of prediction. *Psychological Review, 80,* 237–251.

KAIL, R. (1990). *The development of memory in children* (3rd ed.). New York: Freeman.

KATONA, G. (1940). *Organizing and memorizing.* New York: Columbia University Press.

KATONA, G. (1942). Organizing and memorizing: A reply to Dr. Melton. *American Journal of psychology, 55,* 273–275.

KAYE, D. B., POST, T., HALL, V. C., & DINEEN, J. T. (1986). Emergence of information-retrieval strategies in numerical cognition: A developmental study. *Cognition and Instruction, 3,* 127–150.

KEENAN, J. M., BAILLET, S. D., & BROWN, P. (1984). The effects of causal cohesion on comprehension and memory. *Journal of Verbal Learning and Verbal Behavior, 23,* 115–126.

KENDLER, H. H., & D'AMATO, M. F. (1955). A comparison of reversal and nonreversal shifts in human concept information. *Journal of Experimental Psychology, 49,* 165–174.

KENDLER, H. H., & KENDLER, T. S. (1962a). Vertical and horizontal processes in problem solving. *Psychological Review, 69,* 1–16.

KENDLER, H. H., & KENDLER, T. S. (1975). From discrimination learning to cognitive development: A neobehavioristic odyssey. In W. K. Estes (Ed.), *Handbook of learning and cognitive processes* (Vol. 1). Hillsdale, NJ: Erlbaum.

KENDLER, T. S., & KENDLER, H. H. (1959). Reversal and nonreversal shifts in kindergarten children. *Journal of Experimental Psychology, 58,* 56–60.

KENDLER, T. S., & KENDLER, H. H. (1962b). Inferential behavior as a function of subgoal constancy and age. *Journal of Experimental Psychology, 64,* 460–466.

KINSBOURNE, M. (1972). Eye and head turning indicates cerebral lateralization. *Science,* 176, 539–541.

KINTSCH, W. (1974). *The representation of meaning in memory.* Hillsdale, NJ: Erlbaum.

KINTSCH, W. (1976). Memory for prose. In C. N. Cofer (Ed.), *The structure of human memory.* San Francisco: Freeman, 1976.

KINTSCH, W. (1980). Semantic memory: A tutorial. In R. S. Nickerson (Ed.), *Attention and performance VIII.* Hillsdale, NJ: Erlbaum.

KINTSCH, W., & GREENO, J. G. (1985). Understanding and solving word arithmetic problems. *Psychological Review, 92,* 109–129.

KINTSCH, W., & VAN DIJK, T. A. (1978). Toward a model of text comprehension and production. *Psychological Review, 85,* 363–394.

KLAHR, D. (1978). Goal formation, planning, and learning by pre-school problem solvers or "My socks are in the dryer." In R. S. Siegler (Ed.), *Children's thinking: What develops?* Hillsdale, NJ: Erlbaum.

KLAHR, D. (1982). Nonmonotone assessment of monetone develoment: An information processing analysis. In S. Strauss (Ed.), *U-shaped behavioral growth.* New York: Academic Press.

KLAHR, D. (1984). Transition processes in quantitative development. In R. S. Sternberg (Ed.), *Mechanisms of cognitive development.* New York: Freeman.

KLAHR, D., & DUNBAR, K. (1988). Dual space search during scientific reasoning. *Cognitive Science, 12,* 1–48.

KLAHR, D., & ROBINSON, M. (1981). Formal assessment of problem-solving and planning processes in preschool children. *Cognitive Psychology, 13,* 113–148.

KLAHR, D., & WALLACE, J. G. (1976). *Cognitive development: An information processing view.* Hillsdale, NJ: Erlbaum.

KLAHR, D., DUNBAR, K., & FAY, A. L. (1990). Designing good experiments to test bad hypotheses. In J. Shrager & P. Langley (Eds.), *Computational models of scientific discovery and theory formation.* Los Altos, CA: Kaufmann.

KLAHR, D., LANGLEY, P., & NECHES, R. (Eds.). (1987). *Production system models of learning and development.* Cambridge, MA: M.I.T. Press.

KLATZKY, R. (1980). *Human memory* (2nd ed.). San Francisco: Freeman.

KLAYMAN, J., & HA, Y. (1987). Confirmation, disconfirmation and information in hypothesis testing. *Psychological Review, 94,* 211–228.

KLAYMAN, J., & HA, Y. W. (1989). Hypothesis testing in rule discovery: Strategy, structure, and content. *Journal of Experimental Psychology: Learning, Memory, and Cognition, 15,* 596–604.

KNIGHT, R. T. (1984). Decreased response to novel stimuli after prefrontal lessions in man. *Electroencephalography and Clinical Neurophysiology, 59,* 9–20.

KOCEL, K., GALIN, D., ORNSTEIN, R., & MERRIN, R. (1972). Lateral eye movement and cognitive mode. *Psychonomic Science, 27,* 223–224.

KOHLER, W. (1925). *The mentality of apes.* New York: Harcourt Brace Jovanovich.

KOHLER, W. (1929). *Gestalt psychology.* New York: Liveright.

KOLB, B., & WHISHAW, I. Q. (1990). *Fundamentals of human neuropsychology.* New York: Freeman.

KOTOVSKY, K., & SIMON, H. A. (1973). Empirical tests of a theory of human acquisition of concepts for sequential patterns. *Cognitive Psychology, 4,* 399–424.

KUHN, D. (1974). Inducing development experimentally: Components on a research paradigm. *Developmental Psychology, 10,* 590–600.

KULKARI, D., & SIMON, H. A. (1988). The process of scientific discovery: The strategy of experimentation. *Cognitive Science, 12,* 139–175.

KULPE, O. (1964). The modem psychology of thinking. In J. M. Mandler and G. Mandler (Eds.), *Thinking: From association to Gestalt.* New York: Wiley. (Original work published in German 1912)

KUNDEL, H. L., & NODINE, C. F. (1975). Interpreting chest radiographs without visual search. *Radiology, 116,* 527–532.

KUTAS, M., & HILLYARD, S. A. (1984). Event–related potentials in cognitive science. In M. S. Gazzaniga (Ed.), *Handbook of cognitive neuroscience.* New York: Plenum.

LANDAUER, T. K., & MEYER, D. E. (1972). Category size and semantic-memory retrieval. *Journal of Verbal Learning and Verbal Behavior, 11,* 539–549.

LANGLEY, P., SIMON, H. A., BRADSHAW, G. L., & ZYTKOW, J. M. (1987). *Scientific discovery: Computational explorations of the creative processes.* Cambridge, MA: M.I.T. Press.

LARKIN, J. H. (1979). Information processing models and science instruction. In J. Lochhead & J. Clement (Eds.), *Cognitive process instruction.* Philadelphia: Franklin Institute Press.

LARKIN, J. H. (1983). The role of problem representation in physics. In D. Gentner & A. L. Stevens (Eds.), *Mental models.* Hillsdale, NJ: Erlbaum.

LARKIN, J. H., MCDERMOTT, J., SIMON, D. P., & SIMON, H. A. (1980). Expert and novice performance in solving physics problems. *Science, 208,* 1335–1342.

LARKIN, J. H., MCDERMOTT, J., SIMON, D. P., & SIMON, H. A. (1980b). Models of competence in solving physics problems. *Cognitive Science, 4,* 317–348.

LAVE, J. (1988). *Cognition in practice.* Cambridge, England: Cambridge University Press.

LEFFORD, A. (1946). The influence of emotional subject matter on logical reasoning. *Journal of General Psychology, 34,* 127–151.

LENNEBURG, E. H. (1957). A probabilistic approach to language learning. *Behavioral Science, 2,* 1–12.

LESGOLD, A. M. (1984). Acquiring expertise. In J. R. Anderson & S. M. Kosslyn (Eds.), *Tutorials in learning and memory.* New York: Freeman.

LESGOLD, A., RUBINSON, H., FELTOVICH, P., GLASER, R., KLOPFER, D., & WANG, Y. (1988). Expertise in a complex skill: Diagnosing X-ray pictures. In M. T. H. Chi, R. Glaser, & M. J. Farr (Eds.), *The nature of expertise.* Hillsdale, NJ: Erlbaum.

LESTER, F. K. (1983). Trends and issues in mathematical problem solving research. In R. Lesh & M. Landau (Eds.), *Acquisition of mathematics concepts and processes.* New York: Academic Press.

LEVINE, M. (1966). Hypothesis behavior by humans during discrimination learning. *Journal of Experimental Psychology, 71,* 331–338.

LEWIS, A. B. (1989). Training students to represent arithmentic word problems. *Journal of Educational Psychology, 81,* 521–531.

LEWIS, A. B., & MAYER, R. E. (1987). Students' miscomprehension of relational statements in arithmetic word problems. *Journal of Educational Psychology, 79,* 363–371.

LEWIS, C. (1981). Skill in algebra. In J. R. Anderson (Ed.), *Cognitive skills and their acquisition.* Hillsdale, NJ: Erlbaum.

LINDSAY, P. H., & NORMAN, D. A. (1972). *Human information processing: An introduction to psychology.* New York: Academic Press.

LOCHHEAD, J. (1979). An introduction to cognitive process instruction. In J. Lochhead and J. Clement (Eds.), *Cognitive process instruction.* Philadelphia: Franklin Institute Press.

LOCKHART, R. S., LAMON, M., & GICK, M. L. (1988). Conceptual transfer in simple insight problems. *Memory & Cognition, 16,* 36–44.

LUCHINS, A. S. (1942). Mechanization in problem solving. *Psychological Monographs, 54:6,* Whole No. 248.

LUCHINS, A. S., & LUCHINS, E. H. (1950). New experimental attempts at preventing mechanization in problem solving. *Journal of General Psychology, 42,* 279–297.

LUCHINS, A. S., & LUCHINS, E. H. (1970). *Wertheimer's seminars revisited: Problem solving and thinking.* Albany: State University of New York.

LUNG, C., & DOMINOWSKI, R. L. (1985). Effects of strategy instructions and practice on nine dot problem solving. *Journal of Experimental Psychology: Learning, Memory, & Cognition, 11,* 804–811.

MACHADO, L. A. (1981). The development of intelligence: A political outlook. *Intelligence, 5,* 2–4.

MACLEOD, C. M., HUNT, E. B., & MATHEWS, N. N. (1978). Individual differences in the verification of sentence-picture relationships. *Journal of Verbal Learning and Verbal Behavior, 17,* 493–508.

MAIER, N. R. F. (1930). Reasoning in humans I: On direction. *Journal of Comparative Psychology, 10,* 115–143.

MAIER, N. R. F. (1931). Reasoning in humans II: The solution of a problem and its appearance in consciousness. *Journal of Comparative Psychology, 12,* 181–194.

MAIER, N. R. F. (1933). An aspect of human reasoning. *British Journal of Psychology, 14,* 144–155.

MAIER, N. R. F. (1945). Reasoning in humans III: The mechanisms of equivalent stimuli of reasoning. *Journal of Experimental Psychology, 35,* 349–360.

MAIER, N. R. F., & BURKE, R. J. (1967). Response availability as a factor in the problem-solving performance of males and females. *Journal of Personality and Social Psychology, 5,* 304–310.

MALTZMAN, I. (1955). Thinking: From a behavioristic point of view. *Psychological Review, 62,* 275–286.

MALTZMAN, I., & MORRISETT, L. (1952). Different strengths of set in solution of anagrams. *Journal of Experimental Psychology, 44,* 242–246.

MALTZMAN, I., & MORRISETT, L. (1953). Effects of task instructions on solution of different classes of anagrams. *Journal of Experimental Psychology, 45,* 351–354.

MANDLER, J. M., & JOHNSON, N. S. (1977). Remembrance of things parsed: Story structure and recall. *Cognitive Psychology, 9,* 111–151.

MANDLER, J. M., & MANDLER, G. (1964). *Thinking: From association to Gestalt.* New York: Wiley.

MANKTELOW, K. I., & EVANS, J. ST. B. T. (1979). Facilitation of reasoning by realism: Effect or non-effect? *British Journal of Psychology, 70,* 477–488.

MANSFIELD, R. S., BUSSE, T. V., & KREPELKA, E. J. (1978). The effectiveness of creativity training. *Review of Educational Research, 48,* 517–536.

MARBE, K. (1964). The psychology of judgments. In J. M. Mandler and G. Mandler (Eds.), *Thinking: From association to Gestalt.* New York: Wiley. (Original work published in German 1901)

MARKMAN, E. (1979). Realizing that you don't understand: Elementary school children's awareness of inconsistencies. *Child Development, 50,* 643–655.

MARKOVITS, H. (1987). Incorrect conditional reasoning: Competence or performance? *British Journal of Psychology, 76,* 241–247.

MARKOVITS, H. (1988). Conditional reasoning, representation, and empirical evidence on a concrete task. *Quarterly Journal of Experimental Psychology, 40A,* 483–495.

MARKOVITS, H., & NANTEL, G. (1989). The belief-bias in the production and evaluation of logical conclusions. *Memory & Cognition, 17,* 11–17.

MARR, D. (1982). *Vision.* New York: Freeman.

MARTIN, E., & ROBERTS, K. H. (1967). Sentence length and sentence retention in the free-learning situation. *Psychonomic Science, 8,* 535–536.

MAX, L. W. (1935). Experimental study of the motor theory of consciousness: III. Action-current responses in deaf-mutes during sleep, sensory stimulation, and dreams. *Journal of Comparative Psychology, 19,* 469–486.

MAX, L. W. (1937). Experimental study of the motor theory of consciousness: IV. Action-current responses in the deaf during awakening, kinesthetic imagery and abstract thinking. *Journal of Comparative Psychology, 24,* 301–344.

MAYER, R. E. (1975). Different problem-solving competencies established in learning computer programming with and without meaningful models. *Journal of Educational Psychology, 67,* 725–734.

MAYER, R. E. (1979). Qualitatively different encoding strategies for linear reasoning premises: Evidence for single association and distance theories. *Journal of Experimental Psychology: Human Learning and Memory, 5,* 1–10.

MAYER, R. E. (1981a). Frequency norms and structural analysis of algebra story problems into families, categories, and templates. *Instructional Science, 10,* 135–175.

MAYER, R. E. (1981b). *The promise of cognitive psychology.* New York: Freeman.

MAYER, R. E. (1982a). Different problem-solving strategies for algebra word and equation problems. *Journal of Experimental Psychology: Learning, Memory, and Cognition, 8,* 448–462.

MAYER, R. E. (1982b). Memory for algebra story problems. *Journal of Educational Psychology, 74,* 199–216.

MAYER, R. E. (1983). Can you repeat that? Qualitative effects of repetition and advance organizers on learning from science prose. *Journal of Educational Psychology, 75,* 40–49.

MAYER, R. E. (1985a). Learning in complex domains: A cognitive analysis of computer programming. In G. Bower (Ed.), *Psychology of learning and motivation* (Vol. 19). Orlando, FL: Academic Press.

MAYER, R. E. (1985b). Mathematical ability. In R. J. Sternberg (Ed.), *Human abilities: An information processing approach.* New York: Freeman.

MAYER, R. E. (1987a). *Educational psychology: A cognitive approach.* Boston: Little, Brown.

MAYER, R. E. (1987b). The elusive search for teachable aspects of problem solving. In J. Glover & R. Ronning (Eds.), *Historical foundations of educational psychology.* New York: Plenum.

MAYER, R. E. (1988). From novice to expert. In M. Helander (Ed.), *Handbook of human-computer interaction.* Amsterdam: Elsevier.

MAYER, R. E. (1989a). *Teaching for thinking: Research on the teachability of thinking skills.* In I. S. Cohen (Ed.), *The G. Stanley Hall Lecture Series* (Vol. 9). Washington, DC: American Psychological Association.

MAYER, R. E. (1989b). Introduction to special issue on cognition and instruction in mathematics. *Journal of Educational Psychology, 81,* 452–456.

MAYER, R. E., & GALLINI, J. (1990). When is an illustration worth ten thousand words? *Journal of Educational Psychology, 82,* 715–726.

MAYER, R. E., & GREENO, J. G. (1972). Structural differences between learning outcomes produced by different instructional methods. *Journal of Educational Psychology, 63,* 165–173.

MAYER, R. E., LARKIN, J. H., & KADANE, J. (1983). A cognitive analysis of mathematical problem solving ability. In R. Sternberg (Ed.), *Advances in the psychology of human intelligence* (Vol. 2). Hillsdale, NJ: Erlbaum.

MAYZNER, M. S., & TRESSELT, M. E. (1958). Anagram solution times: A function of letter-order and word frequency. *Journal of Experimental Psychology, 56,* 350–376.

MAYZNER, M. S., & TRESSELT, M. E. (1959). Anagram solution times: A function of transition probabilities. *Journal of Psychology, 47,* 117–125.

MAYZNER, M. S., & TRESSELT, M. E. (1962). Anagram solution times: A function of word transition probabilities. *Journal of Experimental Psychology, 63,* 510–513.

MAYZNER, M. S., & TRESSELT, M. E. (1963). Anagram solution times: A function of word length and letter position variables. *Journal of Psychology, 55,* 469–475.

MAYZNER, M. S., & TRESSELT, M. E. (1966). Anagram solution times: A function of multiple-solution anagrams. *Journal of Experimental Psychology, 71,* 66–73.

MCCLELLAND, J. L., RUMELHART, D. E., & THE PDP RESEARCH GROUP. (Eds.). (1986). *Parallel distributed processing: Explorations in the microstructure of cognition* (Vol. 2). Cambridge, MA: M.I.T. Press.

MCGUIGAN, F. J. (1966). *Thinking: Studies of convert language processes.* New York: Appleton-Century-Crofts.

MCGUIGAN, F. J. (1973). Electrical measurement of covert processes as an explication of "higher mental events." In F. J. McGuigan & R. A. Schoonover (Eds.), *The psychobiology of thinking.* New York: Academic Press.

MCGUIGAN, F. J., KELLER, B., & STANTON, E. (1964). Covert language responses during silent reading. *Journal of Educational Psychology, 55,* 339–343.

MCGUIRE, W. J. (1960). A syllogistic analysis of cognitive relationships. In M. J. Rosenberg and C. I. Hovland (Eds.), *Attitude organization and change.* New Haven, CT: Yale University Press.

MCKEACHIE, W. J., & DOYLE, C. L. (1970). *Psychology.* Reading, MA: Addison-Wesley, 1970.

MCKEITHEN, K. B., REITMAN, J. S., RUETER, H. H., & HIRTLE, S. C. (1981). Knowledge organization and skill differences in computer programmers. *Cognitive Psychology, 13,* 307–325.

MCLEOD, D. B., & ADAMS, V. M. (Eds.). (1989). *Affect and mathematical problem solving.* New York: Springer-Verlag.

MEDIN, D. L., & SMITH, E. E. (1984). Concepts and concept formation. *Annual Review of Psychology, 35,* 113–138.

MEHLER, J. (1963). Some effects of grammar transformations on the recall of English sentences. *Journal of Verbal Learning and Verbal Behavior, 2,* 346–351.

MESSER, A. (1964). Experimental-psychological investigations on thinking. In J. M. Mandler & G. Mandler (Eds.), *Thinking: From association to Gestalt.* New York: Wiley. (Original work published in German 1906)

METCALFE, J. (1986a). Feeling of knowing in memory and problem solving. *Journal of Experimental Psychology: Learning, Memory, and Cognition, 12,* 288–294.

METCALFE, J. (1986b). Premonitions of insight predict impending error. *Journal of Experimental Psychology: Learning, Memory, and Cognition, 12,* 623–634.

METCALFE, J., & WIEBE, D. (1987). Intuition in insight and noninsight problem solving. *Memory & Cognition, 15,* 238–246.

METZLER, J., & SHEPARD, R. N. (1974). Transformational studies of the internal representation of three-dimensional objects. In R. L. Solso (Ed.), *Theories in cognitive psychology: The Loyola Symposium.* Hillsdale, NJ: Erlbaum.

MEYER, B. J. F. (1975). *The organization of prose and its effects on memory*. Amsterdam: North-Holland.

MEYER, B. J. F. (1977). The structure of prose: Effects on learning and memory and implications for educational practice. In R. C. Anderson, R. J. Spiro, and W. E. Montague (Eds.), *Schooling and the acquisition of knowledge*. Hillsdale, NJ: Erlbaum.

MEYER, B. J. F., & MCCONKIE, G. W. (1973). What is recalled after hearing a passage? *Journal of Educational Psychology, 65,* 109–117.

MEYER, D. E. (1970). On the representation and retrieval of stored semantic information. *Cognitive Psychology, 1,* 242–300.

MILLER, G. A. (1962). Some psychological studies of grammar. *American Psychologist, 17,* 748–762.

MILLER, G. A., GALANTER, E., & PRIBRAM, K. H. (1960). *Plans and the structure of behavior*. New York: Holt, Rinehart and Winston.

MINSKY, M. (1975). A framework for representing knowledge. In P. H. Winston (Ed.), *The psychology of computer vision*. New York: McGraw-Hill.

MOELY, B. E., OLSON, F. A., HALWES, T. G., & FLAVELL, J. H. (1969). Production deficiency in young children's clustered recall. *Developmental Psychology, 1,* 26–34.

MORGAN, J. J. B., & MORTON, J. T. (1944). The distortion of syllogistic reasoning produced by personal convictions. *Journal of Social Psychology, 20,* 39–59.

MURRAY, F. B. (1978). Teaching strategies and conservation training. In A. M. Lesgold, J. W. Pellegrino, S. D. Fokkema, & R. Glaser (Eds.), *Cognitive psychology and instruction*. New York: Plenum.

MYERS, R. E., & TORRANCE, E. P. (1964). *Invitations to thinking and doing*. Boston: Ginn.

MYLES-WORSLEY, M., JOHNSON, W. A., & SIMONS, M. A. (1988). The influence of expertise on X-ray image processing. *Journal of Experimental Psychology: Learning, Memory, and Cognition, 14,* 553–557.

NAIR, P. (1963). *An experiment in conservation*. Cambridge, MA: Harvard University Center for Cognitive Studies, Annual Report.

NATIONAL COUNCIL OF TEACHERS OF MATHEMATICS. (1980). *An agenda for action: Recommendations for school mathematics of the 1980s*. Reston, VA: National Council of Teachers of Mathematics.

NATIONAL EDUCATIONAL ASSOCIATION. (1961). *The central purpose of American education*. Washington, DC: National Educational Association. (Also reprinted in A. E. Lawson. *The psychology of thinking for thinking and creativity*. Columbus, OH: ERIC Clearinghouse for Science, Mathematics, and Environmental Education, 1979.)

NEIMARK, E. D., & SANTA, J. L. (1975). Thinking and concept attainment. In M. R. Rosenzweig & L. W. Porter (Eds.), *Annual Review of Psychology* (Vol. 26). Palo Alto, CA: Annual Reviews.

NEISSER, U. (1976). *Cognition and reality: Principles and implications of cognitive psychology*. New York: Freeman.

NEISSER, U., & LAZAR, R. (1964). Searching for novel targets. *Perceptual Motor Skills, 19,* 427–432.

NEISSER, U., NOVICK, R., & LAZAR, R. (1963). Searching for ten targets simultaneously. *Perceptual Motor Skills, 17,* 955–961.

NEUMANN, P. G. (1977). Visual prototype formation with discontinuous representation of dimensions of variability. *Memory and Cognition, 5,* 187–197.

NEWELL, A., & SIMON, H. A. (1972). *Human problem solving.* Englewood Cliffs, NJ: Prentice-Hall.

NEWELL, A., SHAW, J. C., & SIMON, H. A. (1958). Chess-playing programs and the problem of complexity. *IBM Journal of Research and Development, 2,* 320–335.

NEWELL, A., SHAW, J. C., & SIMON, H. A. (1957). Empirical exploration of the logic theory machine: A case study in heuristics. *Proceedings of the joint computer conference,* 218–230.

NEWPORT, E. L., & BELLUGI, U. (1978). Linguistic expression of category levels in a visual-gestural language: A flower is a flower is a flower. In E. Rosch & B. B. Lloyd (Eds.), *Cognition and categorization.* Hillsdale, NJ: Erlbaum.

NICKERSON, R. S., PERKINS, D. N., & SMITH, E. E. (1985). *The teaching of thinking.* Hillsdale, NJ: Erlbaum.

NOELTING, G. (1980). The development of proportional reasoning and the ratio concept. *Educational Studies in Mathematics, 11,* 217–253, 331–363.

NORMAN, D. A. (1980). Cognitive engineering and education. In D. T. Tuma and F. Reif (Eds.), *Problem solving and education: Issues in teaching and learning.* Hillsdale, NJ: Erlbaum.

NOVICK, L. R. (1988). Analogical transfer, problem similarity, and expertise. *Journal of Experimental Psychology: Learning, Memory, and Cognition, 14,* 510–520.

OAKHILL, J. V., & JOHNSON-LAIRD, P. N. (1985). The effects of belief on the spontaneous production of syllogistic conclusions. *Quarterly Journal of Experimental Psychology, 37A,* 553–569.

OHLSSON, S. (1984a). Restructuring revisited: I. A summary and critique of the Gestalt theory of problem solving. *Scandinavian Journal of Psychology, 25,* 65–78.

OHLSSON, S. (1984b). Restructuring revisited: II. An information processing theory of restructuring and insight. *Scandinavian Journal of Psychology, 25,* 117–129.

OLTON, R. M. (1979). Experimental studies of incubation: Searching for the elusive. *Journal of Creative Behavior, 13,* 9–22.

OLTON, R. M., & CRUTCHFIELD, R. S. (1969). Developing the skills of productive thinking. In P. Mussen, J. Langer, & M. V. Covington (Eds.), *New directions in developmental psychology.* New York: Holt, Rinehart and Winston.

OLTON, R. M., & JOHNSON, D. M. (1976). Mechanisms of incubation in creative problem solving. *American Journal of Psychology, 89,* 616–630.

OLVER, R. R., & HORNSBY, J. R. (1966). On equivalence. In J. S. Bruner, R. R. Olver, & P. M. Greenfield (Eds.), *Studies in cognitive growth.* New York: Wiley.

OSBORN, A. F. (1963). *Applied imagination.* New York: Scribner's.

OSGOOD, C. E. (1957). A behavioral analysis of perception and language as cognitive phenomena. In J. S. Bruner (Ed.), *Contemporary approaches to cognition.* Cambridge, MA: Harvard University Press.

OSGOOD, C. E. (1966). Meaning cannot be an r_m? *Journal of Verbal Learning and Verbal Behavior, 5,* 402–407.

OSLER, S. F., & FIVEL, M. W. (1961). Concept attainment: 1. The role of age and intelligence in concept attainment by induction. *Journal of Experimental Psychology, 62,* 1–8.

PAIGE, J. M., & SIMON, H. A. (1966). Cognitive processes in solving algebra word problems. In B. Kleinmuntz (Ed.), *Problem solving: Research, method and theory.* New York: Wiley.

PAIVIO, A. (1971). *Imagery and verbal processes.* New York: Holt, Rinehart and Winston.

PAIVIO, A. (1990). *Mental representations: A dual coding approach.* New York: Oxford University Press.

PALERMO, D. S. (1963). Word associations and children's verbal behavior. In L. P. Lipsitt & C. C. Spiker (Eds.), *Advances in child development and behavior* (Vol. 1). New York: Academic Press.

PALERMO, D. S., & JENKINS, J. J. (1963). *Word association norms: Grade school through college.* Minneapolis: University of Minnesota Press.

PARIS, S. G., & LINDAUER, B. K. (1976). The role of inference in children's comprehension and memory for sentences. *Cognitive Psychology, 8,* 217–227.

PARIS, S. G., LINDAUER, B. K., & COX, G. L. (1977). The development of inferential comprehension. *Child Development, 48,* 1728–1733.

PARNES, S. J. (1967). *Creative behavior guidebook.* New York: Scribner's.

PARROTT, G. L. (1969). The effects of instructions, transfer, and content on reasoning time. Unpublished doctoral dissertation, Michigan State University.

PASCAUL-LEONE, J. (1970). A mathematical model for the transition rule in Piaget's developmental stages. *Acta Psychologica, 32,* 301–345.

PATEL, V., & GROEN, G. J. (1986). Knowledge based solution strategies in medical reasoning. *Cognitive Science, 10,* 91–116.

PELLEGRINO, J. W. (1985). Inductive reasoning ability. In R. J. Sternberg (Ed.), *Human abilities: An information-processing approach.* New York: Freeman.

PELLEGRINO, J. W., & GLASER, R. (1979). Cognitive correlates and components in the analysis of individual differences. In R. J. Sternberg & D. K. Determan (Eds.), *Human intelligence.* Norwood, NJ: Ablex.

PELLEGRINO, J. W., & LYON, D. R. (1979). The components of a componential analysis. *Intelligence, 3,* 169–186.

PERFETTO, G. A., BRANSFORD, J. D., & FRANKS, J. J. (1983). Constraints on access in a problem-solving context. *Memory & Cognition, 11,* 24–31.

PETERSON, L. R., & PETERSON, M. J. (1959). Short-term retention of individual verbal items. *Journal of Experimental Psychology, 58,* 193–198.

PHILLIPS, J. L. (1969). *The origins of intellect: Piaget's theory.* San Francisco: Freeman.

PIAGET, J. (1932). *The moral judgment of the child.* New York: Harcourt Brace Jovanovich. (M. Gabain, Trans.)

PIAGET, J. (1951). *Play, dreams and imitation in childhood.* New York: Norton. (C. Gattegno & F. M. Hodgson, Trans.; original French edition, 1945)

PIAGET, J. (1952a). *The child's conception of number*. London: Routledge & Kegan Paul. (C. Gattegno & F. M. Hodgson, Trans.; original French edition, 1941)

PIAGET, J. (1952b). *The origins of intelligence in children*. New York: International Universities Press. (M. Cook, Trans.; original French edition, 1936)

PIAGET, J. (1954). *The construction of reality in the child*. New York: Basic Books, 1954. (M. Cook, Trans.; original French edition, 1937)

PIAGET, J., & INHELDER, B. (1956). *The child's conception of space*. London: Routledge & Kegan Paul, 1956. (F. J. Langdon & J. L. Lunzer, Trans.; original French edition, 1948)

PICHERT, J., & ANDERSON, R. C. (1977). Taking different perspectives on a story. *Journal of Educational Psychology, 69*, 309–315.

POINCARÉ, H. (1913). Mathematical creation. In *The foundations of science*. (G. H. Halstead, Trans.) New York: Science Press.

POLSON, P. G., & JEFFRIES, R. (1985). Instruction in general problem-solving: An analysis of four approaches. In J. W. Segal, S. F. Chipman, & R. Glaser (Eds.), *Thinking and learning skills: Vol. 1. Relating instruction to research*. Hillsdale, NJ: Erlbaum.

POLYA, G. (1957). *How to solve it*. Garden City, NY: Doubleday/Anchor. (Originally published by Princeton University Press 1945).

POLYA, G. (1965). Mathematical discovery. Vol. II: *On understanding, learning and teaching problem solving*. New York: Wiley.

POPLE, H. (1977). Problem solving: An exercise in synthetic reasoning. *Proceedings of the fifth international joint conference on artificial intelligence*. Pittsburgh: Carnegie-Mellon University.

POPPER, K. R. (1959). *The logic of scientific discovery*. New York: Harper & Row.

POSNER, M. I. (1969). Abstraction and the process of recognition. In G. H. Bower & J. T. Spence (Eds.), *The psychology of learning and motivation* (Vol. 3). New York: Academic Press.

POSNER, M. I. (1978). *Chronometric explorations of mind*. Hillsdale, NJ: Erlbaum, 1978.

POSNER, M. I. (1988). What is an expert? In M. T. H. Chi, R. Glaser, & M. J. Farr (Eds.), *The nature of expertise*. Hillsdale, NJ: Erlbaum.

POSNER, M. I., BOIES, S. J., EICHELMAN, W. H., & TAYLOR, R. L. (1969). Retention of visual and name codes of single letters. *Journal of Experimental Psychology, 79*, 1–16.

POSNER, M. I., & KEELE, S. W. (1968). On the genesis of abstract ideas. *Journal of Experimental Psychology, 77*, 353–363.

POSNER, M. I., & KEELE, S. W. (1970). Retention of abstract ideas. *Journal of Experimental Psychology, 83*, 304–308.

POSNER, M. I., LEWIS, J., & CONRAD, C. (1972). Component processes in reading: A performance analysis. In J. Kavanaugh & I. Mattingly (Eds.), *Language by ear and by eye*. Cambridge, MA: M.I.T. Press.

POSNER, M. I., & MITCHELL, R. F. (1967). Chronometric analysis of classification. *Psychological Review, 74*, 392–409.

POTTS, G. R. (1972). Information processing strategies used in the encoding of linear orderings. *Journal of Verbal Learning and Verbal Behavior, 11*, 727–740.

POTTS, G. R. (1974). Storing and retrieving information about ordered relationships. *Journal of Experimental Psychology, 103,* 431–439.

POTTS, G. R. (1978). The role of inference in memory for real and artificial information. In R. Revlin & R. E. Mayer (Eds.), *Human reasoning.* Washington, DC: Winston/Wiley.

PRESTON, M. S., GUTHRIE, J. T., & CHILDS, B. (1974). Visual evoked responses in normal and disabled readers. *Psychophysiology, 11,* 452–457.

RAAHEIM, K. (1965). Problem solving and past experience. In P. H. Mussen (Ed.), European research in cognitive development. *Monograph Supplement of the Society for Research on Child Development, 30,* No. 2.

RAEBURN, V. P. (1974). Priorities in item recognition. *Memory and Cognition, 2,* 663–669.

REED, S. K. (1972). Pattern recognition and categorization. *Cognitive Psychology, 3,* 382–407.

REED, S. K. (1987). A structure-mapping model for word problems. *Journal of Experimental Psychology: Learning, Memory, and Cognition, 13,* 124–139.

REED, S. K., DEMPSTER, A., & ETTINGER, M. (1985). Usefulness of analogous solutions for solving algebra word problems. *Journal of Experimental Psychology: Learning, Memory, and Cognition, 11,* 106–125.

REED, S. K., ERNST, G. W., & BANERJI, R. (1974). The role of analogy in transfer between similar problem states. *Cognitive Psychology, 6,* 436–450.

REES, H. J., & ISRAEL, H. E. (1935). An investigation of the establishment and operation of mental sets. *Psychological Monographs, 46,* No. 210.

REITMAN, W. R. (1965). *Cognition and thought: An information processing approach.* New York: Wiley.

RESNICK, L. B. (1976). Task analysis in instructional design: Some cases from mathematics. In D. Klahr (Ed.), *Cognition and instruction.* Hillsdale, NJ: Erlbaum.

RESNICK, L. B. (1987). Learning in school and out. *Educational Researcher, 16(9),* 13–20.

RESNICK, L. B., & FORD, W. (1981). *The psychology of mathematics for instruction.* Hillsdale, NJ: Erlbaum.

RESNICK, L. B., & FORD, W. W. (1981). *The psychology of mathematics for instruction.* Hillsdale, NJ: Erlbaum.

RESTLE, F. (1962). The selection of strategies in cue learning. *Psychological Review 69,* 329–343.

RESTLE, F., & GREENO, J. G. (1970). *Introduction to mathematical psychology.* Reading, MA: Addison-Wesley.

REVLIN, R., & LEIRER, V. O. (1978). The effect of personal biases on syllogistic reasoning: Rational decisions from personalized representations. In R. Revlin & R. E. Mayer (Eds.), *Human reasoning.* Washington, DC: Winston/Wiley.

REVLIN, R., LEIRER, V., YOPP, H., & YOPP, R. (1980). The belief bias effect in formal reasoning: The influence of knowledge on logic. *Memory & Cognition, 8,* 584–592.

REVLIS, R. (1975). Two models of syllogistic reasoning: Feature selection and conversion. *Journal of Verbal Learning and Verbal Behavior, 14,* 180–195.

RILEY, C. A. (1976). The representation of comparative relations and the transitive inference task. *Journal of Experimental Child Psychology, 22,* 1–22.

RILEY, C. A., & TRABASSO, T. (1974). Comparatives, logical structures and encoding in a transitive inference task. *Journal of Experimental Child Psychology, 17,* 187–203.

RILEY, M. S., GREENO, J. G., & HELLER, J. I. (1983). Development of children's problem–solving ability. In H. P. Ginsburg (Ed.), *The development of mathematical thinking.* New York: Academic Press.

RIPPA, S. A. (1980). *Education in a free society: An American history.* New York: Longman.

RIPS, L. J. (1990). Reasoning. *Annual Review of Psychology, 41,* 321–353.

RIPS, L. J., & MARCUS, S. L. (1977). Suppositions and the analysis of conditional sentences. In M. A. Just & P. A. Carpenter (Eds.), *Cognitive processes in comprehension.* Hillsdale, NJ: Erlbaum.

RIPS, L. J., SHOBEN, E. J., & SMITH, E. E. (1973). Semantic distance and the verification of semantic relations. *Journal of Verbal Learning and Verbal Behavior, 12,* 1–20.

ROBITAILLE, D. F., & GARDEN, R. A. (1989). *The IEA study of mathematics II: Contexts and outcomes of school mathematics.* Oxford, England: Pergamon.

ROGERS, C. R. (1961). *On becoming a person: A therapist's view of psychotherapy.* Boston: Houghton Mifflin.

ROGOFF, B. (1984). Introduction: Thinking and learning in social context. In B. Rogoff & J. Lave (Eds.), *Everyday cognition: Its development in social context.* Cambridge, MA: Harvard University Press.

ROGOFF, B. (1990). *Apprenticeship in thinking.* New York: Oxford University Press.

ROGOFF, B., & LAVE, J. (Eds.). (1984). *Everyday cognition: Its development in social context.* Cambridge, MA: Harvard University Press.

ROLAND, P. E., ERIKSSON, L., STONE-ELANDER, S., & WIDEN, L. (1987). Does mental activity change the oxidative metabolism of the brain? *Journal of Neuroscience, 7,* 2372–2389.

ROLAND, P. E., & FRIBERG, L. (1985). Localization of cortical areas activated by thinking. *Journal of Neurophysiology, 53,* 1219–1243.

ROSCH, E. (1975). Cognitive representations of semantic categories. *Journal of Experimental Psychology: General, 104,* 192–233.

ROSCH, E. (1978). Principles of categorization. In E. Rosch & B. B. Lloyd (Eds.), *Cognition and categorization.* Hillsdale, NJ: Erlbaum.

ROSCH, E., & MERVIS, C. B. (1975). Family resemblances: Studies in the internal structure of categories. *Cognitive Psychology, 7,* 573–605.

ROSCH, E. H. (1973). Natural categories. *Cognitive Psychology, 4,* 328–350.

ROSCH, E. H., MERVIS, C. B., GRAY, W. D., JOHNSON, D. M., & BOYES-BRAEM, P. (1976). Basic objects in natural categories. *Cognitive Psychology, 8,* 382–439.

ROSENTHAL, R., & JACOBSON, L. (1968). *Pygmalion in the classroom.* New York: Holt, Rinehart and Winston.

ROSS, B. H. (1984). Remindings and their effects in learning a cognitive skill. *Cognitive Psychology, 16,* 371–416.

ROSS, B. H. (1987). This is like that: The use of earlier problems and the separation of similarity effects. *Journal of Experimental Psychology: Learning, Memory, and Cognition, 13,* 629–639.

ROSS, B. H. (1989). Distinguishing types of superficial similarities: Different effects on the access and use of earlier problems. *Journal of Experimental Psychology: Learning, Memory, and Cognition, 15,* 456–468.

ROUGHEAD, W. G., & SCANDURA, J. M. (1968). What is learned in mathematical discovery. *Journal of Educational Psychology, 59,* 283–289.

RUGER, H. (1910). The psychology of efficiency. *Archives of Psychology,* No. 15.

RUMELHART, D. E. (1975). Notes on a schema for stories. In D. G. Brown & A. Collins (Eds.), *Representation and understanding: Studies in cognitive science.* New York: Academic Press.

RUMELHART, D. E. (1977). *Introduction to human information processing.* New York: Wiley.

RUMELHART, D. E., LINDSAY, P. H., & NORMAN, D. A. (1972). A process model for long-term memory. In E. Tulving & W. Donaldson (Eds.), *Organization of memory.* New York: Academic Press.

RUMELHART, D. E., MCCLELLAND, J. L., & THE PDP RESEARCH GROUP. (Eds.). (1986). *Parallel distributed processing: Explorations in the microstructure of cognition* (Vol. 1). Cambridge, MA: M.I.T. Press.

SACHS, J. D. S. (1967). Recognition memory for syntactic and semantic aspects of connected discourse. *Perception and Psychophysics, 2,* 437–442.

SAFREN, M. A. (1962). Associations, set, and the solution of word problems. *Journal of Experimental Psychology, 64,* 40–45.

SAMUEL, A. L. (1963). Some studies in machine learning using the game of checkers. In E. A. Feigenbaum & J. Feldman (Eds.), *Computers and thought.* New York: McGraw-Hill.

SAPIR, E. (1960). *Culture, language, and personality.* Berkeley: University of California Press.

SAUGSTAD, P., & RAAHEIM, K. (1960). Problem solving, past experience and availability of functions. *British Journal of Psychology, 51,* 97–104.

SAXE, G. B. (1988). Candy selling and math learning. *Educational Researcher, 17*(6), 14–21.

SCHALLERT, D. L. (1976). Improving memory for prose: The relationship between depth of processing and context. *Journal of Verbal Learning and Verbal Behavior, 15,* 621–632.

SCHANK, R. C., & ABELSON, R. P. (1977). *Scripts, plans, goals, and understanding.* Hillsdale, NJ: Erlbaum.

SCHLIEMANN, A. D., & ACIOLY, N. M. (1989). Mathematical knowledge developed at work: The contribution of practice versus the contribution of schooling. *Cognition and Instruction, 6,* 185–221.

SCHOENFELD, A. H. (1985). *Mathematical problem solving.* Orlando, FL: Academic Press.

SCHOENFELD, H. H. (1979). Explicit heuristic training as a variable in problem solving performance. *Journal for Research in Mathematics Education, 10,* 173–187.

SCHOLZ, K. W., & POTTS, G. R. (1974). Cognitive processing of linear orderings. *Journal of Experimental Psychology, 102,* 323–326.

SCRIBNER, S. (1984). Studying working intelligence. In B. Rogoff & J. Lave (Eds.), *Everyday cognition: Its development in social context.* Cambridge, MA: Harvard University Press.

SCRIVEN, M. (1977). Comments. In R. C. Anderson, R. Spiro, and W. E. Montague (Eds.), *Schooling and the acquisition of knowledge.* Hillsdale, NJ: Erlbaum.

SEGAL, J. W., CHIPMAN, S. F., & GLASER, R. (Eds.). (1985). *Thinking and learning skills: Vol. 1. Relating instruction to research*. Hillsdale, NJ: Erlbaum.

SELLS, S. B. (1936). The atmosphere effect: An experimental study of reasoning. *Archives of Psychology*, No. 200.

SELZ, O. (1982a). On the laws of ordered thinking. In N. H. Fridja & A. D. de Groot (Eds.), *Otto Selz: His contributions to psychology*. The Hague: Mouton. (Original work published in German 1913)

SELZ, O. (1982b). On the psychology of productive thinking and of error. In N. H. Fridja & A. D. de Groot (Eds.), *Otto Selz: His contributions to psychology*. The Hague: Mouton. (Original work published in German 1922.)

SHALLICE, T. (1982). Specific impairment of planning. In D. E. Broadbent & L. Weiskrantz (Eds.), *The neuropsychology of cognitive function*. London: The Royal Society.

SHALLICE, T. (1988). *From neuropsychology to mental structure*. Cambridge, England: Cambridge University Press.

SHALLICE, T., & EVANS, M. E. (1978). The involvement of the frontal lobes in cognitive estimation. *Cortex, 14*, 294–303.

SHEPARD, R. (1975). Form, formation, and transformation of internal representations. In R. L. Solso (Ed.), *Information processing and cognition: The Loyola Symposium*. Hillsdale, NJ: Erlbaum.

SHIELDS, D. T. (1973). Brain responses to stimuli in disorders of information processing. *Journal of Learning Disabilities, 6*, 501–505.

SHNEIDERMAN, B. (1976). Exploratory experiments in programmer behavior. *International Journal of Computer and Information Sciences, 5*, 123–143.

SHNEIDERMAN, B. (1980). *Software psychology*. Cambridge, MA: Winthrop.

SHORTLIFFE, E. (1976). *Computer-based medical consultations: MYCIN*. New York: Elsevier.

SHRAGER, J., & KLAHR, D. (1986). Instructionless learning about a complex device. *International Journal of Man-Machine Studies, 25*, 153–189.

SHULMAN, L. S., & KEISLER, E. R. (Eds.). (1966). *Learning by discovery*. Chicago: Rand McNally.

SIEGLER, R. S. (1976). Three aspects of cognitive development. *Cognitive Psychology, 4*, 481–520.

SIEGLER, R. S. (1978). The origins of scientific reasoning. In R. S. Siegler (Ed.), *Children's thinking: What develops?* Hillsdale, NJ: Erlbaum.

SIEGLER, R. S. (1981). Developmental sequences within and between concepts. *Monographs of the Society for Research in Child Development, 46* (No. 189).

SIEGLER, R. S. (1986). *Children's thinking*. Englewood Cliffs, NJ: Prentice-Hall.

SIEGLER, R. S. (1987). The perils of averaging data over strategies: An example from children's addition. *Journal of Experimental Psychology: General, 117*, 258–275.

SIEGLER, R. S. (1989a). Hazards of mental chronometry: An example from children's subtraction. *Journal of Educational Psychology, 81*, 497–506.

SIEGLER, R. S. (1989b). Mechanisms of cognitive growth. *Annual Review of Psychology, 40*, 353–379.

SIEGLER, R. S., & JENKINS, E. (1989). *How children discover new strategies*. Hillsdale, NJ: Erlbaum.

SILVER, E. (1981). Recall of mathematic problem information: Solving related problems. *Journal for Research in Mathematics Education, 12,* 54–64.

SIMON, H. A. (1962). An information processing theory of intellectual development. In W. Kessen & C. Kohlman (Eds.), *Thought in the young child. Society for Research in Child Development Monographs 27*(2), 150–155.

SIMON, H. A. (1969). The architecture of complexity. In H. A. Simon, *The sciences of the artificial.* Cambridge, MA: M.I.T. Press.

SIMON, H. A. (1978). Information processing theory of human problem solving. In W. K. Estes (Ed.), *Handbook of learning and cognitive processes.* Hillsdale, NJ: Erlbaum.

SIMON, H. A. (1979). *Models of thought.* New Haven, CT: Yale University Press.

SIMON, H. A. (1980). Problem solving and education. In D. T. Tuma & F. Reif (Eds.), *Problem solving and education: Issues in teaching and learning.* Hillsdale, NJ: Erlbaum.

SIMON, H. A. (1982). Otto Selz and information-processing psychology. In N. H. Fridja & A. D. de Groot (eds.), *Otto Selz: His contributions to psychology.* The Hague: Mouton.

SIMON, H. A., & HAYES, J. R. (1976). The understanding process: Problem isomorphs. *Cognitive Psychology, 8,* 165–190.

SIMON, H. A., & KOTOVSKY, K. (1963). Human acquisition of concepts for sequential patterns. *Psychological Review, 70,* 534–546.

SIMON, H. A., & REED, S. K. (1976). Modeling strategy shifts in a problem solving task. *Cognitive Psychology, 8,* 86–97.

SINGLEY, M. K., & ANDERSON, J. R. (1989). *The transfer of cognitive skill.* Cambridge, MA: Harvard University Press.

SKEMP, R. R. (1971). *The psychology of learning mathematics.* Harmondsworth, England: Penguin.

SKINNER, B. F. (1957). *Verbal behavior.* New York: Appleton-Century-Crofts.

SMITH, E. E., & MEDIN, D. L. (1981). *Categories and concepts.* Cambridge, MA: Harvard University Press.

SMITH, E. E., SHOBEN, E. J., & RIPS, L. J. (1974). Structure and process in semantic memory: A feature model of semantic decisions. *Psychological Review, 81,* 214–241.

SMITH, M. L., & MILNER, B. (1984). Differential effects of frontal-lobe lesions on cognitive estimation and spatial memory. *Neuropsychologia, 22,* 697–705.

SOLOWAY, E., & EHRLICH, K. (1984). Empirical studies of programming knowledge. *IEEE Transactions on Software Engineering, 10,* 595–609.

SOLOWAY, E., LOCHHEAD, J., & CLEMENT, J. (1982). Does computer programming enhance problem-solving ability? Some positive evidence on algebra word problems. In R. J. Seidel, R. E. Anderson, & B. Hunter (Eds.), *Computer literacy.* New York: Academic Press.

SPEARMAN, C. (1904). General intelligence objectively determined and measured. *American Journal of Psychology, 15,* 201–293.

SPEARMAN, C. (1927). *The abilities of man.* New York: Macmillan.

SQUIRES, N. K., & OLLO, C. (1986). Human evoked potential techniques: Possible applications to neuropsychology. In H. J. Hannay (Ed.), *Experimental techniques in human neuropsychology.* New York: Oxford University Press.

STAUDENMAYER, H. (1975). Understanding conditional reasoning with meaningful propositions. In R. J. Falmagne (Ed.), *Reasoning: Representation and process in children and adults.* Hillsdale, N. J.: Erlbaum.

STAUDENMAYER, H., & BOURNE, L. E. (1978). The nature of denied propositions in the conditional sentence reasoning task: Interpretation and learning. In R. Revlin & R. E. Mayer (Eds.), *Human reasoning.* New York: Wiley/Winston.

STERNBERG, R. J. (1977). *Intelligence, information processing, and analogical reasoning.* Hillsdale, NJ: Erlbaum.

STERNBERG, R. J. (1980a). Componentman as vice-president: A reply to Pellegrino and Lyon's analysis of "The components of a componential analysis." *Intelligence, 4,* 83–95.

STERNBERG, R. J. (1980b). Representation and process in linear syllogistic reasoning. *Journal of Experimental Psychology: General, 109,* 119–159.

STERNBERG, R. J. (1984). *Mechanisms of cognitive development.* New York: Freeman.

STERNBERG, R. J. (1985). *Beyond IQ: A triarchic theory of human intelligence.* Cambridge, England: Cambridge University Press.

STERNBERG, R. J. (1988). *The triarchic mind: A new theory of human intelligence.* New York: Viking.

STERNBERG, R. J. (1990). *Metaphors of mind: Conceptions of the nature of intelligence.* Cambridge, England: Cambridge University Press.

STERNBERG, R. J. (Ed.). (1982). *Handbook of human intelligence.* Cambridge, England: Cambridge University Press.

STERNBERG, R. J., & DETTERMAN, D. K. (Eds.). (1986). *What is intelligence? Contemporary views on its nature and definition.* Norwood, NJ: Ablex.

STERNBERG, R. J., & GARDNER, M. K. (1983). Unities in inductive reasoning. *Journal of Experimental Psychology: General, 112,* 80–116.

STERNBERG, R. J., & KETRON, J. L. (1982). Selection and implementation of strategies in reasoning by analogy. *Journal of Educational Psychology, 74,* 399–413.

STERNBERG, R. J., & NIGRO, G. (1983). Interaction and analogy in the comprehension and appreciation of metaphors. *Quarterly Journal of Experimental Psychology, 35A,* 17–38.

STERNBERG, R. J., & RIVKIN, B. (1979). The development of analogical reasoning processes. *Journal of Experimental Child Psychology, 27,* 195–232.

STERNBERG, R. J., & WEIL, E. M. (1980). An aptitude-strategy interaction in linear syllogistic reasoning. *Journal of Educational Psychology, 72,* 226–234.

STERNBERG, S. (1966). High speed scanning in human memory. *Science, 153,* 652–654.

STERNBERG, S. (1969). The discovery of processing stages: Extensions of Donders' method. *Acta Psychologica, 30,* 276–315.

STERNBERG, S. (1975). Memory scanning: New findings and current controversies. *Quarterly Journal of Experimental Psychology, 27,* 1–32.

STEVENS, A. L., & COLLINS, A. (1980). Multiple conceptual models of a complex system. In R. E. Snow, P. Federico, & W. E. Montague (Eds.), *Aptitude, learning and instruction* (Vol. 2). Hillsdale, NJ: Erlbaum.

STRATTON, R. P. (1967). Atmosphere and conversion errors in syllogistic reasoning with contextual material and the effect of differential training. Unpublished master's thesis, Michigan State University.

STRAUSS, S. (1972). Inducing cognitive development and learning: A review of short-term training experiments. *Cognition, 1,* 329–357.

STUSS, D. T., & BENSON, D. F. (1986). *The frontal lobes.* New York: Raven.

SUCHMAN, J. R. (1960). Inquiry training in the elementary school. *Science Teacher, 27,* 42–47.

SUCHMAN, J. R. (1966). *Inquiry development program in physical science.* Chicago: Science Research Associates.

SUCHMAN, J. R. (1969). *Evaluating inquiry in physical science.* Chicago: Science Research Associates.

SUCHMAN, L. A. (1987). *Plans and situated actions.* Cambridge, England: Cambridge University Press.

SUSSMAN, G. J., & Stallman, R. M. (1975). Heuristic techniques in computer aided circuit analysis. *IEEE Transactions on Circuits and Systems, 22*(11).

SUTTON, S., BRAREN, M., ZUBIN, J., & JOHN, E. R. (1965). Evoked potential correlates of stimulus uncertainty. *Science,* 150, 1187–1188.

TAPLIN, J. E., & STAUDENMAYER, H. (1973). Interpretation of abstract conditional sentences in deductive reasoning. *Journal of Verbal Learning and Verbal Behavior, 12,* 530–542.

TAYLOR, B. (1980). Children's memory for expository text after reading. *Reading Research Quarterly, 15,* 399–411.

TAYLOR, D. T., BERRY, P. C., & BLOCK, C. H. (1958). Does group participation when using brain-storming facilitate or inhibit creative thinking? *Administrator's Science Quarterly, 3,* 23–47.

THOMAS, J. C., JR. (1974). An analysis of behavior in the hobbits-orcs problem. *Cognitive Psychology, 6,* 257–269.

THORNDIKE, E. L. (1898). Animal intelligence: An experimental study of the associative processes in animals. *Psychological Monographs, 2*(8).

THORNDIKE, E. L. (1906). *Principles of teaching.* New York: Lemke & Buechner.

THORNDIKE, E. L. (1911). *Animal intelligence.* New York: Macmillan.

THORNDIKE, E. L. (1922). The effect of changed data upon reasoning. *Journal of Experimental Psychology, 15,* 1–22.

THORNDIKE, E. L., & LORGE, I. (1944). *A teacher's word book of 30,000 words.* New York: Columbia University Press.

THORNDIKE, E. L., & WOODWORTH, R. S. (1901). The influence of improvement in one mental function upon the efficiency of other functions. *Psychological Review, 8,* 247–261.

THORNDYKE, P. W. (1977). Cognitive structures in comprehension and memory of narrative discourse. *Cognitive Psychology, 9,* 77–110.

THURSTONE, L. L. (1938). *Primary mental abilities.* Chicago: University of Chicago Press.

TORRANCE, E. P. (1966). *Torrance tests of creative thinking.* Princeton, NJ: Personnel Press.

TORRANCE, E. P. (1972). Can we teach children to think creatively? *Journal of Creative Behavior, 6,* 114–143.

TORRANCE, E. P. (1984). Some products of 25 years of creativity research. *Educational Perspectives, 22,* 3–8.

TRABASSO, T., ISEN, A. M., DOLECKI, P., MCLANAHAN, A. G., RILEY, C. A., & TUCKER, T. (1978). How do children solve class-inclusion problems? In R. S. Siegler (Ed.), *Children's thinking: What develops?* Hillsdale, NJ: Erlbaum.

TRABASSO, T. R., & BOWER, G. H. (1964). Presolution reversal and dimensional shifts in concept identification. *Journal of Experimental Psychology, 67,* 398–399.

TRABASSO, T. R., & BOWER, G. H. (1968). *Attention in learning.* New York: Wiley.

TRABASSO, T. R., ROLLINS, H., & SHAUGHNESSY, E. (1971). Storage and verification stages in processing concepts. *Cognitive Psychology, 2,* 239–289.

TREFFINGER, D. J., & GOWAN, J. C. (1971). An updated representative list of methods and educational programs for stimulating creativity. *Journal of Creative Behavior, 5,* 127–139.

TRESSELT, M. E., & MAYZNER, M. S. (1966). Normative solution times for a sample of 134 solution words and 378 associated anagrams. *Psychonomic Monograph Supplement No. 15, 1,* 293–298.

TURING, A. M. (1950). Computing machinery and intelligence. *Mind, 59,* 433–450.

TVERSKY, A., & KAHNEMAN, D. (1973). Availability: A heuristic for judging frequency and probability. *Cognitive Psychology, 5,* 207–232.

TVERSKY, A., & KAHNEMAN, D. (1974). Judgment under uncertainty: Heuristics and biases. *Science, 185,* 1124–1131.

TVERSKY, A., & KAHNEMAN, D. (1982). Evidential impact of base rates. In D. Kahneman, P. Slovic, & A. Tversky (Eds.), *Judgment under uncertainty: Heuristics and biases.* Cambridge, England: Cambridge University Press.

TVERSKY, A., & KAHNEMAN, D. (1983). Extensional versus intuitive reasoning: The conjunction fallacy in probability judgment. *Psychological Review, 90,* 293–315.

UNDERWOOD, B. J., & RICHARDSON, J. (1956). Some verbal materials for the study of concept formation. *Psychological Bulletin, 53,* 84–95.

VAN DIJK, T. A., & KINTSCH, W. (1983). *Strategies of discourse comprehension.* New York: Academic Press.

VANLEHN, K. (1986). Arithmetic procedures are induced from examples. In J. Hiebert (Ed.), *Conceptual and procedural knowledge: The case of mathematics.* Hillsdale, NJ: Erlbaum.

VERVALIN, C. H. (1978). Just what is creativity? In G. A. Davis & J. A. Scott (Eds.), *Training creative thinking.* Huntington, NY: Krieger.

VESSEY, I. (1985). Expertise in debugging computer programs: A process analysis. *International Journal of Man-Machine Studies, 23,* 459–494.

VESSEY, I. (1986). Expertise in debugging computer programs: An analysis of the content of verbal protocols. *IEEE Transactions on Systems, Man, and Cybernetics, 16,* 621–637.

VOSNIADOU, S., & ORTONY, A. (Eds.). (1989). *Similarity and analogical reasoning.* Cambridge, England: Cambridge University Press.

VYGOTSKY, L. S. (1978). *Mind in society: The development of higher psychological processes.* Cambridge, MA: Harvard University Press.

WALKER, C. M., & BOURNE, L. E., JR. (1961). The identifications of concepts as a function of amount of relevant and irrelevant information. *American Journal of Psychology, 74,* 410–417.

WALLAS, G. (1926). *The art of thought.* New York: Harcourt Brace Jovanovich.

WASON, P. C. (1960). On the failure to eliminate hypotheses in a conceptual task. *Quarterly Journal of Experimental Psychology, 12,* 129–140.

WASON, P. C. (1966). Reasoning. In B. M. Foss (Ed.), *New Horizons in Psychology.* Harmondsworth, England: Penguin.

WASON, P. C. (1968a). On the failure to eliminate hypotheses: A second look. In P. C. Wason & P. N. Johnson-Laird (Eds.), *Thinking and reasoning.* Middlesex, England: Penguin.

WASON, P. C. (1968b). Reasoning about a rule. *Quarterly Journal of Experimental Psychology, 20,* 273–281.

WASON, P. C. (1977). The theory of formal operations—a critique. In B. A. Gerber (Ed.), *Piaget and knowing: Studies in genetic epistemology.* London: Routledge & Kegan Paul.

WASON, P. C., & JOHNSON-LAIRD, P. N. (1972). *Psychology of reasoning: Structure and content.* Cambridge, MA: Harvard University Press.

WATSON, J. B. (1930). *Behaviorism.* New York: Norton.

WATT, H. J. (1964). Experimental contribution to a theory of thinking. In J. M. Mandler & G. Mandler (Eds.), *Thinking: From association to Gestalt.* New York: Wiley. (Original work published 1905)

WECHSLER, D. (1958). *The measurement and appraisal of adult intelligence.* Baltimore: Williams & Wilkins.

WEINER, N. (1948). *Cybernetics.* New York: Wiley.

WEISBERG, R., DICAMILLO, M., & PHILLIPS, D. (1978). Transferring of associations to new situations: A nonautomatic process. *Journal of Verbal Learning and Verbal Behavior, 17,* 219–228.

WEISBERG, R., & SULS, J. (1973). An information processing model of Duncker's candle problem. *Cognitive Psychology, 4,* 255–276.

WEISBERG, R. W. (1986). *Creativity: Genius and other myths.* New York: Freeman.

WEISBERG, R. W., & ALBA, J. W. (1981). An examination of the alleged role of "fixation" in the solution of several "insight" problems. *Journal of Experimental Psychology: General, 110,* 169–192.

WEISER, M., & SHERTZ, J. (1983). Programming problem representation in novice and expert programmers. *International Journal of Man-Machine Studies, 19,* 391–398.

WEISSKOPF-JOELSON, E., & ELISEO, T. S. (1961). An experimental study of the study of the effectiveness of brainstorming. *Journal of Applied Psychology, 45,* 45–49.

WEIZENBAUM, J. (1968). Contextual understanding by computers. In P. A. Kolers & M. Eden (Eds.), *Recognizing patterns.* Cambridge: M.I.T. Press.

WERNER, H., & KAPLAN, E. (1952). The acquisition of word meanings: A developmental study. *Monographs of the Society for Research in Child Development, 15,* No. 5 1, vii.

WERTHEIMER, M. (1959). *Productive thinking.* New York: Harper & Row.

WERTSCH, J. V. (1985). *Vygotsky and the social formation of mind.* Cambridge, MA: Harvard University Press.

WHITE, B. Y., & FREDERIKSEN, J. R. (1987). Qualitative models and intelligent learning environments. In R. W. Lawler & M. Yazdani (Eds.), *Artificial intelligence and education: Learning environments and tutoring systems.* Norwood, NJ: Ablex.

WHORF, B. (1956). *Language, thought, and reality.* Cambridge, MA: M.I.T. Press.

WICKELGREN, W. A. (1974). *How to solve problems: Elements of a theory of problems and problem solving.* San Francisco: Freeman.

WICKENS, T. D., & MILLWARD, R. B. (1971). Attribute elimination strategies for concept identification with practiced subjects. *Journal of Mathematical Psychology, 8,* 453–480.

WIEDENBECK, S. (1985). Novice/expert differences in programming skills. *International Journal of Man-Machine Studies, 23,* 383–390.

WILKINS, M. C. (1928). The effect of changed material on ability to do formal syllogistic reasoning. *Archives of Psychology,* No. 102.

WILLIS, G. B., & FUSON, K. C. (1988). Teaching children to use schematic drawings to solve addition and subtraction word problems. *Journal of Educational Psychology, 80,* 192–201.

WINOGRAD, T. (1972). A program for understanding natural language. *Cognitive Psychology, 3,* 1–192.

WINOGRAD, T. (1983). *Language as a cognitive process.* Reading, MA: Addison-Wesley.

WINSTON, P. H. (1975). *The psychology of computer vision.* New York: McGraw-Hill.

WINSTON, P. H. (1984). *Artificial intelligenced* (2nd ed.). Reading, MA: Addison-Wesley.

WITTROCK, M. C. (1966). The learning by discovery hypothesis. In L. S. Shulman & E. R. Keisler (Eds.), *Learning by discovery.* Chicago: Rand McNally, 1966.

WITTROCK, M. C. (1980). *The brain and psychology.* New York: Academic Press.

WITTROCK, M. C., MARKS, C., & DOCTOROW, M. (1975). Reading as a generative process. *Journal of Educational Psychology, 67,* 484–489.

WOLF, T. H. (1973). *Alfred Binet.* Chicago: University of Chicago Press.

WOODROW, H., & LOWELL, F. (1916). Children's association frequency tables. *Psychological Monographs, 22*(5) (Whole No. 97).

WOODWORTH, R. S., & SELLS, S. B. (1935). An atmosphere effect in formal syllogistic reasoning. *Journal of Experimental Psychology, 18,* 451–460.

WUNDT, W. (1973). *An introduction to psychology.* New York: Arno Press. (Original work published in German 1911)

YUSSEN, S. R., & LEVY, V. M. JR. (1975). Developmental changes in predicting one's own span of short–term memory. *Journal of Experimental Child Psychology, 19,* 502–508.

ZANGWILL, O. L. (1972). Remembering revisited. *Quarterly Journal of Experimental Psychology, 24,* 123–138.

ZHU, X., & SIMON, H. A. (1987). Learning mathematics from examples and by doing. *Cognition and Instruction, 4,* 137–166.

ZOBRIST, A. L., & CARLSON, F. R. (1973, June). An advice-taking chess computer. *Scientific American,* pp. 92–105.

AUTHOR INDEX

SUBJECT INDEX

accommodation, 288–290, 322
ACT, 194–201, 266
aha!, *See* insight.
algebra problems, 446–448,
    450–452, 475–476
algorithm, 178
ambiguity theory, 122, 126–131
anagram problem, 19–20, 25–29
analogical reasoning, 415–454
analogs, 413–430
analogy problems, 326, 344–353,
    357–358
aphasia, 34
artificial intelligence, 172–173. *See
    also* computer simulation.
arithmetic problems, 69–70,
    479–488, 493–506
assimilation, 230–231, 288–290, 322
associationism, 11–12, 17, 19–38, 42
atmosphere theory, 122–124
atomism, 12, 14
attribute listing, 365–366
automatization, 305–310
availability deficiency, 256, 321
availability heuristic, 109, 112

balance beam problem, 310–315,
    319
Balloons passage, 226–227, 253
base rate fallacy, 111–112
BASIC, 397–398, 400–401
basic level category, 274–275
behaviorism, 7, 16–17

beliefs, 477, 479
belief-bias error, 120–121, 134–138
best-buy problem, 495–500
blockbusting, 73–77
box problem, 57–59, 61–62
brain, 30–36
brain damage, 33–34, 36
brain lateralization, 31, 33–34
brainstorming, 366–367
bug, 485–488
BUGGY, 485–488

candle problem, 61–62
card-turning problem, 142–151
case grammar, 243–244
categorical syllogism, 118–138
categories. *See* concept learning,
    natural categories, schematic
    knowledge.
category size effect, 265
chess, 387–390
choice reaction time, 204–205
circular reactions, 293–294
cognitive components, 326, 328,
    344–353
cognitive correlates, 326, 328,
    334–344
cognitive development, 283–323
cognitive economy, 266
cognitive factors, 325, 328, 329–334
cognitive neuroscience, 34, 38
cognitive psychology, 8, 16–17

(*Note:* The following terms are too
pervasive to be indexed: cognition,
cognitive process, knowledge,
learning, problem solving, strategy,
thinking, understanding.)